NEW PERSPECTIVES

Microsoft® Office 365™ & Office 2016

BRIEF

Ann Shaffer
Patrick Carey
Sasha Vodnik
Katherine T. Pinard

Lisa Ruffolo
Robin M. Romer
June Jamrich Parsons
Dan Oja

Mark Shellman
Gaston College

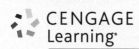

CENGAGE
Learning·

Australia · Brazil · Mexico · Singapore · United Kingdom · United States

New Perspectives Microsoft® Office 365™ &
Office 2016, Brief

SVP, GM Skills & Global Product Management:
    Dawn Gerrain

Product Director: Kathleen McMahon

Senior Product Team Manager: Lauren Murphy

Product Team Manager: Andrea Topping

Associate Product Manager: Melissa Stehler

Senior Director, Development: Marah Bellegarde

Product Development Manager: Leigh Hefferon

Senior Content Developer: Kathy Finnegan

Developmental Editors: Kim T. M. Crowley,
    Jane Pedicini, Robin M. Romer, Mary Pat Shaffer,
    Sasha Vodnik

Product Assistant: Erica Chapman

Marketing Director: Michele McTighe

Marketing Manager: Stephanie Albracht

Senior Production Director: Wendy Troeger

Production Director: Patty Stephan

Senior Content Project Manager:
    Jennifer Goguen McGrail

Art Director: Diana Graham

Text Designer: Althea Chen

Cover Template Designer: Wing-Ip Ngan, Ink
    Design, Inc.

Cover image(s): danielo/Shutterstock.com

Composition: GEX Publishing Services

© 2017 Cengage Learning

For product information and technology assistance, contact us at
Cengage Learning Customer & Sales Support, 1-800-354-9706

For permission to use material from this text or product, submit all requests online at **www.cengage.com/permissions**.
Further permissions questions can be e-mailed to
permissionrequest@cengage.com

Mac users: If you're working through this product using a Mac, some of the steps may vary. Additional information for Mac users is included with the Data Files for this product.

Some of the product names and company names used in this book have been used for identification purposes only and may be trademarks or registered trademarks of their respective manufacturers and sellers.

Windows® is a registered trademark of Microsoft Corporation. © 2012 Microsoft. Microsoft and the Office logo are either registered trademarks or trademarks of Microsoft Corporation in the United States and/or other countries. Cengage Learning is an independent entity from Microsoft Corporation and not affiliated with Microsoft in any manner.

Disclaimer: Any fictional data related to persons or companies or URLs used throughout this text is intended for instructional purposes only. At the time this text was published, any such data was fictional and not belonging to any real persons or companies.

Disclaimer: The material in this text was written using Microsoft Office 365 ProPlus and Microsoft Office 2016 running on Microsoft Windows 10 Professional and was Quality Assurance tested before the publication date. As Microsoft continually updates the Microsoft Office suite and the Windows 10 operating system, your software experience may vary slightly from what is presented in the printed text.

Microsoft product screenshots used with permission from Microsoft Corporation. Unless otherwise noted, all clip art is courtesy of openclipart.org.

Library of Congress Control Number: 2016934397
ISBN: 978-1-305-87918-8

Cengage Learning
20 Channel Center Street
Boston, MA 02210
USA

Cengage Learning is a leading provider of customized learning solutions with employees residing in nearly 40 different countries and sales in more than 125 countries around the world. Find your local representative at **www.cengage.com.**

Cengage Learning products are represented in Canada by Nelson Education, Ltd.

To learn more about Cengage Learning, visit **www.cengage.com**

Purchase any of our products at your local college store or at our preferred online store **www.cengagebrain.com**

Printed in the United States of America
Print Number: 01   Print Year: 2016

TABLE OF CONTENTS

PRODUCTIVITY APPS FOR SCHOOL AND WORK   PA-1

Introduction to OneNote 2016 . . . . PA-2
  Creating a OneNote Notebook PA-2
  Syncing a Notebook to the Cloud PA-2
  Taking Notes PA-3
  Converting Handwriting to Text PA-3
  Recording a Lecture PA-4
  1: Taking Notes for a Week PA-5
  2: Using OneNote to Organize a
  Research Paper PA-5
  3: Planning Your Career PA-5
Introduction to Sway PA-6
  Creating a Sway Presentation PA-6
  Adding Content to Build a Story PA-7
  Designing a Sway PA-8
  Publishing a Sway PA-8
  Sharing a Sway PA-8
  1: Creating a Sway Resume PA-9
  2: Creating an Online Sway Newsletter PA-9
  3: Creating and Sharing a Technology
  Presentation PA-9
Introduction to Office Mix PA-10
  Adding Office Mix to PowerPoint PA-10
  Capturing Video Clips PA-11
  Inserting Quizzes, Live Webpages,
  and Apps PA-12
  Sharing an Office Mix Presentation PA-12
  1: Creating an Office Mix Tutorial
  for OneNote PA-13
  2: Teaching Augmented Reality
  with Office Mix PA-13
  3: Marketing a Travel Destination
  with Office Mix PA-13
Introduction to Microsoft Edge PA-14
  Browsing the Web with Microsoft
  Edge PA-14
  Locating Information with Cortana PA-14
  Annotating Webpages PA-15
  1: Using Cortana in Microsoft Edge PA-16
  2: Viewing Online News with
  Reading View PA-16
  3: Inking with Microsoft Edge PA-16

MANAGING YOUR FILES
Organizing Files and Folders with
Windows 10 . . . . FM 1

Visual Overview:
Files in a Folder Window . . . . FM 2
Organizing Files and Folders . . . . FM 4
  Understanding How to Organize
  Files and Folders . . . . FM 5
Exploring Files and Folders . . . . FM 7
  Navigating to Your Data Files . . . . FM 10
  Changing the View . . . . FM 11
Managing Files and Folders . . . . FM 13
  Opening a File . . . . FM 14
  Saving a File . . . . FM 15
  Creating Folders . . . . FM 17
  Moving and Copying Files and Folders . . . . . . FM 18
  Deleting Files and Folders . . . . FM 23
  Renaming Files . . . . FM 24
Finding Files and Information with Cortana . . . . FM 24
Working with Compressed Files . . . . FM 28
Quick Check . . . . FM 30
Review Assignments . . . . FM 31
Case Problems . . . . FM 31

WORD MODULES

Module 1 Creating and Editing a Document
Writing a Business Letter and Formatting
a Flyer . . . . **WD 1**

Session 1.1 Visual Overview:
The Word Window . . . . WD 2
Starting Word . . . . WD 4
  Working in Touch Mode . . . . WD 5
Setting Up the Word Window . . . . WD 6
Saving a Document . . . . WD 7
Entering Text . . . . WD 10
  Inserting a Date with AutoComplete . . . . WD 10
  Continuing to Type the Block-Style
  Letter . . . . WD 11
  Typing a Hyperlink . . . . WD 12
Using the Undo and Redo Buttons . . . . WD 13
Correcting Errors as You Type . . . . WD 14
Proofreading a Document . . . . WD 17
Adjusting Paragraph and Line Spacing . . . . WD 18

Adjusting the Margins . . . . WD 22
Previewing and Printing a Document . . . . WD 25
Creating an Envelope . . . . WD 26
Session 1.1 Quick Check . . . . WD 29

Session 1.2 Visual Overview:
Formatting a Document . . . . WD 30
Opening an Existing Document . . . . WD 32
Using the Spelling and Grammar
Task Panes . . . . WD 34
Changing Page Orientation. . . . . WD 38
Changing the Font and Font Size . . . . WD 39
Applying Text Effects, Font Colors, and
Font Styles . . . . WD 41
Aligning Text . . . . WD 43
Adding a Paragraph Border and Shading . . . . . . WD 45
Copying Formatting with the Format Painter . . . . WD 47
Working with Pictures . . . . WD 49
Getting Help . . . . WD 52
Session 1.2 Quick Check . . . . WD 54
Review Assignments . . . . WD 55
Case Problems. . . . . WD 56

Module 2 Navigating and Formatting a Document
Editing an Academic Document
According to MLA Style . . . . **WD 61**

Session 2.1 Visual Overview:
Working with Lists and Styles . . . . WD 62
Reviewing the Document . . . . WD 64
Working with Comments. . . . . WD 67
Creating Bulleted and Numbered Lists. . . . . WD 70
Moving Text in a Document . . . . WD 73
    Dragging and Dropping Text. . . . . WD 73
    Cutting or Copying and Pasting Text
    Using the Clipboard . . . . WD 75
Using the Navigation Pane . . . . WD 78
Finding and Replacing Text. . . . . WD 81
Working with Styles. . . . . WD 84
Working with Themes . . . . WD 87
Session 2.1 Quick Check . . . . WD 91

Session 2.2 Visual Overview:
MLA Formatting Guidelines . . . . WD 92
Reviewing the MLA Style. . . . . WD 94
Indenting a Paragraph. . . . . WD 95
Inserting and Modifying Page Numbers. . . . . . . WD 98
Creating Citations and a Bibliography . . . . WD 100
    Creating Citations. . . . . WD 102
    Inserting a Page Break . . . . WD 108

Generating a Bibliography . . . . WD 108
Modifying an Existing Source. . . . . WD 110
Updating and Finalizing a Bibliography . . . . . WD 111
Session 2.2 Quick Check . . . . WD 112
Review Assignments . . . . WD 113
Case Problems. . . . . WD 115

EXCEL MODULES

Module 1 Getting Started with Excel
Creating a Customer Order Report . . . . **EX 1**

Session 1.1 Visual Overview:
The Excel Workbook . . . . EX 2
Introducing Excel and Spreadsheets. . . . . EX 4
    Opening an Existing Workbook. . . . . EX 4
    Using Keyboard Shortcuts to Work Faster. . . . EX 6
    Getting Help. . . . . EX 6
    Using Excel 2016 in Touch Mode . . . . EX 6
Exploring a Workbook. . . . . EX 7
    Changing the Active Sheet. . . . . EX 8
    Navigating Within a Worksheet . . . . EX 9
    Selecting a Cell Range . . . . EX 11
Closing a Workbook . . . . EX 13
Planning a Workbook . . . . EX 13
Starting a New Workbook. . . . . EX 14
    Renaming and Inserting Worksheets . . . . EX 15
    Moving Worksheets . . . . EX 16
    Deleting Worksheets . . . . EX 16
    Saving a Workbook. . . . . EX 17
Entering Text, Dates, and Numbers . . . . EX 17
    Entering Text. . . . . EX 17
    Undoing and Redoing an Action . . . . EX 19
    Editing Cell Content . . . . EX 19
    Understanding AutoComplete. . . . . EX 20
    Displaying Numbers as Text. . . . . EX 21
    Entering Dates . . . . EX 22
    Entering Numbers . . . . EX 24
Resizing Columns and Rows . . . . EX 25
    Changing Column Widths . . . . EX 25
    Wrapping Text Within a Cell . . . . EX 27
    Changing Row Heights. . . . . EX 28
Session 1.1 Quick Check . . . . EX 29

Session 1.2 Visual Overview:
Excel Formulas and Functions. . . . . EX 30
Performing Calculations with Formulas. . . . . EX 32
    Entering a Formula . . . . EX 32
    Copying and Pasting Formulas. . . . . EX 35

Simplifying Formulas with Functions. . . . . EX 36
   Introducing Function Syntax. . . . . EX 36
   Entering Functions with AutoSum . . . . EX 36
Modifying a Worksheet. . . . . EX 39
   Moving and Copying a Cell or Range . . . . EX 39
   Using the COUNT Function . . . . EX 41
   Inserting a Column or Row. . . . . EX 42
   Deleting a Row or Column . . . . EX 44
   Inserting and Deleting a Range . . . . EX 45
Using Flash Fill. . . . . EX 47
Formatting a Worksheet . . . . EX 48
   Adding Cell Borders. EX 49
   Changing the Font Size . . . . EX 50
Printing a Workbook . . . . EX 50
   Changing Worksheet Views . . . . EX 50
   Changing the Page Orientation . . . . EX 52
   Setting the Scaling Options . . . . EX 53
   Setting the Print Options . . . . EX 54
Viewing Worksheet Formulas . . . . EX 55
Saving a Workbook with a New Filename. . . . . . . EX 56
Session 1.2 Quick Check . . . . EX 57
Review Assignments . . . . EX 58
Case Problems. . . . . EX 59

Module 2 Formatting Workbook Text and Data
Creating a Sales Report . . . .**EX 65**

Session 2.1 Visual Overview:
Formatting a Worksheet . . . . EX 66
Formatting Cell Text . . . . EX 68
   Applying Fonts and Font Styles . . . . EX 68
   Applying a Font Color . . . . EX 70
   Formatting Text Selections Within a Cell. . . . . EX 72
Working with Fill Colors and Backgrounds. . . . . . EX 72
   Changing a Fill Color . . . . EX 73
   Adding a Background Image . . . . EX 74
Using Functions and Formulas to Calculate
Sales Data . . . . EX 75
Formatting Numbers. . . . . EX 79
   Applying Number Formats. . . . . EX 79
   Formatting Dates and Times . . . . EX 83
Formatting Worksheet Cells . . . . EX 84
   Aligning Cell Content. . . . . EX 84
   Indenting Cell Content. . . . . EX 85
   Adding Borders to Cells. . . . . EX 85
   Merging Cells . . . . EX 87
   Rotating Cell Contents. . . . . EX 88
Exploring the Format Cells Dialog Box. . . . . EX 89
Session 2.1 Quick Check . . . . EX 93

Session 2.2 Visual Overview:
Designing a Printout . . . . EX 94
Calculating Averages. . . . . EX 96
Applying Cell Styles. . . . . EX 98
Copying and Pasting Formats. . . . . EX 100
   Copying Formats with the Format Painter. . . EX 100
   Copying Formats with the Paste Options
   Button. . . . . EX 101
   Copying Formats with Paste Special . . . . EX 102
Finding and Replacing Text and Formats . . . . . . EX 103
Working with Themes . . . . EX 105
Highlighting Data with Conditional
Formats . . . . EX 107
   Highlighting Cells Based on Their Values. . . . EX 107
   Highlighting Cells with a Top/
   Bottom Rule . . . . EX 109
   Other Conditional Formatting
   Options . . . . EX 111
   Creating a Conditional Formatting
   Legend . . . . EX 111
Formatting a Worksheet for Printing . . . . EX 113
   Using Page Break Preview . . . . EX 113
   Defining the Print Area. . . . . EX 114
   Inserting Page Breaks. . . . . EX 115
   Adding Print Titles . . . . EX 117
   Designing Headers and Footers. . . . . EX 118
   Setting the Page Margins. . . . . EX 120
Session 2.2 Quick Check . . . . EX 122
Review Assignments . . . . EX 123
Case Problems. . . . . EX 125

Module 3 Performing Calculations with Formulas
and Functions
Calculating Farm Yield and Revenue . . . . . .**EX 131**

Session 3.1 Visual Overview:
Formulas and Functions . . . . EX 132
Making Workbooks User-Friendly. . . . . EX 134
   Documenting Formulas . . . . EX 135
   Using Constants in Formulas . . . . EX 136
   Identifying Notes, Input Values, and
   Calculated Values . . . . EX 140
Using Excel Functions . . . . EX 141
   Understanding Function Syntax. . . . . EX 141
   Entering the COUNT function . . . . EX 142
   Nesting the ROUND and AVERAGE
   Functions . . . . EX 143
   Using the Function Library and the Insert
   Function Dialog Box. EX 145

Performing What-If Analyses. . . . . EX 149
    Using Trial and Error. . . . . EX 149
    Using Goal Seek . . . . EX 150
Interpreting Error Values. . . . . EX 151
Session 3.1 Quick Check . . . . EX 153

Session 3.2 Visual Overview:
Cell References and Formulas. . . . . EX 154
AutoFilling Formulas and Data . . . . EX 156
    Filling a Series. . . . . EX 156
    Exploring Auto Fill Options . . . . EX 158
    Filling Formulas. . . . . EX 159
Exploring Cell References . . . . EX 161
    Understanding Relative References . . . . EX 161
    Understanding Absolute References . . . . EX 162
    Understanding Mixed References . . . . EX 163
    Changing Cell References in a
    Formula. . . . . EX 165
Summarizing Data with the Quick
Analysis Tool . . . . EX 167
Working with Dates and Date Functions. . . . . . . EX 169
Using Lookup Functions . . . . EX 171
    Finding an Exact Match with the VLOOKUP
    Function . . . . EX 171
Working with Logical Functions . . . . EX 174
Session 3.2 Quick Check. . . . . EX 180
Review Assignments . . . . EX 181
Case Problems. . . . . EX 182

ACCESS MODULES

Module 1 Creating a Database
*Tracking Animal, Visit, and Billing Data. . . . .***AC 1**

Session 1.1 Visual Overview:
The Access Window . . . . AC 2
Introduction to Database Concepts . . . . AC 4
    Organizing Data . . . . AC 4
    Databases and Relationships . . . . AC 4
    Relational Database Management Systems. . . . . AC 6
Starting Access and Creating a Database. . . . . . . AC 7
    Working in Touch Mode . . . . AC 9
Creating a Table in Datasheet View . . . . AC 11
    Renaming the Default Primary Key Field . . . . . AC 12
    Changing the Data Type of the Default
    Primary Key Field . . . . AC 13
    Adding New Fields. AC 14
    Entering Records . . . . AC 16

Saving a Table. . . . . AC 19
Opening a Table . . . . AC 22
Closing a Table and Exiting Access. . . . . AC 22
Session 1.1 Quick Check . . . . AC 23

Session 1.2 Visual Overview:
The Create Tab Options . . . . AC 24
Copying Records from Another Access
Database . . . . AC 26
Navigating a Datasheet. . . . . AC 29
Creating a Simple Query. . . . . AC 30
Creating a Simple Form. . . . . AC 33
Creating a Simple Report . . . . AC 35
    Printing a Report . . . . AC 39
Viewing Objects in the Navigation Pane. . . . . . . AC 40
Using Microsoft Access Help. . . . . AC 40
Managing a Database . . . . AC 41
    Compacting and Repairing a
    Database. . . . . AC 42
    Backing Up and Restoring a Database. . . . . . . AC 43
Session 1.2 Quick Check . . . . AC 44
Review Assignments . . . . AC 45
Case Problems. . . . . AC 46

**Module 2 Building a Database and Defining Table
Relationships**
*Creating the Billing, Owner, and
Animal Tables. . . . .***AC 51**

Session 2.1 Visual Overview:
Table Window in Design View. . . . . AC 52
Guidelines for Designing Databases. . . . . AC 54
Guidelines for Setting Field Properties. . . . . AC 56
    Naming Fields and Objects . . . . AC 56
    Assigning Field Data Types . . . . AC 56
    Setting Field Sizes . . . . AC 57
    Setting the Caption Property for Fields. . . . . . AC 58
Creating a Table in Design View . . . . AC 59
    Defining Fields . . . . AC 59
    Specifying the Primary Key. . . . . AC 67
    Saving the Table Structure . . . . AC 68
Modifying the Structure of an Access Table . . . . . AC 68
    Moving a Field in Design View . . . . AC 69
    Adding a Field in Design View . . . . AC 69
Modifying Field Properties . . . . AC 71
    Changing the Format Property in
    Datasheet View. . . . . AC 71
    Changing Properties in Design View . . . . AC 73
Session 2.1 Quick Check . . . . AC 75

Session 2.2 Visual Overview:

Modified Visit table in Datasheet view . . . . AC 76

Adding Records to a New Table . . . . AC 78

Importing Data from an Excel Worksheet. . . . . . AC 80

Creating a Table by Importing an Existing Table
or Table Structure . . . . AC 83

    Importing an Existing Table Structure . . . . . . AC 84

    Importing an Existing Table . . . . AC 86

Adding Fields to a Table Using the Data Type
Gallery . . . . AC 86

Modifying the Structure of an Imported
Table . . . . AC 88

    Deleting Fields from a Table Structure. . . . . . AC 88

    Renaming Fields in Design View . . . . AC 90

    Changing the Data Type for a Field in
    Design View . . . . AC 90

Setting the Default Value Property for
a Field . . . . AC 93

Adding Data to a Table by Importing a
Text File . . . . AC 95

Defining Table Relationships. . . . . AC 97

    One-to-Many Relationships . . . . AC 98

    Referential Integrity . . . . AC 99

    Defining a Relationship Between Two
    Tables . . . . AC 99

Session 2.2 Quick Check. . . . . AC 104

Review Assignments . . . . AC 105

Case Problems. . . . . AC 106

Module 3 Maintaining and Querying a Database
*Updating Tables and Retrieving Care
Center Information* . . . .**AC 115**

Session 3.1 Visual Overview:

Query Window in Design View . . . . AC 116

Updating a Database. . . . . AC 118

    Modifying Records . . . . AC 118

    Hiding and Unhiding Fields . . . . AC 119

    Finding Data in a Table. . . . . AC 121

    Deleting Records . . . . AC 122

Introduction to Queries. . . . . AC 124

Creating and Running a Query . . . . AC 125

Updating Data Using a Query. . . . . AC 128

Creating a Multitable Query . . . . AC 129

Sorting Data in a Query . . . . AC 131

    Using an AutoFilter to Sort Data . . . . AC 131

    Sorting on Multiple Fields in
    Design View. . . . . AC 132

Filtering Data. . . . . AC 136

Session 3.1 Quick Check . . . . AC 139

Session 3.2 Visual Overview:

Selection Criteria in Queries . . . . AC 140

Defining Record Selection Criteria for Queries . . . AC 142

    Specifying an Exact Match. . . . . AC 142

    Modifying a Query . . . . AC 144

    Using a Comparison Operator to Match a
    Range of Values . . . . AC 147

Defining Multiple Selection Criteria for
Queries . . . . AC 149

    The And Logical Operator . . . . AC 150

    The Or Logical Operator . . . . AC 152

Changing a Datasheet's Appearance . . . . AC 154

    Modifying the Font Size . . . . AC 154

    Changing the Alternate Row Color in a
    Datasheet . . . . AC 154

Creating a Calculated Field. . . . . AC 156

    Formatting a Calculated Field . . . . AC 160

Using Aggregate Functions. . . . . AC 161

    Working with Aggregate Functions Using
    the Total Row . . . . AC 162

    Creating Queries with Aggregate
    Functions . . . . AC 163

    Using Record Group Calculations . . . . AC 166

Working with the Navigation Pane . . . . AC 167

Session 3.2 Quick Check. . . . . AC 170

Review Assignments . . . . AC 171

Case Problems. . . . . AC 172

POWERPOINT MODULE

Module 1 Creating a Presentation
*Presenting Information About an Event
Venue* . . . . **PPT 1**

Session 1.1 Visual Overview:

The PowerPoint Window . . . . PPT 2

Planning a Presentation. . . . . PPT 4

Starting PowerPoint and Creating a New
Presentation. . . . . PPT 5

    Working in Touch Mode . . . . PPT 6

Creating a Title Slide . . . . PPT 7

Saving and Editing a Presentation . . . . PPT 8

Adding New Slides . . . . PPT 11

Creating Lists. . . . . PPT 14

    Creating a Bulleted List . . . . PPT 14

    Creating a Numbered List . . . . PPT 16

Creating an Unnumbered List . . . . PPT 17

Formatting Text. . . . . PPT 19

Moving and Copying Text. . . . . PPT 22

Converting a List to a SmartArt Diagram . . . . . PPT 24

Manipulating Slides . . . . PPT 28

Closing a Presentation. . . . . PPT 30

Session 1.1 Quick Check . . . . PPT 31

Session 1.2 Visual Overview:

Slide Show and Presenter Views . . . . PPT 32

Opening a Presentation and Saving It with
a New Name . . . . PPT 34

Changing the Theme and the Theme Variant. . . PPT 35

Working with Photos . . . . PPT 38

Inserting Photos Stored on Your Computer
or Network . . . . PPT 39

Cropping Photos. PPT 40

Modifying Photo Compression Options . . . . PPT 42

Resizing and Moving Objects . . . . PPT 44

Resizing and Moving Pictures. . . . . PPT 44

Resizing and Moving Text Boxes . . . . PPT 47

Adding Speaker Notes . . . . PPT 48

Checking Spelling . . . . PPT 50

Running a Slide Show . . . . PPT 52

Using Slide Show View and
Presenter View . . . . PPT 52

Using Reading View . . . . PPT 55

Printing a Presentation . . . . PPT 56

Exiting PowerPoint . . . . PPT 60

Session 1.2 Quick Check . . . . PPT 61

Review Assignments . . . . PPT 62

Case Problems. . . . . PPT 63

COMMUNICATING WITH OUTLOOK 2016

Sending and Receiving Email Messages . . . **OUT 1**

Session 1 Visual Overview:

Outlook Window. . . . . .OUT 2

Exploring Outlook. .OUT 4

Navigating Between Outlook Elements. . . . . .OUT 4

Setting Up Outlook for Email . . . . .OUT 6

Choosing a Message Format . . . . .OUT 7

Adding a Signature. . . . . .OUT 9

Using Stationery and Themes. . . . . .OUT 10

Creating and Sending Email Messages. . . . . . .OUT 10

Setting the Importance and Sensitivity
Levels . . . . .OUT 12

Sending Email. . . . . .OUT 13

Organizing Contact Information . . . . .OUT 15

Creating Contacts . . . . .OUT 15

Switching Contact Views . . . . .OUT 20

Editing Contacts. .OUT 21

Sending Contact Information by Email . . . . .OUT 22

Creating and Modifying a Contact Group . . . . .OUT 22

Modifying a Contact Group . . . . .OUT 24

Session 1 Quick Check . . . . .OUT 25

Session 2 Visual Overview:

Email Messages and Attachments . . . . .OUT 26

Receiving Email . . . . .OUT 28

Replying To and Forwarding Messages . . . . .OUT 29

Printing Messages . . . . .OUT 30

Working with Attachments. . . . . .OUT 31

Flagging and Color Coding Messages. . . . . .OUT 33

Organizing and Managing Messages . . . . .OUT 34

Creating a Folder .OUT 35

Moving Messages into Folders . . . . .OUT 35

Creating Rules. . . . . .OUT 36

Rearranging Messages . . . . .OUT 38

Searching for Messages . . . . .OUT 38

Using Search Folders . . . . .OUT 39

Switching Views and Arrangements. . . . . . . .OUT 40

Sorting Messages. . . . . .OUT 41

Storing Messages . . . . .OUT 42

Saving Messages .OUT 42

Deleting Items and Exiting Outlook . . . . .OUT 43

Session 2 Quick Check . . . . .OUT 45

Review Assignments . . . . .OUT 46

Case Problems. . . . . .OUT 47

INDEX . . . . **REF 1**

Productivity Apps for School and Work

Corinne Hoisington

Lochlan keeps track of his class notes, football plays, and internship meetings with OneNote.

Zoe is using the annotation features of Microsoft Edge to take and save web notes for her research paper.

Nori is creating a Sway site to highlight this year's activities for the Student Government Association.

Hunter is adding interactive videos and screen recordings to his PowerPoint resume.

© Rawpixel/Shutterstock.com

Being computer literate no longer means mastery of only Word, Excel, PowerPoint, Outlook, and Access. To become technology power users, Hunter, Nori, Zoe, and Lochlan are exploring Microsoft OneNote, Sway, Mix, and Edge in Office 2016 and Windows 10.

In this Module

Introduction to OneNote 2016 2
Introduction to Sway 6
Introduction to Office Mix 10
Introduction to Microsoft Edge............. 14

Learn to use productivity apps!
Links to companion **Sways**, featuring **videos** with hands-on instructions, are located on www.cengagebrain.com.

Introduction to OneNote 2016

notebook | section tab | To Do tag | screen clipping | note | template | Microsoft OneNote Mobile app | sync | drawing canvas | inked handwriting | Ink to Text

As you glance around any classroom, you invariably see paper notebooks and notepads on each desk. Because deciphering and sharing handwritten notes can be a challenge, Microsoft OneNote 2016 replaces physical notebooks, binders, and paper notes with a searchable, digital notebook. OneNote captures your ideas and schoolwork on any device so you can stay organized, share notes, and work with others on projects. Whether you are a student taking class notes as shown in **Figure 1** or an employee taking notes in company meetings, OneNote is the one place to keep notes for all of your projects.

Figure 1: OneNote 2016 notebook

Each **notebook** is divided into sections, also called **section tabs**, by subject or topic.

Use **To Do tags**, icons that help you keep track of your assignments and other tasks.

Type on a page to add a **note**, a small window that contains text or other types of information.

Personalize a page with a **template**, or stationery.

Write or draw directly on the page using drawing tools.

Pages can include pictures such as **screen clippings**, images from any part of a computer screen.

Attach files and enter equations so you have everything you need in one place.

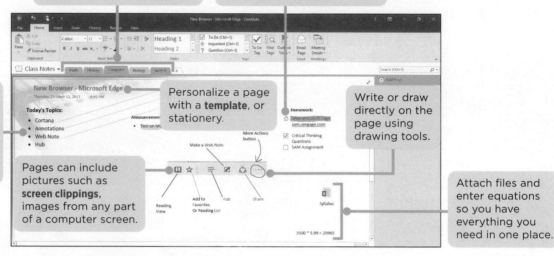

Creating a OneNote Notebook

OneNote is divided into sections similar to those in a spiral-bound notebook. Each OneNote notebook contains sections, pages, and other notebooks. You can use One-Note for school, business, and personal projects. Store information for each type of project in different notebooks to keep your tasks separate, or use any other organization that suits you. OneNote is flexible enough to adapt to the way you want to work.

When you create a notebook, it contains a blank page with a plain white background by default, though you can use templates, or stationery, to apply designs in categories such as Academic, Business, Decorative, and Planners. Start typing or use the buttons on the Insert tab to insert notes, which are small resizable windows that can contain text, equations, tables, on-screen writing, images, audio and video recordings, to-do lists, file attachments, and file printouts. Add as many notes as you need to each page.

Syncing a Notebook to the Cloud

OneNote saves your notes every time you make a change in a notebook. To make sure you can access your notebooks with a laptop, tablet, or smartphone wherever you are, OneNote uses cloud-based storage, such as OneDrive or SharePoint. **Microsoft OneNote Mobile app**, a lightweight version of OneNote 2016 shown in **Figure 2**, is available for free in the Windows Store, Google Play for Android devices, and the AppStore for iOS devices.

If you have a Microsoft account, OneNote saves your notes on OneDrive automatically for all your mobile devices and computers, which is called **syncing**. For example, you can use OneNote to take notes on your laptop during class, and then open OneNote on your phone to study later. To use a notebook stored on your computer with your OneNote Mobile app, move the notebook to OneDrive. You can quickly share notebook content with other people using OneDrive.

Figure 2: Microsoft OneNote Mobile app

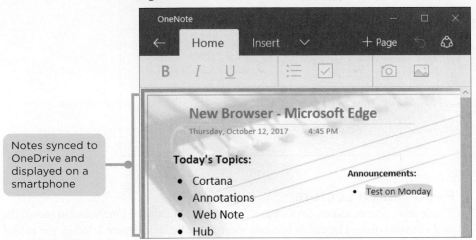

Notes synced to OneDrive and displayed on a smartphone

Taking Notes

Use OneNote pages to organize your notes by class and topic or lecture. Beyond simple typed notes, OneNote stores drawings, converts handwriting to searchable text and mathematical sketches to equations, and records audio and video.

OneNote includes drawing tools that let you sketch freehand drawings such as biological cell diagrams and financial supply-and-demand charts. As shown in **Figure 3**, the Draw tab on the ribbon provides these drawing tools along with shapes so you can insert diagrams and other illustrations to represent your ideas. When you draw on a page, OneNote creates a **drawing canvas**, which is a container for shapes and lines.

On the Job Now

OneNote is ideal for taking notes during meetings, whether you are recording minutes, documenting a discussion, sketching product diagrams, or listing follow-up items. Use a meeting template to add pages with content appropriate for meetings.

Figure 3: Tools on the Draw tab

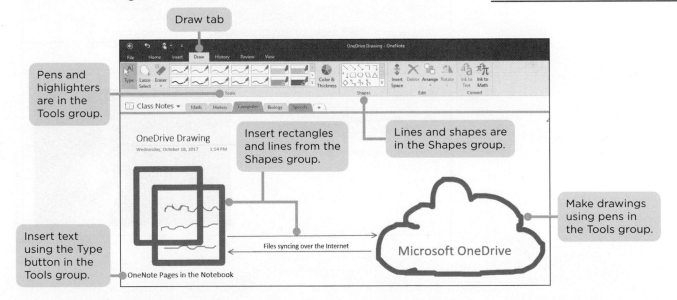

Draw tab

Pens and highlighters are in the Tools group.

Insert rectangles and lines from the Shapes group.

Lines and shapes are in the Shapes group.

Make drawings using pens in the Tools group.

Insert text using the Type button in the Tools group.

Converting Handwriting to Text

When you use a pen tool to write on a notebook page, the text you enter is called **inked handwriting**. OneNote can convert inked handwriting to typed text when you use the **Ink to Text** button in the Convert group on the Draw tab, as shown in **Figure 4**. After OneNote converts the handwriting to text, you can use the Search box to find terms in the converted text or any other note in your notebooks.

Figure 4: Converting handwriting to text

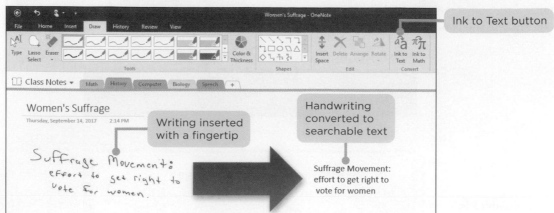

On the Job Now

Use OneNote as a place to brainstorm ongoing work projects. If a notebook contains sensitive material, you can password-protect some or all of the notebook so that only certain people can open it.

Recording a Lecture

If your computer or mobile device has a microphone or camera, OneNote can record the audio or video from a lecture or business meeting as shown in **Figure 5**. When you record a lecture (with your instructor's permission), you can follow along, take regular notes at your own pace, and review the video recording later. You can control the start, pause, and stop motions of the recording when you play back the recording of your notes.

Figure 5: Video inserted in a notebook

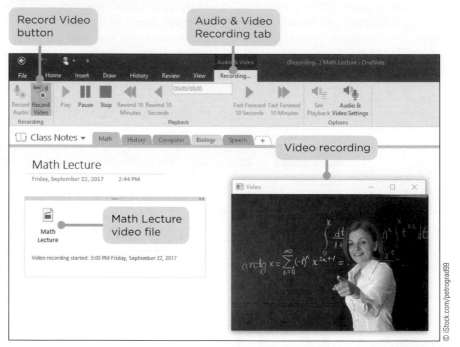

Try This Now

1: Taking Notes for a Week

As a student, you can get organized by using OneNote to take detailed notes in your classes. Perform the following tasks:

    a. Create a new OneNote notebook on your Microsoft OneDrive account (the default location for new notebooks). Name the notebook with your first name followed by "Notes," as in **Caleb Notes**.

    b. Create four section tabs, each with a different class name.

    c. Take detailed notes in those classes for one week. Be sure to include notes, drawings, and other types of content.

    d. Sync your notes with your OneDrive. Submit your assignment in the format specified by your instructor.

2: Using OneNote to Organize a Research Paper

You have a research paper due on the topic of three habits of successful students. Use OneNote to organize your research. Perform the following tasks:

    a. Create a new OneNote notebook on your Microsoft OneDrive account. Name the notebook **Success Research**.

    b. Create three section tabs with the following names:

- **Take Detailed Notes**
- **Be Respectful in Class**
- **Come to Class Prepared**

    c. On the web, research the topics and find three sources for each section. Copy a sentence from each source and paste the sentence into the appropriate section. When you paste the sentence, OneNote inserts it in a note with a link to the source.

    d. Sync your notes with your OneDrive. Submit your assignment in the format specified by your instructor.

3: Planning Your Career

Note: This activity requires a webcam or built-in video camera on any type of device.

Consider an occupation that interests you. Using OneNote, examine the responsibilities, education requirements, potential salary, and employment outlook of a specific career. Perform the following tasks:

    a. Create a new OneNote notebook on your Microsoft OneDrive account. Name the notebook with your first name followed by a career title, such as **Kara - App Developer**.

    b. Create four section tabs with the names **Responsibilities, Education Requirements, Median Salary**, and **Employment Outlook**.

    c. Research the responsibilities of your career path. Using OneNote, record a short video (approximately 30 seconds) of yourself explaining the responsibilities of your career path. Place the video in the Responsibilities section.

    d. On the web, research the educational requirements for your career path and find two appropriate sources. Copy a paragraph from each source and paste them into the appropriate section. When you paste a paragraph, OneNote inserts it in a note with a link to the source.

    e. Research the median salary for a single year for this career. Create a mathematical equation in the Median Salary section that multiplies the amount of the median salary times 20 years to calculate how much you will possibly earn.

    f. For the Employment Outlook section, research the outlook for your career path. Take at least four notes about what you find when researching the topic.

    g. Sync your notes with your OneDrive. Submit your assignment in the format specified by your instructor.

Introduction to Sway

Sway site | responsive design | Storyline | card | Creative Commons license | animation emphasis effects | Docs.com

Expressing your ideas in a presentation typically means creating PowerPoint slides or a Word document. Microsoft Sway gives you another way to engage an audience. Sway is a free Microsoft tool available at Sway.com or as an app in Office 365. Using Sway, you can combine text, images, videos, and social media in a website called a **Sway site** that you can share and display on any device. To get started, you create a digital story on a web-based canvas without borders, slides, cells, or page breaks. A Sway site organizes the text, images, and video into a **responsive design**, which means your content adapts perfectly to any screen size as shown in **Figure 6**. You store a Sway site in the cloud on OneDrive using a free Microsoft account.

Figure 6: Sway site with responsive design

You can display a Sway presentation in a web browser.

Sway uses responsive design to make sure pages fit perfectly on any device.

© iStock.com/marinello, © iStock.com/marekuliasz

Creating a Sway Presentation

You can use Sway to build a digital flyer, a club newsletter, a vacation blog, an informational site, a digital art portfolio, or a new product rollout. After you select your topic and sign into Sway with your Microsoft account, a **Storyline** opens, providing tools and a work area for composing your digital story. See **Figure 7**. Each story can include text, images, and videos. You create a Sway by adding text and media content into a Storyline section, or **card**. To add pictures, videos, or documents, select a card in the left pane and then select the Insert Content button. The first card in a Sway presentation contains a title and background image.

Figure 7: Creating a Sway site

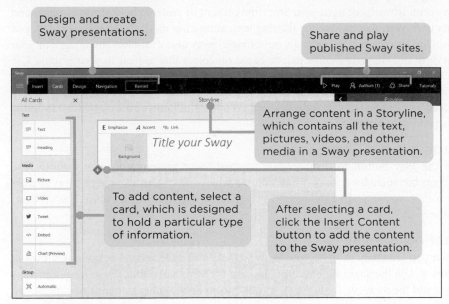

Design and create Sway presentations.

Share and play published Sway sites.

Arrange content in a Storyline, which contains all the text, pictures, videos, and other media in a Sway presentation.

To add content, select a card, which is designed to hold a particular type of information.

After selecting a card, click the Insert Content button to add the content to the Sway presentation.

Adding Content to Build a Story

As you work, Sway searches the Internet to help you find relevant images, videos, tweets, and other content from online sources such as Bing, YouTube, Twitter, and Facebook. You can drag content from the search results right into the Storyline. In addition, you can upload your own images and videos directly in the presentation. For example, if you are creating a Sway presentation about the market for commercial drones, Sway suggests content to incorporate into the presentation by displaying it in the left pane as search results. The search results include drone images tagged with a **Creative Commons license** at online sources as shown in **Figure 8**. A Creative Commons license is a public copyright license that allows the free distribution of an otherwise copyrighted work. In addition, you can specify the source of the media. For example, you can add your own Facebook or OneNote pictures and videos in Sway without leaving the app.

On the Job Now

If you have a Microsoft Word document containing an outline of your business content, drag the outline into Sway to create a card for each topic.

Figure 8: Images in Sway search results

Select the source of media objects

Information about Creative Commons licenses

Storyline title

The Market for Commercial Drones

Drag an image to the picture placeholder box

Suggested images in the search results

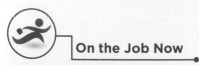

On the Job Now

If your project team wants to collaborate on a Sway presentation, click the Authors button on the navigation bar to invite others to edit the presentation.

Designing a Sway

Sway professionally designs your Storyline content by resizing background images and fonts to fit your display, and by floating text, animating media, embedding video, and removing images as a page scrolls out of view. Sway also evaluates the images in your Storyline and suggests a color palette based on colors that appear in your photos. Use the Design button to display tools including color palettes, font choices, **animation emphasis effects**, and style templates to provide a personality for a Sway presentation. Instead of creating your own design, you can click the Remix button, which randomly selects unique designs for your Sway site.

Publishing a Sway

Use the Play button to display your finished Sway presentation as a website. The Address bar includes a unique web address where others can view your Sway site. As the author, you can edit a published Sway site by clicking the Edit button (pencil icon) on the Sway toolbar.

Sharing a Sway

When you are ready to share your Sway website, you have several options as shown in **Figure 9**. Use the Share slider button to share the Sway site publically or keep it private. If you add the Sway site to the Microsoft **Docs.com** public gallery, anyone worldwide can use Bing, Google, or other search engines to find, view, and share your Sway site. You can also share your Sway site using Facebook, Twitter, Google+, Yammer, and other social media sites. Link your presentation to any webpage or email the link to your audience. Sway can also generate a code for embedding the link within another webpage.

Figure 9: Sharing a Sway site

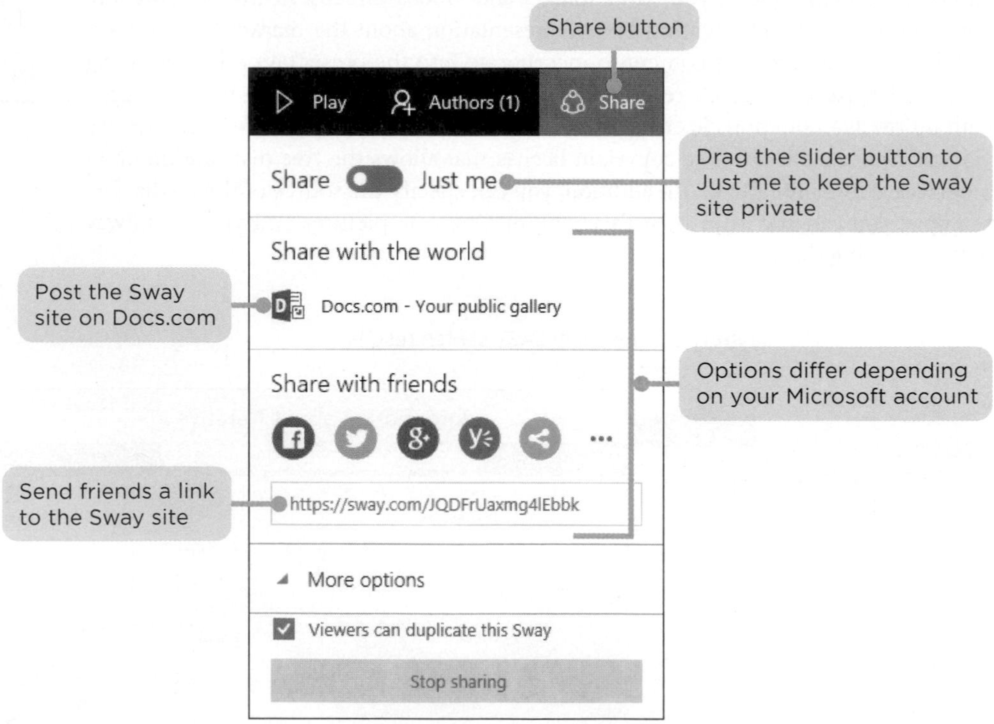

Share button

Play   Authors (1)   Share

Share   Just me

Drag the slider button to Just me to keep the Sway site private

Share with the world

Post the Sway site on Docs.com

Docs.com - Your public gallery

Share with friends

Options differ depending on your Microsoft account

Send friends a link to the Sway site

https://sway.com/JQDFrUaxmg4lEbbk

More options

Viewers can duplicate this Sway

Stop sharing

Try This Now

1: Creating a Sway Resume

Learn to use Sway!
Links to companion **Sways**, featuring **videos** with hands-on instructions, are located on www.cengagebrain.com.

Sway is a digital storytelling app. Create a Sway resume to share the skills, job experiences, and achievements you have that match the requirements of a future job interest. Perform the following tasks:

a. Create a new presentation in Sway to use as a digital resume. Title the Sway Storyline with your full name and then select a background image.
b. Create three separate sections titled **Academic Background, Work Experience**, and **Skills**, and insert text, a picture, and a paragraph or bulleted points in each section. Be sure to include your own picture.
c. Add a fourth section that includes a video about your school that you find online.
d. Customize the design of your presentation.
e. Submit your assignment link in the format specified by your instructor.

2: Creating an Online Sway Newsletter

Newsletters are designed to capture the attention of their target audience. Using Sway, create a newsletter for a club, organization, or your favorite music group. Perform the following tasks:

a. Create a new presentation in Sway to use as a digital newsletter for a club, organization, or your favorite music group. Provide a title for the Sway Storyline and select an appropriate background image.
b. Select three separate sections with appropriate titles, such as Upcoming Events. In each section, insert text, a picture, and a paragraph or bulleted points.
c. Add a fourth section that includes a video about your selected topic.
d. Customize the design of your presentation.
e. Submit your assignment link in the format specified by your instructor.

3: Creating and Sharing a Technology Presentation

To place a Sway presentation in the hands of your entire audience, you can share a link to the Sway presentation. Create a Sway presentation on a new technology and share it with your class. Perform the following tasks:

a. Create a new presentation in Sway about a cutting-edge technology topic. Provide a title for the Sway Storyline and select a background image.
b. Create four separate sections about your topic, and include text, a picture, and a paragraph in each section.
c. Add a fifth section that includes a video about your topic.
d. Customize the design of your presentation.
e. Share the link to your Sway with your classmates and submit your assignment link in the format specified by your instructor.

Introduction to Office Mix

add-in | clip | slide recording | Slide Notes | screen recording | free-response quiz

To enliven business meetings and lectures, Microsoft adds a new dimension to presentations with a powerful toolset called Office Mix, a free add-in for PowerPoint. (An **add-in** is software that works with an installed app to extend its features.) Using Office Mix, you can record yourself on video, capture still and moving images on your desktop, and insert interactive elements such as quizzes and live webpages directly into PowerPoint slides. When you post the finished presentation to OneDrive, Office Mix provides a link you can share with friends and colleagues. Anyone with an Internet connection and a web browser can watch a published Office Mix presentation, such as the one in **Figure 10**, on a computer or mobile device.

Figure 10: Office Mix presentation

Adding Office Mix to PowerPoint

To get started, you create an Office Mix account at the website mix.office.com using an email address or a Facebook or Google account. Next, you download and install the Office Mix add-in (see **Figure 11**). Office Mix appears as a new tab named Mix on the PowerPoint ribbon in versions of Office 2013 and Office 2016 running on personal computers (PCs).

Figure 11: Getting started with Office Mix

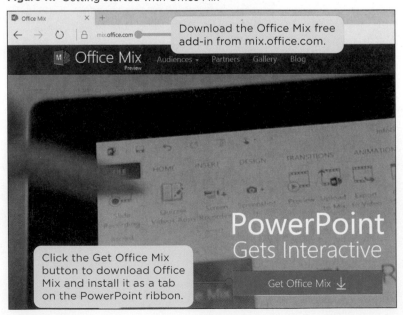

Capturing Video Clips

A **clip** is a short segment of audio, such as music, or video. After finishing the content on a PowerPoint slide, you can use Office Mix to add a video clip to animate or illustrate the content. Office Mix creates video clips in two ways: by recording live action on a webcam and by capturing screen images and movements. If your computer has a webcam, you can record yourself and annotate the slide to create a **slide recording** as shown in **Figure 12**.

Figure 12: Making a slide recording

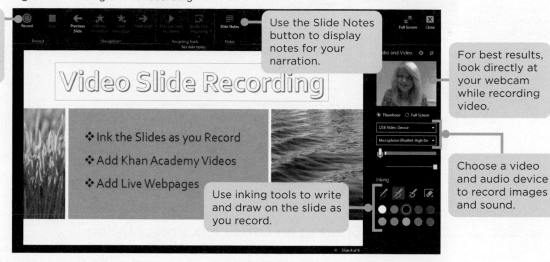

Record your voice; also record video if your computer has a camera.

Use the Slide Notes button to display notes for your narration.

For best results, look directly at your webcam while recording video.

Ink the Slides as you Record

Add Khan Academy Videos

Add Live Webpages

Use inking tools to write and draw on the slide as you record.

Choose a video and audio device to record images and sound.

When you are making a slide recording, you can record your spoken narration at the same time. The **Slide Notes** feature works like a teleprompter to help you focus on your presentation content instead of memorizing your narration. Use the Inking tools to make annotations or add highlighting using different pen types and colors. After finishing a recording, edit the video in PowerPoint to trim the length or set playback options.

The second way to create a video is to capture on-screen images and actions with or without a voiceover. This method is ideal if you want to show how to use your favorite website or demonstrate an app such as OneNote. To share your screen with an audience, select the part of the screen you want to show in the video. Office Mix captures everything that happens in that area to create a **screen recording**, as shown in **Figure 13**. Office Mix inserts the screen recording as a video in the slide.

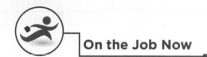
Figure 13: Making a screen recording

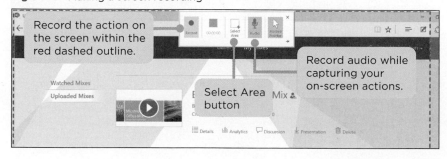

Record the action on the screen within the red dashed outline.

Record audio while capturing your on-screen actions.

Select Area button

Inserting Quizzes, Live Webpages, and Apps

To enhance and assess audience understanding, make your slides interactive by adding quizzes, live webpages, and apps. Quizzes give immediate feedback to the user as shown in **Figure 14**. Office Mix supports several quiz formats, including a **free-response quiz** similar to a short answer quiz, and true/false, multiple-choice, and multiple-response formats.

Figure 14: Creating an interactive quiz

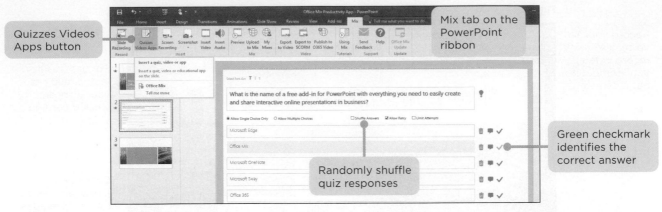

Sharing an Office Mix Presentation

When you complete your work with Office Mix, upload the presentation to your personal Office Mix dashboard as shown in **Figure 15**. Users of PCs, Macs, iOS devices, and Android devices can access and play Office Mix presentations. The Office Mix dashboard displays built-in analytics that include the quiz results and how much time viewers spent on each slide. You can play completed Office Mix presentations online or download them as movies.

Figure 15: Sharing an Office Mix presentation

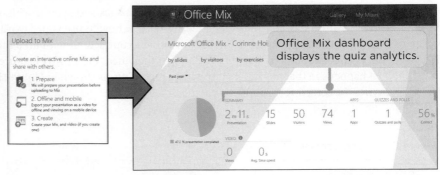

Try This Now

1: Creating an Office Mix Tutorial for OneNote

Note: This activity requires a microphone on your computer.

Office Mix makes it easy to record screens and their contents. Create PowerPoint slides with an Office Mix screen recording to show OneNote 2016 features. Perform the following tasks:

a. Create a PowerPoint presentation with the Ion Boardroom template. Create an opening slide with the title **My Favorite OneNote Features** and enter your name in the subtitle.
b. Create three additional slides, each titled with a new feature of OneNote. Open OneNote and use the Mix tab in PowerPoint to capture three separate screen recordings that teach your favorite features.
c. Add a fifth slide that quizzes the user with a multiple-choice question about OneNote and includes four responses. Be sure to insert a checkmark indicating the correct response.
d. Upload the completed presentation to your Office Mix dashboard and share the link with your instructor.
e. Submit your assignment link in the format specified by your instructor.

2: Teaching Augmented Reality with Office Mix

Note: This activity requires a webcam or built-in video camera on your computer.

A local elementary school has asked you to teach augmented reality to its students using Office Mix. Perform the following tasks:

a. Research augmented reality using your favorite online search tools.
b. Create a PowerPoint presentation with the Frame template. Create an opening slide with the title **Augmented Reality** and enter your name in the subtitle.
c. Create a slide with four bullets summarizing your research of augmented reality. Create a 20-second slide recording of yourself providing a quick overview of augmented reality.
d. Create another slide with a 30-second screen recording of a video about augmented reality from a site such as YouTube or another video-sharing site.
e. Add a final slide that quizzes the user with a true/false question about augmented reality. Be sure to insert a checkmark indicating the correct response.
f. Upload the completed presentation to your Office Mix dashboard and share the link with your instructor.
g. Submit your assignment link in the format specified by your instructor.

3: Marketing a Travel Destination with Office Mix

Note: This activity requires a webcam or built-in video camera on your computer.

To convince your audience to travel to a particular city, create a slide presentation marketing any city in the world using a slide recording, screen recording, and a quiz. Perform the following tasks:

a. Create a PowerPoint presentation with any template. Create an opening slide with the title of the city you are marketing as a travel destination and your name in the subtitle.
b. Create a slide with four bullets about the featured city. Create a 30-second slide recording of yourself explaining why this city is the perfect vacation destination.
c. Create another slide with a 20-second screen recording of a travel video about the city from a site such as YouTube or another video-sharing site.
d. Add a final slide that quizzes the user with a multiple-choice question about the featured city with five responses. Be sure to include a checkmark indicating the correct response.
e. Upload the completed presentation to your Office Mix dashboard and share your link with your instructor.
f. Submit your assignment link in the format specified by your instructor.

Introduction to Microsoft Edge

Reading view | Hub | Cortana | Web Note | Inking | sandbox

Bottom Line
- Microsoft Edge is the name of the new web browser built into Windows 10.
- Microsoft Edge allows you to search the web faster, take web notes, read webpages without distractions, and get instant assistance from Cortana.

Microsoft Edge is the default web browser developed for the Windows 10 operating system as a replacement for Internet Explorer. Unlike its predecessor, Edge lets you write on webpages, read webpages without advertisements and other distractions, and search for information using a virtual personal assistant. The Edge interface is clean and basic, as shown in **Figure 16**, meaning you can pay more attention to the webpage content.

Figure 16: Microsoft Edge tools

Forward button · New tab button · Web address in the Address bar · Add to favorites or reading list button · Reading view button · More button · Back button · Share Web Note button · Make a Web Note button · Refresh (F5) button · Hub (Favorites, reading list, history, and downloads) button

Browsing the Web with Microsoft Edge

One of the fastest browsers available, Edge allows you to type search text directly in the Address bar. As you view the resulting webpage, you can switch to **Reading view**, which is available for most news and research sites, to eliminate distracting advertisements. For example, if you are catching up on technology news online, the webpage might be difficult to read due to a busy layout cluttered with ads. Switch to Reading view to refresh the page and remove the original page formatting, ads, and menu sidebars to read the article distraction-free.

Consider the **Hub** in Microsoft Edge as providing one-stop access to all the things you collect on the web, such as your favorite websites, reading list, surfing history, and downloaded files.

Learn to use Edge!
Links to companion **Sways**, featuring **videos** with hands-on instructions, are located on www.cengagebrain.com.

On the Job Now
Businesses started adopting Internet Explorer more than 20 years ago simply to view webpages. Today, Microsoft Edge has a different purpose: to promote interaction with the web and share its contents with colleagues.

Locating Information with Cortana

Cortana, the Windows 10 virtual assistant, plays an important role in Microsoft Edge. After you turn on Cortana, it appears as an animated circle in the Address bar when you might need assistance, as shown in the restaurant website in **Figure 17**. When you click the Cortana icon, a pane slides in from the right of the browser window to display detailed information about the restaurant, including maps and reviews. Cortana can also assist you in defining words, finding the weather, suggesting coupons for shopping, updating stock market information, and calculating math.

Figure 17: Cortana providing restaurant information

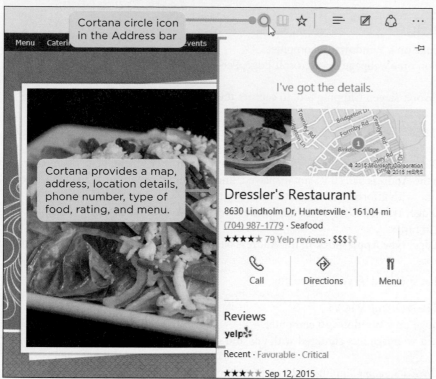

Figure 17: Cortana providing restaurant information

Annotating Webpages

One of the most impressive Microsoft Edge features are the **Web Note** tools, which you use to write on a webpage or to highlight text. When you click the Make a Web Note button, an **Inking** toolbar appears, as shown in **Figure 18**, that provides writing and drawing tools. These tools include an eraser, a pen, and a highlighter with different colors. You can also insert a typed note and copy a screen image (called a screen clipping). You can draw with a pointing device, fingertip, or stylus using different pen colors. Whether you add notes to a recipe, annotate sources for a research paper, or select a product while shopping online, the Web Note tools can enhance your productivity. After you complete your notes, click the Save button to save the annotations to OneNote, your Favorites list, or your Reading list. You can share the inked page with others using the Share Web Note button.

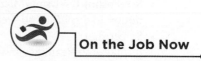

On the Job Now

To enhance security, Microsoft Edge runs in a partial sandbox, an arrangement that prevents attackers from gaining control of your computer. Browsing within the **sandbox** protects computer resources and information from hackers.

Figure 18: Web Note tools in Microsoft Edge

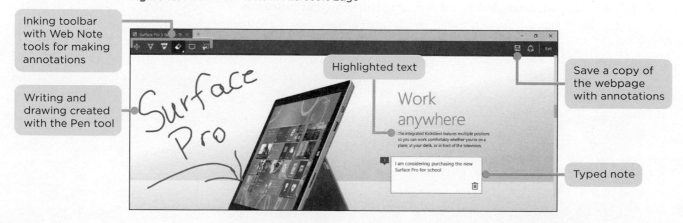

Try This Now

1: Using Cortana in Microsoft Edge

Note: This activity requires using Microsoft Edge on a Windows 10 computer.

Cortana can assist you in finding information on a webpage in Microsoft Edge. Perform the following tasks:

a. Create a Word document using the Word Screen Clipping tool to capture the following screenshots.

- Screenshot A—Using Microsoft Edge, open a webpage with a technology news article. Right-click a term in the article and ask Cortana to define it.
- Screenshot B—Using Microsoft Edge, open the website of a fancy restaurant in a city near you. Make sure the Cortana circle icon is displayed in the Address bar. (If it's not displayed, find a different restaurant website.) Click the Cortana circle icon to display a pane with information about the restaurant.
- Screenshot C—Using Microsoft Edge, type **10 USD to Euros** in the Address bar without pressing the Enter key. Cortana converts the U.S. dollars to Euros.
- Screenshot D—Using Microsoft Edge, type **Apple stock** in the Address bar without pressing the Enter key. Cortana displays the current stock quote.

b. Submit your assignment in the format specified by your instructor.

2: Viewing Online News with Reading View

Note: This activity requires using Microsoft Edge on a Windows 10 computer.

Reading view in Microsoft Edge can make a webpage less cluttered with ads and other distractions. Perform the following tasks:

a. Create a Word document using the Word Screen Clipping tool to capture the following screenshots.

- Screenshot A—Using Microsoft Edge, open the website **mashable.com**. Open a technology article. Click the Reading view button to display an ad-free page that uses only basic text formatting.
- Screenshot B—Using Microsoft Edge, open the website **bbc.com**. Open any news article. Click the Reading view button to display an ad-free page that uses only basic text formatting.
- Screenshot C—Make three types of annotations (Pen, Highlighter, and Add a typed note) on the BBC article page displayed in Reading view.

b. Submit your assignment in the format specified by your instructor.

3: Inking with Microsoft Edge

Note: This activity requires using Microsoft Edge on a Windows 10 computer.

Microsoft Edge provides many annotation options to record your ideas. Perform the following tasks:

a. Open the website **wolframalpha.com** in the Microsoft Edge browser. Wolfram Alpha is a well-respected academic search engine. Type **US$100 1965 dollars in 2015** in the Wolfram Alpha search text box and press the Enter key.

b. Click the Make a Web Note button to display the Web Note tools. Using the Pen tool, draw a circle around the result on the webpage. Save the page to OneNote.

c. In the Wolfram Alpha search text box, type the name of the city closest to where you live and press the Enter key. Using the Highlighter tool, highlight at least three interesting results. Add a note and then type a sentence about what you learned about this city. Save the page to OneNote. Share your OneNote notebook with your instructor.

d. Submit your assignment link in the format specified by your instructor.

OBJECTIVES

- Plan the organization of files and folders
- Use File Explorer to view and manage folders and files
- Open and save files
- Create folders
- Copy and move files and folders
- Find files and information with Cortana
- Compress and extract files

Managing Your Files

Organizing Files and Folders with Windows 10

Case | *Miami Trolleys*

After college, Diego and Anita Marino moved to Miami, Florida, and started Miami Trolleys, a sightseeing company that provides guided tours of Miami on a hop-on, hop-off trolley. As marketing manager, Diego is in charge of creating resources that describe the tours and sights in Miami. He hired you to help him develop marketing materials and use computer tools to organize photos, illustrations, and text documents to promote the business. For your first task, Diego asks you to organize the files on his new computer. Although he has only a few files, he wants to use a logical organization to help him find his work as he stores more files and folders on the computer.

In this module, you'll work with Diego to devise a strategy for managing files. You'll learn how Windows 10 organizes files and folders, and you'll examine Windows 10 file management tools. You'll create folders and organize files within them. You'll also use techniques to display the information you need in folder windows and explore options for working with compressed files.

> **Note:** With the release of Windows 10, Microsoft is taking a new approach to software publication called "Windows as a Service." With this approach, Microsoft is constantly providing updates to Windows instead of releasing new versions periodically. This means that Windows features might change over time, including how they look and how you interact with them. The information provided in this text was accurate at the time this book was published.

STARTING DATA FILES

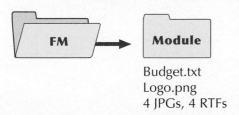

FM →	Module	Review	Case1	Case2
	Budget.txt	Background.png	Designers.txt	Estimate Tips.txt
	Logo.png	Events.xlsx	4 JPGs, 5 RTFs	Plan Projects.txt
	4 JPGs, 4 RTFs	2 JPGs, 3 RTFs		4 RTFs, 6 XLSXs

Visual Overview:

The **Quick Access Toolbar** contains buttons for viewing the properties of a file or folder, creating a new folder, and customizing the toolbar.

The **View tab** provides options for specifying how File Explorer and its contents are displayed.

The **file path** is a notation that indicates a file's location on your computer.

File Explorer includes a ribbon with tools organized on tabs for working with files and folders.

The **Quick access list** shows the folders you used frequently and recently.

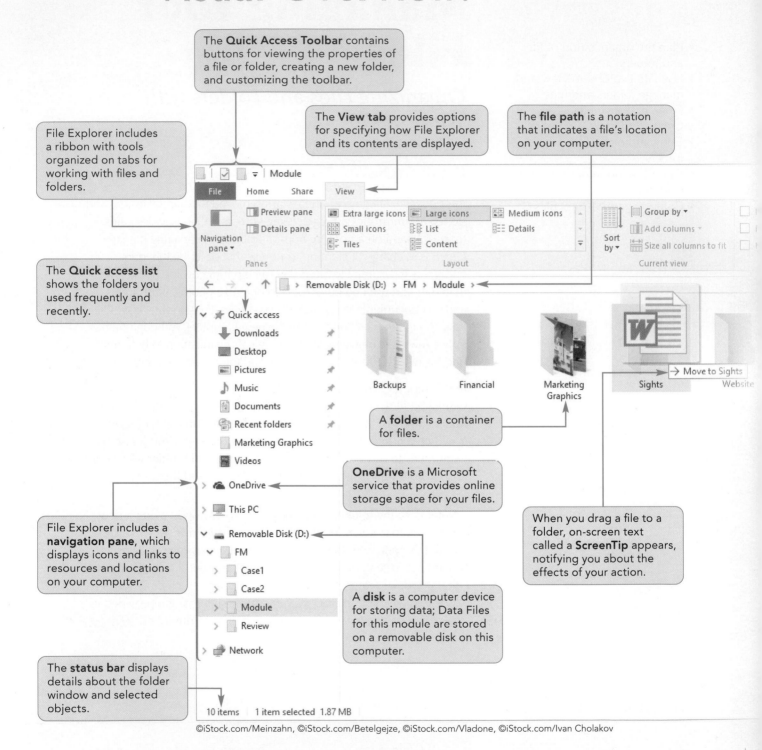

A **folder** is a container for files.

OneDrive is a Microsoft service that provides online storage space for your files.

File Explorer includes a **navigation pane**, which displays icons and links to resources and locations on your computer.

When you drag a file to a folder, on-screen text called a **ScreenTip** appears, notifying you about the effects of your action.

A **disk** is a computer device for storing data; Data Files for this module are stored on a removable disk on this computer.

The **status bar** displays details about the folder window and selected objects.

Files in a Folder Window

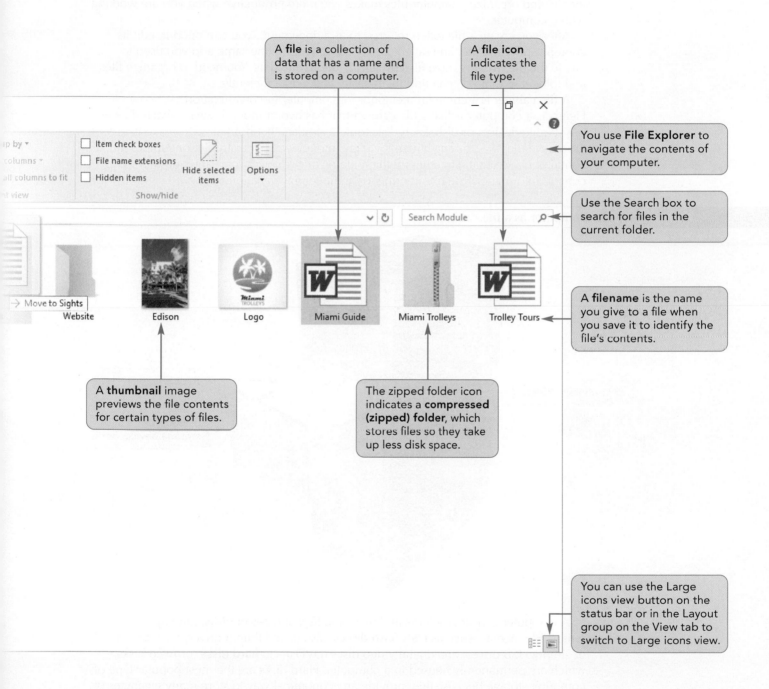

A **file** is a collection of data that has a name and is stored on a computer.

A **file icon** indicates the file type.

You use **File Explorer** to navigate the contents of your computer.

Use the Search box to search for files in the current folder.

A **filename** is the name you give to a file when you save it to identify the file's contents.

A **thumbnail** image previews the file contents for certain types of files.

The zipped folder icon indicates a **compressed (zipped) folder**, which stores files so they take up less disk space.

You can use the Large icons view button on the status bar or in the Layout group on the View tab to switch to Large icons view.

Organizing Files and Folders

Your typical computer session usually begins with starting an app and opening a file. You view, add, or change the file contents, and then save and close the file. Because most of your work involves files, you need to understand how to save and organize files, so you can easily find and open them when necessary. Knowing how to save, locate, and organize computer files makes you more productive when you are working with a computer.

After you create a file (often referred to as a document), you can open it, edit its contents, print the file, and save it again—usually using the same app you used to create the file. You organize files by storing them in folders. You need to organize files and folders so that you can find them easily and work efficiently.

A file cabinet is a common metaphor for computer file organization. As shown in Figure 1, a computer is like a file cabinet that has two or more drawers—each drawer is a storage device, or disk. Each disk contains folders that hold files. To make it easy to retrieve files, you arrange them logically into folders. For example, one folder might contain financial data, another might contain your creative work, and another could contain information you're gathering for an upcoming vacation.

| Figure 1 | Computer as a file cabinet |

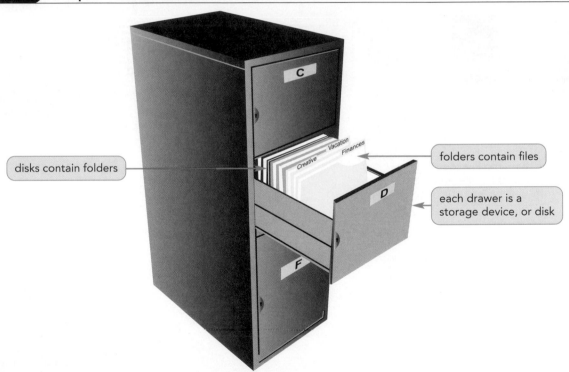

disks contain folders

folders contain files

each drawer is a storage device, or disk

A computer can store folders and files on different types of disks, ranging from removable media—such as **USB flash drives** (also called thumb drives, flash drives, or simply USB drives) and digital video discs (DVDs)—to **hard disks**, or fixed disks, which are permanently housed in a computer. Hard disks are the most popular type of computer storage because they provide an economical way to store many gigabytes of data. (A **gigabyte**, or **GB**, is about 1 billion bytes, with each byte roughly equivalent to a character of data.)

To have your computer access a removable disk, you must insert the disk into a **drive**, which is a device that can retrieve and sometimes record data on a disk. A computer's hard disk is already contained in a drive inside the computer, so you don't need to insert it each time you use the computer.

A computer distinguishes one drive from another by assigning each a drive letter. The hard disk is assigned to drive C. The remaining drives can have any other letters but are usually assigned in the order that the drives were installed on the computer—so your USB drive might be drive D, drive E, or drive F.

If you are using a tablet or a recent-model laptop, it might not have drives for removable disks. Instead, you store files on the hard disk or in the **cloud**, a location on a large computer called a **server**, which you access through the Internet or other network. (A **network** is two or more computers connected together to share resources.) As a Windows 10 user, you probably have OneDrive, a Microsoft service that provides access to a server where you can store your files instead of using a hard disk or removable disk. Your school might also provide a cloud location for storing your files.

Understanding How to Organize Files and Folders

Windows 10 stores thousands of files in many folders on the hard disk of your computer. Windows 10 needs these system files to display the desktop, use drives, and perform other operating system tasks. To keep the system stable and to find files quickly, Windows organizes the folders and files in a hierarchy, or **file system**. At the top of the hierarchy, Windows stores folders and important files that it needs when you turn on the computer. This location, called the **root directory**, is usually drive C (the hard disk). As Figure 2 shows, the root directory contains all the other folders and files on the computer. The figure also shows that folders can contain other folders. An effectively organized computer contains a few folders in the root directory, and those folders contain other folders, also called **subfolders**.

| Figure 2 | Organizing folders and files on a hard disk |

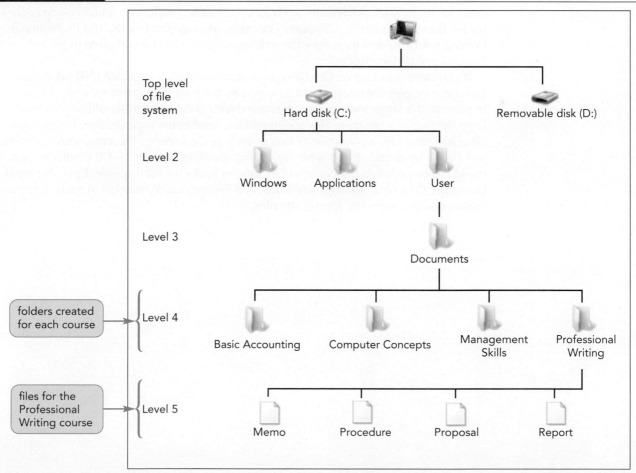

Root Directory in a File System

The root directory in the Windows file system is for system files and folders only. You should not store your own work in the root directory because your files could interfere with Windows or an app. (If you are working in a computer lab, you might not be allowed to access the root directory.)

Do not delete or move any files or folders from the root directory of the hard disk; doing so could disrupt the system so that you can't start or run the computer. In fact, you should not reorganize or change any folder that contains installed software because Windows 10 expects to find the files for specific apps within certain folders.

In Figure 2, folders containing software are stored at level 2 of the file system. If you reorganize or change these folders, Windows 10 can't locate and start the apps stored in those folders. Likewise, you should not make changes to the folder (usually named Windows) that contains the Windows 10 operating system.

Level 2 of the file system also includes a folder for your user account, such as the User folder. This folder contains all of your system settings, preferences, and other user account information. It also contains subfolders, such as the Documents folder, for your personal files.

The folders in level 3 of the file system are designed to contain subfolders for your personal files. You can create as many subfolders at level 4 of the file system as you need to store other folders and files and keep them organized.

Figure 2 shows how you could organize your files on a hard disk if you were taking a full semester of business classes. To duplicate this organization, you would open the main folder for your documents, such as Documents, create four folders—one each for the Basic Accounting, Computer Concepts, Management Skills, and Professional Writing courses—and then store the writing assignments you complete in the Professional Writing folder.

If you store your files on OneDrive or removable media, such as a USB drive, you can use a simpler organization because you do not have to account for system files. In general, the larger the medium, the more levels of folders you should use because large media can store more files and, therefore, need better organization. For example, OneDrive provides a collection of folders such as Documents, Favorites, Music, Pictures, and Public by default. If you were organizing your files on your 15 GB OneDrive, you could create folders in the top-level Documents folder for each course (Basic Accounting, Computer Concepts, Management Skills, and Professional Writing), and each of those folders could contain the appropriate files.

Decision Making: Determining Where to Store Files

When you create and save files on your computer's hard disk, you should store them in subfolders. The top level of the hard disk is off-limits for your files because they could interfere with system files. If you are working on your own computer, store your files within the Documents folder, which is where many apps save your files by default. When you use a computer on the job, your employer might assign a main folder to you for storing your work. In either case, if you simply store all your files in one folder, you will soon have trouble finding the files you want. Instead, you should create subfolders within a main folder to separate files in a way that makes sense for you.

Even if you store most of your files in the cloud, such as on OneDrive, or on removable media, such as USB drives, you still need to organize those files into folders and subfolders. Before you start creating folders in any location, you need to plan the organization you will use. Following your plan increases your efficiency because you don't have to pause and decide which folder to use when you save your files. A file organization plan also makes you more productive in your computer work—the next time you need a particular file, you'll know where to find it.

Exploring Files and Folders

As shown in the Visual Overview, you use File Explorer to explore the files and folders on your computer. File Explorer displays the contents of your computer by using icons to represent drives, folders, and files. When you start File Explorer, it opens to show the contents of the Quick access list, which are the folders and files you used frequently and recently, making it easy to find the files you work with often.

The File Explorer window is divided into two sections, called panes. The left pane is the navigation pane, which contains icons and links to locations on your computer. The right pane displays the contents of the location selected in the navigation pane. If the navigation pane showed all the contents on your computer at once, it could be a very long list. Instead, you open drives and folders only when you want to see what they contain. For example, to display the hierarchy of the folders and other locations on your computer, you select the This PC icon in the navigation pane, and then select the icon for a drive, such as OS (C:) or Removable Disk (D:). (The OS stands for operating system.) You can then open and explore folders on that drive.

If a folder contains undisplayed subfolders, an expand icon appears to the left of the folder icon. (The same is true for drives.) To view the folders contained in an object, you click the expand icon. A collapse icon then appears next to the folder icon; click the collapse icon to hide the folder's subfolders. To view the files contained in a folder, you click the folder icon, and the files appear in the right pane. See Figure 3.

Figure 3	Viewing files in File Explorer

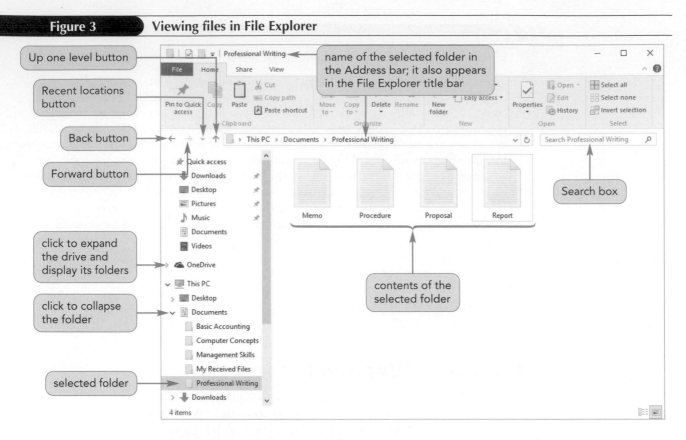

Using the navigation pane helps you explore your computer and orients you to your current location. As you move, copy, delete, and perform other tasks with the files and folders in the right pane of File Explorer, you can refer to the navigation pane to see how your changes affect the overall organization.

In addition to using the navigation pane, you can explore your computer in File Explorer using the following navigation techniques:

- Opening drives and folders in the right pane—To view the contents of a drive or folder, double-click the drive or folder icon in the right pane of File Explorer.
- Using the Address bar—You can use the Address bar to navigate to a different folder. The Address bar displays the file path for your current folder. (Recall that a file path shows the location of a folder or file.) Click a folder name such as Documents in the Address bar to navigate to that folder, or click an arrow button to navigate to a different location in the folder's hierarchy.
- Clicking the Back, Forward, Recent locations, and Up to buttons—Use the Back, Forward, and Recent locations buttons to navigate to other folders you have already opened. Use the Up to button to navigate up to the folder containing the current folder.
- Using the Search box—To find a file or folder stored in the current folder or its subfolders, type a word or phrase in the Search box. The search begins as soon as you start typing. Windows finds files based on text in the filename, text within the file, and other properties of the file.

You'll practice using some of these navigation techniques later in the module. Right now, you'll show Diego how to open File Explorer and then navigate to the Documents folder using the Quick access list and the This PC icon. Your computer should be turned on and displaying the desktop.

To open File Explorer:

1. Click the **File Explorer** button ▢ on the taskbar. The File Explorer window opens, displaying the contents of the Quick access list.

2. Click the **Documents** icon in the navigation pane to display its contents in the right pane. See Figure 4. The contents of your computer will differ.

   Trouble? If your window displays icons in a view different from the one shown in the figure, you can still explore files and folders. The same is true for all figures in this session.

| Figure 4 | Contents of the Documents folder |

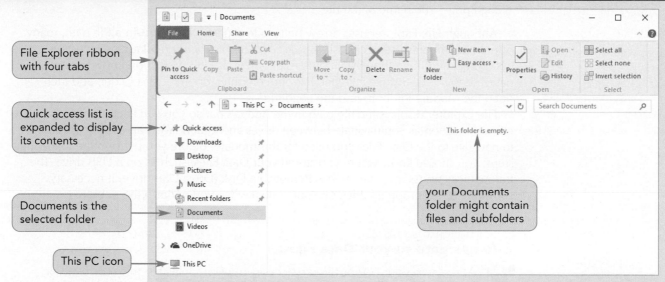

File Explorer ribbon with four tabs

Quick access list is expanded to display its contents

Documents is the selected folder

This PC icon

This folder is empty.

your Documents folder might contain files and subfolders

TIP

When you are working in the navigation pane, you only need to click a folder or drive to open it, not double-click it.

3. In the navigation pane of the open folder window, click the **This PC** icon. The right pane displays the devices and drives on the computer and the locations for storing your work files, including the Documents folder.

4. In the right pane, double-click the **Documents** folder to display its contents.

The Documents folder is designed to store your files—the notes, reports, spreadsheets, presentations, and other files that you create, edit, and manipulate in an app. The Quick access list provides access to folders that most users open frequently. In addition to the Documents folder, This PC displays other default folders, such as the Pictures folder and the Music folder. Although the Pictures folder is designed to store graphics and the Music folder is designed to store music files, you can store graphics, music, or any other type of file in the Documents folder, especially if doing so makes it easier to find these files when you need them. As you create more folders, they are listed in the navigation pane.

Navigating to Your Data Files

To navigate to the files you want, it helps to know the file path because it tells you exactly where the file is stored in the hierarchy of drives and folders on your computer. For example, the Logo file is stored in the Module subfolder of the FM folder. If you are working on a USB drive, for example, the Address bar would show the following file path for the Logo file:

Removable Disk (D:) > FM > Module > Logo.png

This path has four parts, with each part separated by an arrow button:

- Removable Disk (D:)—The drive name, including the drive letter followed by a colon, which indicates a drive rather than a folder
- FM—The top-level folder on drive D
- Module—A subfolder in the FM folder
- Logo.png—The name of the file

Although File Explorer uses arrow buttons to separate locations in a file path, many printed documents use backslashes (\ ). For example, if you read an instruction to open the Logo file in the FM\Module folder on your USB drive, you know you must navigate to the USB drive attached to your computer, open the FM folder, and then open the Module folder to find the Logo file.

File Explorer displays the file path in the Address bar so you can keep track of your current location as you navigate between drives and folders. You can use File Explorer to navigate to the Data Files you need for this module. Before you perform the following steps, you should know where you stored your Data Files, such as on a USB drive. The following steps assume that drive is Removable Disk (D:), a USB drive. If necessary, substitute the appropriate drive on your system when you perform the steps.

To navigate to your Data Files:

1. Make sure your computer can access your Data Files for this module. For example, if you are using a USB drive, insert the drive into the USB port.

   Trouble? If you don't have the starting Data Files, you need to get them before you can proceed. Your instructor will either give you the Data Files or ask you to obtain them from a specified location (such as a network drive). If you have any questions about the Data Files, see your instructor or technical support person for assistance.

2. In the navigation pane of File Explorer, click the **expand** icon ⟩ next to the drive containing your Data Files, such as Removable Disk (D:). A list of the folders on that drive appears below the drive name.

3. If the list of folders does not include the FM folder, continue clicking the **expand** icon ⟩ to navigate to the folder that contains the FM folder.

4. Click the **expand** icon ⟩ next to the FM folder to expand the folder, and then click the **FM** folder so that its contents appear in the navigation pane and in the right pane of the folder window. The FM folder contains the Case1, Case2, Module, and Review folders, as shown in Figure 5. The other folders on your computer might vary.

| Figure 5 | Navigating to the FM folder |

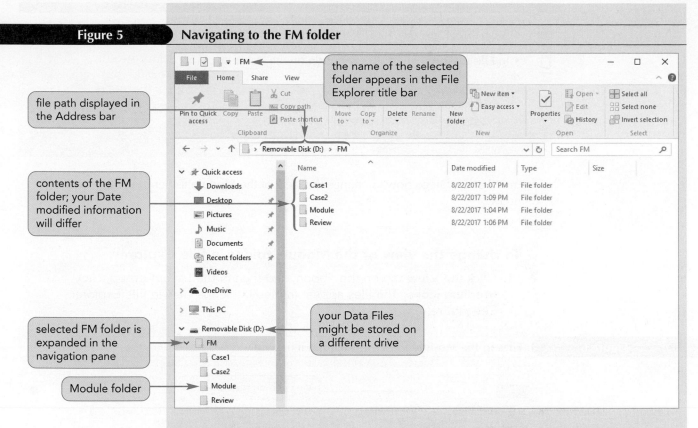

file path displayed in the Address bar

the name of the selected folder appears in the File Explorer title bar

contents of the FM folder; your Date modified information will differ

your Data Files might be stored on a different drive

selected FM folder is expanded in the navigation pane

Module folder

5. In the navigation pane, click the **Module** folder. The files it contains appear in the right pane.

> **Trouble?** If the Module folder does not appear in the navigation pane, you did not click the expand icon next to the FM folder to expand the folder. Click the expand icon [>] next to the FM folder, and then repeat Step 5.

Before you begin working with individual files and folders, you might want to change the appearance of the File Explorer window to suit your preferences. You'll do so next so you can see more details about folders and files.

Changing the View

File Explorer provides eight ways to view the contents of a folder: Extra large icons, Large icons, Medium icons, Small icons, List, Details, Tiles, and Content. For example, the files in the Module folder are currently displayed in Details view, which is the default view for all folders except those stored in the Pictures folder and its subfolders. Details view displays a small icon to identify each file's type and lists file details in columns, such as the date the file was last modified, the file type, and the size of the file. Although only Details view lists the file details, you can also see these details in any other view by pointing to a file to display a ScreenTip.

To change the view of File Explorer to any of the eight views, you use the View tab on the ribbon. To switch quickly between Details view and Large icons view, you can use the view buttons on the status bar.

REFERENCE

Changing the View in File Explorer

• In File Explorer, click a view button on the status bar.

or

• Click the View tab on the ribbon.

• In the Layout group, point to a view option to preview its effect in the folder window, if necessary, and then click a view option.

You'll show Diego how to change the view of the Module folder in the File Explorer window.

To change the view of the Module folder in File Explorer:

1. Click the **View** tab on the ribbon, and then in the Layout group, click **Medium icons**. The files appear in Medium icons view in File Explorer. See Figure 6.

Figure 6	Files in the Module folder in Medium icons view

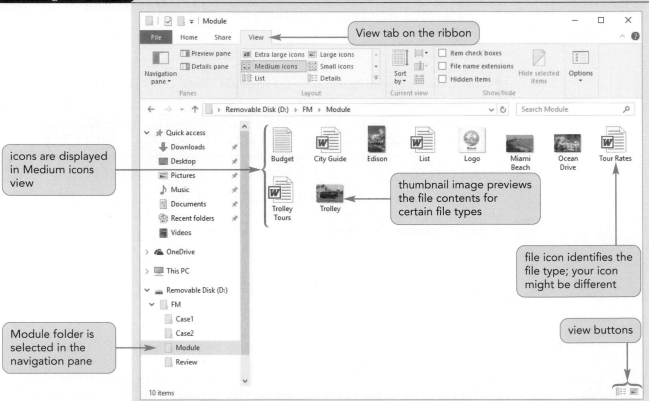

©iStock.com/Meinzahn, ©iStock.com/Betelgejze, ©iStock.com/bosenok, ©iStock.com/Vladone, ©iStock.com/Ivan Cholakov

Trouble? Because the icons used to identify types of files depend on the apps installed on your computer, the file icons that appear in your window might be different.

TIP

When you change the view, it applies only to the current folder.

> **2.** On the status bar, click the **Large icons view** button 🔲. The window shows the files with large icons and no file details.

> **3.** On the status bar, click the **Details view** button 🔡. The window shows the files with small icons and lists the file details.

No matter which view you use, you can sort the file list by the name of the files (the default sort order) or another detail, such as size, type, or date. When you **sort** files, you list them in ascending order (A to Z, 0 to 9, or earliest to latest date) or descending order (Z to A, 9 to 0, or latest to earliest date) by a file detail. If you're viewing music files, you can sort by details such as contributing artists or album title; if you're viewing picture files, you can sort by details such as date taken or size. Sorting can help you find a particular file in a long file listing. For example, suppose you want to work on a document that you know you edited on June 18, 2017, but you can't remember the name of the file. You can sort the file list by date modified to find the file you want.

When you are working in Details view in File Explorer, you sort a list of folders and files by clicking a column heading that appears at the top of the list. In other views, you use the View tab on the ribbon to sort. In the Current view group, click the Sort by button, and then click a file detail.

TIP

To sort by a file detail that does not appear as a column heading, right-click any column heading and then select a file detail on the shortcut menu.

To sort the file list by date modified:

> **1.** At the top of the file list, click the **Date modified** column heading. The down arrow that appears above the label of the column heading indicates that the files are sorted in descending (newest to oldest) order by the date the file was modified. At the top of the list is the List file, which was modified on August 18, 2017.
>
> **Trouble?** If your folder window does not contain a Date modified column, right-click any column heading, click Date modified on the shortcut menu, and then repeat Step 1.

> **2.** Click the **Date modified** column heading again. The up arrow above the Date modified label indicates that the sort order is reversed, with the files listed in ascending (oldest to newest) order.

> **3.** Click the **Name** column heading to sort the files in alphabetical order by name. The Budget file is now listed first.

Now that Diego is comfortable working in File Explorer, you're ready to show him how to manage his files and folders.

Managing Files and Folders

As discussed earlier, you manage your personal files and folders by storing them according to a logical organization so that they are easy to find later. You can organize files as you create, edit, and save them, or you can do so later by creating folders, if necessary, and then moving and copying files into the folders.

To create a file-organization plan for Diego's files, you can begin by reviewing Figure 6 to look for files that logically belong together. In the Module folder, Edison, Logo, Miami Beach, Ocean Drive, and Trolley are all graphics files that Diego uses for marketing Miami Trolleys. The City Guide and Trolley Tours files contain descriptions of sights in Miami for customers. The Budget and Tour Rates files relate to business finances. Diego thinks the List file contains a task list for creating a website, but he isn't sure of its contents. He does recall creating the file using WordPad, a text-editing tool provided with Windows 10.

If the List file does contain a website task list, you can organize the files by creating four folders—one for graphics, one for tours, another for the financial files, and a fourth folder for files about the website. When you create a folder, you give it a name, preferably one that describes its contents. A folder name can have up to 255 characters, and any character is allowed, except / \ : * ? " < > and |. Considering these conventions, you could create four folders to contain Diego's files, as follows:

- Marketing Graphics folder—Edison, Logo, Miami Beach, Ocean Drive, and Trolley files
- Sights folder—City Guide and Trolley Tours files
- Financial folder—Budget and Tour Rates files
- Website folder—List file

Before you start creating folders according to this plan, you need to verify the contents of the List file. You can do so by opening the file.

Opening a File

You can open a file from a running app or from File Explorer. To open a file in a running app, you select the app's Open command to access the Open dialog box, which you use to navigate to the file you want, select the file, and then open it. In the Open dialog box, you use the same tools that are available in File Explorer to navigate to the file you want to open. If the app you want to use is not running, you can open a file by double-clicking it in the right pane of File Explorer. The file usually opens in the app that you used to create or edit it.

Diego says that he might want to edit the List file to add another task. You'll show him how to use File Explorer to open and edit the file in WordPad, which he used to create the file.

TIP

In File Explorer, you can also double-click a file to open it in the default app for that file type.

To open and edit the List file:

1. In the right pane of File Explorer, right-click the **List** file, and then click **Open with** on the shortcut menu to display the How do you want to open this file? dialog box, which lists apps that can open the file.

   Trouble? If a shortcut menu appears when you click Open with, click WordPad and skip Step 2. If WordPad is not an option on the shortcut menu, click Choose another app, click More apps, scroll down the list if necessary to display WordPad, and then continue with Step 2.

2. Click **WordPad** and then click the **OK** button to open the List file in WordPad. The file contains a task list for the Miami Trolleys website, which includes three items.

   Trouble? If the dialog box does not include WordPad, click More apps, scroll down the list, click WordPad, and then click the OK button.

3. Press the **Ctrl+End** keys to move the insertion point to the end of the document, press the **Enter** key if necessary to start a new line, and then type **4. Include tool for customer comments.**

Now that you've added text to the List file, you need to save it to preserve the changes you made.

Saving a File

As you are creating or editing a file, you should save it frequently so you don't lose your work. When you save a file, you need to decide what name to use for the file and where to store it. Most apps provide a default location for saving a file, which makes it easy to find the file again later. However, you can select a different location depending on where you want to store the file.

Besides a storage location, every file must have a filename, which provides important information about the file, including its contents and purpose. A filename such as Miami Tours.docx has the following three parts:

- Main part of the filename—When you save a file, you need to provide only the main part of the filename, such as "Miami Tours."
- Dot—The dot (.) separates the main part of the filename from the filename extension.
- Filename extension—The **filename extension** includes the three or four characters that follow the dot in the filename and identify the file's type, such as .docx.

The main part of a filename can have up to 255 characters. This gives you plenty of room to name your file accurately enough so that you'll recognize the contents of the file just by looking at the filename. You can use spaces and certain punctuation symbols in your filenames. However, filenames cannot contain the symbols / \ : * ? " < > or | because these characters have special meanings in Windows 10.

Windows and other software add the dot and the extension to a filename, although File Explorer does not display them by default. Instead, File Explorer shows the file icon associated with the filename extension or a thumbnail for some types of files, such as graphics.

When you save a newly created file, you use the Save As dialog box to provide a filename and select a location in which to store the file. You can create a folder for the new file at the same time as you save the file. When you edit a file you saved previously, you can use the app's Save command to save the changes you made to the file, keeping the same name and location. If you want to save the edited file with a different name or in a different location, however, you need to use the Save As dialog box to specify the new name or location.

As with the Open dialog box, you specify the file location in the Save As dialog box using the same navigation techniques and tools that are available in File Explorer. To make sure that the Save As dialog box displays these tools, you might need to click the Browse Folders button to expand the dialog box. In addition, the Save As dialog box always includes a File name box where you specify a filename.

INSIGHT

Saving Files on OneDrive

OneDrive is a Microsoft service that provides up to 15 GB of online storage space for your files by default. You can purchase additional storage space if you need it. Some Windows 10 applications, such as Microsoft Office, include OneDrive as a location for saving and opening files. If you have a Microsoft account, you can select a folder on your OneDrive to save the document online. (If you don't have a Microsoft account, you can sign up for one by visiting the OneDrive website.) Because the file is stored online, it takes up no storage space on your computer and is available from any computer with an Internet connection. You access the document by opening it in an Office application or by visiting the OneDrive website (https://onedrive.live.com/about/en-us/) and then signing in to your Microsoft account. Look for a link or button that lets you display your OneDrive. To share the document with other people, you can send them a link to the document via email. They can use the link to access the document even if they do not have a Microsoft account.

One reason that Diego had trouble remembering the contents of the List file is that "List" is not a descriptive name. A better name for this file is Task List. You will save this document in the Module subfolder of the FM folder provided with your Data Files. You will also use the Save As dialog box to specify a new name for the file as you save it.

To save the List file with a new name:

1. In the WordPad window, click the **File** tab on the ribbon to display commands for working with files.

2. Click **Save as** to open the Save As dialog box, as shown in Figure 7. The Module folder is selected as the storage location for this file because you opened the file from this folder.

   Trouble? If the navigation pane does not appear in the Save As dialog box, click the Browse Folders button. The Browse Folders button toggles to become the Hide Folders button.

Figure 7   Saving a file using the Save As dialog box

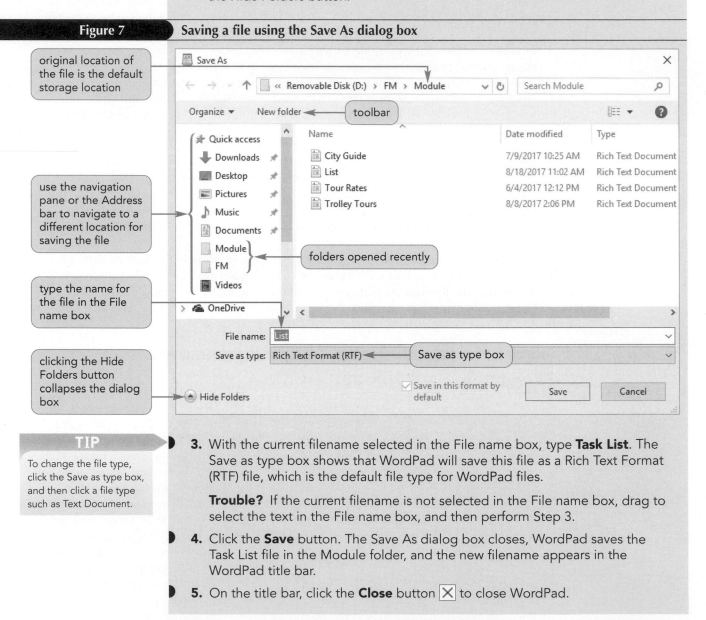

original location of the file is the default storage location

use the navigation pane or the Address bar to navigate to a different location for saving the file

type the name for the file in the File name box

clicking the Hide Folders button collapses the dialog box

toolbar

folders opened recently

Save as type box

TIP

To change the file type, click the Save as type box, and then click a file type such as Text Document.

3. With the current filename selected in the File name box, type **Task List**. The Save as type box shows that WordPad will save this file as a Rich Text Format (RTF) file, which is the default file type for WordPad files.

   Trouble? If the current filename is not selected in the File name box, drag to select the text in the File name box, and then perform Step 3.

4. Click the **Save** button. The Save As dialog box closes, WordPad saves the Task List file in the Module folder, and the new filename appears in the WordPad title bar.

5. On the title bar, click the **Close** button ☒ to close WordPad.

Now you're ready to start creating the folders you need to organize Diego's files.

Creating Folders

You originally proposed creating four new folders for Diego's files: the Marketing Graphics, Sights, Financial, and Website folders. Diego asks you to create these folders now. After that, you'll move his files to the appropriate folders. You create folders in File Explorer using one of three methods: using the New folder button in the New group on the Home tab, using the New folder button on the Quick Access Toolbar, or right-clicking to display a shortcut menu that includes the New command.

INSIGHT

Guidelines for Creating Folders

Keep the following guidelines in mind as you create folders:

- Keep folder names short yet descriptive of the folder's contents. Long folder names can be more difficult to display in their entirety in folder windows, so use names that are short but clear. Choose names that will be meaningful later, such as project names or course numbers.
- Create subfolders to organize files. If a file list in File Explorer is so long that you must scroll the window, you should probably organize those files into subfolders.
- Develop standards for naming folders. Use a consistent naming scheme that is clear to you, such as one that uses a project name as the name of the main folder and includes step numbers in each subfolder name (for example, 1-Outline, 2-First Draft, 3-Final Draft, and so on).

In the following steps, you will create the four folders for Diego in your Module folder. Because it is easier to work with files using large file icons, you'll switch to Large icons view first.

To create folders:

1. On the status bar in the File Explorer window, click the **Large icons view** button 🖿 to switch to Large icons view.

2. Click the **Home** tab on the ribbon.

3. In the New group, click the **New folder** button. A folder icon with the label "New folder" appears in the right pane of the File Explorer window. See Figure 8.

| Figure 8 | Creating a new folder in the Module folder |

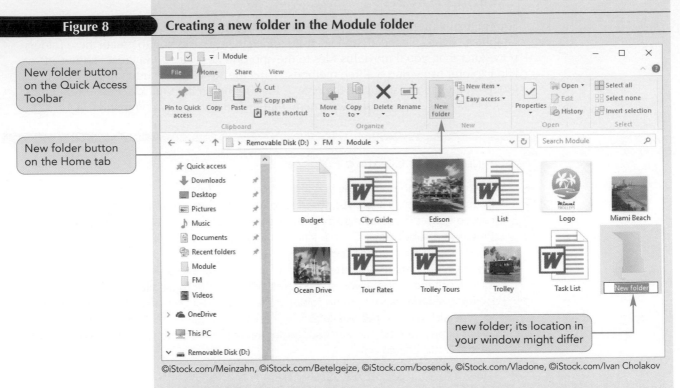

New folder button on the Quick Access Toolbar

New folder button on the Home tab

new folder; its location in your window might differ

©iStock.com/Meinzahn, ©iStock.com/Betelgejze, ©iStock.com/bosenok, ©iStock.com/Vladone, ©iStock.com/Ivan Cholakov

Trouble? If the "New folder" name is not selected, right-click the new folder, click Rename on the shortcut menu, and then continue with Step 4.

Windows uses "New folder" as a placeholder and selects the text so that you can replace it immediately by typing a new name. You do not need to press the Backspace or Delete key to delete the text.

4. Type **Marketing Graphics** as the folder name, and then press the **Enter** key. The new folder is named Marketing Graphics and is the selected item in the right pane. To create a second folder, you can use a shortcut menu.

5. Right-click a blank area in the right pane, point to **New** on the shortcut menu, and then click **Folder**. A folder icon appears in the right pane with the "New folder" text selected.

6. Type **Sights** as the name of the new folder, and then press the **Enter** key. To create the third folder, you can use the Quick Access Toolbar.

7. On the Quick Access Toolbar, click the **New folder** button 🗀, type **Financial**, and then press the **Enter** key to create and name the folder.

8. Using the method you prefer, create the last new subfolder in the Module folder, and name it **Website**.

After creating four folders, you're ready to organize Diego's files by moving them into the appropriate folders.

Moving and Copying Files and Folders

You can either move or copy a file from its current location to a new location. **Moving** a file removes it from its current location and places it in a new location that you specify. **Copying** a file places a duplicate version of the file in a new location that you specify, while leaving the original file intact in its current location. You can also move and copy folders. When you do, you move or copy all the files contained in the folder. (You'll practice moving and copying folders in the Case Problems at the end of this module.)

In File Explorer, you can move and copy files by using the Move to or Copy to buttons in the Organize group on the Home tab, the Copy and Cut commands on a file's shortcut menu, or keyboard shortcuts. When you copy or move files using these methods, you are using the **Clipboard**, a temporary storage area for files and information that you copy or move from one location to place in another.

You can also move files by dragging them in the File Explorer window. You will now organize Diego's files by moving them to the appropriate folders you have created. You'll start by moving the Budget file to the Financial folder by dragging the file.

To move a file by dragging it:

1. In File Explorer, point to the **Budget** file in the right pane, and then press and hold the left mouse button.

2. While still pressing the mouse button, drag the **Budget** file to the **Financial** folder. See Figure 9.

Figure 9	Dragging a file to move it to a folder

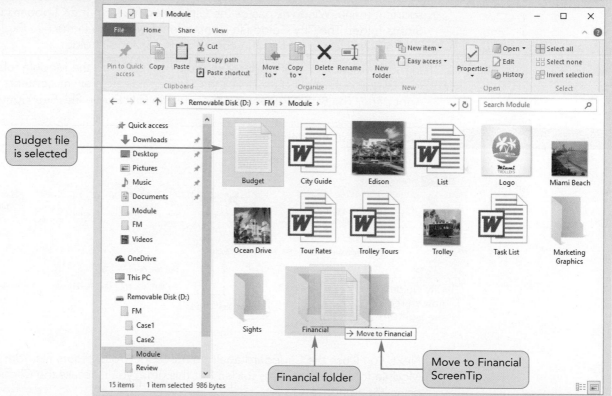

©iStock.com/Meinzahn, ©iStock.com/Betelgejze, ©iStock.com/bosenok, ©iStock.com/Vladone, ©iStock.com/Ivan Cholakov

3. When the Move to Financial ScreenTip appears, release the mouse button. The Budget file is removed from the main Module folder and stored in the Financial subfolder.

   Trouble? If you released the mouse button before the Move to Financial ScreenTip appeared, press the Ctrl+Z keys to undo the move, and then repeat Steps 1–3.

TIP

If you drag a file or folder to a location on a different drive, the file is copied, not moved, to preserve the file in its original location.

Trouble? If you moved a file other than the Budget file, press the Ctrl+Z keys to undo the move, and then repeat Steps 1–3.

4. In the right pane, double-click the **Financial** folder to verify that it contains the Budget file.

    Trouble? If the Budget file does not appear in the Financial folder, you probably moved it to a different folder. Press the Ctrl+Z keys to undo the move, and then repeat Steps 1–4.

5. Click the **Back** button ⬅ in the Address bar to return to the Module folder. Windows sorts the Module folder to list the subfolders first followed by the files.

You'll move the remaining files into the folders using the Clipboard.

To move files using the Clipboard:

1. Right-click the **City Guide** file, and then click **Cut** on the shortcut menu. Although the file icon still appears selected, though dimmed, Windows removes the City Guide file from the Module folder and stores it on the Clipboard.

2. In the right pane, right-click the **Sights** folder, and then click **Paste** on the shortcut menu. Windows pastes the City Guide file from the Clipboard to the Sights folder. The City Guide file icon no longer appears in the File Explorer window, which still displays the contents of the Module folder.

3. In the navigation pane, click the **expand** icon ⟩ next to the Module folder to display its contents, and then click the **Sights** folder to view its contents in the right pane. The Sights folder now contains the City Guide file. See Figure 10.

| Figure 10 | City Guide file in its new location |

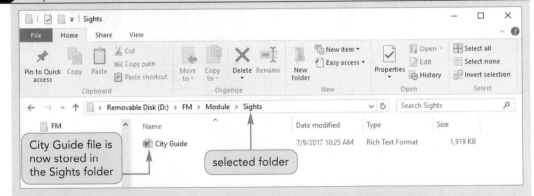

Next, you'll use the Clipboard again to move the Trolley Tours file from the Module folder to the Sights folder. But this time, you'll access the Clipboard using the ribbon.

4. In the Address bar, point to the **Up to** button ⬆ to display its ScreenTip (Up to "Module"), click the **Up to** button ⬆ to return to the Module folder, and then click the **Trolley Tours** file to select it.

    Trouble? If you clicked the Up to button ⬆ twice, click the Module folder in the navigation pane and then click the Trolley Tours file.

5. On the Home tab, in the Clipboard group, click the **Cut** button to remove the Trolley Tours file from the Module folder and temporarily store it on the Clipboard.

▶ **6.** In the navigation pane, click the **Sights** folder to display its contents in the right pane.

▶ **7.** In the Clipboard group, click the **Paste** button to paste the Trolley Tours file in the Sights folder. The Sights folder now contains the City Guide and Trolley Tours files.

Finally, you'll move the Task List file from the Module folder to the Website folder using the Move to button in the Organize group on the Home tab. This button and the Copy to button are ideal when you want to move or copy files without leaving the current folder. When you select a file and then click the Move to or Copy to button, a list of locations appears, including the Windows standard folders (Documents, Pictures, Music, and Videos) and one or more folders you open frequently. You can click a location in the list to move the selected file to that folder. You can also select the Choose location option to open the Move Items or Copy Items dialog box, and then select a location for the file, which you'll do in the following steps.

To move a file using the Move to button:

▶ **1.** In the Address bar, click **Module** to return to the Module folder, and then click the **Task List** file to select it.

▶ **2.** On the Home tab, in the Organize group, click the **Move to** button to display a list of locations to which you can move the selected file. The Website folder is not included on this list because you haven't opened it yet.

▶ **3.** Click **Choose location** to open the Move Items dialog box. See Figure 11. The locations in your Move Items dialog box will differ.

Figure 11　▶　Move Items dialog box

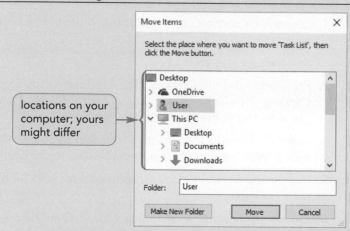

locations on your computer; yours might differ →

▶ **4.** If necessary, scroll the list of locations, and then click the **expand** icon 〉 next to the drive containing your Data Files, such as Removable Disk (D:).

▶ **5.** Navigate to the **FM > Module** folder, and then click the **Website** folder to select it.

▶ **6.** Click the **Move** button to close the dialog box and move the Task List file to the Website folder.

▶ **7.** Open the Website folder to confirm that it contains the Task List file.

One way to save steps when moving or copying multiple files or folders is to select all the files and folders you want to move or copy, and then work with them as a group. You can use several techniques to select multiple files or folders at the same time, which are described in Figure 12.

Figure 12	Selecting multiple files or folders

Items to Select in the Right Pane of File Explorer	Method
Files or folders listed together	Click the first item, press and hold the Shift key, click the last item, and then release the Shift key.
	or
	Drag the pointer to create a selection box around all the items you want to include.
Files or folders not listed together	Press and hold the Ctrl key, click each item you want to select, and then release the Ctrl key.
All files and folders	Click the Select all button in the Select group on the Home tab.

Items to Deselect in the Right Pane of File Explorer	Method
Single file or folder in a selected group	Press and hold the Ctrl key, click each item you want to remove from the selection, and then release the Ctrl key.
All selected files and folders	Click a blank area of the File Explorer window.

Next, you'll copy the five graphics files from the Module folder to the Marketing Graphics folder using the Clipboard. To do this efficiently, you will select multiple files at the same time.

To copy multiple files using the Clipboard:

1. Display the contents of the Module folder in File Explorer.

2. Click the **Edison** file, press and hold the **Shift** key, click the **Trolley** file, and then release the **Shift** key.

3. Press and hold the **Ctrl** key, click the **Tour Rates** file, and then release the **Ctrl** key. Five files—Edison, Logo, Miami Beach, Ocean Drive, and Trolley—are selected in the Module folder window.

4. Right-click one of the selected files, and then click **Copy** on the shortcut menu. Windows copies the selected files to the Clipboard.

5. Right-click the **Marketing Graphics** folder, and then click **Paste** on the shortcut menu.

6. Open the **Marketing Graphics** folder to verify it contains the five files you copied, and then return to the Module folder. The Tour Rates file contains financial information, so you can move it to the Financial folder.

7. Right-click the **Tour Rates** file, and then click **Cut** on the shortcut menu.

8. Double-click the **Financial** folder to open it, right-click a blank area of the right pane, and then click **Paste** on the shortcut menu.

INSIGHT

Duplicating Your Folder Organization

If you work on two computers, such as one computer at an office or school and another computer at home, you can duplicate the folders you use on both computers to simplify the process of transferring files from one computer to another. For example, if you have four folders in your Documents folder on your work computer, copy these four folders to the Documents folder on your OneDrive or USB drive. If you change a file on the hard disk of your home computer, you can copy the most recent version of the file to the corresponding folder on your OneDrive or USB drive so the file is available when you are at work. You also then have a **backup**, or duplicate copy, of important files. Having a backup of your files is invaluable if your computer has a fatal error.

All the files that originally appeared in the Module folder are now stored in appropriate subfolders. You can streamline the organization of the Module folder by deleting the duplicate files you no longer need.

Deleting Files and Folders

TIP

In most cases, a file deleted from a USB drive does not go into the Recycle Bin. Instead, it is deleted when Windows 10 removes its icon, and the file cannot be recovered.

You should periodically delete files and folders you no longer need so that your main folders and disks don't get cluttered. In a folder window, you delete a file or folder by deleting its icon. When you use File Explorer to delete a file from a hard disk, including a OneDrive file, Windows 10 removes the file from the folder but stores the file contents in the Recycle Bin. The Recycle Bin is an area on your hard disk that holds deleted files until you remove them permanently. When you delete a folder from the hard disk, the folder and all of its files are stored in the Recycle Bin. If you change your mind and want to retrieve a deleted file or folder, you can double-click the Recycle Bin, right-click the file or folder you want to retrieve, and then click Restore. However, after you empty the Recycle Bin, you can no longer recover the files it contained.

Because you copied the Edison, Logo, Miami Beach, Ocean Drive, and Trolley files to the subfolders in the Module folder, you can safely delete the original files. As is true for moving, copying, and renaming files and folders, you can delete a file or folder in many ways, including using a shortcut menu or selecting one or more files and then pressing the Delete key.

To delete files in the Module folder:

1. Use any technique you've learned to navigate to and display the **FM > Module** folder.

2. In the right pane, click **Edison**, press and hold the **Shift** key, click **Trolley**, and then release the **Shift** key. All files in the Module folder are now selected. None of the subfolders should be selected.

Make sure you have copied the selected files to the Marketing Graphics folder before completing this step.

3. Right-click the selected files, and then click **Delete** on the shortcut menu. A message box appears, asking if you're sure you want to move these files to the Recycle Bin.

4. Click the **Yes** button to confirm that you want to delete the files.

   Trouble? If you are working with files on a hard disk, Windows does not ask if you want to permanently delete the files. Skip Step 4.

Renaming Files

After creating and naming a file or folder, you might realize that a different name would be more meaningful or descriptive. You can easily rename a file or folder by using the Rename command on the file's shortcut menu.

Now that you've organized Diego's files into folders, he reviews your work and notes that the City Guide file in the Sights folder could contain information about any city. He recommends that you rename that file to give it a more descriptive filename. The City Guide file was originally created to store text specifically about sights on Miami, so you'll rename the file Miami Guide.

To rename the City Guide file:

▶ **1.** In the right pane of the File Explorer window, double-click the **Sights** folder to display its contents.

▶ **2.** Right-click the **City Guide** file, and then click **Rename** on the shortcut menu. The filename is highlighted, and a box appears around it.

▶ **3.** Type **Miami Guide** and then press the **Enter** key. The file now appears with the new name.

Trouble? If you make a mistake while typing and you haven't pressed the Enter key yet, press the Backspace key until you delete the mistake and then complete Step 3. If you've already pressed the Enter key, repeat Steps 2 and 3 to rename the file again.

Trouble? If your computer is set to display filename extensions, a message might appear asking if you are sure you want to change the filename extension. Click the No button and then repeat Steps 2 and 3.

> **TIP**
>
> To rename a file, you can also click the file, pause, click it again to select the filename, and then type to enter a new filename.

Now that the Miami Guide file has a more descriptive name, Diego asks you to copy the Sights folder containing the Miami Guide file to the Documents folder. Anita will need this file the next time she uses Diego's computer. To copy the folder, you'll use the key combinations for copying and pasting. (When you use a **key combination**, you press two or more keys to access a feature or perform a command efficiently.)

To copy the Sights folder using key combinations:

▶ **1.** Return to the Module folder.

▶ **2.** If necessary, click the **Sights** folder to select it, and then press the **Ctrl+C** keys to copy the folder.

▶ **3.** In the navigation pane, click the **Documents** folder, and then press the **Ctrl+V** keys to paste the folder.

▶ **4.** Open each file in the Documents > Sights folder, add your name at the beginning of the file, save the file, and then close it.

> **TIP**
>
> To cut a file or folder and store it on the Clipboard, press the Ctrl+X keys.

Finding Files and Information with Cortana

Cortana is an electronic personal assistant that Windows 10 provides to help you find files, search the web, keep track of information, and answer your questions. For example, you can ask Cortana to tell a joke, remind you about an appointment, or find a document you were working on before you took a break.

Cortana is turned off by default. If you have a Microsoft account, you can turn on Cortana and use it. Turning on Cortana involves agreeing to let it collect information about you. If you use more than one Windows device, Cortana uses the information you provide to keep the devices in sync.

After you turn on Cortana, it responds to text you enter in the Ask me anything box. For example, you can enter the first few characters of a filename to have Cortana display the file in a search results list. Click the file to open it in its default app. If your computer has a microphone, you can also set up Cortana to respond to your voice. You can then say "Hey, Cortana" to let Cortana know you want to find something. Cortana uses the next words you speak as search text. For example, you can say "Find files I edited today" to have Cortana respond appropriately.

If you ask questions, Cortana responds to them based on information stored in its **Notebook**, which is where Cortana keeps track of what you like, such as your interests and favorite places, and what you want it to do, such as display reminders or information that might interest you. Settings in the People and Maps Windows apps also affect Cortana. For example, if you identify a contact as a friend, Cortana can remind you to call that person. As you work in Windows and apps, Cortana can take note of your preferences and what you're doing when you ask for information to give personalized answers and recommendations.

In the following steps, you set up and turn on Cortana for the first time. If your taskbar includes the Ask me anything box, Cortana is already turned on. Skip the following steps and continue with the next set of steps.

To set up and turn on Cortana for the first time:

1. Click the **Search the web and Windows** box on the taskbar. Cortana opens and displays some of the tasks it can do for you. See Figure 13.

Figure 13   **Turning on Cortana**

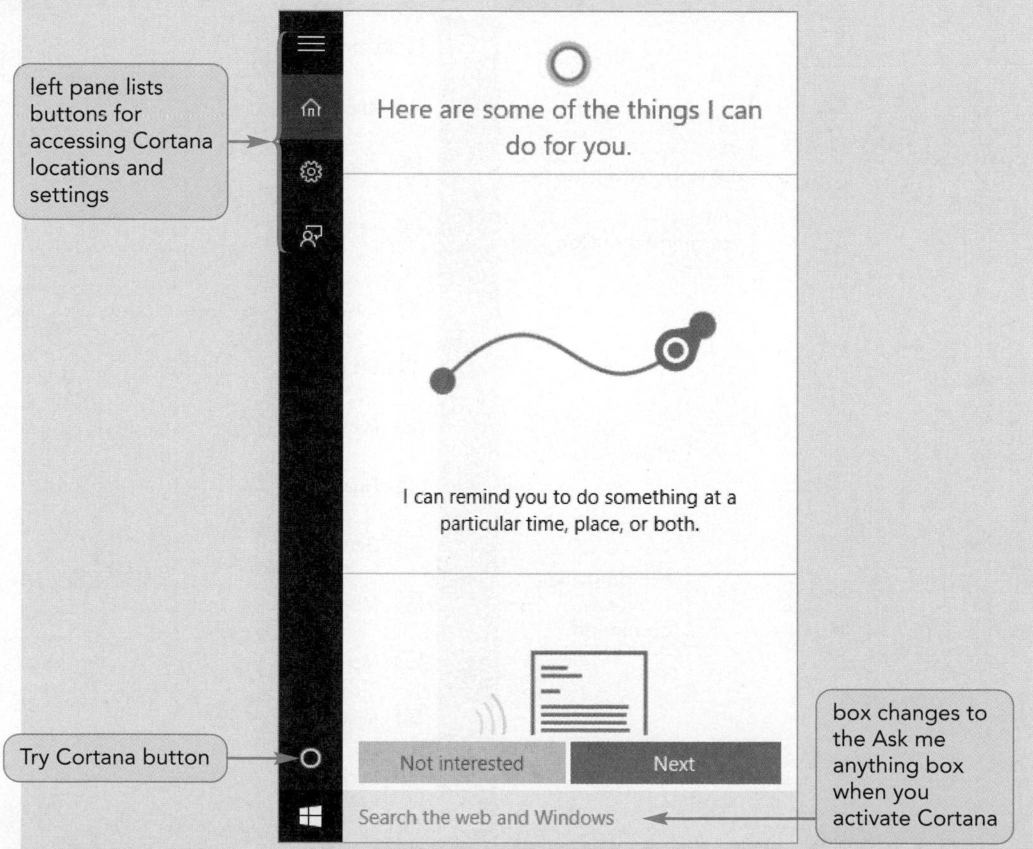

left pane lists buttons for accessing Cortana locations and settings

Here are some of the things I can do for you.

I can remind you to do something at a particular time, place, or both.

Try Cortana button

Not interested   Next

Search the web and Windows

box changes to the Ask me anything box when you activate Cortana

> **Trouble?** If Cortana does not look like Figure 13, click the Try Cortana button ◉ in the left pane.

▶ **2.** Click the **Next** button. A notice appears explaining that Cortana will collect and use information and store it in its Notebook.

▶ **3.** Click the **I agree** button. Cortana asks for a name to use when addressing you.

▶ **4.** Type your first name, and then click the **Next** button. Cortana displays a few starter interests, webpages, and search text that might suit you based on information in your Microsoft account.

▶ **5.** Click the **Got it** button. Cortana stores the webpage information and search text in your Notebook.

You can access the Notebook and configure information about yourself, such as favorite locations, upcoming events, and entertainment preferences. Diego wants to explore his Notebook and learn how to add a reminder for meetings and other events. Before entering a reminder, check to make sure Cortana is set up to store meeting and reminder information.

To access the Cortana Notebook and view reminders:

▶ **1.** In the left pane, click the **Notebook** button 🖳. Cortana displays the Notebook menu. See Figure 14. The top part of the Notebook menu lists categories of general information about you, your accounts, and your settings. The bottom part lists a Cortana setting and categories of interests.

Figure 14   **Cortana Notebook**

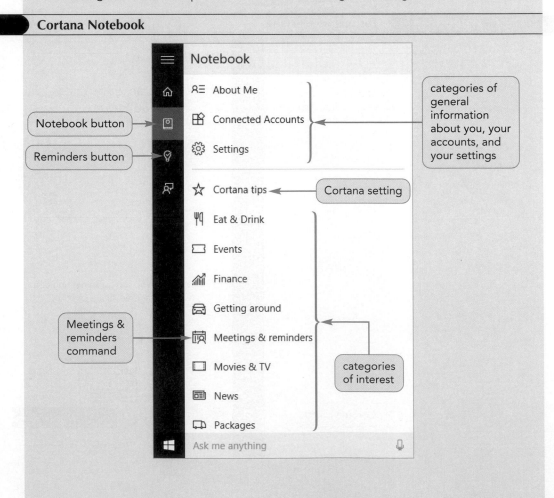

▶ **2.** Click **Meetings & reminders** on the Notebook menu to display the settings for meetings and reminders. All of the settings in this category are activated by default.

▶ **3.** In the left pane, click the **Reminders** button 🔅. The right pane displays tools for entering a reminder.

▶ **4.** Click the **Add** button ➕ to display boxes for entering reminder information. Diego doesn't have all the details for a reminder now, so you can cancel the reminder.

▶ **5.** Click the **Cancel** button.

Finally, you can use Cortana to find files on your computer and information on webpages. By default, Cortana searches the hard drive and OneDrive, but not removable disks, to find files. When you enter text or speak to Cortana, you can use natural language instead of computer commands. For example, you'll show Diego how to find files he added to the Documents folder today.

To use Cortana to find files:

▶ **1.** Click in the **Ask me anything** box.

▶ **2.** Type **find files I added today** and then press the **Enter** key. Cortana displays a list of files added to the hard drive or OneDrive today, including the Miami Guide and Trolley Tours files in the Sights folder on the hard drive. See Figure 15. The files you find and their details might differ.

Figure 15　　**Search results**

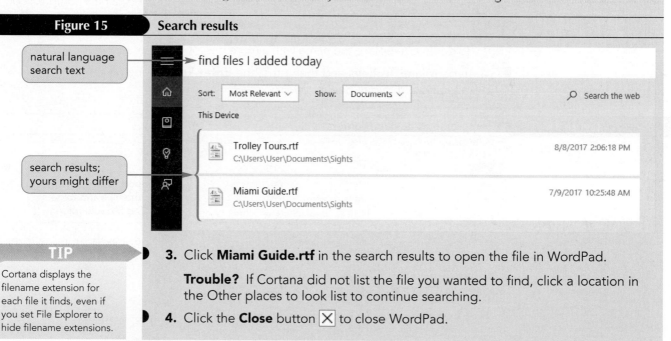

natural language search text

find files I added today

Sort: Most Relevant ∨　　Show: Documents ∨　　🔍 Search the web

This Device

search results; yours might differ

Trolley Tours.rtf
C:\Users\User\Documents\Sights　　8/8/2017 2:06:18 PM

Miami Guide.rtf
C:\Users\User\Documents\Sights　　7/9/2017 10:25:48 AM

TIP

Cortana displays the filename extension for each file it finds, even if you set File Explorer to hide filename extensions.

▶ **3.** Click **Miami Guide.rtf** in the search results to open the file in WordPad.

Trouble? If Cortana did not list the file you wanted to find, click a location in the Other places to look list to continue searching.

▶ **4.** Click the **Close** button ☒ to close WordPad.

INSIGHT

Searching for Files without Cortana

If you are not using Cortana, you can still search for files. Suppose you forgot where you stored a file, what filename you used, or when you last modified the file. You can find the file by clicking in the Search box in File Explorer, typing text that appears at the beginning of the filename, and then using the options on the Search Tools Search tab.

Working with Compressed Files

You compress a file or a folder of files so it occupies less space on the disk. It can be useful to compress files before transferring them from one location to another, such as from your hard disk to a removable disk or vice versa, or from one computer to another via email. You can then transfer the files more quickly. Also, if you or your email contacts can send and receive files only up to a certain size, compressing large files might make them small enough to send and receive.

You can compress one or more files in File Explorer using the Zip button, which is located in the Send group on the Share tab of the ribbon. Windows stores the compressed files in a special type of folder called an **archive**, or a compressed (zipped) folder. File Explorer uses an icon of a folder with a zipper to represent a compressed folder. To compress additional files or folders, you drag them into the compressed folder. You can open a file directly from a compressed folder, although you cannot modify the file. To edit and save a compressed file, you must extract it first. When you **extract** a file, you create an uncompressed copy of the file in a folder you specify. The original file remains in the compressed folder.

You suggest that you compress the files and folders in the Module folder so that Diego can more quickly transfer them to another location.

To compress the folders and files in the Module folder:

TIP

Another way to compress files is to select the files, right-click the selection, point to Send to on the shortcut menu, and then click Compressed (zipped) folder.

1. In File Explorer, navigate to the **FM > Module** folder, and then select all the folders in the Module folder.

2. Click the **Share** tab on the ribbon.

3. In the Send group, click the **Zip** button. After a few moments, a new compressed folder appears in the Module window with the filename selected. By default, File Explorer uses the name of the first selected item as the name of the compressed folder. You'll replace the name with a more descriptive one.

4. Type **Miami Trolleys** and then press the **Enter** key to rename the compressed folder. See Figure 16.

Figure 16   Compressing files and folders

5. Double-click the **Miami Trolleys** compressed folder to open it, open the **Sights** folder, and then note the size of the compressed Miami Guide file, which is 532 KB.

6. Navigate back to the Module folder.

You can move and copy the files and folders from an opened compressed folder to other locations, although you cannot rename the files. More often, you extract all of the files from the compressed folder to a new location that you specify, preserving the files in their original folders as appropriate.

To extract the compressed files:

▶ **1.** If necessary, click the **Miami Trolleys** compressed folder to select it, and then click the **Compressed Folder Tools Extract** tab on the ribbon.

▶ **2.** Click the **Extract all** button. The Extract Compressed (Zipped) Folders Wizard starts and opens the Select a Destination and Extract Files dialog box.

▶ **3.** Press the **End** key to deselect the path in the box and move the insertion point to the end of the path, press the **Backspace** key as many times as necessary to delete the Miami Trolleys text, and then type **Backups**. The final three parts of the path in the box should be FM > Module > Backups. See Figure 17.

Figure 17 **Extracting files from a compressed folder**

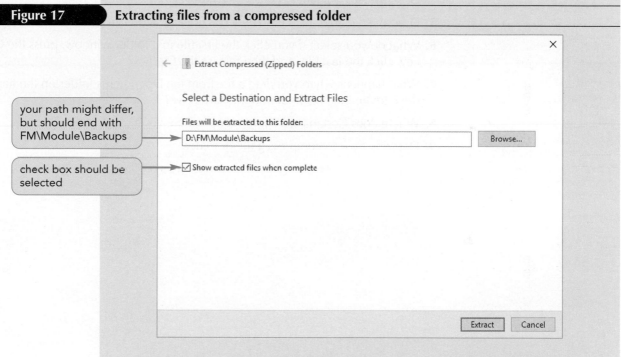

your path might differ, but should end with FM\Module\Backups

check box should be selected

▶ **4.** Make sure the Show extracted files when complete check box is checked, and then click the **Extract** button. Windows extracts the files and then opens the Backups folder, showing the Financial, Marketing Graphics, Sights, and Website folders.

▶ **5.** Open each folder to make sure it contains the files you worked with in this module. When you open the Sights folder, note the uncompressed size of the Miami Guide file, which is 1,932 KB, nearly four times as large as its compressed version.

▶ **6.** Close all open windows.

In this module, you examined the purpose of organizing files and folders, and you planned and created an organization for a set of related files and folders. You also explored your computer using File Explorer and learned how to navigate to your Data Files using the navigation pane. You used File Explorer to manage files and folders by opening and saving files; creating folders; and selecting, moving, and copying files. You also renamed and deleted files according to your organization plan. Finally, you used Cortana to find files and then compressed and extracted files.

REVIEW

Quick Check

1. Why should you take the time to organize files and folders?

2. Windows organizes the folders and files in a hierarchy, or _____.

3. In File Explorer, what does the navigation pane contain?

4. Explain how to use File Explorer to navigate to a file in the following location: D: > Courses > Digital Literacy > Windows.docx.

5. Describe the appearance of file icons in Large icons view.

6. What do you select if you click the first file in a folder window, press the Ctrl key, click the last file, and then release the Ctrl key?

7. What happens when you drag a file from the Documents folder on the hard drive to the Pictures folder on the hard drive?

8. Where does Cortana store information about you?

9. Describe how to compress a file or folder.

Review Assignments

Data Files needed for the Review Assignments: Background.png, Calendar.rtf, Events.xlsx, Skyline.jpg, Visit.rtf, Walking.rtf, Welcome.jpg

Diego has saved a few files from his old computer to a removable disk. He gives you these files in a single, unorganized folder and asks you to organize them logically into subfolders. He needs at least one subfolder for files related to a newsletter he is planning. Devise a plan for managing the files, and then create the subfolders you need. Rename, copy, and move files, and then delete unnecessary or duplicate files. Perform other management tasks to make it easy for Diego to work with these files and folders. Complete the following steps:

1. Use File Explorer to navigate to and open the FM > Review folder provided with your Data Files. Examine the seven files in this folder, and consider the best way to organize the files.
2. Open the **Visit** text file in WordPad, and then add the following line to the end of the document: **Oct - Pleasant**
3. Save the document as **When to Visit** in the Review folder. Close the WordPad window.
4. In the Review folder, create three folders: **Business**, **Newsletter**, and **Tours**.
5. To organize the files into the correct folders:
   - Move the Background and Calendar files from the Review folder to the Business folder.
   - Move the Events and When to Visit files to the Newsletter folder.
   - Move the Skyline, Walking, and Welcome files to the Tours folder.
6. Rename the Walking file in the Tours folder as **Walking Tours**, and then copy the Walking Tours file to the Newsletter folder.
7. Rename the Calendar file in the Business folder as **2017 Calendar**.
8. Delete the **Visit** file from the Review folder.
9. Create a compressed (zipped) folder in the Review folder named **Miami** that contains all the files and folders in the Review folder.
10. Extract the contents of the Miami compressed folder to a new folder named **Miami Backups** in the Review folder. (*Hint*: The file path will end with \FM\Review\Miami Backups.)
11. Close all open windows.

Case Problem 1

Data Files needed for this Case Problem: Advanced Classes.rtf, Beginner Classes.rtf, Designers.txt, Detail.jpg, Intermediate Classes.rtf, Kids Classes.rtf, Lampshade.jpg, Modern.jpg, Round.jpg, Studio.rtf

Art Glass Studio   Shannon Beecher started the Art Glass Studio in Lake George, New York, to provide custom stained-glass works for residential and commercial buildings. The business also holds classes on stained-glass techniques for children and adults. Knowing you are multitalented, Shannon hired you to help her manage the front end of the studio and other parts of her growing business, including electronic business files. Your first task is to organize the files on her new Windows 10 computer. Complete the following steps:

1. Open File Explorer. In the FM > Case1 folder provided with your Data Files, create three folders: **Classes**, **Designs**, and **Marketing**.
2. Move the Advanced Classes, Beginner Classes, Intermediate Classes, and Kids Classes files from the Case1 folder to the Classes folder.
3. Rename the four files in the Classes folder by deleting the word Classes from each name.
4. Move the four JPG files from the Case1 folder to the Designs folder.
5. Copy the remaining two files to the Marketing folder.

6. Copy the Designers file to the Designs folder.

7. Delete the Designers and Studio files from the Case1 folder.

⊕ **Explore** 8. Make a copy of the Designs folder in the Case1 folder. The name of the duplicate folder appears as Designs - Copy. Rename the Designs - Copy folder as **Beecher Designs**.

9. Copy the Advanced file from the Classes folder to the Beecher Designs folder. Rename this file **Classes**.

10. Compress the four photo files in the Beecher Designs folder in a new compressed folder named **Photos**.

11. Move the compressed Photos folder to the Case1 folder.

12. Close File Explorer.

Case Problem 2

Data Files needed for this Case Problem: Estimate Tips.txt, Estimate01.xls, Estimate02.xlsx, Estimate03.xlsx, Planner01.xlsx, Planner02.xlsx, Planner03.xlsx, Project Plans.txt, Steps1.rtf, Steps1 – Copy.rtf, Steps2.rtf, Steps2 – Copy.rtf

Avant Web Design   Dante Havens is the owner of Avant Web Design, a new website design company in Austin, Texas. You work as a part-time technology assistant at the company and spend some of your time organizing business files. Dante recently upgraded to Windows 10 and asks you to examine the folder structure and file system on his computer and then begin organizing the files logically. Complete the following steps:

1. Navigate to the FM > Case2 folder provided with your Data Files, and then examine the files in this folder. Based on the filenames and file types, begin to create an organization plan for the files.

⚙ **Troubleshoot** 2. Open the Steps1 and the Steps1 - Copy files, and consider the problem these files could cause. Close the files and then fix the problem.

⚙ **Troubleshoot** 3. Open the Steps2 and the Steps2 - Copy files, and compare their contents. Change the filenames to clarify the purpose and contents of the files.

4. Complete the organization plan for Dante's files. In the FM > Case2 folder, create the subfolders you need according to your plan.

5. Move the files in the Case2 folder to the subfolders you created. When you finish, the Case2 folder should contain at least two subfolders containing files.

6. Rename the spreadsheet files in each subfolder according to the following descriptions.
   - Estimate01: **Website estimate**
   - Estimate02: **Cost estimates**
   - Estimate03: **Event estimate**
   - Planner01: **Travel expense planner**
   - Planner02: **Project planner**
   - Planner03: **Balance sheet**

⚙ **Troubleshoot** 7. Make sure all files have descriptive names that accurately reflect their contents.

⚙ **Troubleshoot** 8. Based on the work you did in Steps 6 and 7, move files as necessary to improve the file organization.

9. Close File Explorer.

Creating and Editing a Document

Writing a Business Letter and Formatting a Flyer

OBJECTIVES

Session 1.1
- Create and save a document
- Enter text and correct errors as you type
- Use AutoComplete and AutoCorrect
- Select text and move the insertion point
- Undo and redo actions
- Adjust paragraph spacing, line spacing, and margins
- Preview and print a document
- Create an envelope

Session 1.2
- Open an existing document
- Use the Spelling and Grammar task panes
- Change page orientation, font, font color, and font size
- Apply text effects and align text
- Copy formatting with the Format Painter
- Insert a paragraph border and shading
- Delete, insert, and edit a photo
- Use Word Help

Case | *Villa Rio Records*

Villa Rio Records, in Wilmington, Delaware, specializes in vinyl records, which have been making a comeback in the past few years. To replenish the store's stock, the purchasing manager, Leo Barinov, frequently appraises and bids on record collections from around the state. Leo has asked you to create a cover letter to accompany an appraisal that he needs to send to a potential seller and an envelope for sending an appraisal to another potential seller. He also wants your help creating a flyer reminding store customers that Villa Rio Records buys old vinyl records.

You will create the letter and flyer using **Microsoft Office Word 2016** (or simply **Word**), a word-processing program. You'll start by opening Word and saving a new document. Then you'll type the text of the cover letter and print it. In the process of entering the text, you'll learn several ways to correct typing errors and how to adjust paragraph and line spacing. When you create the envelope, you'll learn how to save it as part of a document for later use. As you work on the flyer, you will learn how to open an existing document, change the way text is laid out on the page, format text, and insert and resize a photo. Finally, you'll learn how to use Word's Help system.

STARTING DATA FILES

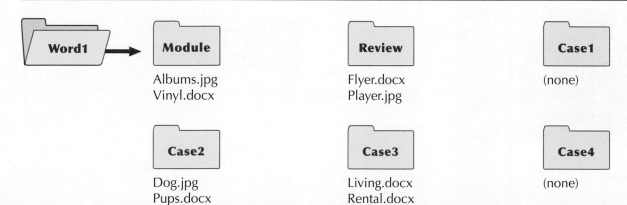

Word1 →	Module	Review	Case1
	Albums.jpg Vinyl.docx	Flyer.docx Player.jpg	(none)
	Case2	Case3	Case4
	Dog.jpg Pups.docx	Living.docx Rental.docx	(none)

Session 1.1 Visual Overview:

The **Quick Access Toolbar** is a collection of buttons that provides one-click access to commonly used commands, such as Save, Undo, and Repeat; you might see additional buttons here.

Each **tab** includes commands related to particular activities or tasks. The Home tab includes options for formatting and editing text.

The **title bar** displays the name of the open file and the program.

The **ribbon** is the main set of buttons and other tools you can use to complete tasks. It is organized into tabs and groups.

The dark gray areas on the ruler represent the document's margins. **Margins** are the blank spaces around the edges of a document's content.

The **insertion point** shows where characters will appear when you start typing.

The **paragraph mark** indicates the end of a paragraph. It is visible only if nonprinting characters are turned on. **Nonprinting characters** appear on the screen but not on the printed page.

Buttons for related commands are organized on a tab in **groups**. The buttons in this group can be used to change the appearance of a paragraph.

The **status bar** provides information about the current document, such as the current page and number of words in the document; it also contains buttons and other controls for working with the document.

You can choose to display the rulers, which help you position elements in a document.

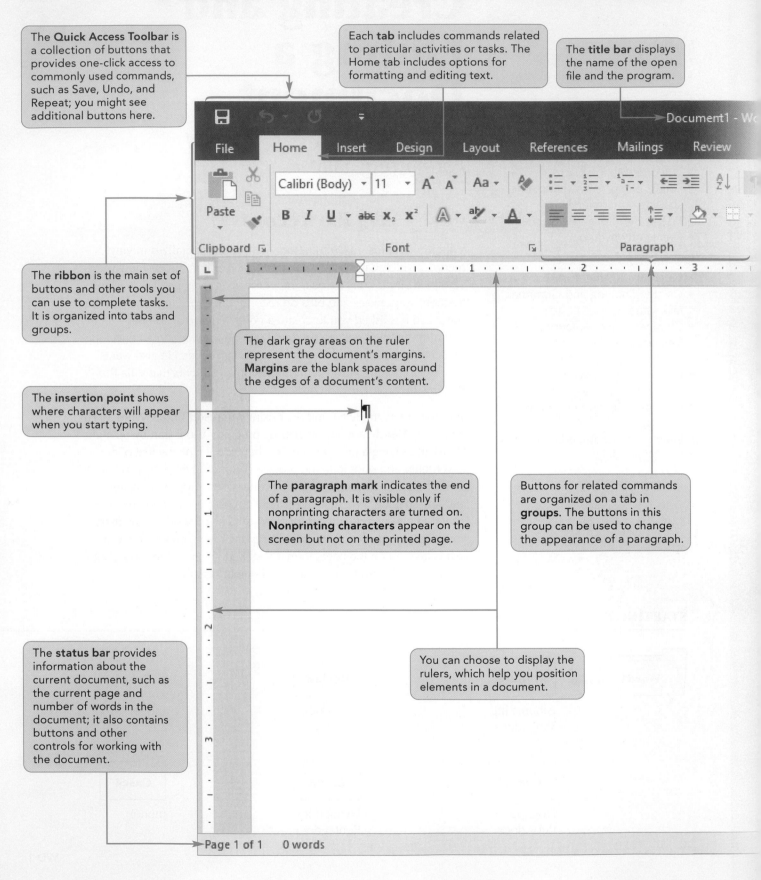

The Word Window

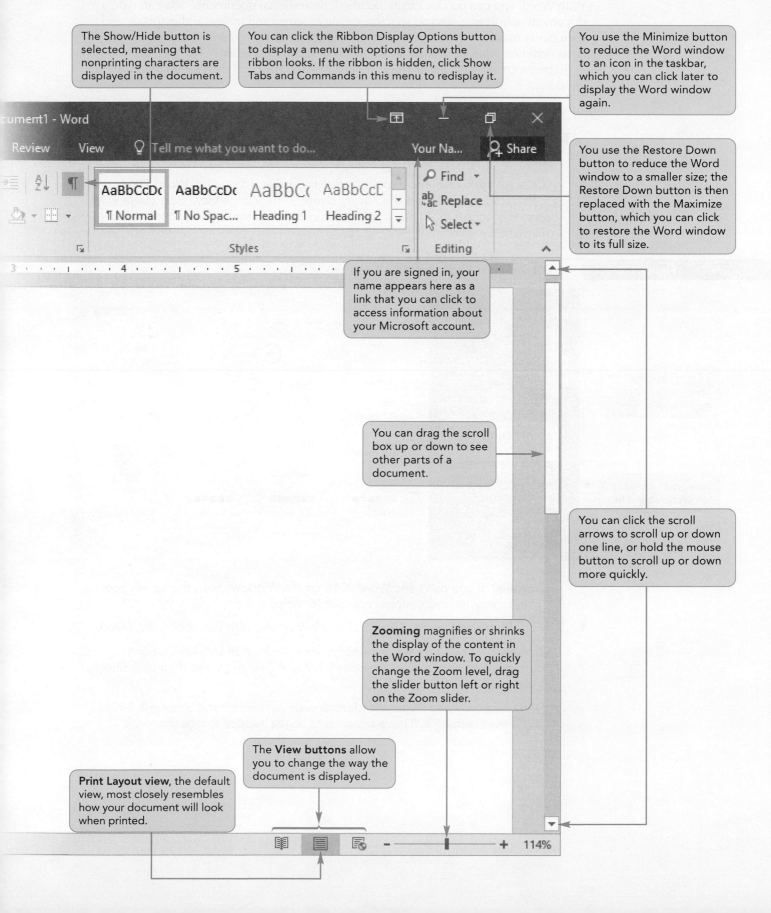

The Show/Hide button is selected, meaning that nonprinting characters are displayed in the document.

You can click the Ribbon Display Options button to display a menu with options for how the ribbon looks. If the ribbon is hidden, click Show Tabs and Commands in this menu to redisplay it.

You use the Minimize button to reduce the Word window to an icon in the taskbar, which you can click later to display the Word window again.

You use the Restore Down button to reduce the Word window to a smaller size; the Restore Down button is then replaced with the Maximize button, which you can click to restore the Word window to its full size.

If you are signed in, your name appears here as a link that you can click to access information about your Microsoft account.

You can drag the scroll box up or down to see other parts of a document.

You can click the scroll arrows to scroll up or down one line, or hold the mouse button to scroll up or down more quickly.

Zooming magnifies or shrinks the display of the content in the Word window. To quickly change the Zoom level, drag the slider button left or right on the Zoom slider.

The **View buttons** allow you to change the way the document is displayed.

Print Layout view, the default view, most closely resembles how your document will look when printed.

Starting Word

With Word, you can quickly create polished, professional documents. You can type a document, adjust margins and spacing, create columns and tables, add graphics, and then easily make revisions and corrections. In this session, you will create one of the most common types of documents—a block-style business letter.

To begin creating the letter, you first need to start Word and then set up the Word window.

To start Microsoft Word:

1. On the Windows taskbar, click the **Start** button ⊞. The Start menu opens.

2. Click **All apps** on the Start menu, scroll the list, and then click **Word 2016**. Word starts and displays the Recent screen in Backstage view. **Backstage view** provides access to various screens with commands that allow you to manage files and Word options. See Figure 1-1.

Figure 1-1   Recent screen in Backstage view

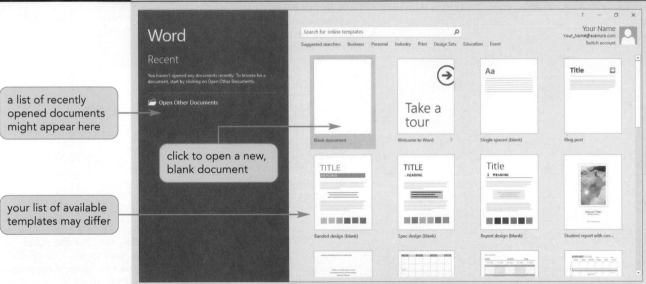

a list of recently opened documents might appear here

click to open a new, blank document

your list of available templates may differ

Trouble? If you don't see Word 2016 on the Windows Start menu, ask your instructor or technical support person for help.

3. Click **Blank document**. The Word window opens, with the ribbon displayed.

Trouble? If you don't see the ribbon, click the Ribbon Display Options button 🔳, as shown in the Session 1.1 Visual Overview, and then click Show Tabs and Commands.

Don't be concerned if your Word window doesn't match the Session 1.1 Visual Overview exactly. You'll have a chance to adjust its appearance shortly.

Working in Touch Mode

You can interact with the Word screen using a mouse, or, if you have a touchscreen, you can work in Touch Mode, using a finger instead of the mouse pointer. In **Touch Mode**, extra space around the buttons on the ribbon makes it easier to tap the specific button you need. The figures in this text show the screen with Mouse Mode on, but it's helpful to learn how to switch back and forth between Touch Mode and Mouse Mode.

Note: The following steps assume that you are using a mouse. If you are instead using a touch device, please read these steps but don't complete them so that you remain working in Touch Mode.

To switch between Touch and Mouse Mode:

1. On the Quick Access Toolbar, click the **Customize Quick Access Toolbar** button ⬇ to open the menu. The Touch/Mouse Mode command near the bottom of the menu does not have a checkmark next to it, indicating that it is currently not selected.

   Trouble? If the Touch/Mouse Mode command has a checkmark next to it, press the Esc key to close the menu, and then skip to Step 3.

2. On the menu, click **Touch/Mouse Mode**. The menu closes, and the Touch/Mouse Mode button 👆 appears on the Quick Access Toolbar.

3. On the Quick Access Toolbar, click the **Touch/Mouse Mode** button 👆. A menu opens with two options—Mouse and Touch. The icon next to Mouse is shaded blue to indicate it is selected.

   Trouble? If the icon next to Touch is shaded blue, press the Esc key to close the menu and skip to Step 5.

4. On the menu, click **Touch**. The menu closes, and the ribbon increases in height so that there is more space around each button on the ribbon. See Figure 1-2.

Figure 1-2   **Word window in Touch Mode**

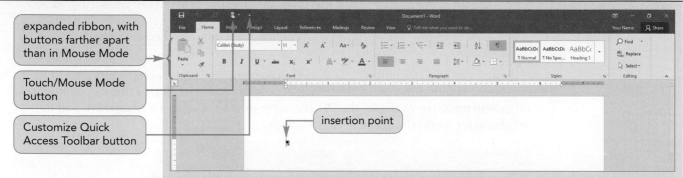

- expanded ribbon, with buttons farther apart than in Mouse Mode
- Touch/Mouse Mode button
- Customize Quick Access Toolbar button
- insertion point

Trouble? If you are working with a touchscreen and want to use Touch Mode, skip Steps 5 and 6.

5. On the Quick Access Toolbar, click the **Touch/Mouse Mode** button 👆, and then click **Mouse**. The ribbon changes back to its Mouse Mode appearance, as shown in the Session 1.1 Visual Overview.

6. On the Quick Access Toolbar, click the **Customize Quick Access Toolbar** button ⬇, and then click **Touch/Mouse Mode** to deselect it. The Touch/Mouse Mode button is removed from the Quick Access Toolbar.

Setting Up the Word Window

Before you start using Word, you should make sure you can locate and identify the different elements of the Word window, as shown in the Session 1.1 Visual Overview. In the following steps, you'll make sure your screen matches the Visual Overview.

To set up your Word window to match the figures in this book:

1. If the Word window does not fill the entire screen, click the **Maximize** button ▣ in the upper-right corner of the Word window.

   The insertion point on your computer should be positioned about an inch from the top of the document, as shown in Figure 1-2, with the top margin visible.

   Trouble? If the insertion point appears at the top of the document, with no white space above it, position the mouse pointer between the top of the document and the horizontal ruler, until it changes to ⇞, double-click, and then scroll up to top of the document.

2. On the ribbon, click the **View** tab. The ribbon changes to show options for changing the appearance of the Word window.

3. In the Show group, click the **Ruler** check box to insert a checkmark, if necessary. If the rulers were not displayed, they are displayed now.

   Next, you'll change the Zoom level to a setting that ensures that your Word window will match the figures in this book. To increase or decrease the screen's magnification, you could drag the slider button on the Zoom slider in the lower-right corner of the Word window. But to choose a specific Zoom level, it's easier to use the Zoom dialog box.

4. In the Zoom group, click the **Zoom** button to open the Zoom dialog box. Double-click the current value in the **Percent** box to select it, type **120**, and then click the **OK** button to close the Zoom dialog box.

5. On the status bar, click the **Print Layout** button 🗐 to select it, if necessary. As shown in the Session 1.1 Visual Overview, the Print Layout button is the middle of the three View buttons located on the right side of the status bar. The Print Layout button in the Views group on the View tab is also now selected.

TIP

Changing the Zoom level affects only the way the document is displayed on the screen; it does not affect the document itself.

Before typing a document, you should make sure nonprinting characters are displayed. Nonprinting characters provide a visual representation of details you might otherwise miss. For example, the (¶) character marks the end of a paragraph, and the (•) character marks the space between words.

To verify that nonprinting characters are displayed:

1. On the ribbon, click the **Home** tab.

2. In the blank Word document, look for the paragraph mark (¶) in the first line of the document, just to the right of the blinking insertion point.

   Trouble? If you don't see the paragraph mark, click the Show/Hide ¶ button ¶ in the Paragraph group.

   In the Paragraph group, the Show/Hide ¶ button should be highlighted in gray, indicating that it is selected, and the paragraph mark (¶) should appear in the first line of the document, just to the right of the insertion point.

Saving a Document

Before you begin working on a document, you should save it with a new name. When you use the Save button on the Quick Access Toolbar to save a document for the first time, Word displays the Save As screen in Backstage view. In the Save As screen, you can select the location where you want to store your document. After that, when you click the Save button, Word saves your document to the same location you specified earlier and with the same name.

To save the document:

▶ **1.** On the Quick Access Toolbar, click the **Save** button 🖫. Word switches to the Save As screen in Backstage view, as shown in Figure 1-3.

Figure 1-3 ▶ **Save As screen in Backstage view**

navigation bar

click to return to the document window

Save As selected in the navigation bar

click to open the Save As dialog box

you might see additional folders here; if you want to save a document in a folder that is listed here, click the folder to open the Save As dialog box with that folder selected

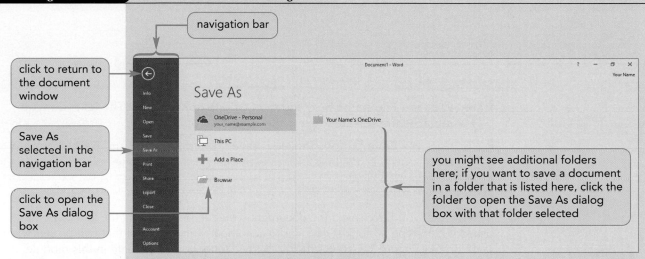

Because a document is now open, more commands are available in Backstage view than when you started Word. The **navigation bar** on the left contains commands for working with the open document and for changing settings that control how Word works.

▶ **2.** Click the **Browse** button. The Save As dialog box opens.

Trouble? If your instructor wants you to save your files to your OneDrive account, click OneDrive - Personal, and then log in to your account.

▶ **3.** Navigate to the location specified by your instructor. The default filename, "Doc1," appears in the File name box. You will change that to something more descriptive. See Figure 1-4.

Figure 1-4	Save As dialog box

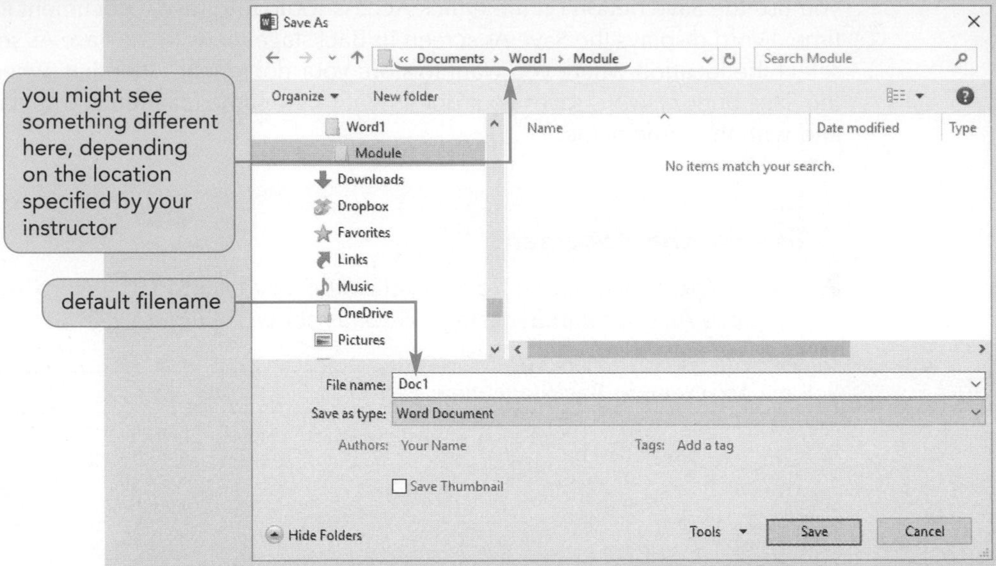

you might see
something different
here, depending
on the location
specified by your
instructor

default filename

Save As dialog box showing Documents > Word1 > Module navigation path, with File name box containing "Doc1" and Save as type set to "Word Document"

4. Click the **File name** box, and then type **Brooks Letter**. The text you type replaces the selected text in the File name box.

5. Click the **Save** button. The file is saved, the dialog box and Backstage view close, and the document window appears again, with the new filename in the title bar.

Now that you have saved the document, you can begin typing the letter. Leo has asked you to type a block-style letter to accompany an appraisal that will be sent to Jayla Brooks. Figure 1-5 shows the block-style letter you will create in this module.

Figure 1-5   Completed block-style letter

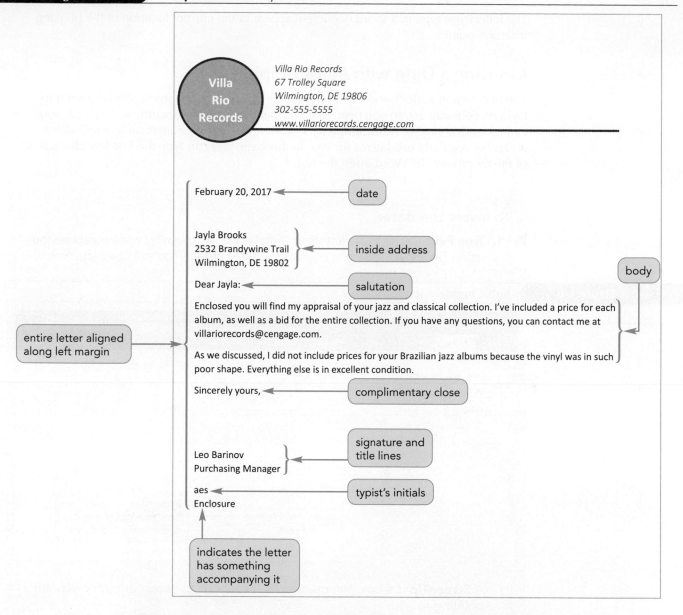

Villa Rio Records
67 Trolley Square
Wilmington, DE 19806
302-555-5555
www.villariorecords.cengage.com

February 20, 2017 ◄───── date

Jayla Brooks
2532 Brandywine Trail ◄───── inside address
Wilmington, DE 19802

Dear Jayla: ◄───── salutation

Enclosed you will find my appraisal of your jazz and classical collection. I've included a price for each album, as well as a bid for the entire collection. If you have any questions, you can contact me at villariorecords@cengage.com.

As we discussed, I did not include prices for your Brazilian jazz albums because the vinyl was in such poor shape. Everything else is in excellent condition.

body

Sincerely yours, ◄───── complimentary close

Leo Barinov
Purchasing Manager ───── signature and title lines

aes ◄───── typist's initials
Enclosure

 indicates the letter has something accompanying it

entire letter aligned along left margin

Written Communication: Creating a Business Letter

PROSKILLS

Several styles are considered acceptable for business letters. The main differences among the styles have to do with how parts of the letter are indented from the left margin. In the block style, which you will use in this module, each line of text starts at the left margin. In other words, nothing is indented. Another style is to indent the first line of each paragraph. The choice of style is largely a matter of personal preference, or it can be determined by the standards used in a particular business or organization. To further enhance your skills in writing business correspondence, you should consult an authoritative book on business writing that provides guidelines for creating a variety of business documents, such as *Business Communication: Process & Product*, by Mary Ellen Guffey.

Entering Text

The letters you type in a Word document appear at the current location of the blinking insertion point.

Inserting a Date with AutoComplete

The first item in a block-style business letter is the date. Leo plans to send the letter to Jayla on February 20, so you need to insert that date into the document. To do so, you can take advantage of **AutoComplete**, a Word feature that automatically inserts dates and other regularly used items for you. In this case, you can type the first few characters of the month and let Word insert the rest.

To insert the date:

1. Type **Febr** (the first four letters of "February"). A ScreenTip appears above the letters, as shown in Figure 1-6, suggesting "February" as the complete word.

Figure 1-6   AutoComplete suggestion

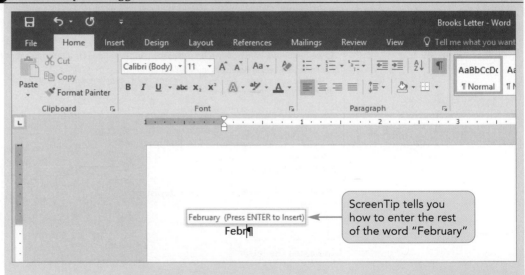

A **ScreenTip** is a box with descriptive text about an object or button you are pointing to.

If you wanted to type something other than "February," you could continue typing to complete the word. In this case, you want to accept the AutoComplete suggestion.

2. Press the **Enter** key. The rest of the word "February" is inserted in the document. Note that AutoComplete works for long month names like February but not shorter ones like May, because "Ma" could be the beginning of many words besides "May."

3. Press the **spacebar**, type **20, 2017** and then press the **Enter** key twice, leaving a blank paragraph between the date and the line where you will begin typing the inside address, which contains the recipient's name and address. Notice the nonprinting character (•) after the word "February" and before the number "20," which indicates a space. Word inserts this nonprinting character every time you press the spacebar.

Trouble? If February happens to be the current month, you will see a second AutoComplete suggestion displaying the current date after you press the spacebar. To ignore that AutoComplete suggestion, continue typing the rest of the date, as instructed in Step 3.

Continuing to Type the Block-Style Letter

In a block-style business letter, the inside address appears below the date, with one blank paragraph in between. Some style guides recommend including even more space between the date and the inside address. But in the short letter you are typing, more space would make the document look out of balance.

To insert the inside address:

1. Type the following information, pressing the **Enter** key after each item:

   Jayla Brooks

   2532 Brandywine Trail

   Wilmington, DE 19802

   Remember to press the Enter key after you type the ZIP code. Your screen should look like Figure 1-7. Don't be concerned if the lines of the inside address seem too far apart. You'll use the default spacing for now, and then adjust it after you finish typing the letter.

| Figure 1-7 | Letter with inside address |

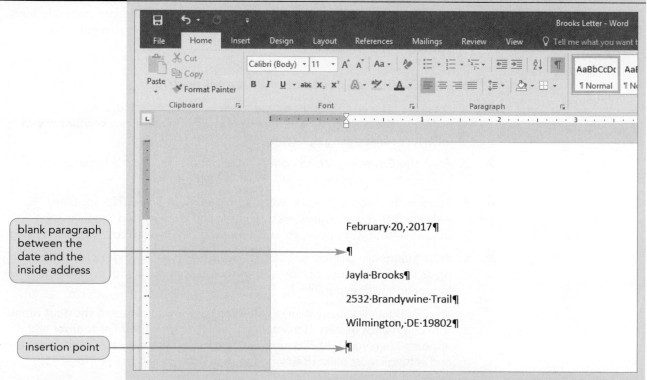

blank paragraph between the date and the inside address

insertion point

Trouble? If you make a mistake while typing, press the Backspace key to delete the incorrect character, and then type the correct character.

Now you can move on to the salutation and the body of the letter. As you type the body of the letter, notice that Word automatically moves the insertion point to a new line when the current line is full.

To type the salutation and the body of the letter:

▶ **1.** Type **Dear Jayla:** and then press the **Enter** key to start a new paragraph for the body of the letter.

▶ **2.** Type the following sentence, including the period: **Enclosed you will find my appraisal of your jazz and classical collection.**

▶ **3.** Press the **spacebar**. Note that you should only include one space between sentences.

▶ **4.** Type the following sentence, including the period: **I've included a price for each album, as well as a bid for the complete collection.**

▶ **5.** On the Quick Access Toolbar, click the **Save** button 🖫. Word saves the document as Brooks Letter to the same location you specified earlier.

The next sentence you need to type includes Leo's email address.

Typing a Hyperlink

When you type an email address and then press the spacebar or the Enter key, Word converts it to a hyperlink, with blue font and an underline. A **hyperlink** is text or a graphic you can click to jump to another file or to somewhere else in the same file. The two most common types of hyperlinks are: 1) an email hyperlink, which you can click to open an email message to the recipient specified by the hyperlink; and 2) a web hyperlink, which opens a webpage in a browser. Hyperlinks are useful in documents that you plan to distribute via email. In printed documents, where blue font and underlines can be distracting, you'll usually want to convert a hyperlink back to regular text.

To add a sentence containing an email address:

▶ **1.** Press the spacebar, and then type the following sentence, including the period: **If you have any questions, you can contact me at villariorecords@cengage.com.**

▶ **2.** Press the **Enter** key. Word converts the email address to a hyperlink, with blue font and an underline.

▶ **3.** Position the mouse pointer over the hyperlink. A ScreenTip appears, indicating that you could press and hold the Ctrl key and then click the link to follow it—that is, to open an email message addressed to Villa Rio Records.

▶ **4.** With the mouse pointer positioned over the hyperlink, right-click—that is, press the right mouse button. A shortcut menu opens with commands related to working with hyperlinks.

You can right-click many items in the Word window to display a **shortcut menu** with commands related to the item you right-clicked. The **Mini toolbar** also appears when you right-click or select text, giving you easy access to the buttons and settings most often used when formatting text. See Figure 1-8.

Figure 1-8   **Shortcut menu**

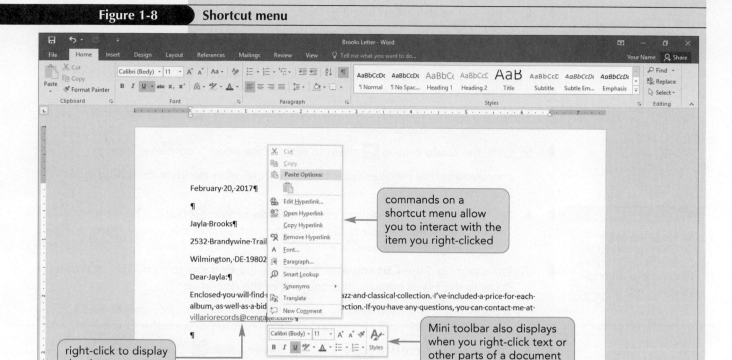

commands on a shortcut menu allow you to interact with the item you right-clicked

Mini toolbar also displays when you right-click text or other parts of a document

right-click to display the shortcut menu

5. Click **Remove Hyperlink** in the shortcut menu. The shortcut menu and the Mini toolbar are no longer visible. The email address is now formatted in black, like the rest of the document text.

6. On the Quick Access Toolbar, click the **Save** button.

Using the Undo and Redo Buttons

To undo (or reverse) the last thing you did in a document, click the Undo button on the Quick Access Toolbar. To restore your original change, click the Redo button, which reverses the action of the Undo button (or redoes the undo). To undo more than your last action, you can continue to click the Undo button, or you can click the Undo button arrow on the Quick Access Toolbar to open a list of your most recent actions. When you click an action in the list, Word undoes every action in the list up to and including the action you clicked.

Leo asks you to change the word "complete" to "entire" in the second-to-last sentence you typed. You'll make the change now. If Leo decides he doesn't like it after all, you can always undo it. To delete a character, space, or blank paragraph to the right of the insertion point, you use the Delete key; or to delete an entire word, you can press the Ctrl+Delete keys. To delete a character, space, or blank paragraph to the left of the insertion point, you use the Backspace key; or to delete an entire word, you can press the Ctrl+Backspace keys.

To change the word "complete":

1. Press the ↑ key once and then press the → key as necessary to move the insertion point to the left of the "c" in the word "complete."

▶ 2. Press and hold the **Ctrl** key, and then press the **Delete** key to delete the word "complete."

▶ 3. Type **entire** as a replacement, and then press the **spacebar**.

 After reviewing the sentence, Leo decides he prefers the original wording, so you'll undo the change.

▶ 4. On the Quick Access Toolbar, click the **Undo** button 🔄. The word "entire" is removed from the sentence.

▶ 5. Click the **Undo** button 🔄 again to restore the word "complete."

 Leo decides that he does want to use "entire" after all. Instead of retyping it, you'll redo the undo.

TIP

You can also press the Ctrl+Z keys to execute the Undo command, and press the Ctrl+Y keys to execute the Redo command.

▶ 6. On the Quick Access Toolbar, click the **Redo** button 🔁 twice. The word "entire" replaces "complete" in the document, so that the phrase reads "…for the entire collection."

▶ 7. Press and hold the **Ctrl** key, and then press the **End** key to move the insertion point to the blank paragraph at the end of the document.

 Trouble? If you are working on a small keyboard, you might need to press and hold a key labeled "Function" or "FN" before pressing the End key.

▶ 8. On the Quick Access Toolbar, click the **Save** button 💾. Word saves your letter with the same name and to the same location you specified earlier.

In the previous steps, you used the arrow keys and a key combination to move the insertion point to specific locations in the document. For your reference, Figure 1-9 summarizes the most common keystrokes for moving the insertion point in a document.

Figure 1-9 **Keystrokes for moving the insertion point**

To Move the Insertion Point	Press
Left or right one character at a time	← or →
Up or down one line at a time	↑ or ↓
Left or right one word at a time	Ctrl+← or Ctrl+→
Up or down one paragraph at a time	Ctrl+↑ or Ctrl+↓
To the beginning or to the end of the current line	Home or End
To the beginning or to the end of the document	Ctrl+Home or Ctrl+End
To the previous screen or to the next screen	Page Up or Page Down
To the top or to the bottom of the document window	Alt+Ctrl+Page Up or Alt+Ctrl+Page Down

Correcting Errors as You Type

As you have seen, you can use the Backspace or Delete keys to remove an error, and then type a correction. In many cases, however, Word's AutoCorrect feature will do the work for you. Among other things, **AutoCorrect** automatically corrects common typing errors, such as typing "adn" instead of "and." For example, you might have noticed AutoCorrect at work if you forgot to capitalize the first letter in a sentence as you typed the letter. After you type this kind of error, AutoCorrect automatically corrects it when you press the spacebar, the Tab key, or the Enter key.

Word draws your attention to other potential errors by marking them with wavy underlines. If you type a word that doesn't match the correct spelling in Word's dictionary, or if a word is not in the dictionary at all, a wavy red line appears beneath it. A wavy red underline also appears if you mistakenly type the same word twice in a row. Misused words (for example, "you're" instead of "your") are underlined with a wavy blue line, as are problems with possessives, punctuation, and plurals.

You'll see how this works as you continue typing the letter and make some intentional typing errors.

To learn more about correcting errors as you type:

1. Type the following sentence, including the errors shown here: **as we discussed, I did not include priices for you're Brazilian jazz albums because teh vynil was in such poor shape. Everything else else is in excellent condition.**

As you type, AutoCorrect changes the lowercase "a" at the beginning of the sentence to uppercase. It also changes "priices" to "prices and "teh" to "the." Also, the incorrectly used word "you're" is marked with a wavy blue underline. The spelling error "vynil" and the second "else" are marked with wavy red underlines. See Figure 1-10.

| Figure 1-10 | **Errors marked in the document** |

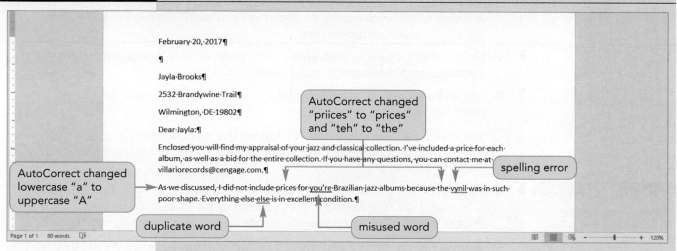

To correct an error marked with a wavy underline, you can right-click the error and then click a replacement in the shortcut menu. If you don't see the correct word in the shortcut menu, click anywhere in the document to close the menu, and then type the correction yourself. You can also bypass the shortcut menu entirely and simply delete the error and type a correction.

To correct the spelling and grammar errors:

▶ **1.** Right-click **you're** to display the shortcut menu shown in Figure 1-11.

Figure 1-11 **Shortcut menu with suggested spelling**

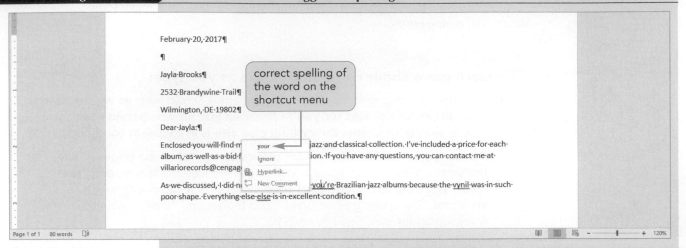

February·20,·2017¶

¶

Jayla·Brooks¶

2532·Brandywine·Trail¶

Wilmington,·DE·19802¶

Dear·Jayla:¶

> correct spelling of the word on the shortcut menu

Enclosed·you·will·find·m[...]jazz·and·classical·collection.·I've·included·a·price·for·each·
album,·as·well·as·a·bid·f[...]ion.·If·you·have·any·questions,·you·can·contact·me·at·
villariorecords@cengag[...]

your
Ignore
Hyperlink...
New Comment

As·we·discussed,·I·did·n[...]·you're·Brazilian·jazz·albums·because·the·vynil·was·in·such·
poor·shape.·Everything·else·else·is·in·excellent·condition.¶

Page 1 of 1   80 words   120%

Trouble? If you see a shortcut menu other than the one shown in Figure 1-11, you didn't right-click exactly on the word "you're." Press the Esc key to close the menu, and then repeat Step 1.

▶ **2.** On the shortcut menu, click **your**. The correct word is inserted into the sentence, and the shortcut menu closes.

▶ **3.** Use a shortcut menu to replace the spelling error "vynil" with the correct word "vinyl."

You could use a shortcut menu to remove the second instance of "else," but in the next step you'll try a different method—selecting the word and deleting it.

▶ **4.** Double-click anywhere in the underlined word **else**. The word and the space following it are highlighted in gray, indicating that they are selected. The Mini toolbar is also visible, but you can ignore it.

Trouble? If the entire paragraph is selected, you triple-clicked the word by mistake. Click anywhere in the document to deselect it, and then repeat Step 4.

▶ **5.** Press the **Delete** key. The second instance of "else" and the space following it are deleted from the sentence.

▶ **6.** On the Quick Access Toolbar, click the **Save** button 🔲.

You can see how quick and easy it is to correct common typing errors with AutoCorrect and the wavy underlines, especially in a short document that you are typing yourself. If you are working on a longer document or a document typed by someone else, you'll also want to have Word check the entire document for errors. You'll learn how to do this in Session 1.2.

Next, you'll finish typing the letter.

To finish typing the letter:

1. Press the **Ctrl+End** keys. The insertion point moves to the end of the document.

2. Press the **Enter** key, and then type **Sincerely yours,** (including the comma).

3. Press the **Enter** key three times to leave space for the signature.

4. Type **Leo Barinov** and then press the **Enter** key. Because Leo's last name is not in Word's dictionary, a wavy red line appears below it. You can ignore this for now.

TIP

You need to include your initials in a letter only if you are typing it for someone else.

5. Type your first, middle, and last initials in lowercase, and then press the **Enter** key. AutoCorrect wrongly assumes your first initial is the first letter of a new sentence and changes it to uppercase. If your initials do not form a word, a red wavy underline appears beneath them. You can ignore this for now.

6. On the Quick Access Toolbar, click the **Undo** button ↶. Word reverses the change, replacing the uppercase initial with a lowercase one.

7. Type **Enclosure**. At this point, your screen should look similar to Figure 1-12.

Figure 1-12	Letter to Jayla Brooks

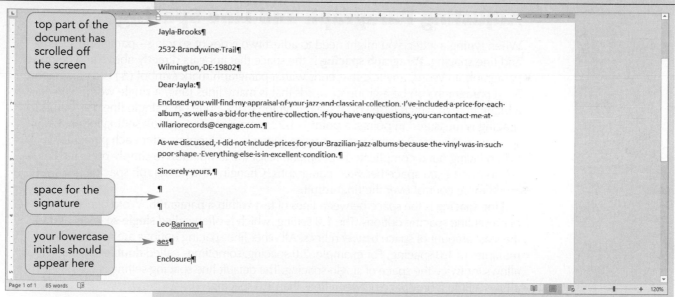

Notice that as you continue to add lines to the letter, the top part of the letter scrolls off the screen. For example, in Figure 1-12, you can no longer see the date.

8. Save the document.

Now that you have finished typing the letter, you need to proofread it.

Proofreading a Document

After you finish typing a document, you need to proofread it carefully from start to finish. Part of proofreading a document in Word is removing all wavy underlines, either by correcting the text or by telling Word to ignore the underlined text because it isn't really an error. For example, Leo's last name is marked as an error, when in fact it is spelled correctly. You need to tell Word to ignore "Barinov" wherever it occurs in the letter. You need to do the same for your initials.

To proofread and correct the remaining marked errors in the letter:

▶ **1.** Right-click **Barinov**. A shortcut menu opens.

▶ **2.** On the shortcut menu, click **Ignore All** to indicate that Word should ignore the word "Barinov" each time it occurs in this document. (The Ignore All option can be particularly helpful in a longer document.) The wavy red underline disappears from below Leo's last name.

▶ **3.** If you see a wavy red underline below your initials, right-click your initials. On the shortcut menu, click **Ignore All** to remove the red wavy underline.

▶ **4.** Read the entire letter to proofread it for typing errors. Correct any errors using the techniques you have just learned.

▶ **5.** Save the document.

The text of the letter is finished. Now you need to think about its appearance—that is, you need to think about the document's **formatting**. First, you need to adjust the spacing in the inside address.

Adjusting Paragraph and Line Spacing

When typing a letter, you might need to adjust two types of spacing—paragraph spacing and line spacing. **Paragraph spacing** is the space that appears directly above and below a paragraph. In Word, any text that ends with a paragraph mark symbol (¶) is a paragraph. So, a **paragraph** can be a group of words that is many lines long, a single word, or even a blank line, in which case you see a paragraph mark alone on a single line. Paragraph spacing is measured in points; a **point** is 1/72 of an inch. The default setting for paragraph spacing in Word is 0 points before each paragraph and 8 points after each paragraph. When laying out a complicated document, resist the temptation to simply press the Enter key to insert extra space between paragraphs. Changing the paragraph spacing gives you much more control over the final result.

Line spacing is the space between lines of text within a paragraph. Word offers a number of preset line spacing options. The 1.0 setting, which is often called **single-spacing**, allows the least amount of space between lines. All other line spacing options are measured as multiples of 1.0 spacing. For example, 2.0 spacing (sometimes called **double-spacing**) allows for twice the space of single-spacing. The default line spacing setting is 1.08, which allows a little more space between lines than 1.0 spacing.

Now consider the line and paragraph spacing in the Brooks letter. The three lines of the inside address are too far apart. That's because each line of the inside address is actually a separate paragraph. Word inserted the default 8 points of paragraph spacing after each of these separate paragraphs. See Figure 1-13.

Figure 1-13   **Line and paragraph spacing in the letter to Jayla Brooks**

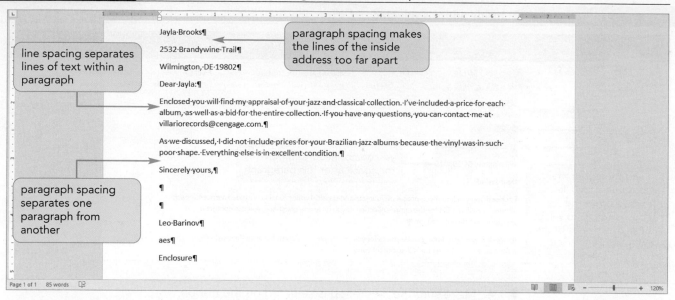

line spacing separates lines of text within a paragraph

paragraph spacing makes the lines of the inside address too far apart

paragraph spacing separates one paragraph from another

Jayla·Brooks¶

2532·Brandywine·Trail¶

Wilmington,·DE·19802¶

Dear·Jayla:¶

Enclosed·you·will·find·my·appraisal·of·your·jazz·and·classical·collection.·I've·included·a·price·for·each· album,·as·well·as·a·bid·for·the·entire·collection.·If·you·have·any·questions,·you·can·contact·me·at· villariorecords@cengage.com.¶

As·we·discussed,·I·did·not·include·prices·for·your·Brazilian·jazz·albums·because·the·vinyl·was·in·such· poor·shape.·Everything·else·is·in·excellent·condition.¶

Sincerely·yours,¶

¶

¶

Leo·Barinov¶

aes¶

Enclosure¶

Page 1 of 1   85 words   120%

To follow the conventions of a block-style business letter, the three paragraphs that make up the inside address should have the same spacing as the lines of text within a single paragraph—that is, they need to be closer together. You can accomplish this by removing the 8 points of paragraph spacing after the first two paragraphs in the inside address. To conform to the block-style business letter format, you also need to close up the spacing between your initials and the word "Enclosure" at the end of the letter.

To adjust paragraph and line spacing in Word, you use the Line and Paragraph Spacing button in the Paragraph group on the Home tab. Clicking this button displays a menu of preset line spacing options (1.0, 1.15, 2.0, and so on). The menu also includes two paragraph spacing options that allow you to add 12 points before a paragraph or remove the default 8 points of space after a paragraph.

Next you'll adjust the paragraph spacing in the inside address and after your initials. In the process, you'll also learn some techniques for selecting text in a document.

To adjust the paragraph spacing in the inside address and after your initials:

1. Move the pointer to the white space just to the left of "Jayla Brooks" until it changes to a right-facing arrow.

2. Click the mouse button. The entire name, including the paragraph symbol after it, is selected.

   Trouble? If the Mini toolbar obscures your view of Jayla's name, move the mouse pointer away from the address to close the Mini toolbar.

3. Press and hold the mouse button, drag the pointer down to select the next paragraph of the inside address as well, and then release the mouse button.

   The name and street address are selected as well as the paragraph marks at the end of each paragraph. You did not select the paragraph containing the city, state, and ZIP code because you do not need to change its paragraph spacing. See Figure 1-14.

TIP

The white space in the left margin is sometimes referred to as the selection bar because you click it to select text.

Figure 1-14   **Inside address selected**

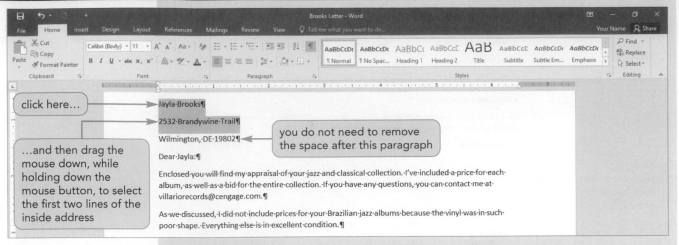

4. Make sure the Home tab is selected on the ribbon.

5. In the Paragraph group on the Home tab, click the **Line and Paragraph Spacing** button ![button]. A menu of line spacing options appears, with two paragraph spacing options at the bottom. See Figure 1-15.

Figure 1-15   **Line and paragraph spacing options**

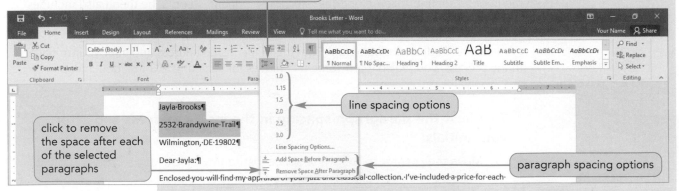

At the moment, you are interested only in the paragraph spacing options. Your goal is to remove the default 8 points of space after the first two paragraphs in the inside address.

6. Click **Remove Space After Paragraph**. The menu closes, and the paragraphs are now closer together.

7. Double-click your initials to select them and the paragraph symbol after them.

8. In the Paragraph group, click the **Line and Paragraph Spacing** button, click **Remove Space After Paragraph**, and then click anywhere in the document to deselect your initials.

Another way to compress lines of text is to press the Shift+Enter keys at the end of a line. This inserts a **manual line break**, also called a **soft return**, which moves the insertion point to a new line without starting a new paragraph. You will use this technique now as you add Leo's title below his name in the signature line.

> ### To use a manual line break to move the insertion point to a new line without starting a new paragraph:
>
> ▶ **1.** Click to the right of the "v" in "Barinov."
>
> ▶ **2.** Press the **Shift+Enter** keys. Word inserts a small arrow symbol ↵ , indicating a manual line break, and the insertion point moves to the line below Leo's name.
>
> ▶ **3.** Type **Purchasing Manager**. Leo's title now appears directly below his name with no intervening paragraph spacing, just like the lines of the inside address.
>
> ▶ **4.** Save the document.

INSIGHT

Understanding Spacing Between Paragraphs

When discussing the correct format for letters, many business style guides talk about single-spacing and double-spacing between paragraphs. In these style guides, to single-space between paragraphs means to press the Enter key once after each paragraph. Likewise, to double-space between paragraphs means to press the Enter key twice after each paragraph. With the default paragraph spacing in Word 2016, however, you need to press the Enter key only once after a paragraph. The space Word adds after a paragraph is not quite the equivalent of double-spacing, but it is enough to make it easy to see where one paragraph ends and another begins. Keep this in mind if you're accustomed to pressing the Enter key twice; otherwise, you could end up with more space than you want between paragraphs.

As you corrected line and paragraph spacing in the previous set of steps, you used the mouse to select text. Word provides multiple ways to select, or highlight, text as you work. Figure 1-16 summarizes these methods and explains when to use them most effectively.

Figure 1-16 Methods for selecting text

To Select	Mouse	Keyboard	Mouse and Keyboard
A word	Double-click the word	Move the insertion point to the beginning of the word, press and hold Ctrl+Shift, and then press →	
A line	Click in the white space to the left of the line	Move the insertion point to the beginning of the line, press and hold Shift, and then press ↓	
A sentence	Click at the beginning of the sentence, then drag the pointer until the sentence is selected		Press and hold Ctrl, then click any location within the sentence
Multiple lines	Click and drag in the white space to the left of the lines	Move the insertion point to the beginning of the first line, press and hold Shift, and then press ↓ until all the lines are selected	
A paragraph	Double-click in the white space to the left of the paragraph, or triple-click at any location within the paragraph	Move the insertion point to the beginning of the paragraph, press and hold Ctrl+Shift, and then press ↓	
Multiple paragraphs	Click in the white space to the left of the first paragraph you want to select, and then drag to select the remaining paragraphs	Move the insertion point to the beginning of the first paragraph, press and hold Ctrl+Shift, and then press ↓ until all the paragraphs are selected	
An entire document	Triple-click in the white space to the left of the document text	Press Ctrl+A	Press and hold Ctrl, and click in the white space to the left of the document text
A block of text	Click at the beginning of the block, then drag the pointer until the entire block is selected		Click at the beginning of the block, press and hold Shift, and then click at the end of the block
Nonadjacent blocks of text			Press and hold Ctrl, then drag the mouse pointer to select multiple blocks of nonadjacent text

Adjusting the Margins

Another important aspect of document formatting is the amount of margin space between the document text and the edge of the page. You can check the document's margins by changing the Zoom level to display the entire page.

To change the Zoom level to display the entire page:

1. On the ribbon, click the **View** tab.

2. In the Zoom group, click the **One Page** button. The entire document is now visible in the Word window. See Figure 1-17.

Figure 1-17   Document zoomed to show entire page

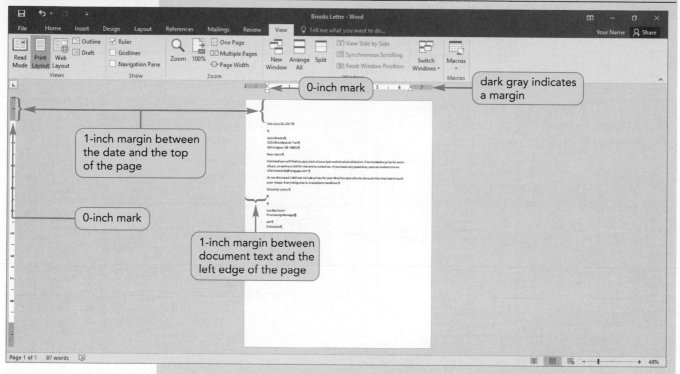

On the rulers, the margins appear dark gray. By default, Word documents include 1-inch margins on all sides of the document. By looking at the vertical ruler, you can see that the date in the letter, the first line in the document, is located 1 inch from the top of the page. Likewise, the horizontal ruler indicates the document text begins 1 inch from the left edge of the page.

Reading the measurements on the rulers can be tricky at first. On the horizontal ruler, the 0-inch mark is like the origin on a number line. You measure from the 0-inch mark to the left or to the right. On the vertical ruler, you measure up or down from the 0-inch mark.

Leo plans to print the letter on Villa Rio Records letterhead, which includes a graphic and the company's address. To allow more blank space for the letterhead, and to move the text down so that it doesn't look so crowded at the top of the page, you need to increase the top margin. The settings for changing the page margins are located on the Layout tab on the ribbon.

To change the page margins:

▶ **1.** On the ribbon, click the **Layout** tab. The Layout tab displays options for adjusting the layout of your document.

▶ **2.** In the Page Setup group, click the **Margins** button. The Margins gallery opens, as shown in Figure 1-18.

Figure 1-18	Margins gallery

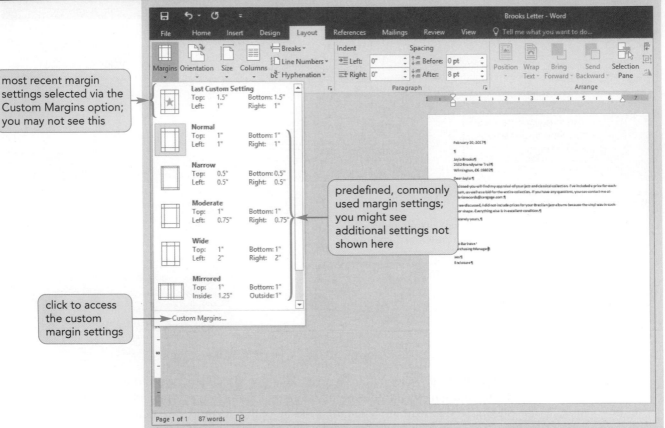

most recent margin settings selected via the Custom Margins option; you may not see this

predefined, commonly used margin settings; you might see additional settings not shown here

click to access the custom margin settings

In the Margins gallery, you can choose from a number of predefined margin options, or you can click the Custom Margins command to select your own settings. After you create custom margin settings, the most recent set appears as an option at the top of the menu. For the Brooks Letter document, you will create custom margins.

▶ **3.** Click **Custom Margins**. The Page Setup dialog box opens with the Margins tab displayed. The default margin settings are displayed in the boxes at the top of the Margins tab. The top margin of 1" is already selected, ready for you to type a new margin setting.

▶ **4.** In the Top box in the Margins section, type **2.5**. You do not need to type an inch mark ("). See Figure 1-19.

| Figure 1-19 | Creating custom margins in the Page Setup dialog box |

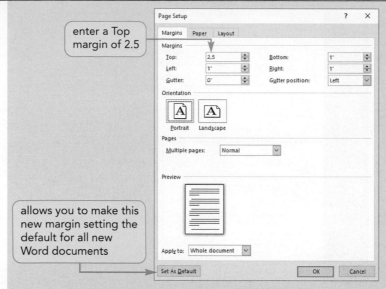

enter a Top margin of 2.5

allows you to make this new margin setting the default for all new Word documents

5. Click the **OK** button. The text of the letter is now lower on the page. The page looks less crowded, with room for the company's letterhead.

6. Change the Zoom level back to **120%**, and then save the document.

For most documents, the Word default of 1-inch margins is fine. In some professional settings, however, you might need to use a particular custom margin setting for all your documents. In that case, define the custom margins using the Margins tab in the Page Setup dialog box, and then click the Set As Default button to make your settings the default for all new documents. Keep in mind that most printers can't print to the edge of the page; if you select custom margins that are too narrow for your printer's specifications, Word alerts you to change your margin settings.

Previewing and Printing a Document

To make sure the document is ready to print, and to avoid wasting paper and time, you should first review it in Backstage view to make sure it will look right when printed. Like the One Page zoom setting you used earlier, the Print option in Backstage view displays a full-page preview of the document, allowing you to see how it will fit on the printed page. However, you cannot actually edit this preview. It simply provides one last opportunity to look at the document before printing.

To preview the document:

1. Proofread the document one last time, and correct any remaining errors.

2. Click the **File** tab to display Backstage view.

3. In the navigation bar, click **Print**.

The Print screen displays a full-page version of your document, showing how the letter will fit on the printed page. The Print settings to the left of the preview allow you to control a variety of print options. For example, you can change the number of copies from the default setting of "1." The 1 Page Per Sheet button opens a menu where you can choose to print multiple pages on a single sheet of paper or to scale the printed page to a particular paper size. You can also use the navigation controls at the bottom of the screen to display other pages in a document. See Figure 1-20.

Figure 1-20 Print settings in Backstage view

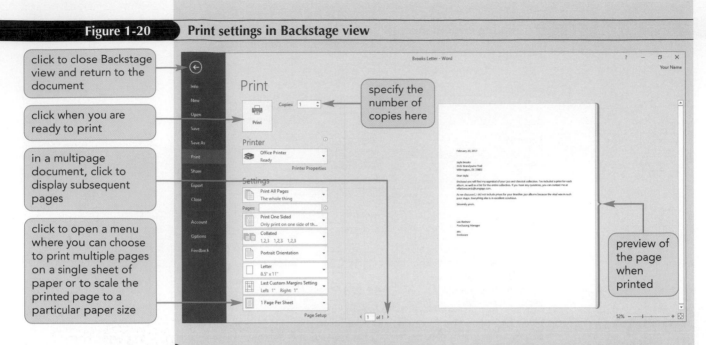

click to close Backstage view and return to the document

click when you are ready to print

in a multipage document, click to display subsequent pages

click to open a menu where you can choose to print multiple pages on a single sheet of paper or to scale the printed page to a particular paper size

specify the number of copies here

preview of the page when printed

4. Review your document and make sure its overall layout matches that of the document in Figure 1-20. If you notice a problem with paragraph breaks or spacing, click the **Back** button ⊖ at the top of the navigation bar to return to the document, make any necessary changes, and then start again at Step 2.

At this point, you can print the document or you can leave Backstage view and return to the document in Print Layout view. In the following steps, you should print the document only if your instructor asks you to. If you will be printing the document, make sure your printer is turned on and contains paper.

To leave Backstage view or to print the document:

1. Click the **Back** button at the top of the navigation bar ⊖ to leave Backstage view and return to the document in Print Layout view, or click the **Print** button. Backstage view closes, and the letter prints if you clicked the Print button.

2. Click the **File** tab, and then click **Close** in the navigation bar to close the document without closing Word.

Next, Leo asks you to create an envelope he can use to send an appraisal to another potential record seller.

Creating an Envelope

Before you can create the envelope, you need to open a new, blank document. To create a new document, you can start with a blank document—as you did with the letter to Jayla Brooks—or you can start with one that already contains formatting and generic text commonly used in a variety of professional documents, such as a fax cover sheet or a memo. These preformatted files are called **templates**. You could use a template to create a formatted envelope, but first you'll learn how to create one on your own in a new, blank document. You'll have a chance to try out a template in the Case Problems at the end of this module.

To create a new document for the envelope:

1. Click the **File** tab, and then click **New** in the navigation bar. The New screen is similar to the one you saw when you first started Word, with a blank document in the upper-left corner, along with a variety of templates. See Figure 1-21.

| Figure 1-21 | New options in Backstage view |

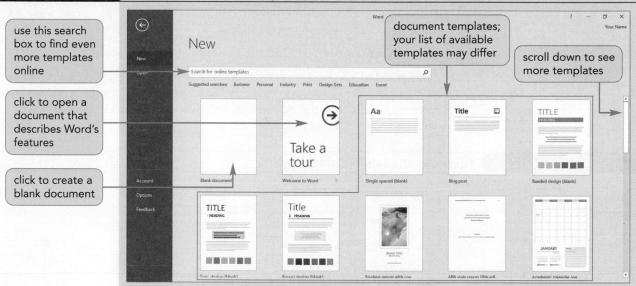

- use this search box to find even more templates online
- document templates; your list of available templates may differ
- scroll down to see more templates
- click to open a document that describes Word's features
- click to create a blank document

2. Click **Blank document**. A new document named Document2 opens in the document window, with the Home tab selected on the ribbon.

3. If necessary, change the Zoom level to **120%**, and display nonprinting characters and the rulers.

4. Save the new document as **Gomez Envelope** in the location specified by your instructor.

To create the envelope:

1. On the ribbon, click the **Mailings** tab. The ribbon changes to display the various Mailings options.

2. In the Create group, click the **Envelopes** button. The Envelopes and Labels dialog box opens, with the Envelopes tab displayed. The insertion point appears in the Delivery address box, ready for you to type the recipient's address. Depending on how your computer is set up, and whether you are working on your own computer or a school computer, you might see an address in the Return address box.

3. In the Delivery address box, type the following address, pressing the Enter key to start each new line:

Alexis Gomez

6549 West 16th Street

Wilmington, DE 19806

Because Leo will be using the store's printed envelopes, you don't need to print a return address on this envelope.

4. Click the **Omit** check box to insert a checkmark, if necessary.

At this point, if you had a printer stocked with envelopes, you could click the Print button to print the envelope. To save an envelope for printing later, you need to add it to the document. Your Envelopes and Labels dialog box should match the one in Figure 1-22.

Figure 1-22	Envelopes and Labels dialog box

select this check box to omit a return address

you might see an address here

if your printer was stocked with envelopes, you could click here to print the envelope immediately

click to save the envelope as part of the document

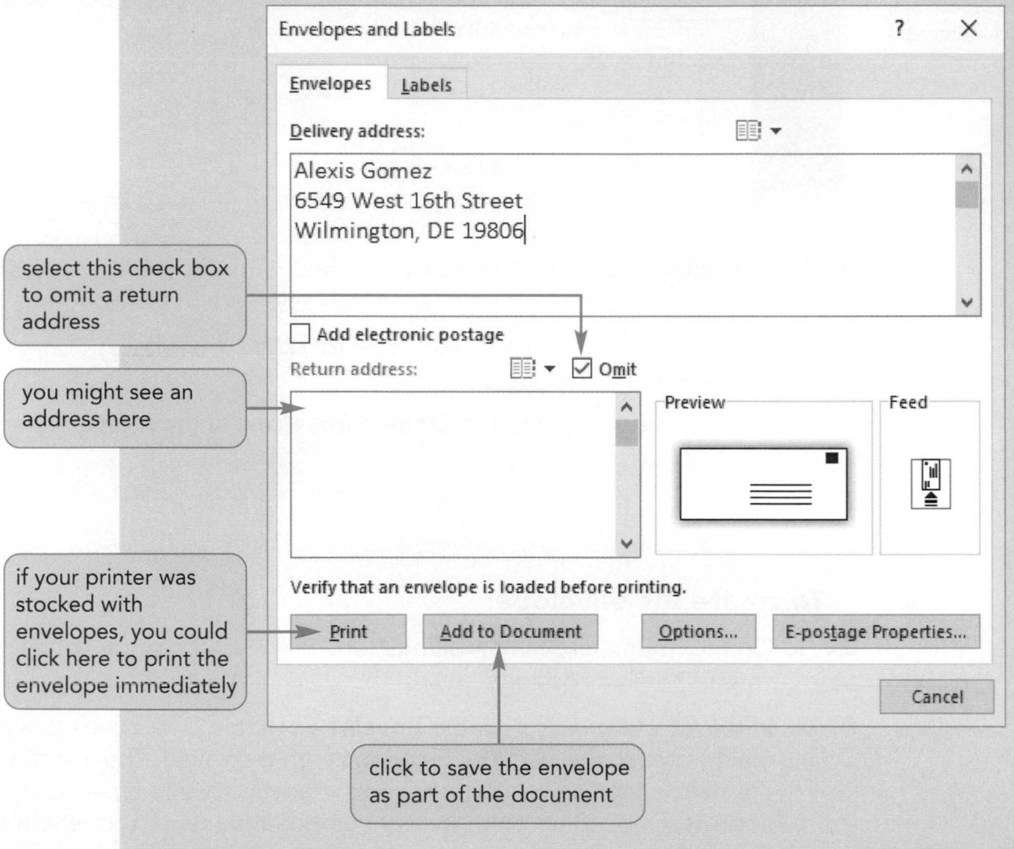

5. Click the **Add to Document** button. The dialog box closes, and you return to the document window. The envelope is inserted at the top of your document, with 1.0 line spacing. The double line with the words "Section Break (Next Page)" is related to how the envelope is formatted and will not be visible when you print the envelope. The envelope will print in the standard business envelope format. In this case, you added the envelope to a blank document, but you could also add an envelope to a completed letter, in which case Word adds the envelope as a new page before the letter.

6. Save the document. Leo will print the envelope later, so you can close the document now.

7. Click the **File** tab, and then click **Close** in the navigation bar. The document closes, but Word remains open.

You're finished creating the cover letter and the envelope. In the next session, you will modify a flyer by formatting the text and adding a photo.

INSIGHT

Creating Documents with Templates

Microsoft offers predesigned templates for all kinds of documents, including calendars, reports, and thank-you cards. You can use the scroll bar on the right of the New screen (shown earlier in Figure 1-21) to scroll down to see more templates, or you can use the Search for online templates box in the New screen to search among thousands of other options available at Office.com. When you open a template, you actually open a new document containing the formatting and text stored in the template, leaving the original template untouched. A typical template includes placeholder text that you replace with your own information.

Templates allow you to create stylish, professional-looking documents quickly and easily. To use them effectively, however, you need to be knowledgeable about Word and its many options for manipulating text, graphics, and page layouts. Otherwise, the complicated formatting of some Word templates can be more frustrating than helpful. As you become a more experienced Word user, you'll learn how to create your own templates.

REVIEW

Session 1.1 Quick Check

1. What Word feature automatically inserts dates and other regularly used items for you?

2. In a block-style letter, does the inside address appear above or below the date?

3. Explain how to display nonprinting characters.

4. Explain how to use a hyperlink in a Word document to open a new email message.

5. Define the term "line spacing."

6. Explain how to display a shortcut menu with options for correcting a word with a wavy red underline.

Session 1.2 Visual Overview:

Alignment buttons control the text's **alignment**—that is, the way it lines up horizontally between the left and right margins. Here, the Center button is selected because the text containing the insertion point is center-aligned.

You can click the Clear All Formatting button to restore selected text to the default font, font size, and color.

Clicking the Format Painter button displays the Format Painter pointer, which you can use to copy formatting from the selected text to other text in the document.

The Font group on the Home tab includes the Font box and the Font size box for setting the text's font and the font size, respectively. A **font** is a set of characters that uses the same typeface.

You click the Shading button arrow to apply a colored background to a selected paragraph.

This document has a landscape orientation, meaning it is wider than it is tall.

You can insert a photo or another type of picture in a document by using the **Pictures button** located on the Insert tab of the ribbon. After you insert a photo or another picture, you can format it with a style that adds a border or a shadow or changes its shape.

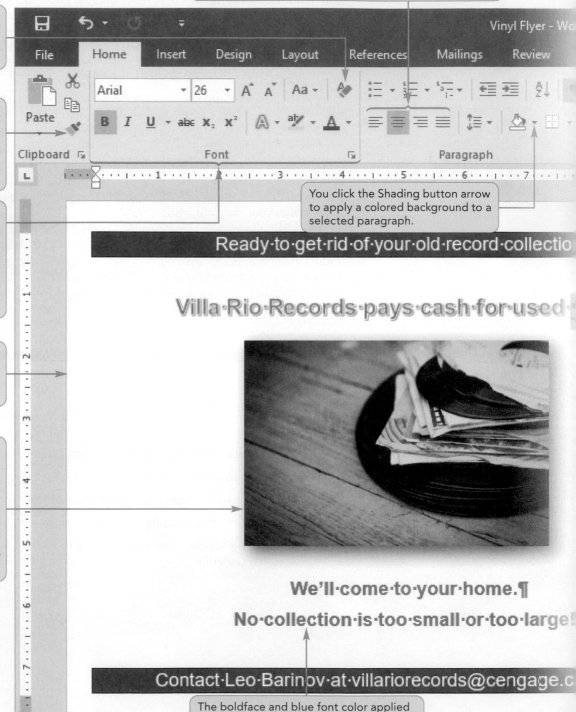

The boldface and blue font color applied to this text are examples of formatting that you should use sparingly to draw attention to a specific part of a document.

Formatting a Document

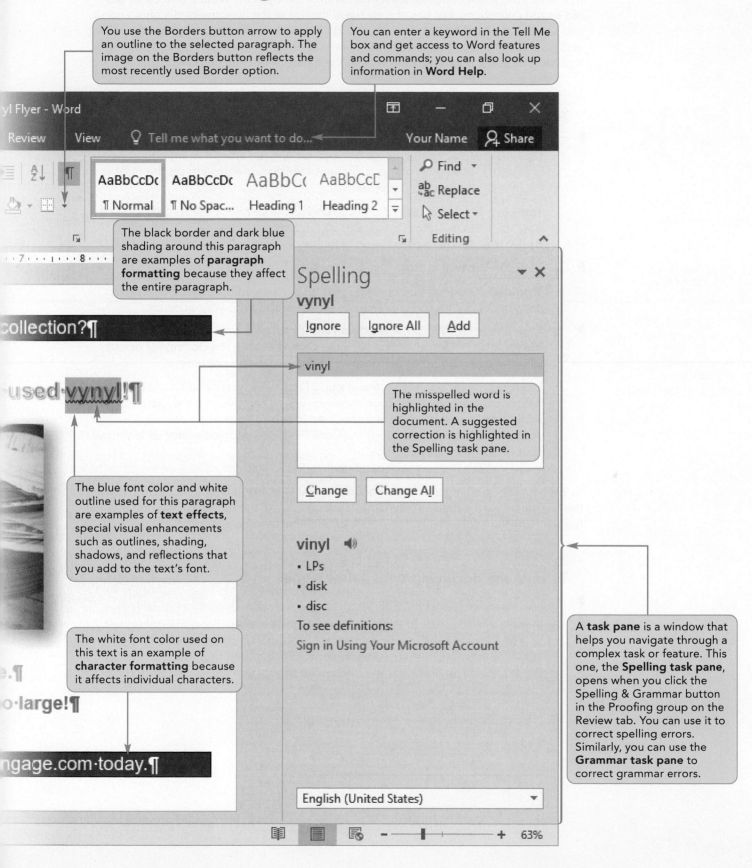

You use the Borders button arrow to apply an outline to the selected paragraph. The image on the Borders button reflects the most recently used Border option.

You can enter a keyword in the Tell Me box and get access to Word features and commands; you can also look up information in **Word Help**.

The black border and dark blue shading around this paragraph are examples of **paragraph formatting** because they affect the entire paragraph.

The misspelled word is highlighted in the document. A suggested correction is highlighted in the Spelling task pane.

The blue font color and white outline used for this paragraph are examples of **text effects**, special visual enhancements such as outlines, shading, shadows, and reflections that you add to the text's font.

The white font color used on this text is an example of **character formatting** because it affects individual characters.

A **task pane** is a window that helps you navigate through a complex task or feature. This one, the **Spelling task pane**, opens when you click the Spelling & Grammar button in the Proofing group on the Review tab. You can use it to correct spelling errors. Similarly, you can use the **Grammar task pane** to correct grammar errors.

Opening an Existing Document

In this session, you'll complete a flyer reminding customers that Villa Rio Records buys old record collections. Leo has already typed the text of the flyer, inserted a photo into it, and saved it as a Word document. He would like you to check the document for spelling and grammar errors, format the flyer to make it eye-catching and easy to read, and then replace the current photo with a new one. You'll start by opening the document.

To open the flyer document:

1. On the ribbon, click the **File** tab to open Backstage view, and then verify that **Open** is selected in the navigation bar. On the left side of the Open screen is a list of places you can go to locate other documents, and on the right is a list of recently opened documents.

    Trouble? If you closed Word at the end of the previous session, start Word now, click Open Other Documents at the bottom of the navigation bar in Backstage view, and then begin with Step 2.

2. Click the **Browse** button. The Open dialog box opens.

    Trouble? If your instructor asked you to store your files to your OneDrive account, click OneDrive - Personal, and then log in to your account.

3. Navigate to the **Word1 > Module folder** included with your Data Files, click **Vinyl** in the file list, and then click the **Open** button. The document opens with the insertion point blinking in the first line of the document.

    Trouble? If you don't have the starting Data Files, you need to get them before you can proceed. Your instructor will either give you the Data Files or ask you to obtain them from a specified location (such as a network drive). If you have any questions about the Data Files, see your instructor or technical support person for assistance.

Before making changes to Leo's document, you will save it with a new name. Saving the document with a different filename creates a copy of the file and leaves the original file unchanged in case you want to work through the module again.

To save the document with a new name:

1. On the ribbon, click the **File** tab.

2. In the navigation bar in Backstage view, click **Save As**. Save the document as **Vinyl Flyer** in the location specified by your instructor. Backstage view closes, and the document window appears again with the new filename in the title bar. The original Vinyl document closes, remaining unchanged.

PROSKILLS

Decision Making: Creating Effective Documents

Before you create a new document or revise an existing document, take a moment to think about your audience. Ask yourself these questions:

- Who is your audience?
- What do they know?
- What do they need to know?
- How can the document you are creating change your audience's behavior or opinions?

Every decision you make about your document should be based on your answers to these questions. To take a simple example, if you are creating a flyer to announce an upcoming seminar on college financial aid, your audience would be students and their parents. They probably all know what the term "financial aid" means, so you don't need to explain that in your flyer. Instead, you can focus on telling them what they need to know—the date, time, and location of the seminar. The behavior you want to affect, in this case, is whether or not your audience will show up for the seminar. By making the flyer professional looking and easy to read, you increase the chance that they will.

You might find it more challenging to answer these questions about your audience when creating more complicated documents, such as corporate reports. But the focus remains the same—connecting with the audience. As you are deciding what information to include in your document, remember that the goal of a professional document is to convey the information as effectively as possible to your target audience.

Before revising a document for someone else, it's a good idea to familiarize yourself with its overall structure.

To review the document:

1. Verify that the document is displayed in Print Layout view and that nonprinting characters and the rulers are displayed. For now, you can ignore the wavy underlines that appear in the document.

2. Change the Zoom level to **120%**, if necessary, and then scroll down, if necessary, so that you can read the last line of the document.

   At this point, the document is very simple. By the time you are finished, it will look like the document shown in the Session 1.2 Visual Overview, with the spelling and grammar errors corrected. Figure 1-23 summarizes the tasks you will perform.

Figure 1-23 Formatting changes requested by Leo

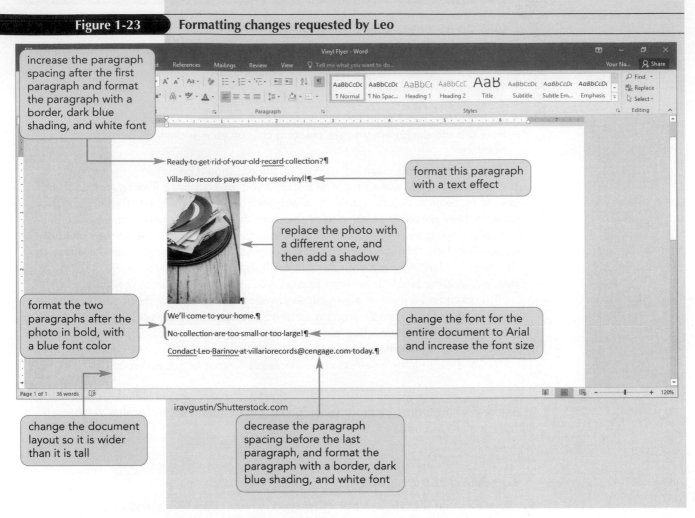

increase the paragraph spacing after the first paragraph and format the paragraph with a border, dark blue shading, and white font

format this paragraph with a text effect

replace the photo with a different one, and then add a shadow

format the two paragraphs after the photo in bold, with a blue font color

change the font for the entire document to Arial and increase the font size

change the document layout so it is wider than it is tall

decrease the paragraph spacing before the last paragraph, and format the paragraph with a border, dark blue shading, and white font

Ready·to·get·rid·of·your·old·recard·collection?¶

Villa·Rio·records·pays·cash·for·used·vinyl!¶

We'll·come·to·your·home.¶

No·collection·are·too·small·or·too·large!¶

Condact·Leo·Barinov·at·villariorecords@cengage.com·today.¶

iravgustin/Shutterstock.com

You will start by correcting the spelling and grammar errors.

Using the Spelling and Grammar Task Panes

Word marks possible spelling and grammatical errors with wavy underlines as you type so that you can quickly go back and correct those errors. A more thorough way of checking the spelling in a document is to use the Spelling and Grammar task panes to check a document word by word for a variety of errors. You can customize the spelling and grammar settings to add or ignore certain types of errors.

Leo asks you to use the Spelling and Grammar task panes to check the flyer for mistakes. Before you do, you'll review the various Spelling and Grammar settings.

To review the Spelling and Grammar settings:

1. On the ribbon, click the **File** tab, and then click **Options** in the navigation bar. The Word Options dialog box opens. You can use this dialog box to change a variety of settings related to how Word looks and works.

2. In the left pane, click **Proofing**.

Note the four selected options in the "When correcting spelling and grammar in Word" section. The first three options tell you that Word will check for misspellings, grammatical errors, and frequently confused words as you type, marking them with wavy underlines as necessary. The fourth option, "Check grammar with spelling," tells you that Word will check both grammar and spelling when you use the Spelling and Grammar task pane. If you want to check only spelling, you could deselect this check box.

3. In the "When correcting spelling and grammar in Word" section, click the **Settings** button. The Grammar Settings dialog box opens. Here you can control the types of grammar errors Word checks for. All of the boxes are selected by default, which is what you want. See Figure 1-24.

Figure 1-24	Grammar Settings dialog box

click to display settings related to proofing a document

deselect if you want to check only spelling

click to recheck words that you chose to ignore in a previous spelling and grammar check

click to display the Grammar Settings dialog box

4. Click the **Cancel** button to close the Grammar Settings dialog box and return to the Word Options dialog box.

Note that the results of the Spelling and Grammar checker are sometimes hard to predict. For example, in some documents Word will mark a misused word or duplicate punctuation as errors and then fail to mark the same items as errors in another document. Also, if you choose to ignore a misspelling in a document, and then, without closing Word, type the same misspelled word in another document, Word will probably not mark it as an error. These issues can be especially problematic when working on a document typed by someone else. So to ensure that you get the best possible results, it's a good idea to click the Recheck Document button before you use the Spelling and Grammar checker.

5. Click the **Recheck Document** button, and then click **Yes** in the warning dialog box.

6. In the Word Options dialog box, click the **OK** button to close the dialog box. You return to the Vinyl Flyer document.

Now you are ready to check the document's spelling and grammar. All errors marked with red underlines are considered spelling errors, while all errors marked with blue underlines are considered grammatical errors.

To check the Vinyl Flyer document for spelling and grammatical errors:

1. Press the **Ctrl+Home** keys, if necessary, to move the insertion point to the beginning of the document, to the left of the "R" in "Ready." By placing the insertion point at the beginning of the document, you ensure that Word will check the entire document from start to finish, without having to go back and check an earlier part.

2. On the ribbon, click the **Review** tab. The ribbon changes to display reviewing options.

3. In the Proofing group, click the **Spelling & Grammar** button.

The Spelling task pane opens on the right side of the Word window, with the word "recard" listed as a possible spelling error. The same word is highlighted in gray in the document. In the task pane's list of possible corrections, the correctly spelled word "record" is highlighted in light blue. See Figure 1-25.

| Figure 1-25 | Spelling task pane |

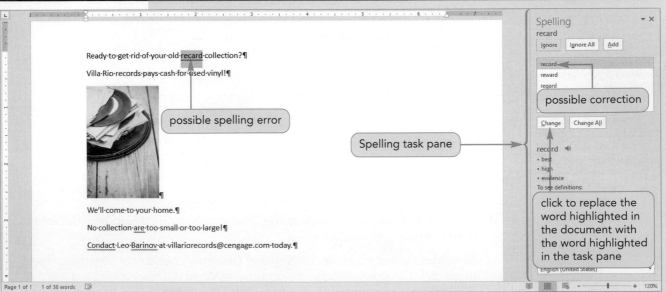

iravgustin/Shutterstock.com

4. In the task pane, click the **Change** button. The misspelled word "recard" is replaced with "record."

Next, Word highlights the second to last sentence, indicating another possible error. The Spelling task pane changes to the Grammar task pane, and the information at the bottom of the task pane explains that the error is related to subject-verb agreement.

5. Verify that "is" is selected in the Grammar task pane, and then click the **Change** button. The first word of the last sentence is now highlighted in the document, and the Grammar task pane changes to the Spelling task pane. You could correct this misspelling by using the options in the Spelling task pane, but this time you'll try typing directly in the document.

6. In the document, click to the right of the "d" in "Condact," press the **Backspace** key, type **t**, and then click the **Resume** button in the Spelling task pane. Leo's last name is now highlighted in the document. Although the Spelling task pane doesn't recognize "Barinov" as a word, it is spelled correctly, so you can ignore it.

7. Click the **Ignore** button in the Spelling task pane. The task pane closes, and a dialog box opens, indicating that the spelling and grammar check is complete.

8. Click the **OK** button to close the dialog box.

PROSKILLS

Written Communication: Proofreading Your Document

Although the Spelling and Grammar task panes are useful tools, they won't always catch every error in a document, and they sometimes flag "errors" that are actually correct. This means there is no substitute for careful proofreading. Always take the time to read through your document to check for errors the Spelling and Grammar task panes might have missed. Keep in mind that the Spelling and Grammar task panes cannot pinpoint inaccurate phrases or poorly chosen words. You'll have to find those yourself. To produce a professional document, you must read it carefully several times. It's a good idea to ask one or two other people to read your documents as well; they might catch something you missed.

You still need to proofread the Vinyl Flyer document. You'll do that next.

To proofread the Vinyl Flyer document:

1. Review the document text for any remaining errors. In the second paragraph, change the lowercase "r" in "records" to an uppercase "R."

2. In the last line of text, replace "Leo Barinov" with your first and last names, and then save the document. Including your name in the document will make it easier for you to find your copy later if you print it on a shared printer.

Now you're ready to begin formatting the document. You will start by turning the page so it is wider than it is tall. In other words, you will change the document's **orientation**.

Changing Page Orientation

Portrait orientation, with the page taller than it is wide, is the default page orientation for Word documents because it is the orientation most commonly used for letters, reports, and other formal documents. However, Leo wants you to format the flyer in **landscape orientation**—that is, with the page turned so it is wider than it is tall—to better accommodate the photo. You can accomplish this task by using the Orientation button located on the Layout tab on the ribbon. After you change the page orientation, you will select narrower margins so you can maximize the amount of color on the page.

To change the page orientation:

▎ **1.** Change the document Zoom level to **One Page** so that you can see the entire document.

▎ **2.** On the ribbon, click the **Layout** tab. The ribbon changes to display options for formatting the overall layout of text and images in the document.

▎ **3.** In the Page Setup group, click the **Orientation** button, and then click **Landscape** on the menu. The document changes to landscape orientation.

▎ **4.** In the Page Setup group, click the **Margins** button, and then click the **Narrow** option on the menu. The margins shrink from 1 inch to .5 inch on all four sides. See Figure 1-26.

Figure 1-26	Document in landscape orientation with narrow margins

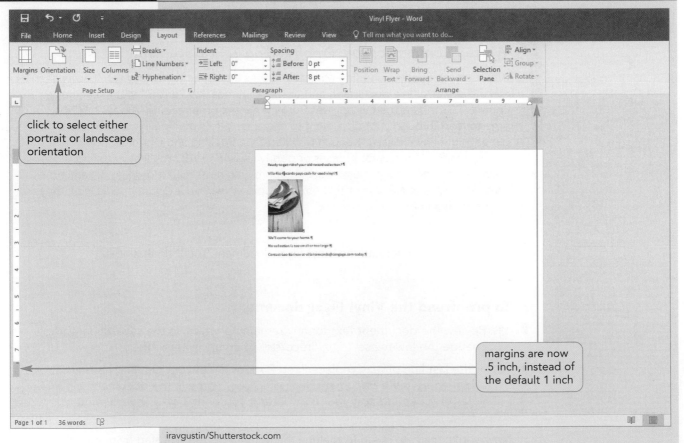

click to select either portrait or landscape orientation

margins are now .5 inch, instead of the default 1 inch

iravgustin/Shutterstock.com

Changing the Font and Font Size

Leo typed the document in the default font size, 11 point, and the default font, Calibri, but he would like to switch to the Arial font instead. Also, he wants to increase the size of all five paragraphs of text. To apply these changes, you start by selecting the text you want to format. Then you select the options you want in the Font group on the Home tab.

To change the font and font size:

▶ **1.** On the ribbon, click the **Home** tab.

▶ **2.** Change the document Zoom level to **120%**.

▶ **3.** To verify that the insertion point is located at the beginning of the document, press the **Ctrl+Home** keys.

▶ **4.** Press and hold the **Shift** key, and then click to the right of the second paragraph marker, at the end of the second paragraph of text. The first two paragraphs of text are selected, as shown in Figure 1-27.

| Figure 1-27 | Selected text, with default font displayed in Font box |

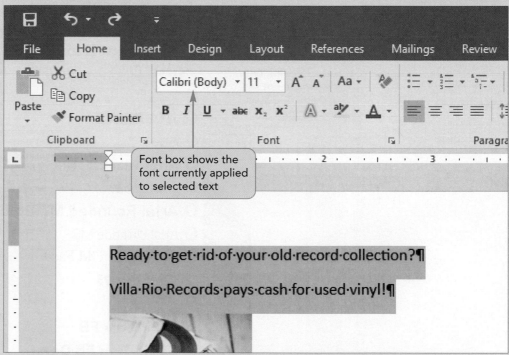

iravgustin/Shutterstock.com

The Font box in the Font group displays the name of the font applied to the selected text, which in this case is Calibri. The word "Body" next to the font name indicates that the Calibri font is intended for formatting body text. **Body text** is ordinary text, as opposed to titles or headings.

▶ **5.** In the Font group on the Home tab, click the **Font** arrow. A list of available fonts appears, with Calibri Light and Calibri at the top of the list. Calibri is highlighted in gray, indicating that this font is currently applied to the selected text. The word "Headings" next to the font name "Calibri Light" indicates that Calibri Light is intended for formatting headings.

Below Calibri Light and Calibri, you might see a list of fonts that have been used recently on your computer, followed by a complete alphabetical list of all available fonts. (You won't see the list of recently used fonts if you just installed Word.) You need to scroll the list to see all the available fonts. Each name in the list is formatted with the relevant font. For example, the name "Arial" appears in the Arial font. See Figure 1-28.

Figure 1-28 **Font list**

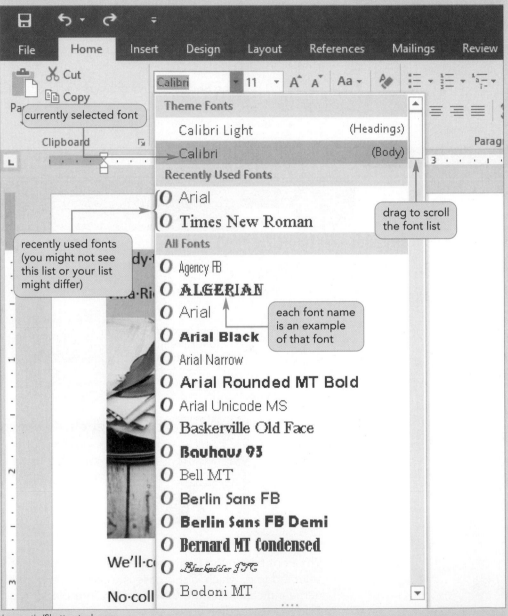

iravgustin/Shutterstock.com

6. Without clicking, move the pointer over a dramatic-looking font in the font list, such as Algerian or Arial Black, and then move the pointer over another font.

The selected text in the document changes to show a Live Preview of the font the pointer is resting on. **Live Preview** shows the results that would occur in your document if you clicked the option you are pointing to.

7. When you are finished reviewing the Font list, click **Arial**. The Font menu closes, and the selected text is formatted in Arial.

    Next, you will make the text more eye-catching by increasing the font size. The Font Size box currently displays the number "11," indicating that the selected text is formatted in 11-point font.

8. Verify that the first two paragraphs are still selected, and then click the **Font Size** arrow in the Font group to display a menu of font sizes. As with the Font menu, you can move the pointer over options in the Font Size menu to see a Live Preview of that option.

9. On the Font Size menu, click **22**. The selected text increases significantly in size, and the Font Size menu closes.

10. Select the three paragraphs of text below the photo, format them in the Arial font, and then increase the paragraph's font size to 22 points.

11. Click a blank area of the document to deselect the text, and then save the document.

TIP

To restore selected text to its default appearance, click the Clear All Formatting button in the Font group on the Home tab.

Leo examines the flyer and decides he would like to apply more character formatting, which affects the appearance of individual characters, in the middle three paragraphs. After that, you can turn your attention to paragraph formatting, which affects the appearance of the entire paragraph.

Applying Text Effects, Font Colors, and Font Styles

To really make text stand out, you can use text effects. You access these options by clicking the Text Effects and Typography button in the Font group on the Home tab. Keep in mind that text effects can be very dramatic. For formal, professional documents, you probably need to use only **bold** or *italic* to make a word or paragraph stand out.

Leo suggests applying text effects to the second paragraph.

To apply text effects to the second paragraph:

1. Scroll up, if necessary, to display the beginning of the document, and then click in the selection bar to the left of the second paragraph. The entire second paragraph is selected.

2. In the Font group on the Home tab, click the **Text Effects and Typography** button [A].

    A gallery of text effects appears. Options that allow you to fine-tune a particular text effect, perhaps by changing the color or adding an even more pronounced shadow, are listed below the gallery. A **gallery** is a menu or grid that shows a visual representation of the options available when you click a button.

3. In the middle of the bottom row of the gallery, place the pointer over the blue letter "A." This displays a ScreenTip with the text effect's full name: Fill - Blue, Accent 1, Outline - Background 1, Hard Shadow - Accent 1. A Live Preview of the effect appears in the document. See Figure 1-29.

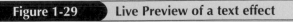

4. In the bottom row of the gallery, click the blue letter "A." The text effect is applied to the selected paragraph and the Text Effects gallery closes. The second paragraph is formatted in blue, as shown in the Session 1.2 Visual Overview. On the ribbon, the Bold button in the Font group is now highlighted because bold formatting is part of this text effect.

Next, to make the text stand out a bit more, you'll increase the font size. This time, instead of using the Font Size button, you'll use a different method.

5. In the Font group, click the **Increase Font Size button** $\boxed{A^{\circ}}$. The font size increases from 22 points to 24 points.

6. Click the **Increase Font Size button** $\boxed{A^{\circ}}$ again. The font size increases to 26 points. If you need to decrease the font size of selected text, you can use the Decrease Font Size button.

Leo asks you to emphasize the third and fourth paragraphs by adding bold and a blue font color.

To apply a font color and bold:

1. Select the third and fourth paragraphs of text, which contain the text "We'll come to your home. No collection is too small or too large!"

2. In the Font group on the Home tab, click the **Font Color button arrow** $\boxed{A \cdot}$. A gallery of font colors appears. Black is the default font color and appears at the top of the Font Color gallery, with the word "Automatic" next to it.

The options in the Theme Colors section of the menu are complementary colors that work well when used together in a document. The options in the Standard Colors section are more limited. For more advanced color options, you could use the More Colors or Gradient options. Leo prefers a simple blue.

Trouble? If the third and fourth paragraphs turned red, you clicked the Font Color button $\boxed{A}$ instead of the arrow next to it. On the Quick Access Toolbar, click the Undo button $\boxed{\leftarrow}$, and then repeat Step 2.

3. In the Theme Colors section, place the mouse pointer over the square that's second from the right in the top row. A ScreenTip with the color's name, "Blue, Accent 5," appears. A Live Preview of the color appears in the document, where the text you selected in Step 1 now appears formatted in blue. See Figure 1-30.

| Figure 1-30 | Font Color gallery showing a Live Preview |

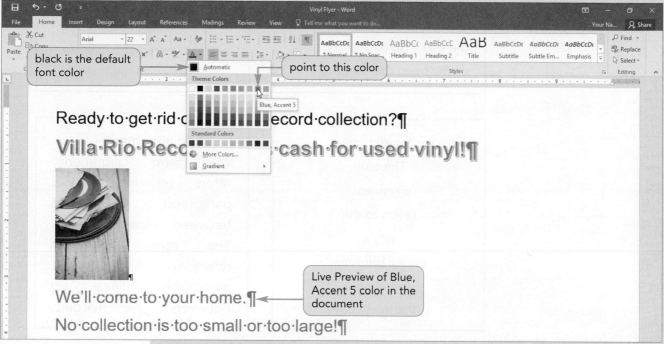

iravgustin/Shutterstock.com

4. Click the **Blue, Accent 5** square. The Font color gallery closes, and the selected text is formatted in blue. On the Font Color button, the bar below the letter "A" is now blue, indicating that if you select text and click the Font Color button, the text will automatically change to blue.

5. In the Font group, click the **Bold** button [B]. The selected text is now formatted in bold, with thicker, darker lettering.

TIP

You can use other buttons in the Font group on the Home tab to apply other character attributes, such as underline, italic, or superscript.

Next, you will complete some paragraph formatting, starting with paragraph alignment.

Aligning Text

Alignment refers to how text and graphics line up between the page margins. By default, Word aligns text along the left margin, with the text along the right margin **ragged**, or uneven. This is called **left alignment**. With **right alignment**, the text is aligned along the right margin and is ragged along the left margin. With **center alignment**, text is centered between the left and right margins and is ragged along both the left and right margins. With **justified alignment**, full lines of text are spaced between both the left and the right margins, and no text is ragged. Text in newspaper columns is often justified. See Figure 1-31.

| Figure 1-31 | Varieties of text alignment |

left alignment

The term "alignment" refers to the way a paragraph lines up between the margins. The term "alignment" refers to the way a paragraph lines up between the margins.

right alignment

The term "alignment" refers to the way a paragraph lines up between the margins. The term "alignment" refers to the way a paragraph lines up between the margins.

center alignment

The term "alignment" refers to the way a paragraph lines up between the margins.

justified alignment

The term "alignment" refers to the way a paragraph lines up between the margins. The term "alignment" refers to the way a paragraph lines up between the margins.

The Paragraph group on the Home tab includes a button for each of the four major types of alignment described in Figure 1-31: the Align Left button, the Center button, the Align Right button, and the Justify button. To align a single paragraph, click anywhere in that paragraph, and then click the appropriate alignment button. To align multiple paragraphs, select the paragraphs first, and then click an alignment button.

You need to center all the text in the flyer now. You can center the photo at the same time.

To center-align the text:

1. Make sure the Home tab is still selected, and press the **Ctrl+A** keys to select the entire document.

2. In the Paragraph group, click the **Center** button ☰, and then click a blank area of the document to deselect the selected paragraphs. The text and photo are now centered on the page, similar to the centered text shown earlier in the Session 1.2 Visual Overview.

3. Save the document.

Use the Ctrl+A keys to select the entire document, instead of dragging the mouse pointer. It's easy to miss part of the document when you drag the mouse pointer.

Adding a Paragraph Border and Shading

A **paragraph border** is an outline that appears around one or more paragraphs in a document. You can choose to apply only a partial border—for example, a bottom border that appears as an underline under the last line of text in the paragraph—or an entire box around a paragraph. You can select different colors and line weights for the border as well, making it more or less prominent as needed. You apply paragraph borders using the Borders button in the Paragraph group on the Home tab. **Shading** is background color that you can apply to one or more paragraphs and can be used in conjunction with a border for a more defined effect. You apply shading using the Shading button in the Paragraph group on the Home tab.

Now you will apply a border and shading to the first paragraph, as shown earlier in the Session 1.2 Visual Overview. Then you will use the Format Painter to copy this formatting to the last paragraph in the document.

To add shading and a paragraph border:

1. Select the first paragraph. Be sure to select the paragraph mark at the end of the paragraph.

2. On the Home tab, in the Paragraph group, click the **Borders button arrow**. A gallery of border options appears, as shown in Figure 1-32. To apply a complete outline around the selected text, you use the Outside Borders option.

Figure 1-32	Border gallery

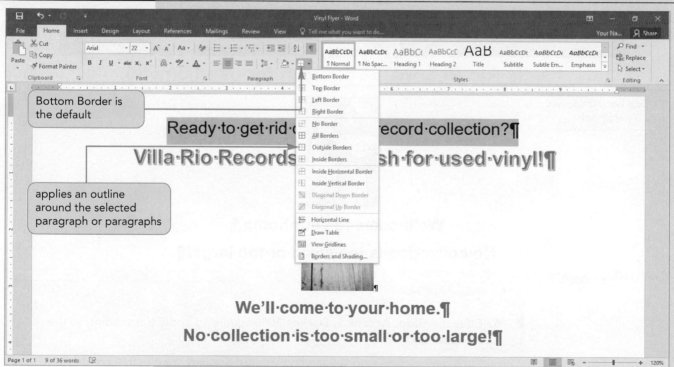

iravgustin/Shutterstock.com

Trouble? If the gallery does not open and instead the paragraph becomes underlined with a single underline, you clicked the Borders button instead of the arrow next to it. On the Quick Access Toolbar, click the Undo button, and then repeat Step 2.

3. In the Border gallery, click **Outside Borders**. The menu closes and a black border appears around the selected paragraph, spanning the width of the page. In the Paragraph group, the Borders button ⊞ changes to show the Outside Borders option.

Trouble? If the border around the first paragraph doesn't extend all the way to the left and right margins and instead encloses only the text, you didn't select the paragraph mark as directed in Step 1. Click the Undo button ⤺ repeatedly to remove the border, and begin again with Step 1.

4. In the Paragraph group, click the **Shading button arrow** ◇▾. A gallery of shading options opens, divided into Theme Colors and Standard Colors. You will use a shade of dark blue in the fifth column from the left.

5. In the bottom row in the Theme Colors section, move the pointer over the square in the fifth column from the left to display a ScreenTip that reads "Blue, Accent 1, Darker 50%." A Live Preview of the color appears in the document. See Figure 1-33.

Figure 1-33	Shading gallery with a Live Preview displayed

iravgustin/Shutterstock.com

6. Click the **Blue, Accent 1, Darker 50%** square to apply the shading to the selected text.

On a dark background like the one you just applied, a white font creates a striking effect. Leo asks you to change the font color for this paragraph to white.

7. Make sure the Home tab is still selected.

8. In the Font group, click the **Font Color button arrow** 🄰▾ to open the Font Color gallery, and then click the **white** square in the top row of the Theme Colors. The Font Color gallery closes, and the paragraph is now formatted with white font.

9. Click a blank area of the document to deselect the text, review the change, and then save the document. See Figure 1-34.

Figure 1-34   **Paragraph formatted with dark blue shading, a black border, and white font**

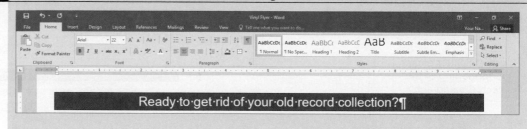

To add balance to the flyer, Leo suggests formatting the last paragraph in the document with the same shading, border, and font color as the first paragraph. You'll do that next.

Copying Formatting with the Format Painter

You could select the last paragraph and then apply the border, shading, and font color one step at a time. But it's easier to copy all the formatting from the first paragraph to the last paragraph using the Format Painter button in the Clipboard group on the Home tab.

REFERENCE

Using the Format Painter

- Select the text whose formatting you want to copy.
- On the Home tab, in the Clipboard group, click the Format Painter button; or to copy formatting to multiple sections of nonadjacent text, double-click the Format Painter button.
- The mouse pointer changes to the Format Painter pointer, the I-beam pointer with a paintbrush.
- Click the words you want to format, or drag to select and format entire paragraphs.
- When you are finished formatting the text, click the Format Painter button again to turn off the Format Painter.

You'll use the Format Painter now.

To use the Format Painter:

1. Change the document Zoom level to One Page so you can easily see both the first and last paragraphs.

2. Select the first paragraph, which is formatted with the dark blue shading, the border, and the white font color.

3. On the ribbon, click the **Home** tab.

4. In the Clipboard group, click the **Format Painter** button to activate, or turn on, the Format Painter.

5. Move the pointer over the document. The pointer changes to the Format Painter pointer 🖌I when you move the mouse pointer near an item that can be formatted. See Figure 1-35.

Figure 1-35   **Format Painter**

Format Painter is turned on

Format Painter copies the formatting of the selected paragraph

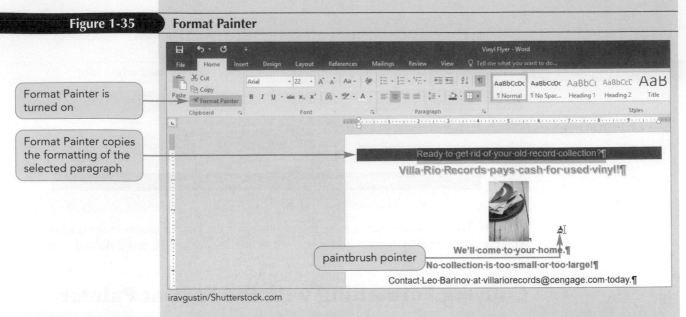

paintbrush pointer

iravgustin/Shutterstock.com

6. Click and drag the Format Painter pointer 📇 to select the last paragraph in the document. The paragraph is now formatted with dark blue shading, a black border, and white font. The mouse pointer returns to its original I-beam shape.

   Trouble? If the text in the newly formatted paragraph wrapped to a second line, replace your full name with your first name, or, if necessary, use only your initials so the paragraph is only one line long.

7. Click anywhere in the document to deselect the text, review the change, and then save the document.

You're almost finished working on the document's paragraph formatting. Your last step is to increase the paragraph spacing below the first paragraph and above the last paragraph. This will give the shaded text even more weight on the page. To complete this task, you will use the settings on the Layout tab, which offer more options than the Line and Paragraph Spacing button on the Home tab.

To increase the paragraph spacing below the first paragraph and above the last paragraph:

1. Click anywhere in the first paragraph, and then click the **Layout** tab. On this tab, the Paragraph group contains settings that control paragraph spacing. Currently, the paragraph spacing for the first paragraph is set to the default 0 points before the paragraph and 8 points after.

2. In the Paragraph group, click the **After** box to select the current setting, type **42**, and then press the **Enter** key. The added space causes the second paragraph to move down 42 points.

3. Click anywhere in the last paragraph.

4. On the Layout tab, in the Paragraph group, click the **Before** box to select the current setting, type **42**, and then press the **Enter** key. The added space causes the last paragraph to move down 42 points.

Formatting Professional Documents

In more formal documents, use color and special effects sparingly. The goal of letters, reports, and many other types of documents is to convey important information, not to dazzle the reader with fancy fonts and colors. Such elements only serve to distract the reader from your main point. In formal documents, it's a good idea to limit the number of colors to two and to stick with left alignment for text. In a document like the flyer you're currently working on, you have a little more leeway because the goal of the document is to attract attention. However, you still want it to look professional.

Finally, Leo wants you to replace the photo with one that will look better in the document's new landscape orientation. You'll replace the photo, and then you'll resize it so that the flyer fills the entire page.

Working with Pictures

A **picture** is a photo or another type of image that you insert into a document. To work with a picture, you first need to select it. Once a picture is selected, a contextual tab—the Picture Tools Format tab—appears on the ribbon, with options for editing the picture and adding effects such as a border, a shadow, a reflection, or a new shape. A **contextual tab** appears on the ribbon only when an object is selected. It contains commands related to the selected object so that you can manipulate, edit, and format the selected object. You can also use the mouse to resize or move a selected picture. To insert a new picture, you use the Pictures button in the Illustrations group on the Insert tab.

To delete the current photo and insert a new one:

▶ **1.** Click the photo to select it.

The circles, called **handles**, around the edge of the photo indicate the photo is selected. The Layout Options button, to the right of the photo, gives you access to options that control how the document text flows around the photo. You don't need to worry about these options now. Finally, note that the Picture Tools Format tab appeared on the ribbon when you selected the photo. See Figure 1-36.

Figure 1-36 **Selected photo**

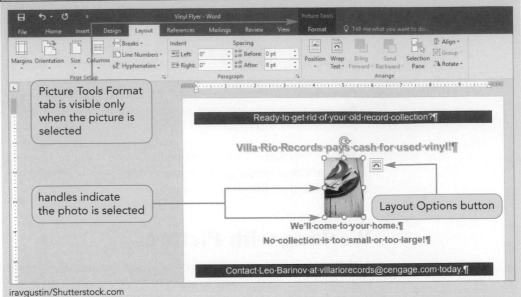

iravgustin/Shutterstock.com

> 2. Press the **Delete** key. The photo is deleted from the document. The insertion point blinks next to the paragraph symbol. You will insert the new photo in that paragraph.

> 3. On the ribbon, click the **Insert** tab. The ribbon changes to display the Insert options.

> 4. In the Illustrations group, click the **Pictures** button. The Insert Picture dialog box opens.

> 5. Navigate to the **Word1 > Module folder** included with your Data Files, and then click **Albums** to select the file. The name of the selected file appears in the File name box.

> 6. Click the **Insert** button to close the Insert Picture dialog box and insert the photo. A different album image, with the albums in the upper-right corner, appears in the document, below the second paragraph. The photo is selected, as indicated by the handles on its border. The newly inserted photo is so large that it appears on a second page.

Now you need to shrink the photo to fit the available space on the first page. You could do so by clicking one of the picture's corner handles, holding down the mouse button, and then dragging the handle to resize the picture. But using the Shape Height and Shape Width boxes on the Picture Tools Format tab gives you more precise results.

To resize the photo:

> 1. Make sure the Picture Tools Format tab is still selected on the ribbon.

> 2. In the Size group on the far right edge of the ribbon, locate the Shape Height box, which tells you that the height of the selected picture is currently 6.67". The Shape Width box tells you that the width of the picture is 10". As you'll see in the next step, when you change one of these measurements, the other changes accordingly, keeping the overall shape of the picture the same. See Figure 1-37.

Figure 1-37   **Shape Height and Shape Width boxes**

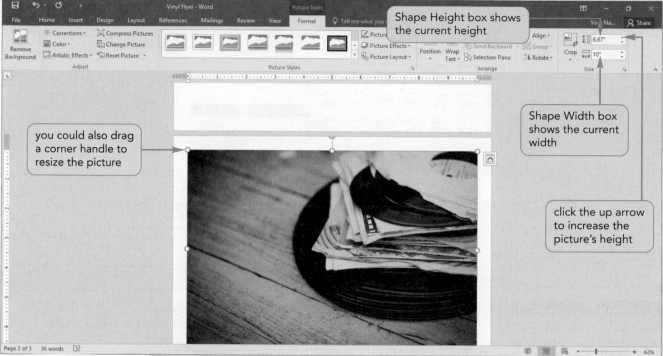

iravgustin/Shutterstock.com

3. Click the **down arrow** in the Shape Height box in the Size group. The photo decreases in size slightly. The measurement in the Shape Height box decreases to 6.6", and the measurement in the Shape Width box decreases to 9.9".

4. Click the **down arrow** in the Shape Height box repeatedly until the picture is 3.3" tall and 4.95" wide. As the photo shrinks, it moves back to page 1, along with the text below it. The entire flyer should again appear on one page.

Finally, to make the photo more noticeable, you can add a **picture style**, which is a collection of formatting options, such as a frame, a rounded shape, and a shadow. You can apply a picture style to a selected picture by clicking the style you want in the Picture Styles gallery on the Picture Tools Format tab. In the following steps, you'll start by displaying the gallery.

To add a style to the photo:

1. Make sure the Picture Tools Format tab is still selected on the ribbon.

2. In the Picture Styles group, click the **More** button to the right of the Picture Styles gallery to open the gallery and display more picture styles. Some of the picture styles simply add a border, while others change the picture's shape. Other styles combine these options with effects such as a shadow or a reflection.

3. Place the mouse pointer over various styles to observe the Live Previews in the document, and then place the mouse pointer over the Drop Shadow Rectangle style, which is the middle style in the top row. See Figure 1-38.

Figure 1-38   Previewing a picture style

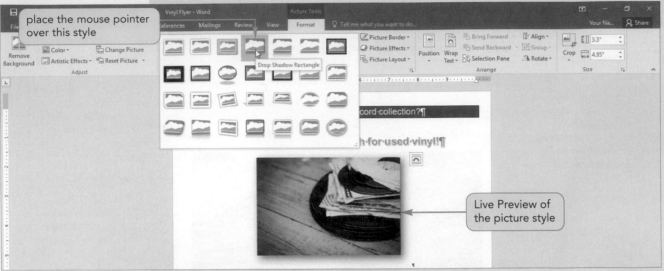

iravgustin/Shutterstock.com

TIP

To return a picture to its original appearance, click the Reset Picture button in the Adjust group on the Picture Tools Format tab.

4. In the gallery, click the **Drop Shadow Rectangle** style to apply it to the photo and close the gallery. The photo is formatted with a shadow on the bottom and right sides, as shown earlier in the Session 1.2 Visual Overview.

5. Click anywhere outside the photo to deselect it, and then save the document.

INSIGHT

Working with Inline Pictures

By default, when you insert a picture in a document, it is treated as an inline object, which means its position changes in the document as you add or delete text. Also, because it is an inline object, you can align the picture just as you would align text, using the alignment buttons in the Paragraph group on the Home tab. Essentially, you can treat an inline picture as just another paragraph.

When you become a more advanced Word user, you'll learn how to wrap text around a picture so that the text flows around the picture—with the picture maintaining its position on the page no matter how much text you add to or delete from the document. The alignment buttons don't work on pictures that have text wrapped around them. Instead, you can drag the picture to the desired position on the page.

The flyer is complete and ready for Leo to print later. Because Leo is considering creating a promotional brochure that would include numerous photographs, he asks you to look up more information about inserting pictures. You can do that using Word's Help system.

Getting Help

To get the most out of Help, your computer must be connected to the Internet so it can access the reference information stored at Office.com. The quickest way to look up information is to use the Tell Me box—which appears with the text "Tell me what you want to do…" within it—on the ribbon. You can also use the Tell Me box to quickly access Word features.

TIP

To search the web for information on a word or phrase in a document, select the text, click the Review tab, and then click the Smart Lookup button in the Insights group.

To look up information in Help:

1. Verify that your computer is connected to the Internet, and then, on the ribbon, click the **Tell Me** box, and type **insert pictures**. A menu of Help topics related to inserting pictures opens. You could click one of the topics in the menu, or you could click the Get Help on "insert pictures" command at the bottom of the menu to open a Word 2016 Help window, where you could continue to search Office.com for more information on inserting pictures. If you prefer to expand your search to the entire web, you could click the Smart Lookup command at the bottom of the menu to open an Insights task pane with links to articles from Wikipedia and other sources. You could also press Enter at this point to open the Insert Pictures dialog box.

2. Click **Get Help on "insert pictures."** After a slight pause, the Word 2016 Help window opens with links to information about inserting pictures. You might see the links shown in Figure 1-39, or you might see other links.

Figure 1-39	Word Help window

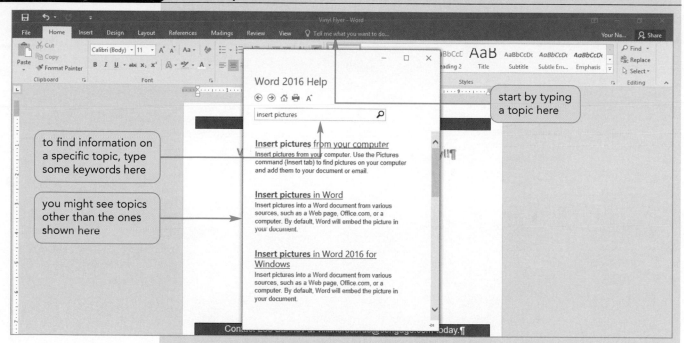

3. Click the first link, and then read the article to see if it contains any information about inserting pictures that might be useful to Leo. Note that to print information about a topic, you can click the Print button near the top of the Word Help window.

4. When you are finished reading the article, click the **Back** button ⬅ near the top of the Word 2016 Help window to return to the previous list of links.

5. Click the **Home** button ⌂ to go to the home page.

6. Click the **Close** button ✕ in the upper-right corner to close the Word 2016 Help window.

7. Click the **File** tab, and then click **Close** in the navigation bar to close the document without closing Word.

Word Help is a great way to learn about and access Word's many features. Articles and videos on basic skills provide step-by-step guides for completing tasks, while more elaborate, online tutorials walk you through more complicated tasks. Be sure to take some time on your own to explore Word Help so you can find the information and features you want when you need it.

REVIEW

Session 1.2 Quick Check

1. Explain how to accept a spelling correction suggested by the Spelling task pane.
2. What orientation should you choose if you want your document to be wider than it is tall?
3. What is the default font size?
4. What is a gallery?
5. What is the default text alignment?
6. Explain two important facts about a picture inserted as an inline object.

PRACTICE

Review Assignments

Data Files needed for the Review Assignments: Flyer.docx, Player.jpg

Leo asks you to write a cover letter to accompany a bid for a collection of reggae albums. After that, he wants you to create an envelope for the letter and to format a flyer reminding customers that Villa Rio Records buys vintage record players in addition to vintage vinyl. Change the Zoom level as necessary while you are working. Complete the following steps:

1. Open a new, blank document and then save the document as **Huang Letter** in the location specified by your instructor.

2. Type the date **February 19, 2017** using AutoComplete for "February."

3. Press the Enter key twice, and then type the following inside address, using the default paragraph spacing and pressing the Enter key once after each line:
   Sabrina Huang
   52 East Dana Parkway
   Wilmington, DE 19802

4. Type **Dear Ms. Huang:** as the salutation, press the Enter key, and then type the following as the body of the letter:
   Enclosed you will find my appraisal of your reggae collection. Please note that you also included some classic rock albums. I've included a separate bid for those titles, as well as a bid for the combined collections.
   I enjoyed our conversation about gospel music of the 1950s. Please let me know if you are looking for more albums from that era. You can see our complete gospel collection online at www.villariorecords.cengage.com.

5. Press the Enter key, type **Sincerely yours,** as the complimentary closing, press the Enter key three times, type **Leo Barinov** as the signature line, insert a manual line break, and type **Purchasing Manager** as his title.

6. Press the Enter key, type your initials, insert a manual line break, and then use the Undo button to make your initials all lowercase, if necessary.

7. Type **Enclosure** and save the document.

8. Scroll to the beginning of the document and proofread your work. Remove any wavy underlines by using a shortcut menu or by typing a correction yourself. Remove the hyperlink formatting from the web address.

9. Remove the paragraph spacing from the first two lines of the inside address.

10. Change the top margin to 2.75 inches. Leave the other margins at their default settings.

11. Save your changes to the letter, preview it, print it if your instructor asks you to, and then close it.

12. Create a new, blank document, and then create an envelope. Use Sabrina Huang's address (from Step 3) as the delivery address. Use your school's name and address for the return address. Add the envelope to the document. If you are asked if you want to save the return address as the new return address, click No.

13. Save the document as **Huang Envelope** in the location specified by your instructor, and then close the document.

14. Open the document **Flyer**, located in the Word1 > Review folder included with your Data Files, and then check your screen to make sure your settings match those in the module.

15. Save the document as **Record Player Flyer** in the location specified by your instructor.

16. Use the Recheck Document button in the Word Options dialog box to reset the Spelling and Grammar checker, and then use the Spelling and Grammar task panes to correct any errors marked with wavy underlines.

17. Proofread the document and correct any other errors. Be sure to change "Today" to "**today**" in the last paragraph.

18. Change the page orientation to Landscape and the margins to Narrow.

19. Format the document text in 22-point Times New Roman font.

20. Center the text and the photo.

21. Format the first paragraph with an outside border, and then add orange shading, using the Orange, Accent 2, Darker 25% color in the Theme Colors section of the Shading gallery. Format the paragraph text in white.

22. Format the last paragraph in the document using the same formatting you applied to the first paragraph.

23. Increase the paragraph spacing after the first paragraph to 42 points. Increase the paragraph spacing before the last paragraph in the document to 42 points.

24. Format the second paragraph with the Fill - Orange, Accent 2, Outline - Accent 2 text effect. Increase the paragraph's font size to 26 points.

25. Format the text in the third and fourth paragraphs (the first two paragraphs below the photo) in orange, using the Orange, Accent 2, Darker 50% font color, and then add bold and italic.

26. Delete the photo and replace it with the **Player.jpg** photo, located in the Word1 > Review folder included with your Data Files.

27. Resize the new photo so that it is 3.8" tall, and then add the Soft Edge Rectangle style in the Pictures Styles gallery.

28. Save your changes to the flyer, preview it, and then close it.

29. Use Word Help to look up the topic **work with pictures**. Read the first article, return to the Help home page, and then close Help.

Case Problem 1

APPLY

There are no Data Files needed for this Case Problem.

Brightly Water Quality Consultants   You are a program administrator at Brightly Water Quality Consultants, in Springfield, Missouri. Over the past few months, you have collected handwritten journals from local residents documenting their daily water use. Now you need to send the journals to the researcher in charge of compiling the information. Create a cover letter to accompany the journals by completing the following steps. Because your office is currently out of letterhead, you'll start the letter by typing a return address. As you type the letter, remember to include the appropriate number of blank paragraphs between the various parts of the letter. Complete the following steps:

1. Open a new, blank document, and then save the document as **Brightly Letter** in the location specified by your instructor. If necessary, change the Zoom level to 120%.

2. Type the following return address, using the default paragraph spacing and replacing [Your Name] with your first and last names:

   [Your Name]
   Brightly Water Quality Consultants
   39985 Pepperdine Avenue, Suite 52
   Springfield, MO 65806

3. Type **November 6, 2017** as the date, leaving a blank paragraph between the last line of the return address and the date.

4. Type the following inside address, using the default paragraph spacing and leaving the appropriate number of blank paragraphs after the date:

   Dr. Albert Strome
   4643 College Drive
   Columbia, MO 65211

5. Type **Dear Dr. Strome:** as the salutation.

6. To begin the body of the letter, type the following paragraph:
   Enclosed please find the journals our participants have completed. I should have thirty more by the end of next month, but I thought you would like to get started on these now. Please review the enclosed journals, and then call or email me with your answers to these questions:

7. Add the following questions as separate paragraphs, using the default paragraph spacing:
   Did the participants include enough helpful information?
   Should we consider expanding the program to additional communities?
   Can you complete your analysis by early March?

8. Insert a new paragraph before the second question, and then add the following as the new second question in the list: **Is the journal format useful, or would you prefer a simple questionnaire?**

9. Insert a new paragraph after the last question, and then type the complimentary closing **Sincerely,** (including the comma).

10. Leave the appropriate amount of space for your signature, type your full name, insert a manual line break, and then type **Program Administrator**.

11. Type **Enclosure** in the appropriate place.

12. Use the Recheck Document button in the Word Options dialog box to reset the Spelling and Grammar checker, and then use the Spelling and Grammar task panes to correct any errors. Instruct the Spelling task pane to ignore the recipient's name.

13. Italicize the four paragraphs containing the questions.

14. Remove the paragraph spacing from the first three lines of the return address. Do the same for the first two paragraphs of the inside address.

15. Center the four paragraphs containing the return address, format them in 16-point font, and then add the Fill – Gray – 50%, Accent 3, Sharp Bevel text effect.

16. Save the document, preview it, and then close it.

17. Create a new, blank document, and create an envelope. Use Dr. Strome's address (from Step 4) as the delivery address. Use the return address shown in Step 2. Add the envelope to the document. If you are asked if you want to save the return address as the new return address, click No.

18. Save the document as **Strome Envelope** in the location specified by your instructor, and then close the document.

Case Problem 2

Data Files needed for this Case Problem: Dog.jpg, Pups.docx

Pups & Pals Pet Care   You work as the sales and scheduling coordinator at Pups & Pals Pet Care, a dog-walking service in San Antonio, Texas. You need to create a flyer promoting the company's services. Complete the following steps:

1. Open the document **Pups** located in the Word1 > Case2 folder included with your Data Files, and then save the document as **Pups & Pals Flyer** in the location specified by your instructor.

2. In the document, replace "Student Name" with your first and last names.

3. Use the Recheck Document button in the Word Options dialog box to reset the Spelling and Grammar checker, and then use the Spelling and Grammar task panes to correct any errors. Instruct the Spelling task pane to ignore your name if Word marks it with a wavy underline.

4. Change the page margins to Narrow.

CREATE

5. Complete the flyer as shown in Figure 1-40. Use the photo **Dog.jpg** located in the Word1 > Case2 folder included with your Data Files. Use the default line spacing and paragraph spacing unless otherwise specified in Figure 1-40.

Figure 1-40	Formatted Pups & Pals flyer

36-point Times New Roman; Fill – Blue, Accent 1, Shadow text effect; center alignment; default paragraph spacing

28-point Arial; Blue Accent 1, Darker 25% font color; bold; right-aligned; 30 points of paragraph spacing before the first item in the list and after third item in the list

24-point Times New Roman; Green, Accent 6, Lighter 40% shading; outside border; Blue, Accent 1, Darker 25% font; center alignment; default paragraph spacing

Centered; height set to 4 inches; Simple Frame, White picture style

24-point Times New Roman; Green, Accent 6, Lighter 40% shading; outside border; Blue, Accent 1, Darker 25% font; center alignment, 6 points of spacing before the paragraph

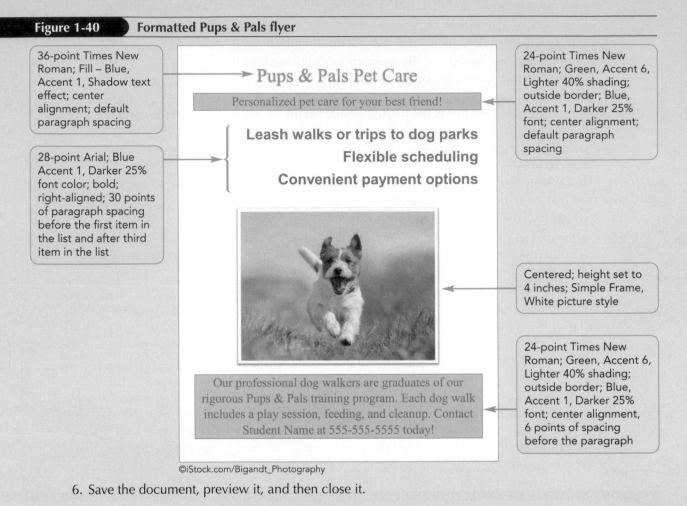

Pups & Pals Pet Care

Personalized pet care for your best friend!

Leash walks or trips to dog parks

Flexible scheduling

Convenient payment options

Our professional dog walkers are graduates of our rigorous Pups & Pals training program. Each dog walk includes a play session, feeding, and cleanup. Contact Student Name at 555-555-5555 today!

©iStock.com/Bigandt_Photography

6. Save the document, preview it, and then close it.

TROUBLESHOOT

Case Problem 3

Data Files needed for this Case Problem: Living.docx, Rental.docx

Salt Lake Synergy Vacation Rentals   You work as the office manager for Salt Lake Synergy Vacation Rentals, a service that rents apartments and houses in Salt Lake City, Utah, to out-of-town visitors. One of the company's rental agents needs to complete a letter to accompany a photo of a rental property. The letter is almost finished, but the agent needs help correcting errors and formatting the text to match the block style. The photo itself is stored in a separate document. The agent mistakenly applied a picture style to the photo that is inappropriate for professional correspondence. She asks you to remove the picture style and then format the page. Complete the following steps:

1. Open the document **Rental** located in the Word1 > Case3 folder included with your Data Files, and then save the document as **Rental Letter** in the location specified by your instructor.

2. Use the Recheck Document button in the Word Options dialog box to reset the Spelling and Grammar checker, and then use the Spelling and Grammar task panes to correct any errors, typing directly in the document as necessary.

⚙ **Troubleshoot** 3. Make any necessary changes to ensure that the letter matches the formatting of a block-style business letter, including the appropriate paragraph spacing. Keep in mind that the letter will include an enclosure. Include your initials where appropriate.

⚙ **Troubleshoot** 4. The letterhead for Salt Lake Synergy Vacation Rentals requires a top margin of 2.5 inches. Determine if the layout of the letter will work with the letterhead, make any necessary changes, and then save the letter.

5. Save the document and preview it.

6. Move the cursor to the beginning of the letter, and then create an envelope. Use the delivery address taken from the letter, but edit the delivery address to remove the salutation, if necessary. Click the Omit check box to deselect it (if necessary), and then, for the return address, type your school's name and address. Add the envelope to the Rental Letter document. If you are asked if you want to save the return address as the new default return address, answer No.

7. Save the document, preview both pages, and then close it.

8. Open the document **Living** located in the Word1 > Case3 folder included with your Data Files, and then save the document as **Living Area Photo** in the location specified by your instructor.

⚙ **Troubleshoot** 9. Reset the picture to its original appearance, before the agent mistakenly added the style with the reflection.

⚙ **Troubleshoot** 10. Modify the page layout and margins and adjust the size of the photo so the photo fills as much of the page as possible without overlapping the page margins.

11. Save the document, preview it, and then close it.

Case Problem 4

There are no Data Files needed for this Case Problem.

CHALLENGE

Palomino Lighting Manufacturers   As an assistant facilities manager at Palomino Lighting Manufacturers, you are responsible for alerting the staff when clients plan to visit the factory. In addition to sending out a company-wide email, you also need to post a memo in the break room. Complete the following steps:

⊕ **Explore** 1. Open a new document—but instead of selecting the Blank document option, search for a memo template online. In the list of search results, click the Memo (Simple design) template, and then click the Create button. (Note: If you don't see that template, pick another with a simple style and the word "Memo" at the top. You will need to adapt the steps in this Case Problem to match the design of the template you use.) A memo template opens in the Word window.

2. Save the document as **Visit Memo** in the location specified by your instructor. If you see a dialog box indicating that the document will be upgraded to the newest file format, click the OK button. Note that of the hundreds of templates available online, only a small portion have been created in the most recent version of Word, so you will often see this dialog box when working with templates.

⊕ **Explore** 3. In the document, click the text "[Company name]." The placeholder text appears in a box with gray highlighting. The box containing the highlighted text (with the small rectangle attached) is called a document control. You can enter text in a document control just as you enter text in a dialog box. Type **Palomino Lighting Manufacturers**, and then press the Tab key. The "[Recipient names]" placeholder text now appears in a document control next to the word "To." (*Hint*: As you work on the memo in the following steps, keep in mind that if you accidentally double-click the word "memo" at the top of the document, you will access the header portion of the document, which is normally closed to editing. In that case, press the Esc key to return to the main document.)

4. Type **All Personnel** and then press the Tab key twice. A document control is now visible to the right of the word "From." Depending on how your computer is set up, you might see your name or another name here, or the document control might be empty. Delete the name, if necessary, and then type your first and last names.

⊕ **Explore** 5. Continue using the Tab key to edit the remaining document controls as indicated below. If you press the Tab key too many times and accidentally skip a document control, you can click the document control to select it.

- In the CC: document control, delete the placeholder text.
- In the Date document control, click the down arrow, and then click the current date in the calendar.
- In the Re: document control, type **Client Visit**.
- In the Comments document control, type **Representatives from Houghton Contractors are scheduled to tour the factory this Tuesday morning. Please greet them warmly, and be prepared to answer any questions they might have.**

6. Use the Recheck Document button in the Word Options dialog box to reset the Spelling and Grammar checker, and then use the Spelling and Grammar task panes to correct any underlined errors. Proofread the document to look for any additional errors.

7. Save the document, preview it, and then close it.

WORD

Navigating and Formatting a Document

Editing an Academic Document According to MLA Style

Case | *Quincy Rivers College*

Carolina Frey, an architecture student at Quincy Rivers College, is doing a student internship at Wilson and Page Design, an architecture firm in Minneapolis, Minnesota. She has written a handout describing the process of acquiring LEED certification, which serves as proof that a home has been constructed according to strict environmental guidelines specified by the U.S. Green Building Council. She asks you to help her finish the handout. The text needs some reorganization and other editing. The handout also needs formatting so the finished document looks professional and is easy to read.

Carolina is also taking an architecture history class and is writing a research paper on the history of architecture. To complete the paper, she needs to follow a set of very specific formatting and style guidelines for academic documents.

Carolina has asked you to help her edit these two very different documents. In Session 2.1, you will review and respond to some comments in the handout and then revise and format that document. In Session 2.2, you will review the MLA style for research papers and then format Carolina's research paper to match the MLA specifications.

STARTING DATA FILES

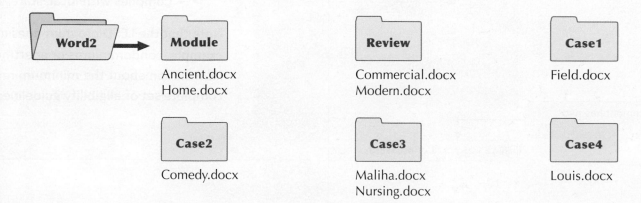

Word2 → Module
Ancient.docx
Home.docx

Review
Commercial.docx
Modern.docx

Case1
Field.docx

Case2
Comedy.docx

Case3
Maliha.docx
Nursing.docx

Case4
Louis.docx

Session 2.1 Visual Overview:

Use the Bullets button to create a bulleted list from selected paragraphs.

Use the Numbering button to create a numbered list from selected paragraphs.

The **Navigation pane** allows you to search for text in the document, with the results highlighted in yellow in the document.

Click the **Search for more things button** to access advanced search tools, or to select something to search for besides text.

You can type the text you want to search for here.

The search text you enter in the Navigation pane is highlighted wherever it appears in the document.

This text is formatted with the Heading 1 style for the Office theme.

The **bullet** before each of these paragraphs identifies the four paragraphs as items in a list.

This document has two pages.

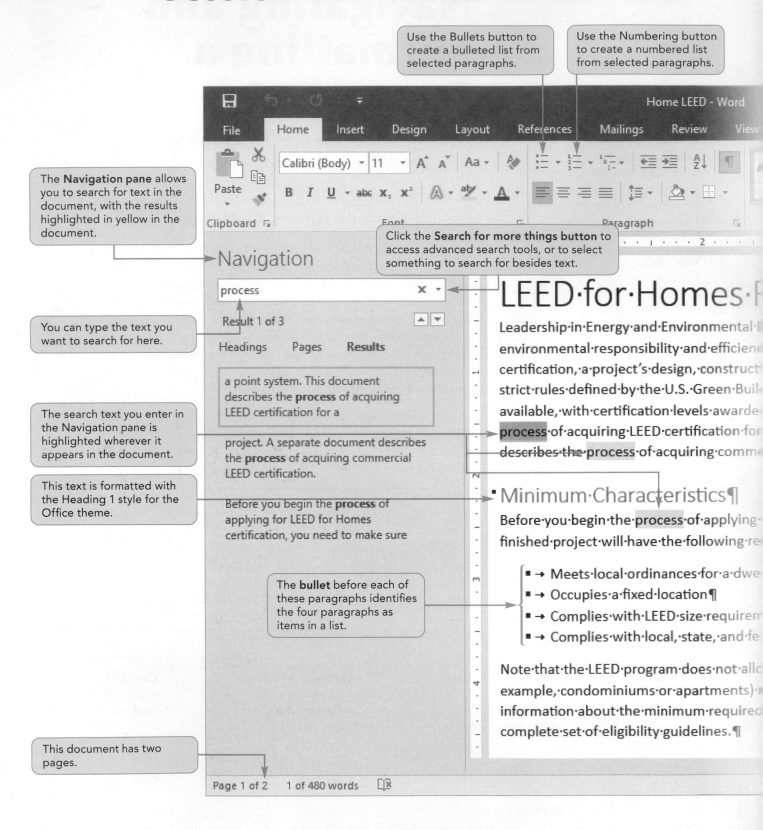

Working with Lists and Styles

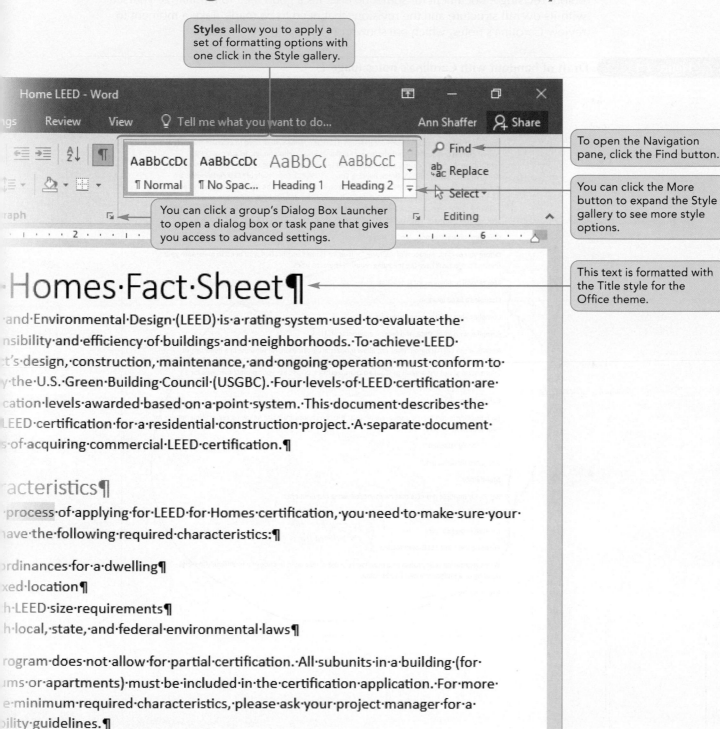

Styles allow you to apply a set of formatting options with one click in the Style gallery.

To open the Navigation pane, click the Find button.

You can click the More button to expand the Style gallery to see more style options.

You can click a group's Dialog Box Launcher to open a dialog box or task pane that gives you access to advanced settings.

This text is formatted with the Title style for the Office theme.

Reviewing the Document

Before revising a document for someone else, it's a good idea to familiarize yourself with its overall structure and the revisions that need to be made. Take a moment to review Carolina's notes, which are shown in Figure 2-1.

Figure 2-1 Draft of handout with Carolina's notes (page 1)

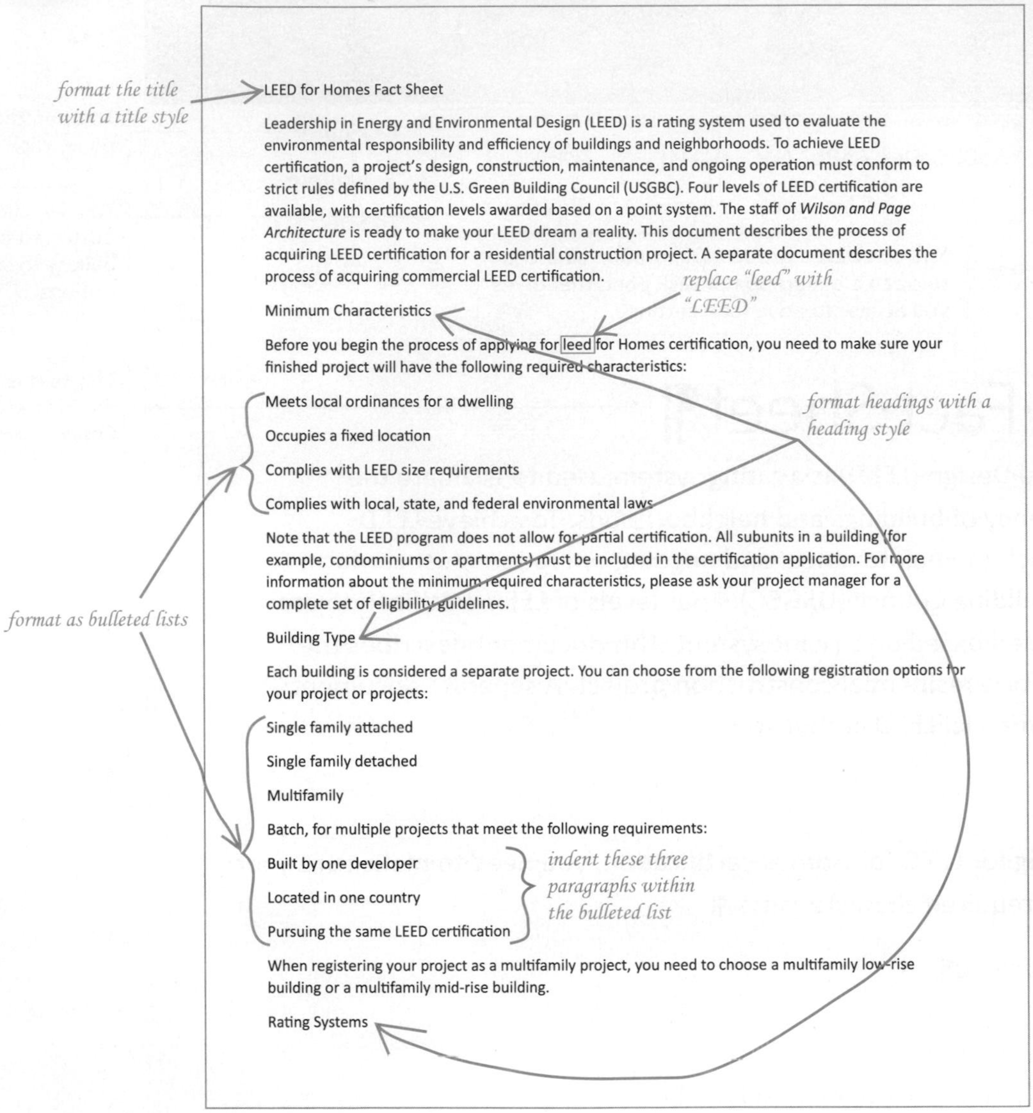

format the title with a title style

LEED for Homes Fact Sheet

Leadership in Energy and Environmental Design (LEED) is a rating system used to evaluate the environmental responsibility and efficiency of buildings and neighborhoods. To achieve LEED certification, a project's design, construction, maintenance, and ongoing operation must conform to strict rules defined by the U.S. Green Building Council (USGBC). Four levels of LEED certification are available, with certification levels awarded based on a point system. The staff of *Wilson and Page Architecture* is ready to make your LEED dream a reality. This document describes the process of acquiring LEED certification for a residential construction project. A separate document describes the process of acquiring commercial LEED certification.

replace "leed" with "LEED"

Minimum Characteristics

Before you begin the process of applying for leed for Homes certification, you need to make sure your finished project will have the following required characteristics:

format headings with a heading style

Meets local ordinances for a dwelling

Occupies a fixed location

Complies with LEED size requirements

Complies with local, state, and federal environmental laws

Note that the LEED program does not allow for partial certification. All subunits in a building (for example, condominiums or apartments) must be included in the certification application. For more information about the minimum required characteristics, please ask your project manager for a complete set of eligibility guidelines.

format as bulleted lists

Building Type

Each building is considered a separate project. You can choose from the following registration options for your project or projects:

Single family attached

Single family detached

Multifamily

Batch, for multiple projects that meet the following requirements:

Built by one developer

Located in one country

Pursuing the same LEED certification

indent these three paragraphs within the bulleted list

When registering your project as a multifamily project, you need to choose a multifamily low-rise building or a multifamily mid-rise building.

Rating Systems

Figure 2-1   Draft of handout with Carolina's notes (page 2)

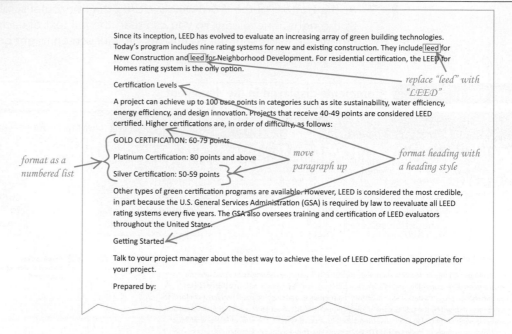

Carolina also included additional guidance in some comments she added to the document file. A **comment** is like an electronic sticky note attached to a word, phrase, or paragraph in a document. Comments appear in the margin, along with the name of the person who added them. Within a single document, you can add new comments, reply to existing comments, and delete comments.

You will open the document now, save it with a new name, and then review Carolina's comments in Word.

To open and rename the document:

1. Open the document **Home** located in the Word2 > Module folder included with your Data Files.

2. Save the document as **Home LEED** in the location specified by your instructor.

3. Verify that the document is displayed in Print Layout view, that the Zoom level is set to **120%**, and that the rulers and nonprinting characters are displayed.

4. On the ribbon, click the **Review** tab to display the tools used for working with comments. Comments can be displayed in several different ways, so your first step is to make sure the comments in the Home LEED document are displayed to match the figures in this book—using Simple Markup view.

5. In the Tracking group, click the **Display for Review** arrow, and then click **Simple Markup** to select it, if necessary. At this point, you might see comment icons to the right of the document text, or you might see the full text of each comment.

6. In the Comments group, click the **Show Comments** button several times to practice displaying and hiding the comments, and then, when you are finished, make sure the Show Comments button is selected so the full text of each comment is displayed.

7. At the bottom of the Word window, drag the horizontal scroll bar all the way to the right, if necessary, so you can read the full text of each comment. See Figure 2-2. Note that the comments on your screen might be a different color than the ones shown in the figure.

Figure 2-2   **Comments displayed in the document**

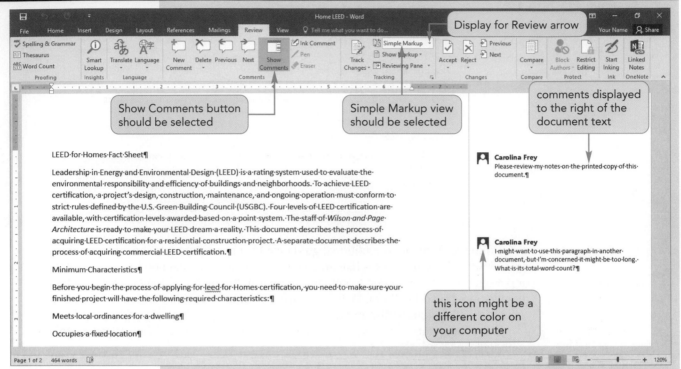

Keep in mind that when working on a small monitor, it can be helpful to switch the document Zoom level to Page Width, in which case Word automatically reduces the width of the document to accommodate the comments on the right.

8. Read the document, including the comments. The handout includes the title "LEED for Homes Fact Sheet" at the top, as well as headings (such as "Minimum Characteristics" and "Building Type") that divide the document into parts. Right now the headings are hard to spot because they don't look different from the surrounding text. Carolina used the default font size, 11-point, and the default font, Calibri (Body), for all the text in the document. Note, too, that the document includes some short paragraphs that would work better as bulleted or numbered lists.

9. Scroll down until you can see the first line on page 2 (which begins "Since its inception…"), and then click anywhere in that sentence. The message "Page 2 of 2" in the status bar, in the lower-left corner of the Word window, tells you that the insertion point is currently located on page 2 of the two-page document. The shaded space between the first and second pages of the document indicates a page break. To hide the top and bottom margins in a document, as well as the space between pages, you can double-click the shaded space between any two pages.

10. Position the mouse pointer over the shaded space between page 1 and page 2 until the pointer changes to ⊢⊣, and then double-click. The shaded space disappears. Instead, the two pages are now separated by a gray, horizontal line.

Trouble? If the Header & Footer Tools Design contextual tab appears on the ribbon, you double-clicked the top or bottom of one of the pages, instead of in the space between them. Click the Close Header and Footer button on the Header & Footer Tools Design tab, and then repeat Step 10.

▶ **11.** Use the ⊞ pointer to double-click the gray horizontal line between pages 1 and 2. The shaded space between the two pages is redisplayed.

Working with Comments

Now that you are familiar with the Home LEED document, you can review and respond to Carolina's comments. The Comment group on the Review tab includes helpful tools for working with comments.

Working with Comments

- On the ribbon, click the Review tab.
- To display comments in an easy-to-read view, in the Tracking group, click the Display for Review button, and then click Simple Markup.
- To see the text of each comment in Simple Markup view, click the Show Comments button in the Comments group.
- To move the insertion point to the next or previous comment in the document, click the Next button or the Previous button in the Comments group.
- To delete a comment, click anywhere in the comment, and then click the Delete button in the Comments group.
- To delete all the comments in a document, click the Delete button arrow in the Comments group, and then click Delete All Comments in Document.
- To add a new comment, select the document text you want to comment on, click the New Comment button in the Comments group, and then type the comment text.
- To reply to a comment, click the Reply button to the right of the comment, and then type your reply.
- To indicate that a comment or an individual reply to a comment is no longer a concern, right-click the comment or reply, and then click Mark Comment Done in the shortcut menu. To mark a comment and all of the replies attached to it as done, right-click the original comment, and then click Mark Comment Done.

To review and respond to the comments in the document:

▶ **1.** Press the **Ctrl+Home** keys to move the insertion point to the beginning of the document.

▶ **2.** On the Review tab, in the Comments group, click the **Next** button. The first comment now has an outline, indicating that it is selected. See Figure 2-3.

Figure 2-3 Comment attached to document text

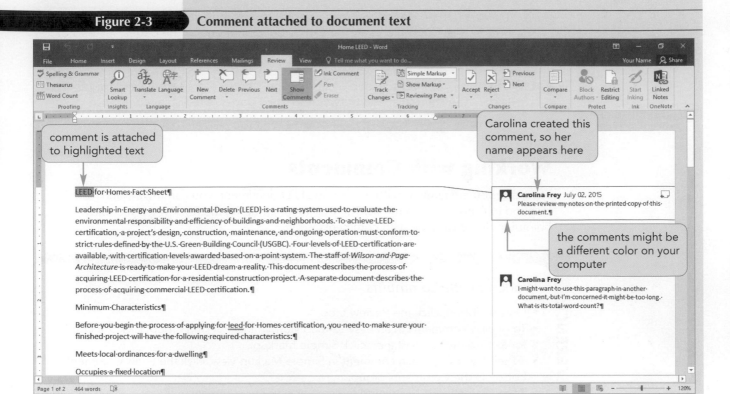

In the document, the text "LEED" is highlighted. A line connects the comment to "LEED," indicating that the comment is attached to that text. Because Carolina created the comment, her name appears at the beginning of the comment, followed by the date on which she created it. The insertion point blinks at the beginning of the comment and is ready for you to edit the comment if you want.

3. Read the comment, and then in the Comments group, click the **Next** button to select the next comment. According to this comment, Carolina wants to know the total word count of the paragraph the comment is attached to. You can get this information by selecting the entire paragraph and locating the word count in the status bar.

4. Triple-click anywhere in the second paragraph of the document (which begins "Leadership in Energy and Environmental Design…") to select the paragraph. In the status bar, the message "105 of 464 words" tells you that 105 of the document's 464 words are currently selected. So the answer to Carolina's question is 105.

5. Point to the second comment to select it again, click the **Reply** button , and then type **105**. Your reply appears below Carolina's original comment.

Trouble? If you do not see the Reply button in the comment box, drag the horizontal scroll bar at the bottom of the Word window to the right until you can see it.

If you are logged in, the name that appears in your reply comment is the name associated with your Microsoft account. If you are not logged in, the name in the Reply comment is taken from the User name box on the General tab of the Word Options dialog box. You can quickly open the General tab of the Word Options dialog box by clicking the Dialog Box Launcher in the

Tracking group on the Review tab, and then clicking Change User Name. From there, you can change the username and the initials associated with your copy of Word. To override the name associated with your Microsoft account and use the name that appears in the User name box in the Word Options dialog box instead, select the "Always use these values regardless of sign in to Office" check box. However, there is no need to change these settings for this module, and you should never change them on a shared computer at school unless specifically instructed to do so by your instructor.

6. In the Comments group, click the **Next** button to move the insertion point to the next comment, which asks you to insert your name after "Prepared by:" at the end of the document.

7. Click after the colon in "Prepared by:", press the **spacebar**, and then type your first and last names. To indicate that you have complied with Carolina's request by adding your name, you could right-click the comment, and then click Mark Comment Done. However, in this case, you'll simply delete the comment. Carolina also asks you to delete the first comment in the document.

8. Click anywhere in the final comment, and then in the Comments group, click the **Delete** button.

9. In the Comments group, click the **Previous** button three times to select the comment at the beginning of the document, and then click the **Delete** button to delete the comment.

As you reviewed the document, you might have noticed that, on page 2, one of the certification levels appears in all uppercase letters. This is probably just a typing mistake. You can correct it and then add a comment that points out the change to Carolina.

To correct the mistake and add a comment:

1. Scroll down to page 2, and then, in the fourth paragraph on the page, select the text **GOLD CERTIFICATION**.

2. On the ribbon, click the **Home** tab.

3. In the Font group, click the **Change Case** button Aa▾, and then click **Capitalize Each Word**. The text changes to read "Gold Certification."

4. Verify that the text is still selected, and then click the **Review** tab on the ribbon.

5. In the Comments group, click the **New Comment** button. A new comment appears, with the insertion point ready for you to begin typing.

6. In the new comment, type **I assumed you didn't want this all uppercase, so I changed it.** and then save the document.

   You can now hide the text of the comments because you are finished working with them.

7. In the Comments group, click the **Show Comments** button. A "See comments" icon now appears in the document margin rather than on the right side of the Word screen. The "See comments" icon alerts you to the presence of a comment without taking up all the space required to display the comment text. You can click a comment icon to read a particular comment without displaying the text of all the comments.

8. Click the **See comments** icon 💬. The comment icon is highlighted, and the full comment is displayed, as shown in Figure 2-4.

Figure 2-4 Document with the See comments icon

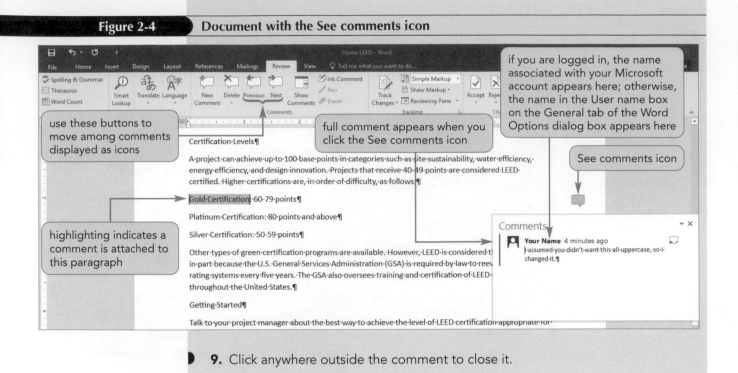

9. Click anywhere outside the comment to close it.

Creating Bulleted and Numbered Lists

A **bulleted list** is a group of related paragraphs with a black circle or other character to the left of each paragraph. For a group of related paragraphs that have a particular order (such as steps in a procedure), you can use consecutive numbers instead of bullets to create a **numbered list**. If you insert a new paragraph, delete a paragraph, or reorder the paragraphs in a numbered list, Word adjusts the numbers to make sure they remain consecutive.

PROSKILLS

Written Communication: Organizing Information in Lists

Bulleted and numbered lists are both great ways to draw the reader's attention to information. But it's important to know how to use them. Use numbers when your list contains items that are arranged by priority in a specific order. For example, in a document reviewing the procedure for performing CPR, it makes sense to use numbers for the sequential steps. Use bullets when the items in the list are of equal importance or when they can be accomplished in any order. For example, in a resume, you could use bullets for a list of professional certifications.

To add bullets to a series of paragraphs, you use the Bullets button in the Paragraph group on the Home tab. To create a numbered list, you use the Numbering button in the Paragraph group instead. Both the Bullets button and the Numbering button have arrows you can click to open a gallery of bullet or numbering styles.

Carolina asks you to format the list of minimum characteristics on page 1 as a bulleted list. She also asks you to format the list of building types on page 1 as a separate bulleted list. Finally, you need to format the list of certification levels on page 2 as a numbered list, in order of difficulty.

To apply bullets to paragraphs:

1. Scroll up until you see the paragraphs containing the list of minimum characteristics (which begins with "Meets local ordinances for a dwelling…"), and then select this paragraph and the three that follow it.

2. On the ribbon, click the **Home** tab.

3. In the Paragraph group, click the **Bullets** button ⬚. Black circles appear as bullets before each item in the list. Also, the bulleted list is indented and the paragraph spacing between the items is reduced.

After reviewing the default, round bullet in the document, Carolina decides she would prefer square bullets.

4. In the Paragraph group, click the **Bullets button arrow** ⬚ ▾. A gallery of bullet styles opens. See Figure 2-5.

| Figure 2-5 | Bullets gallery |

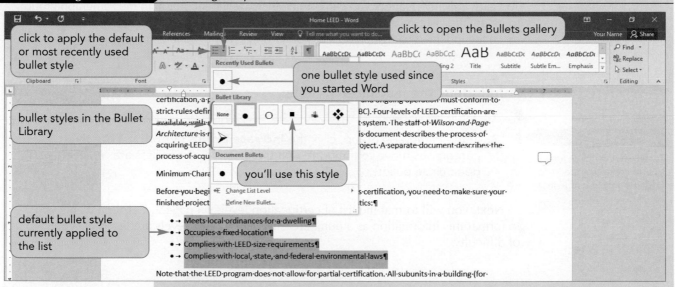

The Recently Used Bullets section appears at the top of the gallery of bullet styles; it displays the bullet styles that have been used since you started Word, which, in this case, is just the round black bullet style that was applied by default when you clicked the Bullets button. The **Bullet Library**, which offers a variety of bullet styles, is shown below the Recently Used Bullets. To create your own bullets from a picture file or from a set of predesigned symbols including diamonds, hearts, or Greek letters, click Define New Bullet, and then click the Symbol button or the Picture button in the Define New Bullet dialog box.

5. Move the mouse pointer over the bullet styles in the Bullet Library to see a Live Preview of the bullet styles in the document. Carolina prefers the black square style.

6. In the Bullet Library, click the **black square**. The round bullets are replaced with square bullets.

Next, you need to format the list of building types on page 1 with square bullets. When you first start Word, the Bullets button applies the default, round bullets you saw earlier. But after you select a new bullet style, the Bullets button applies the last bullet style you used. So, to add square bullets to the decorating styles list, you just have to select the list and click the Bullets button.

To add bullets to the list of building types:

1. Scroll down in the document, and select the paragraphs listing the building types, starting with "Single family attached" and ending with "Pursuing the same LEED certification."

2. In the Paragraph group, click the **Bullets** button [icon]. The list is now formatted with square black bullets.

The list is finished except for one issue. The "Batch" building type has three subrequirements, but that's not clear because of the way the list is currently formatted. To clarify this information, you can use the Increase Indent button in the Paragraph group to indent the last two bullets. When you do this, Word inserts a different style bullet to make the indented paragraphs visually subordinate to the bulleted paragraphs above.

To indent the last three bullets:

1. In the list of building types, select the last three paragraphs.

2. In the Paragraph group, click the **Increase Indent** button [icon]. The three paragraphs move to the right, and the black square bullets are replaced with open circle bullets.

TIP

To remove the indent from selected text, click the Decrease Indent button in the Paragraph group.

Next, you will format the list of certification levels on page 2. Carolina wants you to format this information as a numbered list because the levels are listed in order of difficulty.

To apply numbers to the list of certification levels:

1. Scroll down to page 2 until you see the "Gold Certification: 60-79 points" paragraph. You added a comment to this paragraph earlier, but that will have no effect on the process of creating the numbered list.

2. Select the three paragraphs containing the list of certification levels, starting with "Gold Certification: 60-79 points" and ending with "Silver Certification: 50-59 points."

3. In the Paragraph group, click the **Numbering** button [icon]. Consecutive numbers appear in front of each item in the list. See Figure 2-6.

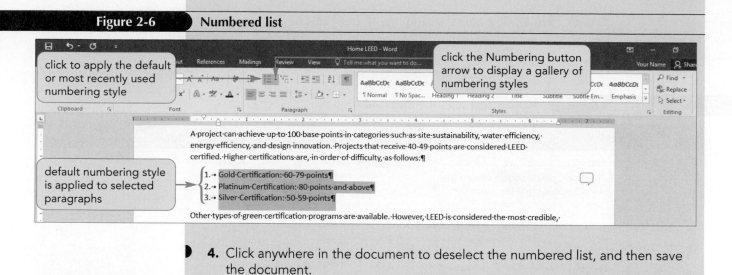

| Figure 2-6 | Numbered list |

4. Click anywhere in the document to deselect the numbered list, and then save the document.

TIP

The Numbering button is a toggle button, which means you can click it to add or remove numbering from selected text.

As with the Bullets button arrow, you can click the Numbering button arrow, and then select from a library of numbering styles. You can also indent paragraphs in a numbered list to create an outline, in which case the indented paragraphs will be preceded by lowercase letters instead of numbers. To apply a different list style to the outline (for example, with Roman numerals and uppercase letters), select the list, click the Multilevel List button in the Paragraph group, and then click a multilevel list style.

Moving Text in a Document

One of the most useful features of a word-processing program is the ability to move text easily. For example, Carolina wants to reorder the information in the numbered list. You could do this by deleting a paragraph and then retyping it at a new location. However, it's easier to select and then move the text. Word provides several ways to move text—drag and drop, cut and paste, and copy and paste.

Dragging and Dropping Text

To move text with **drag and drop**, you select the text you want to move, press and hold the mouse button while you drag the selected text to a new location, and then release the mouse button.

In the numbered list you just created, Carolina wants you to move the paragraph that reads "Silver Certification: 50-59 points" up so it is the first item in the list.

To move text using drag and drop:

1. Select the third paragraph in the numbered list, "Silver Certification: 50-59 points," being sure to include the paragraph marker at the end. The number 3 remains unselected because it's not actually part of the paragraph text.

2. Position the pointer over the selected text. The pointer changes to a left-facing arrow.

3. Press and hold the mouse button, and move the pointer slightly until the drag-and-drop pointer appears. A dark black insertion point appears within the selected text.

4. Without releasing the mouse button, drag the pointer to the beginning of the list until the insertion point is positioned to the left of the "G" in "Gold Certification: 60-79 points." Use the insertion point, rather than the mouse pointer, to guide the text to its new location. See Figure 2-7.

Figure 2-7   Moving text with the drag-and-drop pointer

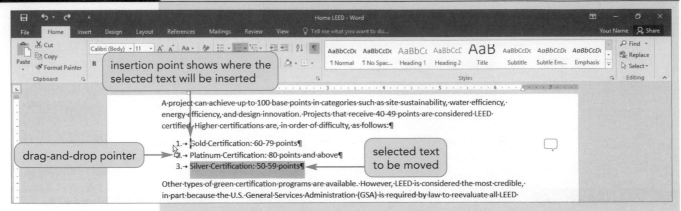

5. Release the mouse button, and then click a blank area of the document to deselect the text. The text "Silver Certification: 50-59 points" is now the first item in the list, and the remaining paragraphs have been renumbered as paragraphs 2 and 3. See Figure 2-8.

Figure 2-8   Text in new location

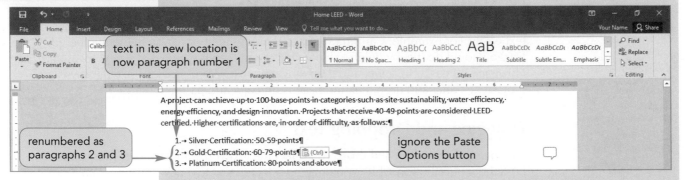

The Paste Options button appears near the newly inserted text, providing access to more advanced options related to pasting text. You don't need to use the Paste Options button right now; it will disappear when you start performing another task.

Trouble? If the selected text moves to the wrong location, click the Undo button 🔄 on the Quick Access Toolbar, and then repeat Steps 2 through 5.

6. Save the document.

Dragging and dropping works well when you are moving text a short distance. When you are moving text from one page to another, it's easier to cut, copy, and paste text using the Clipboard.

Cutting or Copying and Pasting Text Using the Clipboard

The **Office Clipboard** is a temporary storage area on your computer that holds objects such as text or graphics until you need them. To **cut** means to remove text or another item from a document and place it on the Clipboard. Once you've cut something, you can paste it somewhere else. To **copy** means to copy a selected item to the Clipboard, leaving the item in its original location. To **paste** means to insert a copy of whatever is on the Clipboard into the document, at the insertion point. When you paste an item from the Clipboard into a document, the item remains on the Clipboard so you can paste it again somewhere else if you want. The buttons for cutting, copying, and pasting are located in the Clipboard group on the Home tab.

By default, Word pastes text in a new location in a document with the same formatting it had in its old location. To select other ways to paste text, you can use the Paste Options button, which appears next to newly pasted text, or the Paste button arrow in the Clipboard group. Both buttons display a menu of paste options. Two particularly useful paste options are Merge Formatting, which combines the formatting of the copied text with the formatting of the text in the new location, and Keep Text Only, which inserts the text using the formatting of the surrounding text in the new location.

When you need to keep track of multiple pieces of cut or copied text, it's helpful to open the **Clipboard task pane**, which displays the contents of the Clipboard. You open the Clipboard task pane by clicking the Dialog Box Launcher in the Clipboard group on the Home tab. When the Clipboard task pane is displayed, the Clipboard can store up to 24 text items. When the Clipboard task pane is not displayed, the Clipboard can hold only the most recently copied item.

Carolina would like to move the third-to-last sentence under the "LEED for Homes Fact Sheet" heading on page 1. You'll use cut and paste to move this sentence to a new location.

To move text using cut and paste:

1. Make sure the Home tab is selected on the ribbon.

2. Scroll up until you can see the second paragraph in the document, just below the "LEED for Homes Fact Sheet" heading.

3. Press and hold the **Ctrl** key, and then click anywhere in the third-to-last sentence of the second paragraph, which reads "The staff of *Wilson and Page Architecture* is ready to make your LEED dream a reality." The entire sentence and the space following it are selected.

TIP

You can also press the Ctrl+X keys to cut selected text. Press the Ctrl+V keys to paste the most recently copied item.

4. In the Clipboard group, click the **Cut** button. The selected text is removed from the document and copied to the Clipboard.

5. Scroll down to page 2, and then click at the beginning of the second-to-last paragraph in the document, just to the left of the "T" in "Talk to your project manager...."

6. In the Clipboard group, click the **Paste** button. The sentence and the space following it are displayed in the new location. The Paste Options button appears near the newly inserted sentence.

   Trouble? If a menu opens below the Paste button, you clicked the Paste button arrow instead of the Paste button. Press the Esc key to close the menu, and then repeat Step 6, taking care not to click the arrow below the Paste button.

7. Save the document.

Carolina explains that she'll be using some text from the Home LEED document as the basis for another department handout. She asks you to copy that information and paste it into a new document. You can do this using the Clipboard task pane.

To copy text to paste into a new document:

1. In the Clipboard group, click the **Dialog Box Launcher**. The Clipboard task pane opens on the left side of the document window, as shown in Figure 2-9.

Figure 2-9 Clipboard task pane

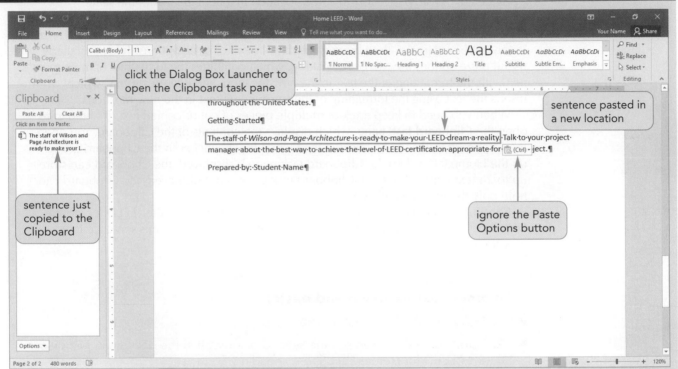

Notice the Clipboard contains the sentence you copied in the last set of steps, although you can see only the first part of the sentence.

2. Scroll up, if necessary, and then locate the first sentence on page 2.

3. Press and hold the **Ctrl** key, and then click anywhere in the first sentence on page 2, which begins "A project can achieve up to 100...." The sentence and the space following it are selected.

4. In the Clipboard group, click the **Copy** button. The first part of the sentence appears at the top of the Clipboard task pane, as shown in Figure 2-10. You can also copy selected text by pressing the Ctrl+C keys.

Figure 2-10   Items in the Clipboard task pane

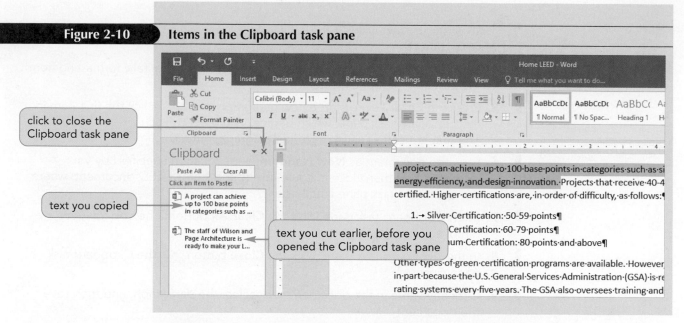

click to close the
Clipboard task pane

text you copied

text you cut earlier, before you
opened the Clipboard task pane

Now you can use the Clipboard task pane to insert the copied text into a new
document.

To insert the copied text into a new document:

1. Open a new, blank document. If necessary, open the Clipboard task pane.

2. In the Clipboard task pane, click the second item in the list of copied items,
   which begins "The staff of *Wilson and Page Architecture* is ready...." The
   text is inserted in the document and the company name, "Wilson and Page
   Architecture," retains its italic formatting.

   Carolina doesn't want to keep the italic formatting in the newly pasted text.
   You can remove this formatting by using the Paste Options button, which is
   visible just below the pasted text.

3. Click the **Paste Options** button in the document. The Paste Options
   menu opens, as shown in Figure 2-11.

Figure 2-11   Paste Options menu

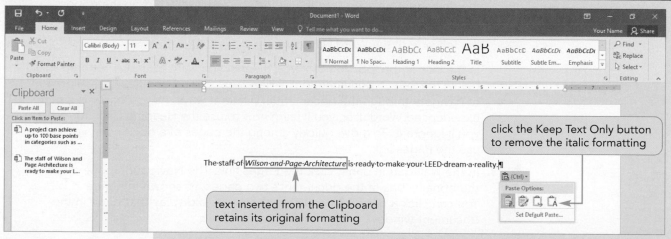

click the Keep Text Only button
to remove the italic formatting

text inserted from the Clipboard
retains its original formatting

To paste the text without the italic formatting, you can click the Keep Text Only button.

TIP

To select a paste option before pasting an item, click the Paste button arrow in the Clipboard group, and then click the paste option you want.

4. Click the **Keep Text Only** button 🄰. Word removes the italic formatting from "Wilson and Page Architecture."

5. Press the **Enter** key to start a new paragraph, and then click the first item in the Clipboard task pane, which begins "A project can achieve up to 100...." The text is inserted as the second paragraph in the document.

6. Save the document as **New Handout** in the location specified by your instructor, and then close it. You return to the Home LEED document, where the Clipboard task pane is still open.

7. In the Clipboard task pane, click the **Clear All** button. The copied items are removed from the Clipboard.

8. In the Clipboard task pane, click the **Close** button ✕. The Clipboard task pane closes.

9. Click anywhere in the document to deselect the paragraph, and then save the document.

Using the Navigation Pane

The Navigation pane simplifies the process of moving through a document page by page. You can also use the Navigation pane to locate a particular word or phrase. You start by typing the text you're searching for—the **search text**—in the Search box at the top of the Navigation pane. As shown in the Session 2.1 Visual Overview, Word highlights every instance of the search text in the document. At the same time, a list of the **search results** appears in the Navigation pane. You can click a search result to go immediately to that location in the document.

To become familiar with the Navigation pane, you'll use it to navigate through the Home LEED document page by page. You'll start by moving the insertion point to the beginning of the document.

To navigate through the document page by page:

1. Press the **Ctrl+Home** keys to move the insertion point to the beginning of the document, making sure the Home tab is still selected on the ribbon.

2. In the Editing group, click the **Find** button. The Navigation pane opens on the left side of the Word window.

   In the box at the top, you can type the text you want to find. The three links below the Search document box—Headings, Pages, and Results—allow you to navigate through the document in different ways. As you become a more experienced Word user, you'll learn how to use the Headings link; for now, you'll ignore it. To move quickly among the pages of a document, you can use the Pages link.

3. In the Navigation pane, click the **Pages** link. The Navigation pane displays thumbnail icons of the document's two pages, as shown in Figure 2-12. You can click a page in the Navigation pane to display that page in the document window.

Figure 2-12	Document pages displayed in the Navigation pane

click to display page thumbnails

Search document box

page 1

page 2

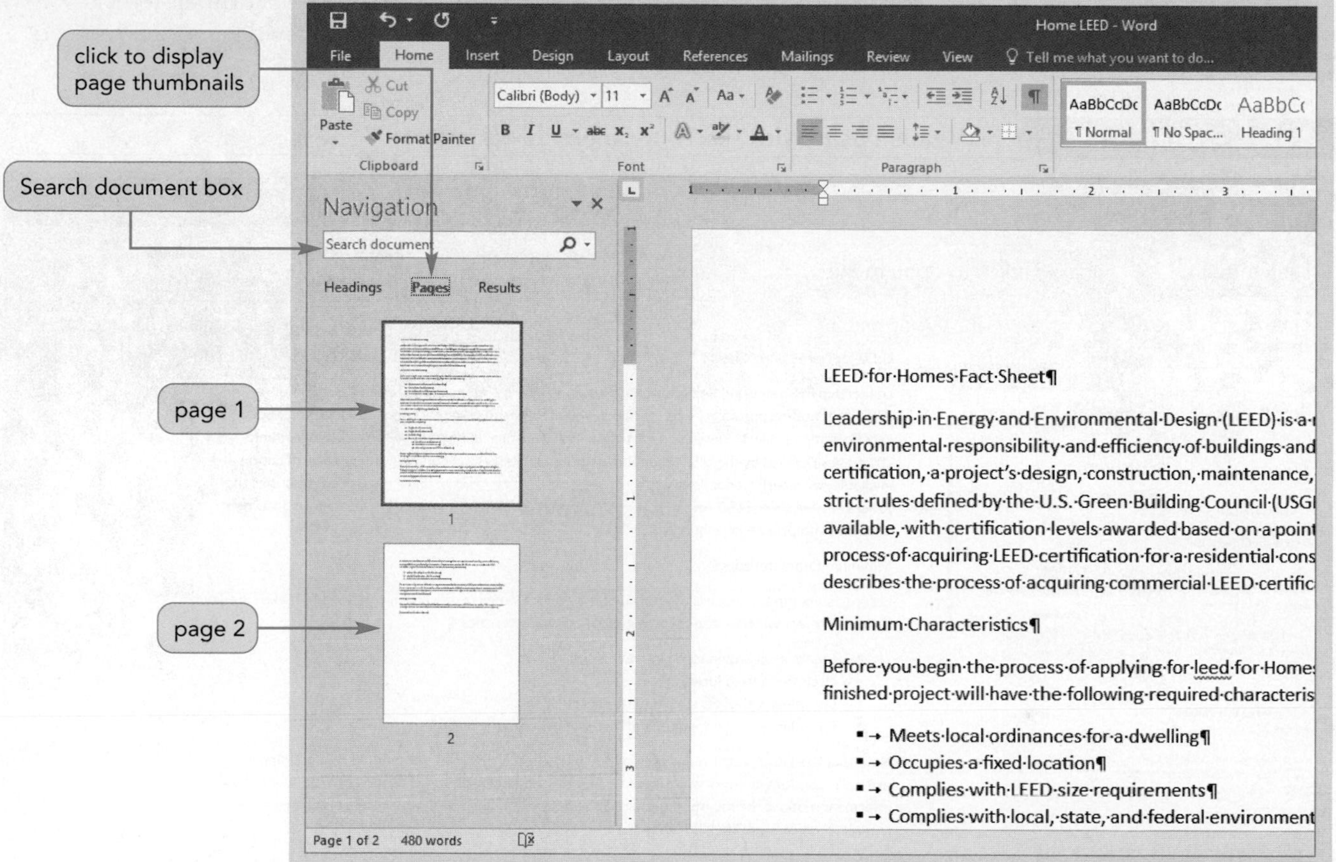

4. In the Navigation pane, click the **page 2** thumbnail. Page 2 is displayed in the document window, with the insertion point blinking at the beginning of the page.

5. In the Navigation pane, click the **page 1** thumbnail to move the insertion point back to the beginning of the document.

Carolina thinks she might have mistakenly used "leed" when she actually meant to use "LEED" in certain parts of the document. She asks you to use the Navigation pane to find all instances of "leed."

To search for "leed" in the document:

1. In the Navigation pane, click the **Results** link, click the **Search document** box, and then type **leed**. You do not have to press the Enter key.

   Every instance of the word "leed" is highlighted in yellow in the document. The yellow highlight is only temporary; it will disappear as soon as you begin to perform any other task in the document. A full list of the 20 search results is displayed in the Navigation pane. Some of the search results contain "LEED" (with all uppercase letters), while others contain "leed" (with all lowercase letters). To narrow the search results, you need to tell Word to match the case of the search text.

2. In the Navigation pane, click the **Search for more things** button ▼. This displays a two-part menu. In the bottom part, you can select other items to search for, such as graphics or tables. The top part provides more advanced search tools. See Figure 2-13.

Figure 2-13   Navigation pane with Search for more things menu

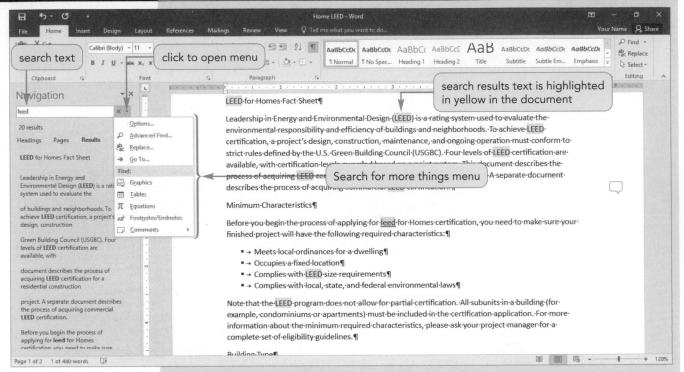

3. At the top of the Search for more things menu, click **Options** to open the Find Options dialog box.

The check boxes in this dialog box allow you to fine-tune your search. For example, to ensure that Word finds the search text only when it appears as a separate word and not when it appears as part of another word, you could select the Find whole words only check box. Right now, you are concerned only with making sure the search results have the same case as the search text.

4. Click the **Match case** check box to select it, and then click the **OK** button to close the Find Options dialog box. Now you can search the document again.

5. Press the **Ctrl+Home** keys to move the insertion point to the beginning of the document, click the **Search document** box in the Navigation pane, and then type **leed**. This time, there are only three search results in the Navigation pane, and they contain the lowercase text "leed."

To move among the search results, you can use the up and down arrows in the Navigation pane.

6. In the Navigation pane, click the **down arrow** button ▼. Word selects the first instance of "leed" in the Navigation pane, as indicated by a blue outline. Also, in the document, the first instance has a gray selection highlight over the yellow highlight. See Figure 2-14.

Figure 2-14   Navigation pane with the first search result selected

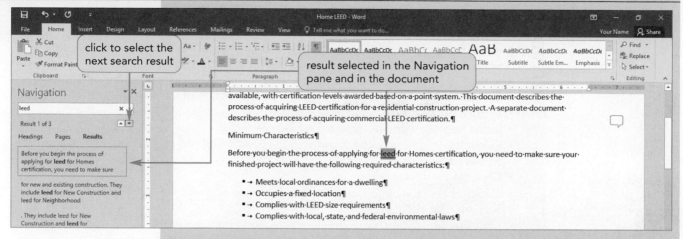

> **Trouble?** If the second instance of "leed" is selected in the Navigation pane, then you pressed the Enter key after typing "leed" in Step 5. Click the up arrow button ▲ to select the first instance.

▶ **7.** In the Navigation pane, click the **down arrow** button ▼. Word selects the second instance of "leed" in the document and in the Navigation pane.

▶ **8.** Click the **down arrow** button ▼ again to select the third search result, and then click the **up arrow** button ▲ to select the second search result again.

You can also select a search result in the document by clicking a search result in the Navigation pane.

▶ **9.** In the Navigation pane, click the **third search result** (which begins ". They include leed for New Construction…"). The third search result is selected in the document and in the Navigation pane.

After reviewing the search results, Carolina decides she would like to replace the three instances of "leed" with "LEED." You can do that by using the Find and Replace dialog box.

Finding and Replacing Text

To open the Find and Replace dialog box from the Navigation pane, click the Search for more things button, and then click Replace. This opens the **Find and Replace dialog box**, with the Replace tab displayed by default. The Replace tab provides options for finding a specific word or phrase in the document and replacing it with another word or phrase. To use the Replace tab, type the search text in the Find what box, and then type the text you want to substitute in the Replace with box. You can also click the More button on the Replace tab to display the Search Options section, which includes the same options you saw earlier in the Find Options dialog box, including the Find whole words only check box and the Match case check box.

After you have typed the search text and selected any search options, you can click the Find Next button to select the first occurrence of the search text; you can then decide whether to substitute the search text with the replacement text.

REFERENCE

Finding and Replacing Text

- Press the Ctrl+Home keys to move the insertion point to the beginning of the document.
- In the Editing group on the Home tab, click the Replace button; or, in the Navigation pane, click the Search for more things button, and then click Replace.
- In the Find and Replace dialog box, click the More button, if necessary, to expand the dialog box and display the Search Options section of the Replace tab.
- In the Find what box, type the search text.
- In the Replace with box, type the replacement text.
- Select the appropriate check boxes in the Search Options section of the dialog box to narrow your search.
- Click the Find Next button.
- Click the Replace button to substitute the found text with the replacement text and find the next occurrence.
- Click the Replace All button to substitute all occurrences of the found text with the replacement text without reviewing each occurrence. Use this option only if you are absolutely certain that the results will be what you expect.

You'll use the Find and Replace dialog box now to replace three instances of "leed" with "LEED."

To replace three instances of "leed" with "LEED":

1. Press the **Ctrl+Home** keys to move the insertion point to the beginning of the document.

2. In the Navigation pane, click the **Search for more things** button ▼ to open the menu, and then click **Replace**. The Find and Replace dialog box opens with the Replace tab on top.

   The search text you entered earlier in the Navigation pane, "leed," appears in the Find what box. If you hadn't already conducted a search, you would need to type your search text now. Because you selected the Match case check box earlier in the Find Options dialog box, "Match Case" appears below the Find what box.

3. In the lower-left corner of the dialog box, click the **More** button to display the search options. Because you selected the Match case check box earlier in the Find Options dialog box, it is selected here.

   Trouble? If you see the Less button instead of the More button, the search options are already displayed.

4. Click the **Replace with** box, and then type **LEED**.

5. Click the **Find Next** button. Word highlights the first instance of "leed" in the document. See Figure 2-15.

Figure 2-15   Find and Replace dialog box

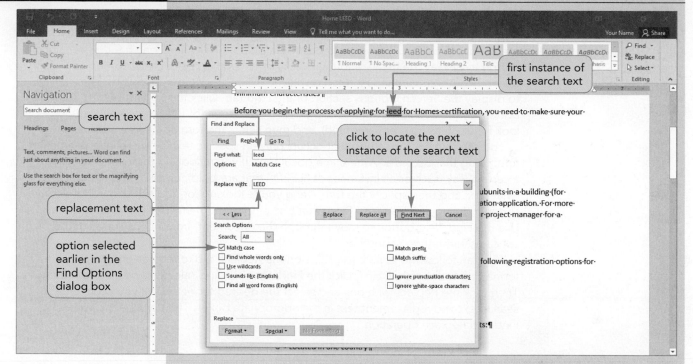

6. Click the **Replace** button. Word replaces "leed" with "LEED," so the text reads "applying for LEED for Homes certification." Then, Word selects the next instance of "leed." If you do not want to make a replacement, you can click the Find Next button to skip the current instance of the search text and move onto the next. In this case, however, you do want to make the replacement.

7. Click the **Replace** button. Word selects the last instance of "leed," which happens to be located in the same sentence.

8. Click the **Replace** button. Word makes the substitution, so the text reads "LEED for Neighborhood Development," and then displays a message box telling you that Word has finished searching the document.

9. Click the **OK** button to close the message box, and then in the Find and Replace dialog box, click the **Close** button.

You are finished with the Navigation pane, so you can close it. But first you need to restore the search options to their original settings. It's a good practice to restore the original search settings so that future searches are not affected by any settings you used for an earlier search.

To restore the search options to their original settings:

1. In the Navigation pane, open the **Find Options** dialog box, deselect the **Match case** check box, and then click the **OK** button to close the Find Options dialog box.

2. Click the **Close** button ☒ in the upper-right corner of the Navigation pane.

3. Save the document.

Searching for Formatting

You can search for formatting just as you can search for text. For example, you might want to check a document to look for text formatted in bold and the Arial font. To search for formatting from within the Navigation pane, click the Search for more things button to display the menu, and then click Advanced Find. The Find and Replace dialog box opens with the Find tab displayed. Click the More button, if necessary, to display the Search Options section of the Find tab. Click the Format button at the bottom of the Search Options section, click the category of formatting you want to look for (such as Font or Paragraph), and then select the formatting you want to find.

You can look for formatting that occurs only on specific text, or you can look for formatting that occurs anywhere in a document. If you're looking for text formatted in a certain way (such as all instances of "LEED" that are bold), enter the text in the Find what box, and then specify the formatting you're looking for. To find formatting on any text in a document, leave the Find what box empty, and then specify the formatting. Use the Find Next button to move through the document, from one instance of the specified formatting to another.

You can follow the same basic steps on the Replace tab to replace one type of formatting with another. First, click the Find what box and select the desired formatting. Then click the Replace with box and select the desired formatting. If you want, type search text and replacement text in the appropriate boxes. Then proceed as with any Find and Replace operation.

Now that the text in the Home LEED document is final, you will turn your attention to styles and themes, which affect the look of the entire document.

Working with Styles

A style is a set of formatting options that you can apply by clicking an icon in the Style gallery on the Home tab. Each style is designed for a particular use. For example, the Title style is intended for formatting the title at the beginning of a document.

All the text you type into a document has a style applied to it. By default, text is formatted in the Normal style, which applies 11-point Calibri font, left alignment, 1.08 line spacing, and a small amount of extra space between paragraphs. In other words, the Normal style applies the default formatting you learned about when you first began typing a Word document.

Note that some styles apply **paragraph-level formatting**—that is, they are set up to format an entire paragraph, including the paragraph and line spacing. The Normal, Heading, and Title styles all apply paragraph-level formatting. Other styles apply **character-level formatting**—that is, they are set up to format only individual characters or words (for example, emphasizing a phrase by adding italic formatting and changing the font color).

One row of the Style gallery is always visible on the Home tab. To display the entire Style gallery, click the More button in the Styles group. After you begin applying styles in a document, the visible row of the Style gallery changes to show the most recently used styles.

You are ready to use the Style gallery to format the document title.

To display the entire Style gallery and then format the document title with a style:

1. Make sure the Home tab is still selected and locate the More button in the Styles group, as shown earlier in the Session 2.1 Visual Overview.

2. In the Styles group, click the **More** button. The Style gallery opens, displaying a total of 16 styles arranged in two rows, as shown in Figure 2-16. If your screen is set at a lower resolution than the screenshots in this book, the Style gallery on your screen might contain more than two rows.

Figure 2-16   Displaying the Style gallery

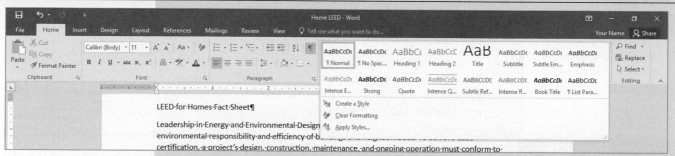

You don't actually need any of the styles in the bottom row now, so you can close the Style gallery.

3. Press the **Esc** key to close the Style gallery.

4. Click anywhere in the first paragraph, "LEED for Homes Fact Sheet," if necessary, and then point to (but don't click) the **Title** style, which is the fifth style from the left in the top row of the gallery. The ScreenTip "Title" is displayed, and a Live Preview of the style appears in the paragraph containing the insertion point, as shown in Figure 2-17. The Title style changes the font to 28-point Calibri Light.

Figure 2-17   Title style in the Style gallery

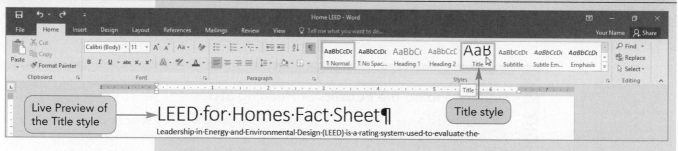

5. Click the **Title** style. The style is applied to the paragraph. To finish the title, you need to center it.

6. In the Paragraph group, click the **Center** button ⬛. The title is centered in the document.

Next, you will format the document headings using the heading styles, which have different levels. The highest level, Heading 1, is used for the major headings in a document, and it applies the most noticeable formatting with a larger font than the other heading styles. (In heading styles, the highest, or most important, level has the lowest number.) The Heading 2 style is used for headings that are subordinate to the highest level headings; it applies slightly less dramatic formatting than the Heading 1 style.

The Home LEED handout only has one level of headings, so you will apply only the Heading 1 style.

To format text with the Heading 1 style:

1. Click anywhere in the "Minimum Characteristics" paragraph.

2. On the Home tab, in the Style gallery, click the **Heading 1** style. The paragraph is now formatted in blue, 16-point Calibri Light. The Heading 1 style also inserts some paragraph space above the heading.

3. Scroll down, click anywhere in the "Building Type" paragraph, and then click the **Heading 1** style in the Style gallery.

4. Repeat Step 3 to apply the Heading 1 style to the "Rating Systems" paragraph, the "Certification Levels" paragraph, and the "Getting Started" paragraph. When you are finished, scroll up to the beginning of the document to review the new formatting. See Figure 2-18.

TIP

On most computers, you can press the F4 key to repeat your most recent action.

Figure 2-18   **Document with Title and Heading 1 styles**

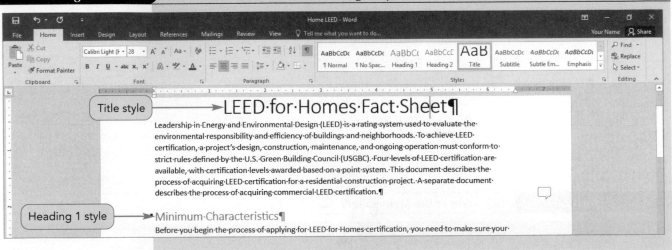

Understanding the Benefits of Heading Styles

By default, the Style gallery offers 16 styles, each designed for a specific purpose. As you gain more experience with Word, you will learn how to use a wider array of styles. You'll also learn how to create your own styles. Styles allow you to change a document's formatting in an instant. But the benefits of heading styles go far beyond attractive formatting. Heading styles allow you to reorganize a document or generate a table of contents with a click of the mouse. Also, heading styles are set up to keep a heading and the body text that follows it together, so a heading is never separated from its body text by a page break. Each Word document includes nine levels of heading styles, although only the Heading 1 and Heading 2 styles are available by default in the Style gallery. Whenever you use the lowest heading style in the Style gallery, the next-lowest level is added to the Style gallery. For example, after you use the Heading 2 style, the Heading 3 style appears in the Styles group in the Style gallery.

INSIGHT

After you format a document with a variety of styles, you can alter the look of the document by changing the document's theme.

Working with Themes

A **theme** is a coordinated collection of fonts, colors, and other visual effects designed to give a document a cohesive, polished look. A variety of themes are installed with Word, with more available online at Templates.office.com. When you open a new, blank document in Word, the Office theme is applied by default. To change a document's theme, you click the Themes button, which is located in the Document Formatting group on the Design tab, and then click the theme you want. Pointing to the Themes button displays a ScreenTip that tells you what theme is currently applied to the document.

When applying color to a document, you usually have the option of selecting a color from a palette of colors designed to match the current theme or from a palette of standard colors. For instance, recall that the colors in the Font Color gallery are divided into Theme Colors and Standard Colors. When you select a Standard Color, such as Dark Red, that color remains the same no matter which theme you apply to the document. But when you click one of the Theme Colors, you are essentially telling Word to use the color located in that particular spot on the Theme Colors palette. Then, if you change the document's theme later, Word substitutes a color from the same location on the Theme Colors palette. This ensures that all the colors in a document are drawn from a group of colors coordinated to look good together. So as a rule, if you are going to use multiple colors in a document (perhaps for paragraph shading and font color), it's a good idea to stick with the Theme Colors.

A similar substitution takes place with fonts when you change the theme. However, to understand how this works, you need to understand the difference between headings and body text. Carolina's document includes the headings "Minimum Characteristics," "Building Type," "Rating Systems," "Certification Levels," and "Getting Started"—all of which you have formatted with the Heading1 style. The title of the document, "LEED for Homes Fact Sheet," is now formatted with the Title style, which is also a type of heading style. Everything else in the Home LEED document is body text.

To ensure that your documents have a harmonious look, each theme assigns a font for headings and a font for body text. Typically, in a given theme, the same font is used for both headings and body text, but not always. In the Office theme, for instance, they are slightly different; the heading font is Calibri Light, and the body font is Calibri. These two fonts appear at the top of the Font list as "Calibri Light (Headings)" and "Calibri (Body)" when you click the Font box arrow in the Font group on the Home tab. When you begin typing text in a new document with the Office theme, the text is formatted as body text with the Calibri font by default.

When applying a font to selected text, you can choose one of the two theme fonts at the top of the Font list, or you can choose one of the other fonts in the Font list. If you choose one of the other fonts and then change the document theme, that font remains the same. But if you use one of the theme fonts and then change the document theme, Word substitutes the appropriate font from the new theme. When you paste text into a document that has a different theme, Word applies the theme fonts and colors of the new document. To retain the original formatting, use the Keep Source Formatting option in the Paste Options menu.

Figure 2-19 compares elements of the default Office theme with the Integral theme. The Integral theme was chosen for this example because, like the Office theme, it has different heading and body fonts.

Figure 2-19   Comparing the Office theme to the Integral theme

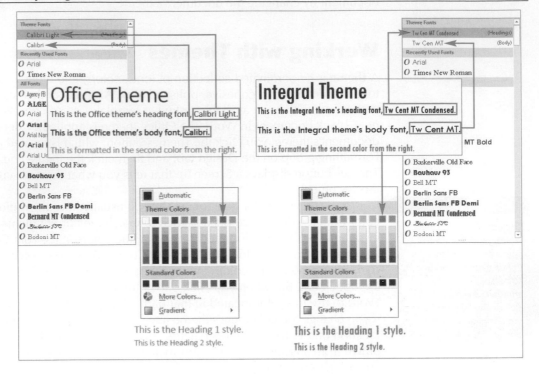

Because Carolina has not yet selected a new theme, the Office theme is currently applied to the Home LEED document. However, she thinks the Berlin theme might be more appropriate for the Home LEED document. She asks you to apply it now.

To change the document's theme:

1. If necessary, press the **Ctrl+Home** keys to move the insertion point to the beginning of the document. With the title and first heading visible, you will more easily see what happens when you change the document's theme.

2. On the ribbon, click the **Design** tab.

3. In the Document Formatting group, point to the **Themes** button. A ScreenTip appears containing the text "Current: Office Theme" as well as general information about themes.

4. In the Document Formatting group, click the **Themes** button. The Themes gallery opens. Because Microsoft occasionally updates the available themes, you might see a different list than the one shown in Figure 2-20.

Figure 2-20   Themes gallery

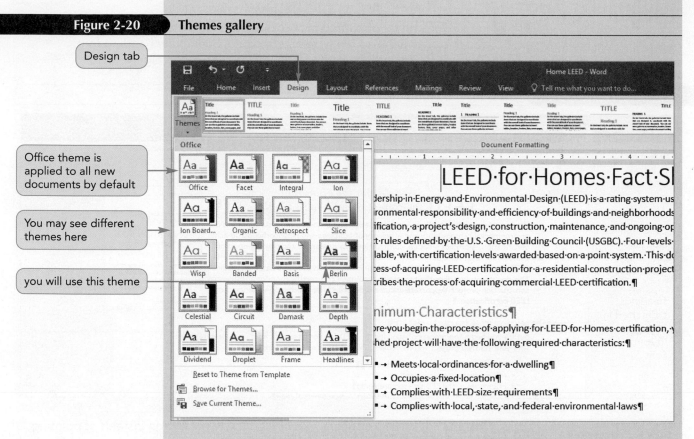

Design tab

Office theme is applied to all new documents by default

You may see different themes here

you will use this theme

5. Move the mouse pointer (without clicking it) over the various themes in the gallery to see a Live Preview of each theme in the document. The heading and body fonts as well as the heading colors change to reflect the fonts associated with the various themes.

6. In the Themes gallery, click the **Berlin** theme. The text in the Home LEED document changes to the body and heading fonts of the Berlin theme, with the headings formatted in dark orange. To see exactly what the Berlin theme fonts are, you can point to the Fonts button in the Document Formatting group.

   Trouble? If you do not see the Berlin theme in your Themes gallery, click a different theme.

7. In the Document Formatting group, point to the **Fonts** button. A ScreenTip appears, listing the currently selected theme (Berlin), the heading font (Trebuchet MS), and the body font (Trebuchet MS). See Figure 2-21.

Figure 2-21 **Fonts for the Berlin theme**

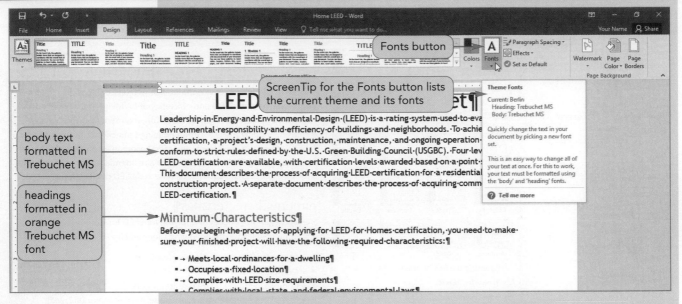

Trouble? If a menu appears, you clicked the Fonts button instead of pointing to it. Press the Esc key, and then repeat Step 7.

8. Save your changes and then close the document.

Carolina's Home LEED document is ready to be handed in to her supervisor. The use of styles, bulleted and numbered lists, and a new theme gives the document a professional look appropriate for use in a business handout.

INSIGHT

Personalizing the Word Interface

The Word Options dialog box allows you to change the look of the Word interface. For starters, you can change the Office Theme from the default setting (Colorful) to Dark Gray or White. Note that in this context, "Office Theme" refers to the colors of the Word interface, and not the colors and fonts used in a Word document. You can also use the Office Background setting to add graphic designs, such as clouds or stars, to the Word interface. To get started, click the File tab, click Options in the navigation bar, and then select the options you want in the Personalize your copy of Microsoft Office section of the Word Options dialog box.

REVIEW

Session 2.1 Quick Check

1. When you reply to a comment, what name appears in the reply?
2. When should you use a numbered list instead of a bulleted list?
3. How can you ensure that the Navigation pane will find instances of "LEED" instead of "leed"?
4. What style is applied to all text in a new document by default?
5. What theme is applied to a new document by default?

Session 2.2 Visual Overview:

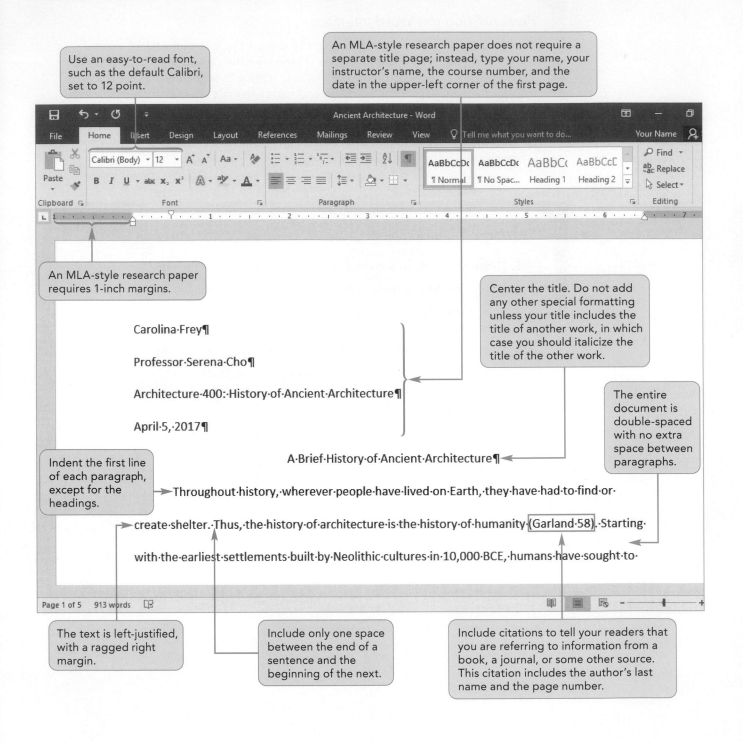

Use an easy-to-read font, such as the default Calibri, set to 12 point.

An MLA-style research paper does not require a separate title page; instead, type your name, your instructor's name, the course number, and the date in the upper-left corner of the first page.

An MLA-style research paper requires 1-inch margins.

Center the title. Do not add any other special formatting unless your title includes the title of another work, in which case you should italicize the title of the other work.

The entire document is double-spaced with no extra space between paragraphs.

Indent the first line of each paragraph, except for the headings.

The text is left-justified, with a ragged right margin.

Include only one space between the end of a sentence and the beginning of the next.

Include citations to tell your readers that you are referring to information from a book, a journal, or some other source. This citation includes the author's last name and the page number.

Carolina·Frey¶

Professor·Serena·Cho¶

Architecture·400:·History·of·Ancient·Architecture¶

April·5,·2017¶

A·Brief·History·of·Ancient·Architecture¶

Throughout·history,·wherever·people·have·lived·on·Earth,·they·have·had·to·find·or·

create·shelter.··Thus,·the·history·of·architecture·is·the·history·of·humanity·(Garland·58).··Starting·

with·the·earliest·settlements·built·by·Neolithic·cultures·in·10,000·BCE,·humans·have·sought·to·

Ancient Architecture - Word

MLA Formatting Guidelines

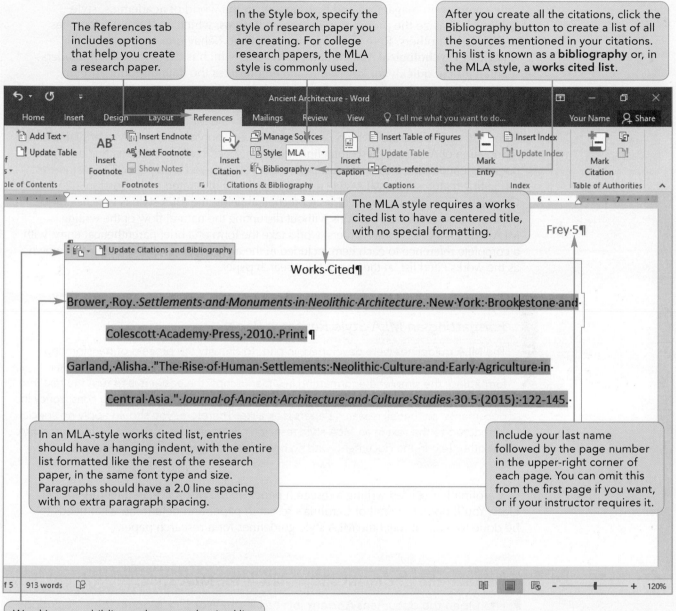

The References tab includes options that help you create a research paper.

In the Style box, specify the style of research paper you are creating. For college research papers, the MLA style is commonly used.

After you create all the citations, click the Bibliography button to create a list of all the sources mentioned in your citations. This list is known as a **bibliography** or, in the MLA style, a **works cited list**.

The MLA style requires a works cited list to have a centered title, with no special formatting.

Update Citations and Bibliography

Frey·5¶

Works·Cited¶

Brower,·Roy.·*Settlements·and·Monuments·in·Neolithic·Architecture.*·New·York:·Brookestone·and·Colescott·Academy·Press,·2010.·Print.¶

Garland,·Alisha.·"The·Rise·of·Human·Settlements:·Neolithic·Culture·and·Early·Agriculture·in·Central·Asia."·*Journal·of·Ancient·Architecture·and·Culture·Studies*·30.5·(2015):·122-145.·

In an MLA-style works cited list, entries should have a hanging indent, with the entire list formatted like the rest of the research paper, in the same font type and size. Paragraphs should have a 2.0 line spacing with no extra paragraph spacing.

Include your last name followed by the page number in the upper-right corner of each page. You can omit this from the first page if you want, or if your instructor requires it.

Word inserts a bibliography, or works cited list, contained in a special feature, known as a **content control**, used to display information that is inserted automatically and that may need to be updated later. You can use the buttons in the content control tab to make changes to material inside the content control.

Reviewing the MLA Style

A **style guide** is a set of rules that describe the preferred format and style for a certain type of writing. People in different fields use different style guides, with each style guide designed to suit the needs of a specific discipline. For example, journalists commonly use the *Associated Press Stylebook*, which focuses on the concise writing style common in magazines and newspapers. In the world of academics, style guides emphasize the proper way to create **citations**, which are formal references to the work of others. Researchers in the social and behavioral sciences use the **American Psychological Association (APA) style**, which is designed to help readers scan an article quickly for key points and emphasizes the date of publication in citations. Other scientific and technical fields have their own specialized style guides.

In the humanities, the **Modern Language Association (MLA) style** is widely used. This is the style Carolina has used for her research paper. She followed the guidelines specified in the *MLA Handbook for Writers of Research Papers*, published by the Modern Language Association of America. These guidelines focus on specifications for formatting a research document and citing the sources used in research conducted for a paper. The major formatting features of an MLA-style research paper are illustrated in the Session 2.2 Visual Overview. Compared to style guides for technical fields, the MLA style is very flexible, making it easy to include citations without disrupting the natural flow of the writing. MLA-style citations of other writers' works take the form of a brief parenthetical entry, with a complete reference to each item included in the alphabetized bibliography, also known as the works cited list, at the end of the research paper.

INSIGHT

Formatting an MLA-Style Research Paper

The MLA guidelines were developed, in part, to simplify the process of transforming a manuscript into a journal article or a chapter of a book. The style calls for minimal formatting; the simpler the formatting in a manuscript, the easier it is to turn the text into a published document. The MLA guidelines were also designed to ensure consistency in documents, so that all research papers look alike. Therefore, you should apply no special formatting to the text in an MLA-style research paper. Headings should be formatted like the other text in the document, with no bold or heading styles.

Carolina has started writing a research paper on the history of architecture for her class. You'll open the draft of Carolina's research paper and determine what needs to be done to make it meet the MLA style guidelines for a research paper.

To open the document and review it for MLA style:

1. Open the document **Ancient** located in the Word2 > Module folder included with your Data Files, and then save the document as **Ancient Architecture** in the location specified by your instructor.

2. Verify that the document is displayed in Print Layout view, and that the rulers and nonprinting characters are displayed. Make sure the Zoom level is set to **120%**.

3. Review the document to familiarize yourself with its structure. First, notice the parts of the document that already match the MLA style. Carolina included a block of information in the upper-left corner of the first page, giving her name, her instructor's name, the course name, and the date. The title at the top of the first page also meets the MLA guidelines in that it is centered and does not have any special formatting. The headings

("Neolithic Settlements," "Egyptian Construction," "The Civic-Minded Greeks," and "Roman Achievement") have no special formatting; but unlike the title, they are left-aligned. Finally, the body text is left-aligned with a ragged right margin, and the entire document is formatted in the same font, Calibri, which is easy to read.

What needs to be changed in order to make Carolina's paper consistent with the MLA style? Currently, the entire document is formatted using the default settings, which are the Normal style for the Office theme. To transform the document into an MLA-style research paper, you need to complete the checklist shown in Figure 2-22.

| Figure 2-22 | Checklist for formatting a default Word document to match the MLA style |

✓ Double-space the entire document.

✓ Remove paragraph spacing from the entire document.

✓ Increase the font size for the entire document to 12 points.

✓ Indent the first line of each body paragraph .5 inch from the left margin.

✓ Add the page number (preceded by your last name) in the upper-right corner of each page. If you prefer, you can omit this from the first page.

You'll take care of the first three items in the checklist now.

To begin applying MLA formatting to the document:

1. Press the **Ctrl+A** keys to select the entire document.

2. Make sure the Home tab is selected on the ribbon.

3. In the Paragraph group, click the **Line and Paragraph Spacing** button 📄, and then click **2.0**.

4. Click the **Line and Spacing** button 📄 again, and then click **Remove Space After Paragraph**. The entire document is now double-spaced, with no paragraph spacing, and the entire document is still selected.

5. In the Font group, click the **Font Size** arrow, and then click **12**. The entire document is formatted in 12-point font.

6. Click anywhere in the document to deselect the text.

7. In the first paragraph of the document, replace Carolina's name with your first and last names, and then save the document.

Now you need to indent the first line of each body paragraph.

Indenting a Paragraph

Word offers a number of options for indenting a paragraph. You can move an entire paragraph to the right, or you can create specialized indents, such as a **hanging indent**, where all lines except the first line of the paragraph are indented from the left margin. As you saw in the Session 2.2 Visual Overview, all the body paragraphs (that is, all the paragraphs except the information in the upper-left corner of the first page, the title, and the headings) have a first-line indent in MLA research papers. Figure 2-23 shows some examples of other common paragraph indents.

Figure 2-23   **Common paragraph indents**

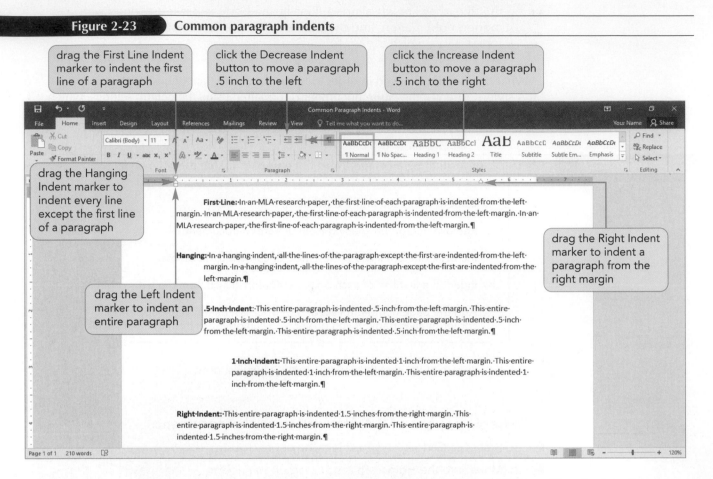

To quickly indent an entire paragraph .5 inch from the left, position the insertion point in the paragraph you want to indent, and then click the Increase Indent button in the Paragraph group on the Home tab. You can continue to indent the paragraph in increments of .5 inch by repeatedly clicking the Increase Indent button. To move an indented paragraph back to the left .5 inch, click the Decrease Indent button.

To create first-line, hanging, or right indents, you can use the indent markers on the ruler. First, click in the paragraph you want to indent or select multiple paragraphs. Then drag the appropriate indent marker to the left or right on the horizontal ruler. The indent markers are small and can be hard to see. As shown in Figure 2-23, the **First Line Indent marker** looks like the top half of an hourglass; the **Hanging Indent marker** looks like the bottom half. The rectangle below the Hanging Indent marker is the **Left Indent marker**. The **Right Indent marker** looks just like the Hanging Indent marker except that it is located on the far-right side of the horizontal ruler.

Note that when you indent an entire paragraph using the Increase Indent button, the three indent markers, shown stacked on top of one another in Figure 2-23, move as a unit along with the paragraphs you are indenting.

In Carolina's paper, you will indent the first lines of the body paragraphs .5 inch from the left margin, as specified by the MLA style.

To indent the first line of each paragraph:

▶ **1.** On the first page of the document, just below the title, click anywhere in the first main paragraph, which begins "Throughout history...."

▶ **2.** On the horizontal ruler, position the mouse pointer over the First Line Indent marker 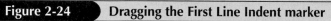. When you see the ScreenTip that reads "First Line Indent," you know the mouse is positioned correctly.

▶ **3.** Press and hold the mouse button as you drag the **First Line Indent** marker to the right, to the .5-inch mark on the horizontal ruler. As you drag, a vertical guideline appears over the document, and the first line of the paragraph moves right. See Figure 2-24.

Figure 2-24	Dragging the First Line Indent marker

First Line Indent marker

.5-inch mark

guideline appears as you drag the indent marker and the first line of the paragraph moves right

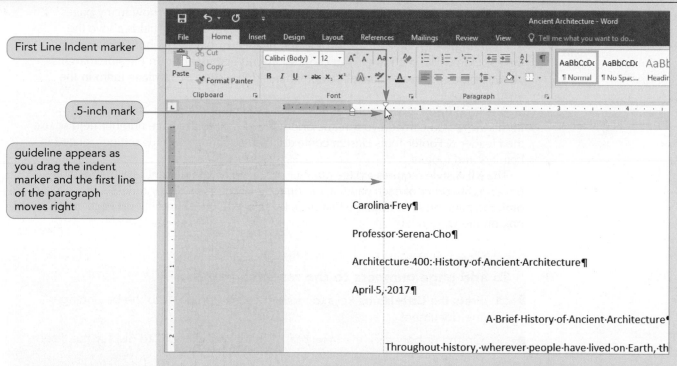

TIP
You can also click the Dialog Box Launcher in the Paragraph group and then adjust the Indentation settings for one or more selected paragraphs.

▶ **4.** When the First Line Indent marker is positioned at the .5-inch mark on the ruler, release the mouse button. The first line of the paragraph containing the insertion point indents .5 inch, and the vertical guideline disappears.

▶ **5.** Scroll down, if necessary, click anywhere in the next paragraph in the document (which begins "In this paper, I will present..."), and then drag the **First Line Indent** marker to the right, to the .5-inch mark on the horizontal ruler. As you move the indent marker, you can use the vertical guideline to ensure that you match the first-line indent of the preceding paragraph.

You could continue to drag the indent marker to indent the first line of the remaining body paragraphs, but it's faster to use the Repeat button on the Quick Access Toolbar.

▶ **6.** Scroll down and click in the paragraph below the "Neolithic Settlements" heading, and then on the Quick Access Toolbar, click the **Repeat** button.

▶ **7.** Click in the next paragraph, at the top of page 2 (which begins "The rise of agriculture introduced..."), and then click the **Repeat** button.

8. Continue using the **Repeat** button ↻ to indent the first line of all of the remaining body paragraphs. Take care not to indent the headings, which in this document are formatted just like the body text.

9. Scroll to the top of the document, verify that you have correctly indented the first line of each body paragraph, and then save the document.

Next, you need to insert page numbers.

Inserting and Modifying Page Numbers

When you insert page numbers in a document, you don't have to type a page number on each page. Instead, you can insert a **page number field**, which is an instruction that tells Word to insert a page number on each page, no matter how many pages you eventually add to the document. Word inserts page number fields above the top margin, in the blank area known as the **header**, or below the bottom margin, in the area known as the **footer**. You can also insert page numbers in the side margins, although for business or academic documents, it's customary to place them in the header or footer.

After you insert a page number field, Word switches to Header and Footer view. In this view, you can add your name or other text next to the page number field or use the Header & Footer Tools Design contextual tab to change various settings related to headers and footers.

The MLA style requires a page number preceded by the student's last name in the upper-right corner of each page. If you prefer (or if your instructor requests it), you can omit the page number from the first page by selecting the Different First Page check box on the Design tab.

To add page numbers to the research paper:

1. Press the **Ctrl+Home** keys to move the insertion point to the beginning of the document.

2. On the ribbon, click the **Insert** tab. The ribbon changes to display the Insert options, including options for inserting page numbers.

3. In the Header & Footer group, click the **Page Number** button to open the Page Number menu. Here you can choose where you want to position the page numbers in your document—at the top of the page, at the bottom of the page, in the side margins, or at the current location of the insertion point.

4. Point to **Top of Page**. A gallery of page number styles opens. You can scroll the list to review the many styles of page numbers. Because the MLA style calls for a simple page number in the upper-right corner, you will use the Plain Number 3 style. See Figure 2-25.

> **TIP**
>
> To remove page numbers from a document, click the Remove Page Numbers command on the Page Number menu.

Figure 2-25   Gallery of page number styles

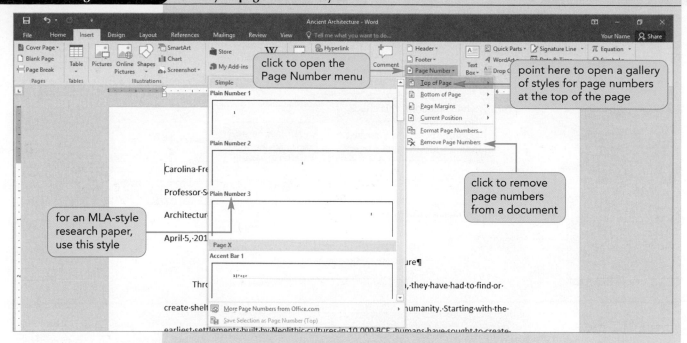

5. In the gallery, click the **Plain Number 3** style. The Word window switches to Header and Footer view, with the page number for the first page in the upper-right corner. The page number has a gray background, indicating that it is actually a page number field and not simply a number that you typed.

   The Header & Footer Tools Design tab is displayed on the ribbon, giving you access to a variety of formatting options. The insertion point blinks to the left of the page number field, ready for you to add text to the header if you wish. Note that in Header and Footer view, you can type only in the header or footer areas. The text in the main document area is a lighter shade of gray, indicating that it cannot be edited in this view.

6. Type your last name, and then press the **spacebar**. If you see a wavy red line below your last name, right-click your name, and then click **Ignore All** on the Shortcut menu.

7. Select your last name and the page number field.

8. In the Mini toolbar, click the **Font Size** button arrow, click **12**, and then click anywhere in the header to deselect it. Now the header's font size matches the font size of the rest of the document. This isn't strictly necessary in an MLA research paper, but some instructors prefer it. The page number no longer has a gray background, but it is still a field, which you can verify by clicking it.

9. Click the **page number field** to display its gray background. See Figure 2-26.

Figure 2-26   **Last name inserted next to the page number field**

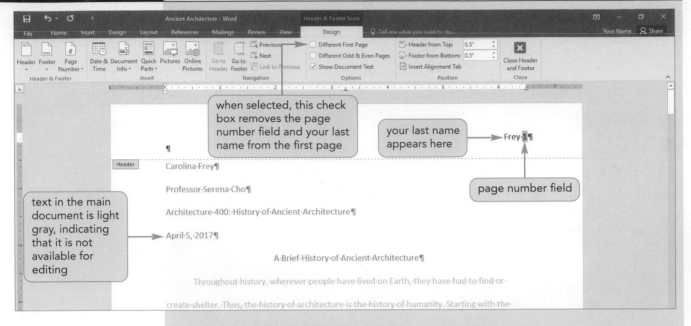

10. Scroll down and observe the page number (with your last name) at the top of pages 2, 3, and 4. As you can see, whatever you insert in the header on one page appears on every page of the document by default.

11. Press the **Ctrl+Home** keys to return to the header on the first page.

12. On the Header & Footer Tools Design tab, in the Options group, click the **Different First Page** check box to insert a check. The page number field and your last name are removed from the first page header. The insertion point blinks at the header's left margin in case you want to insert something else for the first page header. In this case, you don't.

13. In the Close group, click the **Close Header and Footer** button. You return to Print Layout view, and the Header & Footer Tools Design tab is no longer displayed on the ribbon.

14. Scroll down to review your last name and the page number in the headers for pages 2, 3, and 4. In Print Layout view, the text in the header is light gray, indicating that it is not currently available for editing.

TIP

After you insert page numbers, you can reopen Header and Footer view by double-clicking a page number in Print Layout view.

You have finished all the tasks related to formatting the MLA-style research paper. Now Carolina wants your help with creating the essential parts of any research paper—the citations and the bibliography.

Creating Citations and a Bibliography

A bibliography (or, as it is called in the MLA style, the works cited list) is an alphabetical list of all the books, magazine articles, websites, movies, and other works referred to in a research paper. The items listed in a bibliography are known as **sources**. The entry for each source includes information such as the author, the title of the work, the publication date, and the publisher.

Within the research paper itself, you include a parenthetical reference, or citation, every time you quote or refer to a source. Every source included in your citations then has a corresponding entry in the works cited list. A citation should include enough information to identify the quote or referenced material so the reader can easily locate the source in the accompanying works cited list. The exact form for a citation varies depending on the style guide you are using and the type of material you are referencing.

Some style guides are very rigid about the form and location of citations, but the MLA style offers quite a bit of flexibility. Typically, though, you insert an MLA citation at the end of a sentence in which you quote or refer to material from a source. For books or journals, the citation itself usually includes the author's last name and a page number. However, if the sentence containing the citation already includes the author's name, you need to include only the page number in the citation. Figure 2-27 provides some sample MLA citations; the format shown could be used for books or journals. For detailed guidelines, you can consult the *MLA Handbook for Writers of Research Papers, Seventh Edition*, which includes many examples.

Figure 2-27   **MLA guidelines for citing a book or journal**

Citation Rule	Example
If the sentence includes the author's name, the citation should only include the page number.	Peterson compares the opening scene of the movie to a scene from Shakespeare (188).
If the sentence does not include the author's name, the citation should include the author's name and the page number.	The opening scene of the movie has been compared to a scene from Shakespeare (Peterson 188).

Word greatly simplifies the process of creating citations and a bibliography. You specify the style you want to use, and then Word takes care of setting up the citation and the works cited list appropriately. Every time you create a citation for a new source, Word prompts you to enter the information needed to create the corresponding entry in the works cited list. If you don't have all of your source information available, Word also allows you to insert a temporary, placeholder citation, which you can replace later with a complete citation. When you are finished creating your citations, Word generates the bibliography automatically. Note that placeholder citations are not included in the bibliography.

PROSKILLS

Written Communication: Acknowledging Your Sources

A research paper is a means for you to explore the available information about a subject and then present this information, along with your own understanding of the subject, in an organized and interesting way. Acknowledging all the sources of the information presented in your research paper is essential. If you fail to do this, you might be subject to charges of plagiarism, or trying to pass off someone else's thoughts as your own. Plagiarism is an extremely serious accusation for which you could suffer academic consequences ranging from failing an assignment to being expelled from school.

To ensure that you don't forget to cite a source, you should be careful about creating citations in your document as you type. It's very easy to forget to go back and cite all your sources correctly after you've finished typing a research paper. Failing to cite a source could lead to accusations of plagiarism and all the consequences that entails. If you don't have the complete information about a source available when you are typing your paper, you should at least insert a placeholder citation. But take care to go back later and substitute complete citations for any placeholders.

Creating Citations

Before you create citations, you need to select the style you want to use, which in the case of Carolina's paper is the MLA style. Then, to insert a citation, you click the Insert Citation button in the Citations & Bibliography group on the References tab. If you are citing a source for the first time, Word prompts you to enter all the information required for the source's entry in the bibliography or works cited list. If you are citing an existing source, you simply select the source from the Insert Citation menu.

By default, an MLA citation includes only the author's name in parentheses. However, you can use the Edit Citation dialog box to add a page number. You can also use the Edit Citation dialog box to remove, or suppress, the author's name, so only the page number appears in the citation. However, in an MLA citation, Word will replace the suppressed author name with the title of the source, so you need to suppress the title as well, by selecting the Title check box in the Edit Citation dialog box.

REFERENCE

Creating Citations

- On the ribbon, click the References tab. In the Citations & Bibliography group, click the Style button arrow, and then select the style you want.
- Click in the document where you want to insert the citation. Typically, a citation goes at the end of a sentence, before the ending punctuation.
- To add a citation for a new source, click the Insert Citation button in the Citations & Bibliography group, click Add New Source, enter information in the Create Source dialog box, and then click the OK button.
- To add a citation for an existing source, click the Insert Citation button, and then click the source.
- To add a placeholder citation, click the Insert Citation button, click Add New Placeholder, and then, in the Placeholder Name dialog box, type placeholder text, such as the author's last name, that will serve as a reminder about which source you need to cite. Note that a placeholder citation cannot contain any spaces.
- To add a page number to a citation, click the citation in the document, click the Citation Options button, click Edit Citation, type the page number, and then click the OK button.
- To display only the page number in a citation, click the citation in the document, click the Citation Options button, and then click Edit Citation. In the Edit Citation dialog box, select the Author and Title check boxes to suppress this information, and then click the OK button.

So far, Carolina has referenced information from two different sources in her research paper. You'll select a style and then begin adding the appropriate citations.

To select a style for the citation and bibliography:

1. On the ribbon, click the **References** tab. The ribbon changes to display references options.

2. In the Citations & Bibliography group, click the **Style button** arrow, and then click **MLA Seventh Edition** if it is not already selected.

3. Press the **Ctrl+F** keys to open the Navigation pane.

4. Use the Navigation pane to find the phrase "As at least one historian," which appears on page 2, and then click in the document at the end of that sentence (between the end of the word "standing" and the closing period).

5. Close the **Navigation** pane, and then click the **References** tab on the ribbon, if necessary. You need to add a citation that informs the reader that historian Roy Brauer made the observation described in the sentence. See Figure 2-28.

> Be sure to select the correct citation and bibliography style before you begin.

Figure 2-28   **MLA style selected and insertion point positioned for new citation**

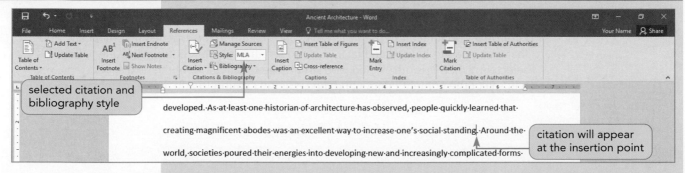

6. In the Citations & Bibliography group, click the **Insert Citation** button to open the menu. At this point, you could click Add New Placeholder on the menu to insert a temporary, placeholder citation. However, because you have all the necessary source information, you can go ahead and create a complete citation.

7. On the menu, click **Add New Source**. The Create Source dialog box opens, ready for you to add the information required to create a bibliography entry for Roy Brauer's book.

8. If necessary, click the **Type of Source** arrow, scroll up or down in the list, and then click **Book**.

9. In the Author box, type **Roy Brauer**.

10. Click in the **Title** box, and then type **Settlements and Monuments in Neolithic Architecture**.

11. Click in the **Year** box, and then type **2010**. This is the year the book was published. Next, you need to enter the name and location of the publisher.

12. Click the **City** box, type **New York**, click the **Publisher** box, and then type **Brookstone and Colescott Academy Press**.

Finally, you need to indicate the medium used to publish the book. In this case, Carolina used a printed copy, so the medium is "Print." For books or journals published online, the correct medium would be "Web."

13. Click the **Medium** box, and then type **Print**. See Figure 2-29.

TIP

When entering information in a dialog box, you can press the Tab key to move the insertion point from one box to another.

| Figure 2-29 | Create Source dialog box with information for the first source |

Create Source   ?   ✕

Type of Source Book ▾

Bibliography Fields for MLA

Author Roy Brauer   Edit

☐ Corporate Author _____

Title Settlements and Monuments in Neolithic Architecture

Year 2010

City New York

Publisher Brookstone and Colescott Academy Press

Medium Print

☐ Show All Bibliography Fields

Tag name   Example: Document

Roy10   OK   Cancel

14. Click the **OK** button. Word inserts the parenthetical "(Brauer)" at the end of the sentence in the document.

Although the citation looks like ordinary text, it is actually contained inside a content control, a special feature used to display information that is inserted automatically and that may need to be updated later. You can see the content control itself only when it is selected. When it is unselected, you simply see the citation. In the next set of steps, you will select the content control and then edit the citation to add a page number.

To edit the citation:

TIP

To delete a citation, click the citation to display the content control, click the tab on the left side of the content control, and then press the Delete key.

1. In the document, click the citation **(Brauer)**. The citation appears in a content control, which is a box with a tab on the left and an arrow button on the right. The arrow button is called the Citation Options button.

2. Click the **Citation Options** button. A menu of options related to editing a citation opens, as shown in Figure 2-30.

Figure 2-30 **Citation Options menu**

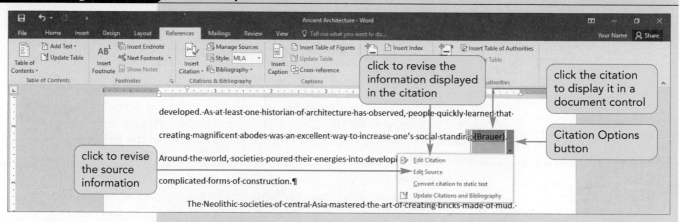

To edit the information about the source, you click Edit Source. To change the information that is displayed in the citation itself, you use the Edit Citation option.

3. On the Citation Options menu, click **Edit Citation**. The Edit Citation dialog box opens, as shown in Figure 2-31.

Figure 2-31 **Edit Citation dialog box**

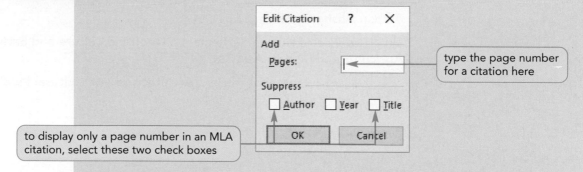

To add a page number for the citation, you type the page number in the Pages box. If you want to display only the page number in the citation (which would be necessary if you already mentioned the author's name in the same sentence in the text), then you would also select the Author and Title check boxes in this dialog box to suppress this information.

4. Type **37** to insert the page number in the Pages box, click the **OK** button to close the dialog box, and then click anywhere in the document outside the citation content control. The revised citation now reads "(Brauer 37)."

Next, you will add two more citations, both for the same journal article.

To insert two more citations:

▶ **1.** Scroll up to display the last paragraph on page 1, and then click at the end of the first sentence in that paragraph (which begins "According to Alisha Garland…"), between the word "animals" and the period. This sentence mentions historian Alisha Garland; you need to add a citation to one of her journal articles.

▶ **2.** In the Citations & Bibliography group, click the **Insert Citation** button to open the Insert Citation menu. Notice that Roy Brauer's book is now listed as a source on this menu. You could click Brauer's book on the menu to add a citation to it, but right now you need to add a new source.

▶ **3.** Click **Add New Source** to open the Create Source dialog box, click the **Type of Source** arrow, and then click **Journal Article**.

The Create Source dialog box displays the boxes, or fields, appropriate for a journal article. The information required to cite a journal article differs from the information you entered earlier for the citation for the Brauer book. For journal articles, you are prompted to enter the page numbers for the entire article. If you want to display a particular page number in the citation, you can add it later.

By default, Word displays boxes, or fields, for the information most commonly included in a bibliography. In this case, you also want to include the volume and issue numbers for Alisha Garland's article, so you need to display more fields.

▶ **4.** In the Create Source dialog box, click the **Show All Bibliography Fields** check box to select this option. The Create Source dialog box expands to allow you to enter more detailed information. Red asterisks highlight the fields that are recommended, but these recommended fields don't necessarily apply to every source.

▶ **5.** Enter the following information, scrolling down to display the necessary boxes:

Author: **Alisha Garland**

Title: **The Rise of Human Settlements: Neolithic Culture and Early Agriculture in Central Asia**

Journal Name: **Journal of Ancient Architecture and Cultural Studies**

Year: **2015**

Pages: **122–145**

Volume: **30**

Issue: **5**

Medium: **Web**

When you are finished, your Create Source dialog box should look like the one shown in Figure 2-32.

Figure 2-32   **Create Source dialog box with information for the journal article**

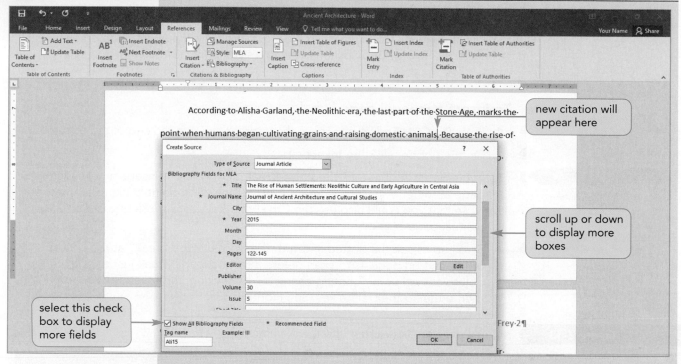

6. Click the **OK** button. The Create Source dialog box closes, and the citation "(Garland)" is inserted in the text. Because the sentence containing the citation already includes the author's name, you will edit the citation to include the page number and suppress the author's name.

7. Click the **(Garland)** citation to display the content control, click the **Citation Options** button , and then click **Edit Citation** to open the Edit Citation dialog box.

8. In the Pages box, type **142**, and then click the **Author** and **Title** check boxes to select them. You need to suppress both the author's name and the title because otherwise Word will replace the suppressed author name with the title. When using the MLA style, you don't ever have to suppress the year because the year is never included as part of an MLA citation. When working in other styles, however, you might need to suppress the year.

9. Click the **OK** button to close the Edit Citation dialog box, and then click anywhere outside the content control to deselect it. The end of the sentence now reads "…raising domestic animals (142)."

10. Use the Navigation pane to find the sentence that begins "The Neolithic societies of central Asia…" on the second page. Click at the end of the sentence, to the left of the period after "mud," and then close the Navigation pane.

11. On the References tab, in the Citations & Bibliography group, click the **Insert Citation** button, and then click the **Garland, Alisha** source at the top of the menu. You want the citation to refer to the entire article instead of just one page, so you will not edit the citation to add a specific page number.

12. Save the document.

You have entered the source information for two sources.

Inserting a Page Break

Once you have created a citation for a source in a document, you can generate a bibliography. In the MLA style, the bibliography (or works cited list) starts on a new page. So your first step is to insert a manual page break. A **manual page break** is one you insert at a specific location; it doesn't matter if the previous page is full or not. To insert a manual page break, use the Page Break button in the Pages group on the Insert tab.

To insert a manual page break:

1. Press the **Ctrl+End** keys to move the insertion point to the end of the document.

2. On the ribbon, click the **Insert** tab.

3. In the Pages group, click the **Page Break** button. Word inserts a new, blank page at the end of the document, with the insertion point blinking at the top. Note that you could also use the Ctrl+Enter keyboard shortcut to insert a manual page break.

4. Scroll up to see the dotted line with the words "Page Break" at the bottom of the text on page 4. You can delete a manual page break just as you would delete any other nonprinting character, by clicking immediately to its left and then pressing the Delete key. See Figure 2-33.

TIP

Use the Blank Page button in the Pages group to insert a new, blank page in the middle of a document.

Figure 2-33	Manual page break inserted into the document

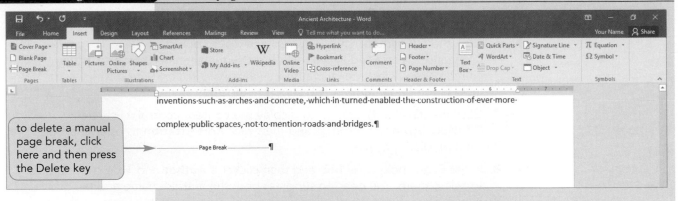

to delete a manual page break, click here and then press the Delete key

Now you can insert the bibliography on the new page 5.

Generating a Bibliography

When you generate a bibliography, Word scans all the citations in the document, collecting the source information for each citation, and then it creates a list of information for each unique source. The format of the entries in the bibliography will reflect the style you specified when you created your first citation, which in this case is the MLA style. The bibliography itself is a **field**, similar to the page number field you inserted earlier in this session. In other words, it is really an instruction that tells Word to display the source information for all the citations in the document. Because it is a field and not actual text, you can easily update the bibliography later to reflect any new citations you might add.

You can choose to insert a bibliography as a field directly in the document, or you can insert a bibliography enclosed within a content control that also includes the heading "Bibliography" or "Works Cited." Inserting a bibliography enclosed in a content control is best because the content control includes a useful button that you can use to update your bibliography if you make changes to the sources.

To insert the bibliography:

1. Scroll down so you can see the insertion point at the top of page 5.

2. On the ribbon, click the **References** tab.

3. In the Citations & Bibliography group, click the **Bibliography** button. The Bibliography menu opens, displaying three styles with preformatted headings—"Bibliography," "References," and "Works Cited." The Insert Bibliography command at the bottom inserts a bibliography directly in the document as a field, without a content control and without a preformatted heading. See Figure 2-34.

Figure 2-34   **Bibliography menu**

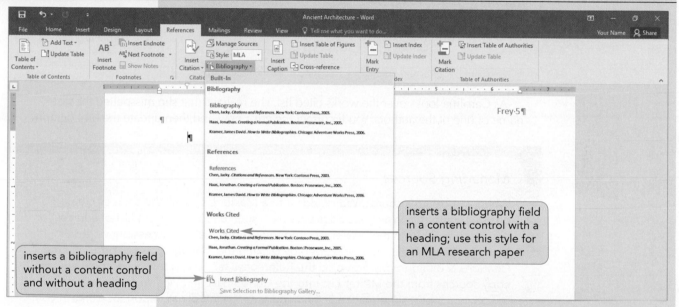

inserts a bibliography field without a content control and without a heading

inserts a bibliography field in a content control with a heading; use this style for an MLA research paper

4. Click **Works Cited**. Word inserts the bibliography, with two entries, below the "Works Cited" heading. The bibliography text is formatted in Calibri, the default font for the Office theme. The "Works Cited" heading is formatted with the Heading 1 style.

   To see the content control that contains the bibliography, you need to select it.

5. Click anywhere in the bibliography. Inside the content control, the bibliography is highlighted in gray, indicating that it is a field and not regular text. The content control containing the bibliography is also now visible in the form of a rectangular border and a tab with two buttons. See Figure 2-35.

Figure 2-35	Bibliography displayed in a content control

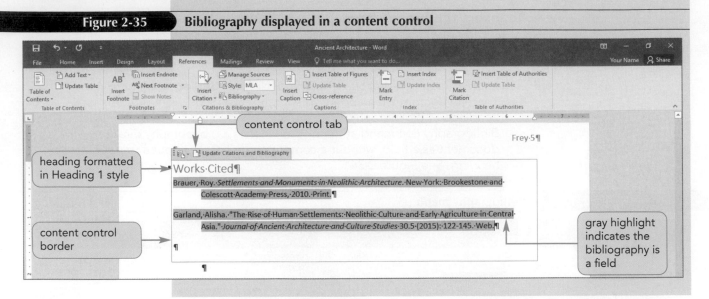

As Carolina looks over the works cited list, she realizes that she misspelled the last name of one of the authors. You'll correct the error now and then update the bibliography.

INSIGHT

Managing Sources

When you create a source, Word adds it to a Master List of all the sources created on your computer. Word also adds each new source to the Current List of sources for that document. Both the Master List and the Current List are accessible via the Source Manager dialog box, which you open by clicking the Manage Sources button in the Citations & Bibliography group on the References tab. Using this dialog box, you can copy sources from the Master List into the Current List and vice versa. As you begin to focus on a particular academic field and turn repeatedly to important works in your chosen field, you'll find this ability to reuse sources very helpful.

Modifying an Existing Source

To modify information about a source, you click a citation to that source in the document, click the Citation Options button on the content control, and then click Edit Source. Depending on how your computer is set up, after you are finished editing the source, Word may prompt you to update the Master List and the source information in the current document. In almost all cases, you should click Yes to ensure that the source information is correct in all the places it is stored on your computer.

To edit a source in the research paper:

1. Click in the blank paragraph below the bibliography content control to deselect the bibliography.

2. Scroll up to display the first paragraph on page 2, and then click the **(Brauer 37)** citation you entered earlier in the second-to-last sentence in the paragraph. The content control appears around the citation.

3. Click the **Citation Options** button ⯆, and then click **Edit Source**. The Edit Source dialog box opens. Note that Word displays the author's last name first in the Author box, just as it would appear in a bibliography.

4. In the **Author** box, double-click **Brauer** to select the author's last name, and then type **Brower**. The author's name now reads "Brower, Roy."

5. Click the **OK** button. The revised author name in the citation now reads "(Brower 37)."

   Trouble? If you see a message dialog box asking if you want to update the master source list and the current document, click the Yes button.

6. Click anywhere on the second page to deselect the citation content control. The revised author name in the citation now reads "(Brower 37)."

7. Save the document.

You've edited the document text and the citation to include the correct spelling of "Brower," but now you need to update the bibliography to correct the spelling.

Updating and Finalizing a Bibliography

The bibliography does not automatically change to reflect edits you make to existing citations or to show new citations. To incorporate the latest information stored in the citations, you need to update the bibliography. To update a bibliography in a content control, click the bibliography, and then, in the content control tab, click Update Citations and Bibliography. To update a bibliography field that is not contained in a content control, right-click the bibliography, and then click Update Field on the shortcut menu.

To update the bibliography:

1. Scroll down to page 5 and click anywhere in the works cited list to display the content control.

2. In the content control tab, click **Update Citations and Bibliography**. The works cited list is updated, with "Brauer" changed to "Brower" in the first entry.

Carolina still has a fair amount of work to do on her research paper. After she finishes writing it and adding all the citations, she will update the bibliography again to include all her cited sources. At that point, you might think the bibliography would be finished. However, a few steps remain to ensure that the works cited list matches the MLA style. To finalize Carolina's works cited list to match the MLA style, you need to make the changes shown in Figure 2-36.

Figure 2-36   Steps for finalizing a Word bibliography to match MLA guidelines for the works cited list

1. Format the "Works Cited" heading to match the formatting of the rest of the text in the document.

2. Center the "Works Cited" heading.

3. Double-space the entire works cited list, including the heading, and remove extra space after the paragraphs.

4. Change the font size for the entire works cited list to 12 points.

To format the bibliography as an MLA-style works cited list:

1. Click in the **Works Cited** heading, and then click the **Home** tab on the ribbon.

2. In the Styles group, click the **Normal** style. The "Works Cited" heading is now formatted in Calibri body font like the rest of the document. The MLA style for a works cited list requires this heading to be centered.

3. In the Paragraph group, click the **Center** button ☰.

4. Select the entire works cited list, including the heading. Change the font size to **12** points, change the line spacing to **2.0**, and then remove the paragraph spacing after each paragraph.

5. Click below the content control to deselect the works cited list, and then review your work. See Figure 2-37.

| Figure 2-37 | MLA-style Works Cited list |

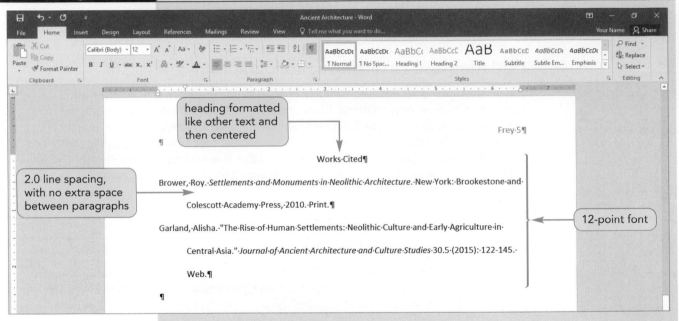

6. Save the document and close it.

Carolina's research paper now meets the MLA style guidelines.

Session 2.2 Quick Check

REVIEW

1. List the five tasks you need to perform to make a default Word document match the MLA style.

2. How can you quickly repeat the action you just performed?

3. Explain how to remove a page number from the first page of a document.

4. What is the default form of an MLA citation in Word?

5. Explain how to edit a citation to display only the page number.

6. Explain how to generate a works cited list.

Review Assignments

Data Files needed for the Review Assignments: Commercial.docx, Modern.docx

Because the Home LEED document turned out so well, Carolina has been asked to create a handout describing LEED certification for commercial buildings. Carolina asks you to help her revise and format the document. She also asks you to create a document listing projects that are suitable for this type of LEED certification. Finally, as part of her architecture history class, Carolina is working on a research paper on the history of modern architecture. She asks you to help her format the paper according to the MLA style and to create some citations and a bibliography. She has inserted the uppercase word "CITATION" wherever she needs to insert a citation. Complete the following steps:

1. Open the document **Commercial** located in the Word2 > Review folder included with your Data Files, and then save the document as **Commercial LEED** in the location specified by your instructor.

2. Read the first comment, which provides an overview of the changes you will be making to the document in the following steps. Perform the task described in the second comment, and then delete both comments.

3. In the middle of page 1, revise the text "SPECIAL PROJECTS" so that only the first letter of each word is capitalized. Attach a comment to this paragraph that explains the change.

4. Near the end of page 2, move the "Getting Started" heading up to position it before the paragraph that begins "Talk to your project manager...."

5. Replace the second instance of "Design" with "design," being sure to match the case.

6. On page 1, format the list of suitable projects as a bulleted list with square bullets, starting with "Schools, including..." and ending with "Clinics, hospitals, and other healthcare facilities." Do the same for the list of special projects, starting with "Mixed-use projects..." and ending with "No larger than 25,000 square feet.") Then indent the three requirements for multiple structures so they are formatted with an open circle bullet.

7. At the top of page 2, format the three steps for developing a certification plan as a numbered list, using the "1), 2), 3)" numbering style.

8. In the numbered list, move paragraph 3 ("Establish target certification level...") up to make it paragraph 2.

9. Format the title "Commercial LEED Fact Sheet" using the Title style. Format the following headings with the Heading 1 style: "Suitable Projects," "Special Projects," "Location," "Developing a Certification Plan," and "Getting Started."

10. Change the document theme to the Ion theme. If the Ion theme isn't included in your Themes gallery, choose a different theme.

11. Display the Clipboard task pane. On page 1, copy the bulleted list of suitable projects (which begins "Schools, including entire college campuses...") to the Clipboard, and then copy the "Suitable Projects" heading to the Clipboard. To ensure that you copy the heading formatting, be sure to select the paragraph mark after "Suitable Projects" before you click the Copy button.

12. Open a new, blank document, and then save the document as **Suitable Projects** in the location specified by your instructor.

13. At the beginning of the document, paste the heading "Suitable Projects," and then, from the Paste Options menu, apply the Keep Source Formatting option. Below the heading, paste the list of suitable projects.

14. At the end of the document, insert a new paragraph, and then type **Prepared by:** followed by your first and last names.

15. Save the Suitable Projects document and close it.

16. In the Commercial LEED document, clear the contents of the Clipboard task pane, close the Clipboard task pane, save the document, and then close it.

17. Open the document **Modern** located in the Word2 > Review folder included with your Data Files.

18. Save the document as **Modern Architecture** in the location specified by your instructor.

19. In the first paragraph, replace Carolina's name with your own.

20. Adjust the font size, line spacing, paragraph spacing, and paragraph indents to match the MLA style.

21. Insert your last name and a page number on every page except the first. Use the same font size as in the rest of the document.

22. If necessary, select MLA Seventh Edition as the citations and bibliography style.

23. Use the Navigation pane to highlight all instances of the uppercase word "CITATION." Keep the Navigation pane open so you can continue to use it to find the locations where you need to insert citations in Steps 24–28.

24. Delete the first instance of "CITATION" and the space before it, and then create a new source with the following information:

    Type of Source: **Book**

    Author: **Lincoln Mayfield**

    Title: **Very Modern Architecture: A History in Words and Photos**

    Year: **2014**

    City: **Cambridge**

    Publisher: **Boston Pines Press**

    Medium: **Print**

25. Edit the citation to add **105** as the page number. Display only the page number in the citation.

26. Delete the second instance of "CITATION" and the space before it, and then create a new source with the following information:

    Type of Source: **Journal Article**

    Author: **Odessa Robinson**

    Title: **Modern Architecture in the Modern World**

    Journal Name: **Atlantis Architecture Quarterly: Criticism and Comment**

    Year: **2015**

    Pages: **68–91**

    Volume: **11**

    Issue: **2**

    Medium: **Web**

27. Edit the citation to add **80** as the page number.

28. Delete the third instance of "CITATION" and the space before it, and then insert a citation for the book by Lincoln Mayfield.

29. At the end of the document, start a new page and insert a bibliography in a content control with the heading "Works Cited."

30. In the second source you created, change "**Robinson**" to "**Robbins**" and then update the bibliography.

31. Finalize the bibliography to create an MLA-style works cited list.

32. Save the Modern Architecture document, and close it.

33. Close any other open documents.

Case Problem 1

APPLY

Data File needed for this Case Problem: Field.docx

Hilltop Elementary School   Crystal Martinez, a fourth-grade teacher at Hilltop Elementary School, created a flyer to inform parents and guardians about an upcoming field trip. It's your job to format the flyer to make it look professional and easy to read. Crystal included comments in the document explaining what she wants you to do. Complete the following steps:

1. Open the document **Field** located in the Word2 > Case1 folder included with your Data Files, and then save the file as **Field Trip Flyer** in the location specified by your instructor.
2. Format the document as directed in the comments. After you complete a task, delete the relevant comment. Respond "Yes" to the comment asking if October 20 is the correct date. When you are finished with the formatting, the comment with the question and the comment with your reply should be the only remaining comments.
3. Move up the second bulleted item (which begins "Email me at...") to make it the first bulleted item in the list.
4. Change the theme to the Slice theme, and then attach a comment to the title listing the heading and body fonts applied by the Slice theme.
5. Save the document, and then close it.

Case Problem 2

APPLY

Data File needed for this Case Problem: Comedy.docx

Frederick Douglass College   Liam Shelton is a student at Frederick Douglass College. He's working on a research paper, which is only partly finished, about the types of comedy used in plays and films. He inserted the uppercase word "CITATION" wherever he needs to insert a citation. Liam asks you to help him format this early draft to match the MLA style. He also asks you to help him create some citations and a first attempt at a bibliography. He will update the bibliography later, after he finishes writing the research paper. Complete the following steps:

1. Open the document **Comedy** located in the Word2 > Case2 folder included with your Data Files, and then save the document as **Comedy Paper** in the location specified by your instructor.
2. In the first paragraph, replace "Liam Shelton" with your name, and then adjust the font size, line spacing, paragraph spacing, and paragraph indents to match the MLA style.
3. Insert your last name and a page number in the upper-right corner of every page except the first page in the document. Use the same font size as in the rest of the document.
4. If necessary, select MLA Seventh Edition as the citations and bibliography style.
5. Use the Navigation pane to find three instances of the uppercase word "CITATION."
6. Delete the first instance of "CITATION" and the space before it, and then create a new source with the following information:
   Type of Source: **Book**
   Author: **Danyl Taylor**
   Title: **Comedy: The Happy Art**
   Year: **2013**
   City: **Chicago**
   Publisher: **Singleton University Press**
   Medium: **Print**
7. Edit the citation to add **135** as the page number. Suppress the author's name and the title.

8. Delete the second instance of "CITATION" and the space before it, and then create a new source with the following information:

   Type of Source: **Sound Recording**

   Performer: **Anne Golden**

   Title: **Slapstick Sample**

   Album Title: **Sounds of the Renaissance**

   Production Company: **Foley Studio Productions**

   Year: **1995**

   Medium: **CD**

   City: **Los Angeles**

9. Edit the citation to suppress the Author and the Year, so that it displays only the title.

10. Delete the third instance of "CITATION" and the space before it, and then insert a second reference to the book by Danyl Taylor.

11. Edit the citation to add **65** as the page number.

12. At the end of the document, start a new page, and then insert a bibliography with the preformatted heading "Works Cited."

13. Edit the last source you created, changing the date to **2000**.

14. Update the bibliography so it shows the revised date.

15. Finalize the bibliography so that it matches the MLA style.

16. Save the Comedy Paper document, and close it.

Case Problem 3

Data Files needed for this Case Problem: Maliha.docx, Nursing.docx

Emergency Room Nurse   Maliha Shadid has more than a decade of experience as a nurse in several different settings. After moving to a new city, she is looking for a job as an emergency room nurse. She has asked you to edit and format her resume. As part of the application process, she will have to upload her resume to employee recruitment websites at a variety of hospitals. Because these sites typically request a simple page design, Maliha plans to rely primarily on heading styles and bullets to organize her information. When the resume is complete, she wants you to remove any color applied by the heading styles. She also needs help formatting a document she created for a nursing organization for which she volunteers. Complete the following steps:

1. Open the document **Maliha** located in the Word2 > Case3 folder included with your Data Files, and then save the file as **Maliha Resume** in the location specified by your instructor.

2. Read the comment included in the document, and then perform the task it specifies.

3. Respond to the comment with the response **I think that's a good choice for the theme.**, and then mark Maliha's comment as done.

4. Replace all occurrences of "Lawrencekansas" with **Lawrence, Kansas**.

5. Format the resume as shown in Figure 2-38. To ensure that the resume fits on one page, pay special attention to the paragraph spacing settings specified in Figure 2-38.

6. In the email address, replace "Maliha Shadid" with your first and last names, separated by an underscore, and then save the document and close it.

Figure 2-38   **Formatting for Maliha Shadid's resume**

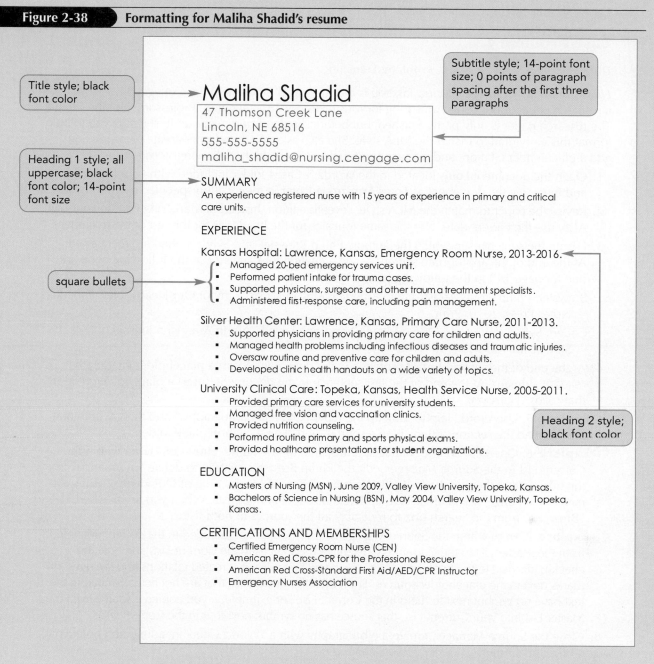

7. Open the document **Nursing** located in the Word2 > Case3 folder included with your Data Files, and then save the file as **Nursing Foundation** in the location specified by your instructor. Search for the text "Your Name", and then replace it with your first and last names.

8. Select the three paragraphs below your name, and then decrease the indent for the selected paragraphs so that they align at the left margin. Create a .5-inch hanging indent for the selected paragraphs.

9. Change the document theme to Facet, and then add a comment to the first word in the document that reads "**I changed the theme to Facet.**" (If Facet is not an option in your Themes gallery, choose a different theme, and then include that theme name in the comment.)

10. Use the Advanced Find dialog box to search for bold formatting. Remove the bold formatting from the fourth bold element in the document, and then add a comment to that element that reads "**I assumed bold here was a mistake, so I removed it.**"

11. Save and close the document.

CHALLENGE

Case Problem 4

Data File needed for this Case Problem: Louis.docx

Elliot Community College   Maria Taketou is a student at Elliot Community College. She's working on a research paper about Louis Armstrong for Music History 201, taught by Professor Delphine Chabot. The research paper is only partly finished, but before she does more work on it, she asks you to help format this early draft to match the MLA style. She also asks you to help her create some citations, add a placeholder citation, and manage her sources. Complete the following steps:

1. Open the document **Louis** located in the Word2 > Case4 folder included with your Data Files, and then save the document as **Louis Armstrong Paper** in the location specified by your instructor.

2. Revise the paper to match the MLA style, seventh edition. Instead of Maria's name, use your own. Also, use the current date. Use the same font size for the header as for the rest of the document.

3. Locate the sentences in which the authors Philip Brewster and Sylvia Cohen are mentioned. At the end of the appropriate sentence, add a citation for page 123 in the following book and one for page 140 in the following journal article:

   Brewster, Philip. Louis Armstrong in America: King of Music, King of Our Hearts. New York: Jazz Notes Press, 2010. Print.

   Cohen, Sylvia. "The New Orleans Louis Armstrong Loved." North American Journal of Jazz Studies (2015): 133–155. Web.

4. At the end of the second-to-last sentence in the document, insert a placeholder citation that reads "Feldman." At the end of the last sentence in the document, insert a placeholder citation that reads "Harrison."

⊕ **Explore** 5. Use Word Help to look up the topic "Create a bibliography," and then, within that article, read the sections titled "Find a source" and "Edit a citation placeholder."

⊕ **Explore** 6. Open the Source Manager, and search for the name "Brewster." From within the Current List in the Source Manager, edit the Philip Brewster citation to delete "in America" from the title, so that the title reads "Louis Armstrong: King of Music, King of Our Hearts." After you make the change, if you are asked, update the source in both lists. When you are finished, delete "Brewster" from the Search box to redisplay all the sources in both lists.

⊕ **Explore** 7. From within the Source Manager, copy a source not included in the current document from the Master List to the Current List. Examine the sources in the Current List, and note the checkmarks next to the two sources for which you have already created citations and the question marks next to the placeholder sources. Sources in the Current list that are not actually cited in the text have no symbol next to them in the Current List. For example, if you copied a source from the Master List into your Current List, that source has no symbol next to it in the Current List.

8. Close the Source Manager, create a bibliography with a "Works Cited" heading, and note which works appear in it.

⊕ **Explore** 9. Open the Source Manager, and then edit the Feldman placeholder source to include the following information about a journal article:

   Feldman, Jamal. "King Joe Oliver, Music Master." Jazz International Journal (2015): 72–89. Web.

10. Update the bibliography.

⊕ **Explore** 11. Open Microsoft Edge, and use the web to research the difference between a works cited list and a works consulted list. If necessary, open the Source Manager, and then delete any uncited sources from the Current List to ensure that your document contains a true works cited list, as specified by the MLA style, and not a works consulted list. (Maria will create a full citation for the "Harrison" placeholder later.)

12. Update the bibliography, finalize it so it matches the MLA style, save the document, and close it.

EXCEL

OBJECTIVES

Session 1.1
- Open and close a workbook
- Navigate through a workbook and worksheet
- Select cells and ranges
- Plan and create a workbook
- Insert, rename, and move worksheets
- Enter text, dates, and numbers
- Undo and redo actions
- Resize columns and rows

Session 1.2
- Enter formulas and the SUM and COUNT functions
- Copy and paste formulas
- Move or copy cells and ranges
- Insert and delete rows, columns, and ranges
- Create patterned text with Flash Fill
- Add cell borders and change font size
- Change worksheet views
- Prepare a workbook for printing
- Save a workbook with a new filename

Getting Started with Excel

Creating a Customer Order Report

Case | *Game Card*

Peter Lewis is part owner of Game Card, a store in Missoula, Montana, that specializes in selling vintage board games. Peter needs to track sales data, generate financial reports, create contact lists for loyal customers, and analyze market trends. He can perform all of these tasks with **Microsoft Excel 2016**, (or just **Excel**), an application used to enter, analyze, and present quantitative data. He wants to create an efficient way of tracking the company inventory and managing customer sales. Peter asks you to use Excel to create a document in which he can enter customer purchases from the store.

STARTING DATA FILES

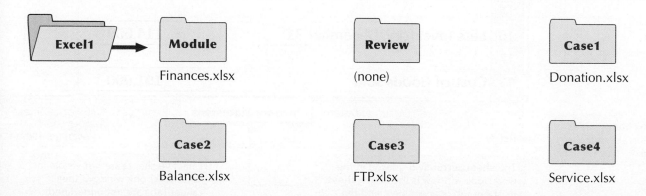

Excel1 → **Module** Finances.xlsx	**Review** (none)	**Case1** Donation.xlsx	
Case2 Balance.xlsx	**Case3** FTP.xlsx	**Case4** Service.xlsx	

Session 1.1 Visual Overview:

The ribbon is organized into tabs. Each **tab** has commands related to particular activities or tasks.

Buttons for related commands are organized on a tab in **groups**.

Excel stores spreadsheets in files called **workbooks**. The name of the current workbook appears in the title bar.

The **ribbon** contains buttons that you click to execute commands to work with Excel.

The **Name box** displays the cell reference of the active cell. In this case, the active cell is cell H12.

The **formula bar** displays the value or formula entered into the active cell.

A group of cells in a rectangular block is called a **cell range** (or **range**). If the blocks are not connected, as shown here, it is a **nonadjacent range**.

The **row headings** are numbers along the left side of the workbook window that identify the different rows of the worksheet.

The **status bar** provides information about the workbook.

The sheet currently displayed in the workbook window is the **active sheet**. Its sheet tab is underlined, and the sheet name is green and bold.

Inactive sheets are not visible in the workbook window; their sheet tabs are not underlined and their sheet name is black.

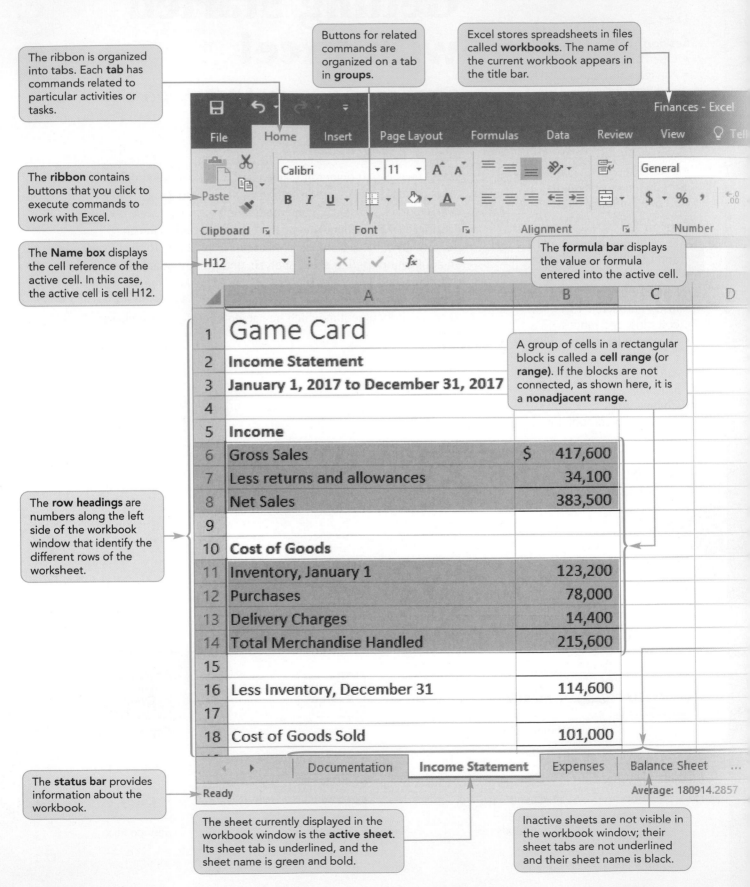

	A	B	C	D
1	Game Card			
2	Income Statement			
3	January 1, 2017 to December 31, 2017			
4				
5	Income			
6	Gross Sales	$ 417,600		
7	Less returns and allowances	34,100		
8	Net Sales	383,500		
9				
10	Cost of Goods			
11	Inventory, January 1	123,200		
12	Purchases	78,000		
13	Delivery Charges	14,400		
14	Total Merchandise Handled	215,600		
15				
16	Less Inventory, December 31	114,600		
17				
18	Cost of Goods Sold	101,000		

Documentation   **Income Statement**   Expenses   Balance Sheet

Ready   Average: 180914.2857

The Excel Workbook

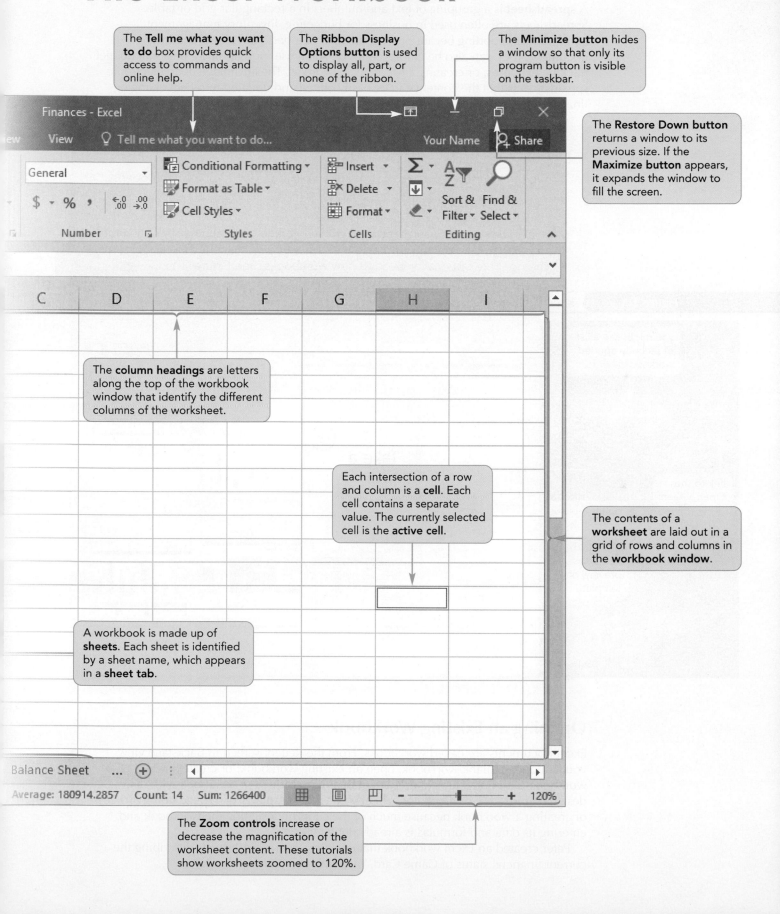

The **Tell me what you want to do** box provides quick access to commands and online help.

The **Ribbon Display Options button** is used to display all, part, or none of the ribbon.

The **Minimize button** hides a window so that only its program button is visible on the taskbar.

The **Restore Down button** returns a window to its previous size. If the **Maximize button** appears, it expands the window to fill the screen.

The **column headings** are letters along the top of the workbook window that identify the different columns of the worksheet.

Each intersection of a row and column is a **cell**. Each cell contains a separate value. The currently selected cell is the **active cell**.

The contents of a **worksheet** are laid out in a grid of rows and columns in the **workbook window**.

A workbook is made up of **sheets**. Each sheet is identified by a sheet name, which appears in a **sheet tab**.

The **Zoom controls** increase or decrease the magnification of the worksheet content. These tutorials show worksheets zoomed to 120%.

Introducing Excel and Spreadsheets

A **spreadsheet** is a grouping of text and numbers in a rectangular grid or table. Spreadsheets are often used in business for budgeting, inventory management, and financial reporting because they unite text, numbers, and charts within one document. They can also be employed for personal use for planning a personal budget, tracking expenses, or creating a list of personal items. The advantage of an electronic spreadsheet is that the content can be easily edited and updated to reflect changing financial conditions.

To start Excel:

1. On the Windows taskbar, click the **Start** button ⊞. The Start menu opens.

2. Click **All Apps** on the Start menu, scroll the list, and then click **Excel 2016**. Excel starts and displays the Recent screen in Backstage view. **Backstage view** provides access to various screens with commands that allow you to manage files and Excel options. On the left is a list of recently opened workbooks. On the right are options for creating new workbooks. See Figure 1-1.

| Figure 1-1 | Recent screen in Backstage view |

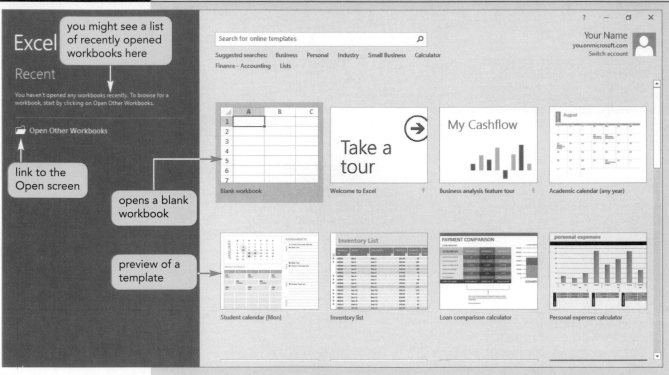

Opening an Existing Workbook

Excel documents are called workbooks. From the Recent screen in Backstage view, you can open a blank workbook, open an existing workbook, or create a new workbook based on a template. A **template** is a preformatted workbook with many design features and some content already filled in. Templates can speed up the process of creating a workbook because much of the effort in designing the workbook and entering its data and formulas is already done for you.

Peter created an Excel workbook that contains several worksheets describing the current financial status of Game Card. You will open that workbook now.

To open the Game Card financial status workbook:

1. In the navigation bar on the Recent screen, click the **Open Other Workbooks** link. The Open screen is displayed and provides access to different locations where you might store files. The Recent Workbooks list shows the workbooks that were most recently opened on your computer.

2. Click the **Browse** button. The Open dialog box appears.

3. Navigate to the **Excel1 > Module** folder included with your Data Files.

   Trouble? If you don't have the starting Data Files, you need to get them before you can proceed. Your instructor will either give you the Data Files or ask you to obtain them from a specified location (such as a network drive). If you have any questions about the Data Files, see your instructor or technical support person for assistance.

4. Click **Finances** in the file list to select it.

5. Click the **Open** button. The workbook opens in Excel.

   Trouble? If you don't see the full ribbon as shown in the Session 1.1 Visual Overview, the ribbon may be partially or fully hidden. To pin the ribbon so that the tabs and groups are fully displayed and remain visible, click the Ribbon Display Options button 🔲, and then click Show Tabs and Commands.

6. If the Excel window doesn't fill the screen, click the **Maximize** button 🔲 in the upper-right corner of the title bar. See Figure 1-2.

Figure 1-2 **Finances workbook**

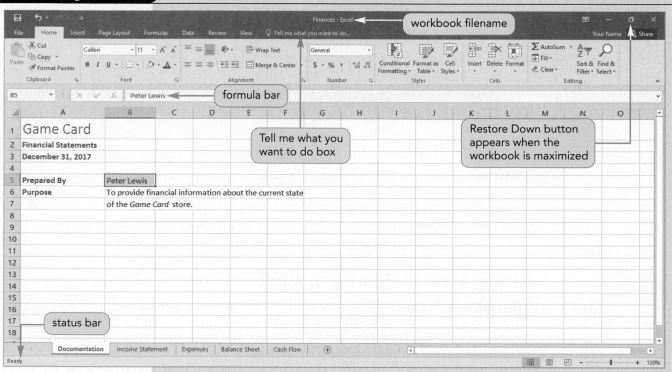

Using Keyboard Shortcuts to Work Faster

Keyboard shortcuts can help you work faster and more efficiently because you can keep your hands on the keyboard. A **keyboard shortcut** is a key or combination of keys that you press to access a feature or perform a command. Excel provides keyboard shortcuts for many commonly used commands. For example, Ctrl+S is the keyboard shortcut for the Save command, which means you hold down the Ctrl key while you press the S key to save the workbook. (Note that the plus sign is not pressed; it is used to indicate that an additional key is pressed.) When available, a keyboard shortcut is listed next to the command's name in a ScreenTip. A **ScreenTip** is a box with descriptive text about a command that appears when you point to a button on the ribbon. Figure 1-3 lists some of the keyboard shortcuts commonly used in Excel. The modules in this text show the corresponding keyboard shortcuts for accomplishing an action when available.

Figure 1-3   Excel keyboard shortcuts

Press	To	Press	To
Alt	Display the Key Tips for the commands and tools on the ribbon	Ctrl+V	Paste content that was cut or copied
Ctrl+A	Select all objects in a range	Ctrl+W	Close the current workbook
Ctrl+C	Copy the selected object(s)	Ctrl+X	Cut the selected object(s)
Ctrl+G	Go to a location in the workbook	Ctrl+Y	Repeat the last command
Ctrl+N	Open a new blank workbook	Ctrl+Z	Undo the last command
Ctrl+O	Open a saved workbook file	F1	Open the Excel Help window
Ctrl+P	Print the current workbook	F5	Go to a location in the workbook
Ctrl+S	Save the current workbook	F12	Save the current workbook with a new name or to a new location

You can also use the keyboard to quickly select commands on the ribbon. First, you press the Alt key to display the **Key Tips**, which are labels that appear over each tab and command on the ribbon. Then, you press the key or keys indicated to access the corresponding tab, command, or button while your hands remain on the keyboard.

Getting Help

If you are unsure about the function of an Excel command or you want information about how to accomplish a particular task, you can use the Help system. To access Excel Help, you either press the F1 key or enter a phrase or keyword into the Tell me what you want to do box next to the tabs on the ribbon. From this search box you can get quick access to detailed information and commands on a wide variety of Excel topics.

Using Excel 2016 in Touch Mode

You can work in Office 2016 with a keyboard and mouse or with touch. If you work with Excel on a touchscreen, you tap objects instead of clicking them. In **Touch Mode**, the ribbon increases in height, the buttons are bigger, and more space appears around each button so you can more easily use your finger or a stylus to tap the button you need.

Although the figures in these modules show the screen with Mouse Mode on, it's helpful to learn how to move between Touch Mode and Mouse Mode. You'll switch to Touch Mode and then back to Mouse Mode. If you are using a touch device, please read these steps, but do not complete them so that you remain working in Touch Mode.

To switch between Touch Mode and Mouse Mode:

▶ **1.** On the Quick Access Toolbar, click the **Customize Quick Access Toolbar** button ![icon]. A menu opens, listing buttons you can add to the Quick Access Toolbar as well as other options for customizing the toolbar.

   Trouble? If the Touch/Mouse Mode command on the menu has a checkmark next to it, press the Esc key to close the menu, and then skip Step 2.

▶ **2.** Click **Touch/Mouse Mode**. The Quick Access Toolbar now contains the Touch/Mouse Mode button ![icon], which you can use to switch between Mouse Mode, the default display, and Touch Mode.

▶ **3.** On the Quick Access Toolbar, click the **Touch/Mouse Mode** button ![icon]. A menu opens listing Mouse and Touch, and the icon next to Mouse is shaded to indicate it is selected.

   Trouble? If the icon next to Touch is shaded, press the Esc key to close the menu and continue with Step 5.

▶ **4.** Click **Touch**. The display switches to Touch Mode with more space between the commands and buttons on the ribbon. See Figure 1-4.

| **Figure 1-4** | **Ribbon displayed in Touch Mode** |

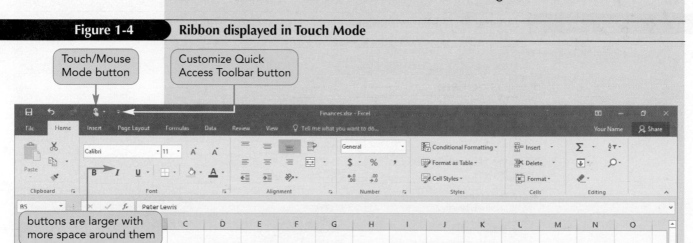

Touch/Mouse Mode button

Customize Quick Access Toolbar button

buttons are larger with more space around them

Next, you will switch back to Mouse Mode. If you are working with a touchscreen and want to use Touch Mode, skip Steps 5 and 6.

▶ **5.** On the Quick Access Toolbar, click the **Touch/Mouse Mode** button ![icon], and then click **Mouse**. The ribbon returns to Mouse Mode, as shown earlier in Figure 1-2.

▶ **6.** On the Quick Access Toolbar, click the **Customize Quick Access Toolbar** button ![icon], and then click **Touch/Mouse Mode** to deselect it. The Touch/Mouse Mode button is removed from the Quick Access Toolbar.

Exploring a Workbook

Workbooks are organized into separate pages called sheets. Excel supports two types of sheets: worksheets and chart sheets. A worksheet contains a grid of rows and columns into which you can enter text, numbers, dates, and formulas and display charts. A **chart sheet** contains a chart that provides a visual representation of worksheet data. The contents of a workbook are shown in the workbook window.

Changing the Active Sheet

The sheets in a workbook are identified in the sheet tabs at the bottom of the workbook window. The Finances workbook for Game Card includes five sheets labeled Documentation, Income Statement, Expenses, Balance Sheet, and Cash Flow. The sheet currently displayed in the workbook window is the active sheet, which in this case is the Documentation sheet. To make a different sheet active and visible, you click its sheet tab. You can tell which sheet is active because its name appears in bold green.

If a workbook includes so many sheets that not all of the sheet tabs can be displayed at the same time in the workbook window, you can use the sheet tab scrolling buttons to scroll through the list of tabs. Scrolling the sheet tabs does not change the active sheet; it changes only which sheet tabs are visible.

You will view the different sheets in the Finances workbook.

To change the active sheet:

▶ 1. Click the **Income Statement** sheet tab. The Income Statement worksheet becomes the active sheet, and its name is in bold green type. See Figure 1-5.

Figure 1-5   **Income Statement worksheet**

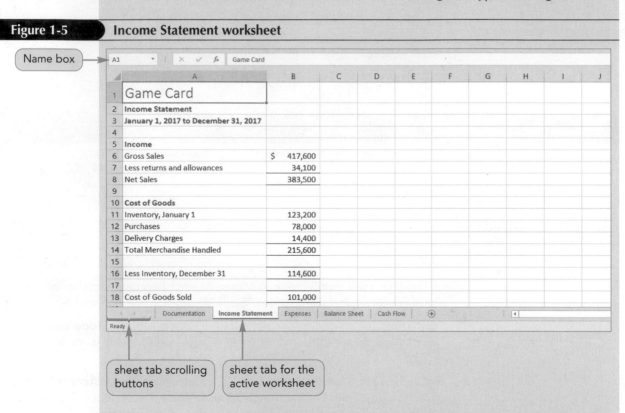

▶ 2. Click the **Expenses** sheet tab to make it the active sheet. The Expenses sheet is an example of a chart sheet containing only an Excel chart. See Figure 1-6.

| Figure 1-6 | Expenses chart sheet |

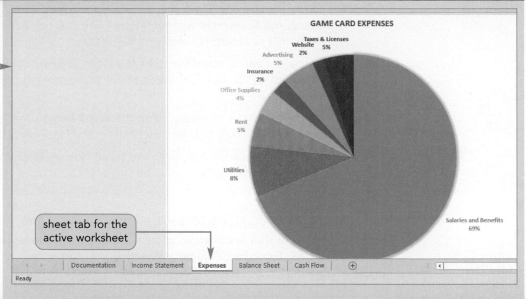

chart sheet contains a chart but no grid of text and data

sheet tab for the active worksheet

TIP
You can move to the previous or next sheet in the workbook by pressing the Ctrl+PgUp or Ctrl+PgDn keys.

3. Click the **Balance Sheet** sheet tab to make it the active sheet. Note that this sheet contains charts embedded into the grid of data values. A worksheet can contain data values, embedded charts, pictures, and other design elements.

4. Click the **Cash Flow** sheet tab. The worksheet with information about the company's cash flow is now active.

5. Click the **Income Statement** sheet tab to make the Income Statement worksheet the active sheet.

Navigating Within a Worksheet

A worksheet is organized into a grid of cells. Each cell is identified by a **cell reference**, which indicates the column and row in which the cell is located. For example, in Figure 1-5, the company name, Game Card, is in cell A1, which is the intersection of column A and row 1. The column letter always appears before the row number in any cell reference. The cell that is currently selected in the worksheet is referred to as the active cell. The active cell is highlighted with a thick green border, its cell reference appears in the Name box, and the corresponding column and row headings are highlighted. The active cell in Figure 1-5 is cell A1.

Row numbers range from 1 to 1,048,576, and column labels are letters in alphabetical order. The first 26 column headings range from A to Z. After Z, the next column headings are labeled AA, AB, AC, and so forth. Excel allows a maximum of 16,384 columns in a worksheet (the last column has the heading XFD). This means that you can create large worksheets whose content extends well beyond what is visible in the workbook window.

To move different parts of the worksheet into view, you can use the horizontal and vertical scroll bars located at the bottom and right edges of the workbook window, respectively. A scroll bar has arrow buttons that you can click to shift the worksheet one column or row in the specified direction, and a scroll box that you can drag to shift the worksheet in the direction you drag.

You will scroll the active worksheet so you can review the rest of the Game Card income statement.

To scroll through the Income Statement worksheet:

▶ **1.** On the vertical scroll bar, click the **down arrow** button ▼ to scroll down the Income Statement worksheet until you see cell B36, which displays the company's net income value of $104,200.

▶ **2.** On the horizontal scroll bar, click the **right arrow** button ▶ three times. The worksheet scrolls three columns to the right, moving columns A through C out of view.

▶ **3.** On the horizontal scroll bar, drag the **scroll box** to the left until you see column A.

▶ **4.** On the vertical scroll bar, drag the **scroll box** up until you see the top of the worksheet and cell A1.

Scrolling the worksheet does not change the location of the active cell. Although the active cell might shift out of view, you can always see the location of the active cell in the Name box. To make a different cell active, you can either click a new cell or use the keyboard to move between cells, as described in Figure 1-7.

Figure 1-7	Excel navigation keys

Press	To move the active cell
↑ ↓ ← →	Up, down, left, or right one cell
Home	To column A of the current row
Ctrl+Home	To cell A1
Ctrl+End	To the last cell in the worksheet that contains data
Enter	Down one row or to the start of the next row of data
Shift+Enter	Up one row
Tab	One column to the right
Shift+Tab	One column to the left
PgUp, PgDn	Up or down one screen
Ctrl+PgUp, Ctrl+PgDn	To the previous or next sheet in the workbook

You will use both your mouse and your keyboard to change the location of the active cell in the Income Statement worksheet.

To change the active cell:

▶ **1.** Move your pointer over cell **A5**, and then click the mouse button. The active cell moves from cell A1 to cell A5. A green border appears around cell A5, the column heading for column A and the row heading for row 5 are both highlighted, and the cell reference in the Name box changes from A1 to A5.

▶ **2.** Press the → key. The active cell moves one cell to the right to cell B5.

▶ **3.** Press the **PgDn** key on your keyboard. The active cell moves down one full screen.

▶ **4.** Press the **PgUp** key. The active cell moves up one full screen, returning to cell B5.

▶ **5.** Press the **Ctrl+Home** keys. The active cell returns to the first cell in the worksheet, cell A1.

The mouse and keyboard provide quick ways to navigate the active worksheet. For larger worksheets that span several screens, you can move directly to a specific cell using the Go To command or by typing a cell reference in the Name box. You will try both of these methods.

To use the Go To dialog box and the Name box:

▶ **1.** On the Home tab, in the Editing group, click the **Find & Select** button, and then click **Go To** on the menu that opens (or press the **Ctrl+G** keys). The Go To dialog box opens.

▶ **2.** Type **B34** in the Reference box. See Figure 1-8.

Figure 1-8   Go To dialog box

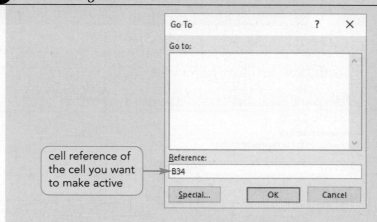

cell reference of the cell you want to make active

▶ **3.** Click the **OK** button. Cell B34 becomes the active cell, displaying 182,000, which is the total expenses for Game Card. Because cell B34 is the active cell, its cell reference appears in the Name box.

▶ **4.** Click in the Name box, type **A1**, and then press the **Enter** key. Cell A1 is again the active cell.

Selecting a Cell Range

Many tasks in Excel require you to work with a group of cells. A group of cells in a rectangular block is called a cell range (or simply a range). Each range is identified with a **range reference** that includes the cell reference of the upper-left cell of the rectangular block and the cell reference of the lower-right cell separated by a colon. For example, the range reference A1:G5 refers to all of the cells in the rectangular block from cell A1 through cell G5.

As with individual cells, you can select cell ranges using your mouse, the keyboard, or commands. You will select a range in the Income Statement worksheet.

To select a cell range:

1. Click cell **A5** to select it, and without releasing the mouse button, drag down to cell **B8**.

2. Release the mouse button. The range A5:B8 is selected. The selected cells are highlighted and surrounded by a green border. The first cell you selected in the range, cell A5, is the active cell in the worksheet. The active cell in a selected range is white. The Quick Analysis button appears, providing options for working with the range; you will use this button in another module. See Figure 1-9.

Figure 1-9 Range A5:B8 selected

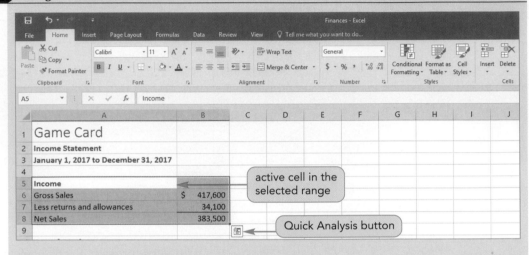

3. Click cell **A1** to deselect the range.

Another type of range is a nonadjacent range, which is a collection of separate rectangular ranges. The range reference for a nonadjacent range includes the range reference to each range separated by a comma. For example, the range reference A1:G5,A10:G15 includes two ranges—the first range is the rectangular block of cells from cell A1 to cell G5, and the second range is the rectangular block of cells from cell A10 to cell G15.

You will select a nonadjacent range in the Income Statement worksheet.

To select a nonadjacent range in the Income Statement worksheet:

1. Click cell **A5**, hold down the **Shift** key as you click cell **B8**, and then release the **Shift** key to select the range A5:B8.

2. Hold down the **Ctrl** key as you drag to select the range **A10:B14**, and then release the **Ctrl** key. The two separate blocks of cells in the nonadjacent range A5:B8,A10:B14 are selected. See Figure 1-10.

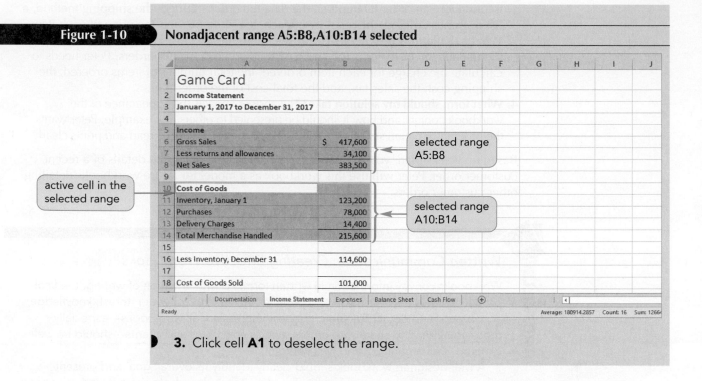

Figure 1-10   Nonadjacent range A5:B8,A10:B14 selected

active cell in the selected range

selected range A5:B8

selected range A10:B14

> **3.** Click cell **A1** to deselect the range.

Closing a Workbook

Once you are finished with a workbook you can close it. When you close a workbook, a dialog box might open, asking whether you want to save any changes you may have made to the document. If you have made changes that you want to keep, you should save the workbook. Since you have finished reviewing the financial workbook for Game Card, you will close it without saving any changes you may have inadvertently made to the document contents.

To close the workbook:

> **1.** On the ribbon, click the **File** tab to display Backstage view, and then click **Close** in the navigation bar (or press the **Ctrl+W** keys).

> **2.** If a dialog box opens, asking whether you want to save your changes to the workbook, click the **Don't Save** button. The workbook closes without saving any changes. Excel remains opens, ready for you to create or open another workbook.

Planning a Workbook

It's good practice to plan out your workbooks before you begin creating them. You can do this by using a planning analysis sheet, which includes the following questions that help you think about the workbook's purpose and how to achieve your desired results:

1. **What problems do I want to solve?** The answer identifies the goal or purpose of the workbook. For example, Peter wants you to record customer orders and be able to analyze details from these orders.
2. **What data do I need?** The answer identifies the type of data that you need to collect and enter into the workbook. For example, Peter needs customer contact

information, an order ID number, the date the order shipped, the shipping method, a list of games ordered, the quantity of each item ordered, and the price of each item.

3. **What calculations do I need?** The answer identifies the formulas you need to apply to the data you have collected and entered. For the customer orders, Peter needs to calculate the charge for each item ordered, the total number of items ordered, the shipping cost, the sales tax, and the total cost of the order.

4. **What form should my solution take?** The answer impacts the appearance of the workbook content and how it should be presented to others. For example, Peter wants the order information stored in a single worksheet that is easy to read and prints clearly.

Based on Peter's plan, you will create a workbook containing the details of a recent customer order. Peter will use this workbook as a model for future workbooks detailing other customer orders.

PROSKILLS

Written Communication: Creating Effective Workbooks

Workbooks convey information in written form. As with any type of writing, the final product creates an impression and provides an indicator of your interest, knowledge, and attention to detail. To create the best impression, all workbooks—especially those you intend to share with others such as coworkers and clients—should be well planned, well organized, and well written.

A well-designed workbook should clearly identify its overall goal and present information in an organized format. The data it includes—both the entered values and the calculated values—should be accurate. The process of developing an effective workbook includes the following steps:

- Determine the workbook's purpose, content, and organization before you start.
- Create a list of the sheets used in the workbook, noting each sheet's purpose.
- Insert a documentation sheet that describes the workbook's purpose and organization. Include the name of the workbook author, the date the workbook was created, and any additional information that will help others to track the workbook to its source.
- Enter all of the data in the workbook. Add labels to indicate what the values represent and, if possible, where they originated so others can view the source of your data.
- Enter formulas for calculated items rather than entering the calculated values into the workbook. For more complicated calculations, provide documentation explaining them.
- Test the workbook with a variety of values; edit the data and formulas to correct errors.
- Save the workbook and create a backup copy when the project is completed. Print the workbook's contents if you need to provide a hard-copy version to others or for your files.
- Maintain a history of your workbook as it goes through different versions, so that you and others can quickly see how the workbook has changed during revisions.

By including clearly written documentation, explanatory text, a logical organization, and accurate data and formulas, you will create effective workbooks that others can use easily.

Starting a New Workbook

You create new workbooks from the New screen in Backstage view. Similar to the Recent screen that opened when you started Excel, the New screen includes templates for a variety of workbook types. You can see a preview of what the different workbooks will look like. You will create a new workbook from the Blank workbook template, in which you can add all of the content and design Peter wants for the Game Card customer order worksheet.

To start a new, blank workbook:

▶ **1.** On the ribbon, click the **File** tab to display Backstage view.

▶ **2.** Click **New** in the navigation bar to display the New screen, which includes access to templates for a variety of workbooks.

▶ **3.** Click the **Blank workbook** tile. A blank workbook opens.

In these modules, the workbook window is zoomed to 120% for better readability. If you want to zoom your workbook window to match the figures, complete Step 4. If you prefer to work in the default zoom of 100% or at another zoom level, read but do not complete Step 4; you might see more or less of the worksheet on your screen, but this will not affect your work in the modules.

▶ **4.** If you want your workbook window zoomed to 120% to match the figures, on the Zoom slider at the bottom-right of the program window, click the **Zoom In** button ⊞ twice to increase the percentage to 120%. The 120% magnification increases the size of each cell but reduces the number of worksheet cells visible in the workbook window. See Figure 1-11.

Figure 1-11 ▶ **Blank workbook**

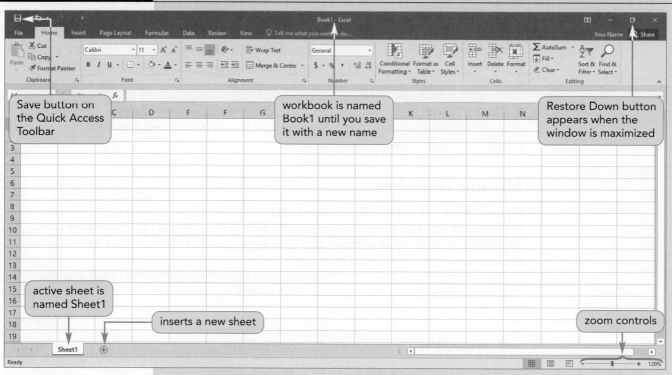

The name of the active workbook, Book1, appears in the title bar. If you open multiple blank workbooks, they are named Book1, Book2, Book3, and so forth until you save them with a more descriptive name.

Renaming and Inserting Worksheets

Blank workbooks open with a single blank worksheet named Sheet1. You can give sheets more descriptive and meaningful names. This is a good practice so that you and others can easily tell what a sheet contains. Sheet names cannot exceed 31 characters, but they can contain blank spaces and include uppercase and lowercase letters.

Because Sheet1 is not a very descriptive name, Peter wants you to rename the worksheet as Customer Order.

To rename the Sheet1 worksheet:

▶ **1.** Double-click the **Sheet1** tab. The Sheet1 label in the tab is selected.

▶ **2.** Type **Customer Order** as the new name, and then press the **Enter** key. The width of the sheet tab expands to fit the longer sheet name.

Many workbooks include multiple sheets so that data can be organized in logical groups. A common business practice is to include a worksheet named Documentation that contains a description of the workbook, the name of the person who prepared the workbook, and the date it was created.

Peter wants you to create two new worksheets. You will rename one worksheet as Documentation and the other worksheet as Customer Contact. The Customer Contact worksheet will be used to store the customer's contact information.

To insert and name the Documentation and Customer Contact worksheets:

▶ **1.** To the right of the Customer Order sheet tab, click the **New sheet** button ⊕. A new sheet named Sheet2 is inserted to the right of the Customer Order sheet.

▶ **2.** Double-click the **Sheet2** sheet tab, type **Documentation** as the new name, and then press the **Enter** key. The worksheet is renamed.

▶ **3.** To the right of the Documentation sheet, click the **New sheet** button ⊕, and then rename the inserted Sheet3 worksheet as **Customer Contact**.

Moving Worksheets

A good practice is to place the most important sheets at the beginning of the workbook (the leftmost sheet tabs) and less important sheets at the end (the rightmost sheet tabs). To change the placement of sheets in a workbook, you drag them by their sheet tabs to the new location.

Peter wants you to move the Documentation worksheet to the front of the workbook, so that it appears before the Customer Order sheet.

To move the Documentation worksheet:

▶ **1.** Point to the **Documentation** sheet tab. The sheet tab name changes to bold.

TIP

To copy a sheet, hold down the Ctrl key as you drag and drop its sheet tab.

▶ **2.** Press and hold the mouse button. The pointer changes to ▯, and a small arrow appears in the upper-left corner of the tab.

▶ **3.** Drag to the left until the small arrow appears in the upper-left corner of the Customer Order sheet tab, and then release the mouse button. The Documentation worksheet is now the first sheet in the workbook.

Deleting Worksheets

In some workbooks, you will want to delete an existing sheet. The easiest way to delete a sheet is by using a **shortcut menu**, which is a list of commands related to a selection that opens when you click the right mouse button. Peter asks you to include the customer's contact information on the Customer Order worksheet so all of the information is on one sheet.

To delete the Customer Contact worksheet from the workbook:

▶ **1.** Right-click the **Customer Contact** sheet tab. A shortcut menu opens.

▶ **2.** Click **Delete**. The Customer Contact worksheet is removed from the workbook.

Saving a Workbook

As you modify a workbook, you should save it regularly—every 10 minutes or so is a good practice. The first time you save a workbook, the Save As dialog box opens so you can name the file and choose where to save it. You can save the workbook on your computer or network or to your account on OneDrive.

To save your workbook for the first time:

▶ **1.** On the Quick Access Toolbar, click the **Save** button 🖫 (or press the **Ctrl+S** keys). The Save As screen in Backstage view opens.

▶ **2.** Click the **Browse** button. The Save As dialog box opens.

▶ **3.** Navigate to the location specified by your instructor.

▶ **4.** In the File name box, select **Book1** (the suggested name) if it is not already selected, and then type **Game Card**.

▶ **5.** Verify that **Excel Workbook** appears in the Save as type box.

▶ **6.** Click the **Save** button. The workbook is saved, the dialog box closes, and the workbook window reappears with the new filename in the title bar.

As you modify the workbook, you will need to resave the file. Because you already saved the workbook with a filename, the next time you save, the Save command saves the changes you made to the workbook without opening the Save As dialog box.

Entering Text, Dates, and Numbers

Workbook content is entered into worksheet cells. Those cells can contain text, numbers, or dates and times. **Text data** is any combination of letters, numbers, and symbols. Text data is often referred to as a **text string** because it contains a series, or string, of text characters. **Numeric data** is any number that can be used in a mathematical calculation. **Date** and **time data** are commonly recognized formats for date and time values. For example, Excel interprets the cell entry April 15, 2017 as a date and not as text. New data is placed into the active cell of the current worksheet. As you enter data, the entry appears in both the active cell and the formula bar. By default, text is left-aligned in cells, and numbers, dates, and times are right-aligned.

Entering Text

Text is often used in worksheets to label other data and to identify areas of a sheet. Peter wants you to enter some of the information from the planning analysis sheet into the Documentation sheet.

To enter text in the Documentation sheet:

1. Go to the **Documentation** sheet, and then click the **Ctrl+Home** keys to make sure cell A1 is the active cell.

2. Type **Game Card** in cell A1. As you type, the text appears in cell A1 and in the formula bar.

3. Press the **Enter** key twice. The text is entered into cell A1, and the active cell moves down two rows to cell A3.

4. Type **Author** in cell A3, and then press the **Tab** key. The text is entered and the active cell moves one column to the right to cell B3.

5. Type your name in cell B3, and then press the **Enter** key. The text is entered and the active cell moves one cell down and to the left to cell A4.

6. Type **Date** in cell A4, and then press the **Tab** key. The text is entered, and the active cell moves one column to the right to cell B4, where you would enter the date you created the worksheet. For now, you will leave the cell for the date blank.

7. Press the **Enter** key to make cell A5 the active cell, type **Purpose** in the cell, and then press the **Tab** key. The active cell moves one column to the right to cell B5.

8. Type **To record customer game orders** in cell B5, and then press the **Enter** key. Figure 1-12 shows the text entered in the Documentation sheet.

| Figure 1-12 | **Text entered in the Documentation sheet** |

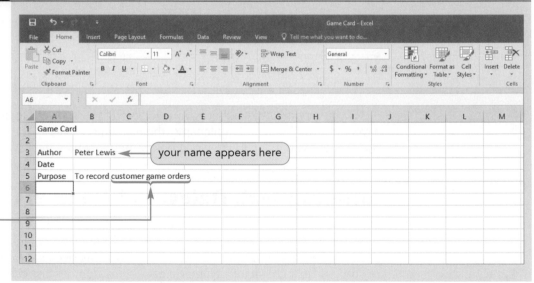

The text strings you entered in cells A1, B3, and B5 are so long that they cover the adjacent cells. Any text you enter in a cell that doesn't fit within that cell will cover the adjacent cells to the right as long as they are empty. If the adjacent cells contain data, only the text that fits into the cell is displayed. The rest of the text entry is hidden from view. The text itself is not affected. The complete text is still entered in the cell; it is just not displayed. (You will learn how to display all text in a cell in the next session.)

Undoing and Redoing an Action

As you enter data in a workbook, you might need to undo a previous action. Excel maintains a list of the actions you performed in the workbook during the current session, so you can undo most of your actions. You can use the Undo button on the Quick Access Toolbar or press the Ctrl+Z keys to reverse your most recent actions one at a time. If you want to undo more than one action, you can click the Undo button arrow and then select the earliest action you want to undo—all of the actions after the earliest action you selected are also undone.

You will undo the most recent change you made to the Documentation sheet— the text you entered into cell B5. Then you will enter more descriptive and accurate description of the worksheet's purpose.

To undo the text entry in cell B5:

1. On the Quick Access Toolbar, click the **Undo** button ↶ (or press the **Ctrl+Z** keys). The last action is reversed, removing the text you entered in cell B5.

2. In cell B5, type **To record purchases of board games from Game Card**, and then press the **Enter** key.

If you want to restore actions you have undone, you can redo them. To redo one action at a time, you can click the Redo button ↷ on the Quick Access Toolbar or press the Ctrl+Y keys. To redo multiple actions at once, you can click the Redo button arrow ↷ ▾ and then click the earliest action you want to redo. After you undo or redo an action, Excel continues the action list starting from any new changes you make to the workbook.

Editing Cell Content

As you continue to create your workbook, you might find mistakes you need to correct or entries that you want to change. To replace all of the content in a cell, you simply select the cell and then type the new entry to overwrite the previous entry. However, if you need to replace only part of a cell's content, you can work in **Edit mode**. To switch to Edit mode, you double-click the cell. A blinking insertion point indicates where the new content you type will be inserted. In the cell or formula bar, the pointer changes to an I-beam, which you can use to select text in the cell. Anything you type replaces the selected content.

Because customers can order more than just games from Game Card, Peter wants you to edit the text in cell B5. You will do that in Edit mode.

To edit the text in cell B5:

1. Double-click cell **B5** to select the cell and switch to Edit mode. A blinking insertion point appears within the text of cell B5. The status bar displays Edit instead of Ready to indicate that the cell is in Edit mode.

2. Press the **arrow keys** to move the insertion point directly to the left of the word "from" in the cell text.

3. Type **and other items** and then press the **spacebar**. The cell now reads "To record purchases of board games and other items from Game Card." See Figure 1-13.

| Figure 1-13 | Edited text in the Documentation sheet |

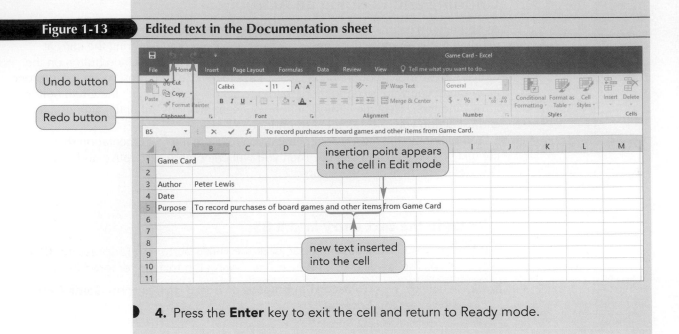

Undo button

Redo button

insertion point appears in the cell in Edit mode

new text inserted into the cell

▶ **4.** Press the **Enter** key to exit the cell and return to Ready mode.

Understanding AutoComplete

As you type text in the active cell, Excel tries to anticipate the remaining characters by displaying text that begins with the same letters as a previous entry in the same column. This feature, known as **AutoComplete**, helps make entering repetitive text easier. To accept the suggested text, press the Tab or Enter key. To override the suggested text, continue to type the text you want to enter in the cell. AutoComplete does not work with dates or numbers or when a blank cell is between the previous entry and the text you are typing.

Next, you will enter the contact information for Leslie Ritter, a customer from Brockton, Massachusetts, who recently placed an order with Game Card. You will enter this information on the Customer Order worksheet.

To enter Leslie Ritter's contact information:

▶ **1.** Click the **Customer Order** sheet tab to make it the active sheet.

▶ **2.** In cell A1, type **Customer Order** as the worksheet title, and then press the **Enter** key twice. The worksheet title is entered in cell A1, and the active cell becomes cell A3.

▶ **3.** Type **Ship To** in cell A3, and then press the **Enter** key. The label is entered in the cell, and the active cell is now cell A4.

▶ **4.** In the range A4:A10, enter the following labels, pressing the **Enter** key after each entry and ignoring any AutoComplete suggestions: **First Name**, **Last Name**, **Address**, **City**, **State**, **Postal Code**, and **Phone**.

▶ **5.** Click cell **B4** to make that cell the active cell.

▶ **6.** In the range B4:B10, enter the following contact information, pressing the **Enter** key after each entry and ignoring any AutoComplete suggestions: **Leslie**, **Ritter**, **805 Mountain St.**, **Brockton**, **MA**, **02302**, and **(508) 555-1072**. See Figure 1-14.

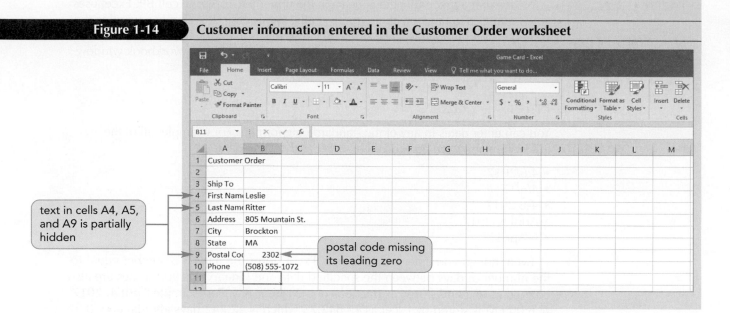

Figure 1-14   Customer information entered in the Customer Order worksheet

text in cells A4, A5, and A9 is partially hidden

postal code missing its leading zero

Displaying Numbers as Text

When you enter a number in a cell, Excel treats the entry as a number and ignores any leading zero. For example, in cell B9, the leading zero in the postal code 02302 is missing. Excel displays 2302 because it treats the postal code as a number, and 2302 and 02302 have the same value. To specify that a number entry should be considered text and all digits should be displayed, you include an apostrophe (') before the numbers.

To enter the postal code as text:

1. Click cell **B9** to select it. Notice that the postal code is right-aligned in the cell, unlike the other text entries, which are left-aligned—another indication that the entry is being treated as a number.

2. Type **'02302** in cell B9, and then press the **Enter** key. The text 02302 appears in cell B9 and is left-aligned in the cell, matching all of the other text entries.

3. Click cell **B9** to select it again. See Figure 1-15.

Figure 1-15   Number entered as text

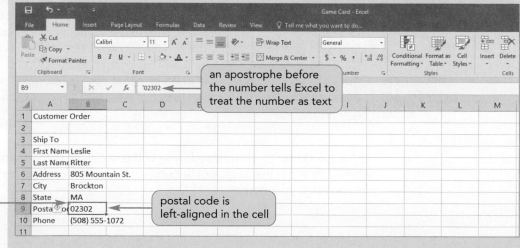

an apostrophe before the number tells Excel to treat the number as text

green triangle flags a potential error

postal code is left-aligned in the cell

TIP

To remove a green triangle, click the cell, click the yellow caution icon that appears to the left of the cell, and then click Ignore Error.

Notice that a green triangle appears in the upper-left corner of cell B9. Excel uses green triangles to flag potential errors in cells. In this case, it is simply a warning that you entered a number as a text string. Because this is intentional, you do not have to edit the cell to fix the "error." Green triangles appear only in the workbook window and not in any printouts of the worksheet.

Entering Dates

You can enter dates in any of the standard date formats. For example, all of the following entries are recognized by Excel as the same date:

- 4/6/2017
- 4/6/17
- 4-6-2017
- April 6, 2017
- 6-Apr-17

Even though you enter a date as text, Excel stores the date as a number equal to the number of days between the specified date and January 0, 1900. Times are also entered as text and stored as fractions of a 24-hour day. For example April 4, 2017 @ 6:00 PM is stored by Excel as 42,842.75 which is 42,842 days after January 0, 1900 plus 3/4 of one day. Dates and times are stored as numbers so that Excel can easily perform date and time calculations, such as determining the elapsed time between one date and another.

Based on the default date format your computer uses, Excel might alter the format of a date after you type it. For example, if you enter the date 4/6/17 into the active cell, Excel might display the date with the four-digit year value, 4/6/2017; if you enter the text April 6, 2017, Excel might change the date format to 6-Apr-17. Changing the date or time format does not affect the underlying date or time value.

INSIGHT

International Date Formats

As business transactions become more international in scope, you may need to adopt international standards for expressing dates, times, and currency values in your workbooks. For example, a worksheet cell might contain 06/05/17. This format could be interpreted as any of the following dates: the 5th of June, 2017; the 6th of May, 2017; and the 17th of May, 2006.

The interpretation depends on which country the workbook has been designed for. You can avoid this problem by entering the full date, as in June 5, 2017. However, this might not work with documents written in foreign languages, such as Japanese, that use different character symbols.

To solve this problem, many international businesses adopt ISO (International Organization for Standardization) dates in the format *yyyy-mm-dd*, where *yyyy* is the four-digit year value, *mm* is the two-digit month value, and *dd* is the two-digit day value. So, a date such as June 5, 2017 is entered as 2017/06/05. If you choose to use this international date format, make sure that people using your workbook understand this format so they do not misinterpret the dates. You can include information about the date format in the Documentation sheet.

For the Game Card workbook, you will enter dates in the format *mm/dd/yyyy*, where *mm* is the two-digit month number, *dd* is the two-digit day number, and *yyyy* is the four-digit year number.

To enter the current date into the Documentation sheet:

▶ **1.** Click the **Documentation** sheet tab to make the Documentation sheet the active worksheet.

▶ **2.** Click cell **B4** to make it the active cell, type the current date in the *mm/dd/yyyy* format, and then press the **Enter** key. The date is entered in the cell.

   Trouble? Depending on your system configuration, Excel might change the date to the date format *dd-mmm-yy*. This difference will not affect your work.

▶ **3.** Click the **Customer Order** sheet tab to return to the Customer Order worksheet.

The next part of the Customer Order worksheet will list the items that customer Leslie Ritter purchased from Game Card. As shown in Figure 1-16, the list includes identifying information about each item, including the item's price, and the quantity of each item ordered.

| Figure 1-16 | Customer order from Leslie Ritter |

Stock ID	Category	Manufacturer	Title	Players	Price	Qty
SG71	Strategy Game	Drebeck Brothers	Kings and Jacks: A Medieval Game of Deception	4	$39.95	2
FG14	Family Game	Misty Games	Twirple, Tweedle, and Twaddle	6	$24.55	1
PG05	Party Game	Parlor Vision	Trivia Connection	8	$29.12	1
SU38	Supplies	Parlor Vision	Box of Dice (10)		$9.95	3
SG29	Strategy Game	Drebeck Brothers	Solar Warfare	2	$35.15	1

You will enter the first four columns of the order into the worksheet.

To enter the first part of the customer order:

▶ **1.** In the Customer Order worksheet, click cell **A12** to make it the active cell, type **Stock ID** as the column label, and then press the **Tab** key to move to cell B12.

▶ **2.** In the range B12:D12, type the following labels, pressing the **Tab** key to move to the next cell: **Category**, **Manufacturer**, and **Title**.

▶ **3.** Press the **Enter** key to go to the next row of the worksheet, making cell A13 the active cell.

▶ **4.** In the range A13:D17, type the Stock ID, Category, Manufacturer, and Title text for the five items purchased by Leslie Ritter listed in Figure 1-16, pressing the **Tab** key to move from one cell to the next, and pressing the **Enter** key to move to a new row. Note that the text in some cells will be partially hidden; you will fix that problem shortly. See Figure 1-17.

Figure 1-17   Partial customer order

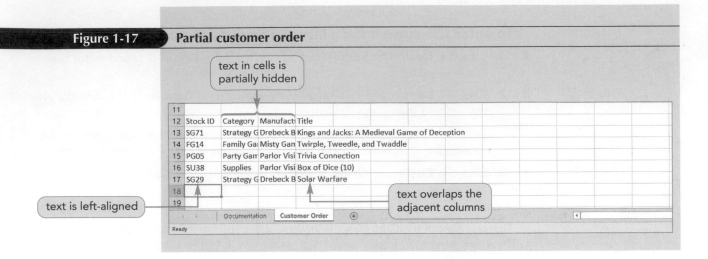

Entering Numbers

TIP

If a number exceeds its cell's width, you see ###### instead of the number. You can display the entire number by increasing the column width.

In Excel, numbers can be integers such as 378, decimals such as 1.95, or negatives such as –5.2. In the case of currency and percentages, you can include the currency symbol and percent sign when you enter the value. Excel treats a currency value such as $87.25 as the number 87.25, and a percentage such as 95% as the decimal 0.95. Much like dates, currency and percentages are formatted in a convenient way for you to read, but only the number is stored within the cell. This makes it easier to perform calculations with currency and percentage values.

You will complete Leslie Ritter's order by entering the players, price, and quantity values.

To enter the rest of the customer order:

1. In the range E12:G12, enter **Players**, **Price**, and **Qty** as the labels.

2. In cell E13, enter **4** as the number of players for the game Kings and Jacks.

3. In cell F13, enter **$39.95** as the price of the game. The game price is stored as a number but displayed with the $ symbol.

4. In cell G13, enter **2** as the quantity of the game ordered by Leslie.

5. In the range E14:G17, enter the remaining number of players, prices, and quantities shown earlier in Figure 1-16. See Figure 1-18.

Figure 1-18   Completed customer order

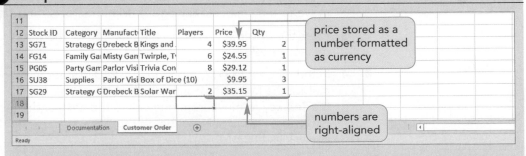

6. On the Quick Access Toolbar, click the **Save** button 🖫 (or press the **Ctrl+S** keys) to save the workbook.

Resizing Columns and Rows

Much of the information in the Customer Order worksheet is difficult to read because of the hidden text. You can display all of the cell contents by changing the size of the columns and rows in the worksheet.

Changing Column Widths

Column widths are expressed as the number of characters the column can contain. The default column width is 8.43 standard-sized characters. In general, this means that you can type eight characters in a cell; any additional text is hidden or overlaps the adjacent cell. Column widths are also expressed in terms of pixels. A **pixel** is a single point on a computer monitor or printout. A column width of 8.43 characters is equivalent to 64 pixels.

INSIGHT

Setting Column Widths

On a computer monitor, pixel size is based on screen resolution. As a result, cell contents that look fine on one screen might appear very different when viewed on a screen with a different resolution. If you work on multiple computers or share your workbooks with others, you should set column widths based on the maximum number of characters you want displayed in the cells rather than pixel size. This ensures that everyone sees the cell contents the way you intended.

You will increase the width of column A so that the contact information labels in cells A4, A5, and A9 are completely displayed.

To increase the width of column A:

1. Point to the **right border** of the column A heading until the pointer changes to ✛.

2. Click and drag to the right until the width of the column heading reaches **15** characters, but do not release the mouse button. The ScreenTip that appears as you resize the column shows the new column width in characters and in pixels. See Figure 1-19.

Figure 1-19   **Width of column A increased to 15 characters**

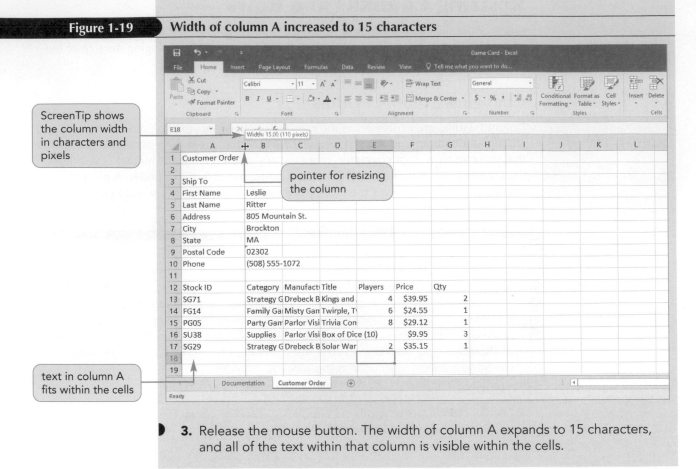

ScreenTip shows the column width in characters and pixels

pointer for resizing the column

text in column A fits within the cells

▶ **3.** Release the mouse button. The width of column A expands to 15 characters, and all of the text within that column is visible within the cells.

You will increase the widths of columns B and C to 18 characters so that their complete entries are visible. Rather than resizing each column separately, you can select both columns and adjust their widths at the same time.

To increase the widths of columns B and C:

▶ **1.** Click the **column B** heading. The entire column is selected.

TIP

To select adjacent columns, you can also click and drag the pointer over multiple column headings.

▶ **2.** Hold down the **Ctrl** key, click the **column C** heading, and then release the **Ctrl** key. Both columns B and C are selected.

▶ **3.** Point to the **right border** of the column C heading until the pointer changes to ╬.

▶ **4.** Drag to the right until the column width changes to **18** characters, and then release the mouse button. Both column widths increase to 18 characters and display all of the entered text.

Using the mouse to resize columns can be imprecise and a challenge to some users with special needs. The Format command on the Home tab gives you precise control over column width and row height settings. You will use the Format command to set the width of column D to exactly 25 characters so that the hidden text is visible.

To set the width of column D using the Format command:

1. Click the **column D** heading. The entire column is selected.

2. On the Home tab, in the Cells group, click the **Format** button, and then click **Column Width.** The Column Width dialog box opens.

3. Type **25** in the Column width box to specify the new column width.

4. Click the **OK** button. The width of column D changes to 25 characters.

5. Click cell **A12** to deselect column D. Figure 1-20 shows the revised column widths for the customer order columns.

Figure 1-20 | **Resized columns**

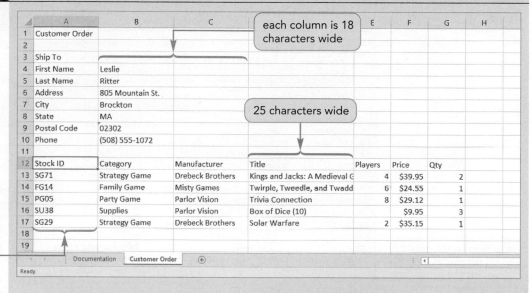

Notice that 25 characters is not wide enough to display all of the characters in each cell of column D. Instead of manually resizing the column width or row height to fit it to the cell contents, you can autofit the column or row. **AutoFit** changes the column width or row height to display the longest or tallest entry within the column or row. You autofit a column or a row by double-clicking the right border of the column heading or the bottom border of the row heading.

TIP

If the row or column is blank, autofitting restores its default height or width.

To autofit the contents of column D:

1. Point to the **right border** of column D until the pointer changes to ✛.

2. Double-click the **right border** of the column D heading. The width of column D increases to about 43 characters so that the longest item title is completely visible.

Wrapping Text Within a Cell

Sometimes, resizing a column width to display all of the text entered in the cells results in a cell that is too wide to read or print nicely. Another way to display long text entries is to wrap text to a new line when it would otherwise extend beyond the cell boundaries. When text wraps within a cell, the row height increases so that all of the text within the cell is displayed.

You will resize column D and then wrap the text entries in the column.

To wrap text in column D:

▶ **1.** Resize the width of column D to **25** characters.

▶ **2.** Select the range **D13:D17**. These cells include the titles that extend beyond the column width.

▶ **3.** On the Home tab, in the Alignment group, click the **Wrap Text** button. The Wrap Text button is toggled on, and text in the selected cells that exceeds the column width wraps to a new line.

▶ **4.** Click cell **A12** to make it the active cell. See Figure 1-21.

Figure 1-21 ▶ **Text wrapped within cells**

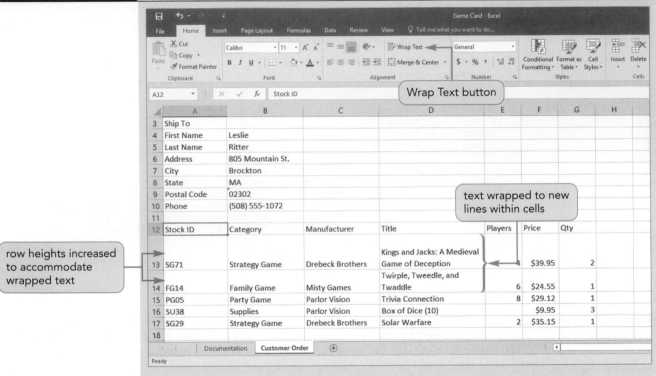

If you want to create a new line within a cell, press the Alt+Enter keys to move the insertion point to the next line within the cell. Whatever you type next will appear on the new line in the cell.

Changing Row Heights

The height of a row is measured in points or pixels. A **point** is approximately 1/72 of an inch. The default row height is 15 points, or 20 pixels. Row heights are set in the same way as column widths. You can drag the bottom border of the row heading to a new row height, specify a row height using the Format command, or autofit the row's height to match its content.

Peter notices that the height of row 13 is a little too tall for its contents. He asks you to change to it 30 points.

To change the height of row 13:

1. Point to the **bottom border** of the row 13 heading until the pointer changes to ✛.

2. Drag the **bottom border** down until the height of the row is equal to **30** points (or **40** pixels), and then release the mouse button. The height of row 13 is set to 30 points.

3. Press the **Ctrl+S** keys to save the workbook.

TIP

You can also set the row height by clicking the Format button in the Cells group on the Home tab and then using the Row Height command.

You have entered most of the data for Leslie Ritter's order at Game Card. In the next session, you will calculate the total charge for the order and print the worksheet.

REVIEW

Session 1.1 Quick Check

1. What are the two types of sheets used in a workbook?
2. What is the cell reference for the cell located in the second column and fifth row of a worksheet?
3. What is the range reference for the block of cells C2 through D10?
4. What is the reference for the nonadjacent block of cells B5 through C10 and cells B15 through D20?
5. What keyboard shortcut makes the active cell to cell A1?
6. What is text data?
7. How do you enter a number so that Excel sees it as text?
8. Cell B2 contains the entry May 3, 2017. Why doesn't Excel consider this a text entry?
9. How do you autofit a column to match the longest cell entry?

Session 1.2 Visual Overview:

The **font size** specifies how big the text is.

The **Page Layout tab** is used to specify how the worksheet will be arranged and printed.

In Excel, every formula begins with an equal sign (=).

When the active cell contains a formula, the formula appears in the formula bar and the result of the formula appears in the cell.

The gridlines that surround cells appear on the worksheet as a guide; they do not print.

A **border** is a line that you add along an edge of a cell. Borders are used to improve the readability of the worksheet.

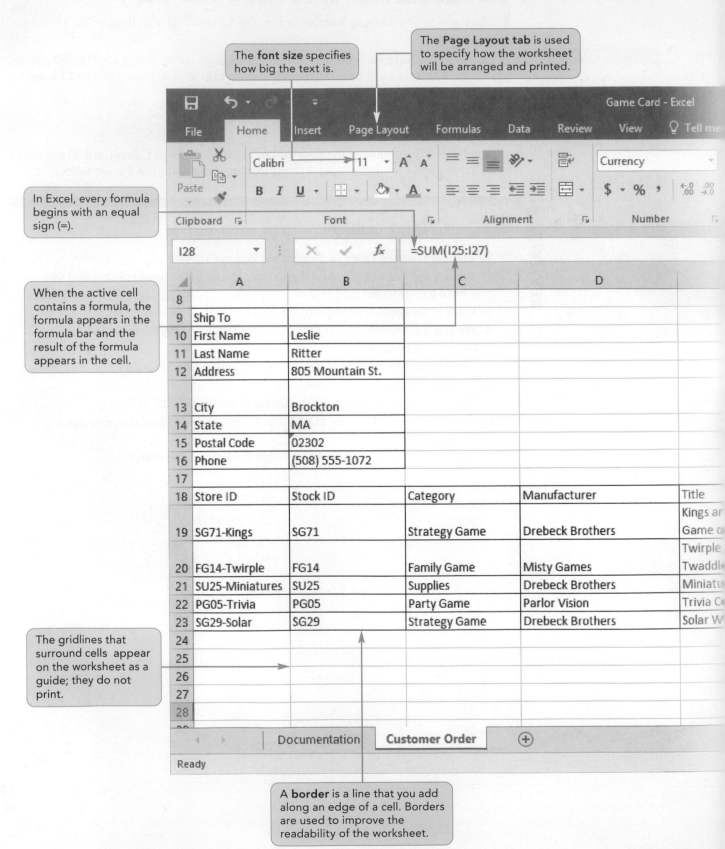

	A	B	C	D
8				
9	Ship To			
10	First Name	Leslie		
11	Last Name	Ritter		
12	Address	805 Mountain St.		
13	City	Brockton		
14	State	MA		
15	Postal Code	02302		
16	Phone	(508) 555-1072		
17				
18	Store ID	Stock ID	Category	Manufacturer	Title
19	SG71-Kings	SG71	Strategy Game	Drebeck Brothers	Kings an / Game o
20	FG14-Twirple	FG14	Family Game	Misty Games	Twirple / Twaddle
21	SU25-Miniatures	SU25	Supplies	Drebeck Brothers	Miniatu
22	PG05-Trivia	PG05	Party Game	Parlor Vision	Trivia C
23	SG29-Solar	SG29	Strategy Game	Drebeck Brothers	Solar W
24				
25				
26				
27				
28				

I28   =SUM(I25:I27)

Game Card - Excel

Documentation   **Customer Order**

Ready

Excel Formulas and Functions

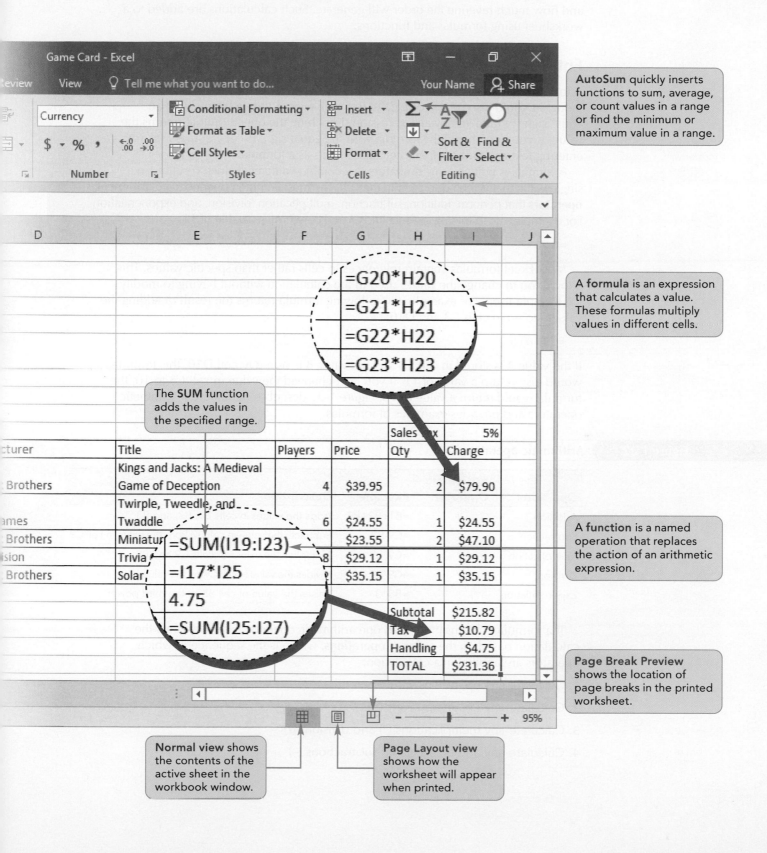

AutoSum quickly inserts functions to sum, average, or count values in a range or find the minimum or maximum value in a range.

A formula is an expression that calculates a value. These formulas multiply values in different cells.

The SUM function adds the values in the specified range.

A function is a named operation that replaces the action of an arithmetic expression.

Page Break Preview shows the location of page breaks in the printed worksheet.

Normal view shows the contents of the active sheet in the workbook window.

Page Layout view shows how the worksheet will appear when printed.

Game Card - Excel

Review   View   Tell me what you want to do...   Your Name   Share

Currency

$ - % ,   .00 .00

Conditional Formatting
Format as Table
Cell Styles

Insert
Delete
Format

Sort & Find &
Filter Select

Number   Styles   Cells   Editing

=G20*H20
=G21*H21
=G22*H22
=G23*H23

		Sales Tax	5%
cturer	Title	Players	Price	Qty	Charge

=SUM(I19:I23)
=I17*I25
4.75
=SUM(I25:I27)

Manufacturer	Title	Players	Price	Qty	Charge
Brothers	Kings and Jacks: A Medieval Game of Deception	4	$39.95	2	$79.90
ames	Twirple, Tweedle, and Twaddle	6	$24.55	1	$24.55
Brothers	Miniatur		$23.55	2	$47.10
ision	Trivia	8	$29.12	1	$29.12
Brothers	Solar		$35.15	1	$35.15
				Subtotal	$215.82
				Tax	$10.79
				Handling	$4.75
				TOTAL	$231.36

95%

Performing Calculations with Formulas

So far you have entered text, numbers, and dates in the worksheet. However, the main reason for using Excel is to perform calculations and analysis on data. For example, Peter wants the workbook to calculate the number of items that the customer ordered and how much revenue the order will generate. Such calculations are added to a worksheet using formulas and functions.

Entering a Formula

A formula is an expression that returns a value. In most cases, this is a number—though it could also be text or a date. In Excel, every formula begins with an equal sign (=) followed by an expression describing the operation that returns the value. If you don't begin the formula with the equal sign, Excel assumes that you are entering text and will not treat the cell contents as a formula.

A formula is written using **operators** that combine different values, resulting in a single value that is then displayed in the cell. The most common operators are **arithmetic operators** that perform addition, subtraction, multiplication, division, and exponentiation. For example, the following formula adds 3 and 8, returning a value of 11:

=3+8

Most Excel formulas contain references to cells rather than specific values. This allows you to change the values used in the calculation without having to modify the formula itself. For example, the following formula returns the result of adding the values stored in cells C3 and D10:

=C3+D10

If the value 3 is stored in cell C3 and the value 8 is stored in cell D10, this formula would also return a value of 11. If you later changed the value in cell C3 to 10, the formula would return a value of 18. Figure 1-22 describes the different arithmetic operators and provides examples of formulas.

Figure 1-22   **Arithmetic operators**

Operation	Arithmetic Operator	Example	Description
Addition	+	=B1+B2+B3	Adds the values in cells B1, B2, and B3
Subtraction	–	=C9-B2	Subtracts the value in cell B2 from the value in cell C9
Multiplication	*	=C9*B9	Multiplies the values in cells C9 and B9
Division	/	=C9/B9	Divides the value in cell C9 by the value in cell B9
Exponentiation	^	=B5^3	Raises the value of cell B5 to the third power

If a formula contains more than one arithmetic operator, Excel performs the calculation based on the **order of operations**, which is the sequence in which operators are applied in a calculation:

1. Calculate any operations within parentheses

2. Calculate any exponentiations (^)

3. Calculate any multiplications (*) and divisions (/)

4. Calculate any additions (+) and subtractions (–)

For example, the following formula returns the value 23 because multiplying 4 by 5 takes precedence over adding 3:

=3+4*5

If a formula contains two or more operators with the same level of priority, the operators are applied in order from left to right. In the following formula, Excel first multiplies 4 by 10 and then divides that result by 8 to return the value 5:

=4*10/8

When parentheses are used, the value inside them is calculated first. In the following formula, Excel calculates (3+4) first, and then multiplies that result by 5 to return the value 35:

=(3+4)*5

Figure 1-23 shows how slight changes in a formula affect the order of operations and the result of the formula.

Figure 1-23   **Order of operations applied to Excel formulas**

Formula	Order of Operations	Result
=50+10*5	10*5 calculated first and then 50 is added	100
=(50+10)*5	(50+10) calculated first and then 60 is multiplied by 5	300
=50/10–5	50/10 calculated first and then 5 is subtracted	0
=50/(10–5)	(10–5) calculated first and then 50 is divided by that value	10
=50/10*5	Two operators are at same precedence level, so the calculation is done left to right with 50/10 calculated first and that value is then multiplied by 5	25
=50/(10*5)	(10*5) is calculated first and then 50 is divided by that value	1

Peter wants the Customer Order worksheet to include the total amount charged for each item ordered. The charge is equal to the number of each item ordered multiplied by each item's price. You already entered this information in columns F and G. Now you will enter a formula to calculate the charge for each set of items ordered in column H.

To calculate the charge for the first item ordered:

1. If you took a break after the previous session, make sure the Game Card workbook is open and the Customer Order worksheet is active.

2. Click cell **H12** to make it the active cell, type **Charge** as the column label, and then press the **Enter** key. The label text is entered in cell H12, and cell H13 is now the active cell.

3. Type **=F13*G13** (the price of the Kings and Jacks game multiplied by the number of that game ordered). As you type the formula, a list of Excel function names appears in a ScreenTip, which provides a quick method for entering functions. The list will close when you complete the formula. You will learn more about Excel functions shortly. Also, after you type each cell reference, Excel color codes each cell reference and its cell. See Figure 1-24.

Figure 1-24 **Figure 1-24** **Formula being entered in a cell**

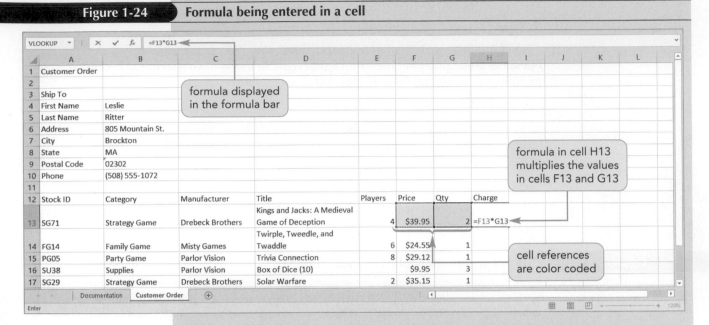

4. Press the **Enter** key. The formula is entered in cell H13 displaying the value $79.90. The result is displayed as currency because cell F13, which is referenced in the formula, contains a currency value.

5. Click cell **H13** to make it the active cell. Note that the cell displays the result of the formula, and the formula bar displays the formula you entered.

For the first item, you entered the formula by typing each cell reference in the expression. You can also insert a cell reference by clicking the cell as you type the formula. This technique reduces the possibility of error caused by typing an incorrect cell reference. You will use this method to enter the formula to calculate the charge for the second item on the order.

Be sure to type = first; otherwise, Excel will not recognize the entry as a formula.

To enter a formula using the mouse:

1. Click cell **H14** to make it the active cell.

2. Type **=**. The equal sign indicates that you are entering a formula. Any cell you click from now on inserts the cell reference of the selected cell into the formula until you complete the formula by pressing the Enter or Tab key.

3. Click cell **F14**. The cell reference is inserted into the formula in the formula bar. At this point, any cell you click changes the cell reference used in the formula. The cell reference isn't locked until you type an operator.

4. Type ***** to enter the multiplication operator. The cell reference for cell F14 is locked in the formula, and the next cell you click will be inserted after the operator.

5. Click cell **G14** to enter its cell reference in the formula. The formula is complete.

6. Press the **Enter** key. Cell H14 displays the value $24.55, which is the charge for the second item ordered.

Copying and Pasting Formulas

Sometimes you will need to repeat the same formula throughout a worksheet. Rather than retyping the formula, you can copy a formula from one cell and paste it into another cell. When you copy a formula, Excel places the formula into the **Clipboard**, which is a temporary storage location for text and graphics. When you paste, Excel takes the formula from the Clipboard and inserts it into the selected cell or range. Excel adjusts the cell references in the formula to reflect the formula's new location in the worksheet. This occurs because you usually want to copy the actions of a formula rather than the specific value the formula generates. In this case, the formula's action is to multiply the price of the item ordered by the quantity. By copying and pasting the formula, you can quickly repeat that action for every item listed in the worksheet.

You will copy the formula you entered in cell H14 to the range H15:H17 to calculate the charges on the remaining three items in Leslie Ritter's order. By copying and pasting the formula, you will save time and avoid potential mistakes from retyping the formula.

To copy and paste the formula:

1. Click cell **H14** to select the cell that contains the formula you want to copy.

2. On the Home tab, in the Clipboard group, click the **Copy** button (or press the **Ctrl+C** keys). Excel copies the formula to the Clipboard. A blinking green box surrounds the cell being copied.

3. Select the range **H15:H17**. You want to paste the formula into these cells.

4. In the Clipboard group, click the **Paste** button (or press the **Ctrl+V** keys). Excel pastes the formula into the selected cells, adjusting each formula so that the charge calculated for each ordered item is based on the corresponding values within that row. A button appears below the selected range, providing options for pasting formulas and values. See Figure 1-25.

| Figure 1-25 | Copied and pasted formula |

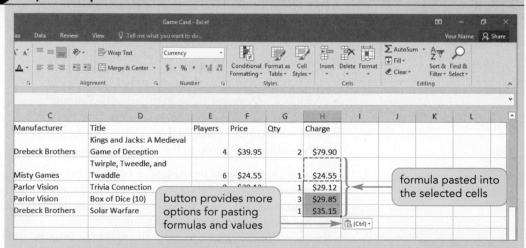

5. Click cell **H15** and verify that the formula =F15*G15 appears in the formula bar. The formula was updated to reflect the cell references in the corresponding row.

6. Click the other cells in column H, and verify that the corresponding formulas are entered in those cells.

Simplifying Formulas with Functions

In addition to cell references and operators, formulas can also contain functions. A function is a named operation that replaces the arithmetic expression in a formula. Functions are used to simplify long or complex formulas. For example, to add the values from cells A1 through A10, you could enter the following long formula:

=A1+A2+A3+A4+A5+A6+A7+A8+A9+A10

Or, you could use the SUM function to calculate the sum of those cell values by entering the following formula:

=SUM(A1:A10)

In both instances, Excel adds the values in cells A1 through A10, but the SUM function is faster and simpler to enter and less prone to a typing error. You should always use a function, if one is available, in place of a long, complex formula. Excel supports more than 300 different functions from the fields of finance, business, science, and engineering, including functions that work with numbers, text, and dates.

Introducing Function Syntax

Every function follows a set of rules, or **syntax**, which specifies how the function should be written. The general syntax of all Excel functions is

FUNCTION(arg1,arg2,…)

where *FUNCTION* is the function name, and *arg1*, *arg2*, and so forth are values used by that function. For example, the SUM function shown above uses a single argument, A1:A10, which is the range reference of the cells whose values will be added. Some functions do not require any arguments and are entered as *FUNCTION()*. Functions without arguments still require the opening and closing parentheses but do not include a value within the parentheses.

Entering Functions with AutoSum

A fast and convenient way to enter commonly used functions is with AutoSum. The AutoSum button includes options to insert the following functions into a select cell or cell range:

- SUM—Sum of the values in the specified range
- AVERAGE—Average value in the specified range
- COUNT—Total count of numeric values in the specified range
- MAX—Maximum value in the specified range
- MIN—Minimum value in the specified range

After you select one of the AutoSum options, Excel determines the most appropriate range from the available data and enters it as the function's argument. You should always verify that the range included in the AutoSum function matches the range that you want to use.

   You will use AutoSum to enter the SUM function to add the total charges for Leslie Ritter's order.

To use AutoSum to enter the SUM function:

1. Click cell **G18** to make it the active cell, type **Subtotal** as the label, and then press the **Tab** key to make cell H18 the active cell.

2. On the Home tab, in the Editing group, click the **AutoSum button arrow**. The button's menu opens and displays five common functions: Sum, Average, Count Numbers, Max (for maximum), and Min (for minimum).

TIP

You can quickly insert the SUM function by pressing the Alt+= keys.

3. Click **Sum** to enter the SUM function. The formula =SUM(H13:H17) is entered in cell H18. The cells being summed are selected and highlighted on the worksheet so you can quickly confirm that Excel selected the appropriate range from the available data. A ScreenTip appears below the formula describing the function's syntax. See Figure 1-26.

Figure 1-26   **SUM function being entered with AutoSum button**

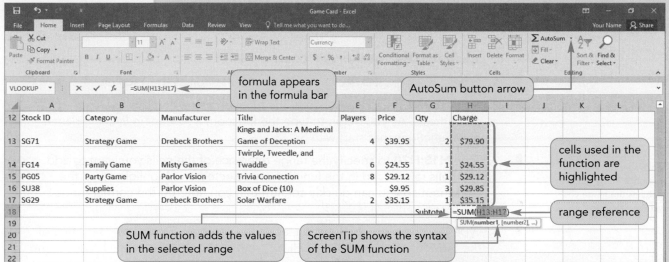

4. Press the **Enter** key to accept the formula. The subtotal of the charges on the order returned by the SUM function is $198.57.

AutoSum makes entering a commonly used formula such as the SUM function fast and easy. However, AutoSum can determine the appropriate range reference to include only when the function is adjacent to the cells containing the values you want to summarize. If you need to use a function elsewhere in the worksheet, you will have to select the range reference to include or type the function yourself.

Each purchase made at Game Card is subject to a 5 percent sales tax and, in the case of online orders, a $4.75 handling fee. You will add these to the Customer Order worksheet so you can calculate the total charge for Leslie Ritter's order.

To add the sales tax and handling fee to the worksheet:

1. Click cell **G11**, type **Sales Tax** as the label, and then press the **Tab** key to make cell H11 the active cell.

2. In cell H11, type **5%** as the sales tax rate, and then press the **Enter** key. The sales tax rate is entered in the cell and can be used in other calculations. The value is displayed with the % symbol but is stored as the equivalent decimal value 0.05.

3. Click cell **G19** to make it the active cell, type **Tax** as the label, and then press the **Tab** key to make cell H19 the active cell.

4. Type **=H11*H18** as the formula to calculate the sales tax on the customer order, and then press the **Enter** key. The formula multiplies the sales tax value in cell H11 by the order subtotal value in cell H18. The value $9.93 is displayed in cell H19, which is 5 percent of the subtotal value of $198.57.

▶ 5. In cell G20, type **Handling** as the label, and then press the **Tab** key to make cell H20 the active cell. You will enter the handling fee in this cell.

▶ 6. Type **$4.75** as the handling fee, and then press the **Enter** key.

The last part of the customer order is to calculate the total cost by adding the subtotal, the tax, and the handling fee. Rather than using AutoSum, you will type the SUM function so you can enter the correct range reference for the function. You can type the range reference or select the range in the worksheet. Remember that you must type parentheses around the range reference.

To calculate the total order cost:

▶ 1. In cell G21, type **TOTAL** as the label, and then press the **Tab** key.

▶ 2. Type **=SUM(** in cell H21 to enter the function name and the opening parenthesis. As you begin to type the function, a ScreenTip lists the names of all functions that start with S.

Make sure the cell reference in the function matches the range you want to calculate.

▶ 3. Type **H18:H20** to specify the range reference of the cells you want to add. The cells referenced in the function are selected and highlighted on the worksheet so you can quickly confirm that you entered the correct range reference.

▶ 4. Type **)** to complete the function, and then press the **Enter** key. The value of the SUM function appears in cell H21, indicating that the total charge for the order is $213.25.

▶ 5. Click cell **H21** to select the cell and its formula. See Figure 1-27.

Figure 1-27 | **Total charge calculated for the order**

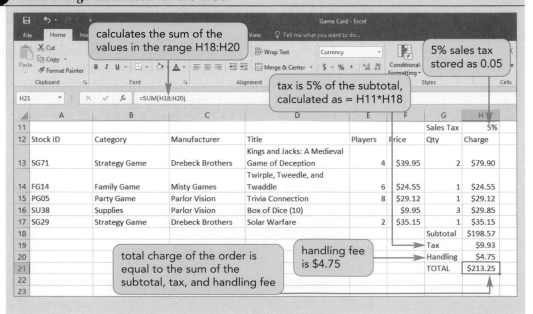

The SUM function makes it simple to quickly add the values in a group of cells.

PROSKILLS

Problem Solving: Writing Effective Formulas

You can use formulas to quickly perform calculations and solve problems. First, identify the problem you need to solve. Then, gather the data needed to solve the problem. Finally, create accurate and effective formulas that use the data to answer or resolve the problem. Follow these guidelines:

- **Keep formulas simple.** Use functions in place of long, complex formulas whenever possible. For example, use the SUM function instead of entering a formula that adds individual cells, which makes it easier to confirm that the formula is making an accurate calculation as it provides answers needed to evaluate the problem.

- **Do not hide data values within formulas.** The worksheet displays formula results, not the actual formula. For example, to calculate a 5 percent interest rate on a currency value in cell A5, you could enter the formula =0.05*A5. However, this doesn't show how the value is calculated. A better approach places the value 0.05 in a cell accompanied by a descriptive label and uses the cell reference in the formula. If you place 0.05 in cell A6, the formula =A6*A5 would calculate the interest value. Other people can then easily see the interest rate as well as the resulting interest, ensuring that the formula is solving the right problem.

- **Break up formulas to show intermediate results.** When a worksheet contains complex computations, other people can more easily comprehend how the formula results are calculated when different parts of the formula are distinguished. For example, the formula =SUM(A1:A10)/SUM(B1:B10) calculates the ratio of two sums but hides the two sum values. Instead, enter each SUM function in a separate cell, such as cells A11 and B11, and use the formula =A11/B11 to calculate the ratio. Other people can see both sums and the value of their ratio in the worksheet and better understand the final result, which makes it more likely that the best problem resolution will be selected.

- **Test formulas with simple values.** Use values you can calculate in your head to confirm that your formula works as intended. For example, using 1s or 10s as the input values lets you easily figure out the answer and verify the formula.

Finding a solution to a problem requires accurate data and analysis. With workbooks, this means using formulas that are easy to understand, clearly showing the data being used in the calculations, and demonstrating how the results are calculated. Only then can you be confident that you are choosing the best problem resolution.

Modifying a Worksheet

As you develop a worksheet, you might need to modify its content and structure to create a more logical organization. Some ways you can modify a worksheet include moving cells and ranges, inserting rows and columns, deleting rows and columns, and inserting and deleting cells.

Moving and Copying a Cell or Range

One way to move a cell or range is to select it, position the pointer over the bottom border of the selection, drag the selection to a new location, and then release the mouse button. This technique is called **drag and drop** because you are dragging the range and dropping it in a new location. If the drop location is not visible, drag the selection to the edge of the workbook window to scroll the worksheet, and then drop the selection.

You can also use the drag-and-drop technique to copy cells by pressing the Ctrl key as you drag the selected range to its new location. A copy of the original range is placed in the new location without removing the original range from the worksheet.

REFERENCE

Moving or Copying a Cell or Range

- Select the cell or range you want to move or copy.
- Move the pointer over the border of the selection until the pointer changes shape.
- To move the range, click the border and drag the selection to a new location (or to copy the range, hold down the Ctrl key and drag the selection to a new location).

or

- Select the cell or range you want to move or copy.
- On the Home tab, in the Clipboard group, click the Cut or Copy button (or right-click the selection, and then click Cut or Copy on the shortcut menu, or press the Ctrl+X or Ctrl+C keys).
- Select the cell or the upper-left cell of the range where you want to paste the content.
- In the Clipboard group, click the Paste button (or right-click the selection and then click Paste on the shortcut menu, or press the Ctrl+V keys).

Peter wants the subtotal, tax, handling, and total values in the range G18:H21 moved down one row to the range G19:H22 to set those calculations off from the list of items in the customer order. You will use the drag-and-drop method to move the range.

To drag and drop the range G18:H21:

1. Select the range **G18:H21**. These are the cells you want to move.

2. Point to the **bottom border** of the selected range so that the pointer changes to ⌖.

3. Press and hold the mouse button to change the pointer to ⬉, and then drag the selection down one row. Do not release the mouse button. A ScreenTip appears, indicating that the new range of the selected cells will be G19:H22. A dark green border also appears around the new range. See Figure 1-28.

Figure 1-28   **Range being moved**

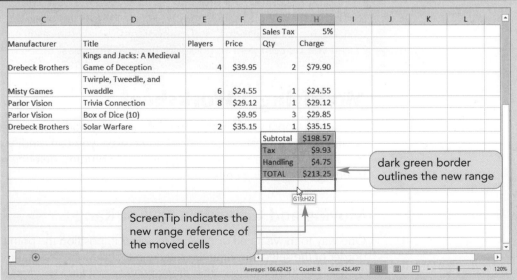

4. Make sure the ScreenTip displays the range G19:H22, and then release the mouse button. The selected cells move to their new location.

Some people find dragging and dropping a select cell range difficult and awkward, particularly if the selected range is large or needs to move a long distance in the worksheet. In those situations, it is often more efficient to cut or copy and paste the cell contents. Cutting moves the selected content, whereas copying duplicates the selected content in the new location.

Peter wants the worksheet to include a summary of the customer order starting in row 3. You will cut the customer contact information and the item listing from range A3:A22 and paste it into range A9:H28, freeing up space for the order information.

To cut and paste the customer contact information:

1. Click cell **A3** to select it.

2. Press the **Ctrl+Shift+End** keys to extend the selection to the last cell in the lower-right corner of the worksheet (cell H22).

3. On the Home tab, in the Clipboard group, click the **Cut** button (or press the **Ctrl+X** keys). The range is surrounded by a moving border, indicating that it has been cut.

4. Click cell **A9** to select it. This is the upper-left corner of the range where you want to paste the range that you cut.

5. In the Clipboard group, click the **Paste** button (or press the **Ctrl+V** keys). The range A3:H22 is pasted into the range A9:H28. Note that the cell references in the formulas were automatically updated to reflect the new location of those cells in the worksheet.

Using the COUNT Function

Sometimes you will want to know how many unique items are included in a range, such as the number of different items in the customer order. To calculate that value, you use the COUNT function

$$=COUNT(range)$$

TIP

To count cells containing non-numeric values, use the COUNTA function.

where *range* is the range of cells containing numeric values to be counted. Note that any cell in the range containing a non-numeric value is not counted in the final tally.

You will include the count of the number of different items from the order in the summary information. The summary will also display the order ID (a unique number assigned by Game Card to identify the order), the shipping date, and the type of delivery (overnight, two-day, or standard) in the freed-up space at the top of the worksheet. In addition, Peter wants the total charge for the order to be displayed with the order summary so that he does not have to scroll to the bottom of the worksheet to find that value.

To add the order summary:

1. Click cell **A3**, type **Order ID** as the label, press the **Tab** key, type **C10489** in cell B3, and then press the **Enter** key. The order ID is entered, and cell A4 is the active cell.

2. Type **Shipping Date** as the label in cell A4, press the **Tab** key, type **4/3/2017** in cell B4, and then press the **Enter** key. The shipping date is entered, and cell A5 is the active cell.

3. Type **Delivery** as the label in cell A5, press the **Tab** key, type **standard** in cell B5, and then press the **Enter** key. The delivery type is entered, and cell A6 is the active cell.

▶ 4. Type **Items Ordered** as the label in cell A6, and then press the **Tab** key. Cell B6 is the active cell. Now you will enter the COUNT function to determine the number of different items ordered.

▶ 5. In cell B6, type **=COUNT(** to begin the function.

▶ 6. With the insertion point still blinking in cell B6, select the range **G19:G23**. The range reference is entered as the argument for the COUNT function.

▶ 7. Type **)** to complete the function, and then press the **Enter** key. Cell B6 displays the value 5, indicating that five items were ordered by Leslie Ritter. Cell A7 is the active cell.

▶ 8. Type **Total Charge** as the label in cell A7, and then press the **Tab** key to make cell B7 the active cell.

▶ 9. Type **=** to start the formula, and then click cell **H28** to enter its cell reference in the formula in cell B7. The formula you created, =H28, tells Excel to display the contents of cell H28 in the current cell.

▶ 10. Press the **Enter** key to complete the formula. The total charge of $213.25 appears in cell B7. See Figure 1-29.

Figure 1-29	Customer order summary

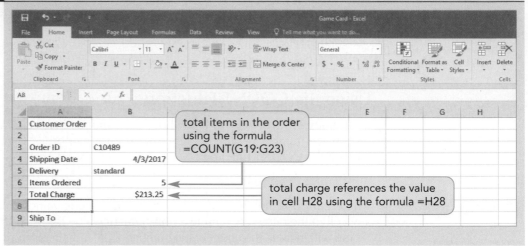

Inserting a Column or Row

You can insert a new column or row anywhere within a worksheet. When you insert a new column, the existing columns are shifted to the right, and the new column has the same width as the column directly to its left. When you insert a new row, the existing rows are shifted down, and the new row has the same height as the row above it. Because inserting a new row or column moves the location of the other cells in the worksheet, any cell references in a formula or function are updated to reflect the new layout.

REFERENCE

Inserting or Deleting a Column or Row

To insert a column or row:

- Select the column(s) or row(s) where you want to insert the new column(s) or row(s). Excel will insert the same number of columns or rows as you select to the left of the selected columns or above the selected rows.
- On the Home tab, in the Cells group, click the Insert button (or right-click a column or row heading or selected column and row headings, and then click Insert on the shortcut menu; or press the Ctrl+Shift+= keys).

To delete a column or row:

- Select the column(s) or row(s) you want to delete.
- On the Home tab, in the Cells group, click the Delete button (or right-click a column or row heading or selected column and row headings, and then click Delete on the shortcut menu; or press the Ctrl+- keys).

Peter informs you that the customer order report for Leslie Ritter is missing an item. You need to insert a new row directly above the entry for the Trivia Connection game in which you'll write the details of the missing item.

TIP

You can insert multiple columns or rows by selecting that number of column or row headings, and then clicking the Insert button or pressing the Ctrl+Shift+= keys.

To insert a row for the missing order item:

1. Click the **row 21** heading to select the entire row.

2. On the Home tab, in the Cells group, click the **Insert** button (or press the **Ctrl+Shift+=** keys). A new row is inserted below row 20 and becomes the new row 21.

3. Enter **SU25** in cell A21, enter **Supplies** in cell B21, enter **Drebeck Brothers** in cell C21, enter **Miniatures Set (12)** in cell D21, leave cell E21 blank, enter **$23.55** in cell F21, and then enter **2** in cell G21.

4. Click cell **H20** to select the cell with the formula for calculating the item charge, and then press the **Ctrl+C** keys to copy the formula in that cell.

5. Click cell **H21** to select the cell where you want to insert the formula, and then press the **Ctrl+V** keys to paste the formula into the cell.

6. Click cell **H26**. See Figure 1-30.

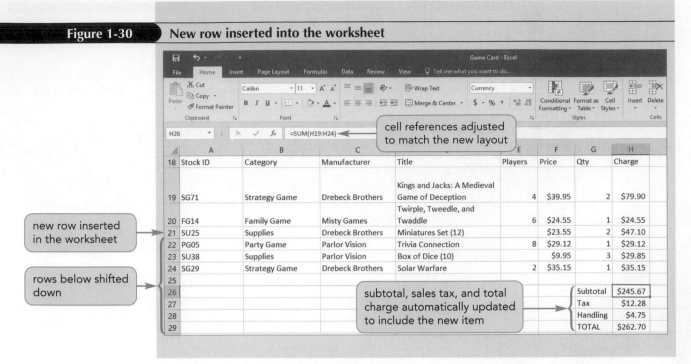

Figure 1-30   **New row inserted into the worksheet**

new row inserted in the worksheet →

rows below shifted down →

cell references adjusted to match the new layout

subtotal, sales tax, and total charge automatically updated to include the new item

Notice that the formula in cell H26 is now =SUM(H19:H24). The range reference was updated to reflect the inserted row. Also, the tax amount increased to $12.28 based on the new subtotal value of $245.67, and the total charge increased to $262.70 because of the added item. Also, the result of the COUNT function in cell B6 increased to 6 to reflect the item added to the order.

Deleting a Row or Column

You can also delete rows or columns from a worksheet. **Deleting** removes the data from the row or column as well as the row or column itself. The rows below the deleted row shift up to fill the vacated space. Likewise, the columns to the right of the deleted column shift left to fill the vacated space. Also, all cell references in the worksheet are adjusted to reflect the change. You click the Delete button in the Cells group on the Home tab to delete selected rows or columns.

Deleting a column or row is not the same as clearing a column or row. **Clearing** removes the data from the selected row or column but leaves the blank row or column in the worksheet. You press the Delete key to clear the contents of the selected row or column, which leaves the worksheet structure unchanged.

Leslie Ritter did not order the box of dice created by Parlor Vision. Peter asks you to delete the row containing this item from the report.

To delete the row containing the box of dice from the order:

1. Click the **row 23** heading to select the entire row.

2. On the Home tab, in the Cells group, click the **Delete** button (or press the **Ctrl+-** keys). Row 23 is deleted, and the rows below it shift up to fill the space.

All of the cell references in the worksheet are again updated automatically to reflect the impact of deleting row 23. The subtotal value in cell H25 is now $215.82, which is the sum of the range H19:H23. The sales tax in cell H26 decreases to $10.79. The total cost of the order decreases to $231.36. Also, the result of the COUNT function in cell B6 decreases to 5 to reflect the item deleted from the order. As you can see, one of the great advantages of using Excel is that it modifies the formulas to reflect the additions and deletions you make to the worksheet.

Inserting and Deleting a Range

You can also insert or delete cell ranges within a worksheet. When you use the Insert button to insert a range of cells, the existing cells shift down when the selected range is wider than it is long, and they shift right when the selected range is longer than it is wide, as shown in Figure 1-31. When you use the Insert Cells command, you specify whether the existing cells shift right or down, or whether to insert an entire row or column into the new range.

| Figure 1-31 | Cells inserted into a worksheet |

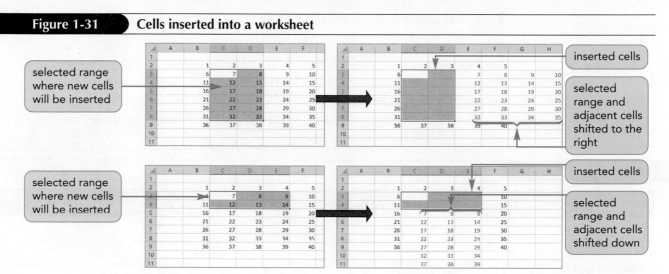

selected range where new cells will be inserted

inserted cells

selected range and adjacent cells shifted to the right

selected range where new cells will be inserted

inserted cells

selected range and adjacent cells shifted down

The process works in reverse when you delete a range. As with deleting a row or column, the cells adjacent to the deleted range either move up or left to fill in the space vacated by the deleted cells. The Delete Cells command lets you specify whether you want to shift the adjacent cells left or up or whether you want to delete the entire column or row.

When you insert or delete a range, cells that shift to a new location adopt the width of the columns they move into. As a result, you might need to resize columns and rows in the worksheet.

REFERENCE

Inserting or Deleting a Range

- Select a range that matches the range you want to insert or delete.
- On the Home tab, in the Cells group, click the Insert button or the Delete button.

or

- Select the range that matches the range you want to insert or delete.
- On the Home tab, in the Cells group, click the Insert button arrow and then click Insert Cells, or click the Delete button arrow and then click Delete Cells (or right-click the selected range, and then click Insert or Delete on the shortcut menu).
- Click the option button for the direction to shift the cells, columns, or rows.
- Click the OK button.

Peter wants you to insert a range into the worksheet for the ID that Game Card uses to identify the items it stocks in its store. You will insert these new cells into the range A17:A28, shifting the adjacent cells to the right.

To insert a range for the store IDs:

▶ **1.** Select the range **A17:A28**.

▶ **2.** On the Home tab, in the Cells group, click the **Insert button arrow**. A menu of insert options appears.

▶ **3.** Click **Insert Cells**. The Insert dialog box opens.

▶ **4.** Verify that the **Shift cells right** option button is selected.

▶ **5.** Click the **OK** button. New cells are inserted into the selected range, and the adjacent cells move to the right. The cell contents do not fit well in the columns and rows they shifted into, so you will resize the columns and rows.

▶ **6.** Resize the width of column E to **25** characters. The text is easier to read in the resized columns.

▶ **7.** Select the row **19** through row **23** headings.

▶ **8.** In the Cells group, click the **Format** button, and then click **AutoFit Row Height**. The selected rows autofit to their contents.

▶ **9.** Resize the height of row 19 to **30 (40 pixels)**. Figure 1-32 shows the revised layout of the customer order.

TIP

You can also autofit by double-clicking the bottom border of row 23.

Figure 1-32	Range added to worksheet

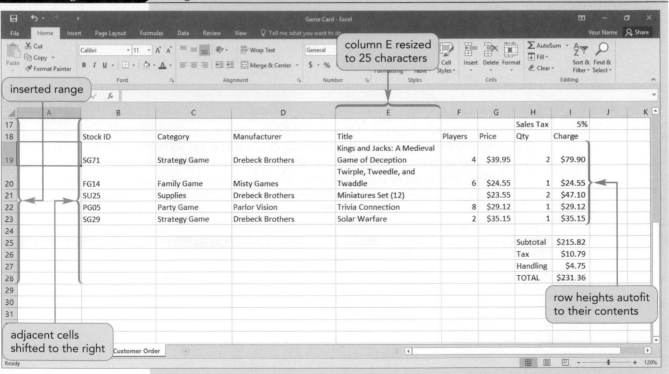

Notice that even though the customer orders will be entered only in the range A18:A23 you selected the range A17:A28 to retain the layout of the page design. Selecting the additional rows ensures that the sales tax and summary values still line up with the Qty and Charge columns. Whenever you insert a new range, be sure to consider its impact on the layout of the entire worksheet.

INSIGHT

Hiding and Unhiding Rows, Columns, and Worksheets

Workbooks can become long and complicated, filled with formulas and data that are important for performing calculations but are of little interest to readers. In those situations, you can simplify these workbooks for readers by hiding rows, columns, and even worksheets. Although the contents of hidden cells cannot be seen, the data in those cells is still available for use in formulas and functions throughout the workbook.

Hiding a row or column essentially decreases that row height or column width to 0 pixels. To a hide a row or column, select the row or column heading, click the Format button in the Cells group on the Home tab, point to Hide & Unhide on the menu that appears, and then click Hide Rows or Hide Columns. The border of the row or column heading is doubled to mark the location of hidden rows or columns.

A worksheet often is hidden when the entire worksheet contains data that is not of interest to the reader and is better summarized elsewhere in the document. To hide a worksheet, make that worksheet active, click the Format button in the Cells group on the Home tab, point to Hide & Unhide, and then click Hide Sheet.

Unhiding redisplays the hidden content in the workbook. To unhide a row or column, click in a cell below the hidden row or to the right of the hidden column, click the Format button, point to Hide & Unhide, and then click Unhide Rows or Unhide Columns. To unhide a worksheet, click the Format button, point to Hide & Unhide, and then click Unhide Sheet. The Unhide dialog box opens. Click the sheet you want to unhide, and then click the OK button. The hidden content is redisplayed in the workbook.

Although hiding data can make a worksheet and workbook easier to read, be sure never to hide information that is important to the reader.

Peter wants you to add the store ID used by Game Card to identify each item it sells. You will use Flash Fill to create these unique IDs.

Using Flash Fill

Flash Fill enters text based on patterns it finds in the data. As shown in Figure 1-33, Flash Fill generates customer names from the first and last names stored in the adjacent columns in the worksheet. To enter the rest of the names, you press the Enter key; to continue typing the names yourself, you press the Esc key.

Figure 1-33   **Text being entered with Flash Fill**

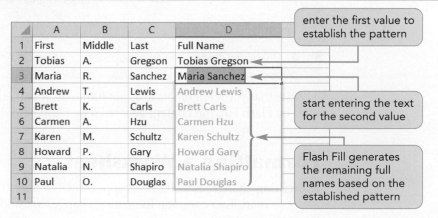

	A	B	C	D
1	First	Middle	Last	Full Name
2	Tobias	A.	Gregson	Tobias Gregson
3	Maria	R.	Sanchez	Maria Sanchez
4	Andrew	T.	Lewis	Andrew Lewis
5	Brett	K.	Carls	Brett Carls
6	Carmen	A.	Hzu	Carmen Hzu
7	Karen	M.	Schultz	Karen Schultz
8	Howard	P.	Gary	Howard Gary
9	Natalia	N.	Shapiro	Natalia Shapiro
10	Paul	O.	Douglas	Paul Douglas
11				

enter the first value to establish the pattern

start entering the text for the second value

Flash Fill generates the remaining full names based on the established pattern

Flash Fill works best when the pattern is clearly recognized from the values in the data. Be sure to enter the data pattern in the column or row right next to the related data. The data used to generate the pattern must be in a rectangular grid and cannot have blank columns or rows.

The store IDs used by Game Card combines the Stock ID and the first name of the item. For example, the Kings and Jacks game has a Stock ID of SG71, so its Store ID is SG71-Kings. Rather than typing this for every item in the customer order, you'll use Flash Fill to complete the data entry.

To enter the Store IDs using Flash Fill:

1. Click cell **A18**, type **Store ID** as the label, and then press the **Enter** key. The label is entered in cell A18, and cell A19 is now the active cell.

2. Type **SG71-Kings** as the Store ID, and then press **Enter** to make cell A20 active.

3. Type **FG** in cell A20. As soon as you complete those two characters Flash Fill generates the remaining entries in the column based on the pattern you entered. See Figure 1-34.

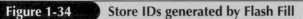

| Figure 1-34 | Store IDs generated by Flash Fill |

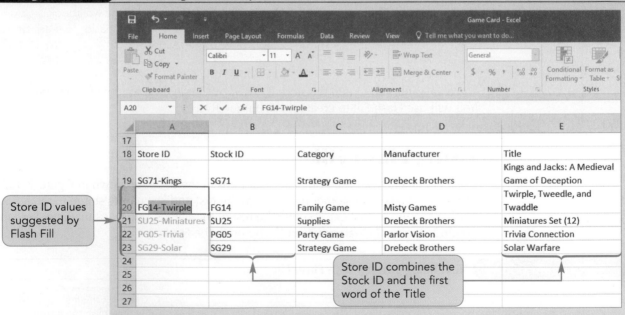

4. Press the **Enter** key to accept the suggested entries.

Note that Flash Fill enters text, not formulas. If you edit or replace an entry originally used by Flash Fill, the content generated by Flash Fill will not be updated.

Formatting a Worksheet

Formatting changes a workbook's appearance to make the content of a worksheet easier to read. Two common formatting changes are adding cell borders and changing the font size of text.

Adding Cell Borders

Sometimes you want to include lines along the edges of cells to enhance the readability of rows and columns of data. You can do this by adding a border to the left, top, right, or bottom edge of a cell or range. You can also specify the thickness of and the number of lines in the border. This is especially helpful when a worksheet is printed because the gridlines that surround the cells are not printed by default; they appear on the worksheet only as a guide.

Peter wants to add borders around the cells that contain content in the Customer Order worksheet to make the content easier to read.

To add borders around the worksheet cells:

1. Select the range **A3:B7**. You will add borders around all of the cells in the selected range.

2. On the Home tab, in the Font group, click the **Borders button arrow** ▦ ▾, and then click **All Borders**. Borders are added around each cell in the range. The Borders button changes to reflect the last selected border option, which in this case is All Borders. The name of the selected border option appears in the button's ScreenTip.

3. Select the nonadjacent range **A9:B16,H17:I17**. You will add borders around each cell in the selected range.

4. In the Font group, click the **All Borders** button ▦ to add borders to all of the cells in the selected range.

5. Select the nonadjacent range **A18:I23,H25:I28**, and then click the **All Borders** button ▦ to add borders to all of the cells in the selected range.

6. Click cell **A28** to deselect the cells. Figure 1-35 shows the borders added to the worksheet cells.

Figure 1-35   Borders added to cells

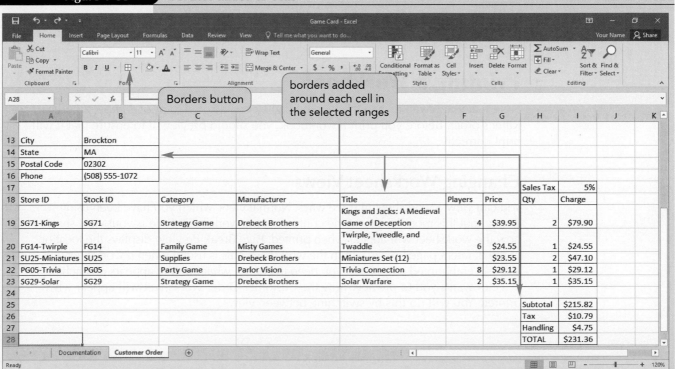

Changing the Font Size

Changing the size of text in a sheet provides a way to identify different parts of a worksheet, such as distinguishing a title or section heading from data. The size of the text is referred to as the font size and is measured in points. The default font size for worksheets is 11 points, but it can be made larger or smaller as needed. You can resize text in selected cells using the Font Size button in the Font group on the Home tab. You can also use the Increase Font Size and Decrease Font Size buttons to resize cell content to the next higher or lower standard font size.

Peter wants you to increase the size of the worksheet title to 26 points to make it more prominent.

To change the font size of the worksheet title:

1. Click cell **A1** to select the cell containing the worksheet title.

2. On the Home tab, in the Font group, click the **Font Size button arrow** [11 ▾] to display a list of font sizes, and then click **28**. The worksheet title changes to 28 points. See Figure 1-36.

Figure 1-36	Font size of the cell increased

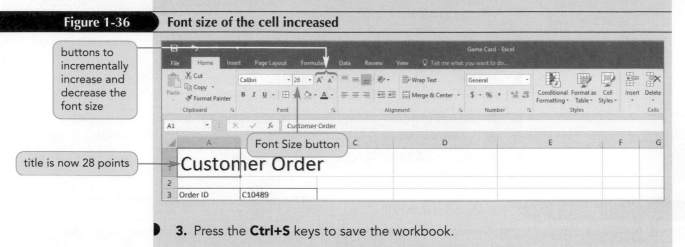

buttons to incrementally increase and decrease the font size

title is now 28 points

3. Press the **Ctrl+S** keys to save the workbook.

Printing a Workbook

Now that you have finished the workbook, Peter wants you to print a copy of Leslie Ritter's order. Before you print a workbook, you should preview it to ensure that it will print correctly.

Changing Worksheet Views

You can view a worksheet in three ways. Normal view, which you have been using throughout this module, shows the contents of the worksheet. Page Layout view shows how the worksheet will appear when printed. Page Break Preview displays the location of the different page breaks within the worksheet. This is useful when a worksheet will span several printed pages, and you need to control what content appears on each page.

Peter wants you to preview how the Customer Order worksheet will appear when printed. You will do this by switching between views.

To switch the Customer Order worksheet to different views:

1. Click the **Page Layout** button on the status bar. The page layout of the worksheet appears in the workbook window.

2. On the Zoom slider, click the **Zoom Out** button until the percentage is **50%**. The reduced magnification makes it clear that the worksheet will spread over two pages when printed. See Figure 1-37.

| Figure 1-37 | Worksheet in Page Layout view |

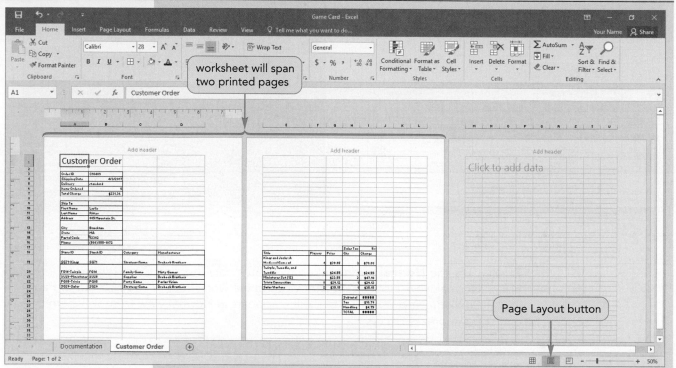

TIP

You can relocate a page break by dragging the dotted blue border in the Page Break Preview window.

3. Click the **Page Break Preview** button on the status bar. The view switches to Page Break Preview, which shows only those parts of the current worksheet that will print. A dotted blue border separates one page from another.

4. Zoom the worksheet to **70%** so that you can more easily read the contents of the worksheet. See Figure 1-38.

Figure 1-38   **Worksheet in Page Break Preview**

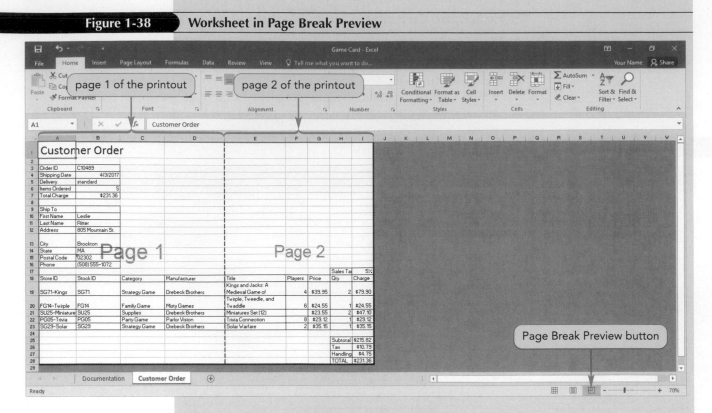

5. Click the **Normal** button ⊞ on the status bar. The worksheet returns to Normal view. Notice that after viewing the worksheet in Page Layout or Page Break Preview, a dotted black line appears in Normal view to show where the page breaks occurs.

Changing the Page Orientation

Page orientation specifies in which direction content is printed on the page. In **portrait orientation**, the page is taller than it is wide. In **landscape orientation**, the page is wider than it is tall. By default, Excel displays pages in portrait orientation. Changing the page orientation affects only the active sheet or sheets.

As you saw in Page Layout view and Page Break Preview, the Customer Order worksheet will print on two pages—columns A through D will print on the first page, and columns E through I will print on the second page, although the columns that print on each page may differ slightly depending on the printer. Peter wants the entire worksheet to print on a single page, so you'll change the page orientation from portrait to landscape.

To change the page orientation of the worksheet:

1. On the ribbon, click the **Page Layout** tab. The tab includes options for changing how the worksheet is arranged.

2. In the Page Setup group, click the **Orientation** button, and then click **Landscape**. The worksheet switches to landscape orientation.

3. Click the **Page Layout** button ▣ on the status bar to switch to Page Layout view. The worksheet will still print on two pages.

Setting the Scaling Options

You can force the printout to a single page by **scaling** the printed output. There are several options for scaling your printout. You can scale the width or the height of the printout so that all of the columns or all of the rows fit on a single page. You can also scale the printout to fit the entire worksheet (both columns and rows) on a single page. If the worksheet is too large to fit on one page, you can scale the print to fit on the number of pages you select. You can also scale the worksheet to a percentage of its size. For example, scaling a worksheet to 50% reduces the size of the sheet by half when it is sent to the printer. When scaling a printout, make sure that the worksheet is still readable after it is resized. Scaling affects only the active worksheet, so you can scale each worksheet to best fit its contents.

Peter asks you to scale the printout so that all of the Customer Order worksheet fits on one page in landscape orientation.

To scale the printout of the Customer Order worksheet:

1. On the Page Layout tab, in the Scale to Fit group, click the **Width** arrow, and then click **1 page** on the menu that appears. All of the columns in the worksheet now fit on one page.

   If more rows are added to the worksheet, Peter wants to ensure that they still fit within a single sheet.

2. In the Scale to Fit group, click the **Height** arrow, and then click **1 page**. All of the rows in the worksheet now fit on one page. See Figure 1-39.

Figure 1-39	Printout scaled to fit on one page

Setting the Print Options

TIP

To print the gridlines or the column and row headings, click the corresponding Print check box in the Sheet Options group on the Page Layout tab.

You can print the contents of a workbook by using the Print screen in Backstage view. The Print screen provides options for choosing where to print, what to print, and how to print. For example, you can specify the number of copies to print, which printer to use, and what to print. You can choose to print only the selected cells, only the active sheets, or all of the worksheets in the workbook that contain data. The printout will include only the data in the worksheet. The other elements in the worksheet, such as the row and column headings and the gridlines around the worksheet cells, will not print by default. The preview shows you exactly how the printed pages will look with the current settings. You should always preview before printing to ensure that the printout looks exactly as you intended and avoid unnecessary reprinting.

Peter asks you to preview and print the customer order workbook now.

Note: Check with your instructor first to make sure you should complete the steps for printing the workbook.

To preview and print the workbook:

1. On the ribbon, click the **File** tab to display Backstage view.

2. Click **Print** in the navigation bar. The Print screen appears with the print options and a preview of the Customer Order worksheet printout. See Figure 1-40.

Figure 1-40   **Print screen in Backstage view**

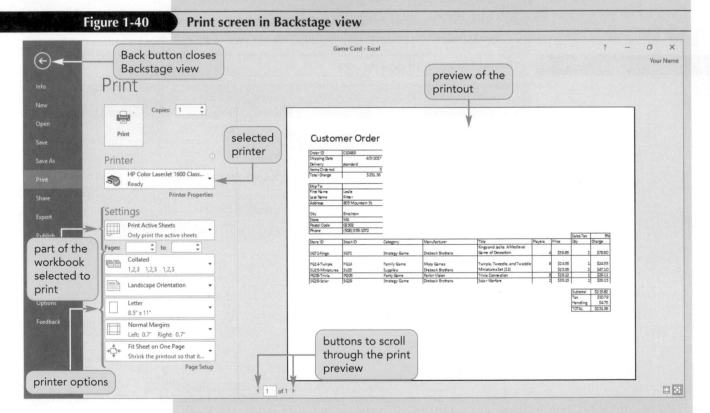

3. Click the **Printer** button, and then click the **printer** to which you want to print, if it is not already selected. By default, Excel will print only the active sheet.

4. In the Settings options, click the top button, and then click **Print Entire Workbook** to print all of the sheets in the workbook—in this case, both the Documentation and the Customer Order worksheets. The preview shows the first sheet in the workbook—the Documentation worksheet. Note that this sheet is still in the default portrait orientation.

5. Below the preview, click the **Next Page** button ▶ to view the Customer Order worksheet. As you can see, the Customer Order worksheet will print on a single page in landscape orientation.

6. If you are instructed to print, click the **Print** button to send the contents of the workbook to the specified printer. If you are not instructed to print, click the **Back** button ⬅ in the navigation bar to exit Backstage view.

Viewing Worksheet Formulas

Most of the time, you will be interested in only the final results of a worksheet, not the formulas used to calculate those results. However, in some cases, you might want to view the formulas used to develop the workbook. This is particularly useful when you encounter unexpected results and you want to examine the underlying formulas, or you want to discuss your formulas with a colleague. You can display the formulas instead of the resulting values in cells.

If you print the worksheet while the formulas are displayed, the printout shows the formulas instead of the values. To make the printout easier to read, you should print the worksheet gridlines as well as the row and column headings so that cell references in the formulas are easy to find in the printed version of the worksheet.

You will look at the Customer Order worksheet with the formulas displayed.

To display the cell formulas:

1. Make sure the Customer Order worksheet is in Page Layout view.

TIP

You can also display formulas in a worksheet by clicking the Show Formulas button in the Formula Auditing group on the Formulas tab.

2. Press the **Ctrl+`** keys (the grave accent symbol ` is usually located above the Tab key). The worksheet changes to display all of the formulas instead of the resulting values. Notice that the columns widen to display all of the formula text in the cells.

3. Look at the entry in cell B4. The underlying numeric value of the shipping date (42828) is displayed instead of the formatted date value (4/3/2017). See Figure 1-41.

| Figure 1-41 | Worksheet with formulas displayed |

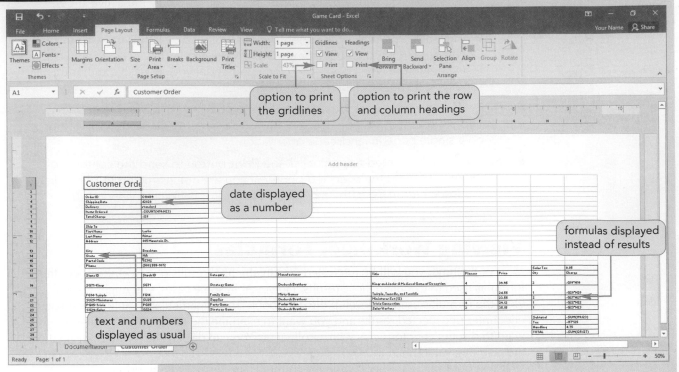

It's good practice to hide the formulas when you are done reviewing them.

▶ **4.** Press the **Ctrl+`** keys to hide the formulas and display the resulting values.

▶ **5.** Click the **Normal** button ▦ on the status bar to return the workbook to Normal view.

Saving a Workbook with a New Filename

Whenever you click the Save button on the Quick Access Toolbar or press the Ctrl+S keys, the workbook file is updated to reflect the latest content. If you want to save a copy of the workbook with a new filename or to a different location, you need to use the Save As command. When you save a workbook with a new filename or to a different location, the previous version of the workbook remains stored as well.

You have completed the customer order workbook for Game Card. Peter wants to use the workbook as a model for other customer order reports. You will save the workbook with a new filename to avoid overwriting the Leslie Ritter order. Then you'll clear the information related to that order, leaving the formulas intact. This new, revised workbook will then be ready for the next customer order.

To save the workbook with a new filename:

▶ **1.** Press the **Ctrl+S** keys to save the workbook. This ensures that the final copy of the workbook contains the formatted version of Leslie Ritter's order.

▶ **2.** On the ribbon, click the **File** tab to display Backstage view, and then click **Save As** on the navigation bar. The Save As screen is displayed.

TIP

Save the workbook with the new name before making changes to avoid inadvertently saving your edits to the wrong file.

3. Click the **Browse** button. The Save As dialog box opens so you can save the workbook with a new filename or to a new location.

4. Navigate to the location specified by your instructor.

5. In the File name box, type **Game Card Order** as the new filename.

6. Click the **Save** button. The workbook is saved with the new filename, and you are returned to the workbook window.

7. Select the range **B3:B5**, right-click the selected range to open the shortcut menu, and then click **Clear Contents** to clear the contents of the order ID, shipping date, and delivery cells.

8. Select the nonadjacent range **B10:B16,A19:H23**, and then press the **Delete** key to clear the contact information for Leslie Ritter and the list of items she ordered.

9. Select cell **I27**, and then clear the handling fee.

10. Click cell **A3** to make that cell the active cell the next time this workbook is opened.

11. Press the **Ctrl+S** keys to save the workbook.

12. Click the **Close** button ☒ on the title bar (or press the **Ctrl+W** keys). The workbook closes, and the Excel program closes.

Peter is pleased with the workbook you created. With the calculations already in place in the new workbook, he will be able to quickly enter new customer orders and see the calculated charges without having to recreate the worksheet.

Session 1.2 Quick Check

REVIEW

1. What formula would you enter to add the values in cells C1, C2, and C3? What function would you enter to achieve the same result?

2. What formula would you enter to count how many numeric values are in the range D21:D72?

3. If you insert cells into the range C1:D10, shifting the cells to the right, what is the new location of the data that was previously in cell F4?

4. Cell E11 contains the formula =SUM(D1:D20). How does this formula change if a new row is inserted above row 5?

5. Describe four ways of viewing the content of a workbook in Excel.

6. How are page breaks indicated in Page Break Preview?

7. What orientation would you use to make the printed page wider than it is tall?

8. How do you display the formulas used in a worksheet instead of the formula results?

Review Assignments

There are no Data Files needed for the Review Assignment.

Game Card also buys and resells used games and gaming supplies. Peter wants to use Excel to record recent used purchases made by the store. The workbook should list every item the company has ordered, provide information about the item, and calculate the total order cost. Complete the following:

1. Create a new, blank workbook, and then save the workbook as **Game List** in the location specified by your instructor.
2. Rename the Sheet1 worksheet as **Documentation**, and then enter the data shown in Figure 1-42 in the specified cells.

Figure 1-42   **Documentation sheet data**

Cell	Text
A1	Game Card
A3	Author
A4	Date
A5	Purpose
B3	*your name*
B4	*current date*
B5	To record game acquisitions for Game Card

---

3. Set the font size of the title text in cell A1 to **28** points.
4. Add a new worksheet after the Documentation sheet, and then rename the sheet as **Game Purchases**.
5. In cell A1, enter the text **Game Purchases**. Set the font size of this text to **28** points.
6. In cell A3, enter the text **Date** as the label. In cell B3, enter the date **4/3/2017**.
7. In the range A5:F10, enter the data shown in Figure 1-43.

Figure 1-43   **Game list**

Purchase Number	Category	Manufacturer	Title	Players	Cost
83	Strategy Game	Drebeck Brothers	Secrets of Flight: Building an Airforce	6	$29.54
84	Family Game	Parlor Vision	Brain Busters and Logic Gaming	8	$14.21
85	Strategy Game	Aspect Gaming	Inspection Deduction	3	$18.91
86	Party Game	Miller Games	Bids and Buys	8	$10.81
87	Family Game	Aspect Gaming	Buzz Up	4	$21.43

---

8. Insert cells into the range A5:A10, shifting the other cells to the right.
9. In cell A5, enter **Stock ID** as the label. In cell A6, enter **SG83** as the first Stock ID, and then type **FG** in cell A7, allowing Flash Fill to enter the remaining Stock IDs.
10. Set the width of column A to **12** characters, columns B through D to **18** characters, and column E to **25** characters.
11. Wrap text in the range E6:E10 so that the longer game titles appear on multiple lines within the cells.

12. Autofit the heights of rows 5 through 10.

13. Move the game list in the range A5:G10 to the range A8:G13.

14. In cell F15, enter **TOTAL** as the label. In cell G15, enter a formula with the SUM function to calculate the sum of the costs in the range G9:G13.

15. In cell A4, enter **Total Items** as the label. In cell B4, enter a formula with the COUNT function to count the number of numeric values in the range G9:G13.

16. In cell A5, enter **Total Cost**. In cell B5, enter a formula to display the value from cell G15.

17. In cell A6, enter **Average Cost** as the label. In cell B6, enter a formula that divides the total cost of the purchased games (listed in cell B5) by the number of games purchased (listed in cell B4).

18. Add borders around each cell in the nonadjacent range A3:B6,A8:G13,F15:G15.

19. For the Game Purchases worksheet, change the page orientation to landscape and scale the worksheet to print on a single page for both the width and the height. If you are instructed to print, print the entire workbook.

20. Display the formulas in the Game Purchases worksheet. If you are instructed to print, print the entire worksheet.

21. Save and close the workbook.

Case Problem 1

Data File needed for this Case Problem: Donation.xlsx

Henderson Pediatric Care Center   Kari Essen is a fundraising coordinator for the Pediatric Care Center located in Henderson, West Virginia. Kari is working on a report detailing recent donations to the center and wants you to enter this data into an Excel workbook. Complete the following:

1. Open the **Donation** workbook located in the Excel1 > Case1 folder included with your Data Files. Save the workbook as **Donation List** in the location specified by your instructor.

2. In the Documentation sheet, enter your name in cell B3 and the date in cell B4.

3. Increase the font size of the text in cell A1 to 28 points.

4. Add a new sheet to the end of the workbook, and rename it as **Donor List**.

5. In cell A1 of the Donor List worksheet, enter **Donor List** as the title, and then set the font size to 28 points.

6. In the range A6:H13, enter the donor information shown in Figure 1-44. Enter the ZIP code data as text rather than as numbers.

Figure 1-44   Donation list

Last Name	First Name	Street	City	State	ZIP	Phone	Donation
Robert	Richards	389 Felton Avenue	Miami	FL	33127	(305) 555-5685	$150
Barbara	Hopkins	612 Landers Street	Caledonia	IL	61011	(815) 555-5865	$75
Daniel	Vaughn	45 Lyman Street	Statesboro	GA	30461	(912) 555-8564	$50
Parker	Penner	209 South Street	San Francisco	CA	94118	(415) 555-7298	$250
Kenneth	More	148 7th Street	Newberry	IN	47449	(812) 555-8001	$325
Robert	Simmons	780 10th Street	Houston	TX	77035	(713) 555-5266	$75
Donna	Futrell	834 Kimberly Lane	Ropesville	TX	79358	(806) 555-6186	$50

7. Set the width of columns A through D to 25 characters. Set the width of column G to 15 characters.

8. In cell A2, enter the text **Total Donors**. In cell A3, enter the text **Total Donations**. In cell A4, enter the text **Average Donation**.

9. In cell B2, enter a formula that counts how many numeric values are in the range H7:H13.

10. In cell B3, enter a formula that calculates the sum of the donations in the range H7:H13.

11. In cell B4, enter a formula that calculates the average donation by dividing the value in cell B3 by the value in cell B2.

12. Add borders around the nonadjacent range A2:B4,A6:H13.

13. Set the page orientation of the Donor List to landscape.

14. Scale the worksheet to print on a single page for both the width and the height. If you are instructed to print the worksheet, print the Donor List sheet.

15. Display the formulas in the Donor List worksheet. If you are instructed to print, print the worksheet.

16. Save and close the workbook.

Case Problem 2

CREATE

Data File needed for this Case Problem: Balance.xlsx

Scott Kahne Tool & Die   Cheryl Hippe is a financial officer at Scott Kahne Tool & Die, a manufacturing company located in Mankato, Minnesota. Every month the company publishes a balance sheet, a report that details the company's assets and liabilities. Cheryl asked you to create the workbook with the text and formulas for this report. Complete the following:

1. Open the **Balance** workbook located in the Excel1 > Case2 folder included with your Data Files. Save the workbook as **Balance Sheet** in the location specified by your instructor.

2. In the Documentation sheet, enter your name in cell B3 and the date in cell B4.

3. Go to the Balance Sheet worksheet. Set the font size of the title in cell A1 to 28 points.

4. In cell A2, enter the text **Statement for March 2017**.

5. Set the width of columns A and E to 30 characters. Set the width of columns B, C, F, and G to 12 characters. Set the width of column D to 4 characters. (*Hint:* Hold down the Ctrl key as you click the column headings to select both adjacent and nonadjacent columns.)

6. Set the font size of the text in cells A4, C4, E4, and G4 to 18 points.

7. Set the font size of the text in cells A5, E5, A11, E11, A14, E15, A19, E20, and A24 to 14 points.

8. Enter the values shown in Figure 1-45 in the specified cells.

Figure 1-45   Assets and liabilities

Current Assets	Cell	Value
Cash	B6	$123,000
Accounts Receivable	B7	$75,000
Inventories	B8	$58,000
Prepaid Insurance	B9	$15,000
Long-Term Investments	**Cell**	**Value**
Available Securities	B12	$29,000
Tangible Assets	**Cell**	**Value**
Land	B15	$49,000
Building and Equipment	B16	$188,000
Less Accumulated Depreciation	B17	-$48,000
Intangible Assets	**Cell**	**Value**
Goodwill	B20	$148,000
Other Assets	B22	$14,000
Current Liabilities	**Cell**	**Value**
Accounts Payable	F6	$62,000
Salaries	F7	$14,000
Interest	F8	$12,000
Notes Payable	F9	$38,000
Long-Term Liabilities	**Cell**	**Value**
Long-Term Notes Payable	F12	$151,000
Mortgage	F13	$103,000
Stockholders' Equity	**Cell**	**Value**
Capital Stock	F16	$178,000
Retained Earnings	F17	$98,000
Comprehensive Income/Loss	F18	-$5,000

9. In cell C9, enter a formula to calculate the sum of the Current Assets in the range B6:B9.
10. In cell C12, enter a formula to display the value of B12.
11. In cell C17, enter a formula to calculate the sum of the Tangible Assets in the range B15:B17.
12. In cells C20 and C22, enter formulas to display the values of cells B20 and B22, respectively.
13. In cell C24, enter a formula to calculate the total assets in the balance sheet by adding cells C9, C12, C17, C20, and C22. Set the font size of the cell to 14 points.
14. In cell G9, enter a formula to calculate the sum of the Current Liabilities in the range F6:F9.
15. In cell G13, enter a formula to calculate the sum of the Long-Term Liabilities in the range F12:F13.
16. In cell G18, enter a formula to calculate the sum of the Stockholders' Equity in the range F16:F18.
17. In cell G20, calculate the Total Liabilities and Equity for the company by adding the values of cells G9, G13, and G18. Set the font size of the cell to 14 points.
18. Check your calculations. In a balance sheet the total assets (cell C24) should equal the total liabilities and equity (cell G20).
19. Set the page layout orientation to landscape and the Balance Sheet worksheet to print to one page for both the width and height.
20. Preview the worksheet on the Print screen in Backstage view, and then save and close the workbook.

Case Problem 3

CHALLENGE

Data File needed for this Case Problem: FTP.xslx

Succeed Gym   Allison Palmer is the owner of Succeed Gym, an athletic club in Austin, Texas, that specializes in coaching men and women aspiring to participate in triathlons, marathons, and other endurance sports. During the winter, Allison runs an indoor cycling class in which she tracks the progress of each student's fitness. One measure of fitness is FTP (Functional Threshold Power). Allison has recorded FTP levels from her students over five races and wants you to use the functions described in Figure 1-46 to analyze this data so that she can track the progress of her class and of individual students.

Figure 1-46   **Excel functions**

Function	Description
=AVERAGE(*range*)	Calculates the average of the values from the specified *range*
=MEDIAN(*range*)	Calculates the median or midpoint of the values from the specified *range*
=MIN(*range*)	Calculates the minimum of the values from the specified *range*
=MAX(*range*)	Calculates the maximum of the values from the specified *range*

Complete the following:

1. Open the **FTP** workbook located the Excel1 > Case3 folder included with your Data Files. Save the workbook as **FTP Report** in the location specified by your instructor.
2. In the Documentation sheet, enter your name in cell B3 and the date in cell B4.
3. Go to the Race Results worksheet. Change the font size of the title in cell A1 to 28 points.
4. Set the width of column A and B to 15 characters. Set the width of column I to 2 characters.
5. In the range J4:M4, enter the labels **Median**, **Average**, **Min**, and **Max**.
⊕ **Explore** 6. In cell J5, use the MEDIAN function to calculate the median (midpoint) of the FTP values of races 1 through 5 for Diana Bartlett in the range D5:H5. Copy the formula in cell J5 to the range J6:J28 to calculate the median FTP values for the other riders.
⊕ **Explore** 7. In cell K5, use the AVERAGE function to calculate the average the FTP value for races 1 through 5 for Diana Bartlett. Copy the formula to calculate the averages for the other riders.
⊕ **Explore** 8. In cell L5, use the MIN function to return the minimum FTP value for Diana Bartlett. Copy the formula to calculate the minimums for the other riders.
⊕ **Explore** 9. In cell M5, use the MAX function to return the maximum FTP value for Diana Bartlett. Copy the formula to calculate the maximums for the other riders.
10. In the range C30:C33, enter the labels **Median**, **Average**, **Min**, and **Max** to record summary information for each of the five races.
11. In cell D30, use the MEDIAN function to calculate the median FTP value from the range D5:D28. Copy the formula to the range E30:H30 to determine the median values for the other four races.
12. In the range D31:H31, use the AVERAGE function to calculate the average FTP value for each race.
13. In the range D32:H32, use the MIN function to calculate the minimum value for each race.
14. In the range D33:H33, use the MAX function to calculate the maximum FTP value for each race.
15. Move the range A4:M33 to the range A10:M39 to create space for additional summary calculations at the top of the worksheet.

16. In the range A3:A7, enter the labels **Class Size**, **Class Average**, **Class Median**, **Class Minimum**, and **Class Maximum**.

✛ **Explore** 17. In cell B3, use the COUNTA function to count the number of entries in the range A11:A34.

18. In cell B4, use the AVERAGE function to calculate the average of all FTP values in the range D11:H34.

19. In cell B5, use the MEDIAN function to calculate the median of all FTP values in the range D11:H34.

20. In cell B6, use the MIN function to calculate the minimum FTP value in the range D11:H34.

21. In cell B7, use the MAX function to calculate the maximum FTP value in the range D11:H34.

22. Set the page layout orientation for the Race Results worksheet to portrait and scale the worksheet so that its width and height fit on one page.

23. View the worksheet in Page Layout view, return to Normal view, and then save and close the workbook.

TROUBLESHOOT

Case Problem 4

Data File needed for this Case Problem: Service.xlsx

Welch Home Appliance Repair Stefan Welch is the owner of Welch Home Appliance Repair in Trenton, New Jersey. Stefan wants to use Excel to record data from his service calls to calculate the total charge on each service call and the total charges from all service calls within a given period. Unfortunately, the workbook he has created contains several errors. He has asked you to fix the errors and complete the workbook. Complete the following:

1. Open the **Service** workbook located in the Excel1 > Case4 folder included with your Data Files. Save the workbook as **Service Calls** in the location specified by your instructor.

2. In the Documentation sheet, enter your name in cell B3 and the date in cell B4.

3. Go to the Call Sheet worksheet. Insert cells in the range A7:A27, shifting the other cells to the right.

4. In cell A7, enter **Cust ID** as the label. In cell A8, enter **Jensen-5864** (the customer's last name and last four digits on the phone number) as the customer ID for Patricia Jensen. Use Flash Fill to enter in the remaining customer IDs in the column.

5. Resize the columns of the Call Sheet worksheet so that all of the column labels and the cell contents are completely displayed.

⚙ **Troubleshoot** 6. There is a problem with the some of the customer ZIP codes. New Jersey ZIP codes begin with a 0, and these leading zeros are not showing up in the contact information. Revise the text of the ZIP code values to correct this problem.

⚙ **Troubleshoot** 7. The formula in cell L8 that calculates the total number of billable hours for the first customer is not correct. Instead of showing the number of hours, it displays the value as a percentage of a day. Fix this problem by revising the formula so that it multiplies the difference between the value in K8 and J8 by 24. (*Hint:* Use parentheses to enclose the expression that calculates the difference between starting and ending times so that the difference is calculated first.)

8. Copy the formula you entered for cell L8 to calculate the total billable hours for the rest of the entries in column L.

9. The total charge for each service call is equal to the hourly rate multiplied by the number of hours plus the charge for parts. In cell O8, enter a formula to calculate the total service charge for the first customer, and then copy that formula to calculate the rest of the service charges in column O.

10. In cell B4, enter a formula that uses the COUNT function to count the total number of service calls.

⚙ **Troubleshoot** 11. In cell B5, Stefan entered a formula to calculate the total charges from all of the service calls. Examine the formula, and correct the expression so that it adds all of the service call charges.

12. Insert two new rows above row 5.

13. In cell A5, enter the label **Total Hours**. In cell B5, enter function to calculate the total number of hours from all of the service calls.

14. In cell A6, enter the label **Average Charge**. In cell B6, enter a formula that calculates the average charge per call by dividing the total charges by the total number of calls.

15. Add borders around the cells in the nonadjacent range A4:B7,A9:O29.

16. Set the page layout of the Call Sheet worksheet so that it prints on a single page in landscape orientation.

17. View the worksheet in Page Break Preview, return to Normal view, and then save and close the workbook.

EXCEL

OBJECTIVES

Session 2.1
- Change fonts, font style, and font color
- Add fill colors and a background image
- Create formulas to calculate sales data
- Format numbers as currency and percentages
- Format dates and times
- Align, indent, and rotate cell contents
- Merge a group of cells

Session 2.2
- Use the AVERAGE function
- Apply cell styles
- Copy and paste formats with the Format Painter
- Find and replace text and formatting
- Change workbook themes
- Highlight cells with conditional formats
- Format a worksheet for printing
- Set the print area, insert page breaks, add print titles, create headers and footers, and set margins

Formatting Workbook Text and Data

Creating a Sales Report

Case | *Morning Bean*

Carol Evans is a sales manager at Morning Bean, a small but growing chain of shops specializing in coffee, tea, and other hot drinks. Carol needs to develop a workbook for the upcoming sales conference that will provide information on sales and profits for stores located in the Northwest region of the country. Carol already started the workbook by entering sales data for the previous years. She wants you to use this financial data to calculate summary statistics and then format the workbook before it's distributed to stockholders attending the conference.

STARTING DATA FILES

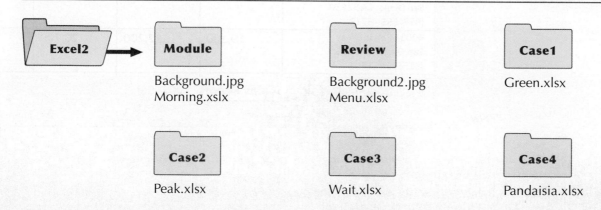

Excel2 →	Module	Review	Case1
	Background.jpg	Background2.jpg	Green.xlsx
	Morning.xslx	Menu.xlsx	

	Case2	Case3	Case4
	Peak.xlsx	Wait.xlsx	Pandaisia.xlsx

Session 2.1 Visual Overview:

The Font group has buttons for setting the font, font size, font color, and **font style**, such as **bold**, *italic*, or underline.

You can format text strings within a cell in Edit mode.

The Alignment group has buttons for setting horizontal and vertical alignment, orientation, and indents; wrapping text in cells; and merging cells.

Accounting format lines up numbers in a column by their currency symbol and decimal point; negative numbers are in parentheses.

A **font** is a set of characters that employ the same typeface, such as Arial, Times New Roman, and Courier.

You can **merge**, or combine, several cells into one cell. This content is centered in the merged range A11:A13.

You can rotate content in a cell.

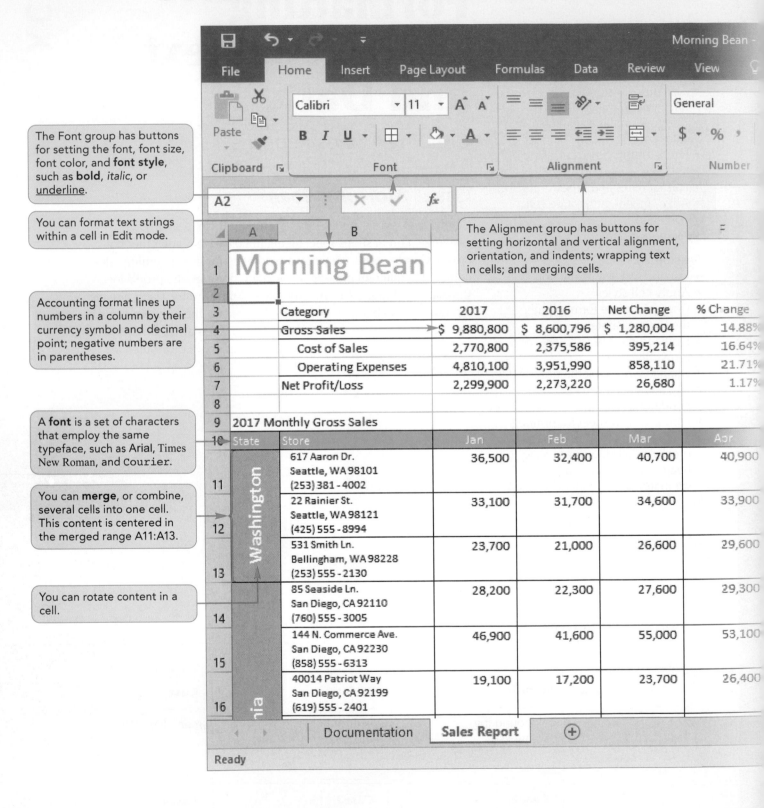

	Category	2017	2016	Net Change	% Change
	Gross Sales	$ 9,880,800	$ 8,600,796	$ 1,280,004	14.88%
	Cost of Sales	2,770,800	2,375,586	395,214	16.64%
	Operating Expenses	4,810,100	3,951,990	858,110	21.71%
	Net Profit/Loss	2,299,900	2,273,220	26,680	1.17%

2017 Monthly Gross Sales

State	Store	Jan	Feb	Mar	Apr
Washington	617 Aaron Dr. Seattle, WA 98101 (253) 381-4002	36,500	32,400	40,700	40,900
	22 Rainier St. Seattle, WA 98121 (425) 555-8994	33,100	31,700	34,600	33,900
	531 Smith Ln. Bellingham, WA 98228 (253) 555-2130	23,700	21,000	26,600	29,600
	85 Seaside Ln. San Diego, CA 92110 (760) 555-3005	28,200	22,300	27,600	29,300
	144 N. Commerce Ave. San Diego, CA 92230 (858) 555-6313	46,900	41,600	55,000	53,100
	40014 Patriot Way San Diego, CA 92199 (619) 555-2401	19,100	17,200	23,700	26,400

Documentation   Sales Report

Ready

Formatting a Worksheet

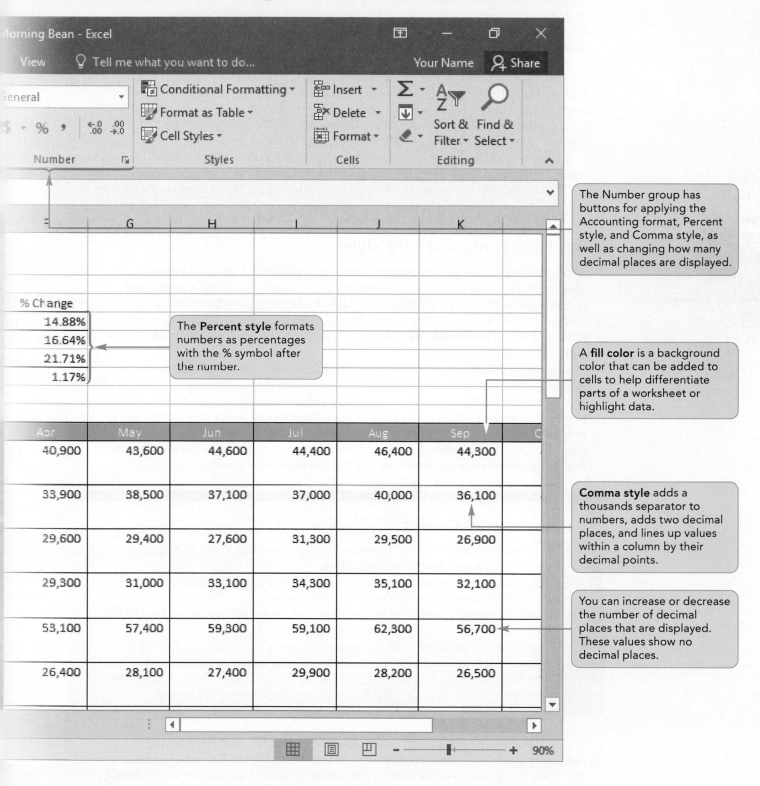

The Number group has buttons for applying the Accounting format, Percent style, and Comma style, as well as changing how many decimal places are displayed.

The **Percent style** formats numbers as percentages with the % symbol after the number.

A **fill color** is a background color that can be added to cells to help differentiate parts of a worksheet or highlight data.

Comma style adds a thousands separator to numbers, adds two decimal places, and lines up values within a column by their decimal points.

You can increase or decrease the number of decimal places that are displayed. These values show no decimal places.

% Change
14.88%
16.64%
21.71%
1.17%

Apr	May	Jun	Jul	Aug	Sep	
40,900	43,600	44,600	44,400	46,400	44,300	
33,900	38,500	37,100	37,000	40,000	36,100	
29,600	29,400	27,600	31,300	29,500	26,900	
29,300	31,000	33,100	34,300	35,100	32,100	
53,100	57,400	59,300	59,100	62,300	56,700	
26,400	28,100	27,400	29,900	28,200	26,500	

Formatting Cell Text

You can improve the readability of workbooks by choosing the fonts, styles, colors, and decorative features that are used in the workbook and within worksheet cells. Formatting changes only the appearance of the workbook data—it does not affect the data itself.

Excel organizes complementary formatting options into themes. A **theme** is a collection of formatting for text, colors, and effects that give a workbook a unique look and feel. The Office theme is applied to workbooks by default, but you can apply another theme or create your own. You can also add formatting to a workbook using colors, fonts, and effects that are not part of the current theme. Note that a theme is applied to the entire workbook and can be shared between workbooks.

To help you choose the best formatting for your workbooks, **Live Preview** shows the results of each formatting option before you apply it to your workbook.

Carol wants you to format the Morning Bean sales report. You'll use Live Preview to see how the workbook looks with different formatting options.

Applying Fonts and Font Styles

A font is a set of characters that share a common appearance by employing the same typeface. Excel organizes fonts into theme and nontheme fonts. A **theme font** is associated with a particular theme and used for headings and body text in the workbook. Theme fonts change automatically when the theme is changed. Text formatted with a **nontheme font** retains its appearance no matter what theme is used with the workbook.

Fonts are classified based on their character style. **Serif fonts**, such as Times New Roman, have extra strokes at the end of each character that aid in reading passages of text. **Sans serif fonts**, such as Arial, do not include these extra strokes. Other fonts are purely decorative, such as a font used for specialized logos. Every font can be further formatted with a font style such as *italic*, **bold**, or ***bold italic***; with <u>underline</u>; and with special effects such as ~~strikethrough~~ and color. You can also increase or decrease the font size to emphasize the importance of the text within the workbook.

REFERENCE

Formatting Cell Content

- To set the font, select the cell or range. On the Home tab, in the Font group, click the Font arrow, and then select a font.
- To set the font size, select the cell or range. On the Home tab, in the Font group, click the Font Size arrow, and then select a font size.
- To set the font style, select the cell or range. On the Home tab, in the Font group, click the Bold, Italic, or Underline button.
- To set the font color, select the cell or range. On the Home tab, in the Font group, click the Font Color button arrow, and then select a theme or nontheme color.
- To format a text selection, double-click the cell to enter Edit mode, select the text to format, change the font, size, style, or color, and then press the Enter key.

Carol already entered the data and some formulas in her workbook for the upcoming conference. The Documentation sheet describes her workbook's purpose and content. At the top of the sheet is the company name. Carol wants you to format the name in large, bold letters using the default heading font from the Office theme.

To the format the company name:

▶ 1. Open the **Morning** workbook located in the **Excel2 > Module** folder included with your Data Files, and then save the workbook as **Morning Bean** in the location specified by your instructor.

▶ 2. In the Documentation sheet, enter your name in cell B4 and the date in cell B5.

▶ 3. Click cell **A1** to make it the active cell.

▶ 4. On the Home tab, in the Font group, click the **Font button arrow** to display a gallery of fonts available on your computer. Each name is displayed in its font. The first two fonts listed are the theme fonts for headings and body text–Calibri Light and Calibri.

▶ 5. Scroll down the Fonts gallery until you see Bauhaus 93 in the All Fonts list, and then point to **Bauhaus 93** (or another font). Live Preview shows the effect of the Bauhaus 93 font on the text in cell A1. See Figure 2-1.

| Figure 2-1 | Font gallery |

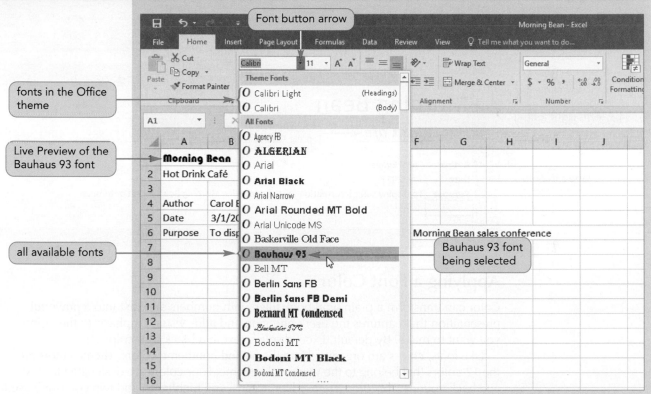

▶ 6. Point to three other fonts in the list to see the Live Preview of how the text in cell A1 would look with that font.

▶ 7. Click **Calibri Light** in the Theme Fonts list. The company name in cell A1 changes to the Calibri Light Font, the default headings font in the current theme.

▶ 8. In the Font group, click the **Font Size button arrow** 11 ▾ to display a list of font sizes, point to **26** to preview the text in that font size, and then click **26**. The company name changes to 26 points.

▶ 9. In the Font group, click the **Bold** button B (or press **Ctrl+B** keys). The text changes to bold.

▶ **10.** Click cell **A2** to make it the active cell. The cell with the company description is selected.

▶ **11.** In the Font group, click the **Font Size button arrow** 11 ▾ , and then click **18**. The company description changes to 18 points.

▶ **12.** In the Font group, click the **Italic** button *I* (or press the **Ctrl+I** keys). The company description in cell A2 is italicized.

▶ **13.** Select the range **A4:A6**, and then press the **Ctrl+B** keys. The text in the selected range changes to bold.

▶ **14.** Click cell **A7** to deselect the range. See Figure 2-2.

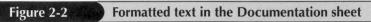

Figure 2-2   **Formatted text in the Documentation sheet**

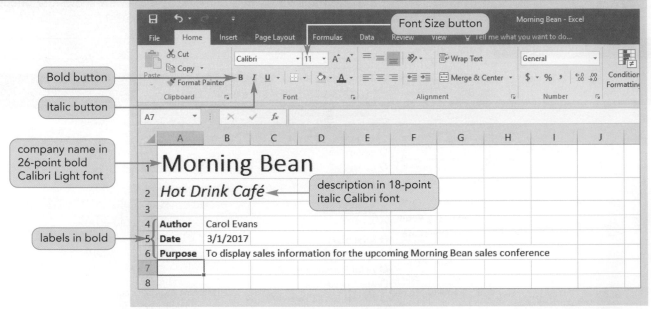

Applying a Font Color

Color can transform a plain workbook filled with numbers and text into a powerful presentation that captures the user's attention and adds visual emphasis to the points you want to make. By default, Excel displays text in a black font color.

Like fonts, colors are organized into theme and nontheme colors. **Theme colors** are the 12 colors that belong to the workbook's theme. Four colors are designated for text and backgrounds, six colors are used for accents and highlights, and two colors are used for hyperlinks (followed and not followed links). These 12 colors are designed to work well together and to remain readable in all combinations. Each theme color has five variations, or accents, in which a different tint or shading is applied to the theme color.

Ten **standard colors**—dark red, red, orange, yellow, light green, green, light blue, blue, dark blue, and purple—are always available regardless of the workbook's theme. You can open an extended palette of 134 standard colors. You can also create a custom color by specifying a mixture of red, blue, and green color values, making available 16.7 million custom colors—more colors than the human eye can distinguish. Some dialog boxes have an automatic color option that uses your Windows default text and background colors, usually black text on a white background.

INSIGHT

Creating Custom Colors

Custom colors let you add subtle and striking colors to a formatted workbook. To create custom colors, you use the **RGB Color model** in which each color is expressed with varying intensities of red, green, and blue. RGB color values are often represented as a set of numbers in the format

`(red, green, blue)`

where `red` is an intensity value assigned to red light, `green` is an intensity value assigned to green light, and `blue` is an intensity value assigned to blue light. The intensities are measured on a scale of 0 to 255—0 indicates no intensity (or the absence of the color) and 255 indicates the highest intensity. So, the RGB color value (255, 255, 0) represents a mixture of high-intensity red (255) and high-intensity green (255) with the absence of blue (0), which creates the color yellow.

To create colors in Excel using the RGB model, click the More Colors option located in a color menu or dialog box to open the Colors dialog box. In the Colors dialog box, click the Custom tab, and then enter the red, green, and blue intensity values. A preview box shows the resulting RGB color.

Carol wants the company name and description in the Documentation sheet to stand out. You will change the text in cell A1 and cell A2 to green.

To change the font color of the company name and description:

1. Select the range **A1:A2**.

2. On the Home tab, in the Font group, click the **Font Color button arrow** to display the gallery of theme and standard colors.

3. In the Standard Colors section, point to the **Green** color (the sixth color). The color name appears in a ScreenTip, and you see a Live Preview of the text with the green font color. See Figure 2-3.

| Figure 2-3 | Font Color gallery |

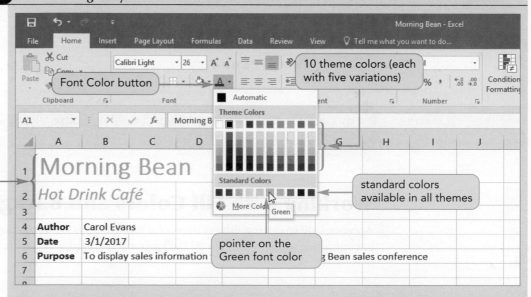

4. Click the **Green** color. The company name and description change to green.

Formatting Text Selections Within a Cell

In Edit mode, you can select and format selections of text within a cell. You can make these changes to selected text from the ribbon or from the Mini toolbar. The **Mini toolbar** contains buttons for common formatting options used for that selection. These same buttons appear on the ribbon.

Carol asks you to format the company name in cell A1 so that the text "Morning" appears in gold.

To format part of the company name in cell A1:

▸ 1. Double-click cell **A1** to select the cell and enter Edit mode (or click cell **A1** and press the **F2** key). The status bar shows Edit to indicate that you are working with the cell in Edit mode. The pointer changes to the I-beam pointer.

▸ 2. Drag the pointer over the word **Morning** to select it. A Mini toolbar appears above the selected text with buttons to change the font, size, style, and color of the selected text in the cell. In this instance, you want to change the font color.

▸ 3. On the Mini toolbar, click the **Font Color button arrow** 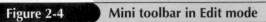, and then in the Themes Colors section, point to the **Gold, Accent 4** color (the eighth color). Live Preview shows the color of the selected text as gold. See Figure 2-4.

Figure 2-4	Mini toolbar in Edit mode

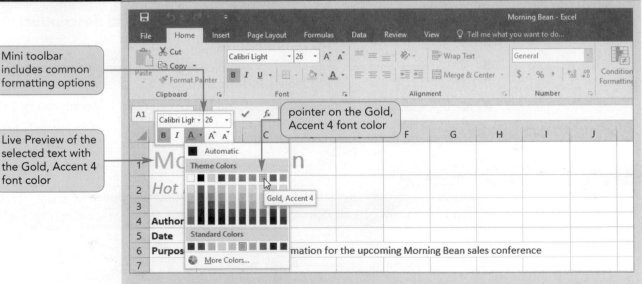

Mini toolbar includes common formatting options

Live Preview of the selected text with the Gold, Accent 4 font color

pointer on the Gold, Accent 4 font color

▸ 4. Click the **Gold, Accent 4** color. The Mini toolbar closes and the selected text changes to the gold color.

Working with Fill Colors and Backgrounds

Another way to distinguish sections of a worksheet is by formatting the cell background. You can fill the cell background with color or an image.

Changing a Fill Color

By default, worksheet cells do not include any background color. But background colors, also known as fill colors, can be helpful for distinguishing different parts of a worksheet or adding visual interest. The same selection of colors used to format the color of cell text can be used to format the cell background.

INSIGHT

Using Color to Enhance a Workbook

When used wisely, color can enhance any workbook. However, when used improperly, color can distract the user, making the workbook more difficult to read. As you format a workbook, keep in mind the following tips:

- Use colors from the same theme to maintain a consistent look and feel across the worksheets. If the built-in themes do not fit your needs, you can create a custom theme.
- Use colors to differentiate types of cell content and to direct users where to enter data. For example, format a worksheet so that formula results appear in cells without a fill color and users enter data in cells with a light gray fill color.
- Avoid color combinations that are difficult to read.
- Print the workbook on both color and black-and-white printers to ensure that the printed copy is readable in both versions.
- Understand your printer's limitations and features. Colors that look good on your monitor might not look as good when printed.
- Be sensitive to your audience. About 8 percent of all men and 0.5 percent of all women have some type of color blindness and might not be able to see the text when certain color combinations are used. Red-green color blindness is the most common, so avoid using red text on a green background or green text on a red background.

Carol wants you to change the background color of the range A4:A6 in the Documentation sheet to green and the font color to white.

To change the font and fill colors in the Documentation sheet:

1. Select the range **A4:A6**.

2. On the Home tab, in the Font group, click the **Fill Color button arrow** ⬙ ⌄, and then click the **Green** color (the sixth color) in the Standard Colors section.

3. In the Font group, click the **Font Color button arrow** 🅰 ⌄, and then click the **White, Background 1** color (the first color) in the Theme Colors section. The labels are formatted as white text on a green background.

4. Select the range **B4:B6**, and then format the cells with the **Green** font color and the **White, Background 1** fill color.

5. Increase the width of column B to **30** characters, and then wrap the text within the selected range.

6. Select the range **A4:B6**, and then add all borders around each of the selected cells.

7. Click cell **A7** to deselect the range. See Figure 2-5.

Figure 2-5   **Font and fill colors in the Documentation sheet**

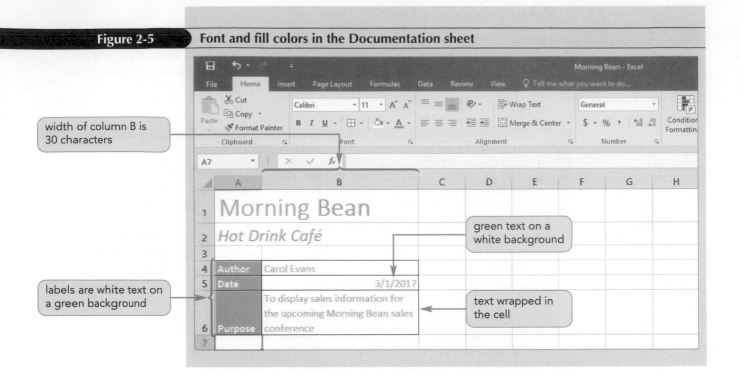

width of column B is 30 characters

green text on a white background

labels are white text on a green background

text wrapped in the cell

Adding a Background Image

Another way to add visual interest to worksheets is with a background image. Many background images are based on textures such as granite, wood, or fibered paper. The image does not need to match the size of the worksheet; a smaller image can be repeated until it fills the entire sheet. Background images do not affect any cell's format or content. Fill colors added to cells appear on top of the image, covering that portion of the image.

Carol has provided an image that she wants you to use as the background of the Documentation sheet.

To add a background image to the Documentation sheet:

1. On the ribbon, click the **Page Layout** tab to display the page layout options.

2. In the Page Setup group, click the **Background** button. The Insert Pictures dialog box opens with options to search for an image file on your computer or local network, or use the Bing Image Search tool.

3. Click the **Browse** button next to the From a file label. The Sheet Background dialog box opens.

4. Navigate to the **Excel2 > Module** folder included with your Data Files, click the **Background** JPEG image file, and then click the **Insert** button. The image is added to the background of the Documentation sheet. The Background button changes to the Delete Background button, which you can click to remove background image. See Figure 2-6.

Figure 2-6   Background image added to the Documentation sheet

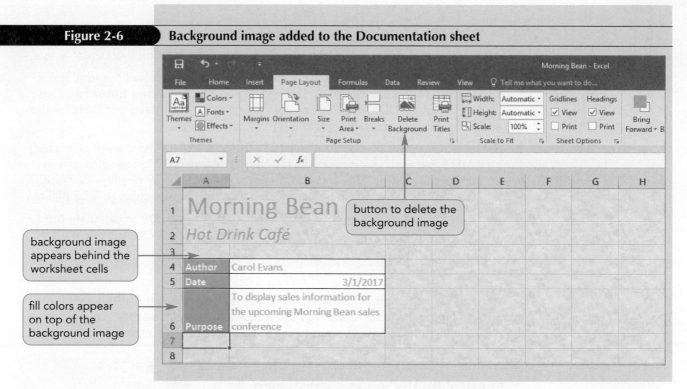

You've completed the formatting the Documentation sheet. Next, you'll work on the Sales Report worksheet.

Using Functions and Formulas to Calculate Sales Data

In the Sales Report worksheet, you will format the data on the gross sales from each of Morning Bean's 20 stores. The worksheet is divided into two areas. The table at the bottom of the worksheet displays gross sales for the past year for each month by store. The section at the top of the worksheet summarizes the sales over the past two years. Carol has compiled the following sales data:

- **Gross Sales**—the total amount of sales at all of the stores
- **Cost of Sales**—the cost of creating Morning Bean products
- **Operating Expenses**—the cost of running the individual stores including the employment and insurance costs
- **Net Profit/Loss**—the difference between the income from the gross sales and the total cost of sales and operating expenses
- **Units Sold**—the total number of menu items sold by Morning Bean during the year
- **Customers Served**—the total number of customers served by Morning Bean during the year

Carol wants you to calculate these sales statistics for the entire company and for each individual store. First, you will calculate Morning Bean's total gross sales from the past year and the company's overall net profit and loss.

To calculate Morning Bean's sales and profit/loss:

▶ 1. Click the **Sales Report** sheet tab to make the Sales Report worksheet active.

▶ 2. Click cell **C6**, type the formula **=SUM(C27:N46)** to calculate the total gross sales from all stores in the previous year, and then press the **Enter** key. Cell C6 displays 9880800, indicating that Morning Bean's total gross sales for the year were more than $9.8 million.

▶ 3. In cell **C9**, enter the formula **=C6-(C7+C8)** to calculate the current year's net profit/loss, which is equal to the difference between the gross sales and the sum of the cost of sales and operating expenses. Cell C9 displays 2299900, indicating that the company's net profit for the year was close to $2.3 million.

▶ 4. Copy the formula in cell **C9**, and then paste it into cell **D9** to calculate the net profit/loss for the previous year. Cell D9 displays 2273220, indicating that the company's net profit for that year was a little less than $2.3 million.

Morning Bean's net profit increased from the previous year, but it also opened two new stores during that time. Carol wants to investigate the sales statistics on a per-store basis by dividing the statistics you just calculated by the number of stores.

To calculate the per-store statistics:

▶ 1. In cell **C16**, enter the formula **=C6/C23** to calculate the gross sales per store for the year. The formula returns 494040, indicating each Morning Bean store had, on average, almost $500,000 in gross sales during the year.

▶ 2. In cell **C17**, enter the formula **=C7/C23** to calculate the cost of sales per store for the year. The formula returns the value 138540, indicating each Morning Bean store had a little more than $138,000 in sales cost.

▶ 3. In cell **C18**, enter the formula **=C8/C23** to calculate the operating expenses per store for the year. The formula returns the value 240505, indicating that operating expense of a typical store was a little more than $240,000.

▶ 4. In cell **C19**, enter the formula **=C9/C23** to calculate the net profit/loss per store for the year. The formula returns the value 114995, indicating that the net profit/loss of a typical store was about $115,000.

▶ 5. In cell **C21**, enter the formula **=C11/C23** to calculate the units sold per store for the year. The formula returns the value 72655, indicating that a typical store sold more than 72,000 units.

▶ 6. In cell **C22**, enter the formula **=C12/C23** to calculate the customers served per store during the year. The formula returns the value 10255, indicating that a typical store served more than 10,000 customers.

▶ 7. Copy the formulas in the range **C16:C22** and paste them into the range **D16:D22**. The cell references in the formulas change to calculate the sales data for the previous year.

▶ 8. Click cell **B24** to deselect the range. See Figure 2-7.

Figure 2-7	Overall and per-store sales statistics

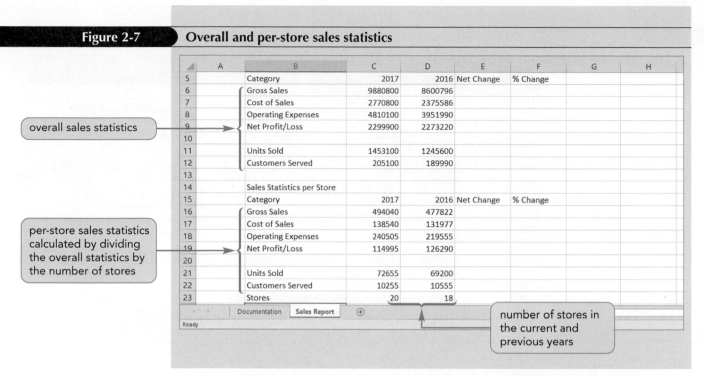

overall sales statistics

per-store sales statistics calculated by dividing the overall statistics by the number of stores

	A	B	C	D	E	F	G	H
5		Category	2017	2016	Net Change	% Change		
6		Gross Sales	9880800	8600796				
7		Cost of Sales	2770800	2375586				
8		Operating Expenses	4810100	3951990				
9		Net Profit/Loss	2299900	2273220				
10								
11		Units Sold	1453100	1245600				
12		Customers Served	205100	189990				
13								
14		Sales Statistics per Store						
15		Category	2017	2016	Net Change	% Change		
16		Gross Sales	494040	477822				
17		Cost of Sales	138540	131977				
18		Operating Expenses	240505	219555				
19		Net Profit/Loss	114995	126290				
20								
21		Units Sold	72655	69200				
22		Customers Served	10255	10555				
23		Stores	20	18				

Documentation   Sales Report   ⊕

Ready

number of stores in the current and previous years

Carol also wants to report how the company's sales and expenses have changed from the previous year to the current year. To do this, you will calculate the net change in the sales statistics as well as the percent change. The percent change is calculated using the following formula:

$$\text{percent change} = \frac{\text{current year value} - \text{previous year value}}{\text{previous year value}}$$

You will calculate the net change and percentage for all of the statistics in the Sales Report worksheet.

To calculate the net and percent changes:

1. In cell **E6**, enter the formula **=C6–D6** to calculate the difference in gross sales between the previous year and the current year. The formula returns 1280004, indicating that gross sales increased by about $1.28 million.

Be sure to include the parentheses as shown to calculate the percent change correctly.

2. In cell **F6**, enter the formula **=(C6–D6)/D6** to calculate the percent change in gross sales from the previous year to the current year. The formula returns 0.1488239, indicating an increase in gross sales of about 14.88 percent.

Next, you'll copy and paste the formulas in cells E6 and F6 to the rest of the sales data to calculate the net change and percent change from the previous year to the current year.

3. Select the range **E6:F6**, and then copy the selected range. The two formulas are copied to the Clipboard.

4. Select the nonadjacent range **E7:F9,E11:F12,E16:F19,E21:F23**, and then paste the formulas from the Clipboard into the selected range. The net and percent changes are calculated for the remaining sales data.

5. Click cell **B24** to deselect the range, and then scroll the worksheet up to display row 5. See Figure 2-8.

Figure 2-8	Net change and percent change from 2016 to 2017

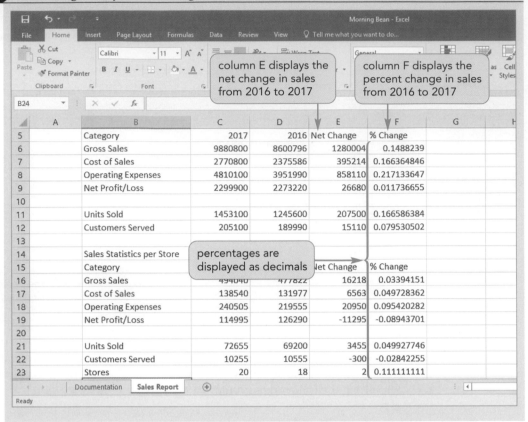

The bottom part of the worksheet contains the sales for each cafe from the current year. You will use the SUM function to calculate the total gross sales for each store during the entire year, the total monthly sales of all 20 stores, and the total gross sales of all stores and months.

To calculate different subtotals of the gross sales:

1. Click in the **Name** box to select the current cell reference, type **O26**, and then press the **Enter** key. Cell O26 is selected.

2. Type **TOTAL** as the label, and then press the **Enter** key. Cell O27 is now the active cell.

3. On the ribbon, click the **Home** tab, if necessary.

4. In the Editing group, click the **AutoSum** button, and then press the **Enter** key to accept the suggested range reference and enter the formula =SUM(C27:N27) in cell O27. The cell displays 370000, indicating gross sales in 2017 for the 85 Seaside Lane store in San Diego were $370,000.

5. Copy the formula in cell **O27**, and then paste that formula into the range **O28:O46** to calculate the total sales for each of the remaining 19 stores in the Morning Bean chain.

6. Click cell **B47**, type **TOTAL** as the label, and then press the **Tab** key. Cell C47 is now the active cell.

7. Select the range **C47:O47** so that you can calculate the total monthly sales for all of the stores.

> **8.** On the Home tab, in the Editing group, click the **AutoSum** button to calculate the total sales for each month as well as the total sales for all months. For example, cell C47 displays 710900, indicating that monthly sales from all stores in January were $710,900.

> **9.** Click cell **O48** to deselect the range. See Figure 2-9.

Figure 2-9   **Gross sales by store and month**

gross sales for each store for all months

	E	F	G	H	I	J	K	L			
42	32100	35400	34000	38800	38100	39600	36700	34100	35000	33000	408600
43	46800	49400	48400	52100	54400	51400	49200	52100	47000	48000	578900
44	51700	56400	58400	59100	58200	62100	55900	57400	51000	53000	655400
45	35800	37300	38700	40300	39700	39700	38600	37600	35300	38000	442000
46	56400	55500	58600	57100	61900	61100	58800	60800	53000	57000	675800
47	795500	820000	861600	872900	903000	920000	859800	866200	788900	833100	9880800
48											
49											
50											

gross sales for each month for all stores

gross sales for all months and all stores

The Sales Report worksheet contains a lot of information that is difficult to read in its current form. You can improve the readability of the data by adding number formats.

Formatting Numbers

The goal in formatting any workbook is to make the content easier to interpret. For numbers, this can mean adding a comma to separate thousands, setting the number of decimal places, and using percentage and currency symbols to make numbers easier to read and understand. Changing the number format does not affect the value itself, only how that value is displayed in the worksheet.

Applying Number Formats

Cells start out formatted with the **General format**, which, for the most part, displays numbers exactly as they are typed. If a value is calculated from a formula or function, the General format displays as many digits after the decimal point as will fit in the cell and rounds the last digit. Calculated values that are too large to fit into the cell are displayed in scientific notation.

The General format is fine for small numbers, but some values require additional formatting to make the numbers easier to interpret. For example, you might want to:

- Change the number of digits displayed to the right of the decimal point
- Add commas to separate thousands in large numbers
- Include currency symbols to numbers to identify the monetary unit being used
- Identify percentages using the % symbol

TIP

To apply the Currency format, click the Number Format button arrow and click Currency, or press the Ctrl+Shift+$ keys.

Excel supports two monetary formats—currency and accounting. Both formats add a thousands separator to the currency values and display two digits to the right of the decimal point. However, the **Currency format** places a currency symbol directly to the left of the first digit of the currency value and displays negative numbers with a negative sign. The **Accounting format** fixes a currency symbol at the left edge of the column, and displays negative numbers within parentheses and zero values with a dash. It also slightly indents the values from the right edge of the cell to allow room for parentheses around negative values. Figure 2-10 compares the two formats.

Figure 2-10 **Currency and Accounting number formats**

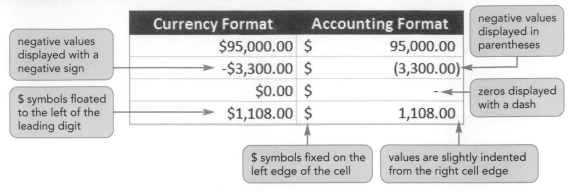

When choosing between the Currency format and the Accounting format for your worksheets, you should consider accounting principles that govern how financial data should be formatted and displayed.

Written Communication: Formatting Monetary Values

PROSKILLS

Spreadsheets commonly include monetary values. To make these values simpler to read and comprehend, keep in mind the following guidelines when formatting the currency data in a worksheet:

- **Format for your audience.** For general financial reports, round values to the nearest hundred, thousand, or million. Investors are generally more interested in the big picture than in exact values. However, for accounting reports, accuracy is important and often legally required. So, for those reports, be sure to display the exact monetary value.

- **Use thousands separators.** Large strings of numbers can be challenging to read. For monetary values, use a thousands separator to make the amounts easier to comprehend.

- **Apply the Accounting format to columns of monetary values.** The Accounting format makes columns of numbers easier to read than the Currency format. Use the Currency format for individual cells that are not part of long columns of numbers.

- **Use only two currency symbols in a column of monetary values.** Standard accounting format displays one currency symbol with the first monetary value in the column and optionally displays a second currency symbol with the last value in that column. Use the Accounting format to fix the currency symbols, lining them up within the column. Following these standard accounting principles will make your financial data easier to read both on the screen and in printouts.

Carol wants you to format the gross sales amounts in the Accounting format so that they are easier to read.

To format the gross sales in the Accounting format:

1. Select the range **C6:E6** containing the gross sales.

TIP

You can click the Accounting Number Format button arrow, and then click a different currency symbol.

2. On the Home tab, in the Number group, click the **Accounting Number Format** button $. The numbers are formatted in the Accounting format. You cannot see the format because the cells display ##########.

The cells display ########## because the formatted numbers don't fit into the columns. One reason for this is that monetary values, by default, show both dollars and cents in the cell. However, you can increase or decrease the number of decimal places displayed in a cell. The displayed value might then be rounded. For example, the stored value 11.7 will appear in the cell as 12 if no decimal places are displayed to the right of the decimal point. Changing the number of decimal places displayed in a cell does not change the value stored in the cell.

Because the conference attendees are interested only in whole dollar amounts, Carol wants you to hide the cents values of the gross sales by decreasing the number of decimal places to zero.

To decrease the number of decimal places displayed in the gross sales:

1. Make sure the range **C6:E6** is still selected.

2. On the Home tab, in the Number group, click the **Decrease Decimal** button twice. The cents are hidden for gross sales.

3. Click cell **C4** to deselect the range. See Figure 2-11.

Figure 2-11   **Formatted gross sales values**

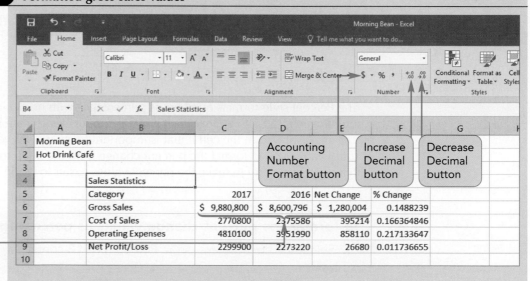

	A	B	C	D	E	F	G
1	Morning Bean						
2	Hot Drink Café						
3							
4		Sales Statistics					
5		Category	2017	2016	Net Change	% Change	
6		Gross Sales	$ 9,880,800	$ 8,600,796	$ 1,280,004	0.1488239	
7		Cost of Sales	2770800	2375586	395214	0.166364846	
8		Operating Expenses	4810100	3951990	858110	0.217133647	
9		Net Profit/Loss	2299900	2273220	26680	0.011736655	
10							

gross sales displayed in the Accounting format with no decimal places

The Comma style is identical to the Accounting format except that it does not fix a currency symbol to the left of the number. The advantage of using the Comma style and the Accounting format together is that the numbers will be aligned in the column.

Carol asks you to apply the Comma style to the remaining sales statistics.

To apply the Comma style to the sales statistics:

▶ **1.** Select the nonadjacent range **C7:E9,C11:E12** containing the sales figures for all stores in 2016 and 2017.

▶ **2.** On the Home tab, in the Number group, click the **Comma Style** button. In some instances, the number is now too large to be displayed in the cell.

▶ **3.** In the Number group, click the **Decrease Decimal** button twice to remove two decimal places. Digits to the right of the decimal point are hidden for all of the selected cells, and all of the numbers are now visible.

▶ **4.** Click cell **C13** to deselect the range. See Figure 2-12.

Figure 2-12 **Formatted sales values**

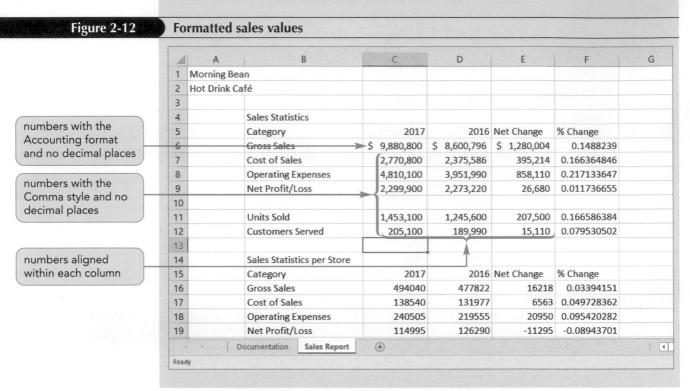

numbers with the Accounting format and no decimal places

numbers with the Comma style and no decimal places

numbers aligned within each column

	A	B	C	D	E	F	G
1	Morning Bean						
2	Hot Drink Café						
3							
4		Sales Statistics					
5		Category	2017	2016	Net Change	% Change	
6		Gross Sales	$ 9,880,800	$ 8,600,796	$ 1,280,004	0.1488239	
7		Cost of Sales	2,770,800	2,375,586	395,214	0.166364846	
8		Operating Expenses	4,810,100	3,951,990	858,110	0.217133647	
9		Net Profit/Loss	2,299,900	2,273,220	26,680	0.011736655	
10							
11		Units Sold	1,453,100	1,245,600	207,500	0.166586384	
12		Customers Served	205,100	189,990	15,110	0.079530502	
13							
14		Sales Statistics per Store					
15		Category	2017	2016	Net Change	% Change	
16		Gross Sales	494040	477822	16218	0.03394151	
17		Cost of Sales	138540	131977	6563	0.049728362	
18		Operating Expenses	240505	219555	20950	0.095420282	
19		Net Profit/Loss	114995	126290	-11295	-0.08943701	

Documentation   Sales Report   ⊕

Ready

The Percent style formats numbers as percentages with no decimal places so that a number such as 0.124 appears as 12%. You can always change how many decimal places are displayed in the cell if that is important to show with your data.

Carol wants you to format the percent change from the 2016 to 2017 sales statistics with a percent symbol to make the percent values easier to read.

To format the percent change values as percentages:

▶ **1.** Select the nonadjacent range **F6:F9,F11:F12** containing the percent change values.

▶ **2.** On the Home tab, in the Number group, click the **Percent Style** button (or press the **Ctrl+Shift+%** keys). The values are displayed as percentages with no decimal places.

▶ **3.** In the Number group, click the **Increase Decimal** button twice. The displayed number includes two decimal places.

▶ **4.** Click cell **F13** to deselect the range. See Figure 2-13.

Figure 2-13	Formatted percent change values

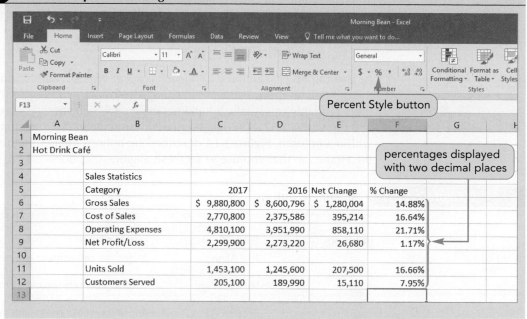

With the data reformatted, the worksheet clearly shows that Morning Bean's gross sales increased from 2016 to 2017 by almost 15 percent, but the company's net profit increased by only 1.17 percent due to increasing expenses in sales costs and operations of 16.64 percent and 21.71 percent, respectively. This type of information is very important to Morning Bean investors and to the company executives as plans are made for the upcoming year.

Formatting Dates and Times

TIP

To view the underlying date and time value, apply the General format to the cell or display the formulas instead of the formula results.

Because Excel stores dates and times as numbers and not as text, you can apply different date formats without affecting the underlying date and time value. The abbreviated format, *mm/dd/yyyy*, entered in the Documentation sheet is referred to as the **Short Date format**. You can also apply a **Long Date format** that displays the day of the week and the full month name in addition to the day of the month and the year. Other built-in formats include formats for displaying time values in 12- or 24-hour time format.

Carol asks you to change the date in the Documentation sheet to the Long Date format.

To format the date in the Long Date format:

1. Go to the **Documentation** sheet, and then select cell **B5**.

2. On the Home tab, in the Number group, click the **Number Format button arrow** to display a list of number formats, and then click **Long Date**. The date is displayed with the weekday name, month name, day, and year. Notice that the date in the formula bar did not change because you changed only the display format, not the date value.

Formatting Worksheet Cells

You can format the appearance of individual cells by modifying the alignment of text within the cell, indenting cell text, or adding borders of different styles and colors.

Aligning Cell Content

By default, text is aligned with the left edge of the cell, and numbers are aligned with the right edge. You might want to change the alignment to make the text and numbers more readable or visually appealing. In general, you should center column titles, left-align other text, and right-align numbers to keep their decimal places lined up within a column. Figure 2-14 describes the buttons located in the Alignment group on the Home tab that you use to set these alignment options.

Figure 2-14   **Alignment buttons**

Button	Name	Description
	Top Align	Aligns the cell content with the cell's top edge
	Middle Align	Vertically centers the cell content within the cell
	Bottom Align	Aligns the cell content with the cell's bottom edge
	Align Left	Aligns the cell content with the cell's left edge
	Center	Horizontally centers the cell content within the cell
	Align Right	Aligns the cell content with the cell's right edge
	Decrease Indent	Decreases the size of the indentation used in the cell
	Increase Indent	Increases the size of the indentation used in the cell
	Orientation	Rotates the cell content to any angle within the cell
	Wrap Text	Forces the cell text to wrap within the cell borders
	Merge & Center	Merges the selected cells into a single cell

The date in the Documentation sheet is right-aligned within cell B5 because Excel treats dates and times as numbers. Carol wants you to left-align the date from the Documentation sheet and center the column titles in the Sales Report worksheet.

To left-align the date and center the column titles:

1. In the Documentation sheet, make sure cell **B5** is still selected.

2. On the Home tab, in the Alignment group, click the **Align Left** button ▤. The date shifts to the left edge of the cell.

3. Go to the **Sales Report** worksheet.

4. Select the range **C5:F5** containing the column titles.

5. In the Alignment group, click the **Center** button ▤. The column titles are centered in the cells.

Indenting Cell Content

Sometimes you want a cell's content moved a few spaces from the cell's left edge. This is particularly useful to create subsections in a worksheet or to set off some entries from others. You can increase the indent to shift the contents of a cell away from the left edge of the cell, or you can decrease the indent to shift a cell's contents closer to the left edge of the cell.

Carol wants you to indent the Cost of Sales and Operating Expenses labels in the sales statistics table from the other labels because they represent expenses to the company.

To indent the expense categories:

▸ **1.** Select the range **B7:B8** containing the expense categories.

▸ **2.** On the Home tab, in the Alignment group, click the **Increase Indent** button 🔲 twice to indent each label two spaces in its cell.

Adding Borders to Cells

Borders are another way to make financial data easier to interpret. Common accounting practices provide guidelines on when to add borders to cells. In general, a single black border should appear above a subtotal, a single bottom border should be added below a calculated number, and a double black bottom border should appear below the total.

Carol wants you to follow common accounting practices in the Sales Report worksheet. You will add borders below the column titles and below the gross sales values. You will add a top border to the net profit/loss values. Finally, you will add a top and bottom border to the Units Sold and Customers Served rows.

To add borders to the sales statistics data:

▸ **1.** Select the range **B5:F5** containing the cell headings.

▸ **2.** On the Home tab, in the Font group, click the **Borders button arrow** 🔲 ⋅, and then click **Bottom Border**. A border is added below the column titles.

▸ **3.** Select the range **B6:F6** containing the gross sales amounts.

▸ **4.** In the Font group, click the **Bottom Border** button 🔲 to add a border below the selected gross sales amounts.

▸ **5.** Select the range **B9:F9**, click the **Borders button arrow** 🔲 ⋅, and then click **Top Border** to add a border above the net profit/loss amounts.

The Units Sold and Customers Served rows do not contain monetary values as the other rows do. You will distinguish these rows by adding a top and bottom border.

▸ **6.** Select the range **B11:F12**, click the **Borders button arrow** 🔲 ⋅, and then click **Top and Bottom Border** to add a border above the number of units sold and below the number of customers served.

▸ **7.** Click cell **B3** to deselect the range. See Figure 2-15.

Figure 2-15   **Borders, indents, and alignment added to the sales data**

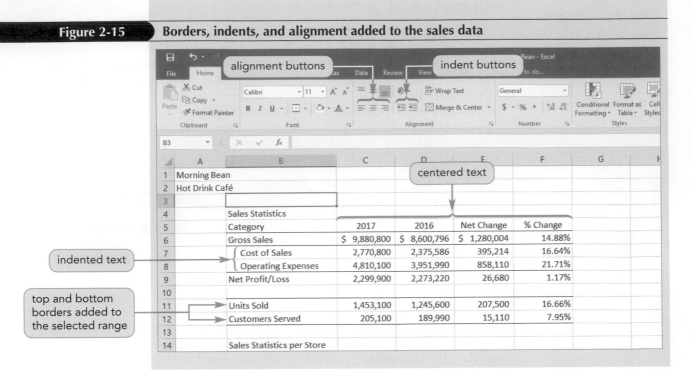

You can apply multiple formats to the same cell to create the look that best fits the data. For example, one cell might be formatted with a number format, alignments, borders, indents, fonts, font sizes, and so on. The monthly sales data needs to be formatted with number styles, alignments, indents, and borders. You'll add these formats now.

To format the monthly sales table:

1. Click in the **Name** box, type **C27:O47**, and then press the **Enter** key. The range C27:O47, containing the monthly gross sales for each store, is selected.

2. On the Home tab, in the Number group, click the **Comma Style** button ⁹ to add a thousands separator to the values.

3. In the Number group, click the **Decrease Decimal** button ⟶.0 twice to hide the cents from the sales results.

4. In the Alignment group, click the **Top Align** button ≡ to align the sales numbers with the top of each cell.

5. Select the range **C26:O26** containing the labels for the month abbreviations and the TOTAL column.

6. In the Alignment group, click the **Center** button ≡ to center the column labels.

7. Select the range **B27:B46** containing the store addresses.

8. Reduce the font size of the store addresses to **9** points.

9. In the Alignment group, click the **Increase Indent** button ≥≡ to indent the store addresses.

10. In the Alignment group, click the **Top Align** button ≡ to align the addresses at the top of each cell.

11. Select the range **B47:O47** containing the monthly totals.

12. In the Font group, click the **Borders button arrow** ⊞ ▾, and then click **All Borders** to add borders around each monthly totals cell.

13. Select the range **O26:O46** containing the annual totals for each restaurant, and then click the **All Borders** button ⊞ to add borders around each restaurant total.

14. Click cell **A24** to deselect the range. See Figure 2-16.

Figure 2-16   **Formatted monthly gross sales**

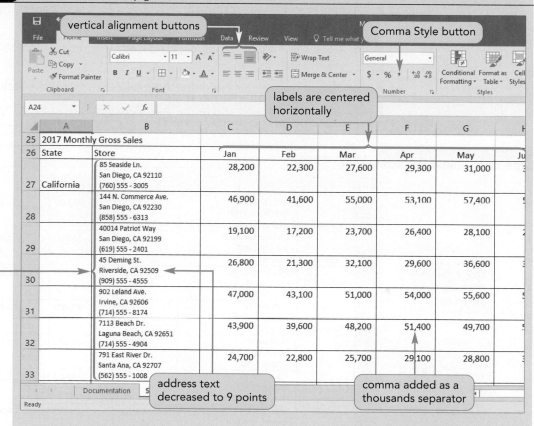

Merging Cells

You can merge, or combine, several cells into one cell. A merged cell contains two or more cells with a single cell reference. When you merge cells, only the content from the upper-left cell in the range is retained. The cell reference for the merged cell is the upper-left cell reference. So, if you merge cells A1 and A2, the merged cell reference is cell A1. After you merge cells, you can align the content within the merged cell. The Merge & Center button in the Alignment group on the Home tab includes the following options:

- **Merge & Center**—merges the range into one cell and horizontally centers the content
- **Merge Across**—merges each row in the selected range across the columns in the range
- **Merge Cells**—merges the range into a single cell but does not horizontally center the cell content
- **Unmerge Cells**—reverses a merge, returning the merged cell to a range of individual cells

The first column of the monthly sales data lists the states in which Morning Bean has stores. You will merge the cells for each state name into a single cell.

To merge the state name cells:

1. Select the range **A27:A33** containing the cells for the California stores. You will merge these seven cells into a single cell.

2. On the Home tab, in the Alignment group, click the **Merge & Center** button. The range A27:A33 merges into one cell with the cell reference A27, and the text is centered and bottom-aligned within the cell.

3. Select the range **A34:A36**, and then click the **Merge & Center** button to merge and center the cells for stores in the state of Washington.

4. Select the range **A37:A40**, and then merge and center the cells for the Oregon stores.

5. Click cell **A41**, and then click the **Center** button ≡ to center the Idaho text horizontally in the cell.

6. Merge and center the range **A42:A43** containing the Nevada cells.

7. Merge and center the range **A44:A46** containing the Colorado cells. See Figure 2-17.

Figure 2-17	Merged cells

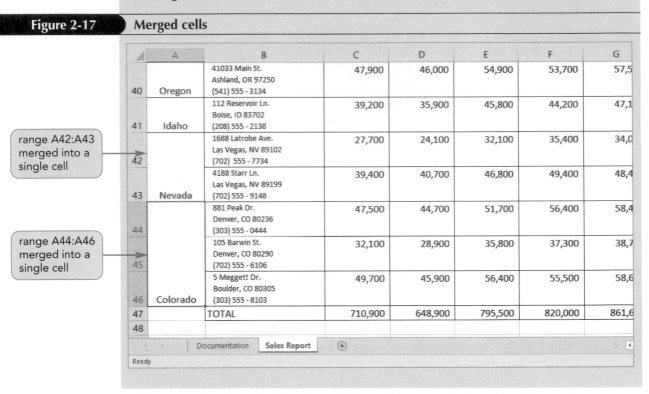

range A42:A43 merged into a single cell

range A44:A46 merged into a single cell

The merged cells make it easier to distinguish restaurants in each state. Next, you will rotate the cells so that the state name rotates up the merged cells.

Rotating Cell Contents

Text and numbers are displayed horizontally within cells. However, you can rotate cell text to any angle to save space or to provide visual interest to a worksheet. The state names at the bottom of the merged cells would look better and take up less room if they were rotated vertically within their cells. Carol asks you to rotate the state names.

To rotate the state names:

1. Select the merged cell **A27**.

2. On the Home tab, in the Alignment group, click the **Orientation** button ≫ - to display a list of rotation options, and then click **Rotate Text Up**. The state name rotates 90 degrees counterclockwise.

3. In the Alignment group, click the **Middle Align** button ≣ to vertically center the rotated text in the merged cell.

4. Select the merged cell range **A34:A46**, and then repeat Steps 2 and 3 to rotate and vertically center the rest of the state names in their cells.

5. Reduce the width of column A to **7** characters because the rotated state names take up less space.

6. Select cell **A47**. See Figure 2-18.

Figure 2-18   Rotated cell content

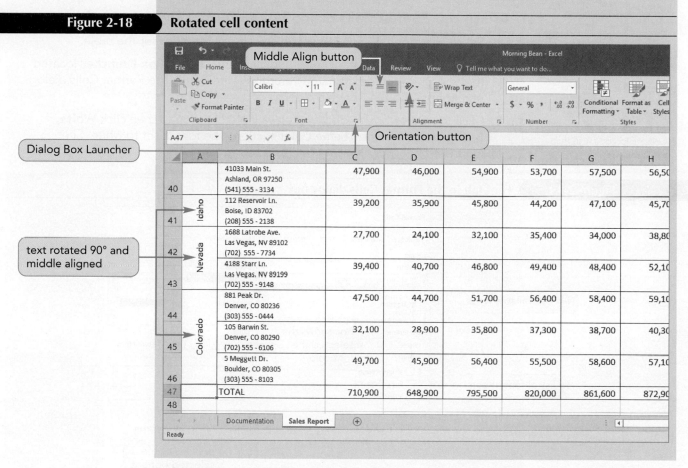

In addition to using the ribbon to apply formatting to a worksheet, you can also use the Format Cells dialog box to apply formatting.

Exploring the Format Cells Dialog Box

The buttons on the Home tab provide quick access to the most commonly used formatting choices. For more options, you can use the Format Cells dialog box. You can apply the formats in this dialog box to the selected worksheet cells. The Format Cells dialog box has six tabs, each focusing on a different set of formatting options, as described below:

- **Number**—provides options for formatting the appearance of numbers, including dates and numbers treated as text such as telephone or Social Security numbers
- **Alignment**—provides options for how data is aligned within a cell
- **Font**—provides options for selecting font types, sizes, styles, and other formatting attributes such as underlining and font colors

- **Border**—provides options for adding and removing cell borders as well as selecting a line style and color
- **Fill**—provides options for creating and applying background colors and patterns to cells
- **Protection**—provides options for locking or hiding cells to prevent other users from modifying their contents

Although you have applied many of these formats from the Home tab, the Format Cells dialog box presents them in a different way and provides more choices. You will use the Font and Fill tabs to format the column titles with a white font on a green background.

To use the Format Cells dialog box to format the column titles:

1. Select the range **A26:O26** containing the column titles for the table.

2. On the Home tab, in the Font group, click the **Dialog Box Launcher** located to the right of the group name (refer to Figure 2-18). The Format Cells dialog box opens with the Font tab displayed.

3. Click the **Color** box to display the available colors, and then click **White, Background 1** in the Theme Color section. The font is set to white. See Figure 2-19.

Figure 2-19   **Font tab in the Format Cells dialog box**

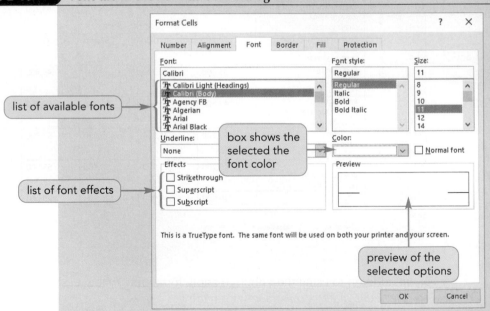

4. Click the **Fill** tab to display background options.

5. In the Background Color section, click the **green** standard color (the sixth color in the last row). The background is set to green, as you can see in the Sample box.

6. Click the **OK** button. The dialog box closes, and the font and fill options you selected are applied to the column titles.

You will also use the Format Cells dialog box to change the appearance of the row titles. You'll format them to be displayed in a larger white font on a gold background.

To format the row titles:

1. Select the range **A27:A46** containing the rotated state names.

2. Right-click the selected range, and then click **Format Cells** on the shortcut menu. The Format Cells dialog box opens with the last tab used displayed—in this case, the Fill tab.

3. In the Background Color section, click the **gold** theme color (the eighth color in the first row). Its preview is shown in the Sample box.

4. Click the **Font** tab to display the font formatting options.

5. Click the **Color** box, and then click the **White, Background 1** theme color to set the font color to white.

6. In the Size box, click **14** to set the font size to 14 points.

7. In the Font style box, click **Bold** to change the font to boldface.

8. Click the **OK** button. The dialog box closes, and the font and fill formats are applied to the state names.

9. Scroll up and click cell **A24** to deselect the A27:A46 range. See Figure 2-20.

Figure 2-20   **Formatted worksheet cells**

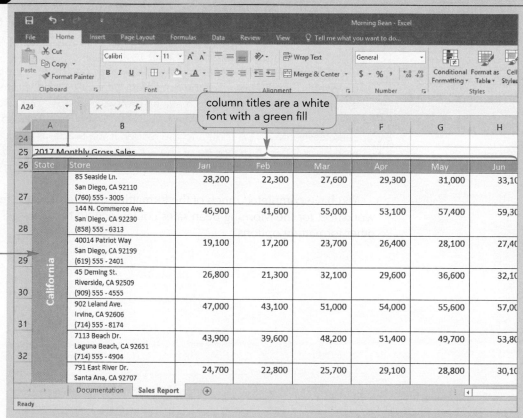

10. Save the workbook.

With the formats you have added to the Sales Report worksheet, readers will be able to more easily read and interpret the large table of store sales.

PROSKILLS

Written Communication: Formatting Workbooks for Readability and Appeal

Designing a workbook requires the same care as designing any written document or report. A well-formatted workbook is easy to read and establishes a sense of professionalism with readers. Do the following to improve the appearance of your workbooks:

- **Clearly identify each worksheet's purpose.** Include column or row titles and a descriptive sheet name.
- **Include only one or two topics on each worksheet.** Don't crowd individual worksheets with too much information. Place extra topics on separate sheets. Readers should be able to interpret each worksheet with a minimal amount of horizontal and vertical scrolling.
- **Place worksheets with the most important information first in the workbook.** Position worksheets summarizing your findings near the front of the workbook. Position worksheets with detailed and involved analysis near the end as an appendix.
- **Use consistent formatting throughout the workbook.** If negative values appear in red on one worksheet, format them in the same way on all sheets. Also, be consistent in the use of thousands separators, decimal places, and percentages.
- **Pay attention to the format of the printed workbook.** Make sure your printouts are legible with informative headers and footers. Check that the content of the printout is scaled correctly to the page size and that page breaks divide the information into logical sections.

Excel provides many formatting tools. However, too much formatting can be intrusive, overwhelm data, and make the document difficult to read. Remember that the goal of formatting is not simply to make a "pretty workbook" but also to accentuate important trends and relationships in the data. A well-formatted workbook should seamlessly convey your data to the reader. If the reader is thinking about how your workbook looks, it means he or she is not thinking about your data.

You have completed much of the formatting that Carol wants in the Sales Report worksheet for the Morning Bean sales conference. In the next session, you will explore other formatting options.

Session 2.1 Quick Check

REVIEW

1. What is the difference between a serif font and a sans serif font?

2. What is the difference between a theme color and a standard color?

3. A cell containing a number displays #######. Why does this occur, and what can you do to fix it?

4. What is the General format?

5. Describe the differences between Currency format and Accounting format.

6. The range B3:B13 is merged into a single cell. What is its cell reference?

7. How do you format text so that it is set vertically within the cell?

8. Where can you access all the formatting options for worksheet cells?

Session 2.2 Visual Overview:

The Page Layout tab has options for setting how the worksheet will print.

The **Format Painter** copies and pastes formatting from one cell or range to another without duplicating any data.

Print titles are rows and/or columns that are included on every page of the printout. In this case, the text in rows 1 and 2 will print on every page.

A **manual page break** is a page break that you set to indicate where a new page of the printout should start and is identified by a solid blue line.

File	Home	Insert	Page Layout	Formulas	Data	Review	View

Tw Cen MT   26   A A   General

B I U $ %

Clipboard   Font   Alignment   Numb

A1   Morning Bean

	A	B	C	D	E	F	G
1	**Morning Bean**						
2	*Hot Drink Café*						
3							
4		Sales Statistics					
5		Category	2017	2016	Net Change	% Change	
6		Gross Sales	$ 9,880,800	$ 8,600,796	$ 1,280,004	14.88%	
7		Cost of Sales	2,770,800	2,375,586	395,214	16.64%	
8		Operating Expenses	4,810,100	3,951,990	858,110	21.71%	
9		Net Profit/Loss	2,299,900	2,273,220	26,680	1.17%	
10							
11		Units Sold	1,453,100	1,245,600	207,500	16.66%	
12		Customers Served	215,100	189,990	25,110	13.22%	
13							
14		Sales Statistics per Store					
15		Category	2017	2016	Net Change	% Change	
16		Gross Sales	$ 494,040	$ 477,822	$ 16,218	3.39%	
17		Cost of Sales	138,540	131,977	6,563	4.97%	
18		Operating Expenses	240,505	219,555	20,950	9.54%	
19		Net Profit/Loss	114,995	126,290	(11,295)	-8.94%	
20							
21		Units Sold	72,655	69,200	3,455	4.99%	
22		Customers Served	10,755	10,555	200	1.89%	
23		Stores	20	18	2	11.11%	
24							
25		2017 Monthly Gross Sales					
26	State	Store	Jan	Feb	Mar	Apr	Ma
27		85 Seaside Lane San Diego, CA 92110 (760) 555 - 3005	28,200	22,300	27,600	29,300	3
28		144 N. Commerce Avenue San Diego, CA 92230 (858) 555 - 6313	46,900	41,600	55,000	53,100	5
		40014 Patriot Way	19,100	17,200	23,700	26,400	2

Page 1

| Documentation | **Sales Report** | + |

Ready

Designing a Printout

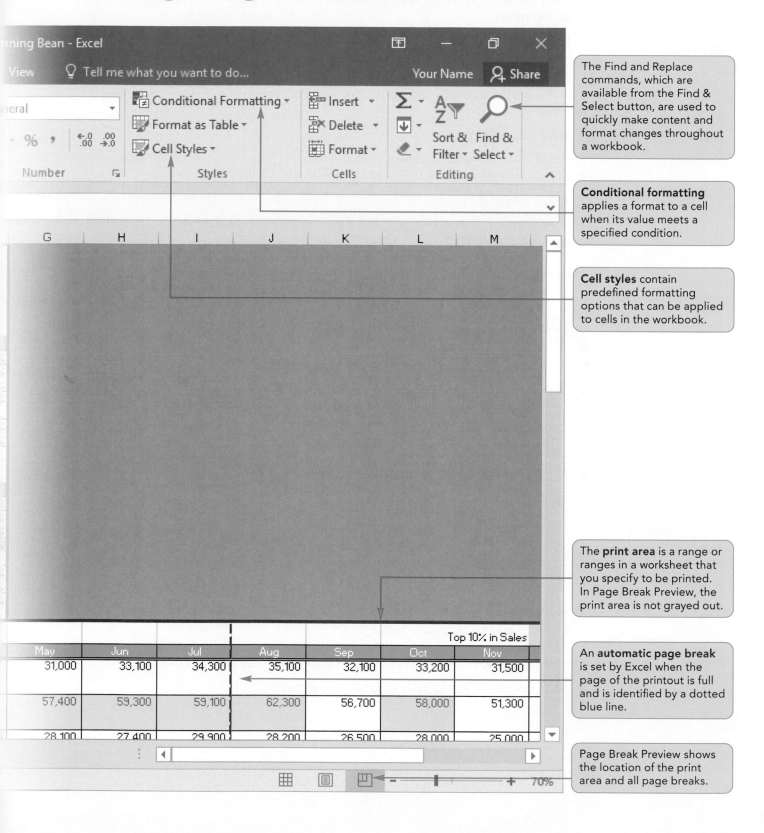

The Find and Replace commands, which are available from the Find & Select button, are used to quickly make content and format changes throughout a workbook.

Conditional formatting applies a format to a cell when its value meets a specified condition.

Cell styles contain predefined formatting options that can be applied to cells in the workbook.

The **print area** is a range or ranges in a worksheet that you specify to be printed. In Page Break Preview, the print area is not grayed out.

An **automatic page break** is set by Excel when the page of the printout is full and is identified by a dotted blue line.

Page Break Preview shows the location of the print area and all page breaks.

Calculating Averages

The **AVERAGE function** calculates the average value from a collection of numbers. It has the syntax

    AVERAGE(number1,number2,number3,…)

where *number1*, *number2*, *number3*, and so forth are either numbers or cell references to the cells or a range where the numbers are stored. For example, the following formula uses the AVERAGE function to calculate the average of 1, 2, 5, and 8, returning the value 4:

    =AVERAGE(1,2,5,8)

However, functions usually reference values entered in a worksheet. So, if the range A1:A4 contains the values 1, 2, 5, and 8, the following formula also returns the value 4:

    =AVERAGE(A1:A4)

The advantage of using cell references is that the values used in the function are visible and can be easily edited.

Carol wants you to calculate the average monthly sales for each of the 20 Morning Bean stores. You will use the AVERAGE function to calculate these values.

To calculate the average monthly sales for each store:

1. If you took a break after the previous session, make sure the Morning Bean workbook is open and the Sales Report worksheet is active.

2. In cell **P26**, enter **AVERAGE** as the column title. The cell is formatted with a green fill and white font color, matching the other column titles.

3. In cell **P27**, enter the formula **=AVERAGE(C27:N27)** to calculate the average of the monthly gross sales values entered in the range C27:N27. The formula returns the value 30,833, which is the average monthly gross sales for the store on 85 Seaside Lane in San Diego, California.

4. Copy the formula in cell **P27**, and then paste the copied formula in the range **P28:P47** to calculate the average monthly gross sales for each of the remaining Morning Bean stores as well as the average monthly sales from all stores. The average monthly gross sales for individual stores range from $25,408 to $56,317. The monthly gross sales from all stores is $823,400.

5. Select the range **P27:P47**. You will format this range of sales statistics.

6. On the Home tab, in the Alignment group, click the **Top Align** button ▤ to align each average value with the top edge of its cell.

7. In the Font group, click the **Borders button arrow** ⊞ ⋅, then click **All Borders** to add borders around every cell in the selected range.

8. Click cell **P27** to deselect the range. See Figure 2-21.

Figure 2-21 Average sales results

AVERAGE function used to calculate the average monthly sales

average monthly sales for each store

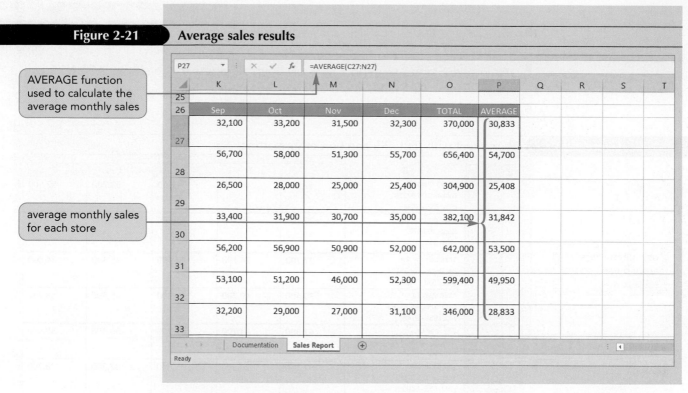

With so many values in the data, Carol wants you to insert double borders around the sales values for each state. The Border tab in the Format Cells dialog box provides options for changing the border style and color and placement.

To add a double border to the state results:

1. Select the range **A27:N33** containing the California monthly sales totals.

2. Open the Format Cells dialog box, and then click the **Border** tab.

3. In the Line section, click the **double line** in the lower-right corner of the Style box.

4. In the Presets section, click the **Outline** option. The double border appears around the selected cells in the Border preview. See Figure 2-22.

Figure 2-22 Border tab in the Format Cells dialog box

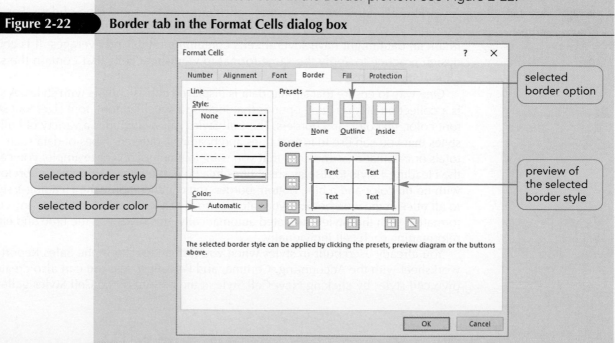

5. Click the **OK** button. The selected border is applied to the California monthly sales.

6. Repeat Steps 2 through 5 to apply double borders to the ranges **A34:N36**, **A37:N40**, **A41:N41**, **A42:N43**, and **A44:N46**.

7. Click cell **A48** to deselect the range. See Figure 2-23.

Figure 2-23   Worksheet with font, fill, and border formatting

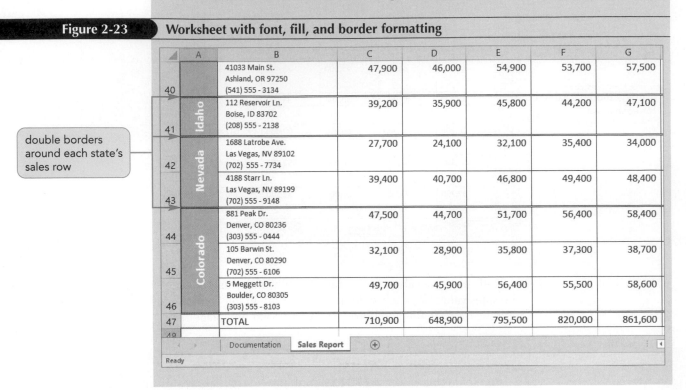

double borders around each state's sales row

Another way to format worksheet cells is with styles.

Applying Cell Styles

A workbook often contains several cells that store the same type of data. For example, each worksheet might have a cell displaying the sheet title, or a range of financial data might have several cells containing totals and averages. It is good design practice to apply the same format to worksheet cells that contain the same type of data.

One way to ensure that similar data is displayed consistently is with styles. A **style** is a collection of formatting options that include a specified font, font size, font styles, font color, fill color, and borders. The Cell Styles gallery includes a variety of built-in styles that you can use to format titles and headings, different types of data such as totals or calculations, and cells that you want to emphasize. For example, you can use the Heading 1 style to display sheet titles in a bold, blue-gray, 15-point Calibri font with no fill color and a blue bottom border. You can then apply the Heading 1 style to all titles in the workbook. If you later revise the style, the appearance of any cell formatted with that style is updated automatically. This saves you the time and effort of reformatting each cell individually.

You already used built-in styles when you formatted data in the Sales Report worksheet with the Accounting, Comma, and Percent styles. You can also create your own cell styles by clicking New Cell Style at the bottom of the Cell Styles gallery.

REFERENCE

Applying a Cell Style

- Select the cell or range to which you want to apply a style.
- On the Home tab, in the Styles group, click the Cell Styles button.
- Point to each style in the Cell Styles gallery to see a Live Preview of that style on the selected cell or range.
- Click the style you want to apply to the selected cell or range.

Carol wants you to add more color and visual interest to the Sales Report worksheet. You'll use the styles in the Cell Styles gallery to do this.

To apply cell styles to the Sales Report worksheet:

1. Click cell **B4** containing the text "Sales Statistics."

2. On the Home tab, in the Styles group, click the **Cell Styles** button. The Cell Styles gallery opens.

3. Point to the **Heading 1** style in the Titles and Headings section. Live Preview shows cell B4 in a 15-point, bold font with a solid blue bottom border. See Figure 2-24.

Figure 2-24   Cell Styles gallery

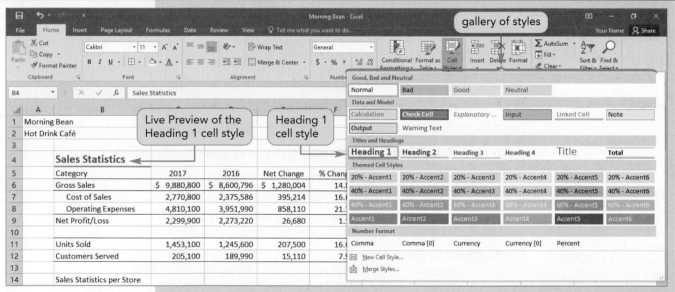

4. Move the pointer over different styles in the Cell Styles gallery to see cell B4 with a Live Preview of each style.

5. Click the **Title** style. The Title style—18-point, Blue-Gray, Text 2 Calibri Light font—is applied to cell B4.

6. Select the range **B5:F5** containing the column titles for the Sales Statistics data.

7. In the Styles group, click the **Cell Styles** button, and then click the **Accent4** style in the Themed Cell Styles section of the Cell Styles gallery.

8. Click cell **A25** containing the text "2017 Monthly Gross Sales," and then apply the **Title** cell style to the cell.

> **9.** Click cell **A3**. See Figure 2-25.

Figure 2-25   Cell styles applied to the worksheet

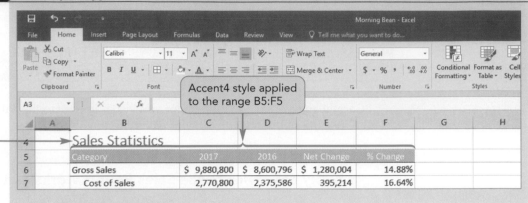

Copying and Pasting Formats

Large workbooks often use the same formatting on similar data throughout the workbook, sometimes in widely scattered cells. Rather than repeating the same steps to format these cells, you can copy the format of one cell or range and paste it to another.

Copying Formats with the Format Painter

The Format Painter provides a fast and efficient way of copying and pasting formats, ensuring that a workbook has a consistent look and feel. The Format Painter does not copy formatting applied to selected text within a cell, and it does not copy data.

Carol wants the Sales Report worksheet to use the same formats you applied to the Morning Bean company name and description in the Documentation sheet. You will use the Format Painter to copy and paste the formats.

To use the Format Painter to copy and paste a format:

> **1.** Go to the **Documentation** worksheet, and then select the range **A1:A2**.

TIP

To paste the same format multiple times, double-click the Format Painter button. Click the button again or press the Esc key to turn it off.

> **2.** On the Home tab, in the Clipboard group, click the **Format Painter** button. The formats from the selected cells are copied to the Clipboard, a flashing border appears around the selected range, and the pointer changes to ⊹▚

> **3.** Go to the **Sales Report** worksheet, and then click cell **A1**. The formatting from the Documentation worksheet is removed from the Clipboard and applied to the range A1:A2. Notice that gold font color you applied to the text selection "Morning" was not included in the pasted formats.

> **4.** Double-click cell **A1** to enter Edit mode, select **Morning**, and then change the font color to the **Gold, Accent 4** theme color. The format for the company title now matches what you applied earlier in the Documentation sheet.

> **5.** Press the **Enter** key to exit Edit mode and select cell A2.

You can use the Format Painter to copy all of the formats within a selected range and then apply those formats to another range that has the same size and shape by clicking the upper-left cell of the range. Carol wants you to copy all of the formats that you applied to the Sales Statistics data to the sales statistics per store data.

To copy and paste multiple formats:

1. Select the range **B4:F12** in the Sales Report worksheet.

2. On the Home tab, in the Clipboard group, click the **Format Painter** button.

3. Click cell **B14**. All of the number formats, cell borders, fonts, and fill colors are pasted in the range B14:F22.

4. Select the range **C23:E23**. You'll format this data.

5. On the Home tab, in the Number group, click the **Comma Style** button ▸, and then click the **Decrease Decimal** button twice to remove the decimal places to the right of the decimal point. The numbers are now vertically aligned in their columns.

6. Click cell **F23**.

7. In the Number group, click the **Percent Style** button % to change the number to a percentage, and then click the **Increase Decimal** button twice to display two decimal places in the percentage. The value is now formatted to match the other percentages.

8. Click cell **B24**. See Figure 2-26.

TIP

If the range you paste the formats in is bigger than the range you copied, Format Painter will repeat the copied formats to fill the pasted range.

Figure 2-26   **Formatting copied and pasted between ranges**

	A	B	C	D	E	F	G
4		Sales Statistics					
5		Category	2017	2016	Net Change	% Change	
6		Gross Sales	$ 9,880,800	$ 8,600,796	$ 1,280,004	14.88%	
7		Cost of Sales	2,770,800	2,375,586	395,214	16.64%	
8		Operating Expenses	4,810,100	3,951,990	858,110	21.71%	
9		Net Profit/Loss	2,299,900	2,273,220	26,680	1.17%	
10							
11		Units Sold	1,453,100	1,245,600	207,500	16.66%	
12		Customers Served	205,100	189,990	15,110	7.95%	
13							
14		Sales Statistics per Store					
15		Category	2017	2016	Net Change	% Change	
16		Gross Sales	$ 494,040	$ 477,822	$ 16,218	3.39%	
17		Cost of Sales	138,540	131,977	6,563	4.97%	
18		Operating Expenses	240,505	219,555	20,950	9.54%	
19		Net Profit/Loss	114,995	126,290	(11,295)	-8.94%	
20							
21		Units Sold	72,655	69,200	3,455	4.99%	

copied formats → (row 8)

pasted formats → (row 17)

B24

Documentation | Sales Report | ⊕

Ready

Copying Formats with the Paste Options Button

Another way to copy and paste formats is with the Paste Options button, which provides options for pasting only values, only formats, or some combination of values and formats. Each time you paste, the Paste Options button appears in the lower-right corner of the pasted cell or range. You click the Paste Options button to open a list of pasting options, shown in Figure 2-27, such as pasting only the values or only the formatting. You can also click the Transpose button to paste the column data into a row, or to paste the row data into a column.

Figure 2-27   Paste Options button

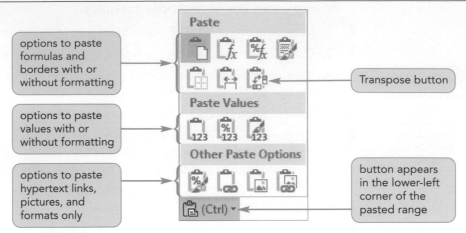

options to paste formulas and borders with or without formatting

Transpose button

options to paste values with or without formatting

button appears in the lower-left corner of the pasted range

options to paste hypertext links, pictures, and formats only

Copying Formats with Paste Special

The Paste Special command provides another way to control what you paste from the Clipboard. To use Paste Special, select and copy a range, select the range where you want to paste the Clipboard contents, click the Paste button arrow in the Clipboard group on the Home tab, and then click Paste Special to open the dialog box shown in Figure 2-28.

Figure 2-28   Paste Special dialog box

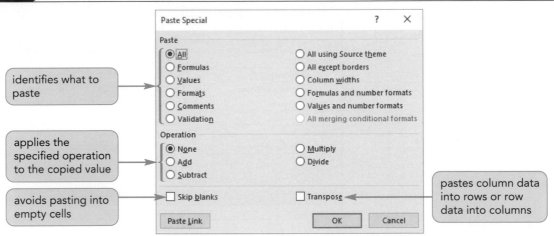

identifies what to paste

applies the specified operation to the copied value

avoids pasting into empty cells

pastes column data into rows or row data into columns

From the Paste Special dialog box, you can control exactly how to paste the copied range.

Finding and Replacing Text and Formats

The Find and Replace commands let you make content and design changes to a worksheet or the entire workbook quickly. The Find command searches through the current worksheet or workbook for the content or formatting you want to locate, and the Replace command then substitutes it with the new content or formatting you specify.

The Find and Replace commands are versatile. You can find each occurrence of the search text one at a time and decide whether to replace it. You can highlight all occurrences of the search text in the worksheet. Or, you can replace all occurrences at once without reviewing them.

Carol wants you to replace all the street title abbreviations (such as Ave.) in the Sales Report with their full names (such as Avenue). You will use Find and Replace to make these changes.

To find and replace the street title abbreviations:

▸ **1.** On the Home tab, in the Editing group, click the **Find & Select** button, and then click **Replace** (or press the **Ctrl+H** keys). The Find and Replace dialog box opens.

▸ **2.** Type **Ave.** in the Find what box.

▸ **3.** Press the **Tab** key to move the insertion point to the Replace with box, and then type **Avenue**. See Figure 2-29.

| Figure 2-29 | Find and Replace dialog box |

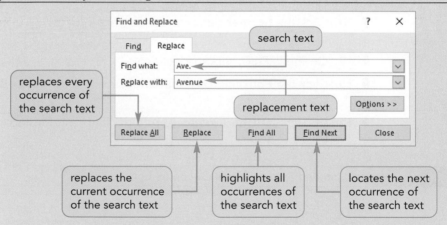

▸ **4.** Click the **Replace All** button to replace all occurrences of the search text without reviewing them. A dialog box opens, reporting that three replacements were made in the worksheet.

▸ **5.** Click the **OK** button to return to the Find and Replace dialog box.

Next, you will replace the other street title abbreviations.

▸ **6.** Repeat Steps 2 through 5 to replace all occurrences of each of the following: **St.** with **Street**, **Ln.** with **Lane,** and **Dr.** with **Drive**.

▸ **7.** Click the **Close** button to close the Find and Replace dialog box.

▸ **8.** Scroll through the Sales Report worksheet to verify that all street title abbreviations were replaced with their full names.

The Find and Replace dialog box can also be used to replace one format with another or to replace both text and a format simultaneously. Carol wants you to replace all occurrences of the white text on a gold fill in the Sales Report worksheet with blue text on a gold fill. You'll use the Find and Replace dialog box to make this formatting change.

To replace white text with blue text:

1. On the Home tab, in the Editing group, click the **Find & Select** button, and then click **Replace** (or press the **Ctrl+H** keys). The Find and Replace dialog box opens.

2. Delete the search text from the Find what and Replace with boxes, leaving those two boxes empty. By not specifying a text string to find and replace, the dialog box will search through all cells regardless of their content.

3. Click the **Options** button to expand the dialog box.

4. Click the **Format** button in the Find what row to open the Find Format dialog box, which is similar to the Format Cells dialog box you used earlier to format a range.

5. Click the **Font** tab to make it active, click the **Color** box, and then click the **White, Background 1** theme color.

6. Click the **Fill** tab, and then in the Background Color section, click the **gold** color (the eighth color in the first row).

7. Click the **OK** button to close the Find Format dialog box and return to the Find and Replace dialog box.

8. Click the **Format** button in the Replace with row to open the Replace Format dialog box.

9. On the Fill tab, click the **gold** color.

10. Click the **Font** tab, click the **Color** box, and then click **Blue** in the Standard Colors section.

11. Click the **OK** button to return to the Find and Replace dialog box. See Figure 2-30.

Figure 2-30 **Expanded Find and Replace dialog box**

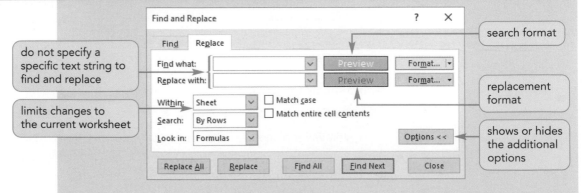

12. Click the **Replace All** button to replace all occurrences of white text on a gold fill in the Sales Report worksheet with blue text on a gold fill. A dialog box opens, reporting that 16 replacements were made.

13. Click the **OK** button to return to the Find and Replace dialog box.

It is a good idea to clear the find and replace formats after you are done so that they won't affect any future searches and replacements. Carol asks you to remove the formats from the Find and Replace dialog box.

To clear the options from the Find and Replace dialog box:

1. In the Find and Replace dialog box, click the **Format button arrow** in the Find what row, and then click **Clear Find Format**. The search format is removed.

2. Click the **Format button arrow** in the Replace with row, and then click **Clear Replace Format**. The replacement format is removed.

3. Click the **Close** button. The Find and Replace dialog box closes.

Another way to make multiple changes to the formats used in your workbook is through themes.

Working with Themes

Recall that a theme is a coordinated selection of fonts, colors, and graphical effects that are applied throughout a workbook to create a specific look and feel. When you switch to a different theme, the theme-related fonts, colors, and effects change throughout the workbook to reflect the new theme. The appearance of nontheme fonts, colors, and effects remains unchanged no matter which theme is applied to the workbook.

Most of the formatting you have applied to the Sales Report workbook is based on the Office theme. Carol wants you to change the theme to see how it affects the workbook's appearance.

To change the workbook's theme:

1. On the ribbon, click the **Page Layout** tab.

2. In the Themes group, click the **Themes** button. The Themes gallery opens. Office—the current theme—is the default.

3. Point to different themes in the Themes gallery using Live Preview to preview the impact of each theme on the fonts and colors used in the worksheet.

4. Click the **Droplet** theme to apply that theme to the workbook. See Figure 2-31.

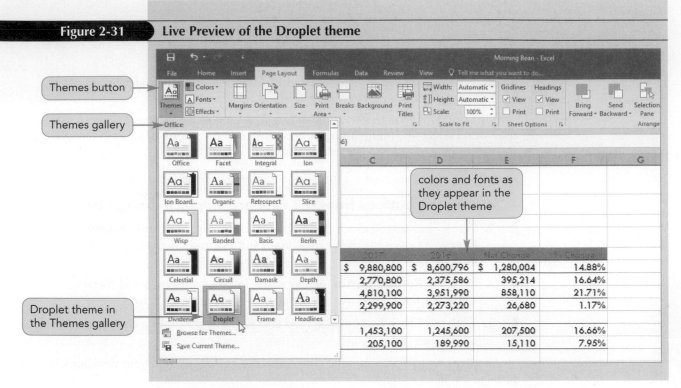

Figure 2-31 Live Preview of the Droplet theme

Changing the theme made a significant difference in the worksheet's appearance. The most obvious changes to the worksheet are the fill colors and the fonts. Only formatting options directly tied to a theme change when you select a different theme. Any formatting options you selected that were not theme-based remain unaffected by the change. For example, using a standard color or a nontheme font will not be affected by the choice of theme. In the Sales Report worksheet, the standard green color used for the font of the company description and the fill of the column title cells in the 2017 Monthly Gross Sales data didn't change because that green is not a theme color.

Sharing Styles and Themes

Using a consistent look and feel for all the files you create in Microsoft Office is a simple way to project a professional image. This consistency is especially important when a team is collaborating on a set of documents. When all team members work from a common set of style and design themes, readers will not be distracted by inconsistent or clashing formatting.

To quickly copy the styles from one workbook to another, open the workbook with the styles you want to copy, and then open the workbook in which you want to copy those styles. On the Home tab, in the Styles group, click the Cell Styles button, and then click Merge Styles. The Merge Styles dialog box opens, listing the currently open workbooks. Select the workbook with the styles you want to copy, and then click the OK button to copy those styles into the current workbook. If you modify any styles, you must copy the styles to the other workbook; Excel does not update styles between workbooks.

Because other Office files, including those created with Word or PowerPoint, use the same file format for themes, you can create one theme to use with all your Office files. To save a theme, click the Themes button in the Themes group on the Page Layout tab, and then click Save Current Theme. The Save Current Theme dialog box opens. Select a save location, type a name in the File name box, and then click the Save button. If you saved the theme file in a default Theme folder, the theme appears in the Themes gallery and affects any Office file that uses that theme.

Highlighting Data with Conditional Formats

Conditional formatting is often used to help analyze data. Conditional formatting applies formatting to a cell when its value meets a specified condition. For example, conditional formatting can be used to format negative numbers in red and positive numbers in black. Conditional formatting is dynamic, which means that the formatting can change when the cell's value changes. Each conditional format has a set of rules that define how the formatting should be applied and under what conditions the format will be changed.

REFERENCE

Highlighting Cells with Conditional Formatting

- Select the range in which you want to highlight cells.
- On the Home tab, in the Styles group, click the Conditional Formatting button, point to Highlight Cells Rules or Top/Bottom Rules, and then click the appropriate rule.
- Select the appropriate options in the dialog box.
- Click the OK button.

Excel has four types of conditional formatting—data bars, highlighting, color scales, and icon sets. In this module, you will use conditional formatting to highlight cells.

Highlighting Cells Based on Their Values

Cell highlighting changes the cell's font color or fill color based on the cell's value, as described in Figure 2-32. You can enter a value or a cell reference if you want to compare other cells with the value in a certain cell.

Figure 2-32   Highlight Cells rules

Rule	Highlights Cell Values
Greater Than	Greater than a specified number
Less Than	Less than a specified number
Between	Between two specified numbers
Equal To	Equal to a specified number
Text that Contains	That contain specified text
A Date Occurring	That contain a specified date
Duplicate Values	That contain duplicate or unique values

Carol wants to highlight important trends and sales values in the Sales Report worksheet. She asks you to highlight sales statistics that show a negative net change or negative percent change from the previous year to the current year. You will use conditional formatting to highlight the negative values in red.

To highlight negative values in red:

1. In the Sales Report worksheet, select the range **E6:F12,E16:F22** containing the net and percent changes overall and per store from the previous year to the current year.

2. On the ribbon, click the **Home** tab.

3. In the Styles group, click the **Conditional Formatting** button, and then point to **Highlight Cells Rules** to display a menu of the available rules.

4. Click **Less Than**. The Less Than dialog box opens so you can select the value and formatting to highlight negative values.

5. Make sure the value in the first box is selected, and then type **0** so that cells in the selected range that contain values that are less than 0 are formatted with a light red fill and dark red text. Live Preview shows the conditional formatting applied to the cells with negative numbers. See Figure 2-33.

Figure 2-33   **Live Preview of the Less Than conditional format**

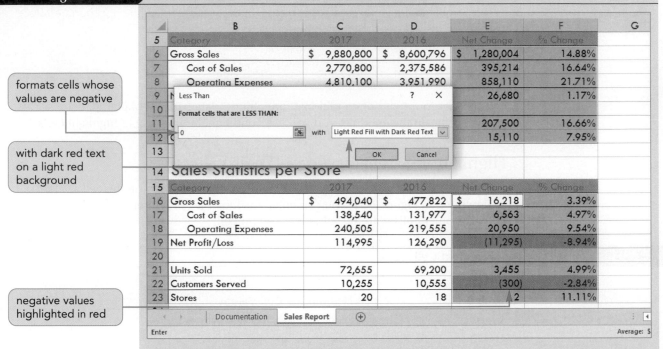

formats cells whose values are negative

with dark red text on a light red background

negative values highlighted in red

6. Click the **OK** button to apply the highlighting rule.

The conditional formatting highlights that Morning Bean showed a decline from the previous year to the current year for two statistics: The net profit per store declined $11,295 or 8.94 percent, and the number of customers served per store declined by 300 persons or 2.84 percent. These declines occurred because the two new stores that Morning Bean opened in 2017 are still finding a market, resulting in lower profit and customer served per store for the entire franchise.

Conditional formatting is dynamic, which means that changes in the values affect the format of those cells. The total number of customers served in 2017 was incorrectly entered in cell C12 as 205,100. The correct value is 215,100. You will make this change and view its impact on the cells highlighted with conditional formatting.

To view the impact of changing values on conditional formatting:

1. Click cell **C12** to select it.

2. Type **215,100** as the new value, and then press the Enter key. The conditional formatting changes based on the new value. See Figure 2-34.

Figure 2-34   **Cells with conditional formatting**

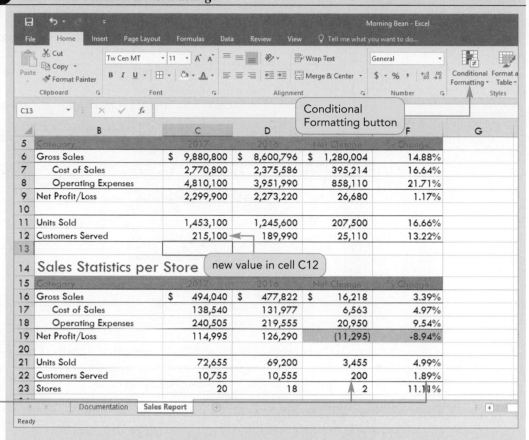

cells E22 and F22 are no longer formatted with red

By changing the value in cell C12 to 215,100, the net change in customers served per store in cell E22 is now 200 and the percentage change in cell F22 is now 1.89%. Because both of these values are now positive, the cells are no longer highlighted in red.

Highlighting Cells with a Top/Bottom Rule

Another way of applying conditional formatting is with the Quick Analysis tool. The **Quick Analysis tool**, which appears whenever you select a range of cells, provides access to the most common tools for data analysis and formatting. The Formatting category includes buttons for the Greater Than and Top 10% conditional formatting rules. You can highlight cells based on their values in comparison to other cells. For example, you can highlight cells with the 10 highest or lowest values in a selected range, or you can highlight the cells with above-average values in a range.

Carol wants to know which stores and which months rank in the top 10 percent of sales. She wants to use this information to identify the most successful stores and learn which months those stores show the highest sales volume. You'll highlight those values using the Quick Analysis tool.

To use a Top/Bottom Rule to highlight stores with the highest average sales:

1. Select the range **C27:N46** containing the monthly sales values for each of the 20 Morning Bean stores.

2. Click the **Quick Analysis** button 📊, and then point to **Top 10%**. Live Preview formats the cells in the top 10 percent with red font and a red fill. See Figure 2-35.

Figure 2-35   Quick Analysis tool applying conditional formatting

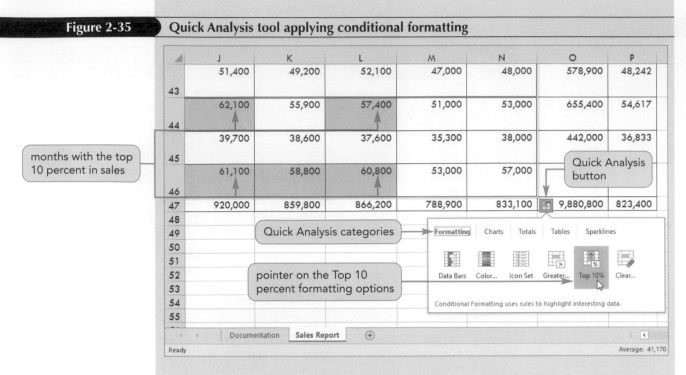

months with the top 10 percent in sales

Quick Analysis button

Quick Analysis categories

pointer on the Top 10 percent formatting options

Carol doesn't like the default format used by the Quick Analysis tool because red is usually applied to negative values and results. Instead, she wants to format the top 10 percent values in green.

3. Press the **Esc** key to close the Quick Analysis tool without applying the conditional format. The range C27:N46 remains selected.

> **Trouble?** If the conditional formatting was applied to the worksheet, press the Ctrl+Z keys to undo the format, and then continue with Step 4.

4. On the Home tab, in the Styles group, click the **Conditional Formatting** button, and then point to **Top/Bottom Rules** to display a list of available rules.

5. Click **Top 10%** to open the Top 10% dialog box.

6. Click the **with** arrow box and click **Green Fill with Dark Green Text** to apply green to cells with sales value in the top 10 percent. See Figure 2-36.

Figure 2-36   Top 10% dialog box

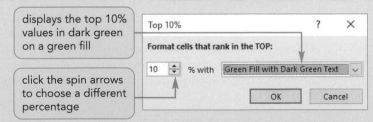

displays the top 10% values in dark green on a green fill

click the spin arrows to choose a different percentage

7. Click the **OK** button, and then click cell **A24** to deselect the cells. Monthly sales that rank in the top 10 percent are formatted with green.

8. Zoom the worksheet to **40%** so you can view all of the monthly gross sales and more easily see the sales pattern. See Figure 2-37.

Figure 2-37   Top 10 percent highlighted with green conditional formatting

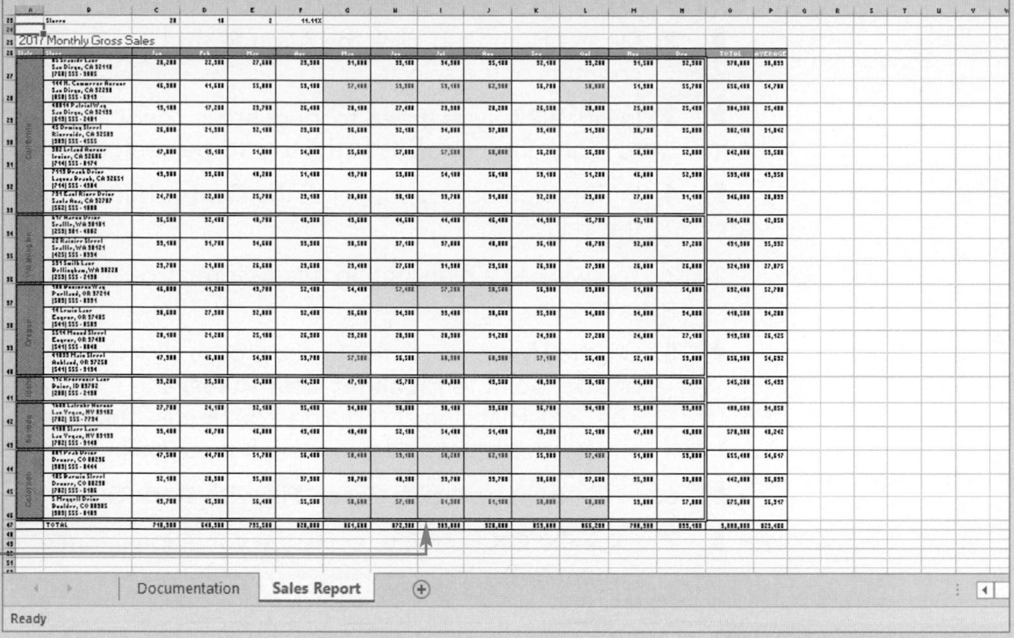

top 10 percent sales occur between May and October and are found in six stores

9. Return the zoom to **120%** or whatever zoom is appropriate for your monitor.

The top 10 percent in monthly sales comes from six stores located in San Diego, Irvine, Portland, Ashland, Denver, and Boulder. The highest sales appear to be centered around the months from May to October. This information will be valuable to Carol as she compares the sales performance of different stores and projects monthly cash flows for the company.

Other Conditional Formatting Options

To create dynamic conditional formats that are based on cell values rather than a constant value, you can enter a cell reference in the conditional format dialog box. For example, you can highlight all cells whose value is greater than the value in cell B10. For this type of conditional format, enter the formula =$B$10 in the conditional formatting dialog box. Note that the $ character keeps the cell reference from changing if that formula moves to another cell.

You can remove a conditional format at any time without affecting the underlying data by selecting the range containing the conditional format, clicking the Conditional Formatting button, and then clicking the Clear Rules command. A menu opens, providing options to clear the conditional formatting rules from the selected cells or the entire worksheet. You can also click the Quick Analysis button that appears in the lower-right corner of the selected range and then click the Clear Format button in the Formatting category. Note that you might see only "Clear..." as the button name.

Creating a Conditional Formatting Legend

When you use conditional formatting to highlight cells in a worksheet, the purpose of the formatting is not always immediately apparent. To ensure that everyone knows why certain cells are highlighted, you should include a **legend**, which is a key that identifies each format and its meaning.

Carol wants you to add a legend to the Sales Report worksheet to document the two conditional formatting rules you created in the worksheet.

To create a conditional formatting legend:

1. In cell **M25**, enter the text **Top 10% in Sales**, and then select cell **M25** again.

2. On the Home tab, click the **Align Right** button ☰ to right-align the cell contents of the selected cell.

3. In cell **N25**, type **green** to identify the conditional formatting color you used to highlight the values in the top 10 percent, and then select cell **N25** again.

4. In the Alignment group, click the **Center** button ☰ to center the contents of the cell.

   You will use a highlighting rule to format cell N25 using dark green text on a green fill.

5. On the Home tab, in the Styles group, click the **Conditional Formatting** button, point to **Highlight Cells Rules**, and then click **Text that Contains**. The Text That Contains dialog box opens. The text string "green" is automatically entered into the left input box.

6. In the right box, click **Green Fill with Dark Green Text**.

7. Click the **OK** button to apply the conditional formatting to cell N25. See Figure 2-38.

Figure 2-38	Conditional formatting legend

legend explains the purpose of the conditional formatting

	J	K	L	M	N	O	P	Q
22								
23								
24								
25				Top 10% in Sales	green			
26	Aug	Sep	Oct	Nov	Dec	TOTAL	AVERAGE	
	35,100	32,100	33,200	31,500	32,300	370,000	30,833	
27								
	62,300	56,700	58,000	51,300	55,700	656,400	54,700	
28								
	28,200	26,500	28,000	25,000	25,400	304,900	25,408	
29								
	37,800	33,400	31,900	30,700	35,000	382,100	31,842	
30								
	60,800	56,200	56,900	50,900	52,000	642,000	53,500	
31								
	56,100	53,100	51,200	46,000	52,300	599,400	49,950	

Documentation   Sales Report   ⊕

Ready

You've completed formatting the appearance of the workbook for the computer screen. Next you'll explore how to format the workbook for the printer.

Written Communication: Using Conditional Formatting Effectively

Conditional formatting is an excellent way to highlight important trends and data values to clients and colleagues. However, be sure to use it judiciously. Overusing conditional formatting might obscure the very data you want to emphasize. Keep in mind the following tips as you make decisions about what to highlight and how it should be highlighted:

- **Document the conditional formats you use.** If a bold, green font means that a sales number is in the top 10 percent of all sales, include that information in a legend in the worksheet.
- **Don't clutter data with too much highlighting.** Limit highlighting rules to one or two per data set. Highlights are designed to draw attention to points of interest. If you use too many, you will end up highlighting everything—and, therefore, nothing.
- **Use color sparingly in worksheets with highlights.** It is difficult to tell a highlight color from a regular fill color, especially when fill colors are used in every cell.
- **Consider alternatives to conditional formats.** If you want to highlight the top 10 sales regions, it might be more effective to simply sort the data with the best-selling regions at the top of the list.

Remember that the goal of highlighting is to provide a strong visual clue to important data or results. Careful use of conditional formatting helps readers to focus on the important points you want to make rather than distracting them with secondary issues and facts.

Formatting a Worksheet for Printing

You should format any worksheets you plan to print so that they are easy to read and understand. You can do this using the print settings, which enable you to set the page orientation, the print area, page breaks, print titles, and headers and footers. Print settings can be applied to an entire workbook or to individual sheets. Because other people will likely see your printed worksheets, you should format the printed output as carefully as you format the electronic version.

Carol wants you to format the Sales Report worksheet so she can distribute the printed version at the upcoming sales conference.

Using Page Break Preview

Page Break Preview shows only those parts of the active sheet that will print and how the content will be split across pages. A dotted blue border indicates a page break, which separates one page from another. As you format the worksheet for printing, you can use this view to control what content appears on each page.

Carol wants to know how the Sales Report worksheet would print in portrait orientation and how many pages would be required. You will look at the worksheet in Page Break Preview to find these answers.

To view the Sales Report worksheet in Page Break Preview:

1. Click the **Page Break Preview** button on the status bar. The worksheet switches to Page Break Preview.

2. Change the zoom level of the worksheet to **30%** so you can view the entire contents of this large worksheet. See Figure 2-39.

Figure 2-39   **Sales Report worksheet in Page Break preview**

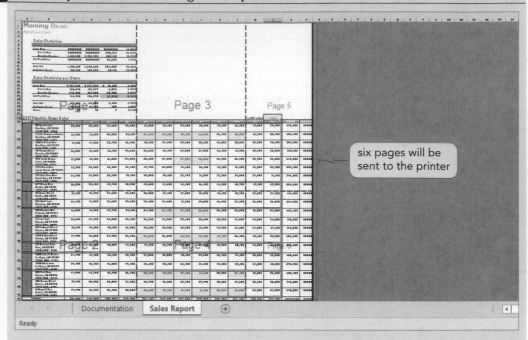

Trouble? If you see a different page layout or the worksheet is split onto a different number of pages, don't worry. Each printer is different, so the layout and pages might differ from what is shown in Figure 2-39.

Page Break Preview shows that a printout of the Sales Report worksheet requires six pages in portrait orientation, and that pages 3 and 5 would be mostly blank. Note that each printer is different, so your Page Break Preview might show a different number of pages. With this layout, each page would be difficult to interpret because the data is separated from the descriptive labels. Carol wants you to fix the layout so that the contents are easier to read and understand.

Defining the Print Area

By default, all cells in a worksheet containing text, formulas, or values are printed. If you want to print only part of a worksheet, you can set a print area, which is the region of the worksheet that is sent to the printer. Each worksheet has its own print area. Although you can set the print area in any view, Page Break Preview shades the areas of the worksheet that are not included in the print area, making it simple to confirm what will print.

Carol doesn't want the empty cells in the range G1:P24 to print, so you will set the print area to exclude those cells.

To set the print area of the Sales Report worksheet:

1. Change the zoom level of the worksheet to **80%** to make it easier to select cells and ranges.

2. Select the nonadjacent range **A1:F24,A25:P47** containing the cells with content.

3. On the ribbon, click the **Page Layout** tab.

4. In the Page Setup group, click the **Print Area** button, and then click **Set Print Area**. The print area changes to cover only the nonadjacent range A1:F24,A25:P47. The rest of the worksheet content is shaded to indicate that it will not be part of the printout.

5. Click cell **A1** to deselect the range.

6. Change the zoom level to **50%** so you can view more of the worksheet. See Figure 2-40.

Figure 2-40   **Print area set for the Sales Report worksheet**

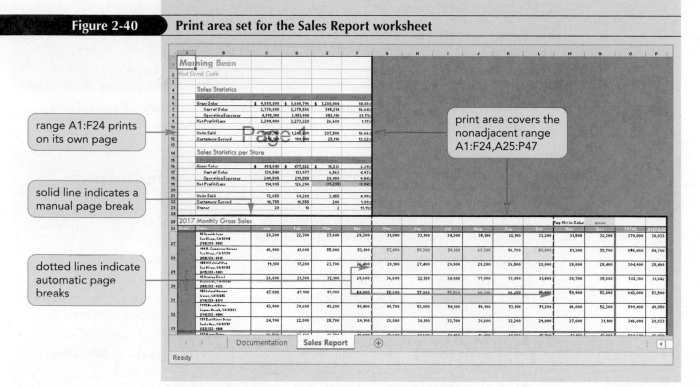

range A1:F24 prints on its own page

print area covers the nonadjacent range A1:F24,A25:P47

solid line indicates a manual page break

dotted lines indicate automatic page breaks

Inserting Page Breaks

Often, the contents of a worksheet will not fit onto a single printed page. When this happens, Excel prints as much of the content that fits on a single page without resizing, and then inserts automatic page breaks to continue printing the remaining worksheet content on successive pages. The resulting printouts might split worksheet content in awkward places, such as within a table of data.

To split the printout into logical segments, you can insert manual page breaks. Page Break Preview identifies manual page breaks with a solid blue line and automatic page breaks with a dotted blue line. When you specify a print area for a nonadjacent range, as you did for the Sales Report worksheet, you also insert manual page breaks around the adjacent ranges. So a manual page break already appears in the print area you defined (see Figure 2-40). You can remove a page break in Page Break Preview by dragging it out of the print area.

TIP

When you remove a page break, Excel will automatically rescale the printout to fit into the allotted pages.

REFERENCE

Inserting and Removing Page Breaks

To insert a page break:
- Click the first cell below the row where you want to insert a page break, click a column heading, or click a row heading.
- On the Page Layout tab, in the Page Setup group, click the Breaks button, and then click Insert Page Break.

To remove a page break:
- Select any cell below or to the right of the page break you want to remove.
- On the Page Layout tab, in the Page Setup group, click the Breaks button, and then click Remove Page Break.

or

- In Page Break Preview, drag the page break line out of the print area.

The Sales Report worksheet has automatic page breaks along columns F and L. Carol wants you to remove these automatic page breaks from the Sales Report worksheet.

To remove the automatic page breaks and insert manual page breaks:

1. Point to the dotted blue page break directly to the right of column L in the 2017 Monthly Gross Sales table until the pointer changes to ↔.

2. Drag the page break to the right and out of the print area. The page break is removed from the worksheet.

3. Point to the page break that is located in column F so that the pointer changes to ↔, and then drag the page break to the right and out of the print area.

4. Click the **I** column heading to select the entire column. You will add a manual page break between columns H and I to split the monthly gross sales data onto two pages so the printout will be larger and easier to read.

5. On the Page Layout tab, in the Page Setup group, click the **Breaks** button, and then click **Insert Page Break**. A manual page break is added between columns H and I, forcing the monthly gross sales onto a new page after the June data.

6. Click cell **A1** to deselect the column. The printout of the Sales Report worksheet is now limited to three pages. However, the gross sales data in the range A25:P47 is split across pages. See Figure 2-41.

Figure 2-41   **Manual page break in the print area**

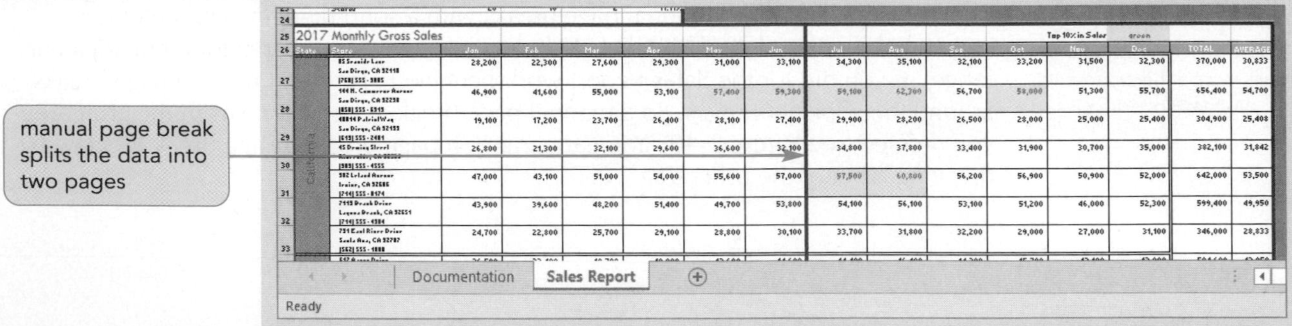

manual page break splits the data into two pages

Adding Print Titles

It is a good practice to include descriptive information such as the company name, logo, and worksheet title on each page of a printout in case a page becomes separated from the other pages. You can repeat information, such as the company name, by specifying which rows or columns in the worksheet act as print titles. If a worksheet contains a large table, you can print the table's column headings and row headings on every page of the printout by designating those columns and rows as print titles.

In the Sales Report worksheet, the company name appears on the first page of the printout but does not appear on subsequent pages. Also, the descriptive row titles for the monthly sales table in column A do not appear on the third page of the printout. You will add print titles to fix these issues.

To set the print titles:

TIP

You can also open the Page Setup dialog box by clicking the Dialog Box Launcher in the Page Setup group on the Page Layout tab.

1. On the Page Layout tab, in the Page Setup group, click the **Print Titles** button. The Page Setup dialog box opens with the Sheet tab displayed.

2. In the Print titles section, click the **Rows to repeat at top** box, move the pointer over the worksheet, and then select the range **A1:A2**. A flashing border appears around the first two rows of the worksheet to indicate that the contents of the first two rows will be repeated on each page of the printout. The row reference $1:$2 appears in the Rows to repeat at top box.

3. Click the **Columns to repeat at left** box, and then select columns A and B from the worksheet. The column reference $A:$B appears in the Columns to repeat at left box. See Figure 2-42.

Figure 2-42   **Sheet tab in the Page Setup dialog box**

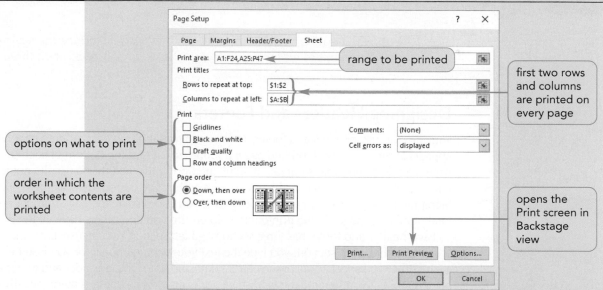

You will next rescale the worksheet so that it doesn't appear too small in the printout.

4. In the Page Setup dialog box, click the **Page** tab.

5. In the Scaling section, change the Adjust to amount to **60%** of normal size.

6. Click the **Print Preview** button to preview the three pages of printed material on the Print screen in Backstage view.

7. Verify that each of the three pages has the Morning Bean title at the top of the page and that the state and store names appear in the leftmost columns of pages 2 and 3. See Figure 2-43.

Figure 2-43 **Print titles on page 3 of the printout**

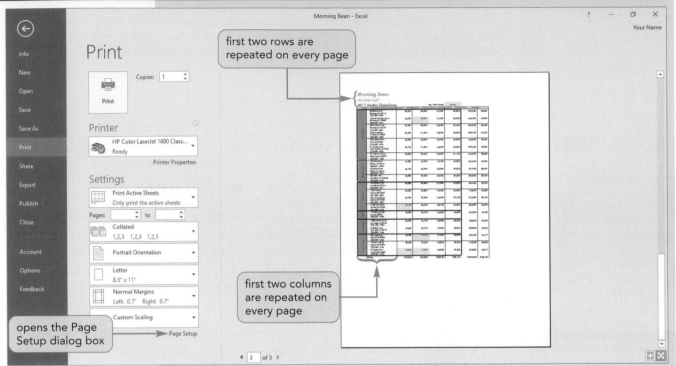

Trouble? If your printout doesn't fit on three pages, reduce the scaling factor from 60 percent to a slightly lower percentage until it does fit on three pages.

Designing Headers and Footers

You can also use headers and footers to repeat information on each printed page. A **header** appears at the top of each printed page; a **footer** appears at the bottom of each printed page. Headers and footers contain helpful and descriptive text that is usually not found within the worksheet, such as the workbook's author, the current date, or the workbook's filename. If the printout spans multiple pages, you can display the page number and the total number of pages in the printout to help ensure you and others have all the pages.

Each header and footer has three sections—a left section, a center section, and a right section. Within each section, you type the text you want to appear, or you insert elements such as the worksheet name or the current date and time. These header and footer elements are dynamic; if you rename the worksheet, for example, the name is automatically updated in the header or footer. Also, you can create one set of headers and footers for even and odd pages, and you can create another set for the first page in the printout.

Carol wants the printout to display the workbook's filename in the header's left section, and the current date in the header's right section. She wants the center footer to display the page number and the total number of pages in the printout, and the right footer to display your name as the workbook's author.

To set up the page header:

1. Near the bottom of the Print screen, click the **Page Setup** link. The Page Setup dialog box opens.

2. Click the **Header/Footer** tab to display the header and footer options.

3. Click the **Different first page** check box to select it. This lets you create one set of headers and footers for the first page, and one set for the rest of the pages.

4. Click the **Custom Header** button to open the Header dialog box. The dialog box contains two tabs—Header and First Page Header—because you selected the Different first page option.

5. On the Header tab, in the Left section box, type **Filename:**, press the **spacebar**, and then click the **Insert File Name** button. The code &[File], which displays the filename of the current workbook, is added to the left section of the header.

6. Press the **Tab** key twice to move to the right section of the header, and then click the **Insert Date** button. The code &[Date] is added to the right section of the header. See Figure 2-44.

Figure 2-44 Header dialog box

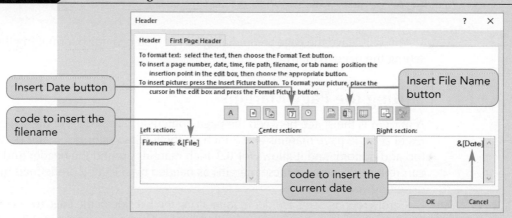

7. Click the **OK** button to return to the Header/Footer tab in the Page Setup dialog box.

You did not define a header for the first page of the printout, so no header information will be added to that page. Next, you will format the footer for all pages of the printout.

To create the page footer:

1. On the Header/Footer tab of the Page Setup dialog box, click the **Custom Footer** button. The Footer dialog box opens.

2. On the Footer tab, click the **Center section** box, type **Page**, press the **spacebar**, and then click the **Insert Page Number** button. The code &[Page], which inserts the current page number, appears after the label "Page."

3. Press the **spacebar**, type **of**, press the **spacebar**, and then click the **Insert Number of Pages** button. The code &[Pages], which inserts the total number of pages in the printout, is added to the Center section box. See Figure 2-45.

Figure 2-45   **Footer dialog box**

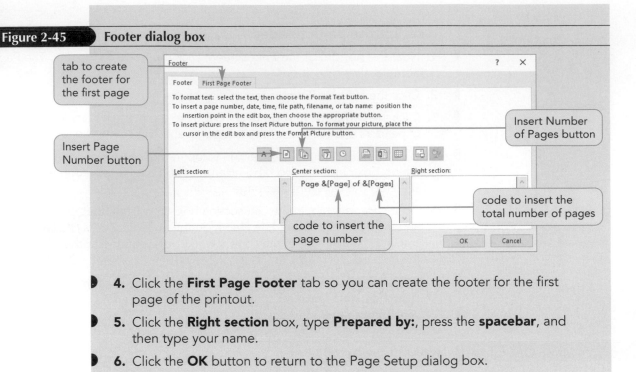

- tab to create the footer for the first page
- Insert Page Number button
- Insert Number of Pages button
- code to insert the total number of pages
- code to insert the page number

4. Click the **First Page Footer** tab so you can create the footer for the first page of the printout.

5. Click the **Right section** box, type **Prepared by:**, press the **spacebar**, and then type your name.

6. Click the **OK** button to return to the Page Setup dialog box.

You will leave the Page Setup dialog box so you can finish formatting the printout by setting the page margins.

Setting the Page Margins

A **margin** is the space between the page content and the edges of the page. By default, Excel sets the page margins to 0.7 inch on the left and right sides, and 0.75 inch on the top and bottom; and it allows for 0.3-inch margins around the header and footer. You can reduce or increase these margins as needed by selecting predefined margin sizes or setting your own.

Carol's reports need a wider margin along the left side of the page to accommodate the binding. She asks you to increase the left margin for the printout from 0.7 inch to 1 inch.

To set the left margin:

1. Click the **Margins** tab in the Page Setup dialog box to display options for changing the page margins.

2. Double-click the **Left** box to select the setting, and then type **1** to increase the size of the left margin to 1 inch. See Figure 2-46.

TIP

To select preset margins, click the Margins button in the Page Setup group on the Page Layout tab.

Figure 2-46   **Margins tab in the Page Setup dialog box**

sets the size of individual page margins

centers the printout horizontally and/or vertically on the page

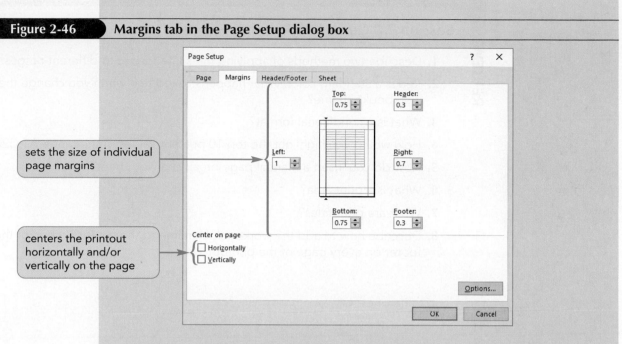

3. Click the **OK** button to close the dialog box. You can see the margin change in the preview on the Print screen in Backstage view.

Now that you have formatted the printout, you can print the final version of the worksheet.

To save and print the workbook:

1. With the workbook still in the Print screen in Backstage view, click the first box in the Settings section, and then click **Print Entire Workbook**.

Both the Sales Report worksheet and the Documentation sheet appear in the preview. As you can see, the printout will include a header with the filename and date on every page except the first page and a footer with your name on the first page and the page number along with the total number of pages on subsequent pages.

2. If you are instructed to print, print the entire workbook.

3. Click the **Back** button ⊖ from the Backstage View navigation bar to return to the workbook window.

4. Click the **Normal** button ▦ on the status bar to return the view of the workbook to normal.

5. Save the workbook, and then close it.

Carol is pleased with the worksheet's appearance and the layout of the printout. The formatting has made the contents easier to read and understand.

REVIEW

Session 2.2 Quick Check

1. Describe two methods of applying the same format to different ranges.

2. Red is a standard color. What happens to red text when you change the workbook's theme?

3. What is a conditional format?

4. How would you highlight the top 10 percent values of the range A1:C20?

5. How do you insert a manual page break in a worksheet?

6. What is a print area?

7. What are print titles?

8. Describe how to add the workbook filename to the center section of the footer on every page of the printout.

Review Assignments

Data Files needed for the Review Assignments: Menu.xlsx, Background2.jpg

Carol created a workbook that tracks the sales of individual items from the Morning Bean menu to share at an upcoming conference. She has already entered most of the financial formulas but wants you to calculate some additional values. She also asks you to format the workbook so that it will look professional and be easy to read and understand. Complete the following:

1. Open the **Menu** workbook located in the Excel2 > Review folder included with your Data Files, and then save the workbook as **Menu Sales** in the location specified by your instructor.
2. In the Documentation sheet, enter your name in cell B4 and the date in cell B5.
3. Change the theme of the workbook to Retrospect.
4. Make the following formatting changes to the Documentation sheet:
   a. Set the background image to the **Background2** JPEG file located in the Excel2 > Review folder.
   b. Format the text in cell A1 in a 26-point bold Calibri Light.
   c. In cell A1, change the font color of the word "Morning" to the Orange, Accent 1 theme color and change the font color of the word "Bean" to the Brown, Accent 3 theme color.
   d. Format the text in cell A2 in 18-point, italic, and change the font color to the Brown, Accent 3 theme color.
   e. Format the range A4:A6 with the Accent 3 cell style.
   f. Change the font color of the range B4:B6 to the Brown, Accent 3 theme color, and change the fill color to the White, Background 1 theme color.
   g. In cell B5, format the date in the Long Date format and left-align the cell contents.
5. Use the Format Painter to copy the formatting in the range A1:A2 in the Documentation sheet and paste it to the same range in the Menu Items worksheet. Change the font colors in cell A1 of the Menu Items worksheet to match the colors used in cell A1 of the Documentation sheet.
6. Apply the Title cell style to cells B4, B12, and A20.
7. Make the following changes to the Units Sold table in the range B5:F10:
   a. Apply the Accent3 cell style to the headings in the range B5:F5. Center the headings in the range C5:F5.
   b. In cell C6, use the SUM function to calculate the total number of specialty drinks sold by the company (found in the range C22:N31 in the Units Sold per Month table). In cell C7, use the SUM function to calculate the total number of smoothies sold (in the range C32:N36). In cell C8, use the SUM function calculate the total number of sandwiches sold (in the range C37:N41). In cell C9, calculate the total number of soups sold (in the range C42:N45).
   c. In cell C10, use the SUM function to calculate the total units sold from all menu types in 2017 (based on the range C6:C9). Copy the formula to cell D10 to calculate the total units sold in 2016.
   d. In each cell of the range E6:E10, calculate the change in units sold between the 2017 and 2016 values. In each cell of the range F6:F10, calculate the percent change from 2016 to 2017. (*Hint*: The percent change is the net change divided by the 2016 value.)
   e. Format the range C6:E10 with the Comma style and no decimal places.
   f. Format the range F6:F10 with the Percent style and two decimal places.
   g. Add a top border to the range B10:F10.
8. Make the following changes to the Gross Sales table in the range B13:F18:
   a. In cells C18 and D18, use the SUM function to calculate the totals of the 2017 and 2016 sales.
   b. In the range E14:F18, enter formulas to calculate the net change and the percent change in sales.
   c. Use the Format Painter to copy the formatting from the range B5:F10 to the range B13:F18.
   d. Format the ranges C14:E14 and C18:E18 with Accounting format and no decimal places.

9. Make the following changes to the Units Sold per Month table in the range A21:O46:

   a. In the range O22:O45, use the SUM function to calculate the total units sold for each menu item. In the range C46:O46, use the SUM function to calculate the total items sold per month and overall.

   b. Format the headings in the range A21:O21 with the Accent3 cell style. Center the headings in the range C21:O21.

   c. Format the units sold values in the range C22:O46 with the Comma style and no decimal places.

   d. Change the fill color of the subtotals in the range O22:O45,C46:N46 to the White, Background 1, Darker 15% theme color (the first color in the third row).

   e. Merge each of the menu categories in the ranges A22:A31, A32:A36, A37:A41, and A42:A45 into single cells. Rotate the text of the cells up, and middle-align the cell contents.

   f. Format cell A22 with the Accent1 cell style. Format cell A32 with the Accent2 cell style. Format cell A37 with the Accent3 cell style. Format cell A42 with the Accent4 cell style. Change the font size of these four merged cells to 14 points.

   g. Add thick outside borders around each category of menu item in the ranges A22:O31, A32:O36, A37:O41, and A42:O45.

10. Use conditional formatting to highlight negative values in the range E6:F10,E14:F18 with a light red fill with dark red text to highlight which menu categories showed a decrease in units sold or gross sales from 2016 to 2017.

11. Use conditional formatting to format cells that rank in the top 10 percent of the range C22:N45 with a green fill with dark green text to highlight the menu items and months that are in the top 10 percent of units sold.

12. Create a legend for the conditional formatting you added to the worksheet. In cell O20, enter the text **Top Sellers**. Add thick outside borders around the cell, and then use conditional formatting to display this text with a green fill with dark green text.

13. Set the following print formats for the Menu Items worksheet:

   a. Set the print area to the nonadjacent range A1:F19,A20:O46.

   b. Switch to Page Break Preview, and then remove any automatic page breaks in the Units Sold per Month table. Insert a manual page break to separate the June and July sales figures. The printout of the Menu Sales worksheet should fit on three pages.

   c. Scale the printout to 70 percent.

   d. Create print titles that repeat the first three rows at the top of the sheet and the first two columns at the left of the sheet.

   e. Increase the left margin of the printout from 0.7 inch to 1 inch.

   f. Create headers and footers for the printout with a different first page.

   g. For the first page header, print **Prepared by** followed by your name in the right section. For every other page, print **Filename:** followed by the filename in the left section and the date in the right section. (*Hint*: Use the buttons in the Header dialog box to insert the filename and date.)

   h. For every footer, including the first page, print **Page** followed by the page number and then **of** followed by the total number of pages in the printout in the center section.

   i. Preview the printout to verify that the company name and description appear on every page of the Menu Items worksheet printout and that the menu category and menu item name appear on both pages with the Units Sold table. If you are instructed to print, print the entire workbook in portrait orientation.

14. Save the workbook, and then close it.

Case Problem 1

Data File needed for this Case Problem: Green.xlsx

Green Clean Homes   Sean Patel is developing a business plan for Green Clean Homes, a new professional home cleaning service in Toledo, Ohio. As part of his business plan, Sean needs to predict the company's annual income and expenses. You will help him finalize and format the Excel workbook containing the projected income statement. Complete the following:

1. Open the **Green** workbook located in the Excel2 > Case1 folder, and then save the workbook as **Green Clean** in the location specified by your instructor.
2. In the Documentation sheet, enter your name in cell B3 and the date in cell B4.
3. Display the date in cell B4 in the Long Date format and left-aligned.
4. Change the theme of the workbook to Facet.
5. Make the following formatting changes to the Documentation sheet:
   a. Merge and center cells A1 and B1.
   b. Apply the Accent2 cell style to the merged cell A1 and to the range A3:A5.
   c. In cell A1, set the font size to 22 points and bold the text. Italicize the word "Clean" in the company name.
   d. Add borders around each cell in the range A3:B5. Top-align the text in the range A3:B5.
   e. Change the font color of the text in the range B3:B5 to Dark Green, Accent 2.
6. In the Income Statement worksheet, merge and center the range A1:C1, and then apply the Accent2 cell style to the merged cell. Change the font size to 24 points and the text style to bold. Italicize the word "Clean" within the company name.
7. Make the following changes to the Income Statement worksheet:
   a. Format the range A3:C3 with the Heading 1 cell style.
   b. Format the range A4:C4,A9:C9 with the 40% - Accent1 cell style.
   c. Format cell B5 in the Accounting style with no decimal places.
   d. Format cell B6 and the range B10:B17 in the Comma style with no decimal places.
8. Add the following calculations to the workbook:
   a. In cell C7, calculate the gross profit, which is equal to the gross sales minus the cost of sales.
   b. In cell C18, calculate the company's total operating expenses, which is equal to the sum of the values in the range B10:B17. Format the value in the Accounting format with no decimal places.
   c. In cell C20, calculate the company's operating profit, which is equal to its gross profit minus its total operating expenses.
   d. In cell C21, calculate the company's incomes taxes by multiplying its total operating profit by the corporate tax rate (cell G25). Format the value in the Accounting format with no decimal places.
   e. In cell C22, calculate the company's net profit, which is equal to the total operating profit minus the income taxes.
9. Finalize the formatting of the Projected Income statement by adding the following:
   a. Add a bottom border to the ranges A6:C6, A17:C17, and A20:C20. Add a single top border and a double bottom border to the range A22:C22.
   b. Indent the expenses categories in the range A10:A17 twice.
10. Format the Financial Assumptions section as follows:
   a. Add borders around all of the cells in the range E4:G25.
   b. Format the range E3:G3 with the Heading 1 cell style.
   c. Merge the cells in the ranges E4:E7, E9:E13, E14:E15, E16:E18, and E20:E22.
   d. Top-align and left-align the range E4:E25.
   e. Change the fill color of the range F4:F25 to Green, Accent 1, Lighter 60%.

11. Use conditional formatting to highlight the net profit (cell C22) if its value is less than $50,000 with a light red fill with dark red text.

12. Change the value in cell G9 from 4 to **5**. Observe the impact that hiring another cleaner has on the projected net profit for the company in cell C22.

13. Format the printed version of the Income Statement worksheet as follows:

    a. Add a manual page break between columns D and E.

    b. For the first page, add a header that prints **Prepared by** followed by your name in the left section of the header and the current date in the right section of the header. Do not display header text on any other page.

    c. For every page, add a footer that prints the workbook filename in the left section, **Page** followed by the page number in the center section, and the worksheet name in the right section.

    d. Set the margins to 1 inch on all four sides of the printout, and center the contents of the worksheet horizontally within the printed page.

14. If you are instructed to print, print the entire contents of the workbook in portrait orientation.

15. Save and close the workbook.

APPLY

Case Problem 2

Data File needed for this Case Problem: Peak.xlsx

Peak Bytes   Peter Taylor is an engineer at Peak Bytes, an Internet service provider located in Great Falls, Montana. Part of Peter's job is to track the over-the-air connection speeds from the company's transmitters. Data from an automated program recording Internet access times has been entered into a workbook, but the data is difficult to interpret. He wants you to edit the workbook so that the data is easier to read and the fast and slow connection times are quickly visible. He also wants the workbook to provide summary statistics on the connection speeds. Complete the following:

1. Open the **Peak** workbook located in the Excel2 > Case2 folder, and then save the workbook as **Peak Bytes** in the location specified by your instructor.

2. In the Documentation sheet, enter your name in cell B3 and the date in cell B4.

3. Apply the Banded theme to the workbook.

4. Format the Documentation sheet as follows:

   a. Apply the Title cell style to cell A1. Change the font style to bold and the font size to 24 points.

   b. Add borders around the range A3:B5.

   c. Apply the Accent4 cell style to the range A3:A5.

   d. Top-align the contents in the range A3:B5.

5. In the Speed Test worksheet, move the data from the range A1:D97 to the range A12:D108.

6. Copy cell A1 from the Documentation sheet, and paste it into cell A1 of the Speed Test worksheet.

7. In cell A2, enter **Internet Speed Test Results**. Apply the Heading 1 cell style to the range A2:D2.

8. In cell A4, enter **Date** and format it using the Accent4 cell style. In cell B4, enter **4/8/2017** and format it using the Long Date format. Add a border around the cells in the range A4:B4.

9. Format the data in the Speed Test worksheet as follows:

   a. In the range A13:A108, format the numeric date and time values with the Time format. (*Hint*: The Time format is in the Number Format box in the Number group on the Home tab.)

   b. In the range C13:D108, show the numbers with three decimal places.

   c. In the range A12:D12, apply the Accent4 cell style and center the text.

   d. In the range A12:D108, add borders around all of the cells.

10. Create a table of summary statistics for the Internet Speed Test as follows:

    a. Copy the headings in the range B12:D12, and paste them into the range B6:D6.

    b. In cell A7, enter **Average**. In cell A8, enter **Minimum**. In cell A9, enter **Maximum**. Format the range A7:A9 with the Accent4 cell style.

   c. In cell B7, use the AVERAGE function to calculate the average ping value of the values in the range B13:B108. In cell B8, use the MIN function to calculate the minimum ping value of the values in the range B13:B108. In cell B9, use the MAX function to calculate the maximum ping value of the values in the range B13:B108.

   d. Copy the formulas from the range B7:B9 to the range C7:D9 to calculate summary statistics for the download and upload speeds from the Internet test.

   e. Format the values in the range B7,C7:D9 to show two decimal places.

   f. Add borders around all of the cells in the range A6:D9.

11. Use conditional formatting to highlight ping values greater than 70 in the range B13:B108 with a light red fill with dark red text to highlight times when the Internet usually appears to be slow.

12. Use conditional formatting to highlight upload values less than 3.5 in the range C13:C108 with a light red fill with dark red text.

13. Use conditional formatting to highlight download values less than 2 in the range D13:D108 with a light red fill with dark red text.

14. In cell D11, enter the text **Slow Connection**. Use conditional formatting to display this text string with a light red fill with dark red text. Center the text, and add a border around cell D11.

15. Set the print titles to repeat the first 12 rows at the top of every page of the printout.

16. For the first page of the printout, add a header that prints **Prepared by** followed by your name in the left section of the header and the current date in the right section of the header. Do not display header text on any other page.

17. For every page, add a footer that prints the workbook filename in the left section, **Page** followed by the page number followed by **of** followed by the number of pages in the center section, and then the worksheet name in the right section.

18. If you are instructed to print, print the entire contents of the workbook in portrait orientation.

19. Save and close the workbook.

Case Problem 3

Data File needed for this Case Problem: Wait.xlsx

YuriTech   Kayla Schwartz is the customer service manager at YuriTech, an electronics and computer firm located in Scottsdale, Arizona. Kayla is analyzing the calling records for technical support calls to YuriTech to determine which times are understaffed, resulting in unacceptable wait times. She has compiled several months of data and calculated the average wait times in one-hour intervals for each day of the week. You will format Kayla's workbook to make it easier to determine when YuriTech should hire more staff to assist with customer support requests. Complete the following:

1. Open the **Wait** workbook located in the Excel2 > Case3 folder, and then save the workbook as **Wait Times** in the location specified by your instructor.

2. In the Documentation sheet, enter your name in cell B3 and the date in cell B4.

3. Apply the Ion theme to the workbook.

4. Format the Documentation sheet as follows:

   a. Format the title in cell A1 using a 36-point Impact font with the Purple, Accent 6 font color.

   b. Format the range A3:A5 with the Accent6 cell style.

   c. Add a border around the cells in the range A3:B5. Wrap the text within each cell, and top-align the cell text.

5. Copy the format you used in cell A1 of the Documentation sheet, and paste it to cell A1 of the Wait Times worksheet.

CHALLENGE

6. Format the text in cell A2 with 14-point bold font and the Purple, Accent6 font color.

7. In the range A14:H39, format the average customer wait times for each hour and day of the week data as follows:

   a. Merge and center the range A14:H14, and apply the Title cell style to the merged contents.

   b. Change the number format of the data in the range B16:H39 to show one decimal place.

   c. Format the column and row labels in the range A15:H15,A16:A39 with the Accent6 cell style. Center the column headings in the range B15:H15.

8. In cell B5, enter the value **22** as an excellent wait time. In cell B6, enter **34** as a good wait time. In cell B7, enter **45** as an acceptable wait time. In cell B8, enter **60** as a poor wait time. In cell B9, enter **78** as a very poor wait time. In cell B10, enter **90** as an unacceptable wait time.

9. In the range A4:C10, apply the following formats to the wait time goals:

   a. Merge and center the range A4:C4, and apply the Accent6 cell style to the merged cells.

   b. Add borders around the cells in the range A4:C10.

10. In cell E4, enter the label **Average Wait Time (All Days)**. In cell E7, enter the label **Average Wait Time (Weekdays)**. In cell E10, enter the label **Average Wait Time (Weekends)**.

11. Merge and center the range E4:F6, wrap the text in the merged cell, center the cell content both horizontally and vertically, and then apply the Accent6 cell style to the merged cell.

12. Copy the format from the merged cell E4:F6 to cells E7 and E10.

13. In cell G4, enter a formula to calculate the average of the wait times in the range B16:H39. In cell G7, enter a formula to calculate the average weekday wait times in the range C16:G39. In cell G10, calculate the average weekend rate times in the range B16:B39,H16:H39.

14. Merge and center the ranges G4:G6, G7:G9, and G10:G12, and then center the calculated averages vertically within each merged cell.

15. Add borders around the cells in the range E4:G12.

16. Change the fill color of the range A5:C5 to a medium green, the fill color of the range A6:C6 to a light green, the fill color of the range A7:C7 to a light gold, the fill color of the range A8:C8 to a light red, and the fill color of the range A9:C9 to a medium red. Format the range A10:C10 with white text on a black background.

✛ **Explore** 17. Use conditional formatting to highlight cells with custom formats as follows:

   a. Select the range G4:G12,B16:H39. Use conditional formatting to highlight cells with values less than 22 with a custom format that matches the fill color used in the range A5:C5.

   b. Use conditional formatting to highlight cells with values greater than 90 in the range G4:G12,B16:H39 with a custom format of a white font on a black fill.

   c. Use conditional formatting to highlight cells with values between 22 and 34 in the range G4:G12,B16:H39 with a custom format that matches the fill color used in the range A6:C6.

   d. Use conditional formatting to highlight cells with values between 34 and 60 in the range G4:G12,B16:H39 with a light gold fill color that matches the cells in the range A7:C7.

   e. Use conditional formatting to highlight cells with values between 60 and 78 in the range G4:G12,B16:H39 with light red, matching the fill color of the cells in the range A8:C8.

   f. Use conditional formatting to highlight cells with values between 78 and 90 in the range G4:G12,B16:H39 with medium red, matching the fill color of the cells in the range A9:C9.

18. In cell A41, enter the label **Notes** and then format it with the Title cell style.

19. Merge the range A42:H50. Top- and left-align the contents of the cell. Turn on text wrapping within the merged cell. Add a thick outside border to the merged cell.

20. Within the merged cell in the range A42:H50, summarize your conclusions about the wait times. Answer whether the wait times are within acceptable limits on average for the entire week, on weekdays, and on weekends. Also indicate whether there are times during the week that customers are experience very poor to unacceptable delays.

21. Format the printed version of the Wait Times worksheet as follows:

   a. Scale the sheet so that it fits on a single page in portrait orientation.

   b. Center the sheet on the page horizontally and vertically.

c. Add the header **Prepared by** followed by your name in the right section.

d. Add a footer that prints the filename in the left section, the worksheet name in the center section, and the date in the right section.

22. If you are instructed to print, print the entire contents of the workbook.

23. Save and close the workbook.

Case Problem 4

CREATE

Data File needed for this Case Problem: Pandaisia.xlsx

Pandaisia Chocolates   Anne Ambrose is the owner and head chocolatier of Pandaisia Chocolates, a chocolate shop located in Essex, Vermont. Anne has asked you to create an Excel workbook in which she can enter customer orders. She wants the workbook to be easy to use and read. The final design of the order form is up to you. One possible solution is shown in Figure 2-47.

Figure 2-47   Pandaisia Chocolates order form

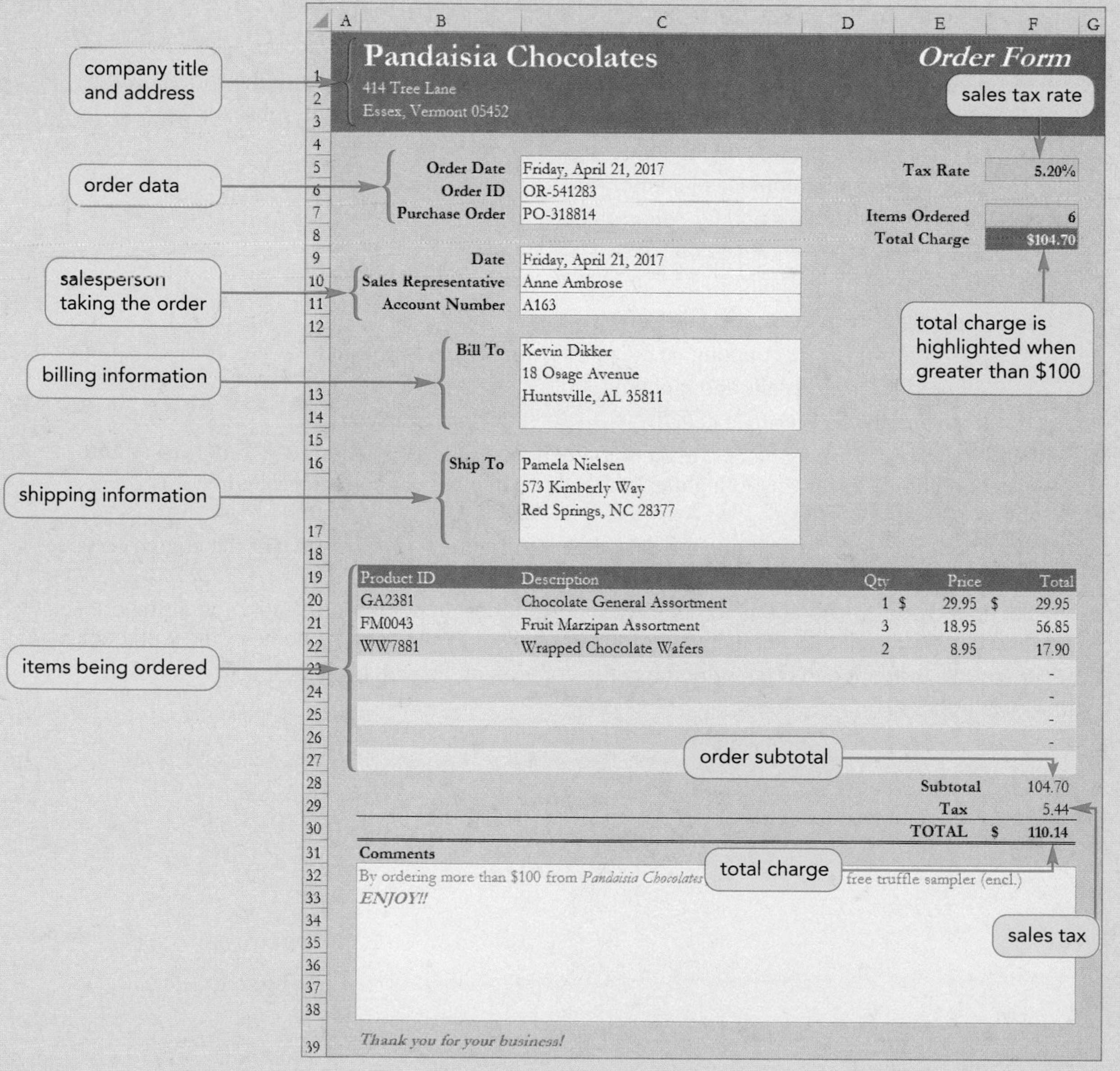

Complete the following:

1. Open the **Pandaisia** workbook located in the Excel2 > Case3 folder, and then save the workbook as **Pandaisia Order** in the location specified by your instructor.

2. In the Documentation sheet, enter your name in cell B3 and the date in cell B4.

3. Insert a worksheet named **Order Form** after the Documentation worksheet.

4. Enter the following information in the order form:

    • The title and address of Pandaisia Chocolates
    • The order date, order ID, and purchase order ID
    • The date, sales representative, and account number for the order
    • The billing address of the order
    • The shipping address of the order
    • A table listing every item ordered including the item's product ID, description, quantity ordered, price, and total charge for the item(s)
    • A comment box where Anne can insert additional information about the order

5. Include formulas in the order form to do the following:

    a. For each item ordered, calculate the cost of the item(s), which is equal to the quantity multiplied by the price.
    b. Calculate the subtotal of the costs for every item ordered by the customer.
    c. Calculate the sales tax for the order, which is equal to 5.2 percent times the subtotal value.
    d. Calculate the total cost of the order, which is equal to the subtotal plus the sale tax.

6. Format the order form by doing the following:

    a. Apply a different built-in Excel theme.
    b. Change the font colors and fill colors.
    c. Format a text string within a cell.
    d. Align content within cells.
    e. Format dates with the Long Date format.
    f. Apply the Percent, Accounting, and Currency formats as appropriate.
    g. Add borders around cells and ranges.
    h. Merge a range into a single cell.

7. Pandaisia Chocolates includes a free complimentary truffle sample for every order over $100. Use conditional formatting to highlight the total charge in bold colored font when it is greater than $100.

8. Test your order form by entering the data shown in Figure 2-47. Confirm that the charge on your order matches that shown in the figure.

9. Set up the print version of the order form so that it prints in portrait orientation on a single sheet. Add a header and/or footer that includes your name, the date, and the name of the workbook.

10. If you are instructed to print, print the entire contents of the workbook.

11. Save and close the workbook.

OBJECTIVES

Session 3.1
- Document formulas and data values
- Explore function syntax
- Insert functions from the Formula Library
- Perform a what-if analysis

Session 3.2
- AutoFill series and formulas
- Use relative and absolute cell references
- Use the Quick Analysis tool
- Work with dates and Date functions
- Find values with Lookup functions
- Work with Logical functions

Performing Calculations with Formulas and Functions

Calculating Farm Yield and Revenue

Case | *Wingait Farm*

Jane Wingait is the owner and operator of Wingait Farm, a small farm located outside of Cascade, Iowa. Jane's cash crop is corn, and she has planted almost 140 acres of the sweet corn variety for the past 11 years. Near harvest time every year Jane samples and analyzes a portion of her crop to estimate her farm's total yield for the year. She wants you to help her design an Excel workbook that will calculate her corn yield. As Jane prepares for next year's crop, she also wants to use Excel to track her corn's growth from planting to harvesting. As you create the workbook, you will explore how Jane can use Excel formulas to help her in running her farm.

STARTING DATA FILES

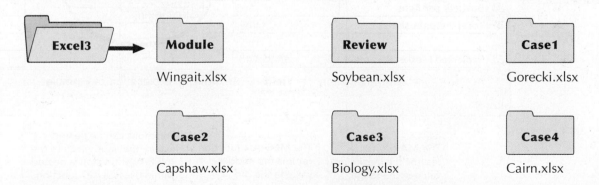

Excel3 → Module	Review	Case1
Wingait.xlsx	Soybean.xlsx	Gorecki.xlsx

Case2	Case3	Case4
Capshaw.xlsx	Biology.xlsx	Cairn.xlsx

Session 3.1 Visual Overview:

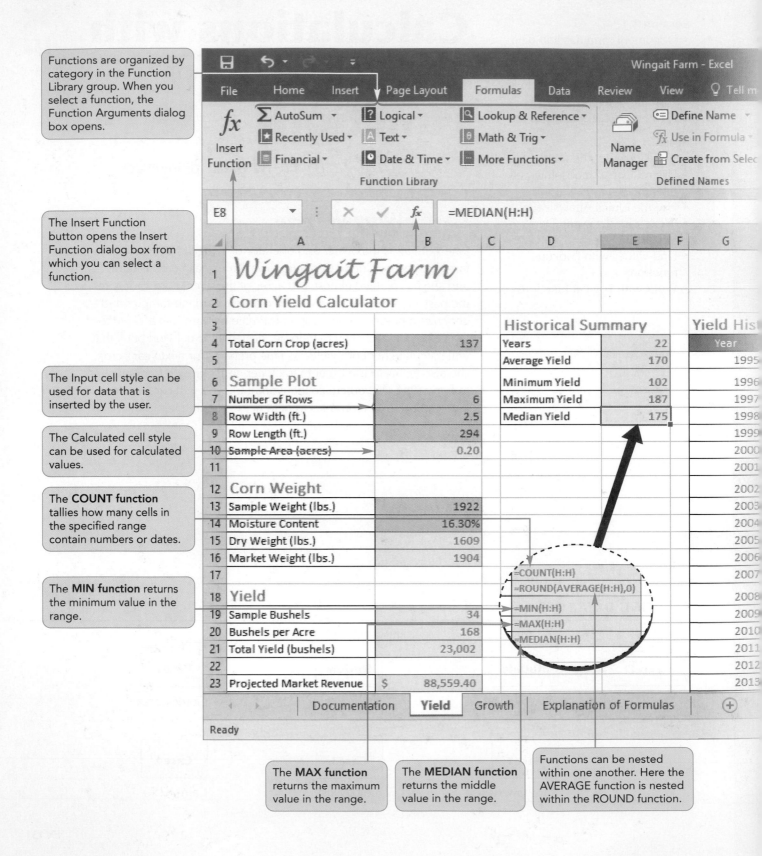

Functions are organized by category in the Function Library group. When you select a function, the Function Arguments dialog box opens.

The Insert Function button opens the Insert Function dialog box from which you can select a function.

The Input cell style can be used for data that is inserted by the user.

The Calculated cell style can be used for calculated values.

The **COUNT function** tallies how many cells in the specified range contain numbers or dates.

The **MIN function** returns the minimum value in the range.

The **MAX function** returns the maximum value in the range.

The **MEDIAN function** returns the middle value in the range.

Functions can be nested within one another. Here the AVERAGE function is nested within the ROUND function.

Formulas and Functions

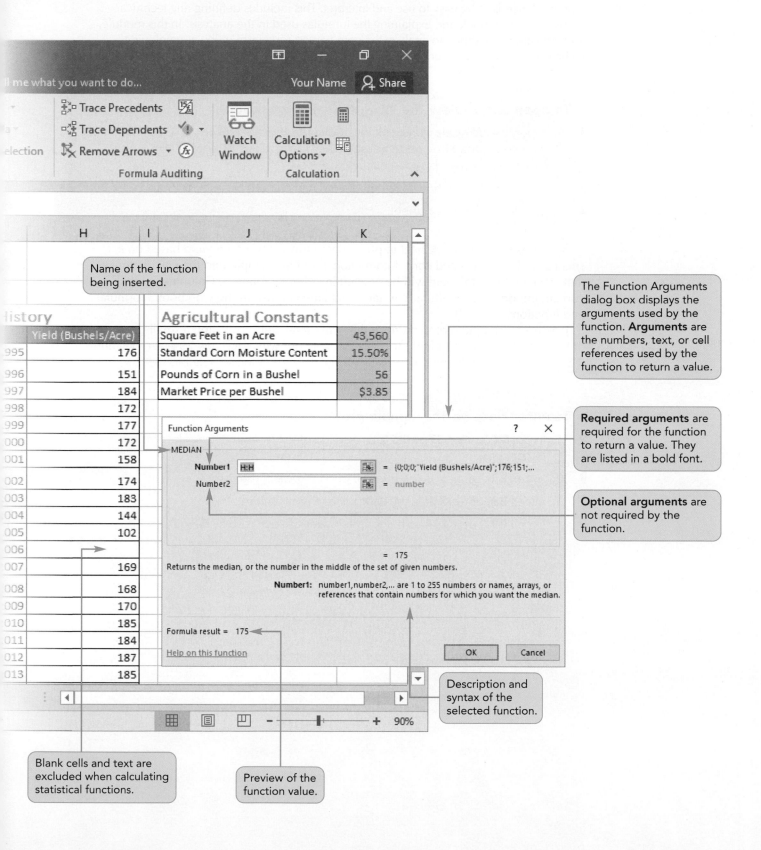

Name of the function being inserted.

The Function Arguments dialog box displays the arguments used by the function. **Arguments** are the numbers, text, or cell references used by the function to return a value.

Required arguments are required for the function to return a value. They are listed in a bold font.

Optional arguments are not required by the function.

Description and syntax of the selected function.

Blank cells and text are excluded when calculating statistical functions.

Preview of the function value.

Agricultural Constants

Square Feet in an Acre	43,560
Standard Corn Moisture Content	15.50%
Pounds of Corn in a Bushel	56
Market Price per Bushel	$3.85

History

	Yield (Bushels/Acre)
995	176
996	151
997	184
998	172
999	177
000	172
001	158
002	174
003	183
004	144
005	102
006	
007	169
008	168
009	170
010	185
011	184
012	187
013	185

Function Arguments

MEDIAN

Number1 H:H = {0;0;0;"Yield (Bushels/Acre)";176;151;...
Number2   = number

= 175

Returns the median, or the number in the middle of the set of given numbers.

Number1: number1,number2,... are 1 to 255 numbers or names, arrays, or references that contain numbers for which you want the median.

Formula result = 175

Help on this function

OK   Cancel

90%

Making Workbooks User-Friendly

Excel is a powerful application for interpreting a wide variety of data used in publications from financial reports to scientific articles. To be an effective tool for data analysis, a workbook needs to be easy to use and interpret. This includes defining any technical terms in the workbook and explaining the formulas used in the analysis. In this module, you'll create a workbook to analyze the corn harvest for a farm in Iowa, employing techniques to make the workbook easily accessible to other users.

To open and review the Wingait Farms workbook:

▶ **1.** Open the **Wingait** workbook located in the **Excel3 > Module** folder included with your Data Files, and then save the workbook as **Wingait Farm** in the location specified by your instructor.

▶ **2.** In the Documentation sheet, enter your name in cell B3 and the date in cell B4.

▶ **3.** Go to the **Yield** worksheet.

Jane uses the Yield worksheet to project her farm's entire corn yield based on a small sample of harvested corn. Information about the sample and the calculations that estimate the total yield will be entered in columns A and B. Columns D and E contain important agricultural constants that Jane will use in the workbook's formulas and functions.

Jane uses a sample plot to estimate the farm's total yield. This plot, a small portion of Jane's 137-acre farm, is laid out in six rows of corn with each row 294 feet long and 2.5 feet wide. You will enter information about the size of the sample plot.

To enter data on the sample plot:

▶ **1.** In cell **B4**, enter **137** as the total acreage of the farm that Jane devotes to sweet corn.

▶ **2.** In cell **B7**, enter **6** as the number of corn rows in the sample plot.

▶ **3.** In cell **B8**, enter **2.5** as the width of each row in feet.

▶ **4.** In cell **B9**, enter **294** as the length in feet of each row. See Figure 3-1.

| Figure 3-1 | Sample plot data entered |

size of the farm in acres

dimensions of the sample plot

constants used in agricultural calculations

	A	B	C	D	E	F
1	*Wingait Farm*					
2	Corn Yield Calculator					
3						
4	Total Corn Crop (acres)	137				
5						
6	Sample Plot			Agricultural Constants		
7	Number of Rows	6		Square Feet in an Acre	43,560	
8	Row Width (ft.)	2.5		Standard Corn Moisture Content	15.50%	
9	Row Length (ft.)	294		Pounds of Corn in a Bushel	56	
10	Sample Area (acres)			Market Price per Bushel	$3.85	
11						
12	Corn Weight					
13	Sample Weight (lbs.)					
14	Moisture Content					
15	Dry Weight (lbs.)					
16	Market Weight (lbs.)					
17						

Documentation Yield Yield History Growth Explanation of Formulas ⊕

Ready

The width and length of the sample rows are measured in feet, but Jane needs the total area expressed in acres. To calculate the area of the sample being tested, you need to refer to the agricultural equations that Jane documented for you.

Documenting Formulas

Documenting the contents of a workbook helps to avoid errors and confusion. It also makes it easier for others to interpret the analysis in the workbook. For workbooks that include many calculations, such as the Wingait Farm workbook, it is helpful to explain the formulas and terms used in the calculations. Such documentation also can serve as a check that the equations are accurate.

Jane has included explanations of equations you'll use in developing her workbook. Before proceeding, you'll review this documentation.

To review the documentation in Wingait Farm workbook:

1. Go to the **Explanation of Formulas** worksheet.

2. Read the worksheet contents, reviewing the descriptions of common agricultural constants and formulas. As you continue developing the Wingait Farm workbook, you'll learn about these terms and formulas in more detail.

3. Go to the **Yield** worksheet.

Using Constants in Formulas

One common skill you need when creating a workbook is being able to translate an equation into an Excel formula. Some equations use **constants**, which are terms in a formula that don't change their value.

The first equation Jane wants you to enter calculates the size of the sample plot in acres, given the number of corn rows and the width and length of each row. The formula is

$$area = \frac{2 \times rows \times width \times length}{43560}$$

where *rows* is the number of corn rows, *width* is the width of the sample rows measured in feet, and *length* is the length of the sample rows measured in feet. In this equation, 43560 is a constant because that value never changes when calculating the sample area.

INSIGHT

Deciding Where to Place a Constant

Should a constant be entered directly into the formula or placed in a separate worksheet cell and referenced in the formula? The answer depends on the constant being used, the purpose of the workbook, and the intended audience. Placing constants in separate cells that you reference in the formulas can help users better understand the worksheet because no values are hidden within the formulas. Also, when a constant is entered in a cell, you can add explanatory text next to each constant to document how it is being used in the formula. On the other hand, you don't want a user to inadvertently change the value of a constant and throw off all the formula results. You will need to evaluate how important it is for other people to immediately see the constant and whether the constant requires any explanation for other people to understand the formula.

To convert the area equation to an Excel formula, you'll replace the *row, width,* and *length* values with references to the cells B7, B8, and B9, and you'll replace 43560 with a reference to cell E7. These cells provide the number of rows in the sample plot, the row width in feet, the row length in feet, and the number of square feet in one acre of land.

To calculate the area of the sample plot:

1. In cell **B10**, enter the formula **=2*B7*B8*B9/E7** to calculate the area of the sample plot. The formula returns 0.202479339.

   Trouble? If your result differs from 0.202479339, you probably entered the formula incorrectly. Edit the formula you entered in cell B10 as needed so that the numbers and cell references match those shown in the formula in Step 1.

   Jane does not need to see the acreage of the sample plot with eight decimal places.

2. Click cell **B10**, and then decrease the number of decimal places to **2**. The area of the sample plot is displayed as 0.20 acres. See Figure 3-2.

TIP

Decreasing the number decimals places rounds the displayed value; the stored value remains unchanged.

Figure 3-2   Calculated size of the sample plot in acres

formula to calculate the size of the sample plot

size of the sample plot in acres

worksheet describing the agricultural formulas

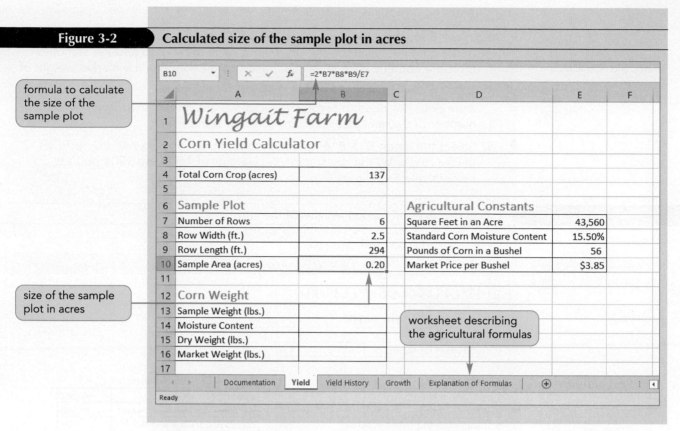

When Jane harvests the corn from the sample plot, she measures the total weight of the corn, which includes its moisture content. She then analyzes the corn to determine what percentage of its weight is due to moisture. The total weight of the corn is 1,922 pounds of which 16.3 percent is moisture. To sell the corn, Jane needs to calculate the dry weight of the corn without the moisture. She can do this with the formula

$$dry\ weight = total\ weight \times (1 - moisture)$$

where *total weight* is the weight of the corn and *moisture* is the percentage of the weight due to moisture. Market prices for corn are standardized at a moisture percentage of 15.5 percent, so to get the correct market weight of her corn, Jane uses the following formula:

$$market\ weight = \frac{dry\ weight}{1 - 0.155}$$

You will enter these two formulas in Jane's workbook to calculate the market weight of the corn she harvested from the sample plot.

To calculate the market weight of the corn:

1. In cell **B13**, enter **1922** as the total weight of the corn sample.

2. In cell **B14**, enter **16.3%** as the moisture content.

3. In cell **B15**, enter the formula **=B13*(1-B14)** to calculate the dry weight of the corn kernels. Based on the formula, the dry weight of the corn harvested from the sample plot is 1608.714 pounds.

Because the expression requires dividing by two terms, you must enclose those terms within parentheses.

4. In cell **B16**, enter the formula **=B15/(1-E8)** to calculate the market weight of the corn kernels using the dry weight value in cell B15 and the standard moisture content value in cell E8. Based on the formula, the market weight of the corn is 1903.80355 pounds.

Jane does not need to see such precise weight values, so you will reduce the number of decimal places displayed in the worksheet.

5. Select the range **B15:B16**, and then format the numbers with no decimals places to display the dry and market weights of 1609 and 1904 pounds, respectively. See Figure 3-3.

Figure 3-3   **Calculated dry and market weights of the corn**

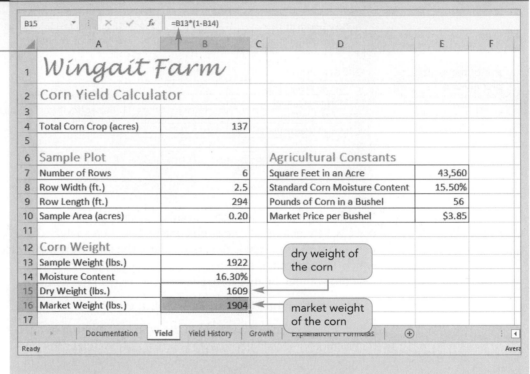

formula to calculate the dry corn weight

dry weight of the corn

market weight of the corn

Corn is not sold by the pound but rather by the bushel where 1 bushel contains 56 pounds of corn. You will calculate the number of bushels of corn in the sample plot and then use this number to estimate the farm's total yield and revenue.

To project the farm's total yield and revenue:

1. In cell **B19**, enter the formula **=B16/E9** to convert the market weight to bushels. In this case, the market weight is equal to 33.99649197 bushels.

2. In cell **B19**, format the number with no decimals places. The number is rounded to 34 bushels.

3. In cell **B20**, enter the formula **=B19/B10** to divide the number of bushels in the sample plot by the size of the plot in acres. Based on this calculation, this year's crop has yielded 167.901042 bushels per acre.

4. In cell **B20**, format the number with no decimals places. This year's crop yielded about 168 bushels per acre.

Assuming that the rest of the farm is as productive as the sample plot, you can calculate the total bushels that the farm can produce by multiplying the bushels per acre by the total acreage of the farm.

5. In cell **B21**, enter the formula **=B20*B4** to multiply the bushels per acre by the total acreage of the farm. Assuming that the rest of the farm is as productive as the sample plot, the total bushels that the farm can produce is 23002.44275 bushels.

6. Format cell B21 using the Comma style with no decimal places. Cell B21 displays 23,002.

7. In cell **B23**, enter the formula **=B21*E10** to calculate the revenue Jane can expect by selling all of the farm's corn at the market price of $3.85 per bushel.

8. Format cell B23 with the Accounting style. The formula result is displayed as $88,559.40. See Figure 3-4.

| Figure 3-4 | Projected yield and revenue from the corn harvest |

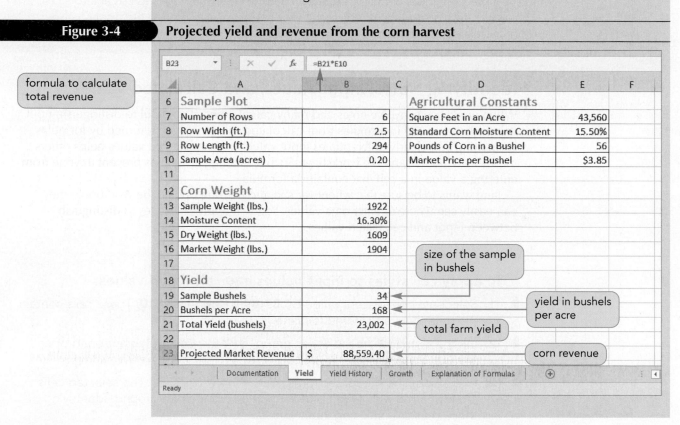

Based on your calculations, Jane projects an income of almost $90,000 from this year's corn crop.

PROSKILLS

Written Communication: Displaying Significant Digits

Excel stores numbers with up to 15 digits and displays as many digits as will fit into the cell. So even the result of a simple formula such as =10/3 will display 3.33333333333333 if the cell is wide enough.

A number with 15 digits is difficult to read, and calculations rarely need that level of accuracy. Many scientific disciplines, such as chemistry or physics, have rules for specifying exactly how many digits should be displayed with any calculation. These digits are called **significant digits** because they indicate the accuracy of the measured and calculated values. For example, an input value of 19.32 has four significant digits.

The rules are based on several factors and vary from one discipline to another. Generally, a calculated value should display no more digits than are found in any of the input values. For example, because the input value 19.32 has four significant digits, any calculated value based on that input should have no more than four significant digits. Showing more digits would be misleading because it implies a level of accuracy beyond that which was actually measured.

Because Excel displays calculated values with as many digits as can fit into a cell, you need to know the standards for your profession and change the display of your calculated values accordingly.

Identifying Notes, Input Values, and Calculated Values

When worksheets involve notes and many calculations, it is useful to distinguish input values that are used in formulas from calculated values that are returned by formulas. Formatting that clearly differentiates input values from calculated values helps others more easily understand the worksheet. Such formatting also helps prevent anyone from entering a value in a cell that contains a formula.

Jane wants to be sure that whenever she and her staff update the workbook, they can easily see where to enter data values. You will apply cell styles to distinguish between input and calculated values.

To apply cell styles to input values and calculated values:

1. Select the nonadjacent range **B4,B7:B9,B13:B14,E7:E10**. These cells contain the data that you entered for Jane.

2. On the Home tab, in the Styles group, click the **Cell Styles** button to open the Cell Styles gallery.

3. In the Data and Model section, click the **Input** cell style. The selected cells are formatted with a light blue font on an orange background, identifying those cells as containing input values.

4. Select the nonadjacent range **B10,B15:B16,B19:B21,B23**. These cells contain the formulas for calculating the weight, yield, and revenue values.

5. Format the selected cells with the **Calculation** cell style located in the Data and Model section of the Cell Styles gallery. The cells with the calculated values are formatted with a bold orange font on a light gray background.

6. Click cell **D12** to deselect the range. See Figure 3-5.

| Figure 3-5 | Input and calculated values formatted with cell styles |

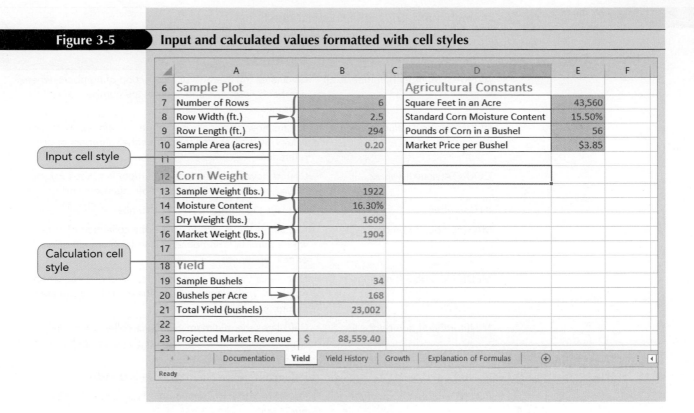

	A	B	C	D	E	F
6	Sample Plot			Agricultural Constants		
7	Number of Rows	6		Square Feet in an Acre	43,560	
8	Row Width (ft.)	2.5		Standard Corn Moisture Content	15.50%	
9	Row Length (ft.)	294		Pounds of Corn in a Bushel	56	
10	Sample Area (acres)	0.20		Market Price per Bushel	$3.85	
11						
12	Corn Weight					
13	Sample Weight (lbs.)	1922				
14	Moisture Content	16.30%				
15	Dry Weight (lbs.)	1609				
16	Market Weight (lbs.)	1904				
17						
18	Yield					
19	Sample Bushels	34				
20	Bushels per Acre	168				
21	Total Yield (bushels)	23,002				
22						
23	Projected Market Revenue	$ 88,559.40				

Input cell style

Calculation cell style

Documentation | Yield | Yield History | Growth | Explanation of Formulas | (+)

Ready

Using Excel Functions

Excel functions can be used in place of long and complicated formulas to simplify your worksheet. Jane wants to compare the estimated yield for this year's crop to historic trends. To make that comparison, you'll work with some Excel functions.

Understanding Function Syntax

Before you use functions, you should understand the function syntax. Recall that the syntax of an Excel function follows the general pattern

    FUNCTION(argument1,argument2,...)

where *FUNCTION* is the name of the function, and *argument1*, *argument2*, and so forth are arguments used by the function. An argument can be any type of value including text, numbers, cell references, or even other formulas or functions. Not all functions require arguments.

Some arguments are optional and can be included with the function or omitted altogether. Most optional arguments will have default values, so that if you omit an argument value, Excel will automatically apply the default. The convention is to show optional arguments within square brackets along with the argument's default value (if any), as

    FUNCTION(argument1[,argument2=value2,...])

where *argument1* is a required argument, *argument2* is optional, and *value2* is the default value for argument2. As you work with specific functions, you will learn which arguments are required and which are optional as well as any default values associated with those optional arguments.

Figure 3-6 describes some of the more commonly used Math, Trig, and Statistical functions and provides the syntax of those functions, including any optional arguments.

TIP

Optional arguments are always placed last in the argument list.

Figure 3-6   **Common Math, Trig, and Statistical functions**

Function	Description
AVERAGE(*number1*[,*number2*,...])	Calculates the average of a collection of numbers, where *number1*, *number2*, and so forth are numbers or cell references
COUNT(*value1*[,*value2*,...])	Counts how many cells in a range contain numbers, where *value1*, *value2*, and so forth are either numbers or cell references
COUNTA(*value1*[,*value2*,...])	Counts how many cells are not empty in ranges *value1*, *value2*, and so forth including both numbers and text entries
INT(*number*)	Displays the integer portion of *number*
MAX(*number1*[,*number2*,...])	Calculates the maximum value of a collection of numbers, where *number1*, *number2*, and so forth are either numbers or cell references
MEDIAN(*number1*[,*number2*,...])	Calculates the median, or middle, value of a collection of numbers, where *number1*, *number2*, and so forth are either numbers or cell references
MIN(*number1*[,*number2*,...])	Calculates the minimum value of a collection of numbers, where *number1*, *number2*, and so forth are either numbers or cell references
RAND()	Returns a random number between 0 and 1
ROUND(*number*,*num_digits*)	Rounds *number* to the number of digits specified by *num_digits*
SUM(*number1*[,*number2*,...])	Adds a collection of numbers, where *number1*, *number2*, and so forth are either numbers or cell references

Entering the COUNT function

The following COUNT function is used by Excel to count how many cells in a range contain numbers. The COUNT function syntax is

```
COUNT(value1[,value2,…])
```

where `value1` is either a cell reference, range reference, or a number, and `value2` and so on are optional arguments that provide additional cell references, range references, or numbers. There are no default values for the optional arguments.

The COUNT function does not include blank cells or cells that contain text in its tally. For example, the following function counts how many cells in the range A1:A10, the range C1:C5, and cell E5 contain numbers or dates:

```
COUNT(A1:A10,C1:C5,E5)
```

The COUNT function is especially helpful when data in the ranges are regularly updated.

> **INSIGHT**
>
> *Counting Text*
>
> Excel has another important function for counting cells—the **COUNTA function**. This function counts the number of cells that contain any entries, including numbers, dates, or text. The syntax of the COUNTA function is
>
> COUNTA(*value1*[,*value2*,...])
>
> where *value1* is the first item or cell reference containing the entries you want to count. The remaining optional value arguments are used primarily when you want to count entries in nonadjacent ranges. The COUNTA function should be used for text data or for data in which you need to include blanks as part of the total.

You'll use the COUNT function to tally how many years of data are included in the corn yield history.

To count the number of years in the corn yield history:

1. Go to the **Yield History** worksheet, and then click cell **B5**. You'll enter the COUNT function in this cell.

2. Type **=COUNT(** to begin entering the COUNT function. The first argument, which is the only required argument, is the cell or range reference for the cells to be counted.

   The yield values are stored in the range E5:F27. Instead of referencing this range, you will use column E as the argument for the COUNT function because Jane plans to add data to this column each year as she continues to track the farm's annual corn yield.

3. Click the **E** column heading to select the entire column. The column reference E:E is inserted into the function as the first argument.

4. Type **)** to end the function, and then press the **Enter** key. The formula =COUNT(E:E) is entered in cell B5 and returns 22, which is the number of years for which Jane has corn yield data.

Nesting the ROUND and AVERAGE Functions

One function can be placed inside, or **nested**, within another function. When a formula contains more than one function, Excel first evaluates the innermost function and then moves outward to evaluate the next function. The inner function acts as an argument value for the outer function. For example, the following expression nests the AVERAGE function within the ROUND function.

ROUND(AVERAGE(A1:A100),0)

> **TIP**
>
> The ROUND function changes the value stored in the cell, not the number of decimal places displayed in the cell.

Excel first uses the AVERAGE function to calculate the average of the values in the range A1:A100 and then uses the ROUND function to round that average to the nearest integer (where the number of digits to the right of the decimal point is 0.)

One challenge of nested functions is being sure to include all of the parentheses. You can check this by counting the number of opening parentheses and making sure that number matches the number of closing parentheses. Excel also displays each level of nested parentheses in different colors to make it easier for you to match the opening and closing parentheses. If the number of parentheses doesn't match, Excel will not accept the formula and will provide a suggestion for how to rewrite the formula so the number of opening and closing parentheses does match.

Jane wants you to analyze the corn yield history at Wingait Farm. You'll use the COUNT function to tally the number of years in the historical sample and then use the AVERAGE function to calculate the average yield during those years. Because Jane doesn't need the exact corn yield values, you'll use the ROUND function to round that calculated average to the nearest integer.

To analyze the corn yield history:

1. Click cell **B6**. You want to enter the nested function in this cell.

2. Type **=ROUND(** to begin the formula with the ROUND function.

3. Type **AVERAGE(E:E)** to enter the AVERAGE function as the first argument of the ROUND function.

4. Type **,** (a comma) to separate the first and second arguments.

5. Type **0)** to specify the number of decimal places to include in the results. In this case, Jane doesn't want to include any decimal places.

6. Press the **Enter** key. The nested functions first calculate the average value of the numbers in column E and then round that number to the nearest integer. The formula returns 170, which is the average annual yield of Wingait Farm in bushels per acre rounded to the nearest integer. See Figure 3-7.

Figure 3-7   Nested functions calculate the average annual yield

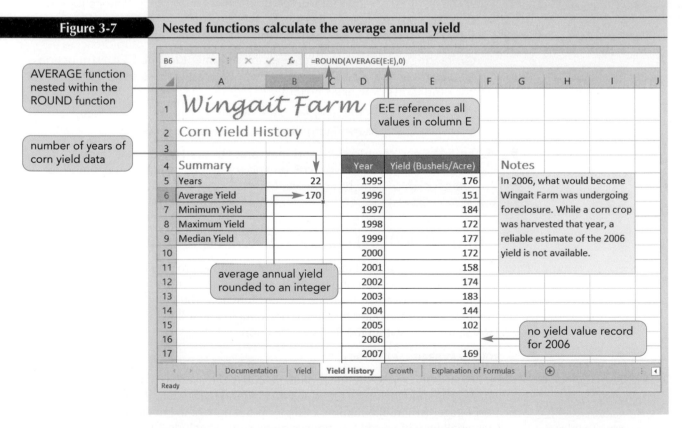

Based on values from 22 seasons of data, Jane expects her farm to yield 170 bushels of corn per acre each year.

Note that in 2006, no data on corn yield was available. Excel ignores nonnumeric data and blank cells when calculating statistical functions such as COUNT and AVERAGE. So, the count and average values in cells B5 and B6 represent only those years containing recorded corn yields. Keep in mind that a blank cell is not the same as a zero value in worksheet calculations. Figure 3-8 shows how function results differ when a zero replaces a blank in the selected range.

Figure 3-8	Calculations with blank cells and zero values

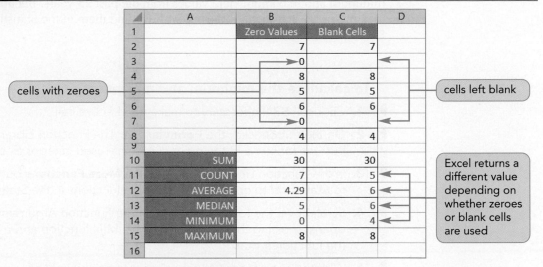

cells with zeroes

cells left blank

Excel returns a different value depending on whether zeroes or blank cells are used

Whether you use a blank or zero depends on what you're trying to measure. For example, if Jane were to calculate average hours worked per day at the Wingait farm store, she could enter 0 for the holidays on which the store is closed, or she could enter a blank and thus calculate the average only for days in which the store is open.

Using the Function Library and the Insert Function Dialog Box

With so many Excel functions, it can difficult to locate the function you want to use for a particular application. Excel organizes its function into the 13 categories described in Figure 3-9. These function categories are available in the Function Library group on the Formulas tab and in the Insert Function dialog box.

Figure 3-9	Excel function categories

Category	Description
Compatibility	Functions from Excel 2010 or earlier, still supported to provide backward compatibility
Cube	Retrieve data from multidimensional databases involving online analytical processing (OLAP)
Database	Retrieve and analyze data stored in databases
Date & Time	Analyze or create date and time values and time intervals
Engineering	Analyze engineering problems
Financial	Analyze information for business and finance
Information	Return information about the format, location, or contents of worksheet cells
Logical	Return logical (true-false) values
Lookup & Reference	Look up and return data matching a set of specified conditions from a range
Math & Trig	Perform math and trigonometry calculations
Statistical	Provide statistical analyses of data sets
Text	Return text values or evaluate text
Web	Provide information on web-based connections

Once you select a function either from the Function Library or the Insert Function dialog box, the Function Arguments dialog box opens, listing all of the arguments associated with that function. Required arguments are in bold type; optional arguments are in normal type.

Jane wants to know the range of annual corn yields, so she asks you to calculate the minimum and maximum yield values from the past 23 years. Because minimums and maximums are statistical measures, you will find them in the Statistics category in the Function Library.

To calculate the minimum and maximum yield:

1. Click cell **B7** if necessary to make it the active cell.

2. On the ribbon, click the **Formulas** tab. The Function Library group has buttons for some of the more commonly used categories of functions.

3. In the Function Library group, click the **More Functions** button, and then point to **Statistical** to open a list of all of the functions in the Statistical category.

4. Scroll down the list, and click **MIN**. The Function Arguments dialog box opens, showing the arguments for the MIN function and a brief description of the function syntax.

5. With the entry for the Number1 argument highlighted, click the **E** column heading to select the entire column and insert the cell reference **E:E** into the Number1 input box. See Figure 3-10.

Figure 3-10 **MIN function in the Function Arguments dialog box**

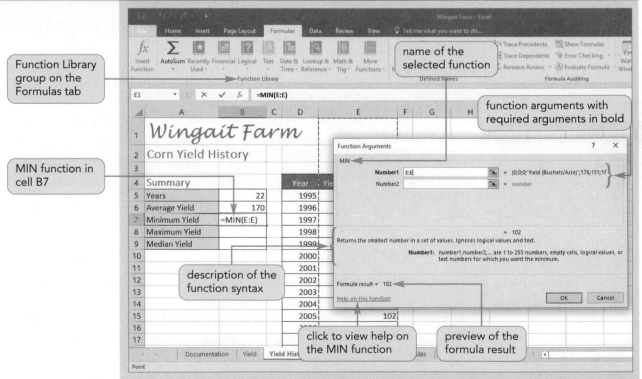

Trouble? You can click and drag the title bar in the Function Arguments dialog box to move it out of the way of the column E heading.

6. Click the **OK** button to insert the formula =MIN(E:E) into cell B7. The formula returns 102, which is the minimum value in column E.

7. Click cell **B8**, and then repeat Steps 3 through 6, selecting the **MAX** function from the Statistical category. The formula =MAX(E:E) entered in cell B8, and returns 187, which is the maximum value in column E. See Figure 3-11.

| Figure 3-11 | Results of the MIN and MAX functions |

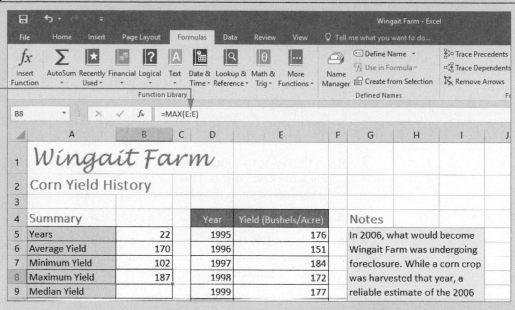

formula to calculate the maximum value in column E

Note that like the COUNT and AVERAGE functions, the MIN and MAX functions ignore cells with text or blank cells in the selected range.

The average is one way of summarizing data from a sample. However, averages are susceptible to the effects of extremely large or extremely small values. For example, imagine calculating the average net worth of 10 people when one of them is a billionaire. An average would probably not be a good representation of the typical net worth of that group. To avoid the effect of extreme values, statisticians often use the middle, or median, value in the sample.

Jane wants you to include the median corn yield value from the farm's history. Rather than inserting the function from the Function Library, you'll search for this function in the Insert Function dialog box.

To find the median corn yield:

1. Click cell **B9** to make it the active cell.

2. Click the **Insert Function** button f_x located to the left of the formula bar. The Insert Function dialog box opens.

3. In the Search for a function box, type **middle value** as the search description, and then click the **Go** button. A list of functions matching that description appears in the Select a function box. See Figure 3-12.

Figure 3-12	Search results in the Insert Function dialog box

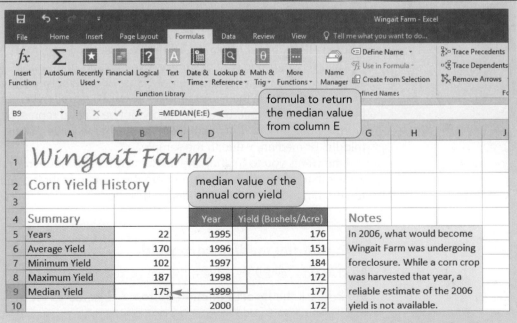

description of the function you want to find

click to search for the function

functions matching the search description

4. In the Select a function box, click **MEDIAN** to select that function, and then click the **OK** button. The Function Arguments dialog box opens with the insertion point in the Number1 box.

5. Click the **E** column heading to insert the reference E:E in the Number1 box.

6. Click the **OK** button. The formula =MEDIAN(E:E) is entered in cell B9. The formula returns 175, which is the middle value from the list of annual corn yields in the farm's history. See Figure 3-13.

Figure 3-13	Median function finds the middle corn yield value

The median estimate of 175 bushels per acre is higher than the average value of 170 bushels per acre. This is due in part to the extremely low yield of 102 bushels per acre in 2005, which brought the overall average value down. Because of this, 175 bushels per acre might be a more reliable estimate of the farm's productivity.

Methods of Rounding

For cleaner and neater workbooks, you will often want to round your values. There is little need for a large corporation to show revenue to the nearest cents at the annual stockholders' convention. Excel provides several methods for rounding data values. One method is to decrease the number of decimal places displayed in the cell, leaving the underlying value unchanged but rounding the displayed value to a specified number of digits.

Another approach is to use the ROUND function, which rounds the value itself to a specified number of digits. The ROUND function also accepts negative values for the number of digits in order to round the value to the nearest multiple of 10, 100, 1000, and so forth. The formula

```
=ROUND(5241,-2)
```

returns a value of 5200, rounding the value to the nearest hundred. For rounding to the nearest of multiple of a given number, use the function

```
MROUND(number,multiple)
```

where *number* is the number to be rounded and *multiple* is the multiple that the number should be rounded to. For example, the formula

```
=MROUND(5241,25)
```

rounds 5241 to the nearest multiple of 25, returning 5250. Remember though that when you use these rounding methods, you should always have access to the original, unrounded data, in case you need to audit your calculations in the future.

Next Jane wants to explore how to increase the farm's corn revenue in future seasons. You can explore the possibilities with a what-if analysis.

Performing What-If Analyses

A **what-if analysis** explores the impact that changing input values has on calculated values. For example, Jane wants to increase the farm's total revenue from corn, which you calculated as $88,559.40 for the current year, to at least $100,000. The most obvious way to increase the farm's corn revenue is to plant and then harvest more corn. Jane asks you to perform a what-if analysis to determine how many acres of corn would be needed to generate $100,000 of income, assuming conditions remain the same as the current year in which the farm yielded 168 bushels per acre at a selling price of $3.85 per bushel.

Using Trial and Error

One way to perform a what-if analysis is with **trial and error** where you change one or more of the input values to see how they affect the calculated results. Trial and error requires some guesswork as you estimate which values to change and by how much. You will use the trial and error to study the impact of changing the cornfield acreage on the total revenue generated for the farm.

To use trial and error to find how many acres of corn will generate $100,000 revenue:

1. Go to the **Yield** worksheet containing calculations for determining the farm's current corn revenue.

▶ **2.** In cell **B4**, change the farm acreage from 137 to **150**. Cell B23 shows that with 150 acres of corn sold at $3.85 per bushel, the farm's revenue from corn sales would increase from $88,559.40 to $96,962.85.

▶ **3.** In cell **B4**, change the farm acreage from 150 to **175**. Cell B23 shows that if the farm plants 175 acres of corn, the revenue would increase to $113,123.33.

▶ **4.** In cell **B4**, change the farm acreage back to **137**, which is the current acreage of corn on Wingait Farm.

To find the exact acreage that would result in $100,000 of revenue, you would have to continue trying different values in cell B4, gradually closing in on the correct value. This is why the method is called "trial and error." For some calculations, trial and error can be a very time-consuming way to locate the exact input value. A more direct approach to this problem is to use Goal Seek.

Using Goal Seek

TIP

Goal Seek can be used only with calculated numbers, not with text.

Goal Seek automates the trial-and-error process by allowing you to specify a value for a calculated item, which Excel uses to determine the input value needed to reach that goal. In this case, because Jane wants $100,000 of revenue, the question that Goal Seek answers is: "How many acres of corn are needed to generate $100,000?" Goal Seek starts by setting the calculated value and automatically works backward to determine the correct input value.

REFERENCE

Performing What-If Analysis and Goal Seek

To perform a what-if analysis by trial and error:
- Change the value of a worksheet cell (the input cell).
- Observe its impact on one or more calculated cells (the result cells).
- Repeat until the desired results are achieved.

To perform a what-if analysis using Goal Seek:
- On the Data tab, in the Forecast group, click the What-If Analysis button, and then click Goal Seek.
- Select the result cell in the Set cell box, and then specify its value (goal) in the To value box.
- In the By changing cell box, specify the input cell.
- Click the OK button. The value of the input cell changes to set the value of the result cell.

You will use Goal Seek to find how much acreage Wingait Farms must plant with corn to achieve $100,000 of revenue.

To use Goal Seek to find how many acres of corn will generate $100,000 revenue:

▶ **1.** On the ribbon, click the **Data** tab.

▶ **2.** In the Forecast group, click the **What-If Analysis** button, and then click **Goal Seek**. The Goal Seek dialog box opens.

▶ **3.** With Set cell box selected, click cell **B23** in the Yield worksheet. The cell reference $B$23 appears in the Set cell box. The set cell is the calculated value you want Goal Seek to change to meet your goal. (You'll learn about $ symbols in cell references in the next session.)

▶ **4.** Press the **Tab** key to move the insertion point to the To value box, and then type **100000** indicating that you want Goal Seek to set the value in cell B23 value to 100,000.

▶ **5.** Press the **Tab** key to move the insertion point to the By changing cell box.

There are often many possible input values you can change to meet a goal. In this case, you want to change the size of the farm acreage in cell B4.

▶ **6.** Click cell **B4**. The cell reference $B$4 appears in the By changing cell box. See Figure 3-14.

Figure 3-14	Goal Seek dialog box

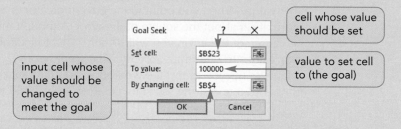

▶ **7.** Click the **OK** button. The Goal Seek dialog box closes, and the Goal Seek Status dialog box opens, indicating that Goal Seek found a solution.

▶ **8.** Click the **OK** button. The value in cell B4 changes to 154.6984204, and the value of cell B23 changes to $100,000.

If Jane increases the acreage devoted to corn production to almost 155 acres, the farm would produce a total revenue from corn of $100,000, assuming a yield of 168 bushels per acre sold at $3.85 per bushel. If the yield or market price increases, the revenue would also increase.

Interpreting Error Values

As you add formulas and values to a workbook, you might make a mistake such as mistyping a formula or entering data as the wrong type. When such errors occur, Excel displays an error value in the cell. An **error value** indicates that some part of a formula is preventing Excel from returning a value. Figure 3-15 lists the common error values you might see in place of calculated values from Excel formulas and functions. For example, the error value #VALUE! indicates that the wrong type of value is used in a function or formula.

Figure 3-15 Excel error values

Error Value	Description
#DIV/0!	The formula or function contains a number divided by 0.
#NAME?	Excel doesn't recognize text in the formula or function, such as when the function name is misspelled.
#N/A	A value is not available to a function or formula, which can occur when a workbook is initially set up prior to entering actual data values.
#NULL!	A formula or function requires two cell ranges to intersect, but they don't.
#NUM!	Invalid numbers are used in a formula or function, such as text entered in a function that requires a number.
#REF!	A cell reference used in a formula or function is no longer valid, which can occur when the cell used by the function was deleted from the worksheet.
#VALUE!	The wrong type of argument is used in a function or formula. This can occur when you reference a text value for an argument that should be strictly numeric.

Error values themselves are not particularly descriptive or helpful. To help you locate the error, an error indicator appears in the upper-left corner of the cell with the error value. When you point to the error indicator, a ScreenTip appears with more information about the source of the error. Although the ScreenTips provide hints as to the source of the error, you will usually need to examine the formulas in the cells with error values to determine exactly what went wrong.

Jane wants you to test the workbook. You'll change the value of cell B4 from a number to a text string, creating an error in the Yield worksheet.

To create an error value:

1. In cell **B4**, enter the text string **137 acres**. After you press the Enter key, the #VALUE! error value appears in cells whose formulas use the value in cell B4 either directly or indirectly, indicating that the wrong type of argument is used in a function or formula. In the Yield worksheet, the value in cell B4 affects the values of cells B21 and B23. See Figure 3-16.

Figure 3-16 Error value in the worksheet

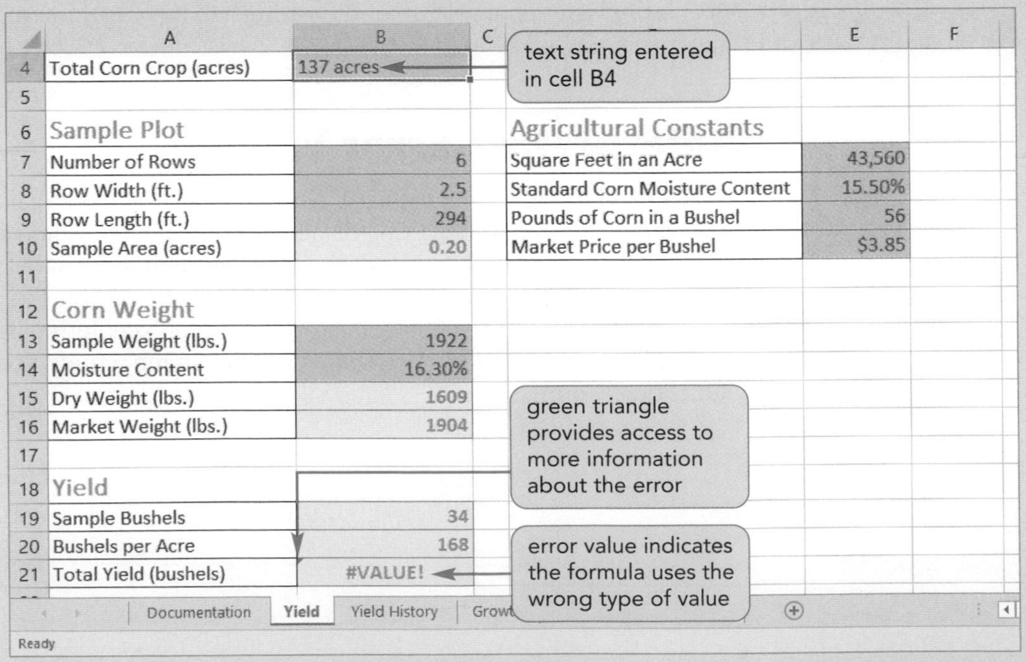

▶ **2.** Click cell **B21**, and then point to the button that appears to the left of the cell. A ScreenTip appears, providing useful information about the cause of the error value. In this case, the ScreenTip is, "A value used in the formula is of the wrong data type."

▶ **3.** Click cell **B4**, enter **137** to change the value back to the current acreage that Wingait Farm devotes to corn. After you press the Enter key, the error values disappear, the total yield in cell B21 returns to 23,002, and the projected revenue in cell B23 returns to $88,559.40.

▶ **4.** Save the workbook.

So far, you have used formulas and functions to analyze the current and past season's crop yield at Wingait Farm. In the next session, you'll use additional formulas and functions to analyze the growth of Wingait Farm's corn crop from planting to harvesting.

REVIEW

Session 3.1 Quick Check

1. Convert the following equation into an Excel formula where the *radius* value is stored in cell E31 and the value of π is stored in cell D12:

$$area = \pi \times radius^2$$

2. In Excel, the PI() function returns the decimal value of π. Rewrite your answer for the previous formula using this function.

3. Write a formula to round the value in cell A5 to the fourth decimal place.

4. Write a formula to return the middle value from the values in the range Y1:Y100.

5. The range of a set of values is defined as the maximum value minus the minimum value. Write a formula to calculate the range of values in the range Y1:Y100 and then to round that value to the nearest integer.

6. Explain the difference between the COUNT function and the COUNTA function.

7. Stephen is entering hundreds of temperature values into an Excel worksheet for a climate research project, and he wants to speed up data entry by leaving freezing point values as blanks rather than typing zeroes. Explain why this will cause complications if he later tries to calculate the average temperature from those data values.

8. What is the difference between a what-if analysis by trial and error and by Goal Seek?

9. Cell B2 contains the formula =SUME(A1:A100) with the name of the SUM function misspelled as SUME. What error value will appear in the cell?

Session 3.2 Visual Overview:

The **VLOOKUP function** returns values from a vertical lookup table by specifying the value to be matched, the location of the lookup table, and the column containing the return values.

The **TODAY function** returns the current date.

A **relative cell reference** is used for references that change when the formula is moved to a new location. For example, E15 is a relative cell reference.

An **absolute cell reference** is used for references that do not change when the formula is moved to a new location. Absolute references have "$" before the row and column components. For example, $O$7 is an absolute cell reference.

Wingait Farm - Excel

File · Home · Insert · Page Layout · Formulas · Data · Review · View · Tell m

B13 · fx =VLOOKUP($B$12,$N$17:$O$19,2,FALSE)

=TODAY()

	A	B	C	D	E	F	G	H	I
1	Wingait Farm								
2	Corn Growth Calculator								
3									
4	Current Date	11/15/2017		Day	Lo		Tmin	Tmax	GDD	Cum
5				Day 1	45	52	50	52	1.0	
6	Estimated Stage Dates			Day 2	42	64	50	64	7.0	
7	Planting Date	4/25/2017		Day 3	38	70	50	70	10.0	
8	Emergence	4/30/2017		Day 4	43	76	50	76	13.0	
9	First Leaf	5/3/2017		Day 5	47	74	50	74	12.0	
10				Day 6	45	74	50	74	12.0	
11	Hybrid Summary			Day 7	47	71	50	71	10.5	
12	Corn Hybrid	CS6489		Day 8	56	68	56	68	12.0	
13	Maturity (GDD)	2920		Day 9	60	85	60	85	22.5	
14		=MAX(E14,$O		Day 10	61	71	61	71	16.0	
15	Harvesting		=MAX(E15,$O$7)		62	80	62	80	21.0	
16	Harvest Date	9/	=MAX(E16,$O$7)		79	65	79	22.0		
17			=MAX(E17,$O$7)		67	80	67	80	23.5	
18			MAX(E18,O		56	70	56	70	13.0	
19					53	75	53	75	14.0	
20				Day 16	59	73	59	73	16.0	

Documentation · Yield · Yield History · **Growth** · Explanation o ...

Ready

Cell References and Formulas

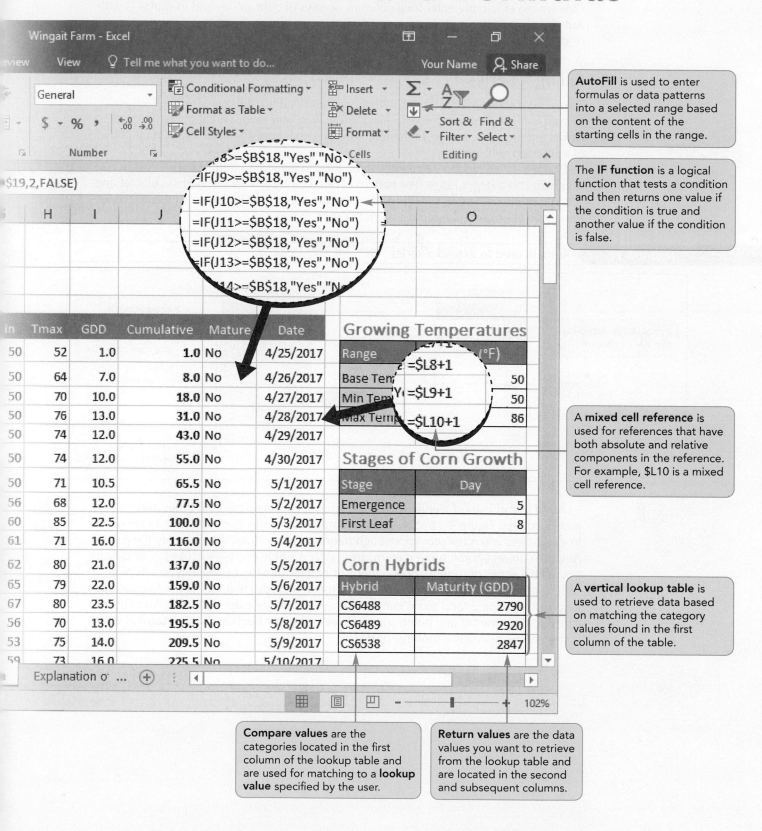

AutoFill is used to enter formulas or data patterns into a selected range based on the content of the starting cells in the range.

The **IF function** is a logical function that tests a condition and then returns one value if the condition is true and another value if the condition is false.

A **mixed cell reference** is used for references that have both absolute and relative components in the reference. For example, $L10 is a mixed cell reference.

A **vertical lookup table** is used to retrieve data based on matching the category values found in the first column of the table.

Compare values are the categories located in the first column of the lookup table and are used for matching to a **lookup value** specified by the user.

Return values are the data values you want to retrieve from the lookup table and are located in the second and subsequent columns.

AutoFilling Formulas and Data

One way to efficiently enter long columns or rows of data values and formulas is with AutoFill. AutoFill extends formulas or data patterns that were entered in a selected cell or range into adjacent cells. AutoFill is faster than copying and pasting.

Filling a Series

To extend a series of data values with a particular pattern, you enter enough values to establish the pattern, next you select those cells, and then you drag the fill handle across additional cells. The **fill handle** is the box that appears in the lower-right corner of a selected cell or range.

Figure 3-17 shows how AutoFill can be used to extend an initial series of odd numbers into a larger range. The pattern of odd numbers is established in cells A2 and A3. When the user drags the fill handle over the range A4:A9, Excel extends the series into those cells using the same pattern of odd numbers.

Figure 3-17   AutoFill used to extend a series

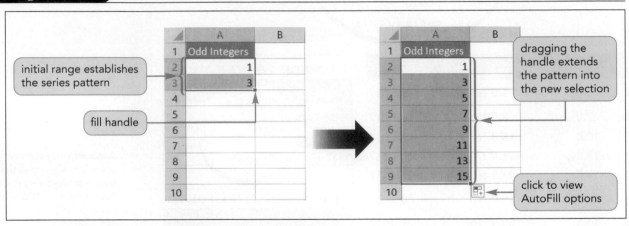

AutoFill can extend a wide variety of series, including dates and times and patterned text. Figure 3-18 shows some examples of series that AutoFill can generate. In each case, you must provide enough information for AutoFill to identify the pattern. AutoFill can recognize some patterns from only a single entry—such as Jan or January to create a series of month abbreviations or names, or Mon or Monday to create a series of the days of the week. A text pattern that includes text and a number such as Region 1, Region 2, and so on can also be automatically extended using AutoFill. You can start the series at any point, such as Weds, June, or Region 10, and AutoFill will complete the next days, months, or text.

Figure 3-18   Series patterns extended with AutoFill

Type	Initial Values	Extended Values
Numbers	1, 2, 3	4, 5, 6, ..
	2, 4, 6	8, 10, 12, ...
Dates and Times	Jan	Feb, Mar, Apr, ...
	January	February, March, April, ...
	15-Jan, 15-Feb	15-Mar, 15-Apr, 15-May, ...
	12/30/2017	12/31/2017, 1/1/2018, 1/2/2018, ...
	12/31/2017, 1/31/2018	2/29/2018, 3/31/2018, 4/30/2018, ...
	Mon	Tue, Wed, Thu, ...
	Monday	Tuesday, Wednesday, Thursday, ...
	11:00AM	12:00PM, 1:00PM, 2:00PM, ...
Patterned Text	1st period	2nd period, 3rd period, 4th period, ...
	Region 1	Region 2, Region 3, Region 4, ...
	Quarter 3	Quarter 4, Quarter 1, Quarter 2, ...
	Qtr3	Qtr4, Qtr1, Qtr2, ...

With AutoFill, you can quickly fill a range with a series of numbers, dates and times, and patterned text.

REFERENCE

Creating a Series with AutoFill

- Enter the first few values of the series into a range.
- Select the range, and then drag the fill handle of the selected range over the cells you want to fill.
- To copy only the formats or only the formulas, click the Auto Fill Options button and select the appropriate option.

or

- Enter the first few values of the series into a range.
- Select the entire range into which you want to extend the series.
- On the Home tab, in the Editing group, click the Fill button, and then click Down, Right, Up, Left, Series, or Justify to set the direction in which you want to extend the series.

Jane wants you to complete the worksheet she started to explore the growth of the Wingait Farm corn crop from planting through harvesting. You need to create a column that labels each day of corn growth starting with Day 1, Day2, and so forth through the end of the season. You will create these labels using AutoFill.

To use AutoFill to extend a series of labels:

1. If you took a break after the previous session, make sure the Wingait Farm workbook is open.

2. Go to the **Growth** worksheet.

3. In cell **D5**, enter the text string **Day 1**. This is the initial label in the series.

4. Click cell **D5** to select the cell, and then drag the **fill handle** (located in the bottom-right corner of the cell) down over the range **D5:D163**.

TIP

You can also fill a series down by selecting the entire range including the initial cell(s) that establish the pattern, and then pressing the Ctrl+D keys.

5. Release the mouse button. AutoFill enters the labels Day1 through Day 159 in the selected range. See Figure 3-19.

Figure 3-19   **Farm Day pattern extended with AutoFill**

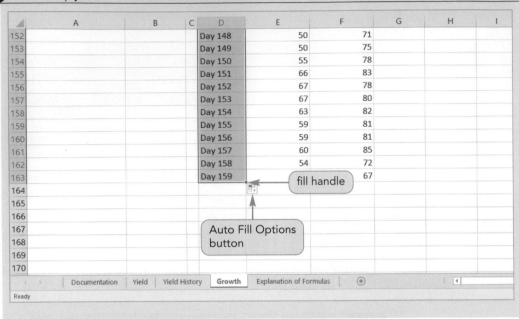

Exploring Auto Fill Options

By default, AutoFill copies both the content and the formatting of the original range to the selected range. However, sometimes you might want to copy only the content or only the formatting. The Auto Fill Options button that appears after you release the mouse button lets you specify what is copied. Figure 3-20 shows the Auto Fill Options menu for an extended series of patterned text.

Figure 3-20   **Auto Fill Options menu**

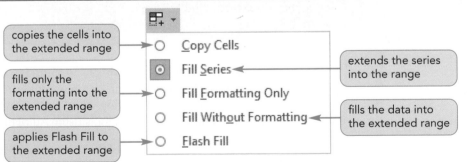

The Copy Cells option copies both the cell content and formatting but does not extend a series based on the initial values. The Fill Series option (the default) extends the initial series values into the new range. Other options allow you to fill in the values with or without the formatting used in the initial cells. Additional options (not shown in Figure 3-20) are provided when extending date values, allowing AutoFill to extend the initial dates by days, weekdays, months, or years.

The Series dialog box provides other options for how AutoFill is applied. To open the Series dialog box, click the Fill button in the Editing group on the Home tab, and then click Series. You can specify a linear or growth series for numbers; a date series for dates that increase by day, weekday, month, or year; or an AutoFill series for patterned text. With numbers, you can also specify the step value (how much each number increases over the previous entry) and a stop value (the endpoint for the entire series). See Figure 3-21.

Figure 3-21 | **Series dialog box**

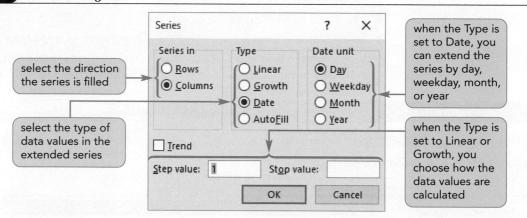

when the Type is set to Date, you can extend the series by day, weekday, month, or year

select the direction the series is filled

select the type of data values in the extended series

when the Type is set to Linear or Growth, you choose how the data values are calculated

Filling Formulas

You can also use AutoFill to extend formulas into a range. AutoFill copies the formula in the initial cell or range into the extended range. Excel modifies the cell references in the formulas based on the location of the cells in the extended range.

Jane wants the Growth worksheet to include the date of each growing day starting from the planting date and extending to the last day of recorded data. Because dates are stored as numbers, you can fill in the calendar days by adding 1 to the date displayed in the previous row. Jane wants to use the date 4/15/2017 as the starting date of when the farm began planting corn.

To copy the formula with the dates for the growing season with AutoFill:

1. In cell **B7**, enter the date **4/15/2017** as the starting date of when the farm began planting corn.

2. In cell **L5**, enter the formula **=B7**. After you press the Enter key, cell L5 displays 4/15/2017, which is the first date of the growing season for corn.

3. In cell **L6**, enter the formula **=L5+1** to add one day to the date in cell L5. After you press the Enter key, the date 4/16/2017 appears in cell L6.

4. Click cell **L6** to select it, and then drag the fill handle over the range **L6:L163**. AutoFill copies the formula in cell L6 to the range L7:L163, increasing the date value by one day in each row.

AutoFill extends the formulas to display the date 4/16/2017 in cell L6 through the date 9/20/2017 in cell L163. Each date is calculated by increasing the value in the cell one row above it by one day. The formulas for these calculations are= L5+1 in cell L6, =L6+1 in cell L7, and so forth up to =L162+1 in cell L163.

Jane wants you to change the planting date to 4/25/2017, which is closer to the final date for planting corn at Wingait Farm.

To change the planting date:

1. Scroll to the top of the workbook.

2. In cell **B7**, change the value from 4/15/2017 to **4/25/2017**. The dates in column L automatically change to reflect the new planting date with the last date in the column changing to 9/30/2017. See Figure 3-22.

Figure 3-22 Date series pattern extended with AutoFill

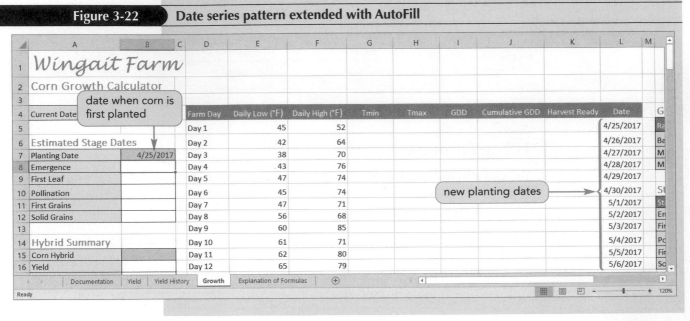

Jane wants to know when the corn crop will reach different stages of growth. In the range N11:O16 of the Growth worksheet, Jane created a table listing the number of days after planting that different growth milestones are reached. For example, the sprouts of the corn plant are often visible five days after planting (cell O12), the first small leaf appears eight days after planting (cell O13), and so forth. You will use the values in the range O12:O16 to estimate the calendar dates for when the first sprouts emerge, the first leaf appears, the corn begins to pollinate, the corn shows its first grains, and finally when the corn shows its solid grains or kernels.

To display the dates for corn growth milestones:

1. In cell **B8**, enter the formula **=B7+O12** to add the number of days until emergence to the planting date. The date 4/30/2017, which is the estimated date when the first corn sprouts will appear, is displayed in cell B8.

2. Click cell **B8** to select it, and then drag the fill handle over the range **B8:B12** to fill in the dates for the other growth milestones. See Figure 3-23.

| Figure 3-23 | Formula extended with AutoFill |

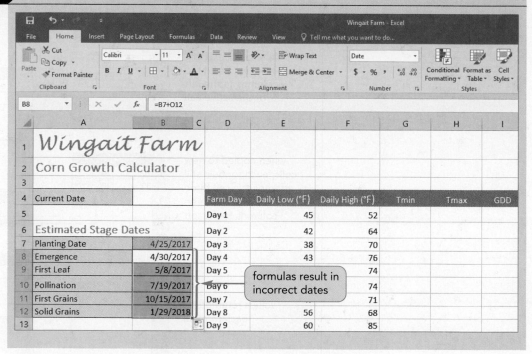

Something is wrong with the formulas that calculate the milestone dates. For example, the date for when the first corn kernels appear is January of the next year. To understand why the formulas resulted in incorrect dates, you need to look at the cell references.

Exploring Cell References

Excel has three types of cell references: relative, absolute, and mixed. Each type of cell reference in a formula is affected differently when the formula is copied and pasted to a new location.

Understanding Relative References

So far, all of the cell references you have worked with are relative cell references. When a formula includes a relative cell reference, Excel interprets the reference to each cell relative to the position of the cell containing the formula. For example, if cell A1 contains the formula =B1+B2, Excel interprets that formula as "Add the value of the cell one column to the right (B1) to the value of the cell one column to the right and one row down (B2)".

This relative interpretation of the cell reference is retained when the formula is copied to a new location. If the formula in cell A1 is copied to cell A3 (two rows down in the worksheet), the relative references also shift two rows down, resulting in the formula =B3+B4.

Figure 3-24 shows another example of how relative references change when a formula is pasted to new locations in the worksheet. In this figure, the formula =A3 entered in cell D6 displays 10, which is the number entered in cell A3. When pasted to a new location, each of the pasted formulas contains a reference to a cell that is three rows up and three rows to the left of the current cell's location.

Figure 3-24   **Formulas using relative references**

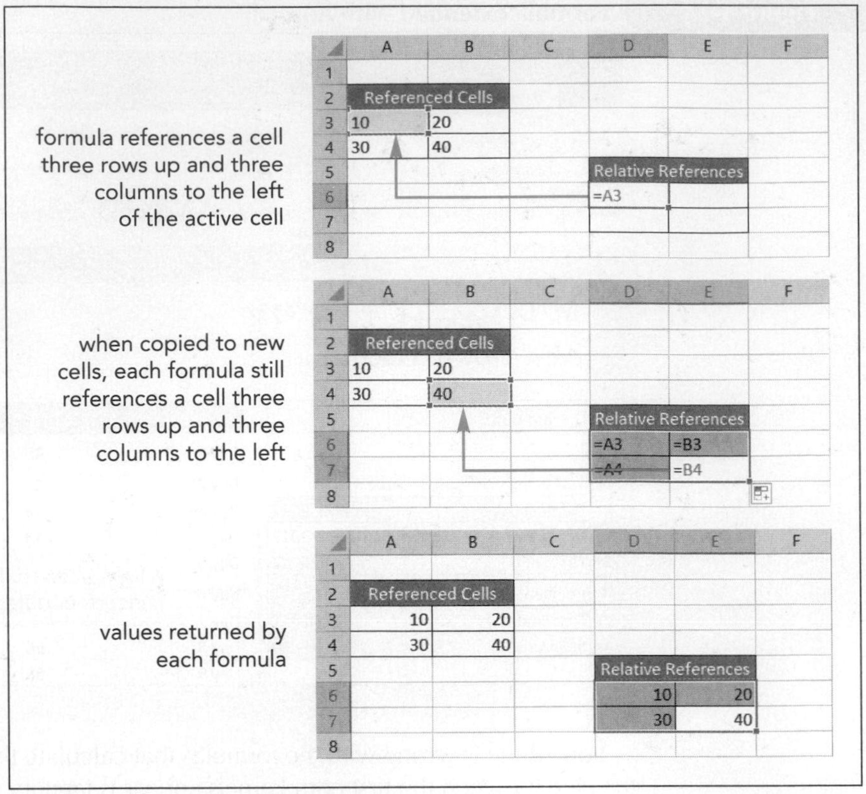

formula references a cell
three rows up and three
columns to the left
of the active cell

when copied to new
cells, each formula still
references a cell three
rows up and three
columns to the left

values returned by
each formula

This explains what happened when you used AutoFill to copy the formula =B7+O12 in cell B8 into the range B9:B12. The formula in cell B9 became =B8+O13, the formula in cell B10 became =B9+O14, the formula in cell B11 became =B10+O15, and the formula in cell B12 became =B11+O16. In each case, the stage days were added to the date in the previous row, not the original planting date entered in cell B7. As a result, date calculation for the appearance of the first solid grains was pushed out to January of the following year.

To correct this, you need a cell reference that remains fixed on cell B7 no matter where the formula is pasted. This can be accomplished with an absolute reference.

Understanding Absolute References

An absolute reference is used for a cell reference that remains fixed even when that formula is copied to a new cell. Absolute references include $ (a dollar sign) before each column and row designation. For example, B8 is a relative reference to cell B8, while $B$8 is an absolute reference to that cell.

Figure 3-25 shows an example of how copying a formula with an absolute reference results in the same cell reference being pasted in different cells regardless of their position compared to the location of the original copied cell. In this example, the formula =$A$3 will always reference cell A3 no matter where the formula is copied to.

Figure 3-25   Formulas using absolute references

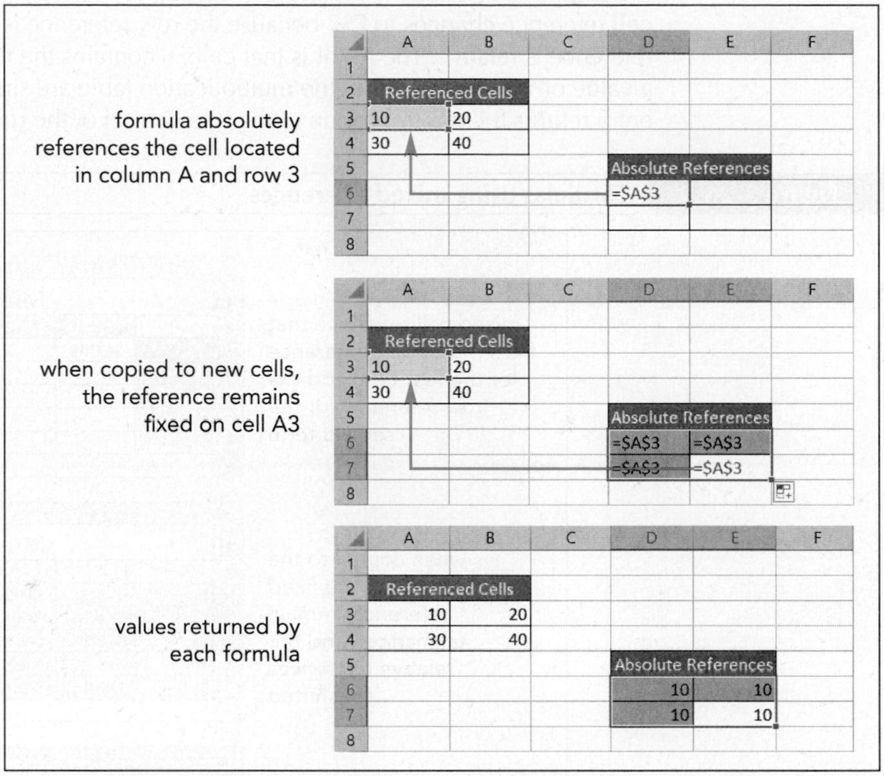

formula absolutely references the cell located in column A and row 3

when copied to new cells, the reference remains fixed on cell A3

values returned by each formula

Sometimes, you'll want only one part of the cell reference to remain fixed. This requires a mixed cell reference.

Understanding Mixed References

A mixed cell reference contains both relative and absolute components. For example, a mixed reference for cell A2 can be either $A2 where the column component is absolute and the row component is relative, or it can be entered as A$2 with a relative column component and a fixed row component. A mixed reference "locks" only one part of the cell reference. When you copy and paste a cell with a mixed reference to a new location, the absolute portion of the cell reference remains fixed, and the relative portion shifts along with the new location of the pasted cell.

Figure 3-26 shows an example of using mixed references to complete a multiplication table. The first cell in the table, cell B3, contains the formula =$A3*B$2, which multiplies the first column entry (cell A3) by the first row entry (cell B2), returning 1. When this formula is copied to another cell, the absolute portions of the cell references remain unchanged, and the relative portions of the references change. For example, if the formula is copied to cell E6, the first mixed cell reference changes to $A6 because the column reference is absolute and the row reference is relative, and the second cell reference changes to E$2 because the row reference is absolute and the column reference is relative. The result is that cell E6 contains the formula =$A6*E$2 and returns a value of 16. Other cells in the multiplication table are similarly modified so that each entry returns the multiplication of the intersection of the row and column headings.

Figure 3-26   **Formulas using mixed references**

mixed cell reference that fixes the column reference for the first term and the row reference for the second term

when copied to the B3:F7 range, the fixed references remain unchanged and the relative references are shifted

values returned by each formula

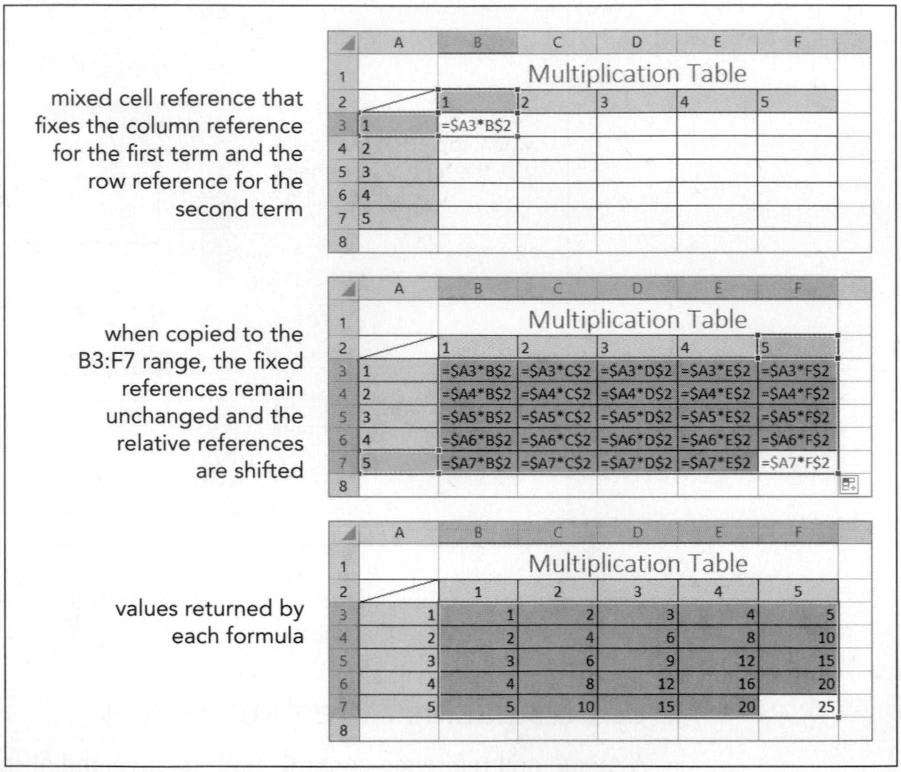

Changing Cell References in a Formula

You can quickly switch a cell reference from relative to absolute or mixed. Rather than retyping the formula, you can select the cell reference in Edit mode and then press the F4 key. As you press the F4 key, Excel cycles through the different reference types—starting with the relative reference, followed by the absolute reference, then to a mixed reference with an absolute row component followed by a mixed reference with an absolute column component.

To calculate the correct stage dates in the Growth worksheet, you will change the formula in cell B8 to use an absolute reference to cell B7 and then use AutoFill to copy that formula into range B9:B12.

To correct the stage dates formulas with absolute cell references:

▶ **1.** Double-click cell **B8** to select it and enter Edit mode.

▶ **2.** In cell B8, double-click the **B7** reference to select it, and then press the **F4** key. Excel changes the formula in cell B8 to =$B$7+O12.

▶ **3.** Press the **Enter** key to enter the formula and exit Edit mode.

▶ **4.** Click cell **B8** to select it, and then drag the fill handle over the range **B8:B12**. Figure 3-27 shows the revised dates for the different stages of corn growth.

| Figure 3-27 | Stage dates calculated with absolute cell references |

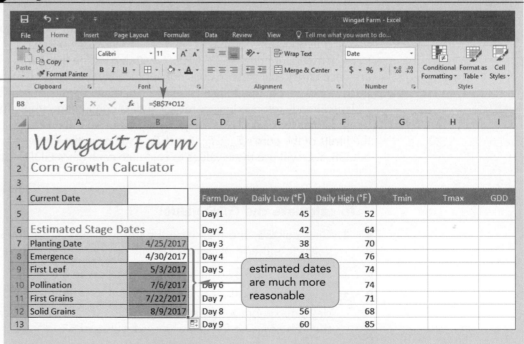

The revised dates for the different stages of the corn maturation are much more reasonable. For example, the date on which solid grains first appear is 8/9/2017, which is more in line with Jane's experience.

PROSKILLS

Problem Solving: When to Use Relative, Absolute, and Mixed References

Part of effective workbook design is knowing when to use relative, absolute, and mixed references. Use relative references when you want to apply the same formula with input cells that share a common layout or pattern. Relative references are commonly used when copying a formula that calculates summary statistics across columns or rows of data values. Use absolute references when you want your copied formulas to always refer to the same cell. This usually occurs when a cell contains a constant value, such as a tax rate, that will be referenced in formulas throughout the worksheet. Mixed references are seldom used other than when creating tables of calculated values such as a multiplication table in which the values of the formula or function can be found at the intersection of the rows and columns of the table.

Calendar days are one way of predicting crop growth, but Jane knows that five days of hot weather will result in more rapid growth than five mild days. A more accurate method to estimate growth is to calculate the crop's Growing Degree Days (GDD), which take into account the range of daily temperatures to which the crop is exposed. GDD is calculated using the formula

$$\text{GDD} = \frac{T_{max} + T_{min}}{2} - T_{base}$$

where T_{max} is the daily high temperature, T_{min} is the daily low temperature, and T_{base} is a baseline temperature for the region. For corn growing in Iowa, T_{min} and T_{max} are limited to the temperature range 50°F to 86°F with a baseline line temperature of 50°F. The limits are necessary because corn does not appreciably grow when the temperature falls below 50°F, nor does a temperature above 86°F increase the rate of growth.

Jane already retrieved meteorological data containing sample low and high temperatures for each day of the growing season in the Cascade, Iowa, region. She stored the limits of the corn's T_{min}, T_{max}, and T_{base} values in the Growth worksheet in the range N5:O8. You will use these values to calculate each day's GDD value for corn growth.

To calculate the GDD value:

1. Click cell **G5**, and then type the formula **=MAX(E5, $O$7)** to set the T_{min} value to either that day's minimum temperature or to 50°F, whichever is larger.

2. Press the **Tab** key. The formula returns a value of 50.

3. In cell H5, type the formula **=MIN(F5, $O$8)** to set the T_{max} value to that day's maximum temperature or to 86°F, whichever is smaller, and then press the **Tab** key. The formula returns a value of 52.

4. In cell I5, enter the formula **=(G5+H5)/2-$O$6** to calculate that day's GDD value using the T_{base} value of 50°F stored in cell O6. The formula returns 1.0, indicating that the GDD value for that day is 1.

   Next you'll use AutoFill to copy these formulas into the range G5:I163. Because you used absolute references in the formulas, the copied formulas will continue to reference cells O7, O8, and O6 in the extended range.

5. Select the range **G5:I5**, and then drag the fill handle down to row **163**. Figure 3-28 shows the first several rows of GDD values for the corn crop's history.

Figure 3-28   GDD values for the corn crop

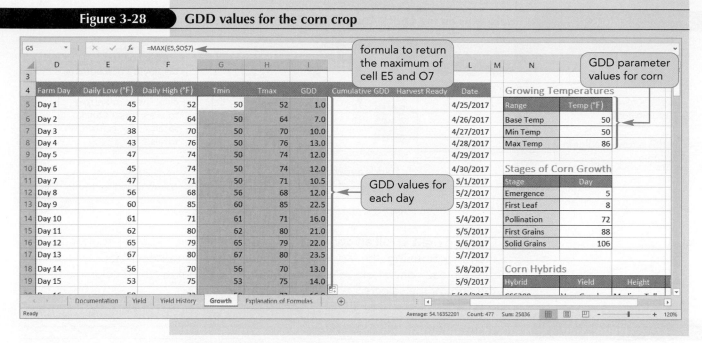

The first GDD values range between 1 and 22.5, but in July and August, GDD routinely reach the upper 20s and lower 30s, indicating that those hot days result in rapid corn growth.

Summarizing Data with the Quick Analysis Tool

The Quick Analysis tool can generate columns and rows of summary statistics and formulas that can be used for analyzing data. GDD is cumulative, which means that as the crop gains more Growing Degree Days, it continues to grow and mature. Jane needs you to calculate a running total of the GDD value for each day in the season. You will enter this calculation using the Quick Analysis tool.

To calculate a running total of GDD:

1. Select the range **I5:I163** containing the GDD values for day of the growing season.

2. Click the **Quick Analysis** button in the lower-right corner of the select range (or press the **Ctrl+Q** keys) to display the menu of Quick Analysis tools.

3. Click **Totals** from the list of tools. The Quick Analysis tools that calculate summary statistics for the selected data appear. See Figure 3-29.

Figure 3-29 Totals tools on the Quick Analysis tool

adds a row displaying column sums

adds a row of column counts

adds a row of column averages

adds a column displaying row sums

click the scroll arrow to view more Quick Analysis tools for row totals

adds a row displaying percent of the totals

adds a row containing column running totals

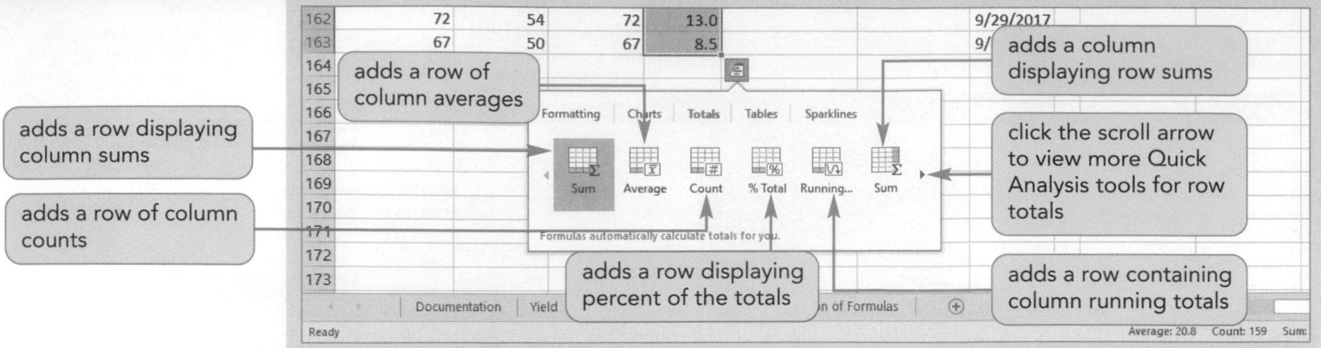

4. Click the **right scroll arrow** ▶ to view additional Quick Analysis tools, and then click **Running** (the last icon in the list). The running total of GDD values through each day of the season appears in a bold font in a new column J to the right of the selected range. See Figure 3-30.

Figure 3-30 Cumulative totals for the GDD values

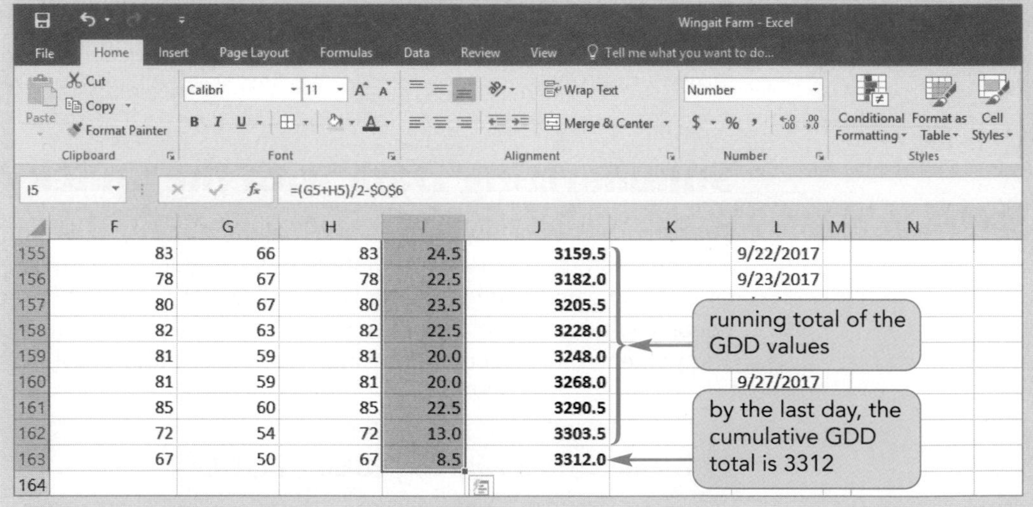

running total of the GDD values

by the last day, the cumulative GDD total is 3312

Based on the running total in column J, Jane projects that by 9/30/2017, the corn crop will have a total of 3312 Growing Degree Days. To create the running total, the Quick Analysis tool added the following formula to cell J5 and then copied that formula over the range J5:J163:

`=SUM($I$5:I5)`

Note that this formula uses a combination of absolute and relative cell references. When copied to cell J6 the formula becomes

`=SUM($I$5:I6)`

and when copied to J7 the formula is

`=SUM($I$5:I7)`

In this formula, the starting cell of the range used with the SUM function is fixed at cell I5, but the ending cell is relative, causing the number of rows in the range to expand to match the cell selection. For the last date in row 163, the formula becomes:

`=SUM($I$5:I163)`

This approach shows how a combination of absolute and relative cell references expands the capability of Excel to create formulas for a variety of ranges.

Working with Dates and Date Functions

Excel has several functions that work with dates and times. These functions are particularly useful in workbooks that involve production schedules and calendars. Figure 3-31 describes some of the commonly used date and time functions.

Figure 3-31   Date functions

Function	Description
DATE(*year,month,day*)	Creates a date value for the date represented by the *year*, *month*, and *day* arguments
DAY(*date*)	Extracts the day of the month from *date*
MONTH(*date*)	Extracts the month number from *date* where 1=January, 2=February, and so forth
YEAR(*date*)	Extracts the year number from *date*
NETWORKDAYS(*start,end*[,*holidays*])	Calculates the number of whole working days between *start* and *end*; to exclude holidays, add the optional *holidays* argument containing a list of holiday dates to skip
WEEKDAY(*date*[,*return_type*])	Calculates the weekday from *date*, where 1=Sunday, 2=Monday, and so forth; to choose a different numbering scheme, set *return_type* to 1 (1=Sunday, 2=Monday, ...), 2 (1=Monday, 2=Tuesday, ...), or 3 (0=Monday, 1=Tuesday, ...)
WORKDAY(*start,days*[,*holidays*])	Returns the workday after *days* workdays have passed since the *start* date; to exclude holidays, add the optional *holidays* argument containing a list of holiday dates to skip
NOW( )	Returns the current date and time
TODAY( )	Returns the current date

Many workbooks include the current date so that any reports generated by the workbook are identified by date. To display the current date, you can use the TODAY function:

`TODAY ( )`

TIP

To display the current date and time, which is updated each time the workbook is reopened, use the NOW function.

Note that although the TODAY function doesn't have any arguments, you still must include the parentheses for the function to work. The date displayed by the TODAY function is updated automatically whenever you reopen the workbook or enter a new calculation.

Jane wants the Growth worksheet to show the current date each time it is used or printed. You will use the TODAY function to display the current date in cell B4.

To display the current date:

1. Scroll to the top of the worksheet, and then click cell **B4**.

2. On the ribbon, click the **Formulas** tab.

3. In the Function Library group, click the **Date & Time** button to display the date and time functions.

4. Click **TODAY**. The Function Arguments dialog box opens and indicates that the TODAY function requires no arguments.

5. Click the **OK** button. The formula =TODAY() is entered in cell B4, and the current date is displayed in the cell.

Note that Excel automatically formats cells containing the TODAY function to display the value in Short Date format.

Date Calculations with Working Days

INSIGHT

Businesspeople are often more interested in workdays rather than in all of the days of the week. For example, to estimate a delivery date in which packages are not shipped or delivered on weekends, it is more useful to know the date of the next weekday rather than the date of the next day.

To display the date of a weekday that is a specified number of weekdays past a start date, Excel provides the **WORKDAY function**

```
WORKDAY(start,days[,holidays])
```

where *start* is a start date, *days* is the number of workdays after that starting date, and *holidays* is an optional list of holiday dates to skip. For example, if cell A1 contains the date 12/20/2018, a Thursday, the following formula displays the date 1/2/2019, a Wednesday that is nine working days later:

```
=WORKDAY(A1,9)
```

The optional *holidays* argument references a series of dates that the WORKDAY function will skip in performing its calculations. So, if both 12/25/2018 and 1/1/2019 are entered in the range B1:B2 as holidays, the following function will return the date 1/4/2019, a Friday that is nine working days, excluding the holidays, after 12/20/2018:

```
=WORKDAY(A1,9,B1:B2)
```

To reverse the process and calculate the number of working days between two dates, use the NETWORKDAYS function

```
NETWORKDAYS(start,end[,holidays])
```

where *start* is the starting date and *end* is the ending date. So, if cell A1 contains the date 12/20/2018 and cell A2 contains the date 1/3/2019, the following function returns 9, indicating that there are nine working days between the start and ending, excluding the holidays specified in the range B1:B2:

```
=NETWORKDAYS(A1,A2,B1:B2)
```

For international applications in which the definition of working day differs between one country and another, Excel supports the WORKDAY.INTL function. See Excel Help for more information.

Corn seed is sold in a wide variety of hybrids used to create corn of different quality, size, resistance to parasites, and growth rates. Jane wants the Growth worksheet to display data about the corn hybrid she chose for Wingait Farm. You can retrieve that data using a lookup function.

Using Lookup Functions

A **lookup function** retrieves values from a table of data that match a specified condition. For example, a lookup function can be used to retrieve a tax rate from a tax table for a given annual income or to retrieve shipping rates for different delivery options.

The table that stores the data you want to retrieve is called a **lookup table**. The first row or column of the table contains compare values, which are the values that are being looked up. If the compare values are in the first row, the table is a **horizontal lookup table**; if the compare values are in the first column, the table is a vertical lookup table. The remaining rows or columns contain the return values, which are the data values being retrieved by the lookup function.

Figure 3-32 shows the range N19:Q27 in the Growth worksheet containing information about different corn hybrids. This information is a vertical lookup table because the first column of the table containing the names of the hybrids stores the compare values. The remaining columns containing type of yield, height of the corn stalk, and GDD units until the hybrid reaches maturity are the return values. To look up the Growing Degree Days required until the corn hybrid CS6478 reaches maturity, Excel scans the first column of the lookup table until it finds the entry for CS6478. Excel then moves to the right to the column containing information that needs to be returned.

Figure 3-32   Finding an exact match from a lookup table

Lookup tables can be constructed for exact match or approximate match lookups. In an **exact match lookup**, the lookup value must exactly match one of the compare values in the first row or column of the lookup table. Figure 3-32 is an exact match lookup because the name of the corn hybrid must match one of the compare values in the table. An **approximate match lookup** is used when the lookup value falls within a range of compare values. You will work with exact match lookups in this module.

Finding an Exact Match with the VLOOKUP Function

To retrieve the return value from a vertical lookup table, you use the VLOOKUP function

```
VLOOKUP(comp_value,table_array,col_index_num[,range_lookup=TRUE])
```

where $comp\_value$ is the compare value to find in the first column of the lookup table, $table\_array$ is the range reference to the lookup table, and col_index_num is the number of the column in the lookup table that contains the return value. Keep in mind that col_index_num refers to the number of the column within the lookup table, not the worksheet column. So, a col_index_num of 2 refers to the lookup table's second column. Finally, *range_lookup* is an optional argument that specifies whether the lookup should be done as an exact match or an approximate match. For an exact match, you set the *range_lookup* value to FALSE. For approximate match lookups, you set the *range_lookup* value to TRUE. The default is to assume an approximate match.

For example, the following formula performs an exact match lookup using the text "CS6478" as the compare value and the data in the range N20:Q27 (shown in Figure 3-32) as the lookup table:

```
=VLOOKUP("CS6478",N20:Q27,4,FALSE)
```

The function looks through the compare values in the first column of the table to locate the "CS6478" entry. When the exact entry is found, the function returns the corresponding value in the fourth column of the table, which in this case is 2795.

Jane wants you to retrieve information about the CS6478 hybrid she uses at Wingait Farm and then display that information in the range B16:B18 on the Growth worksheet. You'll use a VLOOKUP function to retrieve yield information about the hybrid.

To use the VLOOKUP function to find yield information for hybrid CS6478:

1. In cell **B15**, enter the hybrid **CS6478**.

2. Click cell **B16**, and then click the **Insert Function** button f_x to the left of the formula bar. The Insert Function dialog box opens.

3. Click the **Or select a category** box, and then click **Lookup & Reference** in the list of function categories.

4. Scroll down the Select a function box, and then double-click **VLOOKUP**. The Function Arguments dialog box for the VLOOKUP function opens.

5. In the Lookup_value box, type **$B$15** as the absolute reference to the hybrid name, and then press the **Tab** key. The insertion point moves to the Table_array box.

6. In the Growth worksheet, select the range **N20:Q27** as the Table_array value, press the **F4** key to change the range reference to the absolute reference **$N$20:$Q$27**.

7. Press the **Tab** key. The insertion point moves to the Col_index_num box. Yield information is stored in the second column of the lookup table.

8. Type **2** in the Col_index_num box to return information from the second column of the lookup table, and then press the **Tab** key. The insertion point moves to the Range_lookup box.

9. Type **FALSE** in the Range_lookup box to perform an exact match lookup. See Figure 3-33.

Figure 3-33   Function Arguments dialog box for the VLOOKUP function

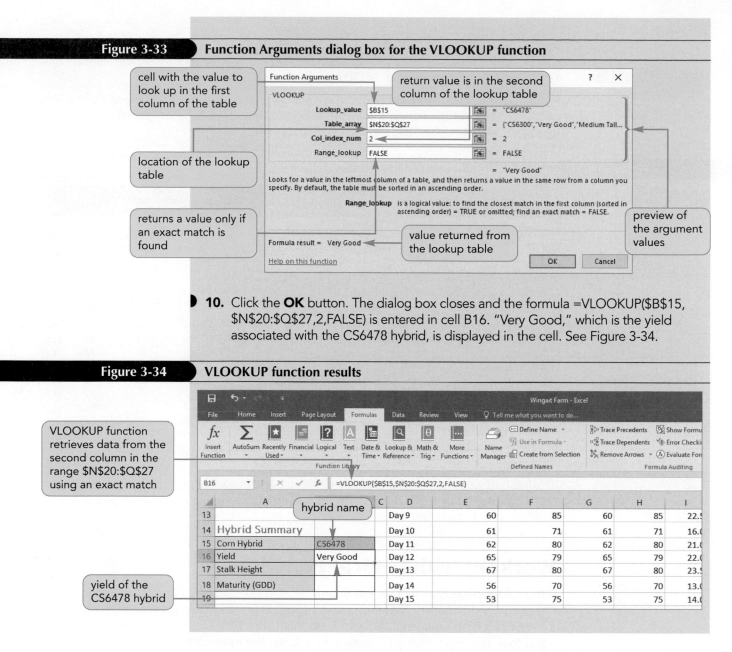

10. Click the **OK** button. The dialog box closes and the formula =VLOOKUP($B$15, $N$20:$Q$27,2,FALSE) is entered in cell B16. "Very Good," which is the yield associated with the CS6478 hybrid, is displayed in the cell. See Figure 3-34.

Figure 3-34   VLOOKUP function results

Jane wants to see the stalk height and the GDD information about the hybrid CS6478. You will use AutoFill to copy the VLOOKUP function into the other cells in the Hybrid Summary table.

To display other information about the hybrid CS6478:

1. Click cell **B16** to select it, and then drag the fill handle over the range **B16:B18** to copy the VLOOKUP formula into cells B17 and B18. The text "Very Good" appears in cells B17 and B18, because the formula is set up to retrieve text from the second column of the lookup table.

   You need to edit the formulas in cells B17 and B18 to retrieve information from the third and fourth columns of the lookup table, respectively.

2. Double-click cell **B17** to enter into Edit mode, change the third argument from 2 to **3**, and then press the **Enter** key. The value Medium for the hybrid's stalk height appears in cell B17.

3. Double-click cell **B18** to enter Edit mode, change the third argument from 2 to **4**, and then press the **Enter** key. The value 2795 for the hybrid's GDD appears in cell B18. See Figure 3-35.

Figure 3-35   **VLOOKUP function results for other columns**

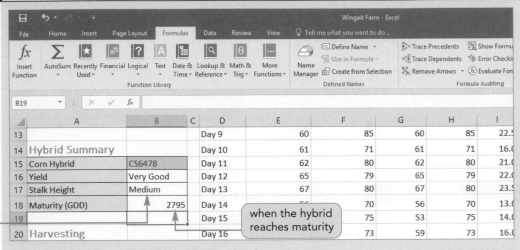

stalk height for the CS6478 hybrid

when the hybrid reaches maturity

Based on the values in the lookup table, the CS6478 hybrid will reach maturity and be ready for harvesting after 2795 Growing Degree Days. Jane wants you to add a column of values to the growth table that indicates for each date, whether the corn crop has reached maturity and is ready for harvesting. To create this column, you will need to use a logical function.

Working with Logical Functions

A **logical function** is a function that returns a different value depending on whether the given condition is true or false. That condition is entered as an expression, such as A5=3. If cell A5 is equal to 3, this expression and condition are true; if cell A5 is not equal to 3, this expression and condition are false. The most commonly used logical function is the IF function. The syntax of the IF function is

`IF(condition,value_if_true,value_if_false)`

where `condition` is an expression that is either true or false, `value_if_true` is the value returned by the function if the expression is true, and `value_if_false` is the value returned if the expression is false.

The value returned by the IF function can be a number, text, a date, a cell reference, or a formula. For example, the following formula tests whether the value in cell A1 is equal to the value in cell B1, returning 100 if those two cells are equal and 50 if they're not.

`=IF(A1=B1,100,50)`

TIP

To apply multiple logical conditions, you can nest one IF function within another.

In many cases, you will use cell references instead of values in the IF function. The following formula, for example, uses cell references, returning the value of cell C1 if A1 equals B1; otherwise, it returns the value of cell C2:

```
=IF(A1=B1,C1,C2)
```

The = symbol in these formulas is a **comparison operator** that indicates the relationship between two parts of the logical function's condition. Figure 3-36 describes other comparison operators that can be used within logical functions.

Figure 3-36 **Logical comparison operators**

Operator	Expression	Tests
=	A1 = B1	If the value in cell A1 is equal to the value in cell B1
>	A1 > B1	If the value in cell A1 is greater than the value in cell B1
<	A1 < B1	If the value in cell A1 is less than the value in cell B1
>=	A1 >= B1	If the value in cell A1 is greater than or equal to the value in cell B1
<=	A1 <= B1	If the value in cell A1 is less than or equal to the value in cell B1
<>	A1 <> B1	If the value in cell A1 is not equal to the value in cell B1

The IF function also works with text. For example, the following formula tests whether the value of cell A1 is equal to "yes":

```
=IF(A1="yes","done","restart")
```

If the condition is true (the value of cell A1 is equal to "yes"), then the formula returns the text "done"; otherwise, it returns the text "restart".

For each date in the growth record of the corn crop, Jane wants to know whether the cumulative GDD value is greater than or equal to the GDD value on which the hybrid reaches maturity and is ready for harvesting. If the crop is ready for harvesting, she wants the cell to display the text "Yes"; otherwise, it should display the text "No". You'll use the IF function to do this.

To enter the IF function to specify whether the corn is ready for harvesting:

▶ 1. Click cell **K5** to select it. You'll enter the IF function in this cell.

▶ 2. On the Formulas tab, in the Function Library group, click the **Logical** button to display the list of logical functions, and then click **IF**. The Function Arguments dialog box for the IF function opens.

▶ 3. In the Logical_test box, enter the expression **J5>=$B$18** to test whether the cumulative GDD value is greater than the maturity value in cell B18.

▶ 4. Press **Tab** key to move the insertion point to the Value_if_true box, and then type **"Yes"** as the value if the logical test is true.

▶ 5. Press **Tab** key to move the insertion point to the Value_if_false box, and then type **"No"** as the value if the logical test is false. See Figure 3-37.

Figure 3-37   **Function Arguments dialog box for the IF function**

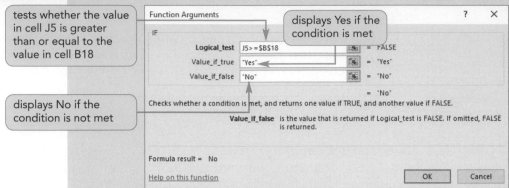

tests whether the value in cell J5 is greater than or equal to the value in cell B18

displays Yes if the condition is met

displays No if the condition is not met

6. Click the **OK** button. The formula =IF(J5>=$B$18,"Yes","No") is entered in cell K5. The cell displays the text "No," indicating that the crop is not harvest ready on this day (a logical result because this is the day when the farm starts planting the corn).

7. Click cell **K5**, and then drag fill handle to select the range **K5:K163**. The formula with the IF function is applied to the remaining days of the growing season. As shown in Figure 3-38, by the end of the growing season, the crop is ready for harvesting because the cumulative GDD value for the hybrid CS6478 has exceeded 2795.

Figure 3-38   **IF function evaluates whether the crop is harvest ready**

IF function testing whether cell J5 is greater than or equal to cell B18

=IF(J5>=$B$18,"Yes","No")

	D	E	F	G	H	I	J	K	L	M	N	O	P
154	Day 150	55	78	55	78	16.5	3135.0	Yes	9/21/2017				
155	Day 151	66	83	66	83	24.5	3159.5	Yes	9/22/2017				
156	Day 152	67	78	67	78	22.5	3182.0	Yes	9/23/2017				
157	Day 153	67	80	67	80	23.5	3205.5	Yes	9/24/2017				
158	Day 154	63	82	63	82	22.5	3228.0	Yes	9/25/2017				
159	Day 155	59	81	59	81	20.0	3248.0	Yes	9/26/2017				
160	Day 156	59	81	59	81	20.0	3268.0	Yes	9/27/2017				
161	Day 157	60	85	60	85	22.5	3290.5	Yes	9/28/2017				
162	Day 158	54	72	54	72	13.0	3303.5	Yes	9/29/2017				
163	Day 159	47	67	50	67	8.5	3312.0	Yes	9/30/2017				
164													

Yes values indicate that the corn is ready to be harvested

By scrolling up and down the Growth worksheet you can locate the row in which the value in the Harvest Ready column switches from No to Yes. For this data, the switch occurs in row 138 where the cumulative GDD value is equal to 2814, exceeding the minimum GDD value required for this particular hybrid to reach maturity.

Rather than scrolling through the worksheet, Jane wants the worksheet to display the calendar date on which the crop reaches maturity and is ready for harvesting. You can obtain this information by using columns K and L as a lookup table. Recall that Excel scans a lookup table from the top to the bottom and stops when it reaches the first value in the compare column that matches the lookup value. You can use this fact to find the first location in column K where the Harvest Ready value is equal to "Yes" and then apply the VLOOKUP function to return the corresponding calendar date in column L.

To display the harvest date for the corn crop:

▶ **1.** Near the top of the worksheet, click cell **B21** to select it.

▶ **2.** Click the **Insert Function** button *fx* to the left of the formula bar. The Insert Function dialog box opens.

▶ **3.** Click the **Or select a category box arrow**, and then click **Most Recently Used** to display a list of the functions you have used most recently.

▶ **4.** Double-click **VLOOKUP** in the list. The Function Arguments dialog box for the VLOOKUP function opens.

▶ **5.** In the Lookup_value box, type **"Yes"** and then press the **Tab** key. The insertion point moves to the Table_array box.

▶ **6.** Select the **K** and **L** column headings to insert the reference K:L in the Table_array box, and then press the **Tab** key. The insertion point moves to the Col_index_num box.

▶ **7.** Type **2** in the Col_index_num box to retrieve the value from the second column in the lookup table, and then press the **Tab** key. The insertion point moves to the Range_lookup box.

Use FALSE to perform an exact match lookup.

▶ **8.** Type **FALSE** in the Range_lookup box to apply an exact match lookup. See Figure 3-39.

Figure 3-39   **Function Arguments for the VLOOKUP function**

looks for cell values equal to "Yes"

uses columns K and L as the lookup table

returns the value from the second column of the lookup table

uses an exact match lookup

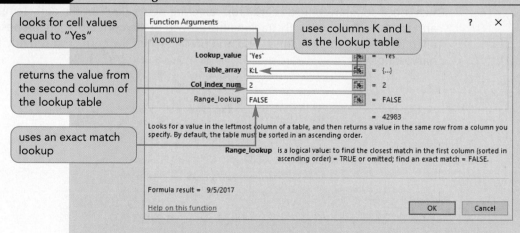

▶ **9.** Click the **OK** button. The formula =VLOOKUP("Yes",K:L,2,FALSE) is entered in cell B21. The cell displays 9/5/2017, which is the date when the corn crop has reached maturity and is ready for harvesting to begin.

Jane can view the impact of different hybrids on the harvest date by changing the value of cell B15.

▸ **10.** Click cell **B15**, and then change the corn hybrid from CS6478 to **CS6489**. The results from the lookup and IF functions in the worksheet change to reflect the corn hybrid CS6489. This hybrid has excellent yield and tall stalks and is ready for harvesting on 9/10/2017, five days later than the corn hybrid CS6478. See Figure 3-40.

Figure 3-40 **Summary and harvesting data for the hybrid CS6489**

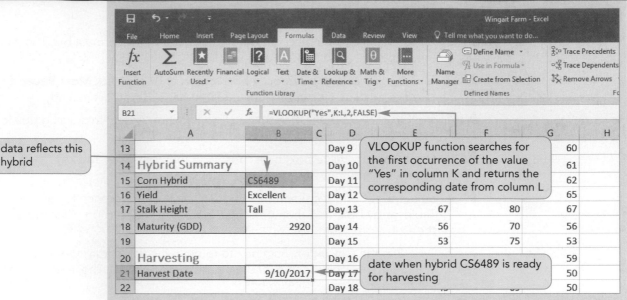

▸ **11.** Save the workbook.

You've completed your work on the Wingait Farm workbook. Jane will use this workbook to analyze next year's crop, entering new values for the daily temperatures and for the hybrid types. By tracking the growth of the corn crop, Jane hopes to more effectively increase her farm's yield and predict when the corn crop is ready for harvesting.

INSIGHT

Managing Error Values with the IF Function

An error value does not mean that you must correct the cell's formula or function. Some error values appear simply because you have not yet entered any data into the workbook. For example, if you use the VLOOKUP function without a lookup value, the #N/A error value appears because Excel cannot look up an empty value. However, as soon as you enter a lookup, the #N/A error value disappears, replaced with the result of the VLOOKUP function.

Error values of this type can make your workbook difficult to read and can confuse other users. One way to avoid error values resulting from missing input values is to nest formulas within an IF function. For example, the following formula first tests whether a value has been entered into cell B2 before attempting to use that cell as a lookup value in the VLOOKUP function:

```
=IF(B2="","",VLOOKUP(B2,$E1:$G$10,3,FALSE)
```

Note that "" is used to represent an empty text string or value. If the IF condition is true because no value has been entered into cell B2, the formula will return an empty text string instead of an error value, but if B2 has a value, the VLOOKUP function is applied using cell B2 as the lookup value. The result is a cleaner workbook that is easier for other people to read and use.

Jane appreciates all of the work you have done in developing the Wingait Farm workbook. She will continue to study the document and get back to you with future projects at the farm.

REVIEW

Session 3.2 Quick Check

1. If 4/30/2017 and 5/31/2017 are the initial values, what are the next two values AutoFill will insert?

2. You need to reference cell Q57 in a formula. What is its relative reference? What is its absolute reference? What are the two mixed references?

3. If cell R10 contains the formula =R1+R2, which is then copied to cell S20, what formula is entered in cell S20?

4. If cell R10 contains the formula =$R1+R$2, which is then copied to cell S20, what formula is entered in cell S20?

5. Explain how to use the Quick Analysis tool to calculate a running total of the values in the range D1:D10.

6. Write the formula to display the current date in the worksheet.

7. Write the formula to display a date that is four workdays after the date in cell A5. Do not assume any holidays in your calculation.

8. Write the formula to perform an exact match lookup with the lookup value from cell G5 using a vertical lookup table located in the range A1:F50. Return the value from the third column of the table.

9. If cell Q3 is greater than cell Q4, you want to display the text "OK"; otherwise, display the text "RETRY". Write the formula that accomplishes this.

Review Assignments

Data File needed for the Review Assignments: Soybean.xlsx

Another cash crop grown at Wingait Farm is soybeans. Jane wants you to create a workbook for the soybean crop similar to the workbook you created for the corn crop. The workbook should estimate the total yield and revenue from a small plot sample and compare that yield to the farm's historic norms. The workbook should also track the soybean growth from planting to harvest. Complete the following:

1. Open the **Soybean** workbook located in the Excel3 > Review folder, and then save the workbook as **Soybean Crop** in the location specified by your instructor.

2. In the Documentation worksheet, enter your name in cell B3 and the date in cell B4.

3. The size of the soybean crop is **72** acres. Enter this value in cell B4 of the Yield worksheet.

4. The soybean sample comes from a plot of **4** rows each **7.5** inches wide and **21** inches long. Enter these values in the range B7:B9.

5. Within the plot, the farm has harvested **400** soybean pods with an average of **2.5** soybeans per pod. Enter these values in the B14:B15 range.

6. Apply the Input cell style to cells B4, B7:B9, and B14:B15.

7. Using the equations described in the Formulas worksheet, enter the following calculations:
   a. In cell B10, calculate the area of the plot sample in inches.
   b. In cell B11, convert the sample area to acres by dividing the value in cell B10 by the number of square inches in an acre (cell H4). Display the result to four decimal places.
   c. In cell B16, calculate the total number of seeds harvested in the sample.
   d. In cell B17, calculate the weight of the sample in pounds by dividing the number of seeds by the number of seeds in one pound (cell H5). Display the value to two decimal places.
   e. In cell B18, convert the weight to bushels by dividing the weight in pounds by the number of pounds of soybeans in one bushel (cell H6). Display the value to four decimal places.
   f. In cell B19, estimate the farm's soybean yield in bushels per acre by dividing the number of bushels in the plot sample by the area of the sample in acres. Display the value as an integer.

8. Calculate the following values for soybean yield and revenue:
   a. In cell B20, calculate the farm's average soybean yield using the values in column E. Use the ROUND function to round that average value to the nearest integer.
   b. In cell B21, calculate the farm's median soybean yield from the values in column E.
   c. In cell B24, calculate the farm's total production of soybeans in bushels by multiplying the bushels per acre value by the total number of acres that the farm devotes to soybeans. Display the value as an integer.
   d. In cell B25, calculate the total revenue from the soybean crop by multiplying the total bushels harvested by the current price per bushel (cell H7). Display the value using the Accounting format style.

9. Apply the Calculation style to the range B10:B11,B16:B21,B24:B25.

10. Use Goal Seek to determine what value in cell B4 (the number of acres devoted to soybeans) will result in a total soybean revenue of $40,000.

11. In the Growth worksheet, in cell B5, enter a formula with a function to display the current date.

12. Use AutoFill to insert the text strings Day 1 through Day 112 in the range D5:D116.

13. In cell G5, calculate the Growing Degree Days (GDD) for the first day of the season using the formula described in the Formulas worksheet and the temperature range values in the range L6:M9. (*Hint*: Use the same formula used in the tutorial for corn, but enter the T_{min}, T_{max}, and *base* values directly in the formula. Be sure to use absolute references for the temperature range values.)

14. Copy the formula in cell G5 to the range G5:G112.

15. Use the Quick Analysis tool to calculate the cumulative total of the GDD values from the range G5:G112, placing those values in the range H5:H112.

16. In cell B9, enter **5/12/2017**, which is the date the farm will start planting the soybean crop.

17. In cell J5, enter a formula to display the date from cell B9. In cell J6, enter a formula to increase the date in cell J5 by one day. Copy the formula in cell J6 to the range J6:J112 to enter the dates for the growing season.

18. In cell B8, enter **M070** as the maturity group for the current soybean hybrid.

19. In cell B10, use the VLOOKUP function to retrieve the cumulative GDD value for the M070 hybrid. (*Hint:* The range L12:M21 displays the cumulative GDD for each maturity group.)

20. In cell I5, enter an IF function that tests whether the cumulative GDD value in cell H5 is greater than the maturity value in cell B10. Use an absolute reference to cell B10. If the condition is true, return the text string "Ready"; otherwise, return the text "Not Ready". Copy the formula to the range I5:I112.

21. In cell B11, insert a VLOOKUP function using the values in the columns I and J that returns the date on which the Harvest Ready value is first equal to the text string "Ready".

22. In cell B12, calculate the number of days between planting and harvesting by subtracting the planting date (cell B9) from the harvest date (cell B11).

23. Save and close the workbook.

Case Problem 1

Data File needed for this Case Problem: Gorecki.xlsx

Gorecki Construction   Stefan Gorecki is the owner of Gorecki Construction, a small construction firm in Chester, Pennsylvania. He wants to use Excel to track his company's monthly income and expenses and then use that information to create a monthly budget. Stefan has already entered the raw data values but has asked to you to complete the workbook by adding the formulas and functions to perform the calculations. Complete the following:

1. Open the **Gorecki** workbook located in the Excel3 > Case1 folder, and then save the workbook as **Gorecki Budget** in the location specified by your instructor.

2. In the Documentation worksheet, enter your name in cell B3 and the date in cell B4.

3. The budget values are entered based on the end-of-month values. In the Monthly Budget worksheet, enter the date **31-Jan-18** in cell E4 and **28-Feb-18** in cell F4. Use AutoFill to fill in the remaining end-of-month date in the range G4:P4.

4. Calculate the company's total monthly income by selecting the range E6:P7 and using the Quick Analysis tool to insert the SUM function automatically into the range E8:P8.

5. Calculate the company's total cost of goods sold by selecting values in range E10:P11 and using the Quick Analysis tool to insert the SUM function automatically into the range E12:P12.

6. In the range E14:P14, calculate the company's monthly gross profit, which is equal to the difference between the monthly income and the monthly cost of goods sold.

7. Select the expenses entered in the range E17:P26, and use the Quick Analysis tool to insert the sum of the monthly expenses into the range E27:P27.

8. In the range E29:P29, calculate the company's net income equal to the difference between its gross profit and its total expenses.

9. Select the values in the range E29:P29, and then use the Quick Analysis tool to insert a running total of the company's net income into the range E30:P30.

10. Calculate the year-end totals for all financial categories by selecting the range E6:P29 and using the Quick Analysis tool to insert the sum of each row into the range Q6:Q29. Delete the content of any cells that do not contain financial figures.

11. Stefan wants the monthly averages of each financial category to be displayed in range B6:B29. Select cell B6, and then enter a formula that contains a nested function that first calculates the average of the values in the range E6:P6 and then uses the ROUND function to round that average to the nearest 10 dollars. (*Hint*: Use –1 for the value of the num_digits argument.) Use AutoFill to extend formula over the range B6:B29, deleting any cells corresponding to empty values.

12. Save and close the workbook.

Case Problem 2

Data File needed for this Case Problem: Capshaw.xlsx

Capshaw Family Dentistry   Carol Lemke is a new receptionist at Capshaw Dentistry in East Point, Georgia. She wants to get a rough estimate of what her take-home pay would be after deductions for federal and local taxes. She asks you to set up an Excel worksheet to perform the wage calculations for a sample two-week period. Carol already entered the work schedule and several tables containing the federal and state tax rates but needs you to insert the formulas. (*Note:* The tax rate tables and formulas used in this example are a simplified version of the tax code and should not be used to calculate actual taxes.) Complete the following:

1. Open the **Capshaw** workbook located in the Excel3 > Case2 folder, and then save the workbook as **Capshaw Wages** in the location specified by your instructor.

2. In the Documentation worksheet, enter your name in cell B3 and the date in cell B4.

3. In the Work Schedule worksheet, enter the following information in the range B5:B9: Name **Carol Lemke**; Hourly Rate **$16.25**; Federal Marital Status **Single**; State Marital Status **Single**; and Withholding Allowances **1**

4. In cell D6, enter the date **4/10/2017**. Use AutoFill to fill in the next day weekdays in the range D6:D15. (*Hint*: Click the AutoFill options button after dragging the fill handle, and then select the Fill Weekdays option button.)

5. In cell G6, calculate the total hours worked on the first day, which is equal to the difference between cell F6 and cell E6 multiplied by 24.

6. Carol will get overtime wages when she works more than eight hours in a day. Calculate the non-overtime hours in cell H6 by using the MIN function to return the minimum of the value in cell G6 and the value 8.

7. In cell I6, calculate the amount of overtime hours by using the IF function to test whether cell G6 is greater than 8. If it is, return the value cell G6 minus 8; otherwise, return the value 0.

8. In cell J6, calculate the salary due on the first day. The salary due is equal to the Straight Time worked multiplied by the hourly rate in cell B6 plus the Overtime multiplied by the hourly rate times 1.5 (Carol will receive time-and-a-half for each overtime hour.) Use an absolute reference to cell B6.

9. Select the range G6:J6, and then use AutoFill to copy the formulas into the range G7:J15 to calculate the salary for each of the ten days in the table.

10. In cell B11, calculate the total straight time hours worked by summing the values in column H. In cell B12, calculate the total overtime hours by summing the values in column I. In cell B13, calculate the total hours worked by summing the value in column G. In cell B14, calculate the total payments by summing the values in column J.

11. In cell B17, calculate the amount of federal tax by multiplying the Total Pay value in cell B14 by the appropriate federal tax rate for an employee with the marital status in cell B7 and withholding allowances in cell B9. (*Hint*: Use the VLOOKUP function with an exact match lookup for the lookup table in the range L6:W8. For the Col_index_num argument, use the value of cell B9 plus 2.)

12. In cell B18, calculate the Social Security tax equal to the value of cell B14 multiplied by the tax rate in cell M16.

13. In cell B19, calculate the Medicare tax equal to the value of cell B14 multiplied by the tax rate in cell M17.

14. In cell B20, calculate the amount of Georgia state tax by multiplying the value of cell B14 by the appropriate state tax rate in the range L12:W14 lookup table using the state marital status in cell B8 and the withholding allowance in cell B9. (*Hint*: Use the same type of VLOOKUP function as you did in Step 10 to retrieve the correct state tax rate.)

15. In cell B22, calculate the total deduction from pay by summing the values in the range B17:B20. In cell B23, calculate the withholding rate by dividing cell B22 by the total pay in cell B14.

16. In cell B24, calculate the take-home pay from subtracting the total withholding in cell B22 from cell B14.

17. Carol wants her take-home pay for the two weeks that she works in the sample schedule to be $1000. Use Goal Seek to find the hourly rate in cell B6 that will result in a take-home pay value of $1000.

18. Save and close the workbook.

Case Problem 3

Data File needed for this Case Problem: Biology.xlsx

Biology 221   Daivi Emani teaches biology and life sciences at Milford College in White Plains, New York. She wants to use Excel to track the test scores and calculate final averages for the students in her Biology 221 class. She has already entered the homework, quiz, and final exam scores for 66 students. The overall score is based on weighted average of the individual scores with homework accounting for 10 percent of the final grade, each of three quizzes accounting for 20 percent, and the final exam accounting for 30 percent. To calculate a weighted average you can use the SUMPRODUCT function

    SUMPRODUCT(*array1*,*array2*)

where *array1* is the range containing the weights assigned to each score and *array2* is the range containing the scores themselves.

  Daivi also wants you to calculate each student's rank in the class based on the student's weighted average. Ranks are calculated using the RANK function

    RANK(*number*,*ref*[,*order*=0])

where *number* is the value to be ranked, *ref* is a reference to the range containing the values against which the ranking is done, and *order* is an optional argument that specifies whether to rank in descending order or ascending order. The default order value is 0 to rank the values in descending order.

  Finally, you will create formulas that will look up information on a particular student based on that student's ID so that Daivi doesn't have to scroll through the complete class roster to find a particular student. Complete the following:

1. Open the **Biology** workbook located in the Excel3 > Case3 folder, and then save the workbook as **Biology Grades** in the location specified by your instructor.

2. In the Documentation worksheet, enter your name in cell B3 and the date in cell B4.

3. In the Biology Grades worksheet, in cell B5, calculate the number of students in the class by using the COUNTA function to count up the student IDs in the H column and subtracting 1 from that value (so as to not include cell H2 in the count).

4. In the range B8:F8, enter the weight values **10%**, **20%**, **20%**, **20%**, and **30%**.

5. In the range B9:F9, calculate the average of the numbers in columns K, L, M, N, and O.

6. In the range B10:F10, calculate the minimum values in the corresponding student score columns.

CHALLENGE

7. In the range B11:F11, use the MEDIAN function to calculate the midpoint of each of the student scores.

8. In the range B12:F12, calculate the maximum values for each of the student scores.

⊕ **Explore** 9. In cell P3, use the SUMPRODUCT function to calculate the weighted average of the scores for the first student in the list. Use an absolute reference to the range B8:F8 for the *array1* argument, and use the relative reference to the student scores in the range K3:O3 for the *array2* argument.

⊕ **Explore** 10. In cell Q3, use the RANK function to calculate the first student's rank in class. Use cell P3 for the *number* argument and column P for the *ref* argument. You do not to specify a value for the *order* argument.

11. Calculate the weighted average and ranks for all of the students by using AutoFill to copy the formulas in the range P3:Q3 to the range P3:Q68.

12. In cell B15, enter the student ID **602-1-99** for Lawrence Fujita.

13. In cell B16, use the VLOOKUP function with the student ID from cell B15 to look up the first name of the student matching that ID. Use the range H:Q as the reference to the lookup table, and retrieve the third column from the table.

14. In the range B17:B24, use lookup functions to retrieve the other data for the student ID entered in cell B15.

15. Test the VLOOKUP function by adding other student IDs in cell B15 to confirm that you can retrieve the record for any student in class based on his or her student ID.

16. Manuel Harmon was not able to take the final exam because of a family crisis. Daivi is scheduling a makeup exam for him. A weighted average of 92.0 will give Manuel an A for the course. Use Goal Seek to determine what grade he would need on the final to get an A for the course.

17. Save and close the workbook.

Case Problem 4

CHALLENGE

Data File needed for this Case Problem: Cairn.xlsx

Cairn Camping Supplies   Diane Cho is the owner of Cairn Camping Supplies, a small camping store she runs out of her home in Fort Smith, Arkansas. To help her manage her inventory and orders, she wants to develop an Excel worksheet for recording orders. The worksheet needs to calculate the cost of each order, including the cost of shipping and sales tax. Shipping costs vary based on whether the customer wants to use standard, three-day, two-day, or overnight shipping. Diane will also offer free shipping for orders that are more than $250. The shipping form worksheet will use lookup functions so that Diane can enter each product's ID code and have the name and price of the product automatically entered into the form. To keep the worksheet clean without distracting error values when no input values have been entered, you'll use IF functions to test whether the user has entered a required value first before applying a formula using that value. Complete the following:

1. Open the **Cairn** workbook located in the Excel3 > Case4 folder, and then save the workbook as **Cairn Camping** in the location specified by your instructor.

2. In the Documentation worksheet, enter your name in cell B3 and the date in cell B4.

3. In the Order Form worksheet, enter the following sample order data: Customer **Dixie Kaufmann**; Order Number **381**; Order Date **4/5/2018**; Street **414 Topeak Lane**; City **Fort Smith**; State **AK**; ZIP **72914**; Phone **(479) 555-2081**; and Delivery Type **3 Day**.

⊕ **Explore** 4. In cell B17, calculate the number of delivery days for the order. Insert an IF function that first tests whether the value in cell B16 is equal to an empty text string (""). If it is, return an empty text string; otherwise, apply a lookup function to retrieve the lookup value from the table in the range F5:H8 using the value of cell B16 as the lookup value.

⊕ **Explore** 5. In cell B18, estimate the date of weekday delivery by inserting an IF function that tests whether cell B16 is equal to an empty text string. If it is, return an empty text string, otherwise apply the WORKDAY function using the values in cell B6 as the starting date and cell B17 as the number of days.

6. In cell D13, enter **p4981** as the initial item ordered by the customer. In cell G13, enter **2** as the number of items ordered.

7. In cell E13, enter an IF function that tests whether the value in cell D13 is equal to an empty text string. If true, return an empty text string. If false, apply the VLOOKUP function to return the name of the product ID entered into cell D13.

8. In cell F13, enter another IF function that tests whether the value in cell D13 is equal to an empty text string. If true, return an empty text string. If false, return the price of the product ID entered in cell D13.

9. In cell H13, enter another IF function to test whether the value in cell D13 is equal to an empty text string. If true, return an empty text string; otherwise, calculate the value of the price of the item multiplied by the number of items ordered.

10. Copy the formula in the range E13:F13 to the range E13:F20. Use AutoFill to copy the formula from cell H13 into the range H13:H20.

11. In cell H22, calculate the sum of the values in the range H13:H20.

12. In cell H23, calculate the sales tax equal to the total cost of the items ordered multiplied by the sales tax rate in cell G10.

13. In cell H24, calculate the shipping cost of the order by inserting an IF function that tests whether the value of cell B16 is an empty text string. If it is, return the value 0; otherwise, use a lookup function to return the shipping cost for the indicated shipping method.

14. In cell H25, insert an IF function that tests whether the value of cell H22 is greater than 250 (the minimum order needed to qualify for free shipping). If it is, return a value of cell H24; otherwise, return a value of 0.

15. In cell H27, calculate the total cost of the order by summing the values in the range H22:H24 and subtracting the value of cell H25.

16. Complete the customer order by adding the following items: Item **t7829** and Qty **1**; Item **led7331** and Qty **3**; and Item **sb8502** and Qty **5**.

17. Confirm that your worksheet correctly calculates the total cost, and then save your workbook.

18. Save the workbook as **Cairn Order Form** in the location specified by your instructor.

19. Create a blank order form sheet by deleting the input values in the ranges B4:B6, B9:B13, B16, D13:D16, G13:G16. Do *not* delete any formulas in the worksheet. Confirm that the worksheet does not show any error values when the input data is removed.

20. Save and close the workbook.

OBJECTIVES

Session 1.1
- Learn basic database concepts and terms
- Start and exit Access
- Explore the Microsoft Access window and Backstage view
- Create a blank database
- Create and save a table in Datasheet view
- Enter field names and records in a table datasheet
- Open a table using the Navigation Pane

Session 1.2
- Open an Access database
- Copy and paste records from another Access database
- Navigate a table datasheet
- Create and navigate a simple query
- Create and navigate a simple form
- Create, preview, navigate, and print a simple report
- Use Help in Access
- Learn how to compact, back up, and restore a database

Creating a Database

Tracking Animal, Visit, and Billing Data

ACCESS

Case | *Riverview Veterinary Care Center*

Riverview Veterinary Care Center, a veterinary care center in Cody, Wyoming, provides care for pets and livestock in the greater Cody area. In addition to caring for household pets, such as dogs and cats, the center specializes in serving the needs of livestock on ranches in the surrounding area. Kimberly Johnson, the office manager for Riverview Veterinary Care Center, oversees a small staff and is responsible for maintaining the medical records for all of the animals the care center serves.

In order to best manage the center, Kimberly and her staff rely on electronic medical records for information on the animals and their owners, billing, inventory control, purchasing, and accounts payable. Several months ago, the center upgraded to **Microsoft Access 2016** (or simply **Access**), a computer program used to enter, maintain, and retrieve related data in a format known as a database. Kimberly and her staff want to use Access to store information about the animals, their owners, billing, vendors, and products. She asks for your help in creating the necessary Access database.

STARTING DATA FILES

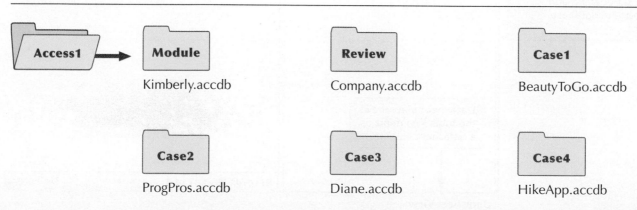

Access1 → Module
Kimberly.accdb

Review
Company.accdb

Case1
BeautyToGo.accdb

Case2
ProgPros.accdb

Case3
Diane.accdb

Case4
HikeApp.accdb

Session 1.1 Visual Overview:

The **Quick Access Toolbar** provides one-click access to commonly used commands, such as Save.

The **Fields tab** provides options for adding, removing, and formatting the fields in a table.

The **Shutter Bar Open/Close Button** allows you to close and open the Navigation Pane; you might want to close the pane so that you have more room on the screen to view the object's contents.

Access assigns the default name "Table1" to the first new table you create. When you save the table, you can give it a more meaningful name.

By default, Access creates the **ID field** as the primary key field for all new tables.

The **Click to Add column** provides another way for you to add new fields to a table.

The **Add & Delete group** contains options for adding different types of fields, including Short Text and Number, to a table.

The **Navigation Pane** lists all the objects (tables, reports, and so on) in the database, and it is the main control center for opening and working with database objects.

Datasheet view shows the table's contents as a datasheet.

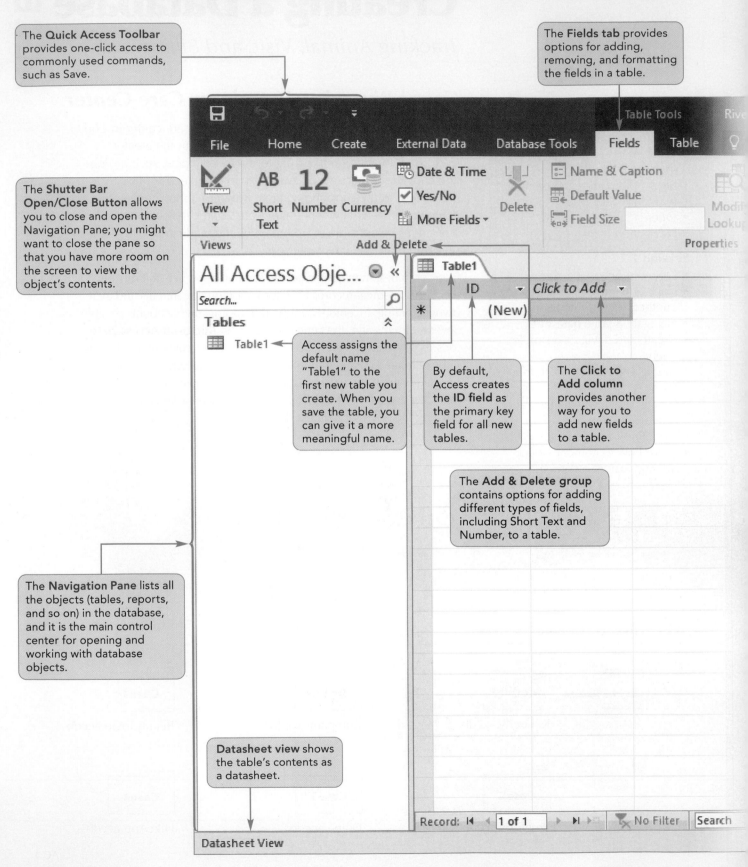

The Access Window

The **Access window** is the program window that appears when you create a new database or open an existing database.

You use the window buttons to minimize, maximize, and close the Access window.

If you are signed in to your Office account, your name appears here. If you are not signed in, the **Sign in link** will appear here, and you can click it to sign into your Office account.

The **ribbon** provides the main Access commands organized by task into tabs and groups.

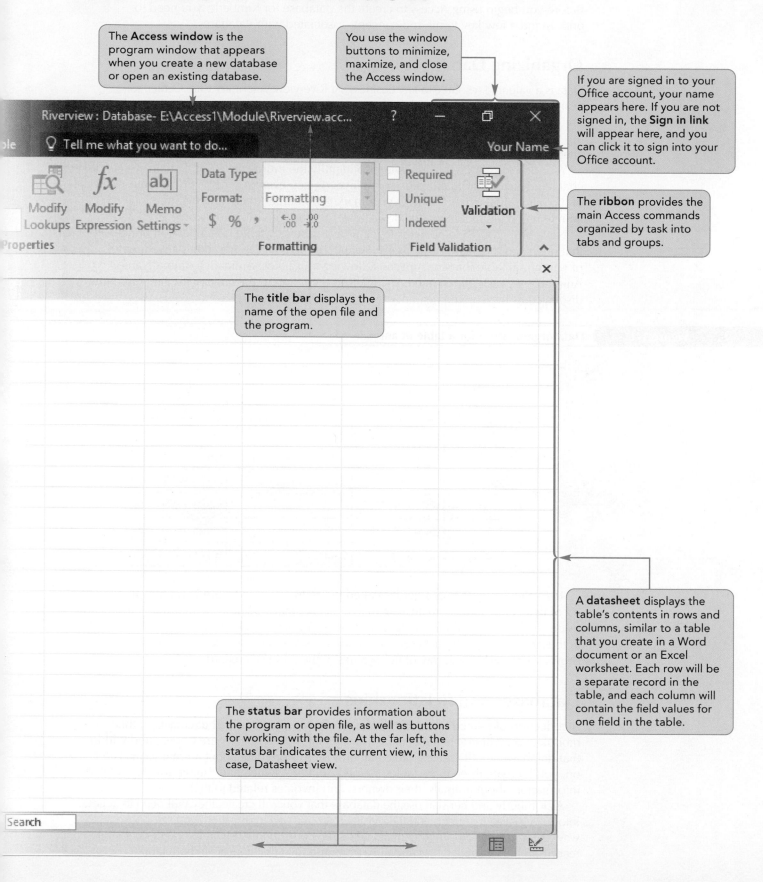

The **title bar** displays the name of the open file and the program.

A **datasheet** displays the table's contents in rows and columns, similar to a table that you create in a Word document or an Excel worksheet. Each row will be a separate record in the table, and each column will contain the field values for one field in the table.

The **status bar** provides information about the program or open file, as well as buttons for working with the file. At the far left, the status bar indicates the current view, in this case, Datasheet view.

Introduction to Database Concepts

Before you begin using Access to create the database for Kimberly, you need to understand a few key terms and concepts associated with databases.

Organizing Data

Data is a valuable resource to any business. At Riverview Veterinary Care Center, for example, important data includes the names of the animals, owners' contact information, visit dates, and billing information. Organizing, storing, maintaining, retrieving, and sorting this type of data are critical activities that enable a business to find and use information effectively. Before storing data on a computer, however, you must organize the data.

Your first step in organizing data is to identify the individual fields. A **field** is a single characteristic or attribute of a person, place, object, event, or idea. For example, some of the many fields that Riverview Veterinary Care Center tracks are the animal ID, animal name, animal type, breed, visit date, reason for visit, and invoice amount.

Next, you group related fields together into tables. A **table** is a collection of fields that describes a person, place, object, event, or idea. Figure 1-1 shows an example of an Animal table that contains the following four fields: AnimalID, AnimalName, AnimalType, and AnimalBreed. Each field is a column in the table, with the field name displayed as the column heading.

Figure 1-1	Data organization for a table of animals

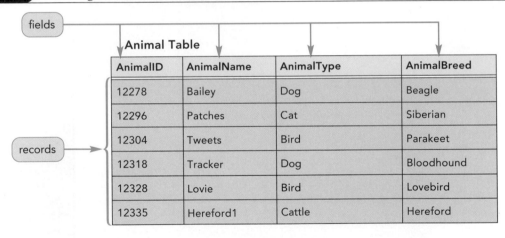

The specific content of a field is called the **field value**. In Figure 1-1, the first set of field values for AnimalID, AnimalName, AnimalType, and AnimalBreed are, respectively: 12278; Bailey; Dog; and Beagle. This set of field values is called a **record**. In the Animal table, the data for each animal is stored as a separate record. Figure 1-1 shows six records; each row of field values in the table is a record.

Databases and Relationships

A collection of related tables is called a **database**, or a **relational database**. In this module, you will create the database for Riverview Veterinary Care Center, and within that database, you'll create a table named Visit to store data about animal visits. Later on, you'll create three more tables, named Animal, Owner, and Billing, to store related information about animals, their owners, and invoices related to their care.

As Kimberly and her staff use the database that you will create, they will need to access information about animals and their visits. To obtain this information, you must have a way to connect records in the Animal table to records in the Visit table. You connect the records in the separate tables through a **common field** that appears in both tables.

In the sample database shown in Figure 1-2, each record in the Animal table has a field named AnimalID, which is also a field in the Visit table. For example, the beagle named Bailey is the first animal in the Animal table and has an AnimalID field value of 12278. This same AnimalID field value, 12278, appears in two records in the Visit table. Therefore, the beagle named Bailey is the animal that was seen at these two visits.

| Figure 1-2 | Database relationship between tables for animals and visits |

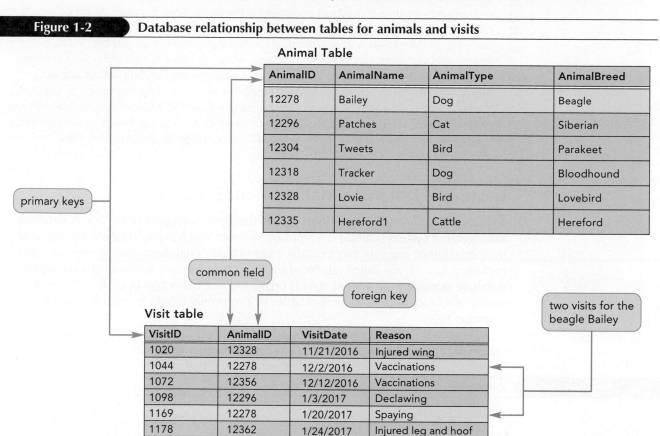

Animal Table

AnimalID	AnimalName	AnimalType	AnimalBreed
12278	Bailey	Dog	Beagle
12296	Patches	Cat	Siberian
12304	Tweets	Bird	Parakeet
12318	Tracker	Dog	Bloodhound
12328	Lovie	Bird	Lovebird
12335	Hereford1	Cattle	Hereford

primary keys

common field

foreign key

two visits for the beagle Bailey

Visit table

VisitID	AnimalID	VisitDate	Reason
1020	12328	11/21/2016	Injured wing
1044	12278	12/2/2016	Vaccinations
1072	12356	12/12/2016	Vaccinations
1098	12296	1/3/2017	Declawing
1169	12278	1/20/2017	Spaying
1178	12362	1/24/2017	Injured leg and hoof

Each AnimalID value in the Animal table must be unique so that you can distinguish one animal from another. These unique AnimalID values also identify each animal's specific visits in the Visit table. The AnimalID field is referred to as the primary key of the Animal table. A **primary key** is a field, or a collection of fields, whose values uniquely identify each record in a table. No two records can contain the same value for the primary key field. In the Visit table, the VisitID field is the primary key because Riverview Veterinary Care Center assigns each visit a unique identification number.

When you include the primary key from one table as a field in a second table to form a relationship between the two tables, it is called a **foreign key** in the second table, as shown in Figure 1-2. For example, AnimalID is the primary key in the Animal table and a foreign key in the Visit table. The AnimalID field must have the same characteristics in both tables. Although the primary key AnimalID contains unique values in the Animal table, the same field as a foreign key in the Visit table does not necessarily contain unique values. The AnimalID value 12278, for example, appears two times in the Visit table because the beagle named Bailey made two visits to the center. Each foreign key value, however, must match one of the field values for the primary key in the other table. In the example shown in Figure 1-2, each AnimalID value in the Visit table must match an AnimalID value in the Animal table. The two tables are related, enabling users to connect the facts about animals with the facts about their visits to the center.

INSIGHT

Storing Data in Separate Tables

When you create a database, you must create separate tables that contain only fields that are directly related to each other. For example, in the Riverview database, the animal and visit data should not be stored in the same table because doing so would make the data difficult to update and prone to errors. Consider the beagle Bailey and her visits to the center, and assume that she has many more than just two visits. If all the animal and visit data was stored in the same table, so that each record (row) contained all the information about each visit and the animal, the animal data would appear multiple times in the table. This causes problems when the data changes. For example, if the phone number of Bailey's owner changed, you would have to update the multiple occurrences of the owner's phone number throughout the table. Not only would this be time-consuming, it would increase the likelihood of errors or inconsistent data.

Relational Database Management Systems

To manage its databases, a company uses a database management system. A **database management system (DBMS)** is a software program that lets you create databases and then manipulate the data they contain. Most of today's database management systems, including Access, are called relational database management systems. In a **relational database management system**, data is organized as a collection of tables. As stated earlier, a relationship between two tables in a relational DBMS is formed through a common field.

A relational DBMS controls the storage of databases and facilitates the creation, manipulation, and reporting of data, as illustrated in Figure 1-3.

Figure 1-3   **Relational database management system**

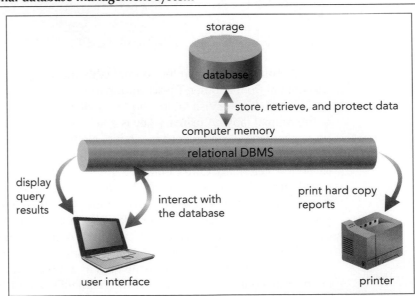

Specifically, a relational DBMS provides the following functions:

- It allows you to create database structures containing fields, tables, and table relationships.
- It lets you easily add new records, change field values in existing records, and delete records.
- It contains a built-in query language, which lets you obtain immediate answers to the questions (or queries) you ask about your data.
- It contains a built-in report generator, which lets you produce professional-looking, formatted reports from your data.
- It protects databases through security, control, and recovery facilities.

An organization such as Riverview Veterinary Care Center benefits from a relational DBMS because it allows users working in different groups to share the same data. More than one user can enter data into a database, and more than one user can retrieve and analyze data that other users have entered. For example, the database for Riverview Veterinary Care Center will contain only one copy of the Visit table, and all employees will use it to access visit information.

Finally, unlike other software programs, such as spreadsheet programs, a DBMS can handle massive amounts of data and can be used to create relationships among multiple tables. Each Access database, for example, can be up to two gigabytes in size, can contain up to 32,768 objects (tables, reports, and so on), and can have up to 255 people using the database at the same time. For instructional purposes, the databases you will create and work with throughout this text contain a relatively small number of records compared to databases you would encounter outside the classroom, which would likely contain tables with very large numbers of records.

Starting Access and Creating a Database

Now that you've learned some database terms and concepts, you're ready to start Access and create the Riverview database for Kimberly.

To start Access:

1. On the Windows taskbar, click the **Start** button ⊞. The Start menu opens.

2. Click **All apps** on the Start menu, and then click **Access 2016**. Access starts and displays the Recent screen in Backstage view. See Figure 1-4.

| Figure 1-4 | Recent screen in Backstage view |

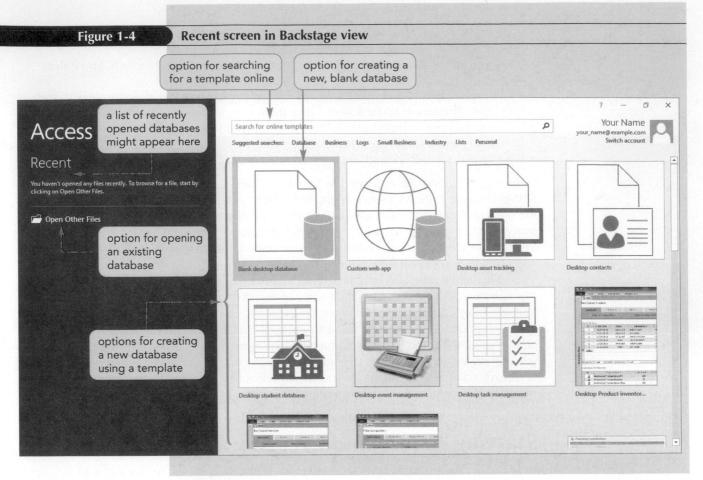

When you start Access, the first screen that appears is Backstage view, which is the starting place for your work in Access. **Backstage view** contains commands that allow you to manage Access files and options. The Recent screen in Backstage view provides options for you to create a new database or open an existing database. To create a new database that does not contain any data or objects, you use the Blank desktop database option. If the database you need to create contains objects that match those found in common databases, such as databases that store data about contacts or tasks, you can use one of the templates provided with Access. A **template** is a predesigned database that includes professionally designed tables, reports, and other database objects that can make it quick and easy for you to create a database. You can also search for a template online using the Search for online templates box.

In this case, the templates provided do not match Kimberly's needs for the center's database, so you need to create a new, blank database from scratch.

To create the new Riverview database:

▶ 1. Make sure you have the Access starting Data Files on your computer.

   Trouble? If you don't have the starting Data Files, you need to get them before you can proceed. Your instructor will either give you the Data Files or ask you to obtain them from a specified location (such as a network drive). If you have any questions about the Data Files, see your instructor or technical support person for assistance.

▶ 2. On the Recent screen, click **Blank desktop database** (see Figure 1-4). The Blank desktop database screen opens.

Be sure to type Riverview or you'll create a database named Database1.

3. In the File Name box, type **Riverview** to replace the selected database name provided by Access, Database1. Next you need to specify the location for the file.

4. Click the **Browse** button ▢ to the right of the File Name box. The File New Database dialog box opens.

5. Navigate to the drive and folder where you are storing your files, as specified by your instructor.

6. Make sure the Save as type box displays "Microsoft Access 2007–2016 Databases."

Trouble? If your computer is set up to show filename extensions, you will see the Access filename extension ".accdb" in the File name box.

7. Click the **OK** button. You return to the Blank desktop database screen, and the File Name box now shows the name Riverview.accdb. The filename extension ".accdb" identifies the file as an Access 2007–2016 database.

8. Click the **Create** button. Access creates the new database, saves it to the specified location, and then opens an empty table named Table1.

Trouble? If you see only ribbon tab names and no buttons, click the Home tab to expand the ribbon, and then in the bottom-right corner of the ribbon, click the Pin the ribbon button ▢.

Refer back to the Session 1.1 Visual Overview and spend some time becoming familiar with the components of the Access window.

INSIGHT

Understanding the Database File Type

Access 2016 uses the .accdb file extension, which is the same file extension used for databases created with Microsoft Access 2007, 2010, and 2013. To ensure compatibility between these earlier versions and the Access 2016 software, new databases created using Access 2016 have the same file extension and file format as Access 2007, Access 2010, and Access 2013 databases. This is why the File New Database dialog box provides the Microsoft Access 2007–2016 Databases option in the Save as type box. In addition, the notation "(Access 2007–2016 file format)" appears in the title bar next to the name of an open database in Access 2016, confirming that database files with the .accdb extension can be used in Access 2007, Access 2010, Access 2013, and Access 2016.

Working in Touch Mode

If you are working on a touch device, such as a tablet, you can switch to Touch Mode in Access to make it easier for you to tap buttons on the ribbon and perform other touch actions. Your screens will not match those shown in the book exactly, but this will not cause any problems.

Note: The following steps assume that you are using a mouse. If you are instead using a touch device, please read these steps but don't complete them, so that you remain working in Touch Mode.

To switch to Touch Mode:

1. On the Quick Access Toolbar, click the **Customize Quick Access Toolbar** button . A menu opens listing buttons you can add to the Quick Access Toolbar as well as other options for customizing the toolbar.

   Trouble? If the Touch/Mouse Mode command on the menu has a checkmark next to it, press the Esc key to close the menu, and then skip to Step 3.

2. Click **Touch/Mouse Mode**. The Quick Access Toolbar now contains the Touch/Mouse Mode button , which you can use to switch between Mouse Mode, the default display, and Touch Mode.

3. On the Quick Access Toolbar, click the **Touch/Mouse Mode** button . A menu opens with two commands: Mouse, which shows the ribbon in the standard display and is optimized for use with the mouse; and Touch, which provides more space between the buttons and commands on the ribbon and is optimized for use with touch devices. The icon next to Mouse is shaded red to indicate that it is selected.

   Trouble? If the icon next to Touch is shaded red, press the Esc key to close the menu and skip to Step 5.

4. Click **Touch**. The display switches to Touch Mode with more space between the commands and buttons on the ribbon. See Figure 1-5.

Figure 1-5   **Ribbon displayed in Touch Mode**

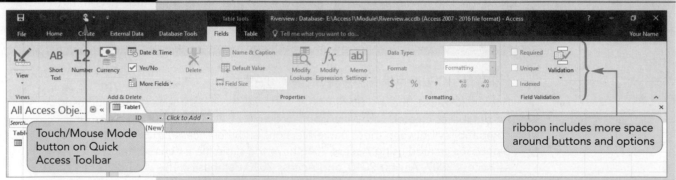

The figures in this text show the standard Mouse Mode display, and the instructions assume you are using a mouse to click and select options, so you'll switch back to Mouse Mode.

   Trouble? If you are using a touch device and want to remain in Touch Mode, skip Steps 5 and 6.

5. On the Quick Access Toolbar, click the **Touch/Mouse Mode** button , and then click **Mouse**. The ribbon returns to the standard display, as shown in the Session 1.1 Visual Overview.

6. On the Quick Access Toolbar, click the **Customize Quick Access Toolbar** button , and then click **Touch/Mouse Mode** to deselect it. The Touch/Mouse Mode button is removed from the Quick Access Toolbar.

Creating a Table in Datasheet View

Tables contain all the data in a database and are the fundamental objects for your work in Access. There are different ways to create a table in Access, including entering the fields and records for the table directly in Datasheet view.

REFERENCE

Creating a Table in Datasheet View

- On the ribbon, click the Create tab.
- In the Tables group, click the Table button.
- Rename the default ID primary key field and change its data type, if necessary; or accept the default ID field with the AutoNumber data type.
- In the Add & Delete group on the Fields tab, click the button for the type of field you want to add to the table (for example, click the Short Text button), and then type the field name; or, in the table datasheet, click the Click to Add column heading, click the type of field you want to add from the list that opens, and then press the Tab or Enter key to move to the next column in the datasheet. Repeat this step to add all the necessary fields to the table.
- In the first row below the field names, enter the value for each field in the first record, pressing the Tab or Enter key to move from one field to the next.
- After entering the value for the last field in the first record, press the Tab or Enter key to move to the next row, and then enter the values for the next record. Continue this process until you have entered all the records for the table.
- On the Quick Access Toolbar, click the Save button, enter a name for the table, and then click the OK button.

For Riverview Veterinary Care Center, Kimberly needs to track information about each animal visit at the center. She asks you to create the Visit table according to the plan shown in Figure 1-6.

Figure 1-6   **Plan for the Visit table**

Field	Purpose
VisitID	Unique number assigned to each visit; will serve as the table's primary key
AnimalID	Unique number assigned to each animal; common field that will be a foreign key to connect to the Animal table
VisitDate	Date on which the animal visited the center or was seen offsite
Reason	Reason/diagnosis for the animal visit
OffSite	Whether the animal visit was offsite at a home or ranch

As shown in Kimberly's plan, she wants to store data about visits in five fields, including fields to contain the date of each visit, the reason for the visit, and if the visit was offsite. These are the most important aspects of a visit and, therefore, must be tracked. Also, notice that the VisitID field will be the primary key for the table; each visit at Riverview Veterinary Care Center has a unique number assigned to it, so this field is the logical choice for the primary key. Finally, the AnimalID field is needed in the Visit table as a foreign key to connect the information about visits to animals. The data about animals, as well as the data about their owners, and the bills for the animals' care, will be stored in separate tables, which you will create later.

Notice the name of each field in Figure 1-6. You need to name each field, table, and object in an Access database.

Decision Making: Naming Fields in Access Tables

One of the most important tasks in creating a table is deciding what names to specify for the table's fields. Keep the following guidelines in mind when you assign field names:

- A field name can consist of up to 64 characters, including letters, numbers, spaces, and special characters, except for the period (.), exclamation mark (!), grave accent ('), and square brackets ([ ]).
- A field name cannot begin with a space.
- Capitalize the first letter of each word in a field name that combines multiple words, for example VisitDate.
- Use concise field names that are easy to remember and reference and that won't take up a lot of space in the table datasheet.
- Use standard abbreviations, such as Num for Number, Amt for Amount, and Qty for Quantity, and use them consistently throughout the database. For example, if you use Num for Number in one field name, do not use the number sign (#) for Number in another.
- Give fields descriptive names so that you can easily identify them when you view or edit records.
- Although Access supports the use of spaces in field names (and in other object names), experienced database developers avoid using spaces because they can cause errors when the objects are involved in programming tasks.

By spending time obtaining and analyzing information about the fields in a table, and understanding the rules for naming fields, you can create a well-designed table that will be easy for others to use.

Renaming the Default Primary Key Field

As noted earlier, Access provides the ID field as the default primary key for a new table you create in Datasheet view. Recall that a primary key is a field, or a collection of fields, whose values uniquely identify each record in a table. However, according to Kimberly's plan, the VisitID field should be the primary key for the Visit table. You'll begin by renaming the default ID field to create the VisitID field.

To rename the ID field to the VisitID field:

1. Right-click the **ID** column heading to open the shortcut menu, and then click **Rename Field**. The column heading ID is selected, so that whatever text you type next will replace it.

2. Type **VisitID** and then click the row below the heading. The column heading changes to VisitID, and the insertion point moves to the row below the heading. The **insertion point** is a flashing cursor that shows where text you type will be inserted. In this case, it is hidden within the selected field value (New). See Figure 1-7.

   Trouble? If you make a mistake while typing the field name, use the Backspace key to delete characters to the left of the insertion point or the Delete key to delete characters to the right of the insertion point. Then type the correct text. To correct a field name by replacing it entirely, press the Esc key, and then type the correct text.

| Figure 1-7 | ID field renamed to VisitID |

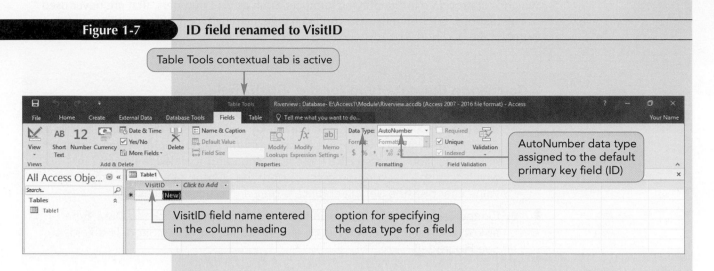

Notice that the Table Tools tab is active on the ribbon. This is an example of a **contextual tab**, which is a tab that appears and provides options for working with a specific object that is selected—in this case, the table you are creating. As you work with other objects in the database, other contextual tabs will appear with commands and options related to each selected object.

You have renamed the default primary key field, ID, to VisitID. However, the VisitID field still retains the characteristics of the ID field, including its data type. Your next task is to change the data type of this field.

Changing the Data Type of the Default Primary Key Field

Notice the Formatting group on the Table Tools Fields tab. One of the options available in this group is the Data Type option (see Figure 1-7). Each field in an Access table must be assigned a data type. The **data type** determines what field values you can enter for the field. In this case, the AutoNumber data type is displayed. Access assigns the AutoNumber data type to the default ID primary key field because the **AutoNumber** data type automatically inserts a unique number in this field for every record, beginning with the number 1 for the first record, the number 2 for the second record, and so on. Therefore, a field using the AutoNumber data type can serve as the primary key for any table you create.

Visit numbers at the Riverview Veterinary Care Center are specific, four-digit numbers, so the AutoNumber data type is not appropriate for the VisitID field, which is the primary key field in the table you are creating. A better choice is the **Short Text** data type, which allows field values containing letters, digits, and other characters, and which is appropriate for identifying numbers, such as visit numbers, that are never used in calculations. So, Kimberly asks you to change the data type for the VisitID field from AutoNumber to Short Text.

To change the data type for the VisitID field:

▸ **1.** Make sure that the VisitID column is selected. A column is selected when you click a field value, in which case the background color of the column heading changes to orange (the default color) and the insertion point appears in the field value. You can also click the column heading to select a column, in which case the background color of both the column heading and the field value changes (the default colors are gray and blue, respectively).

▸ **2.** On the Table Tools Fields tab, in the Formatting group, click the **Data Type arrow**, and then click **Short Text**. The VisitID field is now a Short Text field. See Figure 1-8.

Figure 1-8 **Short Text data type assigned to the VisitID field**

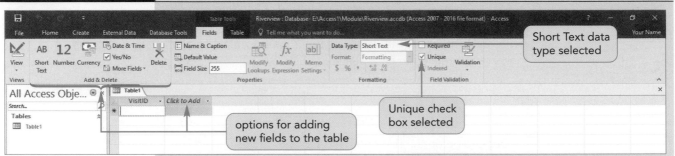

Note the Unique check box in the Field Validation group. This check box is selected because the VisitID field assumed the characteristics of the default primary key field, ID, including the fact that each value in the field must be unique. Because this check box is selected, no two records in the Visit table will be allowed to have the same value in the VisitID field.

With the VisitID field created and established as the primary key, you can now enter the rest of the fields in the Visit table.

Adding New Fields

When you create a table in Datasheet view, you can use the options in the Add & Delete group on the Table Tools Fields tab to add fields to your table. You can also use the Click to Add column in the table datasheet to add new fields. (See Figure 1-8.) You'll use both methods to add the four remaining fields to the Visit table. The next field you need to add is the AnimalID field. Similar to the VisitID field, the AnimalID field will contain numbers that will not be used in calculations, so it should be a Short Text field.

To add the rest of the fields to the Visit table:

▸ **1.** On the Table Tools Fields tab, in the Add & Delete group, click the **Short Text** button. A new field named "Field1" is added to the right of the VisitID field. See Figure 1-9.

| Figure 1-9 | New Short Text field added to the table |

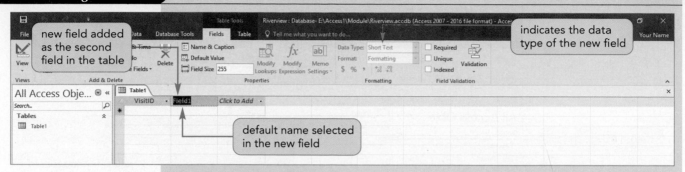

The text "Field1" is selected, so you can simply type the new field name to replace it.

2. Type **AnimalID**. The second field is added to the table. Next, you'll add the VisitDate field. Because this field will contain date values, you'll add a field with the **Date/Time** data type, which allows field values in a variety of date and time formats.

3. In the Add & Delete group, click the **Date & Time** button. Access adds a third field to the table, this time with the Date/Time data type.

4. Type **VisitDate** to replace the selected name "Field1." The fourth field in the Visit table is the Reason field, which will contain brief descriptions of the reason for the visit to the center. You'll add another Short Text field—this time using the Click to Add column.

5. Click the **Click to Add** column heading. Access displays a list of available data types from which you can choose the data type for the new field you're adding.

6. Click **Short Text** in the list. Access adds a fourth field to the table.

7. Type **Reason** to replace the highlighted name "Field1," and then press the **Enter** key. The Click to Add column becomes active and displays the list of field data types.

The fifth and final field in the Visit table is the OffSite field, which will indicate whether or not the visit was at an offsite venue, such as at a home or ranch (that is, not within the center). The **Yes/No** data type is suitable for this field because it is used to define fields that store values representing one of two options—true/false, yes/no, or on/off.

TIP

You can also type the first letter of a data type to select it and close the Click to Add list.

8. Click **Yes/No** in the list, and then type **OffSite** to replace the highlighted name "Field1."

Trouble? If you pressed the Tab or Enter key after typing the OffSite field name, press the Esc key to close the Click to Add list.

9. Click in the row below the VisitID column heading. All five fields are now entered for the Visit table. See Figure 1-10.

Figure 1-10 **Table with all fields entered**

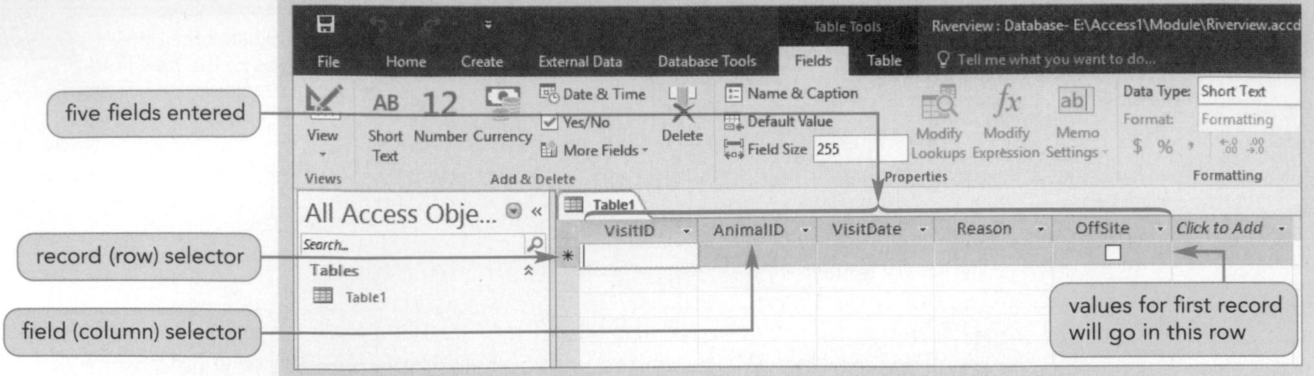

The table contains three Short Text fields (VisitID, AnimalID, and Reason), one Date/Time field (VisitDate), and one Yes/No field (OffSite). You'll learn more about field data types in the next module.

As noted earlier, Datasheet view shows a table's contents in rows (records) and columns (fields). Each column is headed by a field name inside a field selector, and each row has a record selector to its left (see Figure 1-10). Clicking a **field selector** or a **record selector** selects that entire column or row (respectively), which you then can manipulate. A field selector is also called a **column selector**, and a record selector is also called a **row selector**.

Entering Records

With the fields in place for the table, you can now enter the field values for each record. Kimberly requests that you enter eight records in the Visit table, as shown in Figure 1-11.

Figure 1-11 **Visit table records**

VisitID	AmimalID	VisitDate	Reason	OffSite
1072	12356	12/12/2016	Vaccinations	Yes
1169	12278	1/20/2017	Spaying	No
1184	12443	1/25/2017	Neutering	No
1016	12345	11/18/2016	Vaccinations	Yes
1196	12455	2/1/2017	Vaccinations	No
1098	12296	1/3/2017	Declawing	No
1178	12362	1/24/2017	Injured leg and hoof	Yes
1044	12278	12/2/2016	Vaccinations	No

To enter records in a table datasheet, you type the field values below the column headings for the fields. The first record you enter will go in the first row (see Figure 1-10).

Be sure to type the numbers "0" and "1" and not the letters "O" and "I" in the field value.

To enter the first record for the Visit table:

1. In the first row for the VisitID field, type **1072** (the VisitID field value for the first record), and then press the **Tab** key. Access adds the field value and moves the insertion point to the right, into the AnimalID column. See Figure 1-12.

Figure 1-12	First field value entered

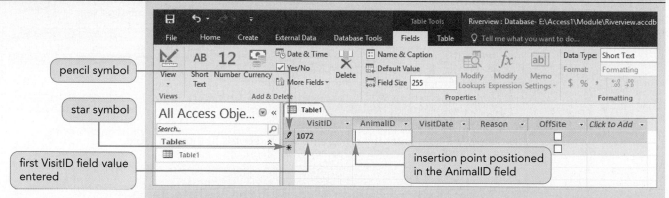

- pencil symbol
- star symbol
- first VisitID field value entered
- insertion point positioned in the AnimalID field

Trouble? If you make a mistake when typing a value, use the Backspace key to delete characters to the left of the insertion point or the Delete key to delete characters to the right of the insertion point. Then type the correct value. To correct a value by replacing it entirely, press the Esc key, and then type the correct value.

Notice the pencil symbol that appears in the row selector for the new record. The **pencil symbol** indicates that the record is being edited. Also notice the star symbol that appears in the row selector for the second row. The **star symbol** identifies the second row as the next row available for a new record.

2. Type **12356** (the AnimalID field value for the first record), and then press the **Tab** key. Access enters the field value and moves the insertion point to the VisitDate column.

3. Type **12/12/16** (the VisitDate field value for the first record), and then press the **Tab** key. Access displays the year as "2016" even though you entered only the final two digits of the year. This is because the VisitDate field has the Date/Time data type, which automatically formats dates with four-digit years.

4. Type **Vaccinations** (the Reason field value for the first record), and then press the **Tab** key to move to the OffSite column.

Recall that the OffSite field is a Yes/No field. Notice the check box displayed in the OffSite column. By default, the value for any Yes/No field is "No"; therefore, the check box is initially empty. For Yes/No fields with check boxes, you press the Tab key to leave the check box unchecked, or you press the spacebar to insert a checkmark in the check box. The record you are entering in the table is for an offsite visit, so you need to insert a checkmark in the check box to indicate "Yes."

TIP

You can also click a check box in a Yes/No field to insert or remove a checkmark.

5. Press the **spacebar** to insert a checkmark, and then press the **Tab** key. The first record is entered into the table, and the insertion point is positioned in the VisitID field for the second record. The pencil symbol is removed from the first row because the record in that row is no longer being edited. The table is now ready for you to enter the second record. See Figure 1-13.

Figure 1-13   Datasheet with first record entered

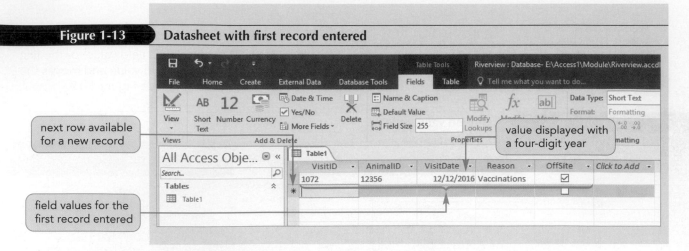

next row available
for a new record

value displayed with
a four-digit year

field values for the
first record entered

Now you can enter the remaining seven records in the Visit table.

To enter the remaining records in the Visit table:

TIP

You can also press the Enter key instead of the Tab key to move from one field to another and to the next row.

1. Referring to Figure 1-11, enter the values for records 2 through 8, pressing the **Tab** key to move from field to field and to the next row for a new record. Keep in mind that you do not have to type all four digits of the year in the VisitDate field values; you can enter only the final two digits, and Access will display all four. Also, for any OffSite field values of "No," be sure to press the Tab key to leave the check box empty.

   Trouble? If you enter a value in the wrong field by mistake, such as entering a Reason field value in the VisitDate field, a menu might open with options for addressing the problem. If this happens, click the "Enter new value" option in the menu. You'll return to the field with the incorrect value selected, which you can then replace by typing the correct value.

   Notice that not all of the Reason field values are fully displayed. To see more of the table datasheet and the full field values, you'll close the Navigation Pane and resize the Reason column.

2. At the top of the Navigation Pane, click the **Shutter Bar Open/Close Button** ⟪. The Navigation Pane closes, and only the complete table datasheet is displayed.

3. Place the pointer on the vertical line to the right of the Reason field name until the pointer changes to ↔, and then double-click the vertical line. All the Reason field values are now fully displayed. See Figure 1-14.

| Figure 1-14 | Datasheet with eight records entered |

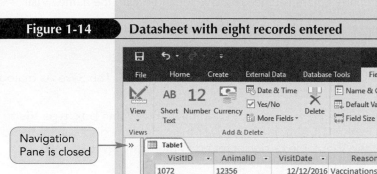

Navigation Pane is closed

field values are completely visible

When you resize a datasheet column by double-clicking the column dividing line, you are sizing the column to its **best fit**—that is, so the column is just wide enough to display the longest visible value in the column, including the field name.

Carefully compare your VisitID and AnimalID values with those in the figure, and correct any errors before continuing.

4. Compare your table to the one in Figure 1-14. If any of the field values in your table do not match those shown in the figure, you can correct a field value by clicking to position the insertion point in the value, and then using the Backspace key or Delete key to delete incorrect text. Then type the correct text and press the Enter key. To correct a value in the OffSite field, simply click the check box to add or remove the checkmark as appropriate. Also, be sure the spelling and capitalization of field names in your table match those shown in the figure exactly and that there are no spaces between words. To correct a field name, double-click it to select it, and then type the correct name; or use the Rename Field option on the shortcut menu to rename a field with the correct name.

Saving a Table

The records you enter are immediately stored in the database as soon as you enter them; however, the table's design—the field names and characteristics of the fields themselves, plus any layout changes to the datasheet—are not saved until you save the table. When you save a new table for the first time, you should give it a name that best identifies the information it contains. Like a field name, a table name can contain up to 64 characters, including spaces.

REFERENCE

Saving a Table

- Make sure the table you want to save is open.
- On the Quick Access Toolbar, click the Save button. The Save As dialog box opens.
- In the Table Name box, type the name for the table.
- Click the OK button.

According to Kimberly's plan, you need to save the table with the name "Visit."

To save and name the Visit table:

1. On the Quick Access Toolbar, click the **Save** button 🔲. The Save As dialog box opens.

2. With the default name Table1 selected in the Table Name box, type **Visit**, and then click the **OK** button. The tab for the table now displays the name "Visit," and the Visit table design is saved in the Riverview database.

Notice that after you saved and named the Visit table, Access sorted and displayed the records in order by the values in the VisitID field because it is the primary key. If you compare your screen to Figure 1-11, which shows the records in the order you entered them, you'll see that the current screen shows the records in order by the VisitID field values.

Kimberly asks you to add two more records to the Visit table. When you add a record to an existing table, you must enter the new record in the next row available for a new record; you cannot insert a row between existing records for the new record. In a table with just a few records, such as the Visit table, the next available row is visible on the screen. However, in a table with hundreds of records, you would need to scroll the datasheet to see the next row available. The easiest way to add a new record to a table is to use the New button, which scrolls the datasheet to the next row available so you can enter the new record.

To enter additional records in the Visit table:

1. If necessary, click the first record's VisitID field value (**1016**) to make it the current record.

2. On the ribbon, click the **Home** tab.

3. In the Records group, click the **New** button. The insertion point is positioned in the next row available for a new record, which in this case is row 9. See Figure 1-15.

Figure 1-15 Entering a new record

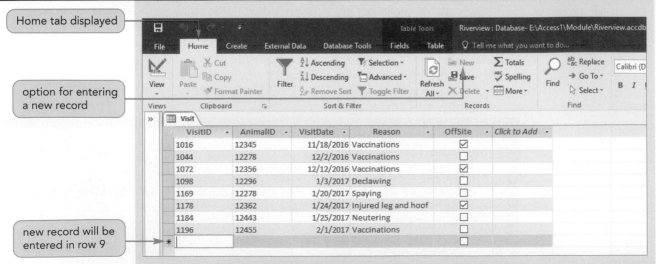

- Home tab displayed
- option for entering a new record
- new record will be entered in row 9

4. With the insertion point in the VisitID field for the new record, type **1036** and then press the **Tab** key.

5. Complete the entry of this record by entering each value shown below, pressing the **Tab** key to move from field to field:

AnimalID = **12294**

VisitDate = **11/29/2016**

Reason = **Declawing**

OffSite = **No (unchecked)**

6. Enter the values for the next new record, as follows, and then press the **Tab** key after entering the OffSite field value:

VisitID = **1152**

AnimalID = **12318**

VisitDate = **1/13/2017**

Reason = **Not eating**

OffSite = **No (unchecked)**

Your datasheet should now look like the one shown in Figure 1-16.

Figure 1-16   **Datasheet with additional records entered**

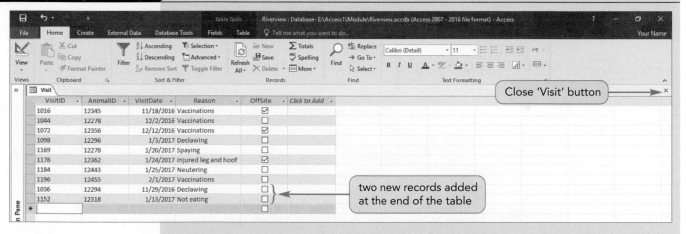

The new records you added appear at the end of the table, and are not sorted in order by the primary key field values. For example, VisitID 1036 should be the second record in the table, placed between VisitID 1016 and VisitID 1044. When you add records to a table datasheet, they appear at the end of the table. The records are not displayed in primary key order until you either close and reopen the table or switch between views.

7. Click the **Close 'Visit'** button ☒ on the object tab (see Figure 1-16 for the location of this button). The Visit table closes, and the main portion of the Access window is now blank because no database object is currently open. The Riverview database file is still open, as indicated by the filename in the Access window title bar.

Opening a Table

The tables in a database are listed in the Navigation Pane. You open a table, or any Access object, by double-clicking the object name in the Navigation Pane. Next, you'll open the Visit table so you can see all the records you've entered in the correct primary key order.

To open the Visit table:

1. On the Navigation Pane, click the **Shutter Bar Open/Close Button** ▶▶ to open the pane. Note that the Visit table is listed.

2. Double-click **Visit** to open the table in Datasheet view. See Figure 1-17.

Figure 1-17   **Table with 10 records entered and displayed in primary key order**

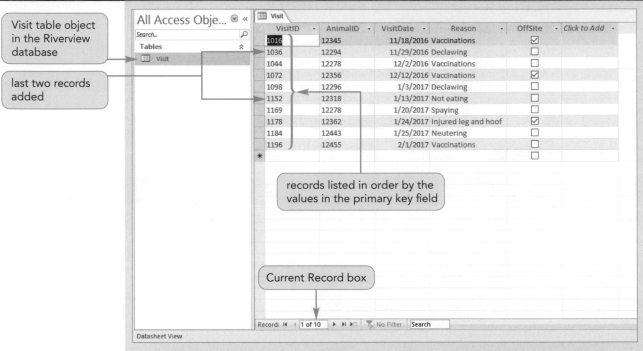

The two records you added, with VisitID field values of 1036 and 1152, now appear in the correct primary key order. The table now contains a total of 10 records, as indicated by the Current Record box at the bottom of the datasheet. The **Current Record box** displays the number of the current record as well as the total number of records in the table.

Each record contains a unique VisitID value because this field is the primary key. Other fields, however, can contain the same value in multiple records; for example, note the four values of "Vaccinations" in the Reason field.

Closing a Table and Exiting Access

When you are finished working in an Access table, it's a good idea to close the table so that you do not make unintended changes to the table data. You can close a table by clicking its Close button on the object tab, as you did earlier. Or, if you want to close the Access program as well, you can click the program's Close button. When you do, any open tables are closed, the active database is closed, and you exit the Access program.

TIP

To close a database without exiting Access, click the File tab to display Backstage view, and then click Close.

To close the Visit table and exit Access:

1. Click the **Close** button ✕ on the program window title bar. The Visit table and the Riverview database close, and then the Access program closes.

INSIGHT

Saving a Database

Unlike the Save buttons in other Office programs, the Save button on the Quick Access Toolbar in Access does not save the active document (database). Instead, you use the Save button to save the design of an Access object, such as a table (as you saw earlier), or to save datasheet format changes, such as resizing columns. Access does not have a button or option you can use to save the active database.

Access saves changes to the active database automatically when you change or add a record or close the database. If your database is stored on a removable storage device, such as a USB drive, you should never remove the device while the database file is open. If you do, Access will encounter problems when it tries to save the database, which might damage the database. Make sure you close the database first before removing the storage device.

Now that you've become familiar with database concepts and Access, and created the Riverview database and the Visit table, Kimberly wants you to add more records to the table and work with the data stored in it to create database objects including a query, form, and report. You'll complete these tasks in the next session.

REVIEW

Session 1.1 Quick Check

1. A(n) _____ is a single characteristic of a person, place, object, event, or idea.

2. You connect the records in two separate tables through a(n) _____ that appears in both tables.

3. The _____, whose values uniquely identify each record in a table, is called a(n) _____ when it is placed in a second table to form a relationship between the two tables.

4. The _____ is the area of the Access window that lists all the objects in a database, and it is the main control center for opening and working with database objects.

5. What is the name of the field that Access creates, by default, as the primary key field for a new table in Datasheet view?

6. Which group on the Fields tab contains the options you use to add new fields to a table?

7. What does a pencil symbol at the beginning of a record represent? What does a star symbol represent?

8. Explain how the saving process in Access is different from saving in other Office programs.

Session 1.2 Visual Overview:

The **Create tab** provides options for creating various database objects, including tables, forms, and reports. The options appear on the tab grouped by object type.

The **Query Wizard button** opens a dialog box with different types of wizards that guide you through the steps to create a query. One of these, the **Simple Query Wizard**, allows you to select records and fields quickly to display in the query results.

You use the options in the Tables group to create a table in Datasheet view or in Design view.

The Forms group contains options for creating a **form**, which is a database object you use to enter, edit, and view records in a database.

Riverview : Database- E:\Access1\Modu e\Riverview.acc

File   Home   Create   External Data   Database Tools   🔎 Tell me what you want

Application Parts ▾ | Table | Table Design | SharePoint Lists ▾ | Query Wizard | Query Design | Form | Form Design | Blank Form | Form Wizard / Navigation ▾ / More Forms

Templates | Tables | Queries | Forms

» Navigation Pane

The **Form tool** quickly creates a form containing all the fields in the table (or query) on which you're basing the form.

The **Form Wizard** guides you through the process of creating a form.

The Queries group contains options for creating a **query**, which is a question you ask about the data stored in a database. In response to a query, Access displays the specific records and fields that answer your question.

Ready

The Create Tab Options

The Reports group contains options for creating a **report**, which is a formatted printout (or screen display) of the contents of one of more tables (or queries) in a database.

The Microsoft Access Help button opens the **Access 2016 Help** window, where you can find information about Access commands and features as well as instructions for using them.

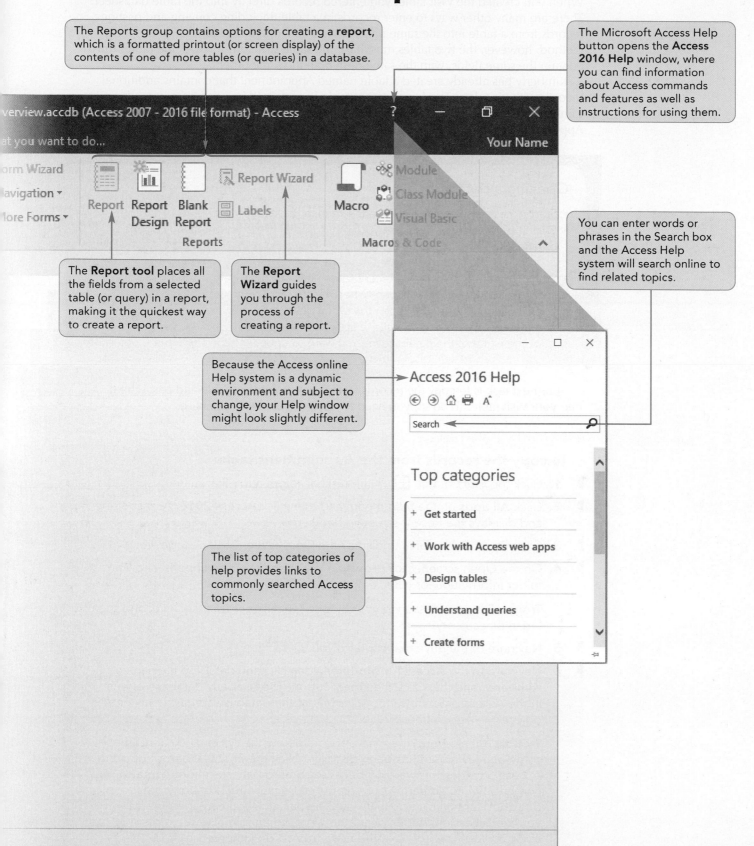

The **Report tool** places all the fields from a selected table (or query) in a report, making it the quickest way to create a report.

The **Report Wizard** guides you through the process of creating a report.

You can enter words or phrases in the Search box and the Access Help system will search online to find related topics.

Because the Access online Help system is a dynamic environment and subject to change, your Help window might look slightly different.

The list of top categories of help provides links to commonly searched Access topics.

Copying Records from Another Access Database

When you created the Visit table, you entered records directly into the table datasheet. There are many other ways to enter records in a table, including copying and pasting records from a table into the same database or into a different database. To use this method, however, the two tables must have the same structure—that is, the tables must contain the same fields, with the same design, in the same order.

Kimberly has already created a table named Appointment that contains additional records with visit data. The Appointment table is contained in a database named Kimberly located in the Access1 > Module folder included with your Data Files. The Appointment table has the same table structure as the Visit table you created.

REFERENCE

Opening a Database

- Start Access and display the Recent screen in Backstage view.
- Click the name of the database you want to open in the list of recently opened databases.

or

- Start Access and display the Recent screen in Backstage view.
- In the navigation bar, click Open Other Files to display the Open screen.
- Click the Browse button to open the Open dialog box, and then navigate to the drive and folder containing the database file you want to open.
- Click the name of the database file you want to open, and then click the Open button.

Your next task is to copy the records from the Appointment table and paste them into your Visit table. To do so, you need to open the Kimberly database.

To copy the records from the Appointment table:

1. Click the **Start** button ⊞ on the taskbar to open the Start menu.

2. Click **All apps** on the Start menu, and then click **Access 2016**. Access starts and displays the Recent screen in Backstage view.

3. Click **Open Other Files** to display the Open screen in Backstage view.

4. On the Open screen, click **Browse**. The Open dialog box opens, showing folder information for your computer.

   Trouble? If you are storing your files on OneDrive, click OneDrive, and then log in if necessary.

5. Navigate to the drive that contains your Data Files.

6. Navigate to the **Access1 > Module** folder, click the database file named **Kimberly**, and then click the **Open** button. The Kimberly database opens in the Access program window. Note that the database contains only one object, the Appointment table.

   Trouble? If a security warning appears below the ribbon indicating that some active content has been disabled, click the Enable Content button. Access provides this warning because some databases might contain content that could harm your computer. Because the Kimberly database does not contain objects that could be harmful, you can open it safely. If you are accessing the file over a network, you might also see a dialog box asking if you want to make the file a trusted document; click Yes.

7. In the Navigation Pane, double-click **Appointment** to open the Appointment table in Datasheet view. The table contains 65 records and the same five fields, with the same characteristics, as the fields in the Visit table. See Figure 1-18.

Figure 1-18   **Appointment table in the Kimberly database**

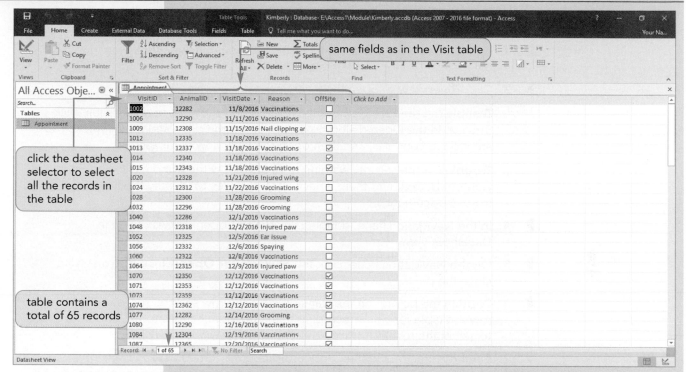

Kimberly wants you to copy all the records in the Appointment table. You can select all the records by clicking the **datasheet selector**, which is the box to the left of the first field name in the table datasheet, as shown in Figure 1-18.

8. Click the **datasheet selector** to the left of the VisitID field. All the records in the table are selected.

9. On the Home tab, in the Clipboard group, click the **Copy** button. All the records are copied to the Clipboard.

10. Click the **Close 'Appointment'** button ☒ on the object tab. A dialog box opens asking if you want to save the data you copied to the Clipboard. This dialog box opens only when you copy a large amount of data to the Clipboard.

11. Click the **Yes** button. The dialog box closes, and then the Appointment table closes.

With the records copied to the Clipboard, you can now paste them into the Visit table. First you need to close the Kimberly database while still keeping the Access program open, and then open the Riverview database.

To close the Kimberly database and then paste the records into the Visit table:

1. Click the **File** tab to open Backstage view, and then click **Close** in the navigation bar to close the Kimberly database. You return to a blank Access program window, and the Home tab is the active tab on the ribbon.

2. Click the **File** tab to return to Backstage view, and then click **Open** in the navigation bar. Recent is selected on the Open screen, and the recently opened database files are listed. This list should include the Riverview database.

3. Click **Riverview** to open the Riverview database file.

   Trouble? If the Riverview database file is not in the list of recent files, click Browse. In the Open dialog box, navigate to the drive and folder where you are storing your files, and then open the Riverview database file.

   Trouble? If the security warning appears below the ribbon, click the Enable Content button, and then, if necessary, click Yes to identify the file as a trusted document.

4. In the Navigation Pane, double-click **Visit** to open the Visit table in Datasheet view.

5. On the Navigation Pane, click the **Shutter Bar Open/Close Button** « to close the pane.

6. Position the pointer on the star symbol in the row selector for row 11 (the next row available for a new record) until the pointer changes to ➡, and then click to select the row.

7. On the Home tab, in the Clipboard group, click the **Paste** button. The pasted records are added to the table, and a dialog box opens asking you to confirm that you want to paste all the records (65 total).

   Trouble? If the Paste button isn't active, click the ➡ pointer on the row selector for row 11, making sure the entire row is selected, and then repeat Step 7.

8. Click the **Yes** button. The dialog box closes, and the pasted records are selected. See Figure 1-19. Notice that the table now contains a total of 75 records—10 records that you entered previously and 65 records that you copied and pasted.

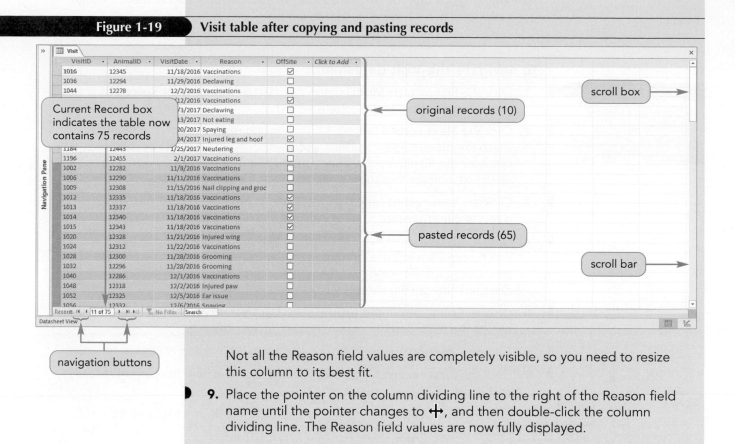

Figure 1-19   **Visit table after copying and pasting records**

Not all the Reason field values are completely visible, so you need to resize this column to its best fit.

9. Place the pointer on the column dividing line to the right of the Reason field name until the pointer changes to ↔, and then double-click the column dividing line. The Reason field values are now fully displayed.

Navigating a Datasheet

The Visit table now contains 75 records, but only some of the records are visible on the screen. To view fields or records not currently visible on the screen, you can use the horizontal and vertical scroll bars to navigate the data. The **navigation buttons**, shown in Figure 1-19 and also described in Figure 1-20, provide another way to move vertically through the records. The Current Record box appears between the two sets of navigation buttons and displays the number of the current record as well as the total number of records in the table. Figure 1-20 shows which record becomes the current record when you click each navigation button. Note the New (blank) record button, which works in the same way as the New button on the Home tab you used earlier to enter a new record in the table.

Figure 1-20   **Navigation buttons**

Navigation Button	Record Selected	Navigation Button	Record Selected
◄	First record	►►	Last record
◄	Previous record	► New	New (blank) record
►	Next record		

Kimberly suggests that you use the various navigation techniques to move through the Visit table and become familiar with its contents.

To navigate the Visit datasheet:

▶ 1. Click the first record's VisitID field value (**1016**). The Current Record box shows that record 1 is the current record.

▶ 2. Click the **Next record** button ▶. The second record is now highlighted, which identifies it as the current record. Also, notice that the second record's value for the VisitID field is selected, and the Current Record box displays "2 of 75" to indicate that the second record is the current record.

▶ 3. Click the **Last record** button ▶|. The last record in the table, record 75, is now the current record.

▶ 4. Drag the scroll box in the vertical scroll bar up to the top of the bar. Notice that record 75 is still the current record, as indicated in the Current Record box. Dragging the scroll box changes the display of the table datasheet, but does not change the current record.

▶ 5. Drag the scroll box in the vertical scroll bar back down until you can see the end of the table and the current record (record 75).

▶ 6. Click the **Previous record** button ◀. Record 74 is now the current record.

▶ 7. Click the **First record** button |◀. The first record is now the current record and is visible on the screen.

Earlier you resized the Reason column to its best fit, to ensure all the field values were visible. However, when you resize a column to its best fit, the column expands to fully display only the field values that are visible on the screen at that time. If you move through the complete datasheet and notice that not all of the field values are fully displayed after conducting the resizing process on the records initially visible, you need to repeat the resizing process.

▶ 8. Scroll down through the records and observe if the field values are fully displayed. In this case, all of the fields are fully visible, so there is no need to resize any of the field columns.

The Visit table now contains all the data about animal visits for Riverview Veterinary Care Center. To better understand how to work with this data, Kimberly asks you to create simple objects for the other main types of database objects—queries, forms, and reports.

Creating a Simple Query

As noted earlier, a query is a question you ask about the data stored in a database. When you create a query, you tell Access which fields you need and what criteria it should use to select the records that will answer your question. Then Access displays only the information you want, so you don't have to navigate through the entire database for the information. In the Visit table, for example, Kimberly might create a query to display only those records for visits that occurred in a specific month. Even though a query can display table information in a different way, the information still exists in the table as it was originally entered.

Kimberly wants to see a list of all the visit dates and reasons for visits in the Visit table. She doesn't want the list to include all the fields in the table, such as AnimalID and OffSite. To produce this list for Kimberly, you'll use the Simple Query Wizard to create a query based on the Visit table.

To start the Simple Query Wizard:

▶ **1.** On the ribbon, click the **Create** tab.

▶ **2.** In the Queries group, click the **Query Wizard** button. The New Query dialog box opens.

▶ **3.** Make sure **Simple Query Wizard** is selected, and then click the **OK** button. The first Simple Query Wizard dialog box opens. See Figure 1-21.

Figure 1-21 ▶ **First Simple Query Wizard dialog box**

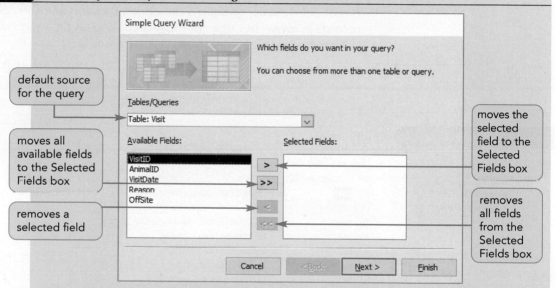

Because the Visit table is the only object in the Riverview database, it is listed in the Tables/Queries box by default. If the database contained more objects, you could click the Tables/Queries arrow and choose another table or a query as the basis for the new query you are creating. The Available Fields box lists all the fields in the Visit table.

You need to select fields from the Available Fields box to include them in the query. To select fields one at a time, click a field and then click the > button. The selected field moves from the Available Fields box on the left to the Selected Fields box on the right. To select all the fields, click the >> button. If you change your mind or make a mistake, you can remove a field by clicking it in the Selected Fields box and then clicking the < button. To remove all fields from the Selected Fields box, click the << button.

Each Simple Query Wizard dialog box contains buttons on the bottom that allow you to move to the previous dialog box (Back button), move to the next dialog box (Next button), or cancel the creation process (Cancel button). You can also finish creating the object (Finish button) and accept the wizard's defaults for the remaining options.

Kimberly wants her query results to list to include data from only the following fields: VisitID, VisitDate, and Reason. You need to select these fields to include them in the query.

To create the query using the Simple Query Wizard:

TIP

You can also double-click a field to move it from the Available Fields box to the Selected Fields box.

1. Click **VisitID** in the Available Fields box to select the field (if necessary), and then click the ⟩ button. The VisitID field moves to the Selected Fields box.

2. Repeat Step 1 for the fields **VisitDate** and **Reason**, and then click the **Next** button. The second, and final, Simple Query Wizard dialog box opens and asks you to choose a name (title) for your query. The suggested name is "Visit Query" because the query you are creating is based on the Visit table. You'll change the suggested name to "VisitList."

3. Click at the end of the suggested name, use the **Backspace** key to delete the word "Query" and the space, and then type **List**. Now you can view the query results.

4. Click the **Finish** button to complete the query. The query results are displayed in Datasheet view, on a new tab named "VisitList." A query datasheet is similar to a table datasheet, showing fields in columns and records in rows—but only for those fields and records you want to see, as determined by the query specifications you select.

5. Place the pointer on the column divider line to the right of the Reason field name until the pointer changes to ↔, and then double-click the column divider line to resize the Reason field. See Figure 1-22.

Figure 1-22   **Query results**

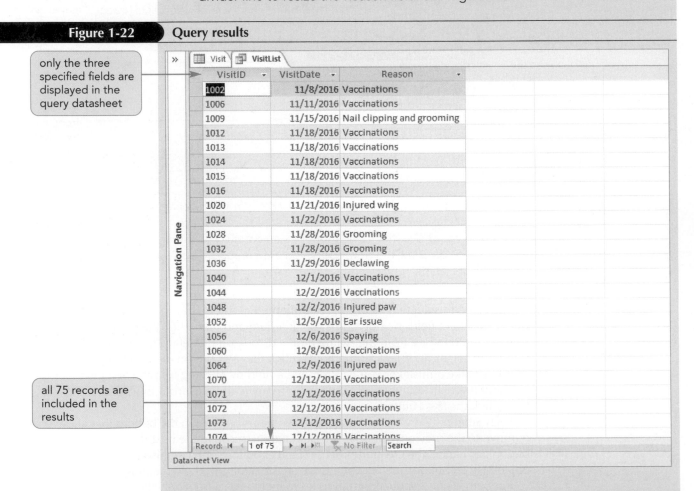

only the three specified fields are displayed in the query datasheet

all 75 records are included in the results

VisitID	VisitDate	Reason
1002	11/8/2016	Vaccinations
1006	11/11/2016	Vaccinations
1009	11/15/2016	Nail clipping and grooming
1012	11/18/2016	Vaccinations
1013	11/18/2016	Vaccinations
1014	11/18/2016	Vaccinations
1015	11/18/2016	Vaccinations
1016	11/18/2016	Vaccinations
1020	11/21/2016	Injured wing
1024	11/22/2016	Vaccinations
1028	11/28/2016	Grooming
1032	11/28/2016	Grooming
1036	11/29/2016	Declawing
1040	12/1/2016	Vaccinations
1044	12/2/2016	Vaccinations
1048	12/2/2016	Injured paw
1052	12/5/2016	Ear issue
1056	12/6/2016	Spaying
1060	12/8/2016	Vaccinations
1064	12/9/2016	Injured paw
1070	12/12/2016	Vaccinations
1071	12/12/2016	Vaccinations
1072	12/12/2016	Vaccinations
1073	12/12/2016	Vaccinations
1074	12/12/2016	Vaccinations

Record: ◄ ◄ 1 of 75 ► ►I ►□   No Filter   Search

Datasheet View

The VisitList query datasheet displays the three fields in the order you selected them in the Simple Query Wizard, from left to right. The records are listed in order by the primary key field, VisitID. Even though the query datasheet displays only the three fields you chose for the query, the Visit table still includes all the fields for all records.

Notice that the navigation buttons are located at the bottom of the window. You navigate a query datasheet in the same way that you navigate a table datasheet.

▶ **6.** Click the **Last record** button ▶▎. The last record in the query datasheet is now the current record.

▶ **7.** Click the **Previous record** button ◀. Record 74 in the query datasheet is now the current record.

▶ **8.** Click the **First record** button ▎◀. The first record is now the current record.

▶ **9.** Click the **Close 'VisitList'** button ✕ on the object tab. A dialog box opens asking if you want to save the changes to the layout of the query. This dialog box opens because you resized the Reason column.

▶ **10.** Click the **Yes** button to save the query layout changes and close the query.

The query results are not stored in the database; however, the query design is stored as part of the database with the name you specified. You can re-create the query results at any time by opening the query again. When you open the query at a later date, the results displayed will reflect up-to-date information to include any new records entered in the Visit table.

Next, Kimberly asks you to create a form for the Visit table so that Riverview Veterinary Care Center staff can use the form to enter and work with data in the table easily.

Creating a Simple Form

As noted earlier, you use a form to enter, edit, and view records in a database. Although you can perform these same functions with tables and queries, forms can present data in many customized and useful ways.

Kimberly wants a form for the Visit table that shows all the fields for one record at a time, with fields listed one below another in a column. This type of form will make it easier for her staff to focus on all the data for a particular visit. You'll use the Form tool to create this form quickly and easily.

To create the form using the Form tool:

▶ **1.** Make sure the Visit table is still open in Datasheet view. The table or other database object you're using as the basis for the form must either be open or selected in the Navigation Pane when you use the Form tool.

Trouble? If the Visit table is not open, click the Shutter Bar Open/Close Button ⏵⏵ to open the Navigation Pane. Then double-click Visit to open the Visit table in Datasheet view. Click the Shutter Bar Open/Close Button ⏴⏴ to close the pane.

▶ **2.** On the ribbon, click the **Create** tab if necessary.

3. In the Forms group, click the **Form** button. The Form tool creates a simple form showing every field in the Visit table and places it on a tab named "Visit" because the form is based on the Visit table. See Figure 1-23.

Figure 1-23 Form created by the Form tool

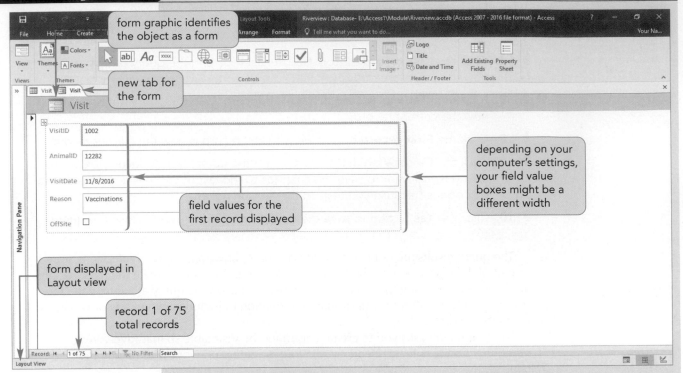

Trouble? Depending on the size of your monitor and your screen resolution settings, the fields in your form might appear in multiple columns instead of a single column. This difference will not present any problems.

The form displays one record at a time in the Visit table, providing another view of the data that is stored in the table and allowing you to focus on the values for one record. Access displays the field values for the first record in the table and selects the first field value (VisitID) as indicated by the border that appears around the value. Each field name appears on a separate line and on the same line as its field value, which appears in a box to the right. Depending on your computer's settings, the field value boxes in your form might be wider or narrower than those shown in the figure. As indicated in the status bar, the form is displayed in Layout view. In **Layout view**, you can make design changes to the form while it is displaying data, so that you can see the effects of the changes you make immediately.

To view, enter, and maintain data using a form, you must know how to move from field to field and from record to record. Notice that the form contains navigation buttons, similar to those available in Datasheet view, which you can use to display different records in the form. You'll use these now to navigate the form; then you'll save and close the form.

To navigate, save, and close the form:

▶ 1. Click the **Next record** button ▶. The form now displays the values for the second record in the Visit table.

▶ 2. Click the **Last record** button ▶| to move to the last record in the table. The form displays the information for VisitID 1196.

▶ 3. Click the **Previous record** button ◀ to move to record 74.

▶ 4. Click the **First record** button |◀ to return to the first record in the Visit table.

▶ 5. Next, you'll save the form with the name "VisitData" in the Riverview database. Then the form will be available for later use.

▶ 6. On the Quick Access Toolbar, click the **Save** button 🖫. The Save As dialog box opens.

▶ 7. In the Form Name box, click at the end of the selected name "Visit," type **Data**, and then press the **Enter** key. The dialog box closes and the form is saved as VisitData in the Riverview database. The tab containing the form now displays the name VisitData.

▶ 8. Click the **Close 'VisitData'** button ✕ on the object tab to close the form.

INSIGHT

Saving Database Objects

In general, it is best to save a database object—query, form, or report—only if you anticipate using the object frequently or if it is time-consuming to create, because all objects use storage space and increase the size of the database file. For example, you most likely would not save a form you created with the Form tool because you can re-create it easily with one mouse click. (However, for the purposes of this text, you usually need to save the objects you create.)

Kimberly would like to see the information in the Visit table presented in a more readable and professional format. You'll help Kimberly by creating a report.

Creating a Simple Report

As noted earlier, a report is a formatted printout (or screen display) of the contents of one or more tables or queries. You'll use the Report tool to quickly produce a report based on the Visit table for Kimberly. The Report tool creates a report based on the selected table or query.

To create the report using the Report tool:

▶ 1. On the ribbon, click the **Create** tab.

▶ 2. In the Reports group, click the **Report** button. The Report tool creates a simple report showing every field in the Visit table and places it on a tab named "Visit" because the object you created (the report) is based on the Visit table. See Figure 1-24.

Figure 1-24   **Report created by the Report tool**

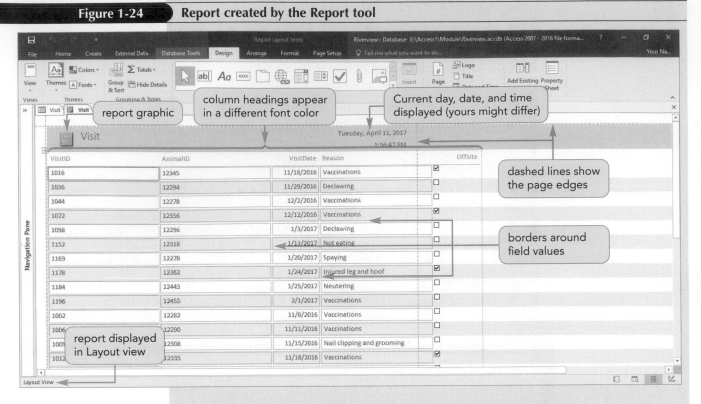

Trouble? The records in your report might appear in a different order from the records shown in Figure 1-24. This difference will not cause any problems.

The report shows each field in a column, with the field values for each record in a row, similar to a table or query datasheet. However, the report offers a more visually appealing format for the data, with the column headings in a different color, borders around each field value, a graphic of a report at the top left, and the current day, date, and time at the top right. Also notice the dashed horizontal and vertical lines on the top and right, respectively; these lines mark the edges of the page and show where text will print on the page.

The report needs some design changes to better display the data. The columns are much wider than necessary for the VisitID and AnimalID fields, and the Reason and OffSite field values and borders are not completely displayed within the page area defined by the dashed lines, which means they would not appear on the same page as the rest of the fields in the printed report. You can resize the columns easily in Layout view.

To resize the VisitID and AnimalID columns:

1. Position the pointer on the right border of any field value in the VisitID column until the pointer changes to ↔.

2. Click and drag the mouse to the left. Notice the dark outlines surrounding the field names and field values indicating the changing column width.

3. Drag to the left until the column is slightly wider than the VisitID field name, and then release the mouse button. The VisitID column is now narrower, and the other four columns have shifted to the left. The Reason and OffSite fields, values, and borders are now completely within the page area. See Figure 1-25.

| Figure 1-25 | Report after resizing the VisitID column |

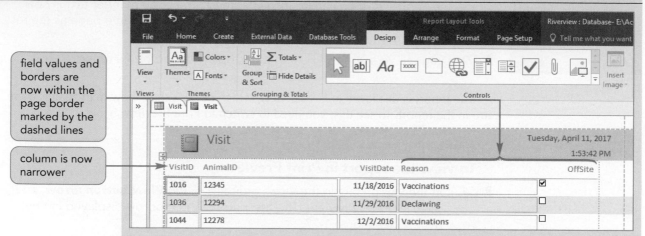

field values and borders are now within the page border marked by the dashed lines

column is now narrower

4. Click the first field value for AnimalID. AnimalID is now the current field.

5. Position the pointer on the right border of the first value in the AnimalID column until the pointer changes to ↔, click and drag to the left until the column is slightly wider than its field name, and then release the mouse button.

6. Drag the scroll box on the vertical scroll bar down to the bottom of the report to check its entire layout.

The Report tool displays the number "75" at the bottom left of the report, showing the total number of records in the report and the table on which it is based—the Visit table. The Report tool also displays the page number at the bottom right, but the text "Page 1 of 1" appears cut off through the vertical dashed line. This will cause a problem when you print the report, so you need to move this text to the left.

7. Click anywhere on the words **Page 1 of 1**. An orange outline appears around the text, indicating it is selected. See Figure 1-26.

| Figure 1-26 | Report page number selected |

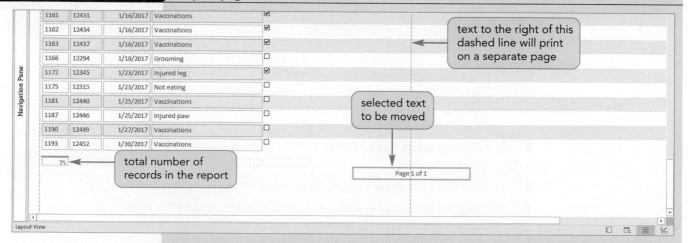

text to the right of this dashed line will print on a separate page

total number of records in the report

selected text to be moved

With the text selected, you can use the keyboard arrow keys to move it.

TIP

You can also use the mouse to drag the selected page number, but the arrow key is more precise.

8. Press the ← key repeatedly until the selected page number is to the left of the vertical dashed line (roughly 35 times). The page number text is now completely within the page area and will print on the same page as the rest of the report.

9. Drag the vertical scroll box up to redisplay the top of the report.

The report is displayed in Layout view, which doesn't show how many pages there are in the report. To see this, you need to switch to Print Preview.

To view the report in Print Preview:

1. On the Design tab, in the Views group, click the **View button arrow**, and then click **Print Preview**. The first page of the report is displayed in Print Preview. See Figure 1-27.

Figure 1-27	First page of the report in Print Preview

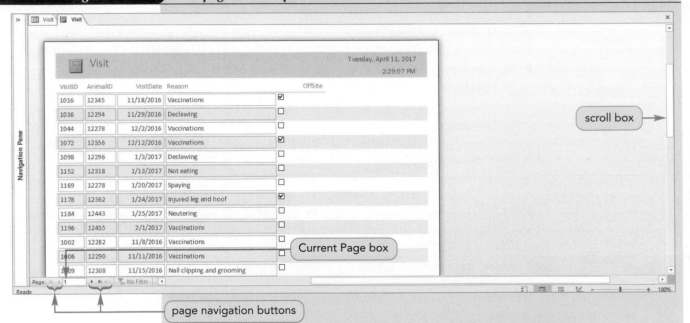

Print Preview shows exactly how the report will look when printed. Notice that Print Preview provides page navigation buttons at the bottom of the window, similar to the navigation buttons you've used to move through records in a table, query, and form.

2. Click the **Next Page** button ▶. The second page of the report is displayed in Print Preview.

3. Click the **Last Page** button ▶I to move to the last page of the report.

4. Drag the scroll box in the vertical scroll bar down until the bottom of the report page is displayed. The notation "Page 3 of 3" appears at the bottom of the page, indicating that you are on page 3 out of a total of 3 pages in the report.

Trouble? Depending on the printer you are using, your report might have more or fewer pages, and some of the pages might be blank. If so, don't worry. Different printers format reports in different ways, sometimes affecting the total number of pages and the number of records printed per page.

5. Click the **First Page** button ◀ to return to the first page of the report, and then drag the scroll box in the vertical scroll bar up to display the top of the report.

Next you'll save the report as VisitDetails, and then print it.

6. On the Quick Access Toolbar, click the **Save** button 🖫. The Save As dialog box opens.

7. In the Report Name box, click at the end of the selected word "Visit," type **Details**, and then press the **Enter** key. The dialog box closes and the report is saved as VisitDetails in the Riverview database. The tab containing the report now displays the name "VisitDetails."

Printing a Report

After creating a report, you might need to print it to distribute it to others who need to view the report's contents. You can print a report without changing any print settings, or display the Print dialog box and select options for printing.

REFERENCE

Printing a Report

- Open the report in any view, or select the report in the Navigation Pane.
- Click the File tab to display Backstage view, click Print, and then click Quick Print to print the report with the default print settings.

or

- Open the report in any view, or select the report in the Navigation Pane.
- Click the File tab, click Print, and then click Print (or, if the report is displayed in Print Preview, click the Print button in the Print group on the Print Preview tab). The Print dialog box opens, in which you can select the options you want for printing the report.

Kimberly asks you to print the entire report with the default settings, so you'll use the Quick Print option in Backstage view.

Note: To complete the following steps, your computer must be connected to a printer. Check with your instructor first to see if you should print the report.

To print the report and then close it:

1. On the ribbon, click the **File** tab to open Backstage view.

2. In the navigation bar, click **Print** to display the Print screen, and then click **Quick Print**. The report prints with the default print settings, and you return to the report in Print Preview.

Trouble? If your report did not print, make sure that your computer is connected to a printer, and that the printer is turned on and ready to print. Then repeat Steps 1 and 2.

3. Click the **Close 'VisitDetails'** button ✕ on the object tab to close the report.

4. Click the **Close 'Visit'** button ✕ on the object tab to close the Visit table.

Trouble? If you are asked to save changes to the layout of the table, click the Yes button.

You can also use the Print dialog box to print other database objects, such as table and query datasheets. Most often, these objects are used for viewing and entering data, and reports are used for printing the data in a database.

Viewing Objects in the Navigation Pane

The Riverview database now contains four objects—the Visit table, the VisitList query, the VisitData form, and the VisitDetails report. When you work with the database file—such as closing it, opening it, or distributing it to others—the file includes all the objects you created and saved in the database. You can view and work with these objects in the Navigation Pane.

To view the objects in the Riverview database:

▶ 1. On the Navigation Pane, click the **Shutter Bar Open/Close Button** ≫ to open the pane. See Figure 1-28.

| Figure 1-28 | First page of the report in Print Preview |

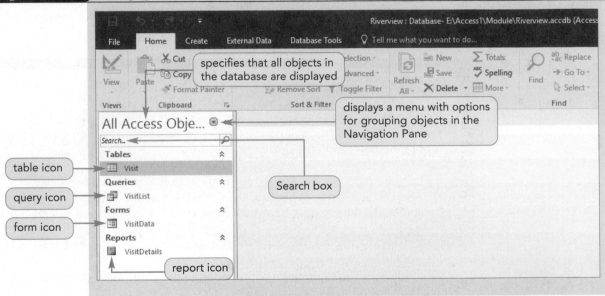

The Navigation Pane currently displays the default category, **All Access Objects**, which lists all the database objects in the pane. Each object type (Tables, Queries, Forms, and Reports) appears in its own group. Each database object (the Visit table, the VisitList query, the VisitData form, and the VisitDetails report) has a unique icon to its left to indicate the type of object. This makes it easy for you to identify the objects and choose which one you want to open and work with.

The arrow on the All Access Objects bar displays a menu with options for various ways to group and display objects in the Navigation Pane. The Search box enables you to enter text for Access to find; for example, you could search for all objects that contain the word "Visit" in their names. Note that Access searches for objects only in the categories and groups currently displayed in the Navigation Pane.

As you continue to build the Riverview database and add more objects to it in later modules, you'll use the options in the Navigation Pane to manage those objects.

Using Microsoft Access Help

Access includes a Help system you can use to search for information about specific program features. You start Help by clicking the Microsoft Access Help button in the top right of the Access window, or by pressing the F1 key.

You'll use Help now to learn more about the Navigation Pane.

To search for information about the Navigation Pane in Help:

TIP

You can also get help by typing keywords in the Tell Me box on the ribbon to access information about topics related to those words in the Access Help window.

1. Click the **Microsoft Access Help** button ❓ on the title bar. The Access 2016 Help window opens, as shown earlier in the Session 1.2 Visual Overview.

2. Click in the **Search** box, type **Navigation Pane**, and then press the **Enter** key. The Access 2016 Help window displays a list of topics related to the Navigation Pane.

3. Click the topic **Manage Access database objects in the Navigation Pane**. The Access Help window displays the article you selected. See Figure 1-29.

Figure 1-29   Article displayed in the Access Help window

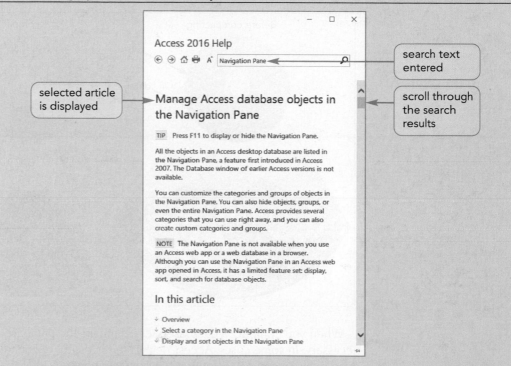

The figure shows the Access 2016 Help window. Callouts: "search text entered" pointing to the search box containing "Navigation Pane"; "scroll through the search results" pointing to the scroll bar; "selected article is displayed" pointing to the article title "Manage Access database objects in the Navigation Pane".

Trouble? If the article on managing database objects is not listed in your Help window, choose another article related to the Navigation Pane to read.

4. Scroll through the article to read detailed information about working with the Navigation Pane.

5. When finished, click the **Close** button ✕ on the Access 2016 Help window to close it.

The Access Help system is an important reference tool for you to use if you need additional information about databases in general, details about specific Access features, or support with problems you might encounter.

Managing a Database

One of the main tasks involved in working with database software is managing your databases and the data they contain. Some of the activities involved in database management include compacting and repairing a database and backing up and restoring a database. By managing your databases, you can ensure that they operate in the most efficient way, that the data they contain is secure, and that you can work with the data effectively.

Compacting and Repairing a Database

Whenever you open an Access database and work in it, the size of the database increases. Further, when you delete records or when you delete or replace database objects—such as queries, forms, and reports—the storage space that had been occupied by the deleted or replaced records or objects does not automatically become available for other records or objects. To make the space available, and also to increase the speed of data retrieval, you must compact the database. **Compacting** a database rearranges the data and objects in a database to decrease its file size, thereby making more storage space available and enhancing the performance of the database. Figure 1-30 illustrates the compacting process.

Figure 1-30 | Compacting a database

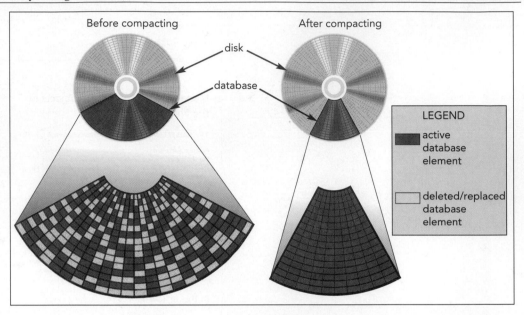

When you compact a database, Access repairs the database at the same time, if necessary. In some cases, Access detects that a database is damaged when you try to open it and gives you the option to compact and repair it at that time. For example, the data in your database might become damaged, or corrupted, if you exit the Access program suddenly by turning off your computer. If you think your database might be damaged because it is behaving unpredictably, you can use the Compact & Repair Database option to fix it.

Compacting and Repairing a Database

- Make sure the database file you want to compact and repair is open.
- Click the File tab to display the Info screen in Backstage view.
- Click the Compact & Repair Database button.

Access also allows you to set an option to compact and repair a database file automatically every time you close it. The Compact on Close option is available in the Current Database section of the Access Options dialog box, which you open from

Backstage view by clicking the Options command in the navigation bar. By default, the Compact on Close option is turned off.

Next, you'll compact the Riverview database manually using the Compact & Repair Database option. This will make the database smaller and allow you to work with it more efficiently. After compacting the database, you'll close it.

To compact and repair the Riverview database:

▶ **1.** On the ribbon, click the **File** tab to open the Info screen in Backstage view.

▶ **2.** Click the **Compact & Repair Database** button. Although nothing visible happens on the screen, the Riverview database is compacted, making it smaller, and repairs it at the same time. The Home tab is again the active tab on the ribbon.

▶ **3.** Click the **File** tab to return to Backstage view, and then click **Close** in the navigation bar. The Riverview database closes.

Backing Up and Restoring a Database

Backing up a database is the process of making a copy of the database file to protect your database against loss or damage. The Back Up Database command enables you to back up your database file from within the Access program, while you are working on your database. To use this option, click the File tab to display the Info screen in Backstage view, click Save As in the navigation bar, click Back Up Database in the Advanced section of the Save Database As pane, and then click the Save As button. In the Save As dialog box that opens, a default filename is provided for the backup copy that consists of the same filename as the database you are backing up (for example, "Riverview"), and an underscore character, plus the current date. This filenaming system makes it easy for you to keep track of your database backups and when they were created. To restore a backup database file, you simply copy the backup from the location where it is stored to your hard drive, or whatever device you use to work in Access, and start working with the restored database file. (You will not actually back up the Riverview database in this module unless directed by your instructor to do so.)

INSIGHT

Planning and Performing Database Backups

Experienced database users make it a habit to back up a database before they work with it for the first time, keeping the original data intact. They also make frequent backups while continuing to work with a database; these backups are generally on flash drives, recordable CDs or DVDs, external or network hard drives, or cloud-based storage (such as OneDrive). Also, it is recommended to store the backup copy in a different location from the original. For example, if the original database is stored on a flash drive, you should not store the backup copy on the same flash drive. If you lose the drive or the drive is damaged, you would lose both the original database and its backup copy.

If the original database file and the backup copy have the same name, restoring the backup copy might replace the original. If you want to save the original file, rename it before you restore the backup copy. To ensure that the restored database has the most current data, you should update the restored database with any changes made to the original between the time you created the backup copy and the time the original database became damaged or lost.

By properly planning for and performing backups, you can avoid losing data and prevent the time-consuming effort required to rebuild a lost or damaged database.

Decision Making: When to Use Access vs. Excel

Using a spreadsheet application like Microsoft Excel to manage lists or tables of information works well when the data is simple, such as a list of contacts or tasks. As soon as the data becomes complex enough to separate into tables that need to be related, you start to see the limitations of using a spreadsheet application. The strength of a database application such as Access is in its ability to easily relate one table of information to another. Consider a table of contacts that includes home addresses, with a separate row for each person living at the same address. When an address changes, it's too easy to make a mistake and not update the home address for each person who lives there. To ensure you have the most accurate data at all times, it's important to have only one instance of each piece of data. By creating separate tables that are related and keeping only one instance of each piece of data, you'll ensure the integrity of the data. Trying to accomplish this in Excel is a complex process, whereas Access is specifically designed for this functionality.

Another limitation of using Excel instead of Access to manage data has to do with the volume of data. Although a spreadsheet can hold thousands of records, a database can hold millions. A spreadsheet containing thousands of pieces of information is cumbersome to use. Think of large-scale commercial applications such as enrollment at a college or tracking customers for a large company. It's hard to imagine managing such information in an Excel spreadsheet. Instead, you'd use a database. Finally, with an Access database, multiple users can access the information it contains at the same time. Although an Excel spreadsheet can be shared, there can be problems when users try to open and edit the same spreadsheet at the same time.

When you're trying to decide whether to use Excel or Access, ask yourself the following questions.

1. Do you need to store data in separate tables that are related to each other?
2. Do you have a very large amount of data to store?
3. Will more than one person need to access the data at the same time?

If you answer "yes" to any of these questions, an Access database is most likely the appropriate application to use.

In the following modules, you'll help Kimberly complete and maintain the Riverview database, and you'll use it to meet the specific information needs of the employees of the care center.

Session 1.2 Quick Check

1. To copy the records from a table in one database to another table in a different database, the two tables must have the same _____.

2. A(n) _____ is a question you ask about the data stored in a database.

3. The quickest way to create a form is to use the _____.

4. Which view enables you to see the total number of pages in a report and navigate through the report pages?

5. In the Navigation Pane, each database object has a unique _____ to its left that identifies the object's type.

6. _____ a database rearranges the data and objects in a database to decrease its file size and enhance the speed and performance of the database.

7. _____ a database is the process of making a copy of the database file to protect the database against loss or damage.

Review Assignments

Data File needed for the Review Assignments: **Company.accdb**

PRACTICE

For Riverview Veterinary Care Center, Kimberly asks you to create a new database to contain information about the vendors that the care center works with to obtain supplies, equipment, and resale items, and the vendors who service and maintain the equipment. Complete the following steps:

1. Create a new, blank database named **Vendor** and save it in the folder where you are storing your files, as specified by your instructor.
2. In Datasheet view for the Table1 table, rename the default ID primary key field to **SupplierID**. Change the data type of the SupplierID field to Short Text.
3. Add the following 10 fields to the new table in the order shown; all of them are Short Text fields *except* InitialContact, which is a Date/Time field: **Company**, **Category**, **Address**, **City**, **State**, **Zip**, **Phone**, **ContactFirst**, **ContactLast**, and **InitialContact**. Resize the columns as necessary so that the complete field names are displayed. Save the table as **Supplier**.
4. Enter the records shown in Figure 1-31 in the Supplier table. For the first record, be sure to enter your first name in the ContactFirst field and your last name in the ContactLast field.
   Note: When entering field values that are shown on multiple lines in the figure, do not try to enter the values on multiple lines. The values are shown on multiple lines in the figure for page spacing purposes only.

Figure 1-31   **Supplier table records**

SupplierID	Company	Category	Address	City	State	Zip	Phone	ContactFirst	ContactLast	InitialContact
YUM345	Yummy Dog Food	Resale	345 Riverside Dr	Charlotte	NC	28201	704-205-8725	Student First	Student Last	2/1/2017
FTS123	Flea & Tick Supplies	Resale	123 Overlook Ln	Atlanta	GA	30301	404-341-2981	Robert	Jackson	3/6/2017
PMC019	Pet Medical	Equipment	19 Waverly Ct	Blacksburg	VA	24061	540-702-0098	Julie	Baxter	2/21/2017
APL619	A+ Labs	Equipment	619 West Dr	Omaha	NE	68022	531-219-7206	Jacques	Dupont	4/10/2017
CWI444	Cat World Inc.	Supplies	444 Boxcar Way	San Diego	CA	92110	619-477-9482	Amelia	Kline	5/1/2017

5. Kimberly created a database named Company that contains a Business table with supplier data. The Supplier table you created has the same design as the Business table. Copy all the records from the **Business** table in the **Company** database (located in the Access1 > Review folder provided with your Data Files) and then paste them at the end of the Supplier table in the Vendor database.
6. Resize all datasheet columns to their best fit, and then save the Supplier table.
7. Close the Supplier table, and then use the Navigation Pane to reopen it. Note that the records are displayed in primary key order by the values in the SupplierID field.
8. Use the Simple Query Wizard to create a query that includes the Company, Category, ContactFirst, ContactLast, and Phone fields (in that order) from the Supplier table. Name the query **SupplierList**, and then close the query.
9. Use the Form tool to create a form for the Supplier table. Save the form as **SupplierInfo**, and then close it.

10. Use the Report tool to create a report based on the Supplier table. In Layout view, resize all fields except the Company field, so that each field is slightly wider than the longest entry (either the field name itself or an entry in the field). Display the report in Print Preview and verify that all the fields fit across one page in the report. Save the report as **SupplierDetails**, and then close it.

11. Close the Supplier table, and then compact and repair the Vendor database.

12. Close the Vendor database.

Case Problem 1

Data File needed for this Case Problem: BeautyToGo.accdb

Beauty To Go Sue Miller, an owner of a nail and hair salon in Orlando, Florida, regularly checks in on her grandmother, who resides in a retirement community. On some of her visits, Sue does her grandmother's hair and nails. Her grandmother recently asked if Sue would also be willing to do the hair and nails of some of her friends in her retirement community and other surrounding communities. She said that these friends would happily pay for her services. Sue thinks this is an excellent way to expand her current business and serve the needs of the retirement community at the same time. In discussing the opportunity with some of the members of the retirement community, she found that the ladies would very much like to pay Sue in advance for her services and have them scheduled on a regular basis; however, the frequency and types of the services vary from person to person. Sue decides to come up with different options that would serve the needs of the ladies in the retirement community. Sue wants to use Access to maintain information about the customers and the types of options offered. She needs your help in creating this database. Complete the following:

1. Create a new, blank database named **Beauty** and save it in the folder where you are storing your files, as specified by your instructor.

2. In Datasheet view for the Table1 table, rename the default primary key ID field to **OptionID**. Change the data type of the OptionID field to Short Text.

3. Add the following three fields to the new table in the order shown: **OptionDescription** (a Short Text field), **OptionCost** (a Currency field), and **FeeWaived** (a Yes/No field). Save the table as **Option**.

4. Enter the records shown in Figure 1-32 in the Option table. *Hint*: When entering the OptionCost field values, you do not have to type the dollar signs, commas, or decimal places; they will be entered automatically.

Figure 1-32 Option table records

when entering currency values, you do not have to type the dollar signs, commas, or decimal places

OptionID	OptionDescription	OptionCost	FeeWaived
136	Wash/cut bi-weekly for 6 months	$500.00	Yes
101	Manicure weekly for 1 month	$125.00	No
124	Manicure/pedicure weekly for 3 months	$700.00	Yes
142	Wash/cut/color monthly for 6 months	$600.00	Yes
117	Pedicure bi-weekly for 3 months	$190.00	No

5. Sue created a database named BeautyToGo that contains a MoreOptions table with plan data. The Option table you created has the same design as the MoreOptions table. Copy all the records from the **MoreOptions** table in the **BeautyToGo** database (located in the Access1 > Case1 folder provided with your Data Files), and then paste them at the end of the Option table in the Beauty database.

6. Resize all datasheet columns to their best fit, and then save the Option table.

7. Close the Option table, and then use the Navigation Pane to reopen it. Note that the records are displayed in primary key order by the values in the OptionID field.

8. Use the Simple Query Wizard to create a query that includes the OptionID, OptionDescription, and OptionCost fields from the Option table. In the second Simple Query Wizard dialog box, select the Detail option if necessary. (This option appears because the query includes a Currency field.) Save the query as **OptionData**, and then close the query.

9. Use the Form tool to create a form for the Option table. Save the form as **OptionInfo**, and then close it.

10. Use the Report tool to create a report based on the Option table. In Layout view, resize the OptionID field so it is slightly wider than the longest entry, which is the field name in this case. Resize the OptionDescription field so there are no entries with multiple lines. Also, resize the box containing the total amount that appears below the OptionCost column by clicking the box and then dragging its bottom border down so that the amount is fully displayed. (The Report Tool calculated this total automatically.) Display the report in Print Preview; then verify that all the fields are within the page area and all field values are fully displayed. Save the report as **OptionList**, print the report (only if asked by your instructor to do so), and then close it.

11. Close the Option table, and then compact and repair the Beauty database.

12. Close the Beauty database.

APPLY

Case Problem 2

Data File needed for this Case Problem: ProgPros.accdb

Programming Pros   While in college obtaining his bachelor's degree in Raleigh, North Carolina, Brent Hovis majored in computer science and learned programming. Brent found that many of his fellow classmates found it difficult to write code, and he was constantly assisting them with helpful tips and techniques. Prior to graduating, Brent began tutoring freshman and sophomore students in programming to make some extra money. As his reputation grew, high school students began contacting him for help with their programming classes. When Brent entered graduate school, he started Programming Pros, a company offering expanded tutoring service for high school and college students through group, private, and semi-private tutoring sessions. As demand for the company's services grew, Brent hired many of his fellow classmates to assist him. Brent wants to use Access to maintain information about the tutors who work for him, the students who sign up for tutoring, and the contracts they sign. He needs your help in creating this database. Complete the following steps:

1. Create a new, blank database named **Programming** and save it in the folder where you are storing your files, as specified by your instructor.

2. In Datasheet view for the Table1 table, rename the default primary key ID field to **TutorID**. Change the data type of the TutorID field to Short Text.

3. Add the following five fields to the new table in the order shown; all of them are Short Text fields *except* HireDate, which is a Date/Time field: **FirstName**, **LastName**, **Major**, **YearInSchool**, **School**, and **HireDate**. Resize the columns, if necessary, so that the complete field names are displayed. Save the table as **Tutor**.

4. Enter the records shown in Figure 1-33 in the Tutor table. For the first record, be sure to enter your first name in the FirstName field and your last name in the LastName field.

Figure 1-33   Tutor table records

TutorID	FirstName	LastName	Major	YearInSchool	School	HireDate
1060	*Student First*	*Student Last*	Computer Science	Senior	Ellings College	2/14/2017
1010	Cathy	Cowler	Computer Engineering	Graduate	Eikenville College	2/1/2017
1051	Donald	Gallager	Computer Science	Graduate	Hogan University	1/18/2017
1031	Nichole	Schneider	Computer Science	Junior	Switzer University	2/28/2017
1018	Fredrik	Karlsson	Mechatronics	Junior	Smith Technical College	2/6/2017

5. Brent created a database named ProgPros that contains a MoreTutors table with tutor data. The Tutor table you created has the same design as the MoreTutors table. Copy all the records from the **MoreTutors** table in the **ProgPros** database (located in the Access1 > Case2 folder provided with your Data Files), and then paste them at the end of the Tutor table in the Programming database.

6. Resize all datasheet columns to their best fit, and then save the Tutor table.

7. Close the Tutor table, and then use the Navigation Pane to reopen it. Note that the records are displayed in primary key order by the values in the TutorID field.

8. Use the Simple Query Wizard to create a query that includes the FirstName, LastName, and HireDate fields from the Tutor table. Save the query as **StartDate**, and then close the query.

9. Use the Form tool to create a form for the Tutor table. Save the form as **TutorInfo**, and then close it.

10. Use the Report tool to create a report based on the Tutor table. In Layout view, resize the TutorID, FirstName, LastName, Major, YearInSchool, School, and HireDate fields so they are slightly wider than the longest entry (either the field name itself or an entry in the field). All seven fields should fit within the page area after you resize the fields. At the bottom of the report, move the text "Page 1 of 1" to the left so it is within the page area. Display the report in Print Preview; then verify that the fields and page number fit within the page area and that all field values are fully displayed. Save the report as **TutorList**, print the report (only if asked by your instructor to do so), and then close it.

11. Close the Tutor table, and then compact and repair the Programming database.

12. Close the Programming database.

Case Problem 3

CHALLENGE

Data File needed for this Case Problem: Diane.accdb

Diane's Community Center   Diane Coleman is a successful businesswoman in Dallas, Georgia, but things were not always that way. Diane experienced trying times and fortunately had people in the community come into her life to assist her and her children when times were difficult. Diane now wants to give back to her community and support those in need, just as she was supported many years ago, by creating a community center in Dallas where those in need can come in for goods and services. Diane plans to open a thrift store as well to sell donated items to support the center. Diane has been contacted by many people in the community wishing to donate materials to the center as well as items to be sold at the thrift store. Diane has asked you to create an Access database to manage information about the center's patrons and donations. Complete the following steps:

1. Create a new, blank database named **Center** and save it in the folder where you are storing your files, as specified by your instructor.

2. In Datasheet view for the Table1 table, rename the default primary key ID field to **PatronID**. Change the data type of the PatronID field to Short Text.

3. Add the following five Short Text fields to the new table in the order shown: **Title**, **FirstName**, **LastName**, **Phone**, and **Email**. Save the table as **Patron**.

4. Enter the records shown in Figure 1-34 in the Patron table. For the first record, be sure to enter your title in the Title field, your first name in the FirstName field, and your last name in the LastName field.

Figure 1-34   **Patron table records**

PatronID	Title	FirstName	LastName	Phone	Email
3001	*Student Title*	*Student First*	*Student Last*	404-987-1234	student@example.com
3030	Mr.	David	Hampton	404-824-3381	thehamptons@example.net
3006	Dr.	Elbert	Schneider	678-492-9101	countrydoc@example.com
3041	Mr.	Frank	Miller	404-824-3431	frankmiller12@example.net
3019	Mrs.	Jane	Michaels	706-489-3310	jjmichaels@example.com

5. Diane created a database named Diane that contains a MorePatrons table with data about additional patrons. The Patron table you created has the same design as the MorePatrons table. Copy all the records from the **MorePatrons** table in the **Diane** database (located in the Access1 > Case3 folder provided with your Data Files), and then paste them at the end of the Patron table in the Center database.

6. Resize all datasheet columns to their best fit, and then save the Patron table.

7. Close the Patron table, and then use the Navigation Pane to reopen it. Note that the records are displayed in primary key order by the values in the PatronID field.

✦ **Explore** 8. Use the Simple Query Wizard to create a query that includes all the fields in the Patron table *except* the Title field. (*Hint*: Use the [>>] and [<] buttons to select the necessary fields.) Save the query using the name **PatronContactList**.

✦ **Explore** 9. The query results are displayed in order by the PatronID field values. You can specify a different order by sorting the query. Display the Home tab. Then, click the insertion point anywhere in the LastName column to make it the current field. In the Sort & Filter group on the Home tab, click the Ascending button. The records are now listed in order by the values in the LastName field. Save and close the query.

✦ **Explore** 10. Use the Form tool to create a form for the Patron table. In the new form, navigate to record 13 (the record with PatronID 3028), and then print the form *for the current record only*. (*Hint*: You must use the Print dialog box in order to print only the current record. Go to Backstage view, click Print in the navigation bar, and then click Print to open the Print dialog box. Click the Selected Record(s) option button, and then click the OK button to print the current record.) Save the form as **PatronInfo**, and then close it.

11. Use the Report tool to create a report based on the Patron table. In Layout view, resize each field so it is slightly wider than the longest entry (either the field name itself or an entry in the field). All six fields should fit within the page area after resizing. At the bottom of the report, move the text "Page 1 of 1" to the left so it is within the page area. Display the report in Print Preview, then verify that the fields and page number fit within the page area and that all field values are fully displayed. Save the report as **PatronList**. Print the report (only if asked by your instructor to do so), and then close it.

12. Close the Patron table, and then compact and repair the Center database.

13. Close the Center database.

Case Problem 4

CHALLENGE

Data File needed for this Case Problem: HikeApp.accdb

Hike Appalachia   Molly and Bailey Johnson grew up in the Blue Ridge Mountains of North Carolina. Their parents were avid outdoors people and loved to take the family on long hikes and teach the girls about the great outdoors. During middle school and high school, their friends would ask them to guide them in the surrounding area because it could be quite dangerous. One summer, the girls had an idea to expand their hiking clientele beyond their friends and help earn money for college; this was the start of their business, which they named Hike Appalachia. The girls advertised in local and regional outdoor magazines and were flooded with requests from people all around the region. They would like you to build an Access database to manage information about the hikers they guide, the tours they provide, and tour reservations. Complete the following:

1. Create a new, blank database named **Appalachia** and save it in the folder where you are storing your files, as specified by your instructor.

2. In Datasheet view for the Table1 table, rename the default primary key ID field to **HikerID**. Change the data type of the HikerID field to Short Text.

3. Add the following seven Short Text fields to the new table in the order shown: **HikerFirst**, **HikerLast**, **Address**, **City**, **State**, **Zip**, and **Phone**. Save the table as **Hiker**.

4. Enter the records shown in Figure 1-35 in the Hiker table. For the first record, be sure to enter your first name in the HikerFirst field and your last name in the HikerLast field.

Figure 1-35 **Hiker table records**

HikerID	HikerFirst	HikerLast	Address	City	State	Zip	Phone
501	*Student First*	*Student Last*	123 Jackson St	Boone	NC	28607	828-497-9128
547	Heather	Smith	412 Sentry Ln	Gastonia	NC	28052	704-998-0987
521	Zack	Hoskins	2 Hope Rd	Atlanta	GA	30301	404-998-2381
535	Elmer	Jackson	99 River Rd	Blacksburg	SC	29702	864-921-2384
509	Sarah	Peeler	32 Mountain Ln	Ridgeview	WV	25169	703-456-9381

5. Molly and Bailey created a database named HikeApp that contains a MoreHikers table with data about hikers. The Hiker table you created has the same design as the MoreHikers table. Copy all the records from the **MoreHikers** table in the **HikeApp** database (located in the Access1 > Case4 folder provided with your Data Files), and then paste them at the end of the Hiker table in the Appalachia database.

6. Resize all datasheet columns to their best fit, and then save the Hiker table.

7. Close the Hiker table, and then use the Navigation Pane to reopen it. Note that the records are displayed in primary key order.

8. Use the Simple Query Wizard to create a query that includes the following fields from the Hiker table, in the order shown: HikerID, HikerLast, HikerFirst, State, and Phone. Name the query **HikerData**.

⊕ **Explore** 9. The query results are displayed in order by the HikerID field values. You can specify a different order by sorting the query. Display the Home tab. Then, click the insertion point anywhere in the State column to make it the current field. In the Sort & Filter group on the Home tab, click the Ascending button. The records are now listed in order by the values in the State field. Save and close the query.

⊕ **Explore** 10. Use the Form tool to create a form for the Hiker table. In the new form, navigate to record 10 (the record with HikerID 527), and then print the form *for the current record only*. (*Hint*: You must use the Print dialog box in order to print only the current record. Go to Backstage view, click Print in the navigation bar, and then click Print to open the Print dialog box. Click the Selected Record(s) option button, and then click the OK button to print the current record.) Save the form as **HikerInfo**, and then close it.

11. Use the Report tool to create a report based on the Hiker table. In Layout view, resize each field so it is slightly wider than the longest entry (either the field name itself or an entry in the field). At the bottom of the report, move the text "Page 1 of 1" to the left so it is within the page area on the report's first page. All fields should fit on one page. Save the report as **HikerList**.

12. Print the report (only if asked by your instructor to do so), and then close it.

    a. Close the Hiker table, and then compact and repair the Appalachia database.

    b. Close the Appalachia database.

OBJECTIVES

Session 2.1
- Learn the guidelines for designing databases and setting field properties
- Create a table in Design view
- Define fields, set field properties, and specify a table's primary key
- Modify the structure of a table
- Change the order of fields in Design view
- Add new fields in Design view
- Change the Format property for a field in Datasheet view
- Modify field properties in Design view

Session 2.2
- Import data from Excel
- Import an existing table structure
- Add fields to a table with the Data Type gallery
- Delete and rename fields
- Change the data type for a field in Design view
- Set the Default Value property for a field
- Import a text file
- Define a relationship between two tables

Building a Database and Defining Table Relationships

Creating the Billing, Owner, and Animal Tables

ACCESS

Case | *Riverview Veterinary Care Center*

The Riverview database currently contains one table, the Visit table. Kimberly Johnson also wants to track information about the clinic's animals, their owners, and the invoices sent to them for services provided by Riverview Veterinary Care Center. This information includes such items as each owner's name and address, animal information, and the amount and billing date for each invoice.

In this module, you'll create three new tables in the Riverview database—named Billing, Owner, and Animal—to contain the additional data Kimberly wants to track. You will use two different methods for creating the tables, and learn how to modify the fields. After adding records to the tables, you will define the necessary relationships between the tables in the Riverview database to relate the tables, enabling Kimberly and her staff to work with the data more efficiently.

STARTING DATA FILES

Access1 ➔ **Module**

AllAnimals.accdb
Invoices.xlsx
Kelly.accdb
Owner.txt
Riverview.accdb (*cont.*)

Review

Supplies.xlsx
Vendor.accdb (*cont.*)

Case1

Beauty.accdb (*cont.*)
Customers.txt

Case2

Agreements.xlsx
Client.accdb
Programming.accdb (*cont.*)
Students.txt

Case3

Auctions.txt
Center.accdb (*cont.*)
Donations.xlsx

Case4

Appalachia.accdb (*cont.*)
Bookings.txt
Travel.accdb

Session 2.1 Visual Overview:

Design view allows you to define or modify a table structure or the properties of the fields in a table.

The default name for a new table you create in Design view is Table1. This name appears on the tab for the new table.

The top portion of the Table window in Design view is called the **Table Design grid**. Here, you enter values for the Field Name, Data type, and Description field properties.

In the Field Name column, you enter the name for each new field in the table. When you first open a new Table window in Design view, Field Name is the current property.

In the Data Type column, you select the appropriate data type for each new field in the table. The data type determines what field values you can enter for a new field and what other properties the field will have. The default data type for a new field is Short Text.

After you assign a data type to a field, the General tab displays additional field properties for that data type. Initially, most field properties are assigned default values.

When defining the fields in a table, you can move from the Table Design grid to the Field Properties pane by pressing the **F6 key**.

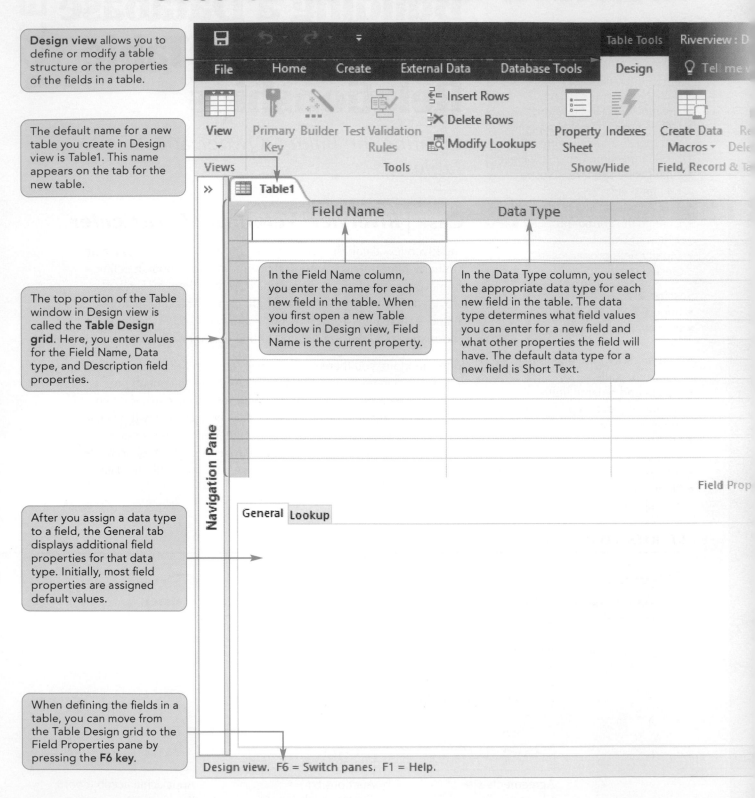

Table Window in Design View

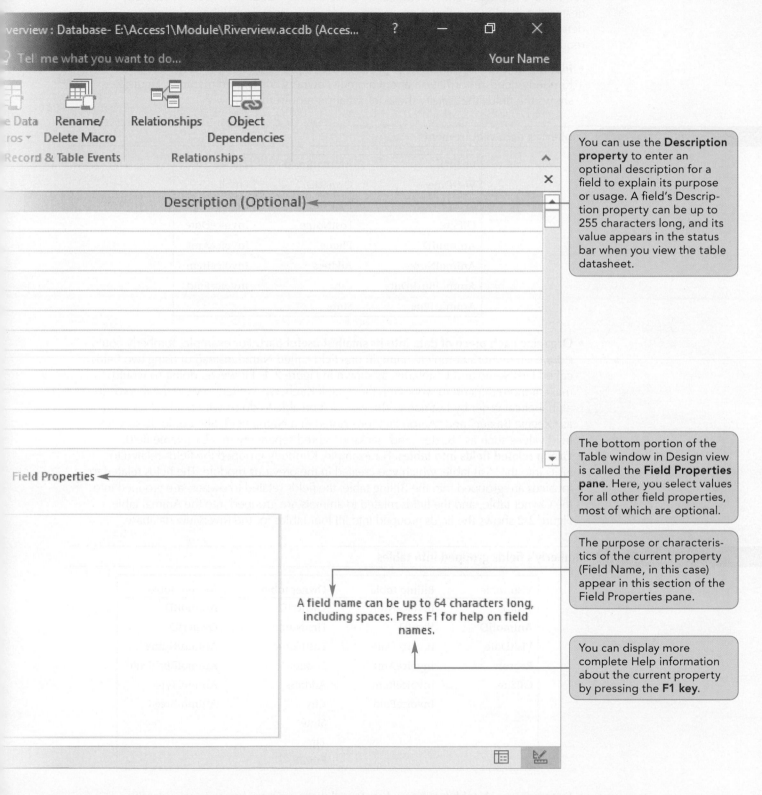

Riverview : Database- E:\Access1\Module\Riverview.accdb (Acces...   ?   —   □   ✕

Tell me what you want to do...   Your Name

Data   Rename/   Relationships   Object
ros ▾   Delete Macro   Dependencies
Record & Table Events   Relationships

Description (Optional)

Field Properties

A field name can be up to 64 characters long,
including spaces. Press F1 for help on field
names.

You can use the **Description property** to enter an optional description for a field to explain its purpose or usage. A field's Description property can be up to 255 characters long, and its value appears in the status bar when you view the table datasheet.

The bottom portion of the Table window in Design view is called the **Field Properties pane**. Here, you select values for all other field properties, most of which are optional.

The purpose or characteristics of the current property (Field Name, in this case) appear in this section of the Field Properties pane.

You can display more complete Help information about the current property by pressing the **F1 key**.

Guidelines for Designing Databases

A database management system can be a useful tool, but only if you first carefully design the database so that it meets the needs of its users. In database design, you determine the fields, tables, and relationships needed to satisfy the data and processing requirements. When you design a database, you should follow these guidelines:

- **Identify all the fields needed to produce the required information.** For example, Kimberly needs information about animals, owners, visits, and invoices. Figure 2-1 shows the fields that satisfy these information requirements.

Figure 2-1	Kimberly's data requirements

VisitID	AnimalBreed	Zip
VisitDate	OwnerID	Email
Reason	FirstName	InvoiceNum
OffSite	LastName	InvoiceDate
AnimalID	Phone	InvoiceAmt
AnimalName	Address	InvoiceItem
AnimalBirthDate	City	InvoicePaid
AnimalType	State	

- **Organize each piece of data into its smallest useful part.** For example, Kimberly could store each owner's complete name in one field called Name instead of using two fields called FirstName and LastName, as shown in Figure 2-1. However, doing so would make it more difficult to work with the data. If Kimberly wanted to view the records in alphabetical order by last name, she wouldn't be able to do so with field values such as "Reggie Baxter" and "Aaron Jackson" stored in a Name field. She could do so with field values such as "Baxter" and "Jackson" stored separately in a LastName field.
- **Group related fields into tables.** For example, Kimberly grouped the fields related to visits into the Visit table, which you created in the previous module. The fields related to invoices are grouped into the Billing table, the fields related to owners are grouped into the Owner table, and the fields related to animals are grouped into the Animal table. Figure 2-2 shows the fields grouped into all four tables for the Riverview database.

Figure 2-2	Kimberly's fields grouped into tables

Visit table	Billing table	Owner table	Animal table
VisitID	InvoiceNum	OwnerID	AnimalID
AnimalID	VisitID	FirstName	OwnerID
VisitDate	InvoiceDate	LastName	AnimalName
Reason	InvoiceAmt	Phone	AnimalBirthDate
OffSite	InvoiceItem	Address	AnimalType
	InvoicePaid	City	AnimalBreed
		State	
		Zip	
		Email	

- **Determine each table's primary key.** Recall that a primary key uniquely identifies each record in a table. For some tables, one of the fields, such as a credit card number, naturally serves the function of a primary key. For other tables, two or more fields might be needed to function as the primary key. In these cases, the primary key is called a **composite key.** For example, a school grade table would use a combination of student number, term, and course code to serve as the primary key. For a third category of tables, no single field or combination of fields can uniquely identify a record in a table. In these cases, you need to add a field whose sole purpose is to serve as the table's primary key. For Kimberly's tables, VisitID is the primary key for the Visit table, InvoiceNum is the primary key for the Billing table, OwnerID is the primary key for the Owner table, and AnimalID is the primary key for the Animal table.

- **Include a common field in related tables.** You use the common field to connect one table logically with another table. For example, Kimberly's Visit and Animal tables include the AnimalID field as a common field. Recall that when you include the primary key from one table as a field in a second table to form a relationship, the field in the second table is called a foreign key; therefore, the AnimalID field is a foreign key in the Visit table. With this common field, Kimberly can find all visits to the clinic made by a particular animal; she can use the AnimalID value for an animal and search the Visit table for all records with that AnimalID value. Likewise, she can determine which animal made a particular visit by searching the Animal table to find the one record with the same AnimalID value as the corresponding value in the Visit table. Similarly, the VisitID field is a common field, serving as the primary key in the Visit table and a foreign key in the Billing table. Since animals have owners responsible for their bills, there must be a relationship between the animals and owners for the clinic to contact; therefore, the OwnerID field is a foreign key in the Animal table.

- **Avoid data redundancy.** When you store the same data in more than one place, **data redundancy** occurs. With the exception of common fields to connect tables, you should avoid data redundancy because it wastes storage space and can cause inconsistencies. An inconsistency would exist, for example, if you type a field value one way in one table and a different way in the same table or in a second table. Figure 2-3, which contains portions of potential data stored in the Animal and Visit tables, shows an example of incorrect database design that has data redundancy in the Visit table. In Figure 2-3, the AnimalName field in the Visit table is redundant, and one value for this field was entered incorrectly, in three different ways.

Figure 2-3	Incorrect database design with data redundancy

AnimalID	AnimalName	AnimalBirthDate	AnimalType
12286	Lady	8/12/2015	Dog
12304	Tweets	11/12/2010	Bird
12332	Smittie	5/19/2014	Cat
12345	Herford5	4/28/2015	Cattle
12359	Merino4	8/2/2014	Sheep

data redundancy

VisitID	AnimalID	AnimalName	VisitDate	OffSite
1202	12500	Bonkers	12/11/2016	No
1250	12332	Smitty	12/19/2016	No
1276	12492	Bessie	1/10/2017	Yes
1308	12332	Smity	1/23/2017	No
1325	12612	Tweets	2/6/2017	No
1342	12595	Angus	2/27/2017	Yes
1367	12332	Smittee	3/7/2017	No

Inconsistent data

- **Determine the properties of each field.** You need to identify the **properties**, or characteristics, of each field so that the DBMS knows how to store, display, and process the field values. These properties include the field's name, data type, maximum number of characters or digits, description, valid values, and other field characteristics. You will learn more about field properties later in this module.

The Billing, Owner, and Animal tables you need to create will contain the fields shown in Figure 2-2. Before creating these new tables in the Riverview database, you first need to learn some guidelines for setting field properties.

Guidelines for Setting Field Properties

As just noted, the last step of database design is to determine which values to assign to the properties, such as the name and data type, of each field. When you select or enter a value for a property, you **set** the property. Access has rules for naming fields and objects, assigning data types, and setting other field properties.

Naming Fields and Objects

You must name each field, table, and other object in an Access database. Access stores these items in the database, using the names you supply. It's best to choose a field or object name that describes the purpose or contents of the field or object so that later you can easily remember what the name represents. For example, the four tables in the Riverview database are named Visit, Billing, Owner, and Animal because these names suggest their contents. Note that a table or query name must be unique within a database. A field name must be unique within a table, but it can be used again in another table.

Assigning Field Data Types

Each field must have a data type, which is either assigned automatically by Access or specifically by the table designer. The data type determines what field values you can enter for the field and what other properties the field will have. For example, the Billing table will include an InvoiceDate field, which will store date values, so you will assign the Date/Time data type to this field. Then Access will allow you to enter and manipulate only dates or times as values in the InvoiceDate field.

Figure 2-4 lists the most commonly used data types in Access, describes the field values allowed for each data type, explains when you should use each data type, and indicates the field size of each data type. You can find more complete information about all available data types in Access Help.

| Figure 2-4 | Common data types |

Data Type	Description	Field Size
Short Text	Allows field values containing letters, digits, spaces, and special characters. Use for names, addresses, descriptions, and fields containing digits that are *not used in calculations*.	0 to 255 characters; default is 255
Long Text	Allows field values containing letters, digits, spaces, and special characters. Use for long comments and explanations.	1 to 65,535 characters; exact size is determined by entry
Number	Allows positive and negative numbers as field values. A number can contain digits, a decimal point, commas, a plus sign, and a minus sign. Use for fields that will be used in calculations, except those involving money.	1 to 15 digits
Date/Time	Allows field values containing valid dates and times from January 1, 100 to December 31, 9999. Dates can be entered in month/day/year format, several other date formats, or a variety of time formats, such as 10:35 PM. You can perform calculations on dates and times, and you can sort them. For example, you can determine the number of days between two dates.	8 bytes
Currency	Allows field values similar to those for the Number data type, but is used for storing monetary values. Unlike calculations with Number data type decimal values, calculations performed with the Currency data type are not subject to round-off error.	Accurate to 15 digits on the left side of the decimal point and to 4 digits on the right side
AutoNumber	Consists of integer values created automatically by Access each time you create a new record. You can specify sequential numbering or random numbering, which guarantees a unique field value, so that such a field can serve as a table's primary key.	9 digits
Yes/No	Limits field values to yes and no, on and off, or true and false. Use for fields that indicate the presence or absence of a condition, such as whether an order has been filled or whether an invoice has been paid.	1 character
Hyperlink	Consists of text used as a hyperlink address, which can have up to four parts: the text that appears in a field or control; the path to a file or page; a location within the file or page; and text displayed as a ScreenTip.	Up to 65,535 characters total for the four parts of the hyperlink

Setting Field Sizes

The **Field Size property** defines a field value's maximum storage size for Short Text, Number, and AutoNumber fields only. The other data types have no Field Size property because their storage size is either a fixed, predetermined amount or is determined automatically by the field value itself, as shown in Figure 2-4. A Short Text field has a default field size of 255 characters; you can also set its field size by entering a number from 0 to 255. For example, the FirstName and LastName fields in the Owner table will be Short Text fields with sizes of 20 characters and 25 characters, respectively. These field sizes will accommodate the values that will be entered in each of these fields.

Decision Making: Specifying the Field Size Property for Number Fields

When you use the Number data type to define a field, you need to decide what the Field Size setting should be for the field. You should set the Field Size property based on the largest value that you expect to store in that field. Access processes smaller data sizes faster, using less memory, so you can optimize your database's performance and its storage space by selecting the correct field size for each field. Field Size property settings for Number fields are as follows:

• **Byte**: Stores whole numbers (numbers with no fractions) from 0 to 255 in one byte
• **Integer**: Stores whole numbers from –32,768 to 32,767 in two bytes
• **Long Integer** (default): Stores whole numbers from –2,147,483,648 to 2,147,483,647 in four bytes
• **Single**: Stores positive and negative numbers to precisely seven decimal places in four bytes
• **Double**: Stores positive and negative numbers to precisely 15 decimal places in eight bytes
• **Replication ID**: Establishes a unique identifier for replication of tables, records, and other objects in databases created using Access 2003 and earlier versions in 16 bytes
• **Decimal**: Stores positive and negative numbers to precisely 28 decimal places in 12 bytes

Choosing an appropriate field size is important to optimize efficiency. For example, it would be wasteful to use the Long Integer field size for a Number field that will store only whole numbers ranging from 0 to 255 because the Long Integer field size uses four bytes of storage space. A better choice would be the Byte field size, which uses one byte of storage space to store the same values. By first gathering and analyzing information about the number values that will be stored in a Number field, you can make the best decision for the field's Field Size property and ensure the most efficient user experience for the database.

Setting the Caption Property for Fields

The **Caption property** for a field specifies how the field name is displayed in database objects, including table and query datasheets, forms, and reports. If you don't set the Caption property, Access displays the field name as the column heading or label for a field. For example, field names such as InvoiceAmt and InvoiceDate in the Billing table can be difficult to read. Setting the Caption property for these fields to "Invoice Amt" and "Invoice Date" would make it easier for users to read the field names and work with the database.

Setting the Caption Property vs. Naming Fields

Although Access allows you to include spaces in field names, this practice is not recommended because the spaces cause problems when you try to perform more complex tasks with the data in your database. Setting the Caption property allows you to follow best practices for naming fields, such as not including spaces in field names, while still providing users with more readable field names in datasheets, forms, and reports.

In the previous module, you created the Riverview database file and, within that file, you created the Visit table working in Datasheet view. According to her plan for the Riverview database, Kimberly also wants to track information about the invoices the care center sends to the owners of the animals. Next, you'll create the Billing table for Kimberly—this time, working in Design view.

Creating a Table in Design View

Creating a table in Design view involves entering the field names and defining the properties for the fields, specifying a primary key for the table, and then saving the table structure. Kimberly documented the design for the new Billing table by listing each field's name and data type; each field's size and description (if applicable); and any other properties to be set for each field. See Figure 2-5.

| Figure 2-5 | Design for the Billing table |

Field Name	Data Type	Field Size	Description	Other
InvoiceNum	Short Text	5	Primary key	Caption = Invoice Num
VisitID	Short Text	4	Foreign key	Caption = Visit ID
InvoiceAmt	Currency			Format = Currency
				Decimal Places = 2
				Caption = Invoice Amt
InvoiceDate	Date/Time			Format = mm/dd/yyyy
				Caption = Invoice Date
InvoicePaid	Yes/No			Caption = Invoice Paid

You'll use Kimberly's design as a guide for creating the Billing table in the Riverview database.

To begin creating the Billing table:

1. Start Access and open the **Riverview** database you created in the previous module.

   Trouble? If the security warning is displayed below the ribbon, click the **Enable Content** button.

2. If the Navigation Pane is open, click the **Shutter Bar Open/Close Button** « to close it.

3. On the ribbon, click the **Create** tab.

4. In the Tables group, click the **Table Design** button. A new table named Table1 opens in Design view. Refer to the Session 2.1 Visual Overview for a complete description of the Table window in Design view.

Defining Fields

When you first create a table in Design view, the insertion point is located in the first row's Field Name box, ready for you to begin defining the first field in the table. You enter values for the Field Name, Data Type, and Description field properties, and then select values for all other field properties in the Field Properties pane. These other properties will appear when you move to the first row's Data Type box.

REFERENCE

Defining a Field in Design View

- In the Field Name box, type the name for the field, and then press the Tab key.
- Accept the default Short Text data type, or click the arrow and select a different data type for the field. Press the Tab key.
- Enter an optional description for the field, if necessary.
- Use the Field Properties pane to type or select other field properties, as appropriate.

The first field you need to define is the InvoiceNum field. This field will be the primary key for the Billing table. Each invoice at Riverview Veterinary Care Center is assigned a specific five-digit number. Although the InvoiceNum field will contain these number values, the numbers will never be used in calculations; therefore, you'll assign the Short Text data type to this field. Any time a field contains number values that will not be used in calculations—such as phone numbers, zip codes, and so on—you should use the Short Text data type instead of the Number data type.

To define the InvoiceNum field:

TIP

You can also press the Enter key to move from one property to the next in the Table Design grid.

1. Type **InvoiceNum** in the first row's Field Name box, and then press the **Tab** key to advance to the Data Type box. The default data type, Short Text, is selected in the Data Type box, which now also contains an arrow, and the field properties for a Short Text field appear in the Field Properties pane. See Figure 2-6.

Figure 2-6 Table window after entering the first field name

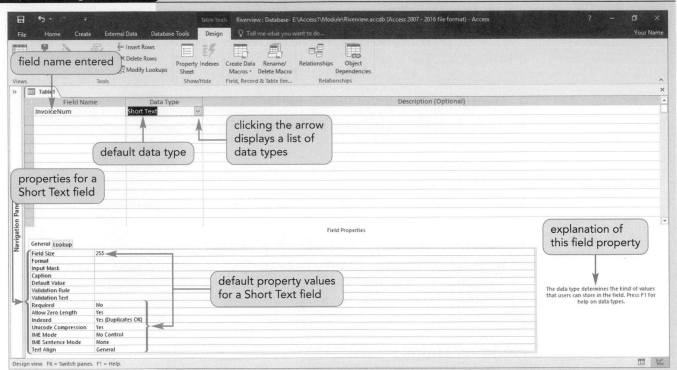

Notice that the right side of the Field Properties pane now provides an explanation for the current property, Data Type.

Trouble? If you make a typing error, you can correct it by clicking to position the insertion point, and then using either the Backspace key to delete characters to the left of the insertion point or the Delete key to delete characters to the right of the insertion point. Then type the correct text.

Because the InvoiceNum field values will not be used in calculations, you will accept the default Short Text data type for the field.

2. Press the **Tab** key to accept Short Text as the data type and to advance to the Description (Optional) box.

3. Next you'll enter the Description property value as "Primary key." The value you enter for the Description property will appear in the status bar when you view the table datasheet. Note that specifying "Primary key" for the Description property does *not* establish the current field as the primary key; you use a button on the ribbon to specify the primary key in Design view, which you will do later in this session.

4. Type **Primary key** in the Description (Optional) box.

    Notice the Field Size property for the field. The default setting of 255 for Short Text fields is displayed. You need to change this number to 5 because all invoice numbers at Riverview Veterinary Care Center contain only five digits.

5. Double-click the number **255** in the Field Size property box to select it, and then type **5**.

    Finally, you need to set the Caption property for the field so that its name appears with a space, as "Invoice Num."

6. Click the **Caption** property box, and then type **Invoice Num**. The definition of the first field is complete. See Figure 2-7.

Figure 2-7   **InvoiceNum field defined**

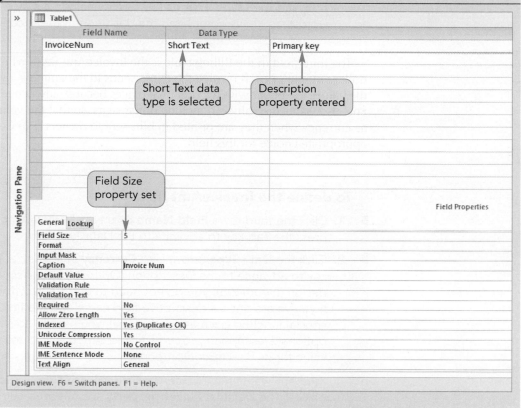

Kimberly's Billing table design (Figure 2-5) shows VisitID as the second field. Because Kimberly and other staff members need to relate information about invoices to the visit data in the Visit table, the Billing table must include the VisitID field, which is the Visit table's primary key. Recall that when you include the primary key from one table as a field in a second table to connect the two tables, the field is a foreign key in the second table. The field must be defined in the same way in both tables—that is, the field properties, including field size and data type, must match exactly.

Next, you will define VisitID as a Short Text field with a field size of 4. Later in this session, you'll change the Field Size property for the VisitID field in the Visit table to 4 so that the field definition is the same in both tables.

To define the VisitID field:

▶ **1.** In the Table Design grid, click the second row's **Field Name** box, type **VisitID**, and then press the **Tab** key to advance to the Data Type box.

▶ **2.** Press the **Tab** key to accept Short Text as the field's data type. Because the VisitID field is a foreign key to the Visit table, you'll enter "Foreign key" in the Description (Optional) box to help users of the database understand the purpose of this field.

▶ **3.** Type **Foreign key** in the Description (Optional) box. Next, you'll change the Field Size property.

▶ **4.** Press the **F6** key to move to the Field Properties pane. The current entry for the Field Size property, 255, is selected.

▶ **5.** Type **4** to set the Field Size property. Finally, you need to set the Caption property for this field.

▶ **6.** Press the **Tab** key three times to position the insertion point in the Caption box, and then type **Visit ID** (be sure to include a space between the two words). You have completed the definition of the second field.

The third field in the Billing table is the InvoiceAmt field, which will display the dollar amount of each invoice the clinic sends to the animals' owners. Kimberly wants the values to appear with two decimal places because invoice amounts include cents. She also wants the values to include dollar signs, so that the values will be formatted as currency when they are printed in bills sent to owners. The Currency data type is the appropriate choice for this field.

To define the InvoiceAmt field:

▶ **1.** Click the third row's **Field Name** box, type **InvoiceAmt** in the box, and then press the **Tab** key to advance to the Data Type box.

▶ **2.** Click the **Data Type** arrow, click **Currency** in the list, and then press the **Tab** key to advance to the Description (Optional) box. According to Kimberly's design (Figure 2-5), you do not need to enter a description for this field. If you've assigned a descriptive field name and the field does not fulfill a special function (such as primary key), you usually do not enter a value for the optional Description property. InvoiceAmt is a field that does not require a value for its Description property.

Kimberly wants the InvoiceAmt field values to be displayed with two decimal places. The **Decimal Places property** specifies the number of decimal places that are displayed to the right of the decimal point.

3. In the Field Properties pane, click the **Decimal Places** box to position the insertion point there. An arrow appears on the right side of the Decimal Places box, which you can click to display a list of options.

4. Click the **Decimal Places** arrow, and then click **2** in the list to specify two decimal places for the InvoiceAmt field values.

5. Press the **Tab** key twice to position the insertion point in the Caption box, and then type **Invoice Amt**. The definition of the third field is now complete. Notice that the Format property is set to "Currency," which formats the values with dollar signs. See Figure 2-8.

| Figure 2-8 | Table window after defining the first three fields |

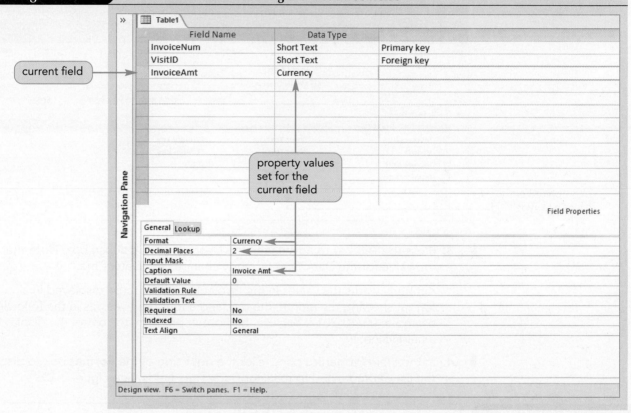

The fourth field in the Billing table is the InvoiceDate field. This field will contain the dates on which invoices are generated for the animals in the care center. You'll define the InvoiceDate field using the Date/Time data type. Also, according to Kimberly's design (Figure 2-5), the date values should be displayed in the format mm/dd/yyyy, which is a two-digit month, a two-digit day, and a four-digit year.

To define the InvoiceDate field:

1. Click the fourth row's **Field Name** box, type **InvoiceDate**, and then press the **Tab** key to advance to the Data Type box.

   You can select a value from the Data Type list as you did for the InvoiceAmt field. Alternately, you can type the property value in the box or type just the first character of the property value.

2. Type **d**. Access completes the entry for the fourth row's Data Type box to "date/Time," with the letters "ate/Time" selected. See Figure 2-9.

Figure 2-9 Selecting a value for the Data Type property

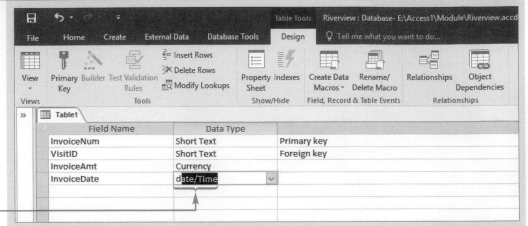

completed entry for Data Type

3. Press the **Tab** key to advance to the Description (Optional) box. Note that the value for the Data Type property changes to "Date/Time."

   Kimberly wants the values in the InvoiceDate field to be displayed in a format showing the month, the day, and a four-digit year, as in the following example: 03/10/2017. You use the Format property to control the display of a field value.

4. In the Field Properties pane, click the right side of the **Format** box to display the list of predefined formats for Date/Time fields. See Figure 2-10.

Figure 2-10 Displaying available formats for Date/Time fields

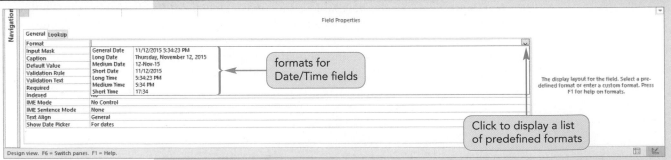

formats for Date/Time fields

Click to display a list of predefined formats

Trouble? If you see an arrow instead of a list of predefined formats, click the arrow to display the list.

As noted in the right side of the Field Properties pane, you can either choose a predefined format or enter a custom format. Even though the Short Date format seems to match the format Kimberly wants, it displays only one digit for months that contain only one digit. For example, it would display the month of March with only the digit "3"—as in 3/10/2017—instead of displaying the month with two digits, as in 03/10/2017.

Because none of the predefined formats matches the exact layout Kimberly wants for the InvoiceDate values, you need to create a custom date format. Figure 2-11 shows some of the symbols available for custom date and time formats.

Figure 2-11   **Symbols for some custom date formats**

Symbol	Description
/	date separator
d	day of the month in one or two numeric digits, as needed (1 to 31)
dd	day of the month in two numeric digits (01 to 31)
ddd	first three letters of the weekday (Sun to Sat)
dddd	full name of the weekday (Sunday to Saturday)
w	day of the week (1 to 7)
ww	week of the year (1 to 53)
m	month of the year in one or two numeric digits, as needed (1 to 12)
mm	month of the year in two numeric digits (01 to 12)
mmm	first three letters of the month (Jan to Dec)
mmmm	full name of the month (January to December)
yy	last two digits of the year (01 to 99)
yyyy	full year (0100 to 9999)

Kimberly wants the dates to be displayed with a two-digit month (mm), a two-digit day (dd), and a four-digit year (yyyy).

5. Click the **Format** arrow to close the list of predefined formats, and then type **mm/dd/yyyy** in the Format box.

6. Press the **Tab** key twice to position the insertion point in the Caption box, and then type **Invoice Date**. See Figure 2-12.

Figure 2-12 **Specifying the custom date format**

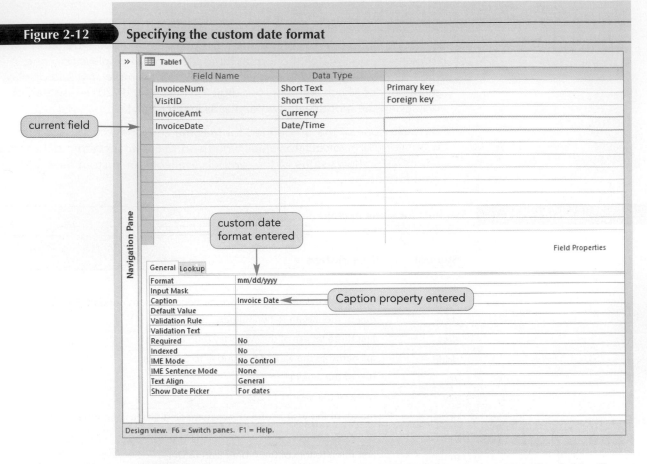

The fifth and final field to be defined in the Billing table is InvoicePaid. This field will be a Yes/No field to indicate the payment status of each invoice record stored in the Billing table. Recall that the Yes/No data type is used to define fields that store true/false, yes/no, and on/off field values. When you create a Yes/No field in a table, the default Format property is set to Yes/No.

To define the InvoicePaid field:

1. Click the fifth row's **Field Name** box, type **InvoicePaid**, and then press the **Tab** key to advance to the Data Type box.

2. Type **y**. Access completes the data type as "yes/No".

3. Press the **Tab** key to select the Yes/No data type and move to the Description (Optional) box. In the Field Properties pane, note that the default format of "Yes/No" is selected, so you do not have to change this property.

4. In the Field Properties pane, click the **Caption** box, and then type **Invoice Paid**.

You've finished defining the fields for the Billing table. Next, you need to specify the primary key for the table.

Specifying the Primary Key

As you learned earlier, the primary key for a table uniquely identifies each record in the table.

Specifying a Primary Key in Design View

- Display the table in Design view.
- Click in the row for the field you've chosen to be the primary key to make it the active field. If the primary key will consist of two or more fields, click the row selector for the first field, press and hold the Ctrl key, and then click the row selector for each additional primary key field.
- In the Tools group on the Table Tools Design tab, click the Primary Key button.

According to Kimberly's design, you need to specify InvoiceNum as the primary key for the Billing table. You can do so while the table is in Design view.

To specify InvoiceNum as the primary key:

1. Click in the row for the InvoiceNum field to make it the current field.

TIP

This button is a toggle; you can click it to remove the key symbol.

2. On the Table Tools Design tab, in the Tools group, click the **Primary Key** button. The Primary Key button in the Tools group is now selected, and a key symbol appears in the row selector for the first row, indicating that the InvoiceNum field is the table's primary key. See Figure 2-13.

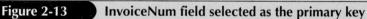

Figure 2-13   InvoiceNum field selected as the primary key

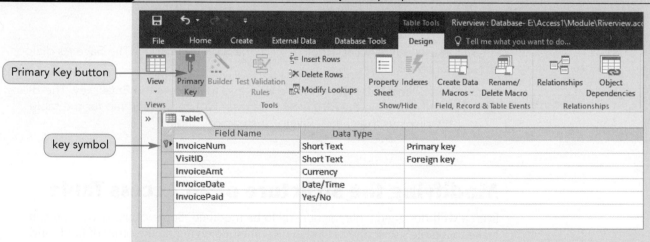

Primary Key button

key symbol

Understanding the Importance of the Primary Key

Although Access does not require a table to have a primary key, including a primary key offers several advantages:

- A primary key uniquely identifies each record in a table.
- Access does not allow duplicate values in the primary key field. For example, if a record already exists in the Visit table with a VisitID value of 1550, Access prevents you from adding another record with this same value in the VisitID field. Preventing duplicate values ensures the uniqueness of the primary key field.
- When a primary key has been specified, Access forces you to enter a value for the primary key field in every record in the table. This is known as **entity integrity**. If you do not enter a value for a field, you have actually given the field a **null value**. You cannot give a null value to the primary key field because entity integrity prevents Access from accepting and processing that record.
- You can enter records in any order, but Access displays them by default in order of the primary key's field values. If you enter records in no specific order, you are ensured that you will later be able to work with them in a more meaningful, primary key sequence.
- Access responds faster to your requests for specific records based on the primary key.

Saving the Table Structure

The last step in creating a table is to name the table and save the table's structure. When you save a table structure, the table is stored in the database file (in this case, the Riverview database file). Once the table is saved, you can enter data into it. According to Kimberly's plan, you need to save the table you've defined as "Billing."

To name and save the Billing table:

1. On the Quick Access Toolbar, click the **Save** button 🖫. The Save As dialog box opens.

2. Type **Billing** in the Table Name box, and then press the **Enter** key. The Billing table is saved in the Riverview database. Notice that the tab for the table now displays the name "Billing" instead of "Table1."

Modifying the Structure of an Access Table

Even a well-designed table might need to be modified. Some changes that you can make to a table's structure in Design view include changing the order of fields and adding new fields.

After meeting with her assistant, Kelly Flannagan, and reviewing the structure of the Billing table, Kimberly has changes she wants you to make to the table. First, she wants the InvoiceAmt field to be moved so that it appears right before the InvoicePaid field. Then, she wants you to add a new Short Text field named InvoiceItem to the table to include information about what the invoice is for, such as office visits, lab work, and so on. Kimberly would like the InvoiceItem field to be inserted between the InvoiceAmt and InvoicePaid fields.

Moving a Field in Design View

To move a field, you use the mouse to drag it to a new location in the Table Design grid. Although you can move a field in Datasheet view by dragging its column heading to a new location, doing so rearranges only the *display* of the table's fields; the table structure is not changed. To move a field permanently, you must move the field in Design view.

Next, you'll move the InvoiceAmt field so that it is before the InvoicePaid field in the Billing table.

To move the InvoiceAmt field:

1. Position the pointer on the row selector for the InvoiceAmt field until the pointer changes to ➡.

2. Click the **row selector** to select the entire InvoiceAmt row.

3. Place the pointer on the row selector for the InvoiceAmt field until the pointer changes to ⬚, press and hold the mouse button and then drag to the row selector for the InvoicePaid field. Notice that as you drag, the pointer changes to ⬚. See Figure 2-14.

Figure 2-14   Moving the InvoiceAmt field in the table structure

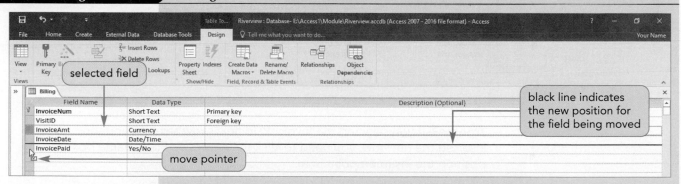

4. Release the mouse button. The InvoiceAmt field now appears between the InvoiceDate and InvoicePaid fields in the table structure.

   Trouble?   If the InvoiceAmt field did not move, repeat Steps 1 through 4, making sure you hold down the mouse button during the drag operation.

Adding a Field in Design View

To add a new field between existing fields, you must insert a row. You begin by selecting the row below where you want the new field to be inserted.

REFERENCE

Adding a Field Between Two Existing Fields

- In the Table window in Design view, select the row below where you want the new field to be inserted.
- In the Tools group on the Table Tools Design tab, click the Insert Rows button.
- Define the new field by entering the field name, data type, optional description, and any property specifications.

Next, you need to add the InvoiceItem field to the Billing table structure between the InvoiceAmt and InvoicePaid fields.

To add the InvoiceItem field to the Billing table:

▸ **1.** Click the **InvoicePaid Field Name** box. You need to establish this field as the current field so that the row for the new record will be inserted above this field.

▸ **2.** On the Table Tools Design tab, in the Tools group, click the **Insert Rows** button. A new, blank row is added between the InvoiceAmt and InvoicePaid fields. The insertion point is positioned in the Field Name box for the new row, ready for you to type the name for the new field. See Figure 2-15.

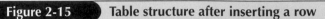

Figure 2-15 Table structure after inserting a row

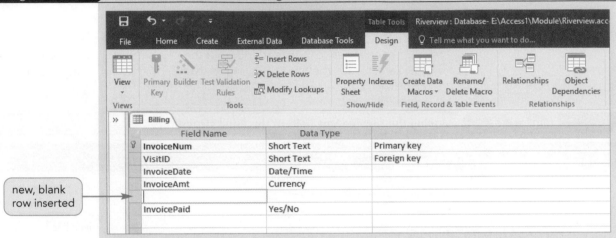

new, blank row inserted

Trouble? If you selected the InvoicePaid field's row selector and then inserted the new row, you need to click the new row's Field Name box to position the insertion point in it.

You'll define the InvoiceItem field in the new row of the Billing table. This field will be a Short Text field with a field size of 40, and you need to set the Caption property to include a space between the words in the field name.

▸ **3.** Type **InvoiceItem**, press the **Tab** key to move to the Data Type property, and then press the **Tab** key again to accept the default Short Text data type.

▸ **4.** Press the **F6** key to select the default field size in the Field Size box, and then type **40**.

▸ **5.** Press the **Tab** key three times to position the insertion point in the Caption box, and then type **Invoice Item**. The definition of the new field is complete. See Figure 2-16.

| Figure 2-16 | InvoiceItem field added to the Billing table |

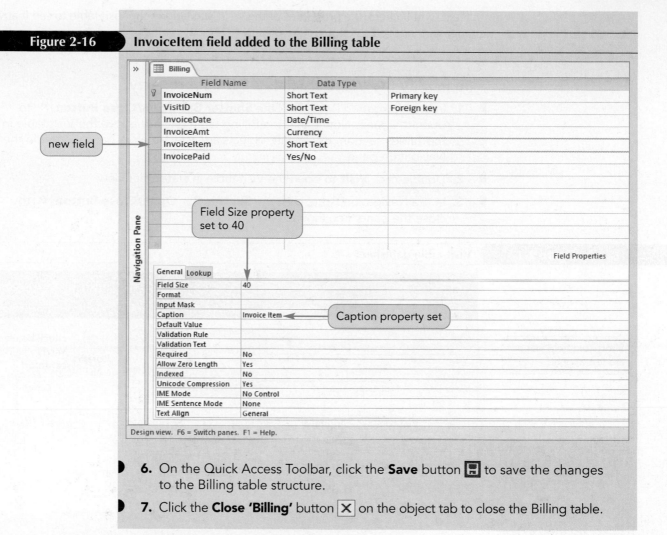

new field

Field Size property set to 40

Caption property set

6. On the Quick Access Toolbar, click the **Save** button 🖫 to save the changes to the Billing table structure.

7. Click the **Close 'Billing'** button ☒ on the object tab to close the Billing table.

Modifying Field Properties

With the Billing table design complete, you can now go back and modify the properties of the fields in the Visit table you created in the previous module, as necessary. You can make some changes to properties in Datasheet view; for others, you'll work in Design view.

Changing the Format Property in Datasheet View

The Formatting group on the Table Tools Fields tab in Datasheet view allows you to modify some formatting for certain field types. When you format a field, you change the way data is displayed, but not the actual values stored in the table.

Next, you'll check the properties of the VisitDate field in the Visit table to see if any changes are needed to improve the display of the date values.

To modify the VisitDate field's Format property:

1. In the Navigation Pane, click the **Shutter Bar Open/Close Button** ⟩⟩ to open the pane. Notice that the Billing table is listed above the Visit table in the Tables section. By default, objects are listed in alphabetical order in the Navigation pane.

2. Double-click **Visit** to open the Visit table in Datasheet view.

3. In the Navigation Pane, click the **Shutter Bar Open/Close Button** ⟨⟨ to close the pane. See Figure 2-17.

| Figure 2-17 | Visit table datasheet |

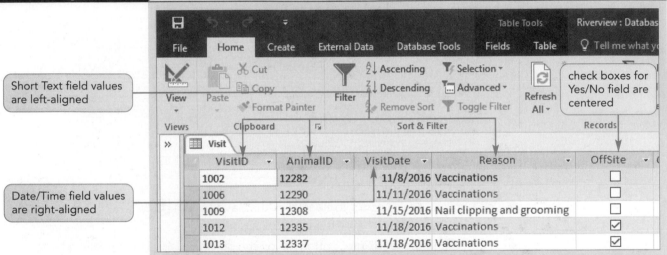

Short Text field values are left-aligned

Date/Time field values are right-aligned

check boxes for Yes/No field are centered

Notice that the values in the three Short Text fields—VisitID, AnimalID, and Reason—appear left-aligned within their boxes, and the values in the Date/Time field (VisitDate) appear right-aligned. In Access, values for Short Text fields are left-aligned, and values for Number, Date/Time, and Currency fields are right-aligned. The Offsite field is a Yes/No field, so its values appear in check boxes that are centered within the column.

4. On the ribbon, click the **Table Tools Fields** tab.

5. Click the **first field value** in the VisitDate column. The Data Type option shows that this field is a Date/Time field.

By default, Access assigns the General Date format to Date/Time fields. Note the Format box in the Formatting group, which you use to set the Format property (similar to how you set the Format property in the Field Properties pane in Design view.) Even though the Format box is empty, the VisitDate field has the General Date format applied to it. The General Date format includes settings for date or time values, or a combination of date and time values. However, Kimberly wants *only date values* to be displayed in the VisitDate field, so she asks you to specify the Short Date format for the field.

6. In the Formatting group, click the **Format** arrow, and then click **Short Date**. See Figure 2-18.

Figure 2-18   **VisitDate field after modifying the format**

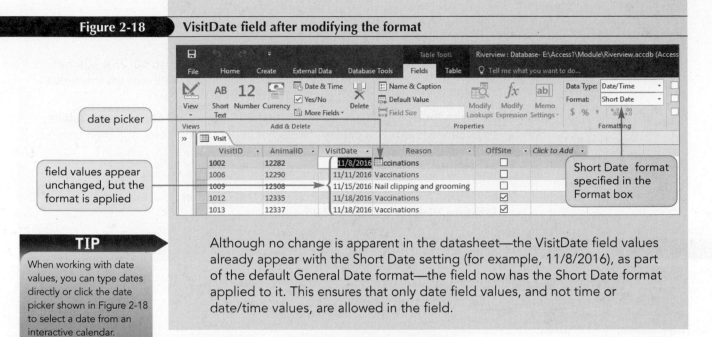

date picker

field values appear unchanged, but the format is applied

Short Date format specified in the Format box

TIP

When working with date values, you can type dates directly or click the date picker shown in Figure 2-18 to select a date from an interactive calendar.

Although no change is apparent in the datasheet—the VisitDate field values already appear with the Short Date setting (for example, 11/8/2016), as part of the default General Date format—the field now has the Short Date format applied to it. This ensures that only date field values, and not time or date/time values, are allowed in the field.

Changing Properties in Design View

Recall that each of the Short Text fields in the Visit table—VisitID, AnimalID, and Reason—still has the default field size of 255, which is too large for the data contained in these fields. Also, the VisitID and AnimalID fields need descriptions to identify them as the primary and foreign keys, respectively, in the table. Finally, each of these fields needs a caption either to include a space between the words in the field name or to make the name more descriptive. You can make all of these property changes more easily in Design view.

To modify the Field Size, Description, and Caption field properties:

TIP

You can also click the Design View button on the far right end of the status bar to switch to Design view.

1. On the Table Tools Fields tab, in the Views group, click the **View** button. The table is displayed in Design view with the VisitID field selected. You need to enter a Description property value for this field, the primary key in the table, and change its Field Size property to 4 because each visit number at Riverview Veterinary Care Center consists of four digits.

2. Press the **Tab** key twice to position the insertion point in the Description (Optional) box, and then type **Primary key**.

3. Press the **F6** key to move to and select the default setting of 255 in the Field Size box in the Fields Properties pane, and then type **4**. Next you need to set the Caption property for this field.

4. Press the **Tab** key three times to position the insertion point in the Caption box, and then type **Visit ID**.

   Next you need to enter a Description property value for the AnimalID field, a foreign key in the table, and set its Field Size property to 5 because each AnimalID number at Riverview Veterinary Care Center consists of five digits. You also need to set this field's Caption property.

5. Click the **VisitDate** Field Name box, click the **Caption** box, and then type **Date of Visit**.

For the Reason field, you will set the Field Size property to 60. This size can accommodate the longer values in the Reason field. You'll also set this field's Caption property to provide a more descriptive name.

6. Click the **Reason** Field Name box, press the **F6** key, type **60**, press the **Tab** key three times to position the insertion point in the Caption box, and then type **Reason/Diagnosis**.

Finally, you'll set the Caption property for the OffSite field.

7. Click the **OffSite** Field Name box, click the **Caption** box, and then type **Off-Site Visit?**. See Figure 2-19.

Figure 2-19	Visit table after modifying field properties

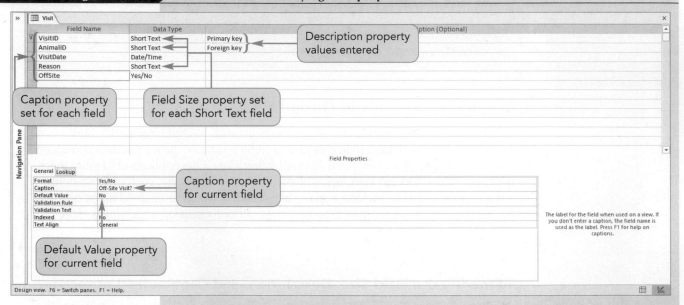

Notice that the OffSite field's Default Value property is automatically set to "No," which means the check box for this field will be empty for each new record. This is the default for this property for any Yes/No field. You can set the Default Value property for other types of fields to make data entry easier. You'll learn more about setting this property in the next session.

The changes to the Visit table's properties are now complete, so you can save the table and view the results of your changes in Datasheet view.

To save and view the modified Visit table:

1. On the Quick Access Toolbar, click the **Save** button 🖫 to save the modified table. A dialog box opens informing you that some data may be lost because you decreased the field sizes. Because all of the values in the VisitID, AnimalID, and Reason fields contain the same number of or fewer characters than the new Field Size properties you set for each field, you can ignore this message.

2. Click the **Yes** button.

3. On the Table Tools Design tab, in the Views group, click the **View** button to display the Visit table in Datasheet view. Notice that each column (field) heading now displays the text you specified in the Caption property for that field. However, now the Off-Site Visit? field caption doesn't fully display.

4. Place the pointer on the column border to the right of the Off-Site Visit? field name until the pointer changes to ┿, and then double-click the column border to fully display this field name. See Figure 2-20.

| Figure 2-20 | Modified Visit table in Datasheet view |

column headings display Caption property values

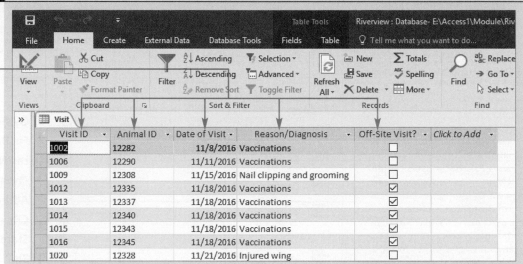

5. Click the **Close 'Visit'** button ✕ on the object tab to close the Visit table, and click **Yes** to save the changes to the Visit table.

6. If you are not continuing to Session 2.2, click the **File** tab, and then click **Close** in the navigation bar of Backstage view to close the Riverview database.

You have created the Billing table and made modifications to its design. In the next session, you'll add records to the Billing table and create the Animal and Owner tables in the Riverview database.

Session 2.1 Quick Check

REVIEW

1. What guidelines should you follow when designing a database?

2. What is the purpose of the Data Type property for a field?

3. The _____ property specifies how a field's name is displayed in database objects, including table and query datasheets, forms, and reports.

4. For which three types of fields can you assign a field size?

5. The default Field Size property setting for a Short Text field is _____.

6. In Design view, which key do you press to move from the Table Design grid to the Field Properties pane?

7. List three reasons why you should specify a primary key for an Access table.

Session 2.2 Visual Overview:

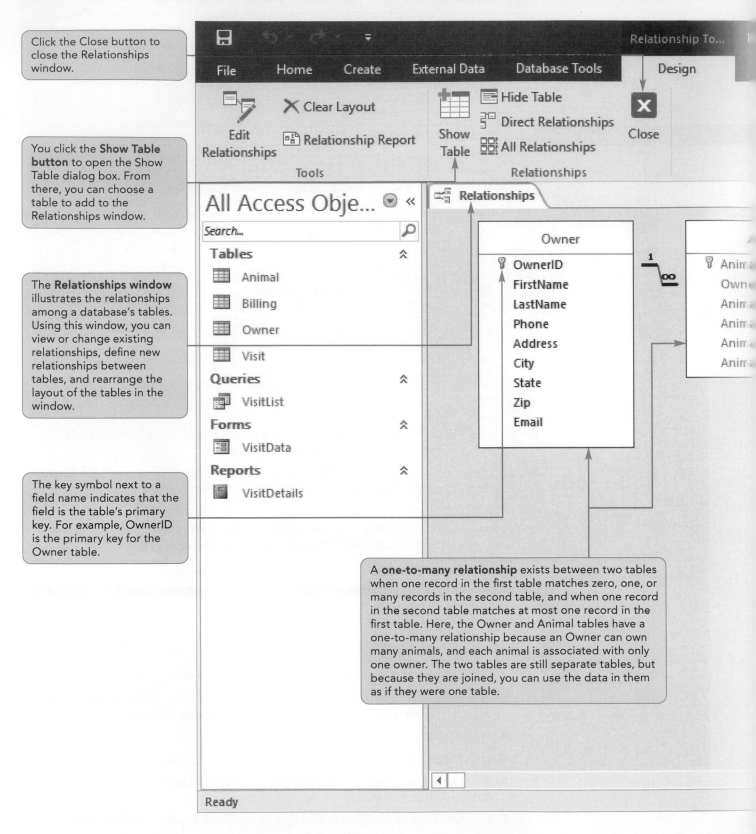

Click the Close button to close the Relationships window.

You click the **Show Table button** to open the Show Table dialog box. From there, you can choose a table to add to the Relationships window.

The **Relationships window** illustrates the relationships among a database's tables. Using this window, you can view or change existing relationships, define new relationships between tables, and rearrange the layout of the tables in the window.

The key symbol next to a field name indicates that the field is the table's primary key. For example, OwnerID is the primary key for the Owner table.

A **one-to-many relationship** exists between two tables when one record in the first table matches zero, one, or many records in the second table, and when one record in the second table matches at most one record in the first table. Here, the Owner and Animal tables have a one-to-many relationship because an Owner can own many animals, and each animal is associated with only one owner. The two tables are still separate tables, but because they are joined, you can use the data in them as if they were one table.

Modified Visit table in Datasheet view

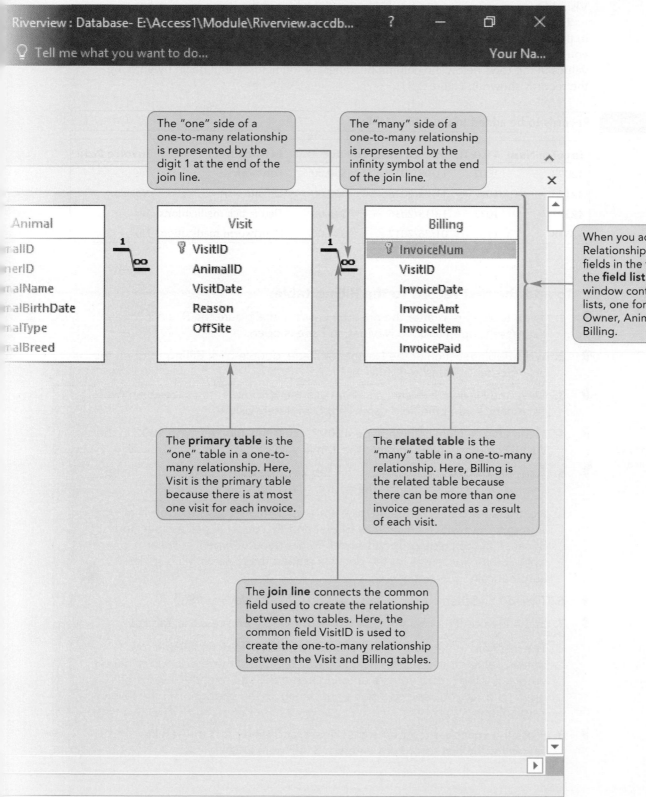

Riverview : Database- E:\Access1\Module\Riverview.accdb...   ?   —   ☐   ✕

♡ Tell me what you want to do...   Your Na...

The "one" side of a one-to-many relationship is represented by the digit 1 at the end of the join line.

The "many" side of a one-to-many relationship is represented by the infinity symbol at the end of the join line.

Animal
- allD
- nerID
- alName
- alBirthDate
- alType
- alBreed

Visit
- 🔑 VisitID
- AnimalID
- VisitDate
- Reason
- OffSite

Billing
- 🔑 InvoiceNum
- VisitID
- InvoiceDate
- InvoiceAmt
- InvoiceItem
- InvoicePaid

When you add a table to the Relationships window, the fields in the table appear in the **field list**. Here, the window contains four field lists, one for each table: Owner, Animal, Visit, and Billing.

The **primary table** is the "one" table in a one-to-many relationship. Here, Visit is the primary table because there is at most one visit for each invoice.

The **related table** is the "many" table in a one-to-many relationship. Here, Billing is the related table because there can be more than one invoice generated as a result of each visit.

The **join line** connects the common field used to create the relationship between two tables. Here, the common field VisitID is used to create the one-to-many relationship between the Visit and Billing tables.

Adding Records to a New Table

Before you can begin to define the table relationships illustrated in the Session 2.2 Visual Overview, you need to finish creating the tables in the Riverview database.

The Billing table design is complete. Now, Kimberly would like you to add records to the table so it will contain the invoice data for Riverview Veterinary Care Center. As you learned earlier, you add records to a table in Datasheet view by typing the field values in the rows below the column headings for the fields. You'll begin by entering the records shown in Figure 2-21.

Figure 2-21   **Records to be added to the Billing table**

Invoice Num	Visit ID	Invoice Date	Invoice Amt	Invoice Item	Invoice Paid
42098	1002	11/09/2016	$50.00	Lab work	Yes
42125	1012	11/21/2016	$50.00	Off-site visit	No
42271	1077	12/15/2016	$45.00	Flea & tick medications	Yes
42518	1181	01/26/2017	$35.00	Heartworm medication	No

To add the first record to the Billing table:

1. If you took a break after the previous session, make sure the Riverview database is open and the Navigation Pane is open.

2. In the Tables section of the Navigation Pane, double-click **Billing** to open the Billing table in Datasheet view.

3. Close the Navigation Pane, and then use the ✛ pointer to resize columns, as necessary, so that the field names are completely visible.

Be sure to type the numbers "0" and "1" and *not* the letters "O" and "I" in the field values.

4. In the Invoice Num column, type **42098**, press the **Tab** key, type **1002** in the Visit ID column, and then press the **Tab** key.

5. Type **11/9/2016** and then press the **Tab** key. The date "11/09/2016" in the Invoice Date column reflects the custom date format you set.

   Next you need to enter the invoice amount for the first record. This is a Currency field with the Currency format and two decimal places specified. Because of the field's properties, you do not need to type the dollar sign, comma, or zeroes for the decimal places; these items will display automatically.

6. Type **50** and then press the **Tab** key. The value displays as "$50.00."

7. In the Invoice Item column, type **Lab work**, and then press the **Tab** key.

   The last field in the table, InvoicePaid, is a Yes/No field. Recall that the default value for any Yes/No field is "No"; therefore, the check box is initially empty. For the record you are entering in the Billing table, the invoice has been paid, so you need to insert a checkmark in the check box in the Invoice Paid column.

8. Press the **spacebar** to insert a checkmark, and then press the **Tab** key. The values for the first record are entered. See Figure 2-22.

| Figure 2-22 | First record entered in the Billing table |

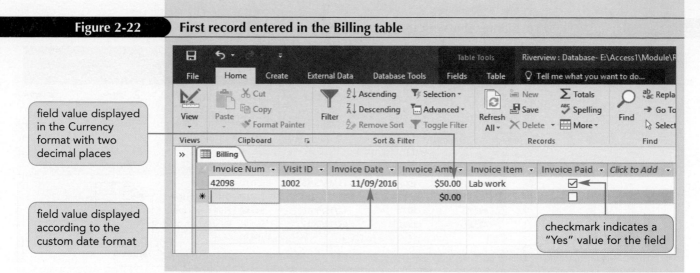

field value displayed in the Currency format with two decimal places

field value displayed according to the custom date format

checkmark indicates a "Yes" value for the field

Now you can add the remaining three records. As you do, you'll learn a keyboard shortcut for inserting the value from the same field in the previous record. A **keyboard shortcut** is a key or combination of keys you press to complete an action more efficiently.

To add the next three records to the Billing table:

1. Refer to Figure 2-21 and enter the values in the second record's Invoice Num, Visit ID, and Invoice Date columns.

   Notice that the value in the second record's Invoice Amt column is $50.00. This value is the exact same value as in the first record. You can quickly insert the value from the same column in the previous record using the Ctrl + ' (apostrophe) keyboard shortcut. To use this shortcut, you press and hold the Ctrl key, press the ' key once, and then release both keys. (The plus sign in the keyboard shortcut indicates you're pressing two keys at once; you do not press the + key.)

2. With the insertion point in the Invoice Amt column, press the **Ctrl + ' keys**. The value "$50.00" is inserted in the Invoice Amt column for the second record.

3. Press the **Tab** key to move to the Invoice Item column, and then type **Off-site visit**.

4. Press the **Tab** key to move to the Invoice Paid column, and then press the **Tab** key to leave the Invoice Paid check box unchecked to indicate the invoice has not been paid. The second record is entered in the Billing table.

5. Refer to Figure 2-21 to enter the values for the third and fourth records. Your table should look like the one in Figure 2-23.

Figure 2-23 **Billing table with four records entered**

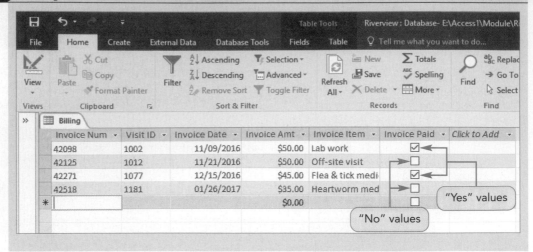

To finish entering records in the Billing table, you'll use a method that allows you to import the data.

Importing Data from an Excel Worksheet

Often, the data you want to add to an Access table exists in another file, such as a Word document or an Excel workbook. You can bring the data from other files into Access in different ways. For example, you can copy and paste the data from an open file, or you can **import** the data, which is a process that allows you to copy the data from a source without having to open the source file.

Kimberly had been using Excel to track invoice data for Riverview Veterinary Care Center and already created a worksheet, named "Invoices," containing this data. You'll import this Excel worksheet into your Billing table to complete the entry of data in the table. To use the import method, the columns in the Excel worksheet must match the names and data types of the fields in the Access table.

The Invoices worksheet contains the following columns: InvoiceNum, VisitID, InvoiceDate, InvoiceAmt, InvoiceItem, and InvoicePaid. These column headings match the field names in the Billing table exactly, so you can import the data. Before you import data into a table, you need to close the table.

To import the Invoices worksheet into the Billing table:

1. Click the **Close 'Billing'** button ⊠ on the object tab to close the Billing table, and then click the **Yes** button in the dialog box asking if you want to save the changes to the table layout.

2. On the ribbon, click the **External Data** tab.

3. In the Import & Link group, click the **Excel** button. The Get External Data - Excel Spreadsheet dialog box opens. See Figure 2-24.

| Figure 2-24 | Get External Data – Excel Spreadsheet dialog box |

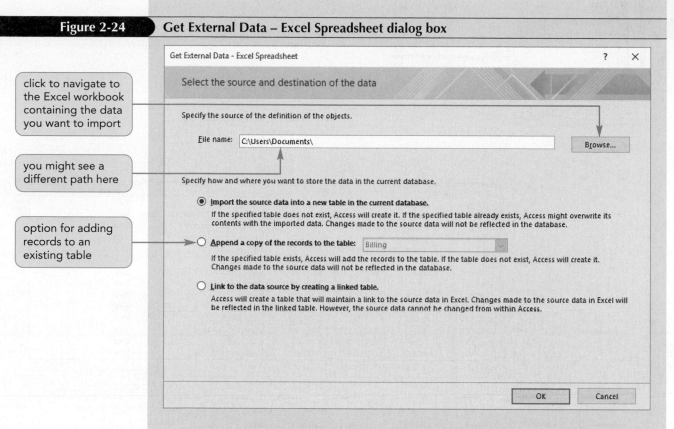

click to navigate to the Excel workbook containing the data you want to import

you might see a different path here

option for adding records to an existing table

The dialog box provides options for importing the entire worksheet as a new table in the current database, adding the data from the worksheet to an existing table, or linking the data in the worksheet to the table. You need to add, or append, the worksheet data to the Billing table.

4. Click the **Browse** button. The File Open dialog box opens. The Excel workbook file is named "Invoices" and is located in the Access1 > Module folder provided with your Data Files.

5. Navigate to the **Access1 > Module** folder, where your Data Files are stored, and then double-click the **Invoices** Excel file. You return to the dialog box.

6. Click the **Append a copy of the records to the table** option button. The box to the right of this option becomes active and displays the Billing table name, because it is the first table listed in the Navigation Pane.

7. Click the **OK** button. The first Import Spreadsheet Wizard dialog box opens. The dialog box confirms that the first row of the worksheet you are importing contains column headings. The bottom section of the dialog box displays some of the data contained in the worksheet. See Figure 2-25.

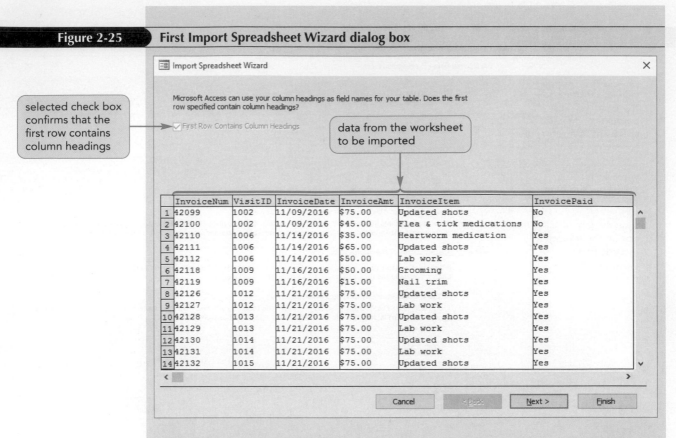

Figure 2-25 First Import Spreadsheet Wizard dialog box

selected check box confirms that the first row contains column headings

data from the worksheet to be imported

8. Click the **Next** button. The second, and final, Import Spreadsheet Wizard dialog box opens. Notice that the Import to Table box shows that the data from the spreadsheet will be imported into the Billing table.

9. Click the **Finish** button. A dialog box opens asking if you want to save the import steps. If you needed to repeat this same import procedure many times, it would be a good idea to save the steps for the procedure. However, you don't need to save these steps because you'll be importing the data only one time. Once the data is in the Billing table, Kimberly will no longer use Excel to track invoice data.

10. Click the **Close** button in the dialog box to close it without saving the steps.

The data from the Invoices worksheet has been added to the Billing table. Next, you'll open the table to view the new records.

To open the Billing table and view the imported data:

1. Open the Navigation Pane, and then double-click **Billing** in the Tables section to open the table in Datasheet view.

2. Resize the Invoice Item column to its best fit, scrolling the worksheet and resizing, as necessary.

▶ **3.** Press the **Ctrl + Home** keys to scroll to the top of the datasheet. Notice that the table now contains a total of 204 records—the four records you entered plus 200 records imported from the Invoices worksheet. The records are displayed in primary key order by the values in the Invoice Num column. See Figure 2-26.

| Figure 2-26 | Billing table after importing data from Excel |

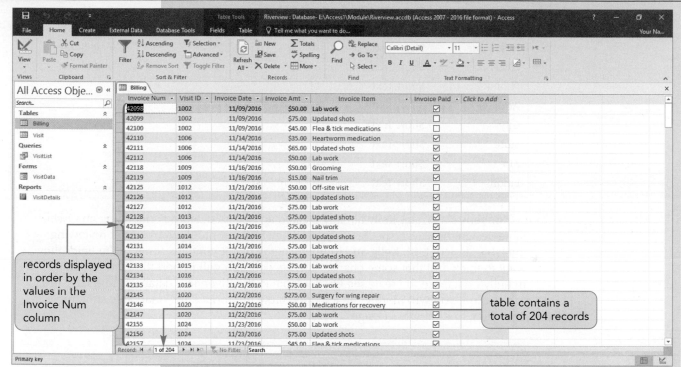

records displayed in order by the values in the Invoice Num column

table contains a total of 204 records

▶ **4.** Save and close the Billing table, and then close the Navigation Pane.

Two of the tables—Visit and Billing—are now complete. According to Kimberly's plan for the Riverview database, you still need to create the Owner and Animal tables. You'll use a different method to create these tables.

Creating a Table by Importing an Existing Table or Table Structure

If another Access database contains a table—or even just the design, or structure, of a table—that you want to include in your database, you can import the table and any records it contains or import only the table structure into your database. To create the new Owner and Animal tables per Kimberly's plan shown in Figure 2-2, you will import a table structure from a different Access database to create the Owner table and an existing table structure and records from another database to create the Animal table.

Importing an Existing Table Structure

Kimberly documented the design for the new Owner table by listing each field's name and data type, as well as any applicable field size, description, and caption property values, as shown in Figure 2-27. Note that each field in the Owner table will be a Short Text field, and the OwnerID field will be the table's primary key.

Figure 2-27	Design for the Owner table

Field Name	Data Type	Field Size	Description	Caption
OwnerID	Short Text	4	Primary key	Owner ID
FirstName	Short Text	20		First Name
LastName	Short Text	25		Last Name
Phone	Short Text	14		
Address	Short Text	35		
City	Short Text	25		
State	Short Text	2		
Zip	Short Text	10		
Email	Short Text	50		

Kimberly's assistant Kelly already created an Access database containing an Owner table design, however, she hasn't entered any records into the table. After reviewing the table design, both Kelly and Kimberly agree that it contains some of the fields they want to track, but that some changes are needed. You will import the table structure in Kelly's database to create the Owner table in the Riverview database, and later in this session, you will modify the imported table to produce the final table structure according to Kimberly's design.

To create the Owner table by importing the structure of another table:

1. Make sure the External Data tab is the active tab on the ribbon.

2. In the Import & Link group, click the **Access** button. The Get External Data - Access Database dialog box opens. This dialog box is similar to the one you used earlier when importing the Excel spreadsheet.

3. Click the **Browse** button. The File Open dialog box opens. The Access database file from which you need to import the table structure is named "Kelly" and is located in the Access1 > Module folder provided with your Data Files.

4. Navigate to the **Access1 > Module** folder, where your Data Files are stored, and then double-click the **Kelly** database file. You return to the dialog box.

5. Make sure the **Import tables, queries, forms, reports, macros, and modules into the current database** option button is selected, and then click the **OK** button. The Import Objects dialog box opens. The dialog box contains tabs for importing all the different types of Access database objects—tables, queries, forms, and so on. The Tables tab is the current tab.

6. Click the **Options** button in the dialog box to see all the options for importing tables. See Figure 2-28.

Figure 2-28   **Import Objects dialog box**

tabs for importing other
types of database objects

table object to be
imported

this option imports
the table structure
and the table

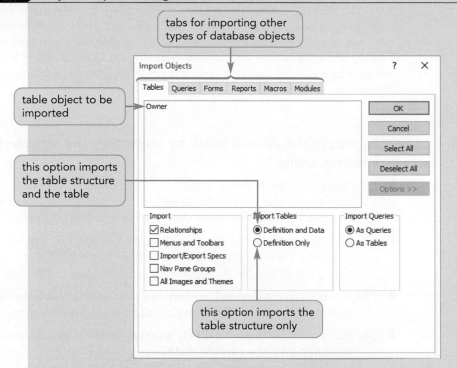

this option imports the
table structure only

▶ **7.** On the Tables tab, click **Owner** to select this table.

▶ **8.** In the Import Tables section of the dialog box, click the **Definition Only** option button, and then click the **OK** button. Access creates the Owner table in the Riverview database using the structure of the Owner table in the Kelly database, and opens a dialog box asking if you want to save the import steps.

▶ **9.** Click the **Close** button to close the dialog box without saving the import steps.

▶ **10.** Open the Navigation Pane, double-click **Owner** in the Tables section to open the table, and then close the Navigation Pane. The Owner table opens in Datasheet view. The table contains no records. See Figure 2-29.

Figure 2-29   **Imported Owner table in Datasheet view**

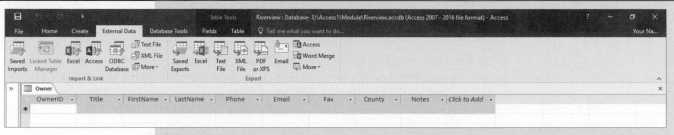

Before you add records to the Owner table and fine-tune its design, you need to first add the Animal table to the Riverview database. You will do this by importing a table and its data from another database.

Importing an Existing Table

Kelly has already created a database called "AllAnimals" that contains a table called "Animal." To import this Animal table into the Riverview database, you will follow the same process you used to import the table structure from the Kelly database to create the Owner table; however, this time you will choose the Definition and Data option, instead of the Definition only option in the Import Objects dialog box. This will import the structure and the data that Kelly has created and verified in the Animal table in the AllAnimals database.

To create the Animal table by importing the structure and data of another table:

▶ 1. Close the Owner table, make sure the External Data tab is the active tab on the ribbon, and then in the Import & Link group, click the **Access** button. The Get External Data - Access Database dialog box opens.

▶ 2. Click the **Browse** button. The File Open dialog box opens. The Access database file from which you need to import the table is named "AllAnimals" and is located in the Access1 > Module folder provided with your Data Files.

▶ 3. Navigate to the **Access1 > Module** folder, where your Data Files are stored, and then double-click the **AllAnimals** database file. You return to the dialog box.

▶ 4. Make sure the **Import tables, queries, forms, reports, macros, and modules into the current database** option button is selected, and then click the **OK** button to open the Import Objects dialog box opens. The Tables tab is the current tab.

▶ 5. Click **Animal** to select this table, click the **Options** button to display the options for importing tables, and then, in the Import Tables section, make sure the **Definition and Data** option button is selected.

▶ 6. Click the **OK** button, and then click the **Close** button to close the dialog box without saving the import steps. Access creates the Animal table in the Riverview database using the records and structure of the Animal table in the AllAnimals database.

▶ 7. Open the Navigation Pane, double-click **Animal** in the Tables section to open the table, and then close the Navigation Pane. The Animal table opens in Datasheet view. Kimberly reviews the new Animal table and is satisfied with its structure and the records it contains, so you can close this table.

▶ 8. Close the Animal table.

Now Kimberly asks you to complete the Owner table. She notes that the table structure you imported earlier for this table contains some of the fields she wants, but not all (see Figure 2-27); it also contains some fields she does not want in the Owner table. You can add the missing fields using the Data Type gallery.

Adding Fields to a Table Using the Data Type Gallery

The **Data Type gallery**, available from the More Fields button located on the Add & Delete group on the Table Tools Fields tab, allows you to add a group of related fields to a table at the same time, rather than adding each field to the table individually.

The group of fields you add is called a **Quick Start selection**. For example, the **Address Quick Start selection** adds a collection of fields related to an address, such as Address, City, State, and so on, to the table at one time. When you use a Quick Start selection, the fields added already have properties set. However, you need to review and possibly modify the properties to ensure the fields match your design needs for the database.

Next, you'll use the Data Type gallery to add the missing fields to the Owner table.

To add fields to the Owner table using the Data Type gallery:

▶ 1. Open the **Owner** table, and then on the ribbon, click the **Table Tools Fields** tab. Before inserting fields from the Data Type gallery, you need to place the insertion point in the field to the right of where you want to insert the new fields. According to Kimberly's design, the Address field should come after the Phone field, so you need to make the next field, Email, the active field.

Make sure the correct field is active before adding new fields.

▶ 2. Click the **first row** in the Email field to make it the active field.

▶ 3. In the Add & Delete group, click the **More Fields** button. The Data Type gallery opens and displays options for different types of fields you can add to your table.

▶ 4. Scroll down the gallery until the Quick Start section is visible. See Figure 2-30.

Figure 2-30   Owner table with the Data Type gallery displayed

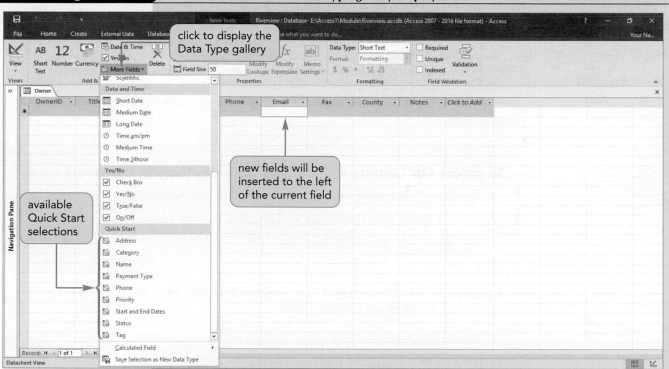

The Quick Start section provides options that will add multiple, related fields to the table at one time. The new fields will be inserted to the left of the current field.

▶ 5. In the Quick Start section, click **Address**. Five fields are added to the table: Address, City, State Province, ZIP Postal, and Country Region. See Figure 2-31.

| Figure 2-31 | Owner table after adding fields from the Data Type gallery |

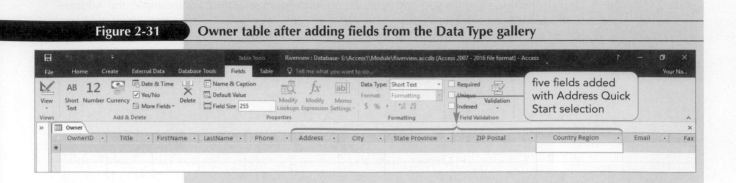

Modifying the Structure of an Imported Table

Refer back to Kimberly's design for the Owner table (Figure 2-27). To finalize the table design, you need to modify the imported table by deleting fields, renaming fields, and changing field data types. You'll begin by deleting fields.

Deleting Fields from a Table Structure

After you've created a table, you might need to delete one or more fields. When you delete a field, you also delete all the values for that field from the table. So, before you delete a field, you should make sure that you want to do so and that you choose the correct field to delete. You can delete fields in either Datasheet view or Design view.

The Address Quick Start selection added a field named "Country Region" to the Owner table. Kimberly doesn't need a field to store country data because all of the owners of the animals that Riverview Veterinary Care Center serves are located in the United States. You'll begin to modify the Owner table structure by deleting the Country Region field.

To delete the Country Region field from the table in Datasheet view:

1. Click the **first row** in the Country Region field (if necessary).

2. On the Table Tools Fields tab, in the Add & Delete group, click the **Delete** button. The Country Region field is removed and the first field, OwnerID, is now the active field.

You can also delete fields from a table structure in Design view. You'll switch to Design view to delete the other unnecessary fields.

To delete the fields in Design view:

1. On the Table Tools Fields tab, in the Views group, click the **View** button. The Owner table opens in Design view. See Figure 2-32.

Figure 2-32   Owner table in Design view

Figure 2-32   Owner table in Design view

click to delete the current field

fields to be deleted

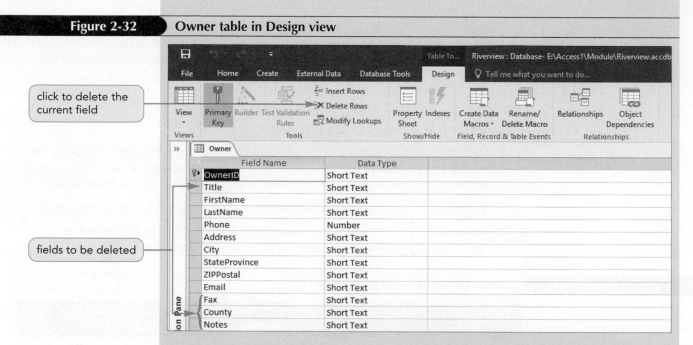

2. Click the **Title** Field Name box to make it the current field.

3. On the Table Tools Design tab, in the Tools group, click the **Delete Rows** button. The Title field is removed from the Owner table structure. You'll delete the Fax, County, and Notes fields next. Instead of deleting these fields individually, you'll select and delete them at the same time.

4. On the row selector for the **Fax** field, press and hold the mouse button and then drag the mouse to select the **County** and **Notes** fields.

5. Release the mouse button. The rows for the three fields are outlined in red, indicating all three fields are selected.

6. In the Tools group, click the **Delete Rows** button. See Figure 2-33.

Figure 2-33   Owner table after deleting fields

fields to be renamed

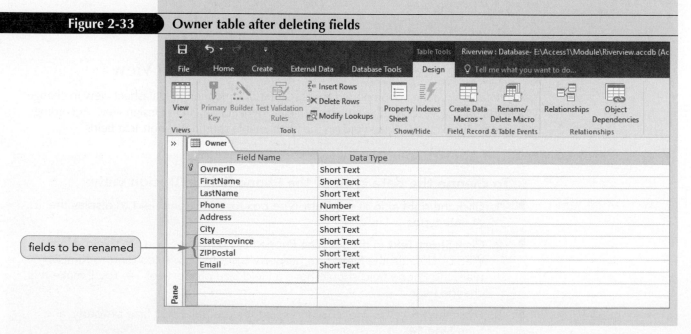

Renaming Fields in Design View

To match Kimberly's design for the Owner table, you need to rename some of the fields. You already have renamed the default primary key field (ID) in Datasheet view in the previous module. You can also rename fields in Design view by simply editing the names in the Table Design grid.

To rename the fields in Design view:

▶ 1. Click to position the insertion point to the right of the text StateProvince in the seventh row's Field Name box, and then press the **Backspace** key eight times to delete the word "Province." The name of the seventh field is now State.

You can also select an entire field name and then type new text to replace it.

▶ 2. In the eighth row's Field Name box, drag to select the text **ZIPPostal**, and then type **Zip**. The text you type replaces the original text. See Figure 2-34.

Figure 2-34   **Owner table after renaming fields**

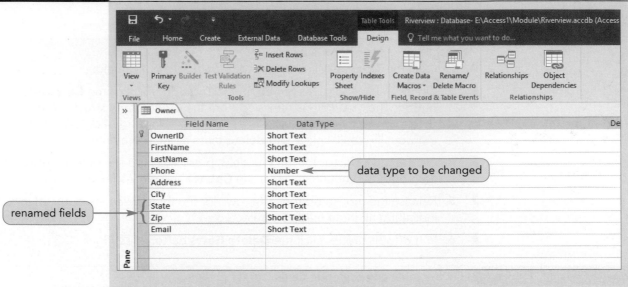

Changing the Data Type for a Field in Design View

In the table structure you imported earlier, you used an option in Datasheet view to change a field's data type. You can also change the data type for a field in Design view. According to Kimberly's plan, all of the fields in the Owner table should be Short Text fields.

To change the data type of the Phone field in Design view:

▶ 1. Click the right side of the Data Type box for the Phone field to display the list of data types.

▶ 2. Click **Short Text** in the list. The Phone field is now a Short Text field. Note that, by default, the Field Size property is set to 255. According to Kimberly's plan, the Phone field should have a Field Size property of 14. You'll make this change next.

▶ 3. Press the **F6** key to move to and select the default Field Size property, and then type **14**.

Each of the remaining fields you added using the Address Quick Start selection—Address, City, State, and Zip—also has the default field size of 255. You need to change the Field Size property for these fields to match Kimberly's design. You'll also delete any Caption property values for these fields because the field names match how Kimberly wants them displayed, so captions are unnecessary.

To change the Field Size and Caption properties for the fields:

1. Click the **Address Field Name** box to make it the current field.

2. Press the **F6** key to move to and select the default Field Size property, and then type **35**. Note that the Caption property setting for this field is the same as the field name. This field doesn't need a caption, so you can delete this value.

3. Press the **Tab** key three times to select Address in the Caption box, and then press the **Delete** key. The Caption property value is removed.

4. Repeat Steps 1 through 3 for the City field to change the Field Size property to **25** and delete its Caption property value.

5. Change the Field Size property for the State field to **2**, and then delete its Caption property value.

6. Change the Field Size property for the Zip field to **10**, and then delete its Caption property value.

7. On the Quick Access Toolbar, click the **Save** button 🖫 to save your changes to the Owner table.

Finally, Kimberly would like you to set the Description property for the OwnerID field and the Caption property for the OwnerID, FirstName, and LastName fields. You'll make these changes now.

To enter the Description and Caption property values:

1. Click the **Description (Optional)** box for the OwnerID field, and then type **Primary key**.

2. In the Field Properties pane, click the **Caption** box.

   After you leave the Description (Optional) box, the Property Update Options button 📝 appears below this box for the OwnerID field. When you change a field's property in Design view, you can use this button to update the corresponding property on forms and reports that include the modified field. For example, if the Riverview database included a form that contained the OwnerID field, you could choose to propagate, or update, the modified Description property in the form by clicking the Property Update Options button, and then choosing the option to make the update everywhere the field is used. The ScreenTip on the Property Update Options button and the options it lists vary depending on the task; in this case, if you click the button, the option is "Update Status Bar Text everywhere OwnerID is used." Because the Riverview database does not include any forms or reports that are based on the Owner table, you do not need to update the properties, so you can ignore the button for now. In most cases, however, it is a good idea to perform the update.

3. In the Caption box for the OwnerID field, type **Owner ID**.

4. Click the **FirstName** Field Name box to make it the current field, click the **Caption** box, and then type **First Name**.

5. Click the **LastName** Field Name box to make it the current field, click the **Caption** box, and then type **Last Name**. See Figure 2-35.

Figure 2-35 Owner table after entering descriptions and captions

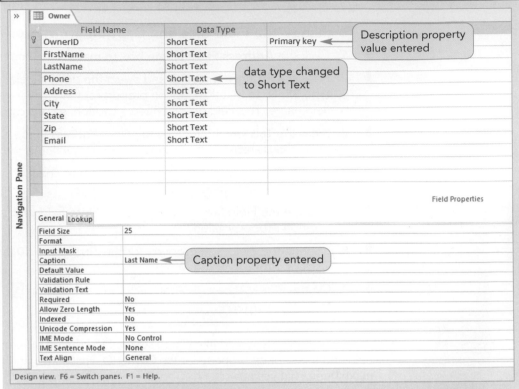

6. On the Quick Access Toolbar, click the **Save** button 🔲 to save your changes to the Owner table.

7. On the Table Tools Design tab, in the Views group, click the **View** button to display the table in Datasheet view.

8. Resize each column to its best fit, and then click in the first row for the **Owner ID** column. See Figure 2-36.

Figure 2-36 Modified Owner table in Datasheet view

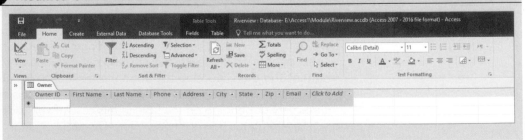

Kimberly feels that data entry would be made easier if the State field value of "WY" was automatically filled in for each new record added to the table, because all of the owners live in Wyoming. You can accomplish this by setting the Default Value property for the field.

Setting the Default Value Property for a Field

The **Default Value property** for a field specifies what value will appear, by default, for the field in each new record you add to a table.

Because all of the owners at Riverview Veterinary Care Center live in Wyoming, you'll specify a default value of "WY" for the State field in the Owner table. With this setting, each new record in the Owner table will have the correct State field value entered automatically.

To set the Default Value property for the State field:

▶ **1.** On the Home tab, in the Views group, click the **View** button to display the Owner table in Design view.

▶ **2.** Click the **State** Field Name box to make it the current field.

▶ **3.** In the Field Properties pane, click the **Default Value** box, type **WY**, and then press the **Tab** key. See Figure 2-37.

Figure 2-37	Specifying the Default Value property for the State field

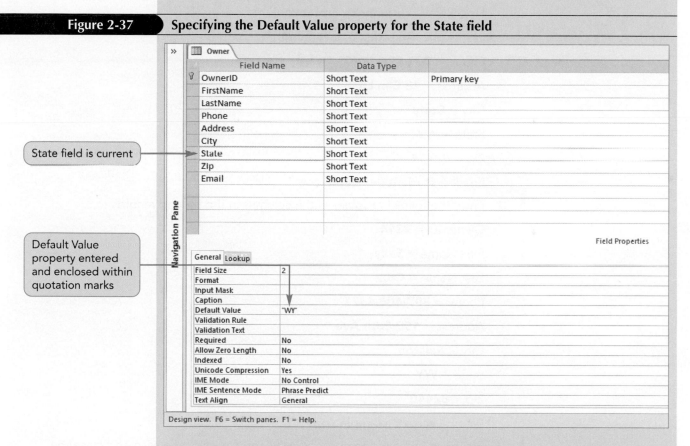

State field is current

Default Value property entered and enclosed within quotation marks

Note that a text entry in the Default Value property must be enclosed within quotation marks. If you do not type the quotation marks, Access adds them for you. However, for some entries, you would receive an error message indicating invalid syntax if you omitted the quotation marks. In such cases, you have to enter the quotation marks yourself.

▶ **4.** On the Quick Access Toolbar, click the **Save** button 🖫 to save your changes to the Owner table.

TIP

You can change the value in a record from the default value to another value, if necessary.

5. Display the table in Datasheet view. Note that the State field for the first row now displays the default value "WY" as specified by the Default Value property. Each new record entered in the table will automatically have this State field value entered.

With the Owner table design set, you can now enter records in it. You'll begin by entering two records, and then you'll use a different method to add the remaining records.

Note: Be sure to enter your last name and first name where indicated.

To add two records to the Owner table:

1. Enter the following values in the columns in the first record; note that you can press **Tab** to move past the default State field value:

   Owner ID = **2310**

   First Name = **[student's first name]**

   Last Name = **[student's last name]**

   Phone = **307-824-1245**

   Address = **12 Elm Ln**

   City = **Cody**

   State = **WY**

   Zip = **82414**

   Email = **student@example.com**

2. Enter the following values in the columns in the second record:

   Owner ID = **2314**

   First Name = **Sally**

   Last Name = **Cruz**

   Phone = **307-406-4321**

   Address = **199 18th Ave**

   City = **Ralston**

   State = **WY**

   Zip = **82440**

   Email = **scruz@example.com**

3. Resize columns to their best fit, as necessary, and then save and close the Owner table.

Before Kimberly decided to store data using Access, Kelly managed the owner data for the care center in a different system. She exported that data into a text file and now asks you to import it into the new Owner table. You can import the data contained in this text file to add the remaining records to the Owner table.

Adding Data to a Table by Importing a Text File

There are many ways to import data into an Access database. So far, you've learned how to add data to an Access table by importing an Excel spreadsheet, and you've created a new table by importing the structure of an existing table. You can also import data contained in text files.

To complete the entry of records in the Owner table, you'll import the data contained in Kelly's text file. The file is named "Owner" and is located in the Access1 > Module folder provided with your Data Files.

To import the data contained in the Owner text file:

1. On the ribbon, click the **External Data** tab.

2. In the Import & Link group, click the **Text File** button. The Get External Data - Text File dialog box opens. This dialog box is similar to the one you used earlier when importing the Excel spreadsheet and the Access table structure.

3. Click the **Browse** button. The File Open dialog box opens.

4. Navigate to the **Access1 > Module** folder, where your Data Files are stored, and then double-click the **Owner** file. You return to the dialog box.

5. Click the **Append a copy of the records to the table** option button. The box to the right of this option becomes active. Next, you need to select the table to which you want to add the data.

6. Click the arrow on the box, and then click **Owner**.

7. Click the **OK** button. The first Import Text Wizard dialog box opens. The dialog box indicates that the data to be imported is in a delimited format. A **delimited text file** is one in which fields of data are separated by a character such as a comma or a tab. In this case, the dialog box shows that data is separated by the comma character in the text file.

8. Make sure the **Delimited** option button is selected in the dialog box, and then click the **Next** button. The second Import Text Wizard dialog box opens. See Figure 2-38.

| Figure 2-38 | Second Import Wizard dialog box |

fields in the text file are separated by commas

preview of the data being imported

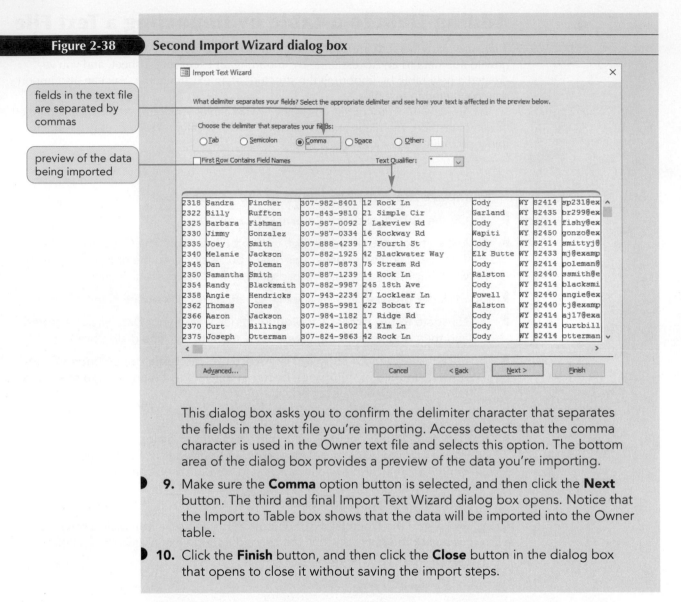

This dialog box asks you to confirm the delimiter character that separates the fields in the text file you're importing. Access detects that the comma character is used in the Owner text file and selects this option. The bottom area of the dialog box provides a preview of the data you're importing.

9. Make sure the **Comma** option button is selected, and then click the **Next** button. The third and final Import Text Wizard dialog box opens. Notice that the Import to Table box shows that the data will be imported into the Owner table.

10. Click the **Finish** button, and then click the **Close** button in the dialog box that opens to close it without saving the import steps.

Kimberly asks you to open the Owner table in Datasheet view so she can see the results of importing the text file.

To view the Owner table datasheet:

1. Open the Navigation Pane, and then double-click **Owner** to open the Owner table in Datasheet view. The Owner table contains a total of 25 records.

2. Close the Navigation Pane, and then resize columns to their best fit, scrolling the table datasheet as necessary, so that all field values are displayed. When finished, scroll back to display the first fields in the table, and then click the first row's **Owner ID** field, if necessary. See Figure 2-39.

Figure 2-39 Owner table after importing data from the text file

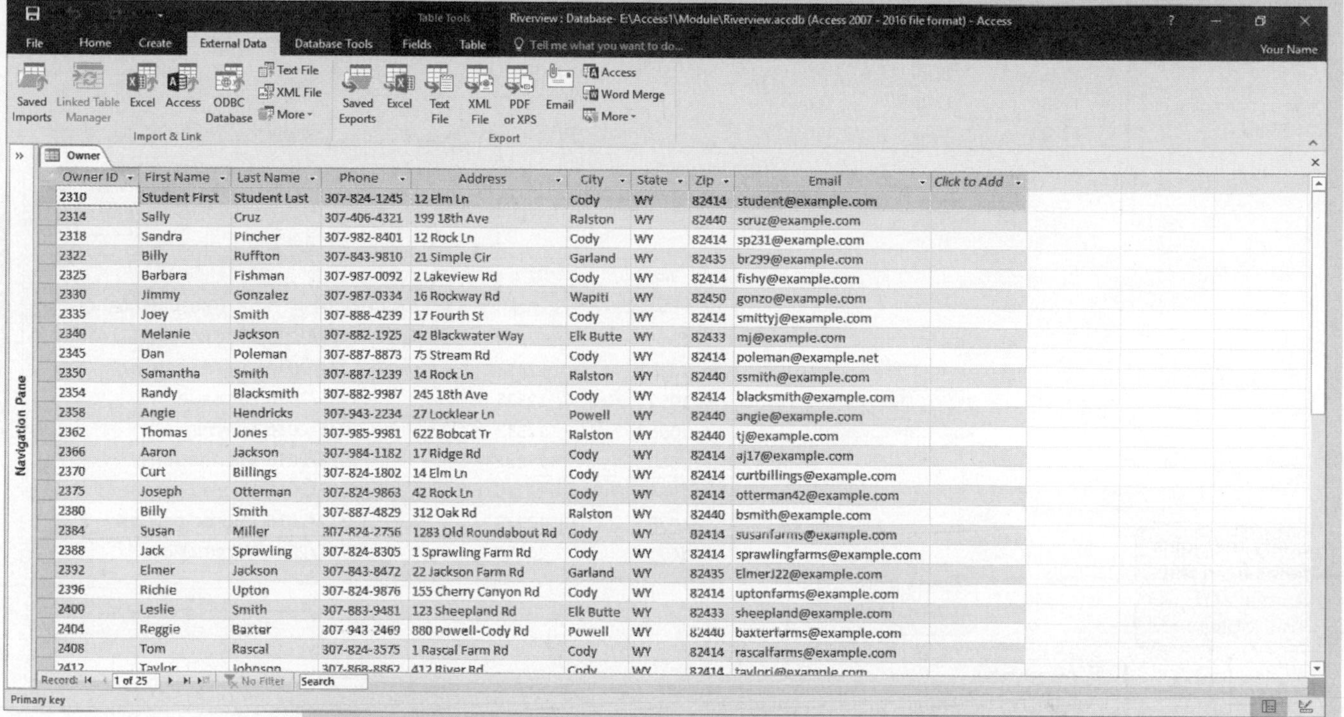

Owner ID	First Name	Last Name	Phone	Address	City	State	Zip	Email	Click to Add
2310	Student First	Student Last	307-824-1245	12 Elm Ln	Cody	WY	82414	student@example.com	
2314	Sally	Cruz	307-406-4321	199 18th Ave	Ralston	WY	82440	scruz@example.com	
2318	Sandra	Pincher	307-982-8401	12 Rock Ln	Cody	WY	82414	sp231@example.com	
2322	Billy	Ruffton	307-843-9810	21 Simple Cir	Garland	WY	82435	br299@example.com	
2325	Barbara	Fishman	307-987-0092	2 Lakeview Rd	Cody	WY	82414	fishy@example.com	
2330	Jimmy	Gonzalez	307-987-0334	16 Rockway Rd	Wapiti	WY	82450	gonzo@example.com	
2335	Joey	Smith	307-888-4239	17 Fourth St	Cody	WY	82414	smittyj@example.com	
2340	Melanie	Jackson	307-882-1925	42 Blackwater Way	Elk Butte	WY	82433	mj@example.com	
2345	Dan	Poleman	307-887-8873	75 Stream Rd	Cody	WY	82414	poleman@example.net	
2350	Samantha	Smith	307-887-1239	14 Rock Ln	Ralston	WY	82440	ssmith@example.com	
2354	Randy	Blacksmith	307-882-9987	245 18th Ave	Cody	WY	82414	blacksmith@example.com	
2358	Angie	Hendricks	307-943-2234	27 Locklear Ln	Powell	WY	82440	angie@example.com	
2362	Thomas	Jones	307-985-9981	622 Bobcat Tr	Ralston	WY	82440	tj@example.com	
2366	Aaron	Jackson	307-984-1182	17 Ridge Rd	Cody	WY	82414	aj17@example.com	
2370	Curt	Billings	307-824-1802	14 Elm Ln	Cody	WY	82414	curtbillings@example.com	
2375	Joseph	Otterman	307-824-9863	42 Rock Ln	Cody	WY	82414	otterman42@example.com	
2380	Billy	Smith	307-887-4829	312 Oak Rd	Ralston	WY	82440	bsmith@example.com	
2384	Susan	Miller	307-824-2756	1283 Old Roundabout Rd	Cody	WY	82414	susanfarms@example.com	
2388	Jack	Sprawling	307-824-8305	1 Sprawling Farm Rd	Cody	WY	82414	sprawlingfarms@example.com	
2392	Elmer	Jackson	307-843-8472	22 Jackson Farm Rd	Garland	WY	82435	ElmerJ22@example.com	
2396	Richie	Upton	307-824-9876	155 Cherry Canyon Rd	Cody	WY	82414	uptonfarms@example.com	
2400	Leslie	Smith	307-883-9481	123 Sheepland Rd	Elk Butte	WY	82433	sheepland@example.com	
2404	Reggie	Baxter	307 943 2469	880 Powell-Cody Rd	Powell	WY	82440	baxterfarms@example.com	
2408	Tom	Rascal	307-824-3575	1 Rascal Farm Rd	Cody	WY	82414	rascalfarms@example.com	
2412	Taylor	Johnson	307-868-8862	412 River Rd	Cody	WY	82414	taylorj@example.com	

3. Save and close the Owner table, and then open the Navigation Pane.

The Riverview database now contains four tables—Visit, Billing, Owner, and Animal—and the tables contain all the necessary records. Your final task is to complete the database design by defining the necessary relationship between its tables.

Defining Table Relationships

One of the most powerful features of a relational database management system is its ability to define relationships between tables. You use a common field to relate one table to another. The process of relating tables is often called performing a **join**. When you join tables that have a common field, you can extract data from them as if they were one larger table. For example, you can join the Animal and Visit tables by using the AnimalID field in both tables as the common field. Then you can use a query, form, or report to extract selected data from each table, even though the data is contained in two separate tables, as shown in Figure 2-40. The AnimalVisits query shown in Figure 2-40 includes the AnimalID, AnimalName, AnimalType, and AnimalBreed fields from the Animal table, and the VisitDate and Reason fields from the Visit table. The joining of records is based on the common field of AnimalID. The Animal and Visit tables have a type of relationship called a one-to-many relationship.

Figure 2-40 One-to-many relationship and sample query

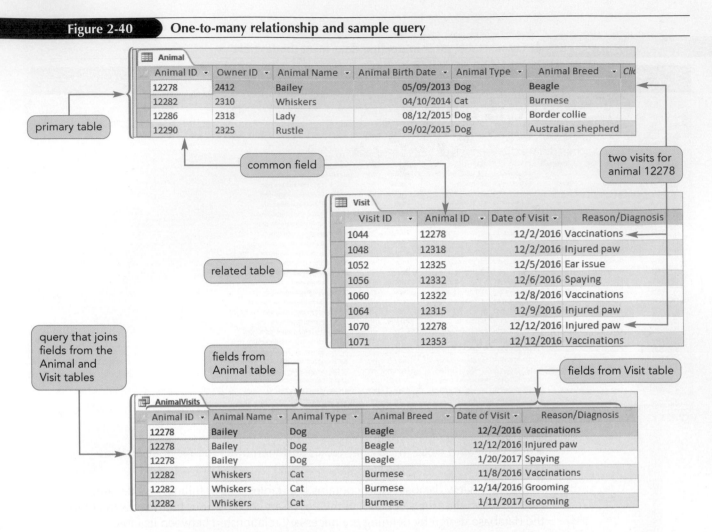

One-to-Many Relationships

As shown earlier in the Session 2.2 Visual Overview, a one-to-many relationship exists between two tables when one record in the first table matches zero, one, or many records in the second table, and when one record in the second table matches at most one record in the first table. For example, as shown in Figure 2-40, Animal 12278 has two visits in the Visit table. Other animals have one or more visits. Every visit has a single matching animal.

In Access, the two tables that form a relationship are referred to as the primary table and the related table. The primary table is the "one" table in a one-to-many relationship; in Figure 2-40, the Animal table is the primary table because there is only one animal for each visit. The related table is the "many" table; in Figure 2-40, the Visit table is the related table because an animal can have zero, one, or many visits.

Because related data is stored in two tables, inconsistencies between the tables can occur. Referring to Figure 2-40, consider the following three scenarios:

- Kimberly adds a record to the Visit table for a new animal, Fluffy (a Siberian cat), using Animal ID 12500. She did not first add the new animal's information to the animal table, so this visit does not have a matching record in the animal table. The data is inconsistent, and the visit record is considered to be an **orphaned record**.
- In another situation, Kimberly changes the AnimalID in the Animal table for Bailey the beagle from 12278 to 12510. Because there is no longer an animal with the AnimalID 12278 in the Animal table, this change creates two orphaned records in the Visit table, and the database is inconsistent.

• In a third scenario, Kimberly deletes the record for Bailey the beagle, Animal 12278, from the Animal table because this animal and its owner have moved and so the animal no longer receives care from Riverview. The database is again inconsistent; two records for Animal 12278 in the Visit table have no matching record in the Animal table.

You can avoid these types of problems and avoid having inconsistent data in your database by specifying referential integrity between tables when you define their relationships.

Referential Integrity

Referential integrity is a set of rules that Access enforces to maintain consistency between related tables when you update data in a database. Specifically, the referential integrity rules are as follows:

• When you add a record to a related table, a matching record must already exist in the primary table, thereby preventing the possibility of orphaned records.
• If you attempt to change the value of the primary key in the primary table, Access prevents this change if matching records exist in a related table. However, if you choose the **Cascade Update Related Fields option**, Access permits the change in value to the primary key and changes the appropriate foreign key values in the related table, thereby eliminating the possibility of inconsistent data.
• When you attempt to delete a record in the primary table, Access prevents the deletion if matching records exist in a related table. However, if you choose the **Cascade Delete Related Records option**, Access deletes the record in the primary table and also deletes all records in related tables that have matching foreign key values. However, you should rarely select the Cascade Delete Related Records option because doing so might cause you to inadvertently delete records you did not intend to delete. It is best to use other methods for deleting records that give you more control over the deletion process.

Defining a Relationship Between Two Tables

At the Riverview Veterinary Care Center, the owners own animals, the animals visit the clinic, and the owner receives the bill for the visits. It is important to understand these relationships in order to determine which owner to send the bill to for the visit each animal makes. Understanding these relationships also allows you to establish relationships between the tables of records in the Riverview database. When two tables have a common field, you can define a relationship between them in the Relationships window, as shown in the Session 2.2 Visual Overview.

Next, you need to define a series of relationships in the Riverview database. First, you will define a one-to-many relationship between the Owner and Animal tables, with Owner as the primary table and Animal as the related table and with OwnerID as the common field (primary key in the Owner table and a foreign key in the Animal table). Second, you will define a one-to-many relationship between the Animal and Visit tables, with Animal as the primary table and Visit as the related table and with AnimalID as the common field (the primary key in the Animal table and a foreign key in the Visit table). Finally, you will define a one-to-many relationship between the Visit and Billing tables, with Visit as the primary table and Billing as the related table and with VisitID as the common field (the primary key in the Visit table and a foreign key in the Billing table).

To define the one-to-many relationship between the Owner and Animal tables:

1. On the ribbon, click the **Database Tools** tab.

2. In the Relationships group, click the **Relationships** button to display the Relationship window and open the Show Table dialog box. See Figure 2-41.

Figure 2-41 **Show Table dialog box**

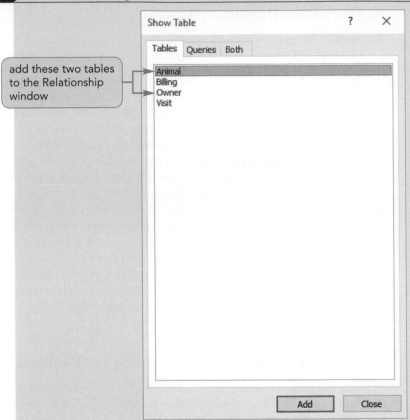

add these two tables to the Relationship window

You must add each table participating in a relationship to the Relationships window. Because the Owner table is the primary table in the relationship, you'll add it first.

TIP

You can also double-click a table in the Show Table dialog box to add it to the Relationships window.

3. Click **Owner**, and then click the **Add** button. The Owner table's field list is added to the Relationships window.

4. Click **Animal**, and then click the **Add** button. The Animal table's field list is added to the Relationships window.

5. Click the **Close** button in the Show Table dialog box to close it.

So that you can view all the fields and complete field names, you'll resize the Owner table field list.

6. Position the mouse pointer on the bottom border of the Owner table field list until it changes to ↕, and then drag the bottom of the Owner table field list to lengthen it until the vertical scroll bar disappears and all the fields are visible.

To form the relationship between the two tables, you drag the common field of OwnerID from the primary table to the related table. Then Access opens the Edit Relationships dialog box, in which you select the relationship options for the two tables.

7. Click **OwnerID** in the Owner field list, and then drag it to **OwnerID** in the Animal field list. When you release the mouse button, the Edit Relationships dialog box opens. See Figure 2-42.

Figure 2-42 **Edit Relationships dialog box**

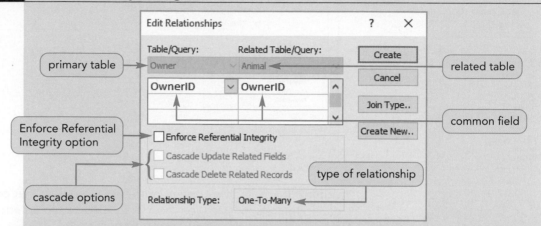

The primary table, related table, common field, and relationship type (One-To-Many) appear in the dialog box. Note that Access correctly identifies the "One" side of the relationship and places the primary table Owner in the Table/Query section of the dialog box; similarly, Access correctly identifies the "Many" side of the relationship and places the related table Animal in the Related Table/Query section of the dialog box.

8. Click the **Enforce Referential Integrity** check box. After you click the Enforce Referential Integrity check box, the two cascade options become available. If you select the Cascade Update Related Fields option, Access will update the appropriate foreign key values in the related table when you change a primary key value in the primary table. You will *not* select the Cascade Delete Related Records option because doing so could cause you to delete records that you do not want to delete; this option is rarely selected.

9. Click the **Cascade Update Related Fields** check box.

10. Click the **Create** button to define the one-to-many relationship between the two tables and to close the dialog box. The completed relationship appears in the Relationships window, with the join line connecting the common field of OwnerID in each table. See Figure 2-43.

Figure 2-43   Defined relationship in the Relationship window

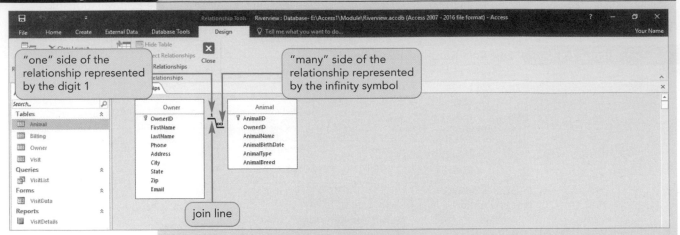

"one" side of the relationship represented by the digit 1

"many" side of the relationship represented by the infinity symbol

join line

Trouble? If a dialog box opens indicating a problem that prevents you from creating the relationship, you most likely made a typing error when entering the two records in the Owner table. If so, click the OK button in the dialog box and then click the Cancel button in the Edit Relationships dialog box. Refer back to the earlier steps instructing you to enter the two records in the Owner table and carefully compare your entries with those shown in the text, especially the OwnerID field values. Make any necessary corrections to the data in the Owner table, and then repeat Steps 7 through 10. If you still receive an error message, ask your instructor for assistance.

The next step is to define the one-to-many relationship between the Animal and Visit tables. In this relationship, Animal is the primary ("one") table because there is at most one animal for each visit. Visit is the related ("many") table because there are zero, one, or many visits that are generated for each animal. Similarly, you need to define the one-to-many relationship between the Visit and Billing tables. In this relationship, Visit is the primary ("one") table because there is at most one visit for each invoice. Billing is the related ("many") table because there are zero, one, or many invoices that are generated for each animal visit. For example, some visits require lab work, which is invoiced separately.

To define the relationship between the Animal and Visit tables and to define the relationship between the Visit and billing tables:

1. On the Relationship Tools Design tab, in the Relationships group, click the **Show Table** button to open the Show Table dialog box.

2. Click **Visit** on the Tables tab, click the **Add** button, and then click the **Close** button to close the Show Table dialog box. The Visit table's field list appears in the Relationships window to the right of the Animal table's field list.

   Because the Animal table is the primary table in this relationship, you need to drag the AnimalID field from the Animal field list to the Visit field list.

3. Drag the **AnimalID** field in the Animal field list to the **AnimalID** field in the Visit field list. When you release the mouse button, the Edit Relationships dialog box opens.

TIP

You can also use the mouse to drag a table from the Navigation Pane to add it to the Relationships window.

4. Click the **Enforce Referential Integrity** check box, click the **Cascade Update Related Fields** check box, and then click the **Create** button. The Edit Relationships dialog box closes and the completed relationship appears in the Relationships window.

Finally, you will define the relationship between the Visit and Billing tables.

5. On the Relationship Tools Design tab, in the Relationships group, click the **Show Table** button to open the Show Table dialog box.

6. Click **Billing** on the Tables tab, click the **Add** button, and then click the **Close** button to close the Show Table dialog box. The Billing table's field list appears in the Relationships window to the right of the Visit table's field list.

7. Click and drag the **VisitID** field in the Visit field list to the **VisitID** field in the Billing field list. The Edit Relationships dialog box opens.

8. In the Edit Relationships dialog box, click the **Enforce Referential Integrity** check box, click the **Cascade Update Related Fields** check box, and then click the **Create** button to define the one-to-many relationship between the two tables and to close the dialog box. The completed relationships for the Riverview database appear in the Relationships window. See Figure 2-44.

| Figure 2-44 | All three relationships now defined |

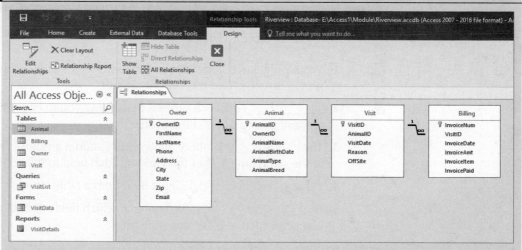

9. On the Quick Access Toolbar, click the **Save** button 🖫 to save the layout in the Relationships window.

10. On the Relationship Tools Design tab, in the Relationships group, click the **Close** button to close the Relationships window.

11. Compact and repair the Riverview database, and then close the database.

Problem Solving: Creating a Larger Database

The Riverview database is a relatively small database containing only a few tables, and the data and the reports you will generate from it will be fairly simple. A larger database would most likely have many more tables and different types of relationships that can be quite complex. When creating a large database, follow this standard process:

• Consult people who will be using the data to gain an understanding of how it will be used. Gather sample reports and representative data if possible.
• Plan the tables, fields, data types, other properties, and the relationships between the tables.
• Create the tables and define the relationships between them.
• Populate the tables with sample data.
• Design some queries, forms, and reports that will be needed, and then test them.
• Modify the database structure, if necessary, based on the results of your tests.
• Enter the actual data into the database tables.

Testing is critical at every stage of creating a database. Once the database is finalized and implemented, it's not actually finished. The design of a database evolves as new functionality is required and as the data that is gathered changes.

Session 2.2 Quick Check

1. What is the keyboard shortcut for inserting the value from the same field in the previous record into the current record?

2. _____ data is a process that allows you to copy the data from a source without having to open the source file.

3. The _____ gallery allows you to add a group of related fields to a table at the same time, rather than adding each field to the table individually.

4. What is the effect of deleting a field from a table structure?

5. A(n) _____ text file is one in which fields of data are separated by a character such as a comma or a tab.

6. The _____ is the "one" table in a one-to-many relationship, and the _____ is the "many" table in the relationship.

7. _____ is a set of rules that Access enforces to maintain consistency between related tables when you update data in a database.

Review Assignments

PRACTICE

Data File needed for the Review Assignments: Vendor.accdb (*cont. from Module 1*) and Supplies.xlsx

In addition to tracking information about the vendors Riverview Veterinary Care Center works with, Kimberly also wants to track information about their products and services. First, Kimberly asks you to modify the necessary properties in the existing Supplier table in the Vendor database; then she wants you to create a new table in the Vendor database to contain product data. Complete the following:

1. Open the **Vendor** database you created in the previous module.
2. Open the **Supplier** table in Design view, and set the field properties as shown in Figure 2-45.

Figure 2-45   **Field properties for the Supplier table**

Field Name	Data Type	Description	Field Size	Other
SupplierID	Short Text	Primary key	6	Caption = Supplier ID
Company	Short Text		50	
Category	Short Text		15	
Address	Short Text		35	
City	Short Text		25	
State	Short Text		2	
Zip	Short Text		10	
Phone	Short Text		14	Caption = Contact Phone
ContactFirst	Short Text		20	Caption = Contact First Name
ContactLast	Short Text		25	Caption = Contact Last Name
InitialContact	Date/Time			Format = Short Date
				Caption = Initial Contact

3. Save the Supplier table. Click the **Yes** button when a message appears, indicating some data might be lost. Switch to Datasheet view and resize columns, as necessary, to their best fit. Then save and close the Supplier table.
4. Create a new table in Design view, using the table design shown in Figure 2-46.

Figure 2-46   **Design for the Product table**

Field Name	Data Type	Description	Field Size	Other
ProductID	Short Text	Primary key	5	Caption = Product ID
SupplierID	Short Text	Foreign key	6	Caption = Supplier ID
ProductName	Short Text		75	Caption = Product Name
Price	Currency			Format = Standard
				Decimal Places = 2
TempControl	Yes/No			Caption = Temp Controlled?
Sterile	Yes/No			Caption = Sterile?
Units	Number		Integer	Decimal Places = 0
				Caption = Units/Case
				Default Value = [no entry]

5. Specify ProductID as the primary key, and then save the table as **Product**.

6. Modify the table structure by adding a new field between the Price and TempControl fields. Name the new field **Weight** (data type: **Number**; field size: **Single**; Decimal Places: **2**; Caption: **Weight in Lbs**; Default Value: [no entry]). Then move the **Units** field so that it is positioned between the Price and Weight fields.

7. Enter the records shown in Figure 2-47 in the Product table. Resize all datasheet columns to their best fit. When finished, save and close the Product table.

Figure 2-47   **Records for the Product table**

Product ID	Supplier ID	Product Name	Price	Units/Case	Weight in Lbs	Temp Controlled?	Sterile?
PT100	KLS321	Paper tape roll	20.00	12	3	No	No
TC050	QLS002	Thermometer covers	27.00	50	1	No	Yes

8. Use the Import Spreadsheet Wizard to add data to the Product table. The data you need to import is contained in the Supplies workbook, which is an Excel file located in the Access1 > Review folder provided with your Data Files.

   a. Specify the Supplies workbook as the source of the data.

   b. Select the option for appending the data.

   c. Select Product as the table.

   d. In the Import Spreadsheet Wizard dialog boxes, make sure Access confirms that the first row contains column headings, and import to the Product table. Do not save the import steps.

9. Open the **Product** table in Datasheet view, and resize columns to their best fit, as necessary. Then save and close the Product table.

10. Define a one-to-many relationship between the primary Supplier table and the related Product table. Resize the table field lists so that all field names are visible. Select the referential integrity option and the cascade updates option for the relationship.

11. Save the changes to the Relationships window and close it, compact and repair the Vendor database, and then close the database.

Case Problem 1

Data Files needed for this Case Problem: Beauty.accdb (cont. from Module 1) and Customers.txt

Beauty To Go   Sue Miller wants to use the Beauty database to track information about customers who subscribe to her business, which provides a variety of salon services on a subscription basis, and the plans in which customers are enrolled. She asks you to help maintain this database. Complete the following:

1. Open the **Beauty** database you created in the previous module, open the **Option** table in Design view, and then change the following field properties:

   a. OptionID: Enter **Primary key** for the description, change the field size to **3**, and enter **Option ID** for the caption.

   b. OptionDescription: Change the field size to **45** and enter **Option Description** for the caption.

   c. OptionCost: Change the format to **Standard**, specify **0** decimal places, enter **Option Cost** for the caption, no default value.

   d. FeeWaived: Enter **Fee Waived** for the caption.

2. Save and close the Option table. Click the Yes button when a message appears, indicating some data might be lost.

3. Create a new table in Design view, using the table design shown in Figure 2-48.

| Figure 2-48 | Design for the Member table |

Field Name	Data Type	Description	Field Size	Other
MemberID	Short Text	Primary key	4	Caption = Member ID
OptionID	Short Text	Foreign key	3	Caption = Option ID
FirstName	Short Text		20	Caption = First Name
LastName	Short Text		25	Caption = Last Name
Phone	Short Text		14	
OptionEnd	Date/Time	Date Option Ends		Format = Short Date
				Caption = Option Ends

4. Specify **MemberID** as the primary key, and then save the table as **Member**.
5. Use the Address Quick Start selection in the Data Type gallery to add five fields between the LastName and Phone fields.
6. Switch to Design view, and then make the following changes to the Member table design:
   a. Address field: Change the name of this field to **Street**, change the field size to **40**, and delete the entry for the caption.
   b. City field: Change the field size to **25**, and delete the entry for the caption.
   c. StateProvince field: Change the name of this field to **State**, change the field size to **2**, delete the entry for the caption, and enter **FL** for the default value.
   d. ZIPPostal field: Change the name of this field to **Zip**, change the field size to **10**, and delete the entry for the caption.
   e. Delete the **CountryRegion** field from the Member table structure.
   f. Between the Phone and OptionEnd fields, add a new field named **OptionBegin** (data type: **Date/Time**; format: **Short Date**; Caption: **Option Begins**).
7. Enter the records shown in Figure 2-49 in the Member table. Resize all datasheet columns to their best fit. When finished, save and close the Member table. Be sure to enter your first and last name in the appropriate fields in the first record.

| Figure 2-49 | Records for the Member table |

Member ID	Option ID	First Name	Last Name	Street	City	State	Zip	Phone	Option Begins	Option Ends
2103	123	*Student First*	*Student Last*	22 Oak St	Orlando	FL	32801	407-832-3944	2/1/17	3/1/17
2118	120	Susan	Reyes	3 Balboa St	Orlando	FL	32804	407-216-0091	11/2/16	2/2/17

8. Use the Import Text File Wizard to add data to the Member table. The data you need to import is contained in the Customers text file, which is located in the Access1 > Case1 folder provided with your Data Files.
   a. Specify the Customers text file as the source of the data.
   b. Select the option for appending the data.
   c. Select Member as the table.
   d. In the Import Text File Wizard dialog boxes, choose the options to import delimited data, to use a comma delimiter, and to import the data into the Member table. Do not save the import steps.
9. Open the **Member** table in Datasheet view and resize columns to their best fit, as necessary. Then save and close the Member table.

10. Define a one-to-many relationship between the primary Option table and the related Member table. Resize the Member table field list so that all field names are visible. Select the referential integrity option and the cascade updates option for this relationship.

11. Save the changes to the Relationships window and close it, compact and repair the Beauty database, and then close the database.

Case Problem 2

APPLY

Data Files needed for this Case Problem: Programming.accdb *(cont. from Module 1)*, **Client.accdb, Students.txt, and Agreements.xlsx**

Programming Pros Brent Hovis plans to use the Programming database to maintain information about the students, tutors, and contracts for his tutoring services company. Brent asks you to help him build the database by updating one table and creating two new tables in the database. Complete the following:

1. Open the **Programming** database you created in the previous module, open the **Tutor** table in Design view, and then set the field properties as shown in Figure 2-50.

Figure 2-50 **Field properties for the Tutor table**

Field Name	Data Type	Description	Field Size	Other
TutorID	Short Text	Primary key	4	Caption = Tutor ID
FirstName	Short Text		20	Caption = First Name
LastName	Short Text		25	Caption = Last Name
Major	Short Text		25	
YearInSchool	Short Text		12	Caption = Year In School
School	Short Text		30	
HireDate	Date/Time			Format = Short Date
				Caption = Hire Date

2. Add a new field as the last field in the Tutor table with the field name **Groups**, the **Yes/No** data type, and the caption **Groups Only**.

3. Save the Tutor table. Click the **Yes** button when a message appears, indicating some data might be lost.

4. In the table datasheet, specify that the following tutors conduct group tutoring sessions only: Carey Billings, Fredrik Karlsson, Ellen Desoto, and Donald Gallager. Close the Tutor table.

5. Brent created a table named Student in the Client database that is located in the Access1 > Case2 folder provided with your Data Files. Import the structure of the Student table in the Client database into a new table named Student in the Programming database. Do not save the import steps.

6. Open the **Student** table in Datasheet view, and then add the following two fields to the end of the table: **BirthDate** (Date/Time field) and **Gender** (Short Text field).

7. Use the Phone Quick Start selection in the Data Type gallery to add four fields related to phone numbers between the Zip and BirthDate fields. (*Hint:* Be sure to make the BirthDate field the active field before adding the new fields.)

8. Display the Student table in Design view, delete the BusinessPhone and FaxNumber fields, and then save and close the Student table.

9. Reopen the Student table and modify its design so that it matches the design in Figure 2-51, *including the revised field names and data types.*

Figure 2-51	Field properties for the Student table

Field Name	Data Type	Description	Field Size	Other
StudentID	Short Text	Primary key	7	Caption = Student ID
LastName	Short Text		25	Caption = Last Name
FirstName	Short Text		20	Caption = First Name
Address	Short Text		35	
City	Short Text		25	
State	Short Text		2	Default Value = NC
Zip	Short Text		10	
HomePhone	Short Text		14	Caption = Home Phone
CellPhone	Short Text		14	Caption = Cell Phone
BirthDate	Date/Time			Format = Short Date
				Caption = Birth Date
Gender	Short Text		1	

10. Move the LastName field so it follows the FirstName field.
11. Save your changes to the table design, and then add the records shown in Figure 2-52 to the Student table.

Figure 2-52	Records for the Student table

Student ID	First Name	Last Name	Address	City	State	Zip	Home Phone	Cell Phone	Date of Birth	Gender
LOP4015	Henry	Lopez	19 8th St	Raleigh	NC	27601	919-264-9981	919-665-8110	2/19/1998	M
PER4055	Rosalyn	Perez	421 Pine Ln	Cary	NC	27511	984-662-4761	919-678-0012	4/12/1996	F

12. Resize the fields to their best fit, and then save and close the Student table.
13. Use the Import Text File Wizard to add data to the Student table. The data you need to import is contained in the Students text file, which is located in the Access1 > Case2 folder provided with your Data Files.

    a. Specify the Students text file as the source of the data.

    b. Select the option for appending the data.

    c. Select Student as the table.

    d. In the Import Text File Wizard dialog boxes, choose the options to import delimited data, to use a comma delimiter, and to import the data into the Student table. Do not save the import steps.

14. Open the **Student** table in Datasheet view, resize columns in the datasheet to their best fit (as necessary), and then save and close the table.
15. Create a new table in Design view, using the table design shown in Figure 2-53.

Figure 2-53	Design for the Contract table

Field Name	Data Type	Description	Field Size	Other
ContractID	Short Text	Primary key	4	Caption = Contract ID
StudentID	Short Text	Foreign key	7	Caption = Student ID
TutorID	Short Text	Foreign key	4	Caption = Tutor ID
SessionType	Short Text		15	Caption = Session Type
Length	Number		Integer	Decimal Places = 0
				Caption = Length (Hrs)
				Default Value = [no entry]
NumSessions	Number		Integer	Decimal Places = 0
				Caption = Number of Sessions
				Default Value = [no entry]
Cost	Currency			Format = Currency
				Decimal Places = 0
				Default Value = [no entry]
Assessment	Yes/No	Pre-assessment exam complete		Caption = Assessment Complete

16. Specify ContractID as the primary key, and then save the table using the name **Contract**.
17. Add a new field to the Contract table, between the TutorID and SessionType fields, with the field name **ContractDate**, the **Date/Time** data type, the description **Date contract is signed**, the **Short Date** format, and the caption **Contract Date**. Save and close the Contract table.
18. Use the Import Spreadsheet Wizard to add data to the Contract table. The data you need to import is contained in the Agreements workbook, which is an Excel file located in the Access1 > Case2 folder provided with your Data Files.
    a. Specify the Agreements workbook as the source of the data.
    b. Select the option for appending the data to the table.
    c. Select Contract as the table.
    d. In the Import Spreadsheet Wizard dialog boxes, choose the Agreements worksheet, make sure Access confirms that the first row contains column headings, and import to the Contract table. Do not save the import steps.
19. Open the **Contract** table, and add the records shown in Figure 2-54. (*Hint:* Use the New (blank) record button in the navigation buttons to add a new record.)

Figure 2-54	Records for the Contract table

Contract ID	Student ID	Tutor ID	Contract Date	Session Type	Length (Hrs)	Number of Sessions	Cost	Assessment Complete
6215	PER4055	1018	7/6/2017	Group	2	5	$400	Yes
6350	LOP4015	1010	10/12/2017	Private	3	4	$720	Yes

20. Resize columns in the datasheet to their best fit (as necessary), and then save and close the Contract table.
21. Define the one-to-many relationships between the database tables as follows: between the primary Student table and the related Contract table, and between the primary Tutor table and the related Contract table. Resize the table field lists so that all field names are visible. Select the referential integrity option and the cascade updates option for each relationship.
22. Save the changes to the Relationships window and close it, compact and repair the Programming database, and then close the database.

Case Problem 3

Data Files needed for this Case Problem: Center.accdb *(cont. from Module 1)***, Donations.xlsx, and Auctions.txt**

Diane's Community Center   Diane Coleman wants to use the Center database to maintain information about the patrons and donations for her not-for-profit community center. Diane asks you to help her maintain the database by updating one table and creating two new ones. Complete the following:

1. Open the **Center** database you created in the previous module, open the **Patron** table in Design view, and then change the following field properties:

   a. PatronID: Enter **Primary key** for the description, change the field size to **5**, and enter **Patron ID** for the caption.

   b. Title: Change the field size to **4**.

   c. FirstName: Change the field size to **20**, and enter **First Name** for the caption.

   d. LastName: Change the field size to **25**, and enter **Last Name** for the caption.

   e. Phone: Change the field size to **14**.

   f. Email: Change field size to **35**.

2. Save and close the Patron table. Click the Yes button when a message appears, indicating some data might be lost.

⊕ **Explore** 3. Use the Import Spreadsheet Wizard to create a table in the Center database. As the source of the data, specify the Donations workbook, which is located in the Access1 > Case3 folder provided with your Data Files. Select the option to import the source data into a new table in the database.

⊕ **Explore** 4. Complete the Import Spreadsheet Wizard dialog boxes as follows:

   a. Select Donation as the worksheet you want to import.

   b. Specify that the first row contains column headings.

   c. Accept the field options suggested by the wizard, and do not skip any fields.

   d. Choose DonationID as your own primary key.

   e. Import the data to a table named **Donation**, and do not save the import steps.

⊕ **Explore** 5. Open the Donation table in Datasheet view. Left-justify the DonationDescription field by clicking the column heading, and then on the Home tab, clicking the Align Left button in the Text Formatting group.

6. Open the Donation table in Design view, and then modify the table so it matches the design shown in Figure 2-55, including changes to data types, field name, and field position. For the Short Text fields, delete any formats specified in the Format property boxes.

Figure 2-55 **Design for the Donation table**

Field Name	Data Type	Description	Field Size	Other
DonationID	Short Text	Primary key	4	Caption = Donation ID
PatronID	Short Text	Foreign key	5	Caption = Patron ID
DonationDate	Date/Time			Format = mm/dd/yyyy
				Caption = Donation Date
Description	Short Text		30	
DonationValue	Currency	Dollar amount or estimated value		Format = Currency
				Decimal Places = 2
				Caption = Donation Value
				Default Value = [no entry]
CashDonation	Yes/No			Caption = Cash Donation?
AuctionItem	Yes/No			Caption = Possible Auction Item?

7. Save your changes to the table design, click Yes for the message about lost data, and then switch to Datasheet view.

8. Resize the columns in the Donation datasheet to their best fit.

⊕ **Explore** 9. Diane decides that the values in the Donation Value column would look better without the two decimal places. Make this field the current field in the datasheet. Then, on the Table Tools Fields tab, in the Formatting group, use the Decrease Decimals button to remove the two decimal places and the period from these values. Switch back to Design view, and note that the Decimal Places property for the DonationValue field is now set to 0.

10. Save and close the Donation table.

11. Use Design view to create a table using the table design shown in Figure 2-56.

Figure 2-56 **Design for the Auction table**

Field Name	Data Type	Description	Field Size	Other
AuctionID	Short Text	Primary key	3	Caption = Auction ID
AuctionDate	Date/Time			Format = mm/dd/yyyy
				Caption = Date of Auction
DonationID	Short Text		4	Caption = Donation ID
MinPrice	Currency			Format = Currency
				Decimal Places = 0
				Caption = Minimum Sale Price
ItemSold	Yes/No			Caption = Item Sold at Auction?

12. Specify **AuctionID** as the primary key, save the table as **Auction**, and then close the table.

13. Use the Import Text File Wizard to add data to the Auction table. The data you need to import is contained in the Auctions text file, which is located in the Access1 > Case3 folder provided with your Data Files.

   a. Specify the Auctions text file as the source of the data.

   b. Select the option for appending the data.

   c. Select Auction as the table.

   d. In the Import Text File Wizard dialog boxes, choose the options to import delimited data, to use a comma delimiter, and to import the data into the Auction table. Do not save the import steps.

14. Open the Auction table in Datasheet view, and resize all columns to their best fit.

15. Display the Auction table in Design view. Move the DonationID field to make it the second field in the table, and enter the description **Foreign key** for the DonationID field. Save the modified Auction table design.

16. Switch to Datasheet view, and then add the records shown in Figure 2-57 to the Auction table. (*Hint:* Use the New (blank) record button in the navigation buttons to add a new record.) Close the table when finished.

Figure 2-57	Records for the Auction table

AuctionID	DonationID	AuctionDate	MinPrice	ItemSold
205	5132	8/12/2017	200	No
235	5217	10/14/2017	150	No

17. Define the one-to-many relationships between the database tables as follows: between the primary Patron table and the related Donation table, and between the primary Donation table and the related Auction table. Resize any field lists so that all field names are visible. Select the referential integrity option and the cascade updates option for each relationship.

18. Save the changes to the Relationships window and close it, compact and repair the Center database, and then close the database.

Case Problem 4

CHALLENGE

Data Files needed for this Case Problem: Appalachia.accdb *(cont. from Module 1)*, Travel.accdb, and Bookings.txt

Hike Appalachia   Molly and Bailey Johnson use the Appalachia database to track the data about the hikers and tours offered through their business. They ask you to help them maintain this database. Complete the following:

1. Open the **Appalachia** database you created in the previous module, open the **Hiker** table in Design view, and then change the following field properties:

   a. HikerID: Enter **Primary key** for the description, change the field size to **3**, and enter **Hiker ID** for the caption.

   b. HikerFirst: Change the field size to **20**, and enter **Hiker First Name** for the caption.

   c. HikerLast: Change the field size to **25**, and enter **Hiker Last Name** for the caption.

   d. Address: Change the field size to **35**.

   e. City: Change the field size to **25**.

   f. State: Change the field size to **2**.

   g. Zip: Change the field size to **10**.

   h. Phone: Change the field size to **14**.

2. Save the Hiker table, click the Yes button when a message appears, indicating some data might be lost, resize the Hiker First Name and Hiker Last Name columns in Datasheet view to their best fit, and then save and close the table.

   a. Import the **Trip** table structure and data from the **Travel** database into a new table in the **Appalachia** database. As the source of the data, specify the Travel database, which is located in the Access1 > Case4 folder provided with your Data Files; select the option button to import tables, queries, forms, reports, macros, and modules into the current database; and in the Import Objects dialog box, select the **Trip** table, click the **Options** button, and then make sure that the correct option is selected to import the table's data and structure (definition).

   b. Do not save your import steps.

✛ **Explore** 3. Using a shortcut menu in the Navigation Pane, rename the Trip table as **Tour** to give this name to the new table in the Appalachia database.

4. Open the **Tour** table in Design view, and then delete the VIPDiscount field.

5. Change the following properties:

   a. TourID: Enter the description **Primary key**, change the field size to **3**, and enter **Tour ID** for the caption.

   b. TourName: Enter **Tour Name** for the caption, and change the field size to **35**.

   c. TourType: Enter **Tour Type** for the caption, and change the field size to **15**.

   d. PricePerPerson: Enter **Price Per Person** for the caption.

6. Save the modified table, click the Yes button when a message appears, indicating some data might be lost, and then display the table in Datasheet view. Resize all datasheet columns to their best fit, and then save and close the table.

7. In Design view, create a table using the table design shown in Figure 2-58.

Figure 2-58   **Design for the Reservation table**

Field Name	Data Type	Description	Field Size	Other
ReservationID	Short Text	Primary key	4	Caption = Reservation ID
HikerID	Short Text	Foreign key	3	Caption = Hiker ID
TourID	Short Text	Foreign key	3	Caption = Tour ID
TourDate	Date/Time			Caption = Tour Date
People	Number		Integer	Decimal Places = 0
				Default Value = [no entry]

8. Specify **ReservationID** as the primary key, and then save the table as **Reservation**.

✛ **Explore** 9. Refer back to Figure 2-11 to review the custom date formats. Change the Format property of the TourDate field to a custom format that displays dates in a format similar to 02/15/17. Save and close the Reservation table.

10. Use the Import Text File Wizard to add data to the Reservation table. The data you need to import is contained in the Bookings text file, which is located in the Access1 > Case4 folder provided with your Data Files.

    a. Specify the Bookings text file as the source of the data.

    b. Select the option for appending the data.

    c. Select Reservation as the table.

    d. In the Import Text File Wizard dialog boxes, choose the options to import delimited data, to use a comma delimiter, and to import the data into the Reservation table. Do not save the import steps.

11. Open the **Reservation** table, and then resize columns in the table datasheet to their best fit (as necessary), verify that the date values in the StartDate field are displayed correctly according to the custom format, and then save and close the table.

12. Define the one-to-many relationships between the database tables as follows: between the primary Hiker table and the related Reservation table, and between the primary Tour table and the related Reservation table. (*Hint:* Place the Reservation table as the middle table in the Relationships window to make it easier to join the tables.) Resize the Hiker field list so that all field names are visible. Select the referential integrity option and the cascade updates option for each relationship.

13. Save the changes to the Relationships window and close it, compact and repair the Appalachia database, and then close the database.

ACCESS

Maintaining and Querying a Database

Updating Tables and Retrieving Care Center Information

Case | *Riverview Veterinary Care Center*

At a recent meeting, Kimberly Johnson and her staff discussed the importance of maintaining accurate information about the animals seen by Riverview Veterinary Care Center, as well as the owners, visits, and invoices, and regularly monitoring the business activities of the care center. For example, Kelly Flannagan, Kimberly's assistant, needs to make sure she has up-to-date contact information, such as phone numbers and email addresses, for the owners of all the animals seen by the care center. The office staff also must monitor billing activity to ensure that invoices are paid on time and in full. In addition, the staff handles marketing efforts for the care center and tracks services provided to develop new strategies for promoting these services. Kimberly is also interested in analyzing other aspects of the business related to animal visits and finances. You can satisfy all these informational needs for Riverview Veterinary Care Center by updating data in the Riverview database and by creating and using queries that retrieve information from the database.

STARTING DATA FILES

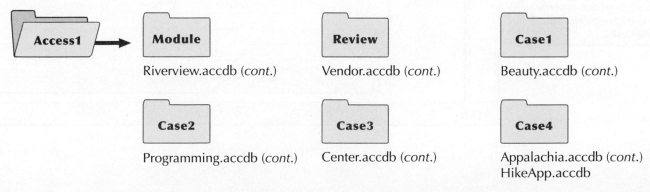

Access1 → Module
Riverview.accdb (*cont.*)

Review
Vendor.accdb (*cont.*)

Case1
Beauty.accdb (*cont.*)

Case2
Programming.accdb (*cont.*)

Case3
Center.accdb (*cont.*)

Case4
Appalachia.accdb (*cont.*)
HikeApp.accdb

Session 3.1 Visual Overview:

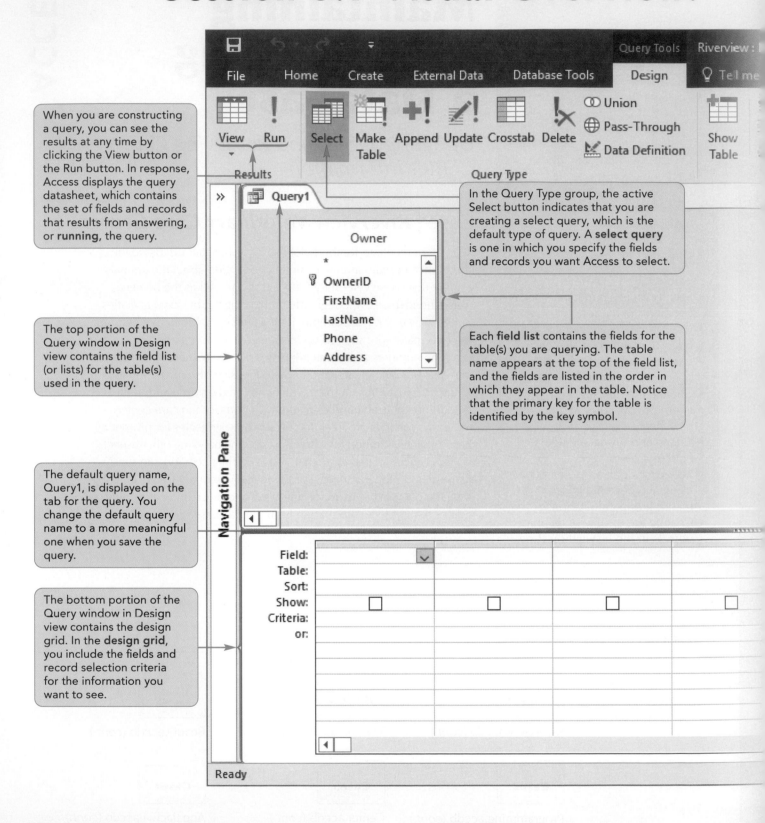

When you are constructing a query, you can see the results at any time by clicking the View button or the Run button. In response, Access displays the query datasheet, which contains the set of fields and records that results from answering, or **running**, the query.

In the Query Type group, the active Select button indicates that you are creating a select query, which is the default type of query. A **select query** is one in which you specify the fields and records you want Access to select.

The top portion of the Query window in Design view contains the field list (or lists) for the table(s) used in the query.

Each **field list** contains the fields for the table(s) you are querying. The table name appears at the top of the field list, and the fields are listed in the order in which they appear in the table. Notice that the primary key for the table is identified by the key symbol.

The default query name, Query1, is displayed on the tab for the query. You change the default query name to a more meaningful one when you save the query.

The bottom portion of the Query window in Design view contains the design grid. In the **design grid**, you include the fields and record selection criteria for the information you want to see.

Query Window in Design View

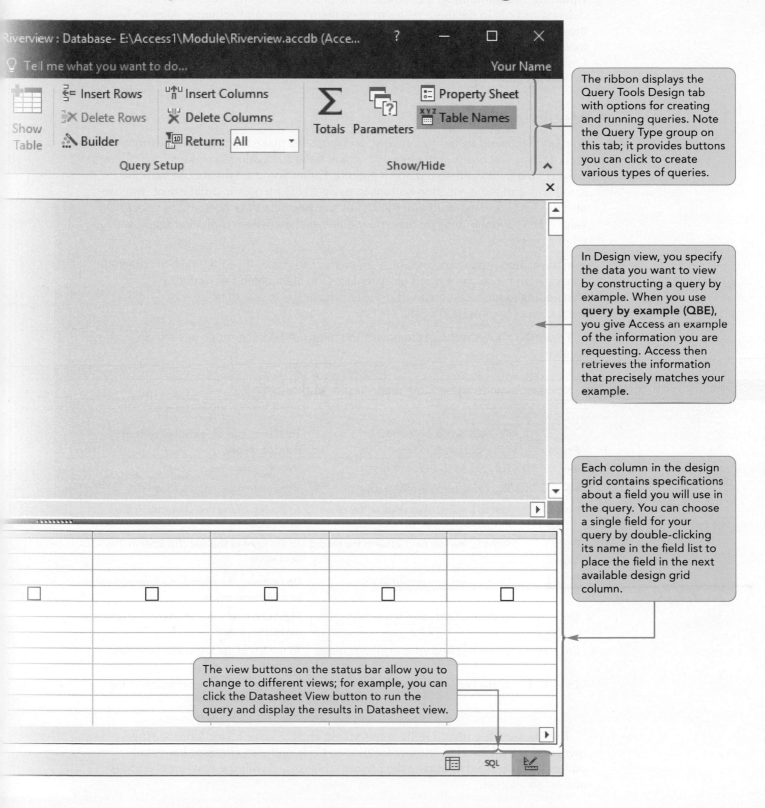

The ribbon displays the Query Tools Design tab with options for creating and running queries. Note the Query Type group on this tab; it provides buttons you can click to create various types of queries.

In Design view, you specify the data you want to view by constructing a query by example. When you use **query by example (QBE)**, you give Access an example of the information you are requesting. Access then retrieves the information that precisely matches your example.

Each column in the design grid contains specifications about a field you will use in the query. You can choose a single field for your query by double-clicking its name in the field list to place the field in the next available design grid column.

The view buttons on the status bar allow you to change to different views; for example, you can click the Datasheet View button to run the query and display the results in Datasheet view.

Updating a Database

Updating, or **maintaining**, a database is the process of adding, modifying, and deleting records in database tables to keep them current and accurate. After reviewing the data in the Riverview database, Kelly identified some changes that need to be made to the data. She would like you to update the field values in one record in the Owner table, correct an error in one record in the Visit table, and then delete a record in the Visit table.

Modifying Records

To modify the field values in a record, you must first make the record the current record. Then you position the insertion point in the field value to make minor changes or select the field value to replace it entirely. Earlier you used the mouse with the scroll bars and the navigation buttons to navigate the records in a datasheet. You can also use keyboard shortcuts and the F2 key to navigate a datasheet and to select field values. The **F2 key** is a toggle that you use to switch between navigation mode and editing mode.

- In **navigation mode**, Access selects an entire field value. If you type while you are in navigation mode, your typed entry replaces the highlighted field value.
- In **editing mode**, you can insert or delete characters in a field value based on the location of the insertion point.

Figure 3-1 shows some of the navigation mode and editing mode keyboard shortcuts.

Figure 3-1 | **Navigation mode and editing mode keyboard shortcuts**

Press	To Move the Selection in Navigation Mode	To Move the Insertion Point in Editing Mode
←	Left one field value at a time	Left one character at a time
→	Right one field value at a time	Right one character at a time
Home	Left to the first field value in the record	To the left of the first character in the field value
End	Right to the last field value in the record	To the right of the last character in the field value
↑ or ↓	Up or down one record at a time	Up or down one record at a time and switch to navigation mode
Tab or Enter	Right one field value at a time	Right one field value at a time and switch to navigation mode
Ctrl + Home	To the first field value in the first record	To the left of the first character in the field value
Ctrl + End	To the last field value in the last record	To the right of the last character in the field value

The Owner table record Kelly wants you to change is for Taylor Johnson. This owner recently moved to another location in Cody and also changed her email address, so you need to update the Owner table record with the new street address and email address.

To open the Owner table in the Riverview database:

▶ **1.** Start Access and open the **Riverview** database you created and worked with earlier.

  Trouble? If the security warning is displayed below the ribbon, click the Enable Content button.

▶ **2.** Open the **Owner** table in Datasheet view.

The Owner table contains many fields. Sometimes, when updating data in a table, it can be helpful to remove the display of some fields on the screen.

Hiding and Unhiding Fields

When you are viewing a table or query datasheet in Datasheet view, you might want to temporarily remove certain fields from the displayed datasheet, making it easier to focus on the data you're interested in viewing. The **Hide Fields** command allows you to remove the display of one or more fields, and the **Unhide Fields** command allows you to redisplay any hidden fields.

To make it easier to modify the owner record, you'll first hide a couple of fields in the Owner table.

To hide fields in the Owner table and modify the owner record:

▶ **1.** Right-click the **State** field name to display the shortcut menu, and then click **Hide Fields**. The State column is removed from the datasheet display.

▶ **2.** Right-click the **Zip** field name, and then click **Hide Fields** on the shortcut menu. The Zip column is removed from the datasheet display.

  With the fields hidden, you can now update the owner record. The record you need to modify is near the end of the table and has an OwnerID field value of 2412.

▶ **3.** Scroll the datasheet until you see the last record in the table.

▶ **4.** Click the OwnerID field value **2412**, for Taylor Johnson. The insertion point appears within the field value, indicating you are in editing mode.

▶ **5.** Press the **Tab** key to move to the First Name field value, Taylor. The field value is selected, indicating you are in navigation mode.

▶ **6.** Press the **Tab** key three times to move to the Address field and select its field value, type **458 Rose Ln**, and then press the **Tab** key twice to move to the Email field.

▶ **7.** Type **taylor.johnson@example.net**, and then press the **Tab** key to move to the insertion point to the OwnerID field in the blank record at the bottom of the table. The changes to the record are complete. See Figure 3-2.

Figure 3-2	Table after changing field values in a record

field values changed

Access saves changes to field values when you move to a new field or another record, or when you close the table. You don't have to click the Save button to save changes to field values or records.

8. Press the **Ctrl+Home** keys to move to the first field value in the first record. With the changes to the record complete, you can unhide the hidden fields.

9. Right-click any field name to display the shortcut menu, and then click **Unhide Fields**. The Unhide Columns dialog box opens. See Figure 3-3.

Figure 3-3   Unhide Columns dialog box

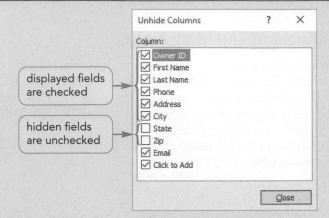

displayed fields are checked

hidden fields are unchecked

All currently displayed fields are checked in this dialog box, and all hidden fields are unchecked. To redisplay them, you simply click their check boxes to select them.

10. In the Unhide Columns dialog box, click the **State** check box to select it, click the **Zip** check box to select it, and then click the **Close** button to close the dialog box. The two hidden fields are now displayed in the datasheet.

11. Close the Owner table, and then click the **No** button in the dialog box that opens, asking if you want to save changes to the layout of the Owner table. This box appears because you hid fields and redisplayed them.

In this case, you can click either the Yes button or the No button, because no changes were actually made to the table layout or design.

Next you need to correct an error in the Visit table for a visit made by Molly, Animal ID 12312. A staff member incorrectly entered "Vaccinations" as the reason for the visit, when the animal actually came to the care center that day for a wellness exam. Ensuring the accuracy of the data in a database is an important maintenance task.

To correct the record in the Visit table:

1. Open the **Visit** table in Datasheet view. The record containing the error is for Visit ID 1024.

2. Scroll the Visit table as necessary until you locate Visit ID **1024**, and then click at the end of the **Reason/Diagnosis** field value "Vaccinations" for this record. You are in editing mode.

▶ **3.** Delete **Vaccinations** from the Reason/Diagnosis field, type **Wellness exam**, and then press the **Enter** key twice. The record now contains the correct value in the Reason/Diagnosis field, and this change is automatically saved in the Visit table.

The next update Kelly asks you to make is to delete a record in the Visit table. The owner of Butch, one of the animals seen by the care center, recently notified Taylor that he received an invoice for a neutering visit, but that he had canceled this scheduled appointment. Because this visit did not take place, the record for this visit needs to be deleted from the Visit table. Rather than scrolling through the table to locate the record to delete, you can use the Find command.

Finding Data in a Table

Access provides options you can use to locate specific field values in a table. Instead of scrolling the Visit table datasheet to find the visit that you need to delete—the record for Visit ID 1128—you can use the Find command to find the record. The **Find command** allows you to search a table or query datasheet, or a form, to locate a specific field value or part of a field value. This feature is particularly useful when searching a table that contains a large number of records.

To search for the record in the Visit table:

TIP

You can click any value in the column containing the field you want to search to make the field current.

▶ **1.** Make sure the VisitID field value **1028** is still selected, and the **Home** tab is selected on the ribbon. You need to search the VisitID field to find the record containing the value 1128, so the insertion point is already correctly positioned in the field you want to search.

▶ **2.** In the Find group, click the **Find** button. The Find and Replace dialog box opens. See Figure 3-4.

Figure 3-4   **Find and Replace dialog box**

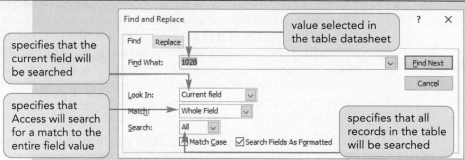

The field value 1028 appears in the Find What box because this value is selected in the table datasheet. You also can choose to search for only part of a field value, such as when you need to find all Visit IDs that start with a certain value. The Search box indicates that all the records in the table will be searched for the value you want to find. You also can choose to search up or down from the currently selected record.

Trouble? Some of the settings in your dialog box might be different from those shown in Figure 3-4 depending on the last search performed on the computer you're using. If so, change the settings so that they match those in the figure.

▶ **3.** Make sure the value 1028 is selected in the Find What box, type **1128** to replace the selected value, and then click the **Find Next** button. Record 50 appears with the field value you specified selected.

▶ **4.** Click the **Cancel** button to close the Find and Replace dialog box.

Deleting Records

To delete a record, you need to select the record in Datasheet view and then delete it using the Delete button in the Records group on the Home tab or the Delete Record option on the shortcut menu.

Deleting a Record

- With the table open in Datasheet view, click the row selector for the record you want to delete.
- In the Records group on the Home tab, click the Delete button (or right-click the row selector for the record, and then click Delete Record on the shortcut menu).
- In the dialog box asking you to confirm the deletion, click the Yes button.

Now that you have found the record with Visit ID 1128, you can delete it. To delete a record, you must first select the entire row for the record.

To delete the record:

▶ **1.** Click the row selector for the record containing the VisitID field value **1128**, which should still be highlighted. The entire row is selected.

▶ **2.** On the Home tab, in the Records group, click the **Delete** button. A dialog box opens indicating that you cannot delete the record because the Billing table contains records that are related to VisitID 1128. Recall that you defined a one-to-many relationship between the Visit and Billing tables and you enforced referential integrity. When you try to delete a record in the primary table (Visit), the enforced referential integrity prevents the deletion if matching records exist in the related table (Billing). This protection helps to maintain the integrity of the data in the database.

To delete the record in the Visit table, you first must delete the related records in the Billing table.

▶ **3.** Click the **OK** button in the dialog box to close it. Notice the plus sign that appears at the beginning of each record in the Visit table. The plus sign, also called the **expand indicator**, indicates that the Visit table is the primary table related to another table—in this case, the Billing table. Clicking the expand indicator displays related records from other tables in the database in a **subdatasheet**.

▶ **4.** Scroll down the datasheet until the selected record is near the top of the datasheet, so that you have room to view the related records for the visit record.

5. Click the **expand indicator** next to VisitID 1128. Two related records from the Billing table for this visit are displayed in the subdatasheet. See Figure 3-5.

Figure 3-5   **Related records from the Billing table in the subdatasheet**

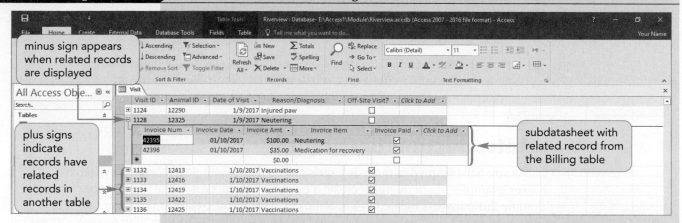

When the subdatasheet is open, you can navigate and update it, just as you can using a table datasheet. The expand indicator for an open subdatasheet is replaced by a minus sign. Clicking the minus sign, or **collapse indicator**, hides the subdatasheet.

You need to delete the records in the Billing table that are related to Visit ID 1128 before you can delete this visit record. The records are for the invoices that were mistakenly sent to the owner of Butch, who had canceled his dog's neutering visit at the care center. You could open the Billing table and find the related records. However, an easier way is to delete the records right in the subdatasheet. The records will be deleted from the Billing table automatically.

6. In the Billing table subdatasheet, click the row selector for invoice number **42395**, and then drag down one row. The rows are selected for both invoice number 42395 and invoice number 42396.

7. On the Home tab, in the Records group, click the **Delete** button. Because the deletion of records is permanent and cannot be undone, a dialog box opens asking you to confirm the deletion of two records.

8. Click the **Yes** button to confirm the deletion and close the dialog box. The records are removed from the Billing table, and the subdatasheet is now empty.

9. Click the **collapse indicator** next to VisitID 1128 to close the subdatasheet.

Now that you have deleted the related records in the Billing table, you can delete the record for Visit ID 1128. You'll use the shortcut menu to do so.

Be sure to select the correct record before deleting it.

10. Right-click the row selector for the record for Visit ID **1128** to select the record and open the shortcut menu.

11. Click **Delete Record** on the shortcut menu, and then click the **Yes** button in the dialog box to confirm the deletion. The record is deleted from the Visit table.

12. Close the Visit table.

Process for Deleting Records

When working with more complex databases that are managed by a database administrator, you typically need special permission to delete records from a table. Many companies also follow the practice of archiving records before deleting them so that the information is still available but not part of the active database.

You have finished updating the Riverview database by modifying and deleting records. Next, you'll retrieve specific data from the database to meet various requests for information about Riverview Veterinary Care Center.

Introduction to Queries

As you have learned, a query is a question you ask about data stored in a database. For example, Kimberly might create a query to find records in the Owner table for only those owners located in a specific city. When you create a query, you tell Access which fields you need and what criteria Access should use to select the records. Access provides powerful query capabilities that allow you to do the following:

- Display selected fields and records from a table
- Sort records
- Perform calculations
- Generate data for forms, reports, and other queries
- Update data in the tables in a database
- Find and display data from two or more tables

Most questions about data are generalized queries in which you specify the fields and records you want Access to select. These common requests for information, such as "Which owners are located in Ralston?" or "How many invoices have been paid?" are select queries. The answer to a select query is returned in the form of a datasheet. The result of a query is also referred to as a **recordset** because the query produces a set of records that answers your question.

Designing Queries vs. Using a Query Wizard

More specialized, technical queries, such as finding duplicate records in a table, are best formulated using a Query Wizard. A **Query Wizard** prompts you for information by asking a series of questions and then creates the appropriate query based on your answers. For example, earlier you used the Simple Query Wizard to display only some of the fields in the Visit table; Access provides other Query Wizards for more complex queries. For common, informational queries, designing your own query is more efficient than using a Query Wizard.

The care center staff is planning an email campaign advertising a microchipping service being offered to animals seen by Riverview Veterinary Care Center. You need to create a query to display the owner ID, last name, first name, city, and email address for each record in the Owner table. You'll open the Query window in Design view to create the query.

To open the Query window in Design view:

▶ **1.** Close the Navigation Pane, and then, on the ribbon, click the **Create** tab.

▶ **2.** In the Queries group, click the **Query Design** button to display the Query window in Design view, with the Show Table dialog box open and the Tables tab selected. See Figure 3-6.

Figure 3-6   Show Table dialog box

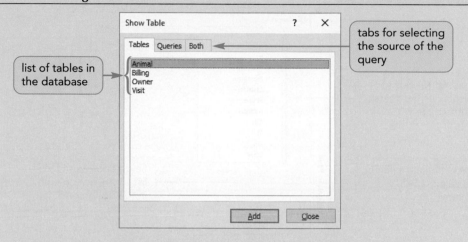

The Show Table dialog box lists all the tables in the Riverview database. You can choose to base a query on one or more tables, on other queries, or on a combination of tables and queries. The query you are creating will retrieve data from the Owner table, so you need to add this table to the Query window.

▶ **3.** In the Tables list, click **Owner**, click the **Add** button, and then click the **Close** button to close the Show Table dialog box. The Owner table's field list appears in the Query window. Refer to the Session 3.1 Visual Overview to familiarize yourself with the Query window in Design view.

Trouble? If you add the wrong table to the Query window, right-click the bar at the top of the field list containing the table name, and then click Remove Table on the shortcut menu. To add the correct table to the Query window, repeat Steps 2 and 3.

Now you'll create and run the query to display selected fields from the Owner table.

Creating and Running a Query

The default table datasheet displays all the fields in the table in the same order as they appear in the table. In contrast, a query datasheet can display selected fields from a table, and the order of the fields can be different from that of the table, enabling those viewing the query results to see only the information they need and in the order they want.

You need the OwnerID, LastName, FirstName, City, and Email fields from the Owner table to appear in the query results. You'll add each of these fields to the design grid. First you'll resize the Owner table field list to display all of the fields.

To select the fields for the query, and then run the query:

1. Drag the bottom border of the Owner field list to resize the field list so that all the fields in the Owner table are visible.

2. In the Owner field list, double-click **OwnerID** to place the field in the design grid's first column Field box. See Figure 3-7.

Figure 3-7 | **Field added to the design grid**

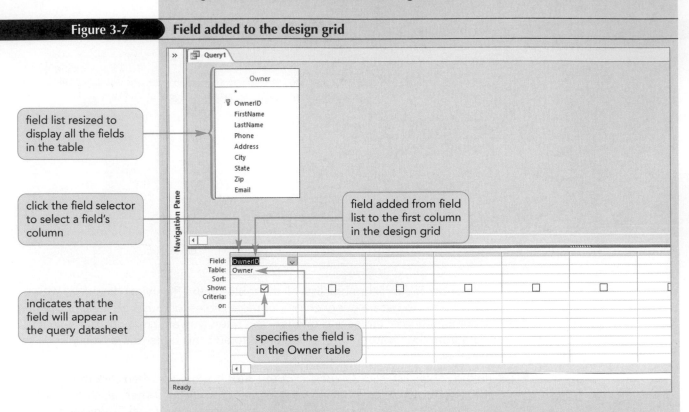

field list resized to display all the fields in the table

click the field selector to select a field's column

field added from field list to the first column in the design grid

indicates that the field will appear in the query datasheet

specifies the field is in the Owner table

In the design grid's first column, the field name OwnerID appears in the Field box, the table name Owner appears in the Table box, and the checkmark in the Show check box indicates that the field will be displayed in the datasheet when you run the query. Sometimes you might not want to display a field and its values in the query results. For example, if you are creating a query to list all owners located in Ralston, and you assign the name "RalstonOwners" to the query, you do not need to include the City field value for each record in the query results—the query design lists only owners with the City field value of "Ralston." Even if you choose not to display a field in the query results, you can still use the field as part of the query to select specific records or to specify a particular sequence for the records in the datasheet. You can also add a field to the design grid using the arrow on the Field box; this arrow appears when you click the Field box, and if you click the arrow or the right side of an empty Field box, a menu of available fields opens.

TIP

You can also use the mouse to drag a field from the field list to a column in the design grid.

3. In the design grid, click the right side of the second column's Field box to display a menu listing all the fields in the Owner table, and then click **LastName** to add this field to the second column in the design grid.

4. Add the **FirstName**, **City**, and **Email** fields to the design grid in that order.

   Trouble? If you accidentally add the wrong field to the design grid, select the field's column by clicking the pointer ↓ on the field selector, which is the thin bar above the Field box, for the field you want to delete, and then press the Delete key (or in the Query Setup group on the Query Tools Design tab, click the Delete Columns button).

   Now that the five fields for the query have been selected, you can run the query.

5. On the Query Tools Design tab, in the Results group, click the **Run** button. Access runs the query and displays the results in Datasheet view. See Figure 3-8.

Figure 3-8   Datasheet displayed after running the query

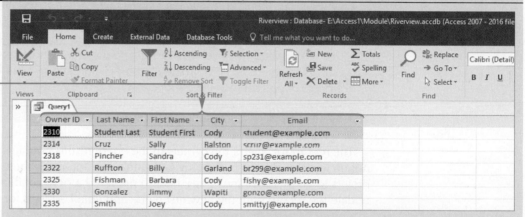

The five fields you added to the design grid appear in the datasheet in the same order as they appear in the design grid. The records are displayed in primary key sequence by OwnerID. The query selected all 25 records from the Owner table for display in the query datasheet. You will save the query as "OwnerEmail" so that you can easily retrieve the same data again.

6. On the Quick Access Toolbar, click the **Save** button 🖫. The Save As dialog box opens.

7. In the Query Name box, type **OwnerEmail** and then press the **Enter** key. The query is saved with the specified name in the Riverview database, and its name appears on the tab for the query.

PROSKILLS

Decision Making: Comparing Methods for Adding All Fields to the Design Grid

If the query you are creating includes every field from the specified table, you can use one of the following three methods to transfer all the fields from the field list to the design grid:

- Double-click (or click and drag) each field individually from the field list to the design grid. Use this method if you want the fields in your query to appear in an order that is different from the order in the field list.
- Double-click the asterisk at the top of the field list. The table name, followed by a period and an asterisk (as in "Owner.*"), appears in the Field box of the first column in the design grid, which signifies that the order of the fields is the same in the query as it is in the field list. Use this method if you don't need to sort the query or specify conditions based on the fields in the table you added in this way (for example, in a query based on more than one table). The advantage of using this method is that you do not need to change the query if you add or delete fields from the underlying table structure. Such changes are reflected automatically in the query.
- Double-click the field list title bar to select all the fields, and then click and drag one of the selected fields to the first column in the design grid. Each field appears in a separate column, and the fields are arranged in the order in which they appear in the field list. Use this method when you need to sort your query or include record selection criteria.

By choosing the most appropriate method to add all the table fields to the query design grid, you can work more efficiently and ensure that the query produces the results you want.

The record for one of the owners in the query results contains information that is not up to date. This owner, Jimmy Gonzalez, had informed the care center that he now prefers to go by the name James; he also provided a new email address. You need to update the record with the new first name and email address for this owner.

Updating Data Using a Query

A query datasheet is temporary, and its contents are based on the criteria in the query design grid; however, you can still update the data in a table using a query datasheet. In this case, you want to make changes to a record in the Owner table. Instead of making the changes in the table datasheet, you can make them in the OwnerEmail query datasheet because the query is based on the Owner table. The underlying Owner table will be updated with the changes you make.

To update data using the OwnerEmail query datasheet:

1. Locate the record with OwnerID 2330, Jimmy Gonzalez (record 6 in the query datasheet).

2. In the First Name column for this record, double-click **Jimmy** to select the name, and then type **James**.

3. Press the **Tab** key twice to move to the Email column, type **thewholething@ example.com** and then press the **Tab** key.

4. Close the OwnerEmail query, and then open the Navigation Pane. Note that the OwnerEmail query is listed in the Queries section of the Navigation Pane.

Now you'll check the Owner table to verify that the changes you made in the query datasheet are reflected in the Owner table.

 5. Open the **Owner** table in Datasheet view, and then close the Navigation Pane.

 6. Locate the record for OwnerID 2330 (record 6). Notice that the changes you made in the query datasheet to the First Name and Email field values were made to the record in the Owner table.

 7. Close the Owner table.

Kelly also wants to view specific information in the Riverview database. She would like to review the visit data for animals while also viewing certain information about them. So, she needs to see data from both the Animal table and the Visit table at the same time.

Creating a Multitable Query

A multitable query is a query based on more than one table. If you want to create a query that retrieves data from multiple tables, the tables must have a common field. Earlier, you established a relationship between the Animal (primary) and Visit (related) tables based on the common AnimalID field that exists in both tables, so you can now create a query to display data from both tables at the same time. Specifically, Kelly wants to view the values in the AnimalType, AnimalBreed, and AnimalName fields from the Animal table and the VisitDate and Reason fields from the Visit table.

To create the query using the Animal and Visit tables:

 1. On the ribbon, click the **Create** tab.

 2. In the Queries group, click the **Query Design** button. The Show Table dialog box opens in the Query window. You need to add the Animal and Visit tables to the Query window.

 3. Click **Animal** in the Tables list, click the **Add** button, click **Visit**, click the **Add** button, and then click the **Close** button to close the Show Table dialog box. The Animal and Visit field lists appear in the Query window.

 4. Resize the Animal and Visit field lists if necessary so that all the fields in each list are displayed.

The one-to-many relationship between the two tables is shown in the Query window in the same way that a relationship between two tables is shown in the Relationships window. Note that the join line is thick at both ends; this signifies that you selected the option to enforce referential integrity. If you had not selected this option, the join line would be thin at both ends, and neither the "1" nor the infinity symbol would appear, even though the tables have a one-to-many relationship.

You need to place the AnimalType, AnimalBreed, and AnimalName fields (in that order) from the Animal field list into the design grid and then place the VisitDate and Reason fields from the Visit field list into the design grid. This is the order in which Taylor wants to view the fields in the query results.

 5. In the Animal field list, double-click **AnimalType** to place this field in the design grid's first column Field box.

6. Repeat Step 5 to add the **AnimalBreed** and **AnimalName** fields from the Animal table to the second and third columns of the design grid.

7. Repeat Step 5 to add the **VisitDate** and **Reason** fields (in that order) from the Visit table to the fourth and fifth columns of the design grid. The query specifications are complete, so you can now run the query.

8. In the Results group on the Query Tools Design tab, click the **Run** button. After the query runs, the results are displayed in Datasheet view. See Figure 3-9.

Figure 3-9   **Datasheet for query based on the Animal and Visit tables**

fields from the Animal table

fields from the Visit table

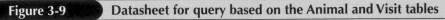

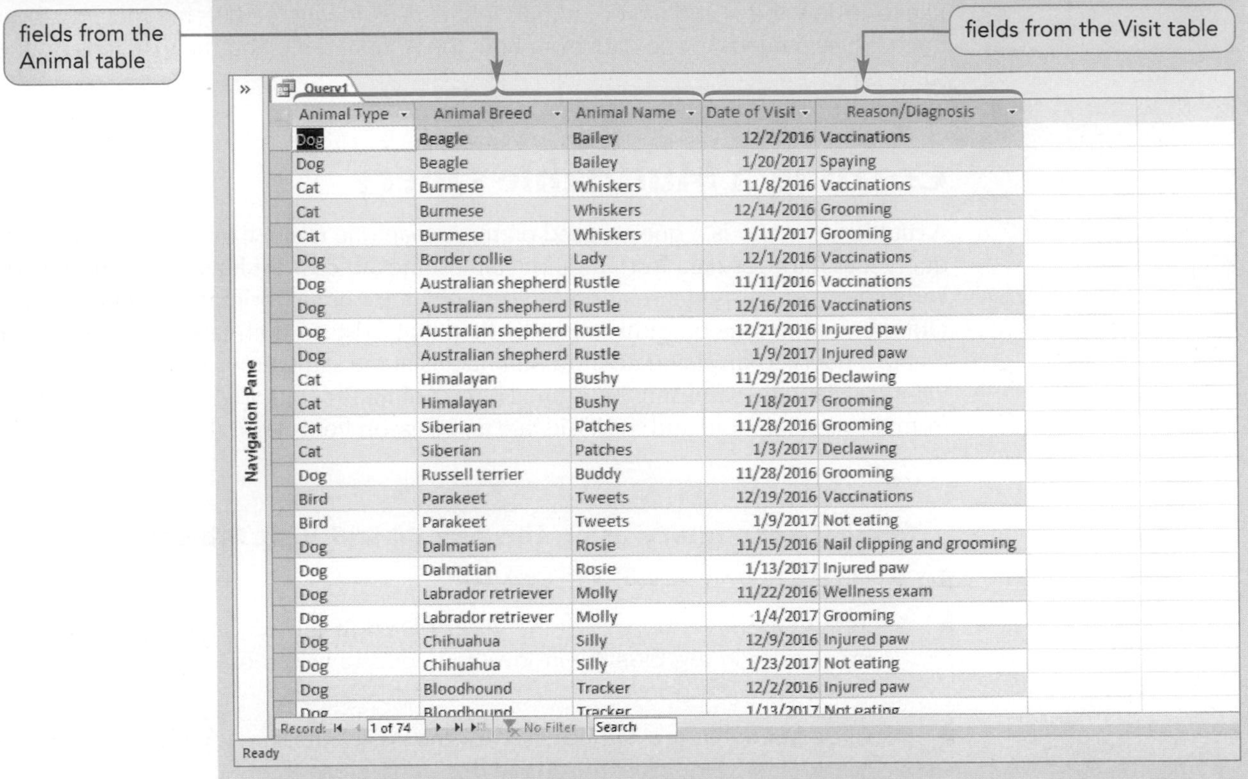

Animal Type	Animal Breed	Animal Name	Date of Visit	Reason/Diagnosis
Dog	Beagle	Bailey	12/2/2016	Vaccinations
Dog	Beagle	Bailey	1/20/2017	Spaying
Cat	Burmese	Whiskers	11/8/2016	Vaccinations
Cat	Burmese	Whiskers	12/14/2016	Grooming
Cat	Burmese	Whiskers	1/11/2017	Grooming
Dog	Border collie	Lady	12/1/2016	Vaccinations
Dog	Australian shepherd	Rustle	11/11/2016	Vaccinations
Dog	Australian shepherd	Rustle	12/16/2016	Vaccinations
Dog	Australian shepherd	Rustle	12/21/2016	Injured paw
Dog	Australian shepherd	Rustle	1/9/2017	Injured paw
Cat	Himalayan	Bushy	11/29/2016	Declawing
Cat	Himalayan	Bushy	1/18/2017	Grooming
Cat	Siberian	Patches	11/28/2016	Grooming
Cat	Siberian	Patches	1/3/2017	Declawing
Dog	Russell terrier	Buddy	11/28/2016	Grooming
Bird	Parakeet	Tweets	12/19/2016	Vaccinations
Bird	Parakeet	Tweets	1/9/2017	Not eating
Dog	Dalmatian	Rosie	11/15/2016	Nail clipping and grooming
Dog	Dalmatian	Rosie	1/13/2017	Injured paw
Dog	Labrador retriever	Molly	11/22/2016	Wellness exam
Dog	Labrador retriever	Molly	1/4/2017	Grooming
Dog	Chihuahua	Silly	12/9/2016	Injured paw
Dog	Chihuahua	Silly	1/23/2017	Not eating
Dog	Bloodhound	Tracker	12/2/2016	Injured paw
Dog	Bloodhound	Tracker	1/13/2017	Not eating

Record: 1 of 74   No Filter   Search

Ready

Only the five selected fields from the Animal and Visit tables appear in the datasheet. The records are displayed in order according to the values in the AnimalID field because it is the primary key field in the primary table, even though this field is not included in the query datasheet.

Kelly plans on frequently tracking the data retrieved by the query, so she asks you to save it as "AnimalVisits."

9. On the Quick Access Toolbar, click the **Save** button. The Save As dialog box opens.

10. In the Query Name box, type **AnimalVisits** and then press the **Enter** key. The query is saved, and its name appears on the object tab.

Kelly decides she wants the records displayed in alphabetical order by animal type. Because the query displays data in order by the field values in the AnimalID field, which is the primary key for the Animal table, you need to sort the records by the AnimalType field to display the data in the order Kelly wants.

Sorting Data in a Query

Sorting is the process of rearranging records in a specified order or sequence. Sometimes you might need to sort data before displaying or printing it to meet a specific request. For example, Kelly might want to review visit information arranged by the VisitDate field because she needs to know which months are the busiest for Riverview Veterinary Care Center in terms of animal visits. Kimberly might want to view billing information arranged by the InvoiceAmt field because she monitors the finances of the care center.

When you sort data in a query, you do not change the sequence of the records in the underlying tables. Only the records in the query datasheet are rearranged according to your specifications.

To sort records, you must select the **sort field**, which is the field used to determine the order of records in the datasheet. In this case, Kelly wants the data sorted alphabetically by animal type, so you need to specify AnimalType as the sort field. Sort fields can be Short Text, Number, Date/Time, Currency, AutoNumber, or Yes/No fields, but not Long Text, Hyperlink, or Attachment fields. You sort records in either ascending (increasing) or descending (decreasing) order. Figure 3-10 shows the results of each type of sort for these data types.

Figure 3-10	Sorting results for different data types

Data Type	Ascending Sort Results	Descending Sort Results
Short Text	A to Z (alphabetical)	Z to A (reverse alphabetical)
Number	lowest to highest numeric value	highest to lowest numeric value
Date/Time	oldest to most recent date	most recent to oldest date
Currency	lowest to highest numeric value	highest to lowest numeric value
AutoNumber	lowest to highest numeric value	highest to lowest numeric value
Yes/No	yes (checkmark in check box) then no values	no then yes values

Access provides several methods for sorting data in a table or query datasheet and in a form. One of the easiest ways is to use the AutoFilter feature for a field.

Using an AutoFilter to Sort Data

As you've probably noticed when working in Datasheet view for a table or query, each column heading has an arrow to the right of the field name. This arrow gives you access to the **AutoFilter** feature, which enables you to quickly sort and display field values in various ways. When you click this arrow, a menu opens with options for sorting and displaying field values. The first two options on the menu enable you to sort the values in the current field in ascending or descending order. Unless you save the datasheet or form after you've sorted the records, the rearrangement of records is temporary.

Next, you'll use an AutoFilter to sort the AnimalVisits query results by the AnimalType field.

To sort the records using an AutoFilter:

1. Click the **arrow** on the Animal Type column heading to display the AutoFilter menu. See Figure 3-11.

Figure 3-11   **Using AutoFilter to sort records in the datasheet**

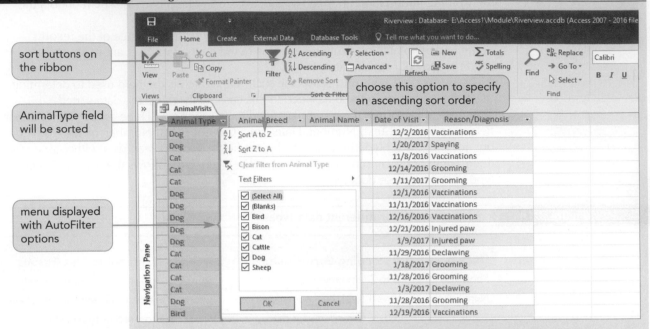

Kelly wants the data sorted in ascending (alphabetical) order by the values in the AnimalType field, so you need to select the first option in the menu.

2. Click **Sort A to Z**. The records are rearranged in ascending alphabetical order by animal type. A small, upward-pointing arrow appears on the right side of the Animal Type column heading. This arrow indicates that the values in the field have been sorted in ascending order. If you used the same method to sort the field values in descending order, a small downward-pointing arrow would appear there instead.

After viewing the query results, Kelly decides that she would also like to see the records arranged by the values in the VisitDate field, so that the data is presented in chronological order. She still wants the records to be arranged by the AnimalType field values as well. To produce the results Kelly wants, you need to sort using two fields.

Sorting on Multiple Fields in Design View

Sort fields can be unique or nonunique. A sort field is **unique** if the value in the sort field for each record is different. The AnimalID field in the Animal table is an example of a unique sort field because each animal record has a different value in this primary key field. A sort field is **nonunique** if more than one record can have the same value for the sort field. For example, the AnimalType field in the Animal table is a nonunique sort field because more than one record can have the same AnimalType value.

TIP

The primary sort field is not the same as a table's primary key. A table has at most one primary key, which must be unique, whereas any field in a table can serve as a primary sort field.

When the sort field is nonunique, records with the same sort field value are grouped together, but they are not sorted in a specific order within the group. To arrange these grouped records in a specific order, you can specify a **secondary sort field**, which is a second field that determines the order of records that are already sorted by the **primary sort field** (the first sort field specified).

In Access, you can select up to 10 different sort fields. When you use the buttons on the ribbon to sort by more than one field, the sort fields must be in adjacent columns in the datasheet. (Note that you cannot use an AutoFilter to sort on more than one field. This method works for a single field only.) You can specify only one type of sort—either ascending or descending—for the selected columns in the datasheet. You select the adjacent columns, and Access sorts first by the first column and then by each remaining selected column in order from left to right.

Kelly wants the records sorted first by the AnimalType field values, as they currently are, and then by the VisitDate values. The two fields are in the correct left-to-right order in the query datasheet, but they are not adjacent, so you cannot use the Ascending and Descending buttons on the ribbon to sort them. You could move the AnimalType field to the left of the VisitDate field in the query datasheet, but both columns would have to be sorted with the same sort order. This is not what Kelly wants—she wants the AnimalType field values sorted in ascending order so that they are in the correct alphabetical order, for ease of reference; and she wants the VisitDate field values to be sorted in descending order, so that she can focus on the most recent animal visits first. To sort the AnimalType and VisitDate fields with different sort orders, you must specify the sort fields in Design view.

In the Query window in Design view, you must arrange the fields you want to sort from left to right in the design grid, with the primary sort field being the leftmost. In Design view, multiple sort fields do not have to be adjacent to each other, as they do in Datasheet view; however, they must be in the correct left-to-right order.

REFERENCE

Sorting a Query Datasheet

- In the query datasheet, click the arrow on the column heading for the field you want to sort.
- In the menu that opens, click Sort A to Z for an ascending sort, or click Sort Z to A for a descending sort.

or

- In the query datasheet, select the column or adjacent columns on which you want to sort.
- In the Sort & Filter group on the Home tab, click the Ascending button or the Descending button.

or

- In Design view, position the fields serving as sort fields from left to right.
- Click the right side of the Sort box for each field you want to sort, and then click Ascending or Descending for the sort order.

To achieve the results Kelly wants, you need to modify the query in Design view to specify the sort order for the two fields.

To select the two sort fields in Design view:

TIP

In Design view, the sort fields do not have to be adjacent, and fields that are not sorted can appear between the sort fields.

1. On the Home tab, in the Views group, click the **View** button to open the query in Design view. The fields are currently in the correct left-to-right order in the design grid, so you only need to specify the sort order for the two fields.

   First, you need to specify an ascending sort order for the AnimalType field. Even though the records are already sorted by the values in this field, you need to modify the query so that this sort order, and the sort order you will specify for the VisitDate field, are part of the query's design. Any time the query is run, the records will be sorted according to these specifications.

2. Click the right side of the **AnimalType Sort** box to display the arrow and the sort options, and then click **Ascending**. You've selected an ascending sort order for the AnimalType field, which will be the primary sort field. The AnimalType field is a Short Text field, and an ascending sort order will display the field values in alphabetical order.

3. Click the right side of the **VisitDate Sort** box, click **Descending**, and then click in one of the empty text boxes below the VisitDate field to deselect the setting. You've selected a descending sort order for the VisitDate field, which will be the secondary sort field because it appears to the right of the primary sort field (AnimalType) in the design grid. The VisitDate field is a Date/Time field, and a descending sort order will display the field values with the most recent dates first. See Figure 3-12.

Figure 3-12   Selecting two sort fields in Design view

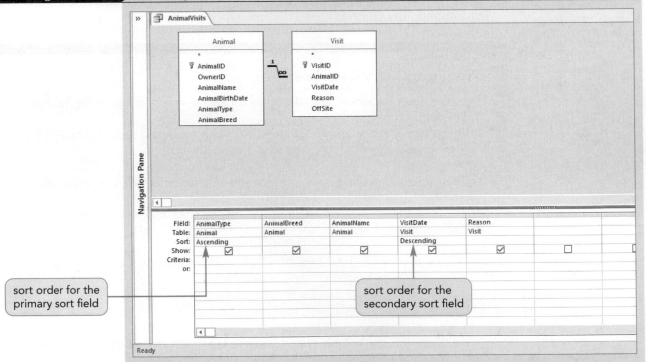

You have finished your query changes, so now you can run the query and then save the modified query with the same name.

4. On the Query Tools Design tab, in the Results group, click the **Run** button. After the query runs, the records appear in the query datasheet in ascending order based on the values in the AnimalType field. Within groups of records with the same AnimalType field value, the records appear in descending order by the values of the VisitDate field. See Figure 3-13.

Figure 3-13   **Datasheet sorted on two fields**

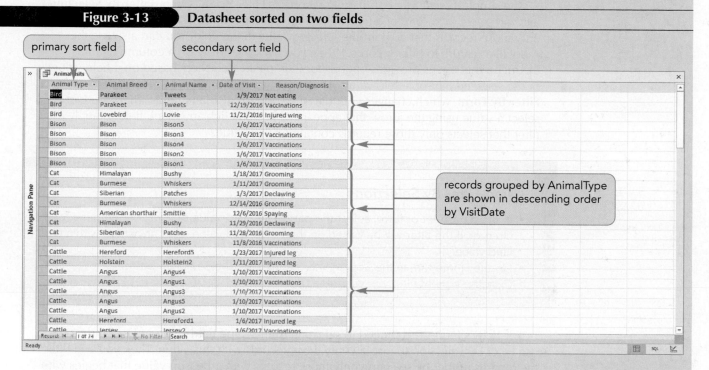

primary sort field   secondary sort field

records grouped by AnimalType are shown in descending order by VisitDate

When you save the query, all of your design changes—including the selection of the sort fields—are saved with the query. The next time Kelly runs the query, the records will appear sorted by the primary and secondary sort fields.

5. On the Quick Access Toolbar, click the **Save** button to save the revised AnimalVisits query.

Kelly knows that Riverview Veterinary Care Center has seen an increase in the number of dogs receiving care. She would like to focus briefly on the information for that animal type only. Also, she is interested in knowing how many dogs have had recent vaccinations. She is concerned that, although more dogs are being brought to the care center, not enough of them are receiving regular vaccinations. Selecting only the records with an AnimalType field value of "Dog" and a Reason field value beginning with "Vaccination" is a temporary change that Kelly wants in the query datasheet, so you do not need to switch to Design view and change the query. Instead, you can apply a filter.

Filtering Data

A **filter** is a set of restrictions you place on the records in an open datasheet or form to *temporarily* isolate a subset of the records. A filter lets you view different subsets of displayed records so that you can focus on only the data you need. Unless you save a query or form with a filter applied, an applied filter is not available the next time you run the query or open the form.

The simplest technique for filtering records is Filter By Selection. **Filter By Selection** lets you select all or part of a field value in a datasheet or form and then display only those records that contain the selected value in the field. You can also use the AutoFilter feature to filter records. When you click the arrow on a column heading, the menu that opens provides options for filtering the datasheet based on a field value or the selected part of a field value. Another technique for filtering records is to use **Filter By Form**, which changes your datasheet to display blank fields. Then you can select a value using the arrow that appears when you click any blank field to apply a filter that selects only those records containing that value.

REFERENCE

Using Filter By Selection

- In the datasheet or form, select the part of the field value that will be the basis for the filter; or, if the filter will be based on the entire field value, click anywhere within the field value.
- On the Home tab, in the Sort & Filter group, click the Selection button.
- Click the type of filter you want to apply.

For Kelly's request, you need to select an AnimalType field value of Dog and then use Filter By Selection to display only those records with this value. Then you will filter the records further by selecting only those records with a Reason value that begins with "Vaccination" (for visits that include a single vaccination or multiple vaccinations).

To display the records using Filter By Selection:

1. In the query datasheet, locate the first occurrence of an AnimalType field containing the value **Dog**, and then click anywhere within that field value.

2. On the Home tab, in the Sort & Filter group, click the **Selection** button. A menu opens with options for the type of filter to apply. See Figure 3-14.

Figure 3-14 **Using Filter By Selection**

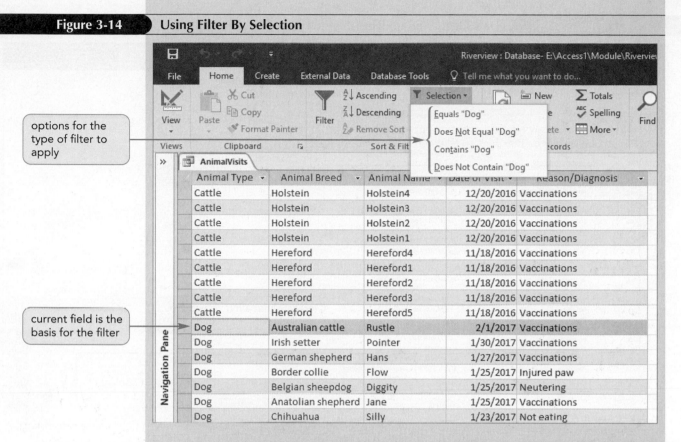

options for the type of filter to apply

current field is the basis for the filter

The menu provides options for displaying only those records with an AnimalType field value that equals the selected value (in this case, Dog); does not equal the value; contains the value somewhere within the field; or does not contain the value somewhere within the field. You want to display all the records whose AnimalType field value equals Dog.

3. In the Selection menu, click **Equals "Dog"**. Only the 25 records that have an AnimalType field value of Dog appear in the datasheet. See Figure 3-15.

Figure 3-15   **Datasheet after applying the filter**

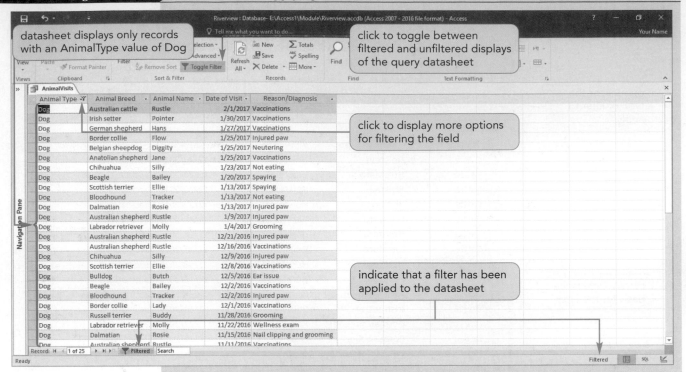

Next, Kelly wants to view only those records with a Reason field value beginning with the word "Vaccination" so she can view the records for visits that involved one or more vaccinations. You need to apply an additional filter to the datasheet.

4. In any Reason field value beginning with the word "Vaccination," select only the text **Vaccination**.

5. In the Sort & Filter group, click the **Selection** button. The same four filter types are available for this selection as when you filtered the AnimalType field.

6. On the Selection menu, click **Begins With "Vaccination"**. The first filter is applied to the query datasheet, which now shows only the nine records for dogs who have had one or more vaccinations at the care center.

   Trouble? If you do not see the Begins With "Vaccination" option, click anywhere in the datasheet to close the Selection menu, and then repeat Steps 4–6, being sure not to select the letter "s" at the end of the word "Vaccination."

   Now you can redisplay all the query records by clicking the Toggle Filter button, which you use to switch between the filtered and unfiltered displays.

TIP

The ScreenTip for this button is Remove Filter.

7. In the Sort & Filter group, click the **Toggle Filter** button. The filter is removed, and all 74 records appear in the query datasheet.

8. Close the AnimalVisits query. A dialog box opens, asking if you want to save your changes to the design of the query—in this case, the filtered display, which is still available through the Toggle Filter button. Kelly does not want the query saved with the filter because she doesn't need to view the filtered information on a regular basis.

9. Click the **No** button to close the query without saving the changes.

10. If you are not continuing to Session 3.2, click the **File** tab, and then click **Close** in the navigation bar to close the Riverview database.

REVIEW

Session 3.1 Quick Check

1. In Datasheet view, what is the difference between navigation mode and editing mode?

2. What command can you use in Datasheet view to remove the display of one or more fields from the datasheet?

3. What is a select query?

4. Describe the field list and the design grid in the Query window in Design view.

5. How are a table datasheet and a query datasheet similar? How are they different?

6. For a Date/Time field, how do the records appear when sorted in ascending order?

7. When you define multiple sort fields in Design view, describe how the sort fields must be positioned in the design grid.

8. A(n) _____ is a set of restrictions you place on the records in an open datasheet or form to isolate a subset of records temporarily.

Session 3.2 Visual Overview:

When creating queries in Design view, you can enter criteria so that only selected records are displayed in the query results.

Field:	AnimalName	AnimalBirthDate	AnimalType	VisitDate	Reason
Table:	Animal	Animal	Animal	Visit	Visit
Sort:					
Show:	☑	☑	☑	☑	☑
Criteria:			"Bird"		
or:					

To define a condition for a field, you place the condition in the field's Criteria box in the design grid.

To indicate which records you want to select, you must specify a condition as part of the query. A **condition** is a criterion, or rule, that determines which records are selected.

Field:	InvoiceNum	InvoiceDate	InvoiceAmt	
Table:	Billing	Billing	Billing	
Sort:				
Show:	☑	☑	☑	☐
Criteria:			>100	
or:				

A condition usually consists of an operator, often a comparison operator, and a value. A **comparison operator** compares the value in a field to the condition value and selects all the records for which the condition is true.

Field:	VisitID	AnimalID	VisitDate	Reason
Table:	Visit	Visit	Visit	Visit
Sort:				
Show:	☑	☑	☑	☑
Criteria:			Between #1/1/2017# And #1/15/2017#	
or:				

Most comparison operators (such as Between...And...) select records that match a range of values for the condition—in this case, all records with dates that fall within the range shown.

Selection Criteria in Queries

The results of a query containing selection criteria include only the records that meet the specified criteria.

BirdAnimalType

Animal Name ▾	Animal Birth Date ▾	Animal Type ▾	Date of Visit ▾
Tweets	11/12/2010	Bird	12/19/2016
Tweets	11/12/2010	Bird	1/9/2017
Lovie	02/03/2002	Bird	11/21/2016
*			

The results of this query show only birds because the condition "Bird" in the AnimalType field's Criteria box specifies that the query should select records only with AnimalType field values of bird. This type of condition is called an **exact match** because the value in the specified field must match the condition exactly in order for the record to be included in the query results.

LargeInvoiceAmts

Invoice Num ▾	Invoice Date ▾	Invoice Amt ▾
42145	11/22/2016	$275.00
42182	11/30/2016	$225.00
42320	01/04/2017	$225.00
42435	01/16/2017	$125.00
42525	01/26/2017	$125.00
*		$0.00

The results of this query show only those invoices with amounts greater than $100 because the condition >100, which uses the greater than comparison operator, specifies that query should select records only with InvoiceAmt field values over $100.

EarlyJanuaryVisits

Visit ID ▾	Animal ID ▾	Date of Visit ▾	Reason/Diagnosis ▾
1098	12296	1/3/2017	Declawing
1101	12312	1/4/2017	Grooming
1120	12304	1/9/2017	Not eating
1124	12290	1/9/2017	Injured paw
1140	12282	1/11/2017	Grooming
1148	12308	1/13/2017	Injured paw
1152	12318	1/13/2017	Not eating
1156	12322	1/13/2017	Spaying
*			

The results of this query show only those visits that took place in the first half of January 2017 because the condition in the VisitDate Criteria box specifies that the query should select records only with a visit date between 1/1/2017 and 1/15/2017.

Defining Record Selection Criteria for Queries

Kimberly is considering offering a workshop on dog care at the care center, with a special emphasis on the needs of older dogs. To prepare for this, she is interested in knowing more about the level of care provided to the dogs that have visited the care center, as well as where these dogs live. For this request, you could create a query to select the correct fields and all records in the Owner, Animal, and Visit tables, select an AnimalType field value of Dog in the query datasheet, and then click the Selection button and choose the appropriate filter option to display the information for only those animals that are dogs. However, a faster way of accessing the data Kimberly needs is to create a query that displays the selected fields and only those records in the Owner, Animal, and Visit tables that satisfy a condition.

Just as you can display selected fields from a database in a query datasheet, you can display selected records. To identify which records you want to select, you must specify a condition as part of the query, as illustrated in the Session 3.2 Visual Overview. A condition usually includes one of the comparison operators shown in Figure 3-16.

Figure 3-16   **Access comparison operators**

Operator	Meaning	Example
=	equal to (optional; default operator)	="Hall"
<>	not equal to	<>"Hall"
<	less than	<#1/1/99#
<=	less than or equal to	<=100
>	greater than	>"C400"
>=	greater than or equal to	>=18.75
Between … And …	between two values (inclusive)	Between 50 And 325
In ()	in a list of values	In ("Hall", "Seeger")
Like	matches a pattern that includes wildcards	Like "706*"

Specifying an Exact Match

For Kimberly's request, you need to first create a query that will display only those records in the Animal table with the value Dog in the AnimalType field. This type of condition is an exact match because the value in the specified field must match the condition exactly in order for the record to be included in the query results. You'll create the query in Design view.

To create the query in Design view:

▶ 1. If you took a break after the previous session, make sure that the Riverview database is open and the Navigation Pane is closed, and then on the ribbon, click the **Create** tab.

▶ 2. In the Queries group, click the **Query Design** button. The Show Table dialog box opens. You need to add the Owner, Animal, and Visit tables to the Query window.

▶ 3. Click **Owner** in the Tables list, click the **Add** button, click **Animal**, click the **Add** button, click **Visit**, click the **Add** button, and then click the **Close** button. The field lists for the Owner, Animal, and Visit tables appear in the top portion of the window, and join lines indicating one-to-many relationships connect the tables.

▶ **4.** Resize all three field lists so that all the fields are displayed.

▶ **5.** Add the following fields from the Animal table to the design grid in this order: **AnimalName**, **AnimalBirthDate**, and **AnimalType**.

Kimberly also wants information from the Visit table and the Owner table included in the query results.

▶ **6.** Add the following fields from the Visit table to the design grid in this order: **VisitDate** and **Reason**.

▶ **7.** Add the following fields from the Owner table to the design grid in this order: **FirstName**, **LastName**, **Phone**, and **Email**. All the fields needed for the query appear in the design grid. See Figure 3-17.

Figure 3-17	Design grid after adding fields from both tables

To display the information Kimberly wants, you need to enter the condition for the AnimalType field in its Criteria box, as shown in Figure 3-17. Kimberly wants to display only those records with an AnimalType field value of Dog.

To enter the exact match condition, and then save and run the query:

▶ **1.** Click the **AnimalType Criteria** box, type **Dog**, and then press the **Enter** key. The condition changes to "Dog".

Access automatically enclosed the condition you typed in quotation marks. You must enclose text values in quotation marks when using them as selection criteria. If you omit the quotation marks, however, Access will include them automatically in most cases. Some words—including "in" and "select"—are special keywords in Access that are reserved for functions and commands. If you want to enter one of these keywords as the condition, you must type the quotation marks around the text or an error message will appear indicating the condition cannot be entered.

▶ **2.** Save the query with the name **DogAnimalType**. The query is saved, and its name is displayed on the object tab.

▶ **3.** Run the query. After the query runs, the selected field values for only those records with an AnimalType field value of Dog are shown. A total of 25 records is selected and displayed in the datasheet. See Figure 3-18.

| Figure 3-18 | Datasheet displaying selected fields and records |

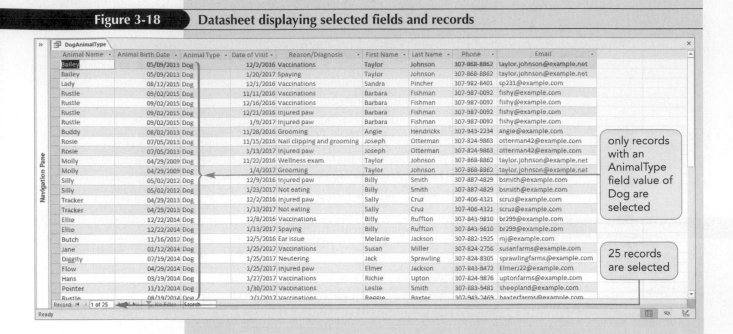

Kimberly realizes that it's not necessary to include the AnimalType field values in the query results. The name of the query, DogAnimalType, indicates that the query design includes all animals with an AnimalType of Dog, so the AnimalType field values are unnecessary and repetitive in the query results. Also, she decides that she would prefer the query datasheet to show the fields from the Owner table first, followed by the Animal table fields and then the Visit table fields. You need to modify the query to produce the results Kimberly wants.

Modifying a Query

After you create a query and view the results, you might need to make changes to the query if the results are not what you expected or require. First, Kimberly asks you to modify the DogAnimalType query so that it does not display the AnimalType field values in the query results.

To remove the display of the AnimalType field values:

1. On the Home tab, in the Views group, click the **View** button. The DogAnimalType query opens in Design view.

   You need to keep the AnimalType field as part of the query design because it contains the defined condition for the query. You only need to remove the display of the field's values from the query results.

2. Click the **AnimalType Show** check box to remove the checkmark. The query will still find only those records with the value Dog in the AnimalType field, but the query results will not display these field values.

Next, you need to change the order of the fields in the query so that the owner information is listed first.

To move the Owner table fields to precede the Animal and Visit table fields:

  1. Position the pointer on the FirstName field selector until the pointer changes to ↓, and then click to select the field. See Figure 3-19.

Figure 3-19   **Selected FirstName field**

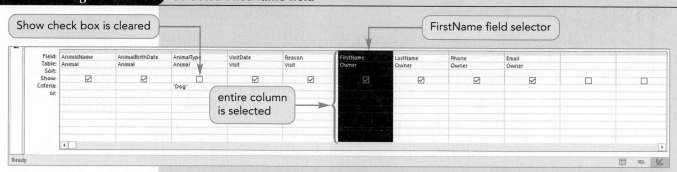

  2. Position the pointer on the FirstName field selector, and then press and hold the mouse button; notice that the pointer changes to ⬚, and a black vertical line appears to the left of the selected field. This line represents the selected field when you drag the mouse to move it.

  3. Drag the pointer to the left until the vertical line representing the selected field is positioned to the left of the AnimalName field. See Figure 3-20.

Figure 3-20   **Dragging the field in the design grid**

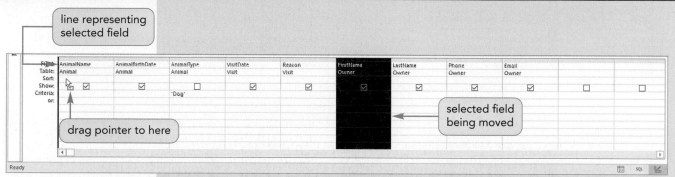

TIP

Instead of moving a field by dragging, you can also delete the field and then add it back to the design grid in the location you want.

  4. Release the mouse button. The FirstName field moves to the left of the AnimalName field.

    You can also select and move multiple fields at once. You need to select and move the LastName, Phone, and Email fields so that they appear directly after the FirstName field in the query design. To select multiple fields, you click and drag the mouse over the field selectors for the fields you want.

  5. Point to the LastName field selector. When the pointer changes to ↓, press and hold the mouse button, drag to the right to select the Phone and Email fields, and then release the mouse button. All three fields are now selected. See Figure 3-21.

Figure 3-21   **Multiple fields selected to be moved**

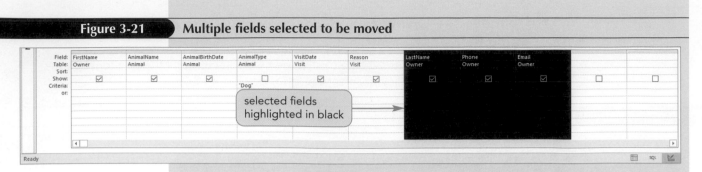

selected fields
highlighted in black

6. Position the pointer on the field selector for any of the three selected fields, press and hold the mouse button, and then drag to the left until the vertical line representing the selected fields is positioned to the left of the AnimalName field.

7. Release the mouse button. The four fields from the Owner table are now the first four fields in the query design.

You have finished making the modifications to the query Kimberly requested, so you can now run the query.

8. Run the query. The results of the modified query are displayed. See Figure 3-22.

Figure 3-22   **Results of the modified query**

fields from the Owner table are now
listed first in the query datasheet

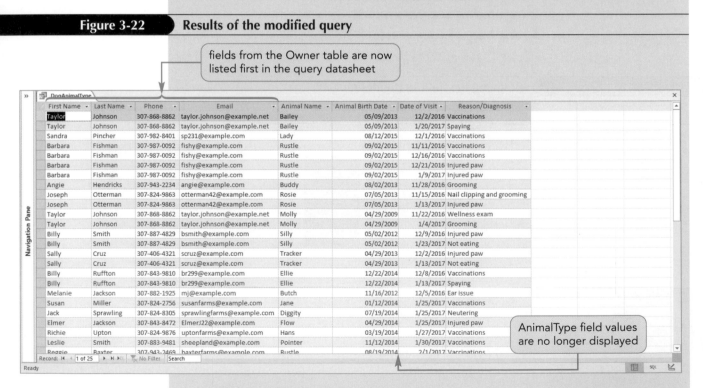

AnimalType field values
are no longer displayed

Note that the AnimalType field values are no longer displayed in the query results.

9. Save and close the DogAnimalType query.

Kimberly asks you to create a new query. She is interested to know which animals of all animal types that have not been to the care center recently, so that her staff can follow up with their owners by sending them reminder notes or emails. To create the query that will produce the results Kimberly wants, you need to use a comparison operator to match a range of values—in this case, any VisitDate value less than 1/1/2017. Because this new query will include information from several of the same fields as the DogAnimalType query, you can use that query as a starting point in designing this new query.

Using a Comparison Operator to Match a Range of Values

As you know, after you create and save a query, you can double-click the query name in the Navigation Pane to run the query again. You can then click the View button to change its design. You can also use an existing query as the basis for creating another query. Because the design of the query you need to create next is similar to the DogAnimalType query, you will copy, paste, and rename this query to create the new query. Using this approach keeps the DogAnimalType query intact.

To create the new query by copying the DogAnimalType query:

▶ **1.** Open the Navigation Pane. Note that the DogAnimalType query is listed in the Queries section.

You need to use the shortcut menu to copy the DogAnimalType query and paste it in the Navigation Pane; then you'll give the copied query a different name.

▶ **2.** In the Queries section of the Navigation Pane, right-click **DogAnimalType** to select it and display the shortcut menu.

▶ **3.** Click **Copy** on the shortcut menu.

▶ **4.** Right-click the empty area near the bottom of the Navigation Pane, and then click **Paste** on the shortcut menu. The Paste As dialog box opens with the text "Copy Of DogAnimalType" in the Query Name box. Because Kimberly wants the new query to show data for animals that have not visited the care center recently, you'll name the new query "EarlierVisits."

▶ **5.** In the Query Name box, type **EarlierVisits** and then press the **Enter** key. The new query appears in the Queries section of the Navigation Pane.

▶ **6.** Double-click the **EarlierVisits** query to open, or run, the query. The design of this query is currently the same as the original DogAnimalType query.

▶ **7.** Close the Navigation Pane.

Next, you need to open the query in Design view and modify its design to produce the results Kimberly wants—to display records for all animals and only those records with VisitDate field values that are earlier than, or less than, 1/1/2017.

To modify the design of the new query:

▶ **1.** Display the query in Design view.

▶ **2.** Click the **VisitDate Criteria** box, type **<1/1/2017** and then press the **Tab** key. Note that Access automatically encloses the date criteria with number signs. The condition specifies that a record will be selected only if its VisitDate field value is less than (earlier than) 1/1/2017. See Figure 3-23.

Figure 3-23 Criteria entered for the VisitDate field

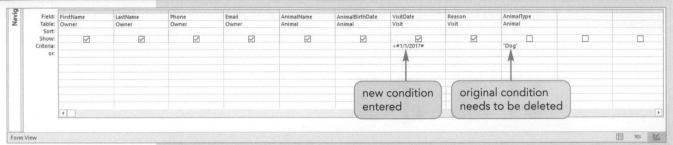

Before you run the query, you need to delete the condition for the AnimalType field. Recall that the AnimalType field is part of the query, but its values are not displayed in the query results. When you modified the query to remove the AnimalType field values from the query results, Access moved the field to the end of the design grid. You need to delete the AnimalType field's condition, specify that the AnimalType field values should be included in the query results, and then move the field back to its original position following the AnimalBirthDate field.

▶ **3.** Press the **Tab** key to select the condition for the AnimalType field, and then press the **Delete** key. The condition for the AnimalType field is removed.

▶ **4.** Click the **Show** check box for the AnimalType field to insert a checkmark so that the field values will be displayed in the query results.

▶ **5.** Use the pointer to select the AnimalType field, drag the selected field to position it to the left of the VisitDate field, and then click in an empty box to deselect the AnimalType field. See Figure 3-24.

Figure 3-24 Design grid after moving the AnimalType field

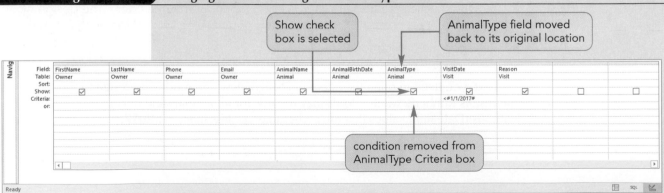

▶ **6.** Run the query. The query datasheet displays the selected fields for only those records with a VisitDate field value less than 1/1/2017, a total of 34 records. See Figure 3-25.

Figure 3-25   **Running the modified query**

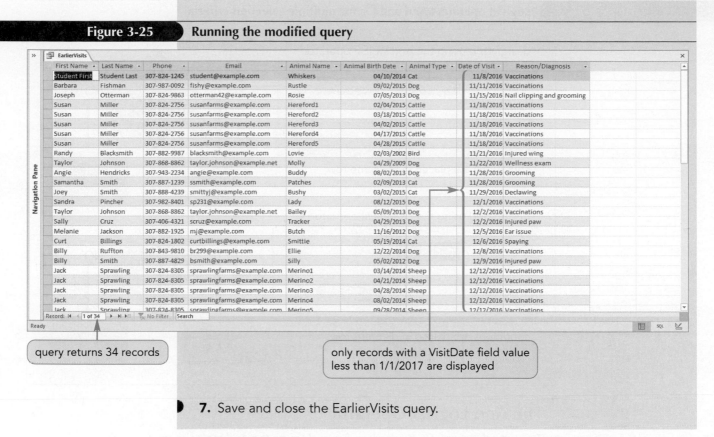

query returns 34 records

only records with a VisitDate field value less than 1/1/2017 are displayed

7. Save and close the EarlierVisits query.

Kimberly continues to analyze animal visits to Riverview Veterinary Care Center. Although the care center offers payment plans and pet insurance options, she realizes that owners of younger animals seen off-site might not see the literature about these options that is available in the care center's waiting room. With this in mind, she would like to see a list of all animals that are less than a year old and that the care center has visited off-site. She wants to track these animals in particular so that her staff can contact their owners to review payment plans and pet insurance options. To produce this list, you need to create a query containing two conditions—one for the animal's date of birth and another for whether each visit was off-site.

Defining Multiple Selection Criteria for Queries

Multiple conditions require you to use **logical operators** to combine two or more conditions. When you want a record selected only if two or more conditions are met, you need to use the **And logical operator**. In this case, Kimberly wants to see only those records with an AnimalBirthDate field value greater than or equal to 7/1/2015 *and* an OffSite field value of "Yes" (indicating a checked box). If you place conditions in separate fields in the *same* Criteria row of the design grid, all conditions in that row must be met in order for a record to be included in the query results. However, if you place conditions in *different* Criteria rows, a record will be selected if at least one of the conditions is met. If none of the conditions are met, Access does not select the record. When you place conditions in different Criteria rows, you are using the **Or logical operator**. Figure 3-26 illustrates the difference between the And and Or logical operators.

Figure 3-26   Logical operators And and Or for multiple selection criteria

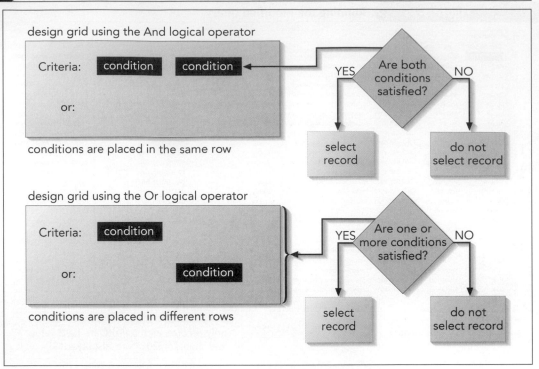

The And Logical Operator

To create the query for Kimberly, you need to use the And logical operator to show only the records for animals that were born on or after 7/1/2015 *and* who have had an off-site visit. You'll create a new query based on the Owner, Animal, and Visit tables to produce the necessary results. In the query design, both conditions you specify will appear in the same Criteria row; therefore, the query will select records only if both conditions are met.

To create a new query using the And logical operator:

1. On the ribbon, click the **Create** tab.

2. In the Queries group, click the **Query Design** button.

3. Add the **Owner**, **Animal**, and **Visit** tables to the Query window in that order, and then close the Show Table dialog box. Resize all three field lists to display all the field names.

4. Add the **AnimalName** and **AnimalBirthDate** fields from the Animal table to the design grid.

5. Add the **FirstName**, **LastName**, and **Phone** fields from the Owner field list to the design grid.

6. Add the **VisitDate** and **OffSite** fields from the Visit table to the design grid.

   Now you need to enter the two conditions for the query.

7. Click the **AnimalBirthDate Criteria** box, and then type **>=7/1/2015**.

8. Press the **Tab** key five times to move to the **OffSite** box, type **Yes**, and then press the **Tab** key. Notice that for a Yes/No field such as OffSite, the criteria value is not automatically enclosed in quotes. See Figure 3-27.

| Figure 3-27 | Query to find younger animals who have had off-site visits |

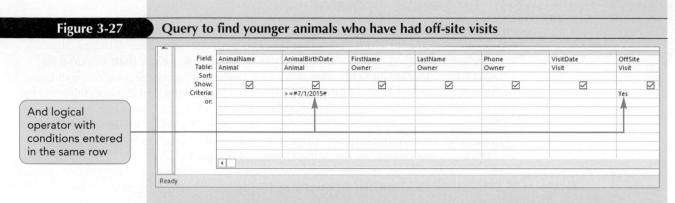

And logical operator with conditions entered in the same row

9. Run the query. The query displays only those records that meet both conditions: an AnimalBirthDate field value greater than or equal to 7/1/2015 *and* an OffSite field value of Yes. 14 records are displayed for 14 different animals. See Figure 3-28.

| Figure 3-28 | Results of query using the And logical operator |

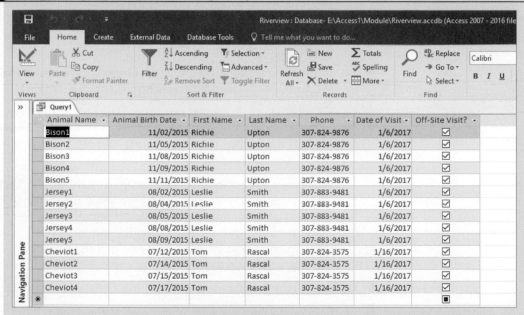

10. On the Quick Access Toolbar, click the **Save** button 💾, and then save the query as **YoungerAndOffsiteAnimals**.

11. Close the query.

Kimberly meets with staff members to discuss the issue of owners with younger animals being informed of the care center's payment plans and insurance options. After viewing the results of the YoungerAndOffsiteAnimals query, the group agrees that the care center should reach out to the owners of all younger animals regarding these services, because first-time owners are more likely to be unaware of the care center's options. In addition, the care center should contact the owner of any animal that has received an off-site visit, because these owners are less likely to have seen the care center's waiting room literature on these payment options. To help with their planning, Kimberly asks you to produce a list of all animals that were born on or after 7/1/2015 or that received an off-site visit. To create this query, you need to use the Or logical operator.

The Or Logical Operator

To create the query that Kimberly requested, your query must select a record when either one of two conditions is satisfied or when both conditions are satisfied. That is, a record is selected if the AnimalBirthDate field value is greater than or equal to 7/1/2015 *or* if the OffSite field value is Yes *or* if both conditions are met. You will enter the condition for the AnimalBirthDate field in the Criteria row and the condition for the OffSite field in the "or" criteria row, thereby using the Or logical operator.

To display the information, you'll create a new query based on the existing YoungerAndOffsiteAnimals query, since it already contains the necessary fields. Then you'll specify the conditions using the Or logical operator.

To create a new query using the Or logical operator:

▶ **1.** Open the Navigation Pane. You'll use the shortcut menu to copy and paste the YoungerAndOffsiteAnimals query to create the new query.

▶ **2.** In the Queries section of the Navigation Pane, right-click **YoungerAndOffsiteAnimals**, and then click **Copy** on the shortcut menu.

▶ **3.** Right-click the empty area near the bottom of the Navigation Pane, and then click **Paste** on the shortcut menu. The Paste As dialog box opens with the text "Copy Of YoungerAndOffsiteAnimals" in the Query Name box. You'll name the new query "YoungerOrOffsiteAnimals."

▶ **4.** In the Query Name box, type **YoungerOrOffsiteAnimals** and then press the **Enter** key. The new query appears in the Queries section of the Navigation Pane.

▶ **5.** In the Navigation Pane, right-click the **YoungerOrOffsiteAnimals** query, click **Design View** on the shortcut menu to open the query in Design view, and then close the Navigation Pane.

The query already contains all the fields Kimberly wants to view, as well as the first condition—a BirthDate field value greater than or equal to 7/1/2015. Because you want records selected if either the condition for the BirthDate field or the condition for the OffSite field is satisfied, you must delete the existing condition for the OffSite field in the Criteria row and then enter this same condition in the "or" row of the design grid for the OffSite field.

▶ **6.** In the design grid, delete **Yes** in the OffSite Criteria box.

▶ **7.** Press the ↓ key to move to the "or" row for the OffSite field, type **Yes**, and then press the **Tab** key. See Figure 3-29.

Figure 3-29	Query window with the Or logical operator

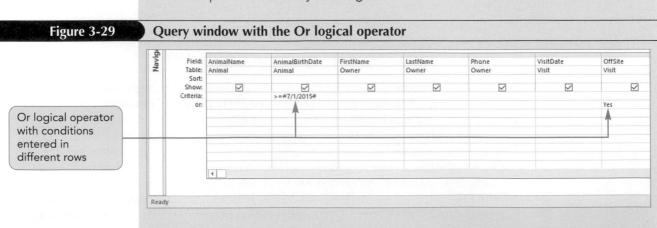

Or logical operator with conditions entered in different rows

Field:	AnimalName	AnimalBirthDate	FirstName	LastName	Phone	VisitDate	OffSite
Table:	Animal	Animal	Owner	Owner	Owner	Visit	Visit
Sort:							
Show:	☑	☑	☑	☑	☑	☑	☑
Criteria:		>=#7/1/2015#					
or:							Yes

To better analyze the data, Kimberly wants the list displayed in descending order by AnimalBirthDate.

8. Click the right side of the **AnimalBirthDate Sort** box, and then click **Descending**.

9. Run the query. The query datasheet displays only those records that meet either condition: a BirthDate field value greater than or equal to 7/1/2015 *or* an OffSite field value of Yes. The query also returns records that meet both conditions. The query displays a total of 43 records. The records in the query datasheet appear in descending order based on the values in the AnimalBirthDate field. See Figure 3-30.

| Figure 3-30 | Results of query using the Or logical operator |

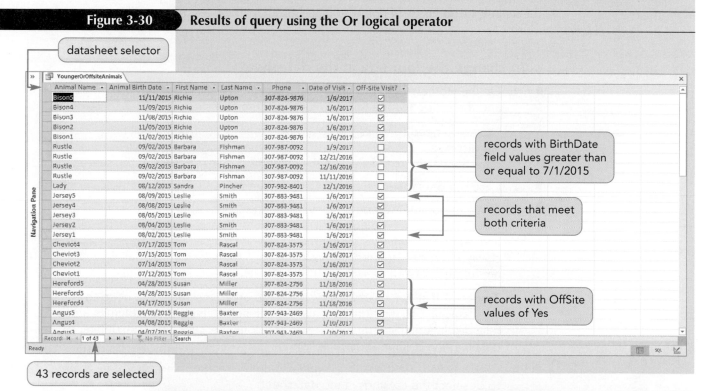

Kimberly would like to spend some time reviewing the results of the YoungerOrOffsiteAnimals query. To make this task easier, she asks you to change how the datasheet is displayed.

INSIGHT

Understanding the Results of Using And vs. Or

When you use the And logical operator to define multiple selection criteria in a query, you *narrow* the results produced by the query because a record must meet more than one condition to be included in the results. For example, the YoungerAndOffsiteAnimals query you created resulted in only 14 records. When you use the Or logical operator, you *broaden* the results produced by the query because a record must meet only one of the conditions to be included in the results. For example, the YoungerOrOffsiteAnimals query you created resulted in 43 records. This is an important distinction to keep in mind when you include multiple selection criteria in queries, so that the queries you create will produce the results you want.

Changing a Datasheet's Appearance

You can make many formatting changes to a datasheet to improve its appearance or readability. Many of these modifications are familiar types of changes you can also make in Word documents or Excel spreadsheets, such as modifying the font type, size, color, and the alignment of text. You can also apply different colors to the rows and columns in a datasheet to enhance its appearance.

Modifying the Font Size

Depending on the size of the monitor you are using or the screen resolution, you might need to increase or decrease the size of the font in a datasheet to view more or fewer columns of data. Kimberly asks you to change the font size in the query datasheet from the default 11 points to 14 points so that she can read the text more easily.

To change the font size in the datasheet:

1. On the Home tab, in the Text Formatting group, click the **Font Size** arrow, and then click **14**. The font size for the entire datasheet increases to 14 points.

   Next, you need to resize the columns to their best fit, so that all field values are displayed. Instead of resizing each column individually, you'll use the datasheet selector to select all the columns and resize them at the same time.

2. Click the **datasheet selector**. All the columns in the datasheet are selected.

3. Move the pointer to one of the vertical lines separating two columns in the datasheet until the pointer changes to ↔, and then double-click the vertical line. All the columns visible on the screen are resized to their best fit. Scroll down and repeat the resizing, as necessary, to make sure that all field values are fully displayed.

   Trouble? If all the columns are not visible on your screen, you need to scroll the datasheet to the right to make sure all field values for all columns are fully displayed. If you need to resize any columns, click a field value first to deselect the columns before resizing an individual column.

4. Click any value in the Animal Name column to make it the current field and to deselect the columns in the datasheet.

Changing the Alternate Row Color in a Datasheet

Access uses themes to format the objects in a database. A **theme** is a predefined set of formats including colors, fonts, and other effects that enhance an object's appearance and usability. When you create a database, Access applies the Office theme to objects as you create them. By default, the Office theme formats every other row in a datasheet with a gray background color to distinguish one row from another, making it easier to view and read the contents of a datasheet. The gray alternate row color provides a subtle difference compared to the rows that have the default white color. You can change the alternate row color in a datasheet to something more noticeable using the Alternate Row Color button in the Text Formatting group on the Home tab. Kimberly suggests that you change the alternate row color in the datasheet to see the effect of using this feature.

To change the alternate row color in the datasheet:

1. On the Home tab, in the Text Formatting group, click the **Alternate Row Color button arrow** to display the gallery of color choices. See Figure 3-31.

Figure 3-31   Gallery of color choices for alternate row color

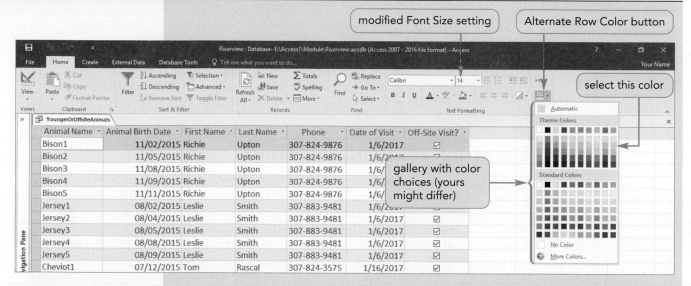

TIP

The name of the color appears in a ScreenTip when you point to a color in the gallery.

The Theme Colors section provides colors from the default Office theme, so that your datasheet's color scheme matches the one in use for the database. The Standard Colors section provides many standard color choices. You might also see a Recent Colors section, with colors that you have recently used in a datasheet. The No Color option, which appears at the bottom of the gallery, sets each row's background color to white. If you want to create a custom color, you can do so using the More Colors option. You'll use one of the theme colors.

2. In the Theme Colors section, click the **Green, Accent 6, Lighter 60%** color (third row, tenth color). The alternate row color is applied to the query datasheet. See Figure 3-32.

Figure 3-32   Datasheet formatted with alternate row color

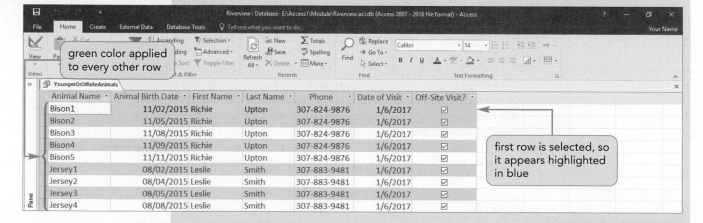

Every other row in the datasheet uses the selected theme color. Kimberly likes how the datasheet looks with this color scheme, so she asks you to save the query.

▶ **3.** Save and close the YoungerOrOffsiteAnimals query. The query is saved with both the increased font size and the green alternate row color.

Next, Kimberly turns her attention to some financial aspects of operating the care center. She wants to use the Riverview database to perform calculations. She is considering imposing a 2% late fee on unpaid invoices and wants to know exactly what the late fee charges would be, should she decide to institute such a policy in the future. To produce the information for Kimberly, you need to create a calculated field.

Creating a Calculated Field

In addition to using queries to retrieve, sort, and filter data in a database, you can use a query to perform calculations. To perform a calculation, you define an **expression** containing a combination of database fields, constants, and operators. For numeric expressions, the data types of the database fields must be Number, Currency, or Date/Time; the constants are numbers such as .02 (for the 2% late fee); and the operators can be arithmetic operators (+ − * /) or other specialized operators. In complex expressions, you can enclose calculations in parentheses to indicate which one should be performed first; any calculation within parentheses is completed before calculations outside the parentheses. In expressions without parentheses, Access performs basic calculations using the following order of precedence: multiplication and division before addition and subtraction. When operators have equal precedence, Access calculates them in order from left to right.

To perform a calculation in a query, you add a calculated field to the query. A **calculated field** is a field that displays the results of an expression. A calculated field that you create with an expression appears in a query datasheet or in a form or report; however, it does not exist in a database. When you run a query that contains a calculated field, Access evaluates the expression defined by the calculated field and displays the resulting value in the query datasheet, form, or report.

To enter an expression for a calculated field, you can type it directly in a Field box in the design grid. Alternately, you can open the Zoom box or Expression Builder and use either one to enter the expression. The **Zoom box** is a dialog box that you can use to enter text, expressions, or other values. To use the Zoom box, however, you must know all the parts of the expression you want to create. **Expression Builder** is an Access tool that makes it easy for you to create an expression; it contains a box for entering the expression, an option for displaying and choosing common operators, and one or more lists of expression elements, such as table and field names. Unlike a Field box, which is too narrow to show an entire expression at one time, the Zoom box and Expression Builder are large enough to display longer expressions. In most cases, Expression Builder provides the easiest way to enter expressions because you don't have to know all the parts of the expression; you can choose the necessary elements from the Expression Builder dialog box, which also helps to prevent typing errors.

REFERENCE

Creating a Calculated Field Using Expression Builder

- Create and save the query in which you want to include a calculated field.
- Open the query in Design view.
- In the design grid, click the Field box in which you want to create an expression.
- In the Query Setup group on the Query Tools Design tab, click the Builder button.
- Use the expression elements and common operators to build the expression, or type the expression directly in the expression box.
- Click the OK button.

To produce the information Kimberly wants, you need to create a new query based on the Billing and Visit tables and, in the query, create a calculated field that will multiply each InvoiceAmt field value by .02 to calculate the proposed 2% late fee.

To create the new query:

▶ **1.** On the ribbon, click the **Create** tab.

▶ **2.** In the Queries group, click the **Query Design** button. The Show Table dialog box opens.

Kimberly wants to see data from both the Visit and Billing tables, so you need to add these two tables to the Query window.

▶ **3.** Add the **Visit** and **Billing** tables to the Query window, and resize the field lists as necessary so that all the field names are visible. The field lists appear in the Query window, and the one-to-many relationship between the Visit (primary) and Billing (related) tables is displayed.

▶ **4.** Add the following fields to the design grid in the order given: **VisitID**, **AnimalID**, and **VisitDate** from the Visit table; and **InvoiceItem**, **InvoicePaid**, and **InvoiceAmt** from the Billing table.

Kimberly is interested in viewing data only for unpaid invoices because a late fee would apply only to them, so you need to enter the necessary condition for the InvoicePaid field. Recall that InvoicePaid is a Yes/No field. The condition you need to enter is the word "No" in the Criteria box for this field, so that Access will retrieve the records for unpaid invoices only.

▶ **5.** In the **InvoicePaid Criteria box**, type **No**. As soon as you type the letter "N," a menu appears with options for entering various functions for the criteria. You don't need to enter a function, so you can close this menu.

▶ **6.** Press the **Esc** key to close the menu.

You must close the menu or you'll enter a function, which will cause an error.

▶ **7.** Press the **Tab** key. The query name you'll use will indicate that the data is for unpaid invoices, so you don't need to include the InvoicePaid values in the query results.

▶ **8.** Click the **InvoicePaid Show** check box to remove the checkmark.

▶ **9.** Save the query with the name **UnpaidInvoiceLateFee**.

Now you can use Expression Builder to create the calculated field for the InvoiceAmt field.

To create the calculated field:

1. Click the blank Field box to the right of the InvoiceAmt field. This field will contain the expression.

2. On the Query Tools Design tab, in the Query Setup group, click the **Builder** button. The Expression Builder dialog box opens.

   The insertion point is positioned in the large box at the top of the dialog box, ready for you to enter the expression. The Expression Categories section of the dialog box lists the fields from the query so you can include them in the expression. The Expression Elements section contains options for including other elements in the expression, including functions, constants, and operators. If the expression you're entering is a simple one, you can type it in the box; if it's more complex, you can use the options in the Expression Elements section to help you build the expression.

   The expression for the calculated field will multiply the InvoiceAmt field values by the numeric constant .02 (which represents a 2% late fee).

3. In the Expression Categories section of the dialog box, double-click **InvoiceAmt**. The field name is added to the expression box, within brackets and with a space following it. In an expression, all field names must be enclosed in brackets.

   Next you need to enter the multiplication operator, which is the asterisk (*), followed by the constant.

4. Type * (an asterisk) and then type **.02**. You have finished entering the expression. See Figure 3-33.

Figure 3-33 **Completed expression for the calculated field**

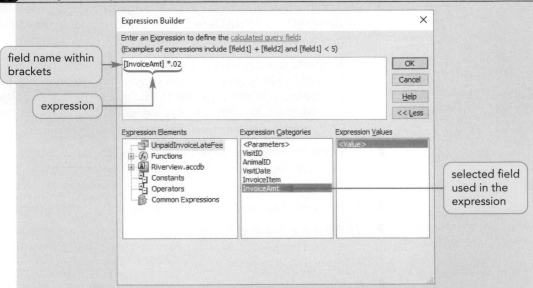

field name within brackets

expression

selected field used in the expression

   If you're not sure which operator to use, you can click Operators in the Expression Elements section to display a list of available operators in the center section of the dialog box.

5. Click the **OK** button. The Expression Builder dialog box closes, and the expression is added to the design grid in the Field box for the calculated field.

When you create a calculated field, Access uses the default name "Expr1" for the field. You need to specify a more meaningful field name so it will appear in the query results. You'll enter the name "LateFee," which better describes the field's contents.

6. Click to the left of the text "Expr1:" at the beginning of the expression, and then press the **Delete** key five times to delete the text **Expr1**. *Do not delete the colon*; it is needed to separate the calculated field name from the expression.

7. Type **LateFee**. Next, you'll set this field's Caption property so that the field name will appear as "Late Fee" in the query datasheet.

8. On the Query Tools Design tab, in the Show/Hide group, click the **Property Sheet** button. The Property Sheet for the current field, LateFee, opens on the right side of the window. See Figure 3-34.

Figure 3-34   Property Sheet for the calculated field

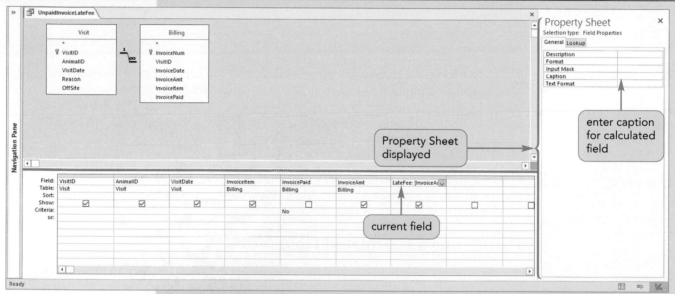

9. In the Property sheet, click in the Caption box, type **Late Fee** and then close the Property Sheet.

10. Run the query. The query datasheet is displayed and contains the specified fields and the calculated field with the caption "Late Fee." See Figure 3-35.

Figure 3-35 Datasheet displaying the calculated field

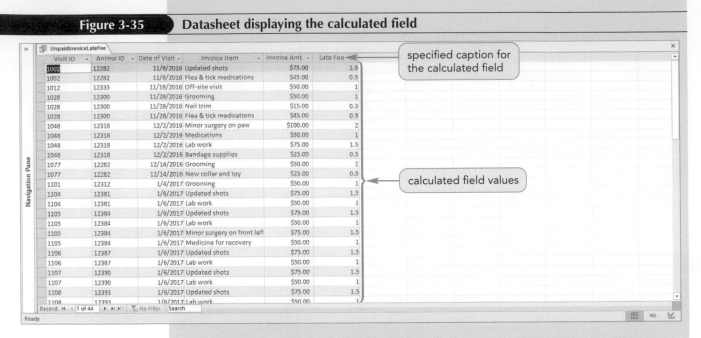

Trouble? If a dialog box opens noting that the expression contains invalid syntax, you might not have included the required colon in the expression. Click the OK button to close the dialog box, resize the column in the design grid that contains the calculated field to its best fit, change your expression to LateFee: [InvoiceAmt]*0.02 and then repeat Step 10.

The LateFee field values are currently displayed without dollar signs and decimal places. Kimberly wants these values to be displayed in the same format as the InvoiceAmt field values for consistency.

Formatting a Calculated Field

You can specify a particular format for a calculated field, just as you can for any field, by modifying its properties. Next, you'll change the format of the LateFee calculated field so that all values appear in the Currency format.

To format the calculated field:

1. Switch to Design view.

2. In the design grid, click in the **LateFee** calculated field to make it the current field, if necessary.

3. On the Query Tools Design tab, in the Show/Hide group, click the **Property Sheet** button to open the Property Sheet for the calculated field.

   You need to change the Format property to Currency, which displays values with a dollar sign and two decimal places.

4. In the Property Sheet, click the right side of the **Format** box to display the list of formats, and then click **Currency**.

5. Close the Property Sheet, and then run the query. The amounts in the LateFee calculated field are now displayed with dollar signs and two decimal places.

6. Save and close the UnpaidInvoiceLateFee query.

PROSKILLS

Problem Solving: Creating a Calculated Field vs. Using the Calculated Field Data Type

You can also create a calculated field using the Calculated Field data type, which lets you store the result of an expression as a field in a table. However, database experts caution users against storing calculations in a table for several reasons. First, storing calculated data in a table consumes valuable space and increases the size of the database. The preferred approach is to use a calculated field in a query; with this approach, the result of the calculation is not stored in the database—it is produced only when you run the query—and it is always current. Second, the Calculated Field data type provides limited options for creating a calculation, whereas a calculated field in a query provides more functions and options for creating expressions. Third, including a field in a table using the Calculated Field data type limits your options if you need to upgrade the database at some point to a more robust DBMS, such as Oracle or SQL Server, that doesn't support this data type; you would need to redesign your database to eliminate this data type. Finally, most database experts agree that including a field in a table whose value is dependent on other fields in the table violates database design principles. To avoid such problems, it's best to create a query that includes a calculated field to perform the calculation you want, instead of creating a field in a table that uses the Calculated Field data type.

To better analyze costs at Riverview Veterinary Care Center, Kimberly wants to view more detailed information about invoices for animal care. Specifically, she would like to know the minimum, average, and maximum invoice amounts. She asks you to determine these statistics from data in the Billing table.

Using Aggregate Functions

You can calculate statistical information, such as totals and averages, on the records displayed in a table datasheet or selected by a query. To do this, you use the Access aggregate functions. **Aggregate functions** perform arithmetic operations on selected records in a database. Figure 3-36 lists the most frequently used aggregate functions.

Figure 3-36   **Frequently used aggregate functions**

Aggregate Function	Determines	Data Types Supported
Average	Average of the field values for the selected records	AutoNumber, Currency, Date/Time, Number
Count	Number of records selected	AutoNumber, Currency, Date/Time, Long Text, Number, OLE Object, Short Text, Yes/No
Maximum	Highest field value for the selected records	AutoNumber, Currency, Date/Time, Number, Short Text
Minimum	Lowest field value for the selected records	AutoNumber, Currency, Date/Time, Number, Short Text
Sum	Total of the field values for the selected records	AutoNumber, Currency, Date/Time, Number

Working with Aggregate Functions Using the Total Row

If you want to quickly perform a calculation using an aggregate function in a table or query datasheet, you can use the Totals button in the Records group on the Home tab. When you click this button, a row labeled "Total" appears at the bottom of the datasheet. You can then choose one of the aggregate functions for a field in the datasheet, and the results of the calculation will be displayed in the Total row for that field.

Kimberly wants to know the total amount of all invoices for the care center. You can quickly display this amount using the Sum function in the Total row in the Billing table datasheet.

To display the total amount of all invoices in the Billing table:

1. Open the Navigation Pane, open the **Billing** table in Datasheet view, and then close the Navigation Pane.

2. Make sure the Home tab is displayed.

3. In the Records group, click the **Totals** button. A row with the label "Total" is added to the bottom of the datasheet.

4. Scroll to the bottom of the datasheet to view the Total row. You want to display the sum of all the values in the Invoice Amt column.

5. In the Total row, click the **Invoice Amt** field. An arrow appears on the left side of the field.

6. Click the **arrow** to display the menu of aggregate functions. The functions displayed depend on the data type of the current field; in this case, the menu provides functions for a Currency field. See Figure 3-37.

Figure 3-37   Using aggregate functions in the Total row

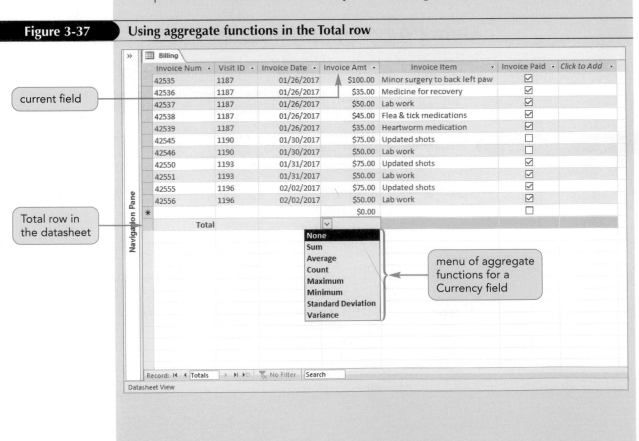

7. Click **Sum** in the menu. All the values in the Invoice Amt column are added, and the total $12,015.00 appears in the Total row for the column.

Kimberly doesn't want to change the Billing table to always display this total. You can remove the Total row by clicking the Totals button again; this button works as a toggle to switch between the display of the Total row with the results of any calculations in the row, and the display of the datasheet without this row.

8. In the Records group, click the **Totals** button. The Total row is removed from the datasheet.

9. Close the Billing table without saving the changes.

Kimberly wants to know the minimum, average, and maximum invoice amounts for Riverview Veterinary Care Center. To produce this information for Kimberly, you need to use aggregate functions in a query.

Creating Queries with Aggregate Functions

Aggregate functions operate on the records that meet a query's selection criteria. You specify an aggregate function for a specific field, and the appropriate operation applies to that field's values for the selected records.

To display the minimum, average, and maximum of all the invoice amounts in the Billing table, you will use the Minimum, Average, and Maximum aggregate functions for the InvoiceAmt field.

To calculate the minimum of all invoice amounts:

1. Create a new query in Design view, add the **Billing** table to the Query window, and then resize the Billing field list to display all fields.

To perform the three calculations on the InvoiceAmt field, you need to add the field to the design grid three times.

2. In the Billing field list, double-click **InvoiceAmt** three times to add three copies of the field to the design grid.

You need to select an aggregate function for each InvoiceAmt field. When you click the Totals button in the Show/Hide group on the Design tab, a row labeled "Total" is added to the design grid. The Total row provides a list of the aggregate functions that you can select.

3. On the Query Tools Design tab, in the Show/Hide group, click the **Totals** button. A new row labeled "Total" appears between the Table and Sort rows in the design grid. The default entry for each field in the Total row is the Group By operator, which you will learn about later in this module. See Figure 3-38.

Figure 3-38 | **Total row inserted in the design grid**

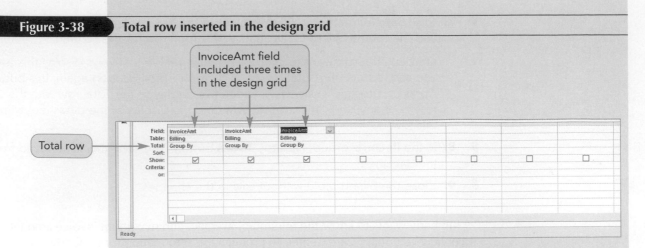

In the Total row, you specify the aggregate function you want to use for a field.

4. Click the right side of the first column's **Total** box, and then click **Min**. This field will calculate the minimum amount of all the InvoiceAmt field values.

When you run the query, Access automatically will assign a datasheet column name of "MinOfInvoiceAmt" for this field. You can change the datasheet column name to a more descriptive or readable name by entering the name you want in the Field box. However, you must also keep the InvoiceAmt field name in the Field box because it identifies the field to use in the calculation. The Field box will contain the datasheet column name you specify followed by the field name (InvoiceAmt) with a colon separating the two names.

5. In the first column's Field box, click to the left of InvoiceAmt, and then type **MinimumInvoiceAmt:** (including the colon).

Be sure to type the colon following the name or the query will not work correctly.

6. Resize the column so that you can see the complete field name, MinimumInvoiceAmt:InvoiceAmt.

Next, you need to set the Caption property for this field so that the field name appears with spaces between words in the query datatsheet.

7. On the Query Tools Design tab, in the Show/Hide group, click the **Property Sheet** button to open the Property Sheet for the current field.

8. In the Caption box, type **Minimum Invoice Amt**, and then close the Property Sheet.

You'll follow the same process to complete the query by calculating the average and maximum invoice amounts.

To calculate the average and maximum of all invoice amounts:

1. Click the right side of the second column's **Total** box, and then click **Avg**. This field will calculate the average of all the InvoiceAmt field values.

2. In the second column's Field box, click to the left of InvoiceAmt, and then type **AverageInvoiceAmt:**.

3. Resize the second column to fully display the field name, AverageInvoiceAmt:InvoiceAmt.

4. Open the Property Sheet for the current field, and then set its Caption property to **Average Invoice Amt**.

5. Click the right side of the third column's **Total** box, and then click **Max**. This field will calculate the maximum amount of all the InvoiceAmt field values.

6. In the third column's Field box, click to the left of InvoiceAmt, and then type **MaximumInvoiceAmt:**.

7. Resize the third column to fully display the field name, MaximumInvoiceAmt:InvoiceAmt.

8. In the Property Sheet, set the Caption property to **Maximum Invoice Amt**, and then close the Property Sheet. See Figure 3-39.

Figure 3-39   **Query with aggregate functions entered**

functions entered and columns resized

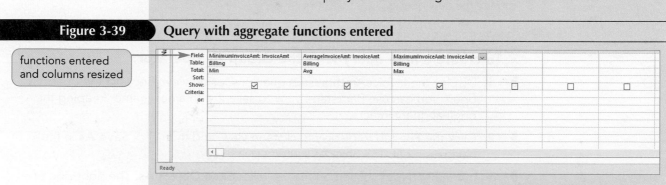

Trouble? Carefully compare your field names to those shown in the figure to make sure they match exactly; otherwise the query will not work correctly.

9. Run the query. One record displays containing the three aggregate function results. The single row of summary statistics represents calculations based on all the records selected for the query—in this case, all 202 records in the Billing table.

10. Resize all columns to their best fit so that the column names are fully displayed, and then click the field value in the first column to deselect the value and view the results. See Figure 3-40.

Figure 3-40   **Result of the query using aggregate functions**

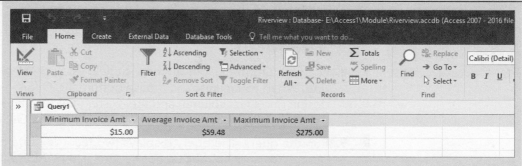

Minimum Invoice Amt ᵛ	Average Invoice Amt ᵛ	Maximum Invoice Amt ᵛ
$15.00	$59.48	$275.00

---

11. Save the query as **InvoiceAmtStatistics**.

Kimberly would like to view the same invoice amount statistics (minimum, average, and maximum) as they relate to both appointments at the care center and off-site visits.

Using Record Group Calculations

In addition to calculating statistical information on all or selected records in selected tables, you can calculate statistics for groups of records. The **Group By operator** divides the selected records into groups based on the values in the specified field. Those records with the same value for the field are grouped together, and the datasheet displays one record for each group. Aggregate functions, which appear in the other columns of the design grid, provide statistical information for each group.

To create a query for Kimberly's latest request, you will modify the current query by adding the OffSite field and assigning the Group By operator to it. The Group By operator will display the statistical information grouped by the values of the OffSite field for all the records in the query datasheet. To create the new query, you will save the InvoiceAmtStatistics query with a new name, keeping the original query intact, and then modify the new query.

To create a new query with the Group By operator:

1. Display the InvoiceAmtStatistics query in Design view. Because the query is open, you can use Backstage view to save it with a new name, keeping the original query intact.

2. Click the **File** tab to display Backstage view, and then click **Save As** in the navigation bar. The Save As screen opens.

3. In the File Types section on the left, click **Save Object As**. The right side of the screen changes to display options for saving the current database object as a new object.

4. Click the **Save As** button. The Save As dialog box opens, indicating that you are saving a copy of the InvoiceAmtStatistics query.

5. Type **InvoiceAmtStatisticsByOffsite** to replace the selected name, and then press the **Enter** key. The new query is saved with the name you specified and appears in Design view.

   You need to add the OffSite field to the query. This field is in the Visit table. To include another table in an existing query, you open the Show Table dialog box.

TIP

You could also open the Navigation Pane and drag the Visit table from the pane to the Query window.

6. On the Query Tools Design tab, in the Query Setup group, click the **Show Table** button to open the Show Table dialog box.

7. Add the **Visit** table to the Query window, and then resize the Visit field list if necessary.

8. Drag the **OffSite** field from the Visit field list to the first column in the design grid. When you release the mouse button, the OffSite field appears in the design grid's first column, and the existing fields shift to the right. Group By, the default option in the Total row, appears for the OffSite field.

9. Run the query. The query displays two records—one for each OffSite group, Yes and No. Each record contains the OffSite field value for the group and the three aggregate function values. The summary statistics represent calculations based on the 202 records in the Billing table. See Figure 3-41.

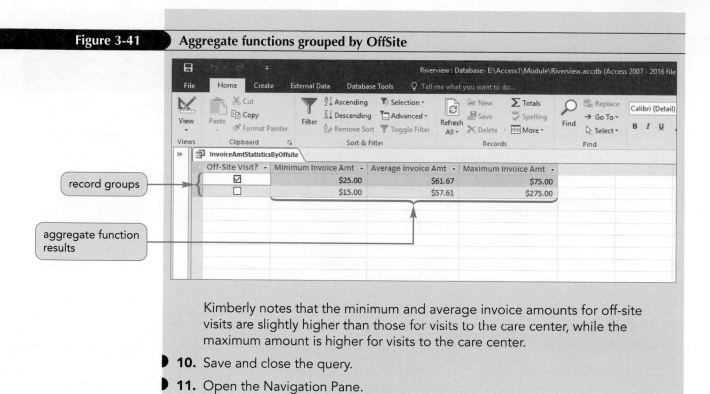

Figure 3-41   Aggregate functions grouped by OffSite

record groups

aggregate function
results

Kimberly notes that the minimum and average invoice amounts for off-site visits are slightly higher than those for visits to the care center, while the maximum amount is higher for visits to the care center.

▶ **10.** Save and close the query.

▶ **11.** Open the Navigation Pane.

You have created and saved many queries in the Riverview database. The Navigation Pane provides options for opening and managing the queries you've created, as well as the other objects in the database, such as tables, forms, and reports.

Working with the Navigation Pane

As noted earlier, the Navigation Pane is the main area for working with the objects in a database. As you continue to create objects in your database, you might want to display and work with them in different ways. The Navigation Pane provides options for grouping database objects in various ways to suit your needs. For example, you might want to view only the queries created for a certain table or all the query objects in the database.

As you know, the Navigation Pane divides database objects into categories. Each category contains groups, and each group contains one or more objects. The default category is **Object Type**, which arranges objects by type—tables, queries, forms, and reports. The default group is **All Access Objects**, which displays all objects in the database. You can also choose to display only one type of object, such as tables.

The default group name, All Access Objects, appears at the top of the Navigation Pane. Currently, each object type—Tables, Queries, Forms, and Reports—is displayed as a heading, and the objects related to each type are listed below the heading. To group objects differently, you can select another category by using the Navigation Pane menu. You'll try this next.

TIP

You can hide the display of a group's objects by clicking the button to the right of the group name; click the button again to expand the group and display its objects.

To group objects differently in the Navigation Pane:

▶ **1.** At the top of the Navigation Pane, click the **All Access Objects** button ⊙. A menu opens with options for choosing different categories and groups. See Figure 3-42.

Figure 3-42 Navigation Pane menu

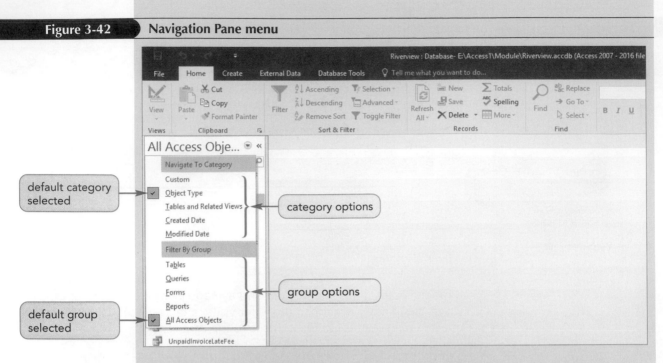

The top section of the menu provides the options for choosing a different category. The Object Type category has a checkmark next to it, signifying that it is the currently selected category. The lower section of the menu provides options for choosing a different group; these options might change depending on the selected category.

2. In the Navigate To Category section, click **Tables and Related Views**. The Navigation Pane is now grouped into categories of tables, and each table in the database—Visit, Billing, Owner, and Animal—is its own group. All database objects related to a table are listed below the table's name. Notice the UnpaidInvoiceLateFee query is based on both the Visit and Billing tables, so it is listed in the group for both tables. See Figure 3-43.

Figure 3-43	Database objects grouped by table in the Navigation Pane

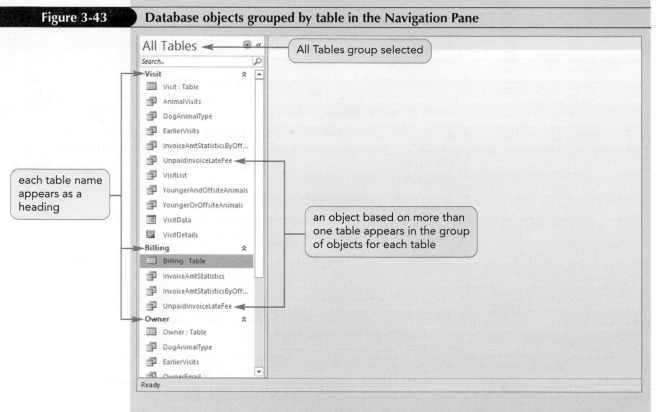

each table name appears as a heading

All Tables group selected

an object based on more than one table appears in the group of objects for each table

You can also choose to display the objects for only one table to better focus on that table.

▶ **3.** At the top of the Navigation Pane, click the **All Tables** button ⊙ to display the Navigation Pane menu, and then click **Owner**. The Navigation Pane now shows only the objects related to the Owner table—the table itself plus the five queries you created that include fields from the Owner table.

▶ **4.** At the top of the Navigation Pane, click the **Owner** button ⊙, and then click **Object Type** to return to the default display of the Navigation Pane.

▶ **5.** Compact and repair the Riverview database, and then close the database.

Trouble? If a dialog box opens and warns that this action will cause Microsoft Access to empty the Clipboard, click the Yes button to continue.

The default All Access Objects category is a predefined category. You can also create custom categories to group objects in the way that best suits how you want to manage your database objects. As you continue to build a database and the list of objects grows, creating a custom category can help you to work more efficiently with the objects in the database.

The queries you've created and saved will help Kimberly and her staff to monitor and analyze the business activity of Riverview Veterinary Care Center and its patients. Now any staff member can run the queries at any time, modify them as needed, or use them as the basis for designing new queries to meet additional information requirements.

Session 3.2 Quick Check

REVIEW

1. A(n) _____ is a criterion, or rule, that determines which records are selected for a query datasheet.

2. In the design grid, where do you place the conditions for two different fields when you use the And logical operator, and where do you place them when you use the Or logical operator?

3. To perform a calculation in a query, you define a(n) _____ containing a combination of database fields, constants, and operators.

4. Which Access tool do you use to create an expression for a calculated field in a query?

5. What is an aggregate function?

6. The _____ operator divides selected records into groups based on the values in a field.

7. What is the default category for the display of objects in the Navigation Pane?

Review Assignments

Data File needed for the Review Assignments: Vendor.accdb *(cont. from Module 2)*

Kimberly asks you to update some information in the Vendor database and also to retrieve specific information from the database. Complete the following:

1. Open the **Vendor** database you created and worked with in previous modules, and then click the Enable Content button next to the security warning, if necessary.

2. Open the **Supplier** table in Datasheet view, and then change the following field values for the record with the Supplier ID GGF099: Address to **738 26th St**, Contact Phone to **321-296-1958**, Contact First Name to **Carmela**, and Contact Last Name to **Montoya**. Close the table.

3. Create a query based on the Supplier table. Include the following fields in the query, in the order shown: Company, Category, ContactFirst, ContactLast, Phone, and City. Sort the query in ascending order based on the Category field values. Save the query as **ContactList**, and then run the query.

4. Use the ContactList query datasheet to update the Supplier table by changing the Phone field value for A+ Labs to **402-495-3957**.

5. Change the size of the font in the ContactList query datasheet to 12 points. Resize columns, as necessary, so that all field values and column headings are visible.

6. Change the alternate row color in the ContactList query datasheet to the Theme Color named Gold, Accent 4, Lighter 60%, and then save and close the query.

7. Create a query based on the Supplier and Product tables. Select the Company, Category, and State fields from the Supplier table, and the ProductName, Price, Units, and Weight fields from the Product table. Sort the query results in descending order based on price. Select only those records with a Category field value of Supplies, but do not display the Category field values in the query results. Save the query as **SupplyProducts**, run the query, and then close it.

8. Create a query that lists all products that cost more than $50 and are temperature controlled. Display the following fields from the Product table in the query results: ProductID, ProductName, Price, Units, and Sterile. (*Hint*: The TempControl field is a Yes/No field that should not appear in the query results.) Save the query as **HighPriceAndTempControl**, run the query, and then close it.

9. Create a query that lists information about suppliers who sell equipment or sterile products. Include the Company, Category, ContactFirst, and ContactLast fields from the Supplier table; and the ProductName, Price, TempControl, and Sterile fields from the Product table. Save the query as **EquipmentOrSterile**, run the query, and then close it.

10. Create a query that lists all resale products, along with a 10% markup amount based on the price of the product. Include the Company field from the Supplier table and the following fields from the Product table in the query: ProductID, ProductName, and Price. Save the query as **ResaleProductsWithMarkup**. Display the discount in a calculated field named **Markup** that determines a 10% markup based on the Price field values. Set the Caption property **Markup** for the calculated field. Display the query results in descending order by Price. Save and run the query.

11. Modify the format of the Markup field in the ResaleProductsWithMarkup query so that it uses the Standard format and two decimal places. Run the query, resize all columns in the datasheet to their best fit, and then save and close the query.

12. Create a query that calculates the lowest, highest, and average prices for all products using the field names **MinimumPrice**, **MaximumPrice**, and **AveragePrice**, respectively. Set the Caption property for each field to include a space between the two words in the field name. Run the query, resize all columns in the datasheet to their best fit, save the query as **PriceStatistics**, and then close it.

13. In the Navigation Pane, copy the PriceStatistics query, and then rename the copied query as **PriceStatisticsBySupplier**.

14. Modify the PriceStatisticsBySupplier query so that the records are grouped by the Company field in the Supplier table. The Company field should appear first in the query datasheet. Save and run the query, and then close it.

15. Compact and repair the Vendor database, and then close it.

Case Problem 1

Data File needed for this Case Problem: Beauty.accdb *(cont. from Module 2)*

Beauty To Go   Sue Miller needs to modify a few records in the Beauty database and analyze the data for customers that subscribe to her business. To help Sue, you'll update the Beauty database and create queries to answer her questions. Complete the following:

1. Open the **Beauty** database you created and worked with in previous modules, and then click the Enable Content button next to the security warning, if necessary.

2. In the **Member** table, find the record for MemberID 2163, and then change the Street value to **844 Sanford Ln** and the Zip to **32804**.

3. In the **Member** table, find the record for MemberID 2169, and then delete the record. Close the Member table.

4. Create a query that lists customers who did not have to pay a fee when they signed up for their current option. In the query results, display the FirstName, LastName, and OptionBegin fields from the Member table, and the OptionCost field from the Option table. Sort the records in ascending order by the option start date. Select records only for customers whose fees were waived. (*Hint*: The FeeWaived field is a Yes/No field that should not appear in the query results.) Save the query as **NoFees**, and then run the query.

5. Use the NoFees query datasheet to update the Member table by changing the Last Name value for Gilda Packson to **Washington**.

6. Use the NoFees query datasheet to display the total Option Cost for the selected members. Save and close the query.

7. Create a query that lists the MemberID, FirstName, LastName, OptionBegin, OptionDescription, and OptionCost fields for customers who signed up with Beauty To Go between January 1, 2017 and January 31, 2017. Save the query as **JanuaryOptions**, run the query, and then close it.

8. Create a query that lists all customers who live in Celebration and whose options end on or after 4/1/2017. Display the following fields from the Member table in the query results: MemberID, FirstName, LastName, Phone, and OptionEnd. (*Hint*: The City field values should not appear in the query results.) Sort the query results in ascending order by last name. Save the query as **CelebrationAndEndDate**, run the query, and then close it.

9. Copy and paste the CelebrationAndEndDate query to create a new query named **CelebrationOrEndDate**. Modify the new query so that it lists all members who live in Celebration or whose memberships expire on or after 4/1/2017. Display the City field values in the query results following the Phone field values, and sort the query results in ascending order by city (this should be the only sort in the query). Save and run the query.

10. Change the size of the font in the CelebrationOrEndDate query datasheet to 14 points. Resize columns, as necessary, so that all field values and column headings are visible.

11. Change the alternate row color in the CelebrationOrEndDate query datasheet to the Theme Color named Green, Accent 6, Lighter 80%, and then save and close the query.

12. Create a query that calculates the lowest, highest, and average cost for all options using the field names **LowestCost**, **HighestCost**, and **AverageCost**, respectively. Set the Caption property for each field to include a space between the two words in the field name. Run the query, resize all columns in the datasheet to their best fit, save the query as **CostStatistics**, and then close it.

13. Copy and paste the CostStatistics query to create a new query named **CostStatisticsByZip**.

14. Modify the CostStatisticsByZip query to display the same statistics grouped by Zip, with Zip appearing as the first field. (*Hint*: Add the Member table to the query.) Run the query, and then save and close it.

15. Compact and repair the Beauty database, and then close it.

Case Problem 2

Data File needed for this Case Problem: Programming.accdb *(cont. from Module 2)*

Programming Pros   After reviewing the Programming database, Brent Hovis wants to modify some records and then view specific information about the students, tutors, and contracts for his tutoring services company. He asks you to update and query the Programming database to perform these tasks. Complete the following:

1. Open the **Programming** database you created and worked with in previous modules, and then click the Enable Content button next to the security warning, if necessary.

2. In the **Tutor** table, change the following information for the record with TutorID 1048: Major is **Computer Science** and Year In School is **Graduate**. Close the table.

3. In the **Student** table, find the record with the StudentID RAM4025, and then delete the related record in the subdatasheet for this student. Delete the record for StudentID RAM4025, and then close the Student table.

4. Create a query based on the Student table that includes the LastName, FirstName, and CellPhone fields, in that order. Save the query as **StudentCellList**, and then run the query.

5. In the results of the StudentCellList query, change the cell phone number for Hidalgo Hickman to **919-301-2209**. Close the query.

6. Create a query based on the Tutor and Contract tables. Display the LastName field from the Tutor table, and the StudentID, ContractDate, SessionType, Length, and Cost fields, in that order, from the Contract table. Sort first in ascending order by the tutor's last name, and then in ascending order by the StudentID. Save the query as **SessionsByTutor**, run the query, and then close it.

7. Copy and paste the SessionsByTutor query to create a new query named **GroupSessions**. Modify the new query so that it displays the same information for records with a Group session type only. Do not display the SessionType field values in the query results. Save and run the query, and then close it.

8. Create and save a query that produces the results shown in Figure 3-44. Close the query when you are finished.

Figure 3-44 **RaleighPrivate query results**

show only records for students from Raleigh who are taking private sessions

sort by Last Name

format with a font size of 12 and the Blue, Accent 5, Lighter 80% alternate row Theme Color

9. Create and save a query that produces the results shown in Figure 3-45. Close the query when you are finished.

Figure 3-45 **CaryOrSemi query results**

show only records for students from Cary or students taking semi-private sessions

sort in descending order by Contract Date

Total row shows the sum of the Cost values

10. Create and save a query to display statistics for the Cost field, as shown in Figure 3-46. Close the query when you are finished.

Figure 3-46 **CostStatistics query results**

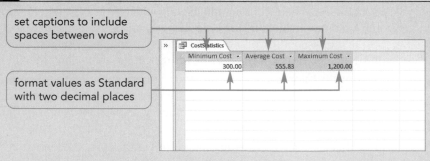

set captions to include spaces between words

format values as Standard with two decimal places

11. Copy and paste the CostStatistics query to create a new query named **CostStatisticsByCity**.

12. Modify the CostStatisticsByCity query to display the same statistics grouped by City, with City appearing as the first field. (*Hint*: Add the Student table to the query.) Run the query, and then save and close it.

13. Compact and repair the Programming database, and then close it.

Case Problem 3

Data File needed for this Case Problem: Center.accdb *(cont. from Module 2)*

CHALLENGE

Diane's Community Center   Diane Coleman needs to modify some records in the Center database, and then she wants to find specific information about the patrons, donations, and auction items for her not-for-profit community center. Diane asks you to help her update the database and create queries to find the information she needs. Complete the following:

1. Open the **Center** database you created and worked with in previous modules, and then click the Enable Content button next to the security warning, if necessary.

2. In the **Patron** table, delete the record with PatronID 3024. (*Hint*: Delete the related records in the Donation subdatasheet first.) Close the Patron table without saving changes to the table layout.

3. Create a query based on the Auction and Donation tables that includes the AuctionID, DonationID, DonationDate, and Description fields, in that order. Save the query as **AuctionItemsByDate**, and then run it.

4. Modify the AuctionItemsByDate query design so that it sorts records in ascending order first by DonationDate and then by Description. Save and run the query.

5. In the AuctionItemsByDate query datasheet, find the record for the auction item with Auction ID 250, and then change the description for this item to **New scooter**. Close the query.

6. Create a query that displays the PatronID, FirstName, and LastName fields from the Patron table, and the Description and DonationValue fields from the Donation table for all donations over $150. Sort the query in ascending order by donation value. Save the query as **LargeDonations**, run the query, and then close it.

7. Copy and paste the LargeDonations query to create a new query named **LargeCashDonations**.

⊕ **Explore** 8. Modify the LargeCashDonations query to display only those records with donations valued at more than $150 in cash. Do not include the Description field values in the query results. Use the query datasheet to calculate the average cash donation. Save and close the query.

9. Create a query that displays the PatronID, FirstName, and LastName fields from the Patron table, and the AuctionID, AuctionDate, and MinPrice fields from the Auction table. Specify that the results show records for only those items with a minimum price greater than $150. Save the query as **ExpensiveAuctionItems**, and then run the query.

10. Filter the results of the ExpensiveAuctionItems query datasheet to display records with an auction date of 10/14/2017 only.

⊕ **Explore** 11. Format the datasheet of the ExpensiveAuctionItems query so that it does not display gridlines, uses an alternate row Standard Color of Maroon 2, and displays a font size of 12. (*Hint*: Use the Gridlines button in the Text Formatting group on the Home tab to select the appropriate gridlines option.) Resize the columns to display the complete field names and values, if necessary. Save and close the query.

✦ **Explore** 12. Create a query that displays the PatronID, FirstName, and LastName fields from the Patron table, and the Description, DonationDate, and DonationValue fields from the Donation table. Specify that the query include records for noncash donations only or for donations made in the month of September 2017. Sort the records first in ascending order by the patron's last name, and then in descending order by the donation value. Save the query as **NonCashOrSeptemberDonations**, run the query, and then close it.

13. Copy and paste the NonCashOrSeptemberDonations query to create a new query named **DonationsAfterStorageCharge**.

✦ **Explore** 14. Modify the DonationsAfterStorageCharge query so that it displays records for noncash donations made on all dates. Create a calculated field named **NetDonation** that displays the results of subtracting $3.50 from the DonationValue field values to account for the cost of storing each noncash donated item. Set the Caption property **Net Donation** for the calculated field. Display the results in ascending order by donation value and not sorted on any other field. Run the query, and then modify it to format both the DonationValue field and the calculated field as Currency with two decimal places. Run the query again, and resize the columns in the datasheet to their best fit, as necessary. Save and close the query.

✦ **Explore** 15. Create a query based on the **Donation** table that displays the sum, average, and count of the DonationValue field for all donations. Then complete the following:

   a. Specify field names of **TotalDonations**, **AverageDonation**, and **NumberOfDonations**. Then specify captions to include spaces between words.

   b. Save the query as **DonationStatistics**, and then run it. Resize the query datasheet columns to their best fit.

   c. Modify the field properties so that the values in the Total Donations and Average Donation columns display two decimal places and the Standard format. Run the query again, and then save and close the query.

   d. Copy and paste the DonationStatistics query to create a new query named **DonationStatisticsByDescription**.

   e. Modify the DonationStatisticsByDescription query to display the sum, average, and count of the DonationValue field for all donations grouped by Description, with Description appearing as the first field. Sort the records in descending order by Total Donations. Save, run, and then close the query.

16. Compact and repair the Center database, and then close it.

TROUBLESHOOT

Case Problem 4

Data Files needed for this Case Problem: Appalachia.accdb *(cont. from Module 2)* **and HikeApp.accdb**

Hike Appalachia   Molly and Bailey Johnson need your help to maintain and analyze data about the hikers, reservations, and tours for their hiking tour business. Additionally, you'll troubleshoot some problems in another database containing tour information. Complete the following:

1. Open the **Appalachia** database you created and worked with in previous modules, and then click the Enable Content button next to the security warning, if necessary.

2. In the **Hiker** table, change the phone number for Wilbur Sanders to **828-910-2058**, and then close the table.

3. Create a query based on the Tour table that includes the TourName, Hours, PricePerPerson, and TourType fields, in that order. Sort in ascending order based on the PricePerPerson field values. Save the query as **ToursByPrice**, and then run the query.

4. Use the ToursByPrice query datasheet to display the total Price Per Person for the tours. Save and close the query.

5. Create a query that displays the HikerLast, City, and State fields from the Hiker table, and the ReservationID, TourDate, and People fields from the Reservation table. Save the query as **HikerTourDates**, and then run the query. Change the alternate row color in the query datasheet to the Theme Color Blue, Accent 1, Lighter 80%. In Datasheet view, use an AutoFilter to sort the query results from oldest to newest Tour Date. Save and close the query.

6. Create a query that displays the HikerFirst, HikerLast, City, ReservationID, TourID, and TourDate fields for all guests from North Carolina (NC). Do not include the State field in the query results. Sort the query in ascending order by the guest's last name. Save the query as **NorthCarolinaHikers** and then run it. Close the query.

7. Create a query that displays data from all three tables in the database as follows: the HikerLast, City, and State fields from the Hiker table; the TourDate field from the Reservation table; and the TourName and TourType fields from the Tour table. Specify that the query select only those records for guests from West Virginia (WV) or guests who are taking climbing tours. Sort the query in ascending order by Tour Name. Save the query as **WestVirginiaOrClimbing** and then run the query. Resize datasheet columns to their best fit, as necessary, and then save and close the query.

8. Copy and paste the **WestVirginiaOrClimbing** query to create a new query named **SouthCarolinaAndSeptember**.

9. Modify the **SouthCarolinaAndSeptember** query to select all guests from South Carolina (SC) who are taking a tour starting sometime in the month of September 2017. Do not include the State field values in the query results. Run the query. Resize datasheet columns to their best fit, as necessary, and then save and close the query.

10. Create a query that displays the ReservationID, TourDate, and People fields from the Reservation table, and the TourName and PricePerPerson fields from the Tour table for all reservations with a People field value greater than 1. Save the query as **ReservationCosts**. Add a field to the query named **TotalCost** that displays the results of multiplying the People field values by the PricePerPerson field values. Set the Caption property **Total Cost** for the calculated field. Display the results in descending order by TotalCost. Run the query. Modify the query by formatting the TotalCost field to show 0 decimal places. Run the query, resize datasheet columns to their best fit, as necessary, and then save and close the query.

11. Create a query based on the Tour table that determines the minimum, average, and maximum price per person for all tours. Then complete the following:

    a. Specify field names of **LowestPrice**, **AveragePrice**, and **HighestPrice**.

    b. Set the Caption property for each field to include a space between the two words in the field name.

    c. Save the query as **PriceStatistics**, and then run the query.

    d. In Design view, specify the Standard format and two decimal places for each column.

    e. Run the query, resize all the datasheet columns to their best fit, save your changes, and then close the query.

    f. Create a copy of the PriceStatistics query named **PriceStatisticsByTourType**.

    g. Modify the PriceStatisticsByTourType query to display the price statistics grouped by TourType, with TourType appearing as the first field. Save your changes, and then run and close the query.

    h. Compact and repair the Appalachia database, and then close it.

☼ **Troubleshoot** 12. Open the **HikeApp** database located in the Access1 > Case4 folder provided with your Data Files, and then click the Enable Content button next to the security warning, if necessary. Run the ReservationByDateAndState query in the HikeApp database. The query is not producing the desired results. Fix the query so that the data from the Reservation table is listed first and the data is sorted only by TourDate in ascending order. Save and close the corrected query.

☼ **Troubleshoot** 13. Run the NCGuestsFewerPeople query, which displays no records in the results. This query is supposed to show data for guests from North Carolina (NC) with fewer than four people in their booking. Find and correct the errors in the query design, run the query, and then close it.

☼ **Troubleshoot** 14. Run the GeorgiaOrOctStart query. This query should display the records for all guests who are from Georgia (GA) or whose tour date is on or after 10/1/2017. Find and correct the errors in the query design, run the query, and then close it.

15. Compact and repair the HikeApp database, and then close it.

POWERPOINT

Creating a Presentation

Presenting Information About an Event Venue

OBJECTIVES

Session 1.1
- Plan and create a new presentation
- Create a title slide and slides with lists
- Edit and format text
- Move and copy text
- Convert a list to a SmartArt diagram
- Duplicate, rearrange, and delete slides
- Close a presentation

Session 1.2
- Open an existing presentation
- Change the theme and theme variant
- Insert and crop photos
- Modify photo compression options
- Resize and move objects
- Create speaker notes
- Check the spelling
- Run a slide show
- Print slides, handouts, speaker notes, and the outline

Case | *Lakeside Event Center*

Lakeside Event Center is a venue in Lake Havasu City, Arizona, that opened in 1981 and is available for functions of all types, including birthdays, bar mitzvahs, corporate events, and weddings. The event center, located on the shore of Lake Havasu, has rooms that can host from 50 to 900 people. The center underwent a recent renovation including planting new gardens and updating the décor inside. Caitlin Keough-Barton was recently hired as the events manager. One of Caitlin's responsibilities is to attract new bookings. Caitlin wants to advertise the hall at upcoming wedding and event-planning conventions.

Microsoft PowerPoint 2016 (or simply **PowerPoint**) is a computer program you use to create a collection of slides that can contain text, charts, pictures, sounds, movies, multimedia, and so on. In this module, you'll use PowerPoint to create a presentation that Caitlin can use to showcase everything Lakeside Event Center has to offer when she attends the Event Planners Association annual convention. After Caitlin reviews it, you'll add graphics and speaker notes to the presentation. Finally, you'll check the spelling, run the slide show to evaluate it, and print the presentation.

STARTING DATA FILES

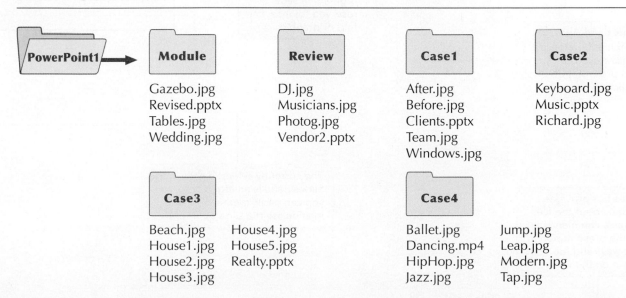

PowerPoint1 →

Module
Gazebo.jpg
Revised.pptx
Tables.jpg
Wedding.jpg

Review
DJ.jpg
Musicians.jpg
Photog.jpg
Vendor2.pptx

Case1
After.jpg
Before.jpg
Clients.pptx
Team.jpg
Windows.jpg

Case2
Keyboard.jpg
Music.pptx
Richard.jpg

Case3
Beach.jpg   House4.jpg
House1.jpg   House5.jpg
House2.jpg   Realty.pptx
House3.jpg

Case4
Ballet.jpg   Jump.jpg
Dancing.mp4   Leap.jpg
HipHop.jpg   Modern.jpg
Jazz.jpg   Tap.jpg

Session 1.1 Visual Overview:

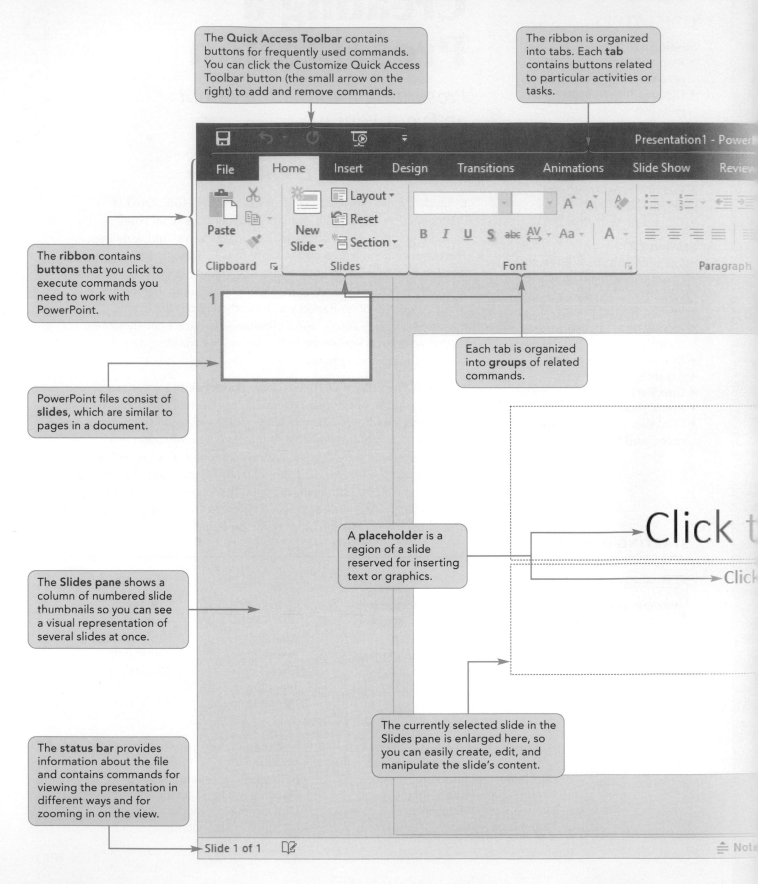

The **Quick Access Toolbar** contains buttons for frequently used commands. You can click the Customize Quick Access Toolbar button (the small arrow on the right) to add and remove commands.

The ribbon is organized into tabs. Each **tab** contains buttons related to particular activities or tasks.

The **ribbon** contains **buttons** that you click to execute commands you need to work with PowerPoint.

PowerPoint files consist of **slides**, which are similar to pages in a document.

Each tab is organized into **groups** of related commands.

The **Slides pane** shows a column of numbered slide thumbnails so you can see a visual representation of several slides at once.

A **placeholder** is a region of a slide reserved for inserting text or graphics.

The **status bar** provides information about the file and contains commands for viewing the presentation in different ways and for zooming in on the view.

The currently selected slide in the Slides pane is enlarged here, so you can easily create, edit, and manipulate the slide's content.

The PowerPoint Window

The title bar contains the filename of the current presentation. A temporary filename "Presentation" followed by a number appears until you save the file.

You click the Ribbon Display Options button to select commands to display and hide the ribbon.

You use the windows buttons to minimize, maximize, and close the PowerPoint window.

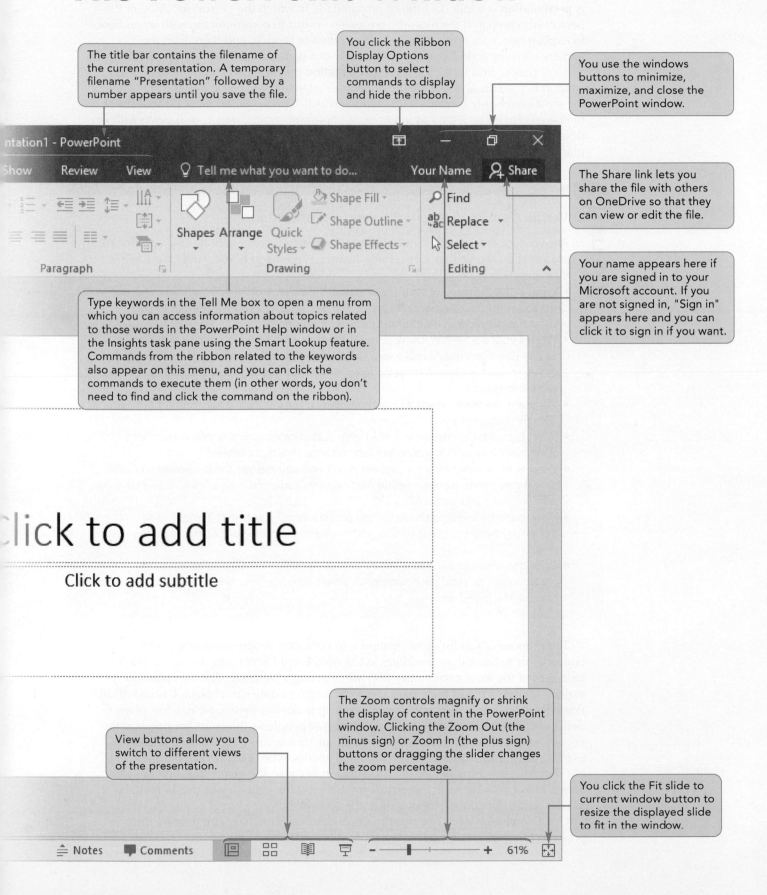

The Share link lets you share the file with others on OneDrive so that they can view or edit the file.

Type keywords in the Tell Me box to open a menu from which you can access information about topics related to those words in the PowerPoint Help window or in the Insights task pane using the Smart Lookup feature. Commands from the ribbon related to the keywords also appear on this menu, and you can click the commands to execute them (in other words, you don't need to find and click the command on the ribbon).

Your name appears here if you are signed in to your Microsoft account. If you are not signed in, "Sign in" appears here and you can click it to sign in if you want.

The Zoom controls magnify or shrink the display of content in the PowerPoint window. Clicking the Zoom Out (the minus sign) or Zoom In (the plus sign) buttons or dragging the slider changes the zoom percentage.

View buttons allow you to switch to different views of the presentation.

You click the Fit slide to current window button to resize the displayed slide to fit in the window.

Planning a Presentation

A **presentation** is a talk (lecture) or prepared file in which the person speaking or the person who prepared the file—the presenter—wants to communicate with an audience to explain new concepts or ideas, sell a product or service, entertain, train the audience in a new skill or technique, or any of a wide variety of other topics.

Most people find it helpful to use **presentation media**—visual and audio aids to support key points and engage the audience's attention. Microsoft PowerPoint is one of the most commonly used tools for creating effective presentation media. The features of PowerPoint make it easy to incorporate photos, diagrams, music, and video with key points of a presentation. Before you create a presentation, you should spend some time planning its content.

PROSKILLS

Verbal Communication: Planning a Presentation

Answering a few key questions will help you create a presentation using appropriate presentation media that successfully delivers its message or motivates the audience to take an action.

- What is the purpose of your presentation? In other words, what action or response do you want your audience to have? For example, do you want them to buy something, follow instructions, or make a decision?
- Who is your audience? Think about the needs and interests of your audience as well as any decisions they'll make as a result of what you have to say. What you choose to say to your audience must be relevant to their needs, interests, and decisions or it will be forgotten.
- What are the main points of your presentation? Identify the information that is directly relevant to your audience.
- What presentation media will help your audience absorb the information and remember it later? Do you need lists, photos, charts, or tables?
- What is the format for your presentation? Will you deliver the presentation orally or will you create a presentation file that your audience members will view on their own, without you present?
- How much time do you have for the presentation? Keep that in mind as you prepare the presentation content so that you have enough time to present all of your key points.
- Consider whether handouts will help your audience follow along with your presentation or steal your audience's attention when you want them to be focused on you, the presenter.

The purpose of Caitlin's presentation is to convince people attending wedding conventions to book their weddings at Lakeside Event Center. Her audience will be members of the local community who are planning a wedding. She also plans to explain the service and price packages from which people can choose. Caitlin will use PowerPoint to display lists and graphics to help make her message clear. She plans to deliver her presentation orally to small groups of people as they visit her booth at the convention, and her presentation will be about 10 minutes long. For handouts, she plans to have flyers available to distribute to anyone who is interested, but she will not distribute anything before her presentation because she wants the audience's full attention to be on her, and the details are not complex enough that the audience will need a written document to refer to as she is speaking.

Once you know what you want to say or communicate, you can prepare the presentation media to help communicate your ideas.

Starting PowerPoint and Creating a New Presentation

Microsoft PowerPoint 2016 is a tool you can use to create and display visual and audio aids on slides to help clarify the points you want to make in your presentation or to create a presentation that people view on their own without you being present.

When PowerPoint starts, the Recent screen in Backstage view is displayed. **Backstage view** contains commands that allow you to manage your presentation files and PowerPoint options. When you first start PowerPoint, the only actions available to you in Backstage view are to open an existing PowerPoint file or create a new file. You'll start PowerPoint now.

To start PowerPoint:

▶ 1. On the Windows taskbar, click the **Start** button ⊞. The Start menu opens.

▶ 2. Click **All apps** on the Start menu, scroll the list, and then click **PowerPoint 2016.** PowerPoint starts and displays the Recent screen in Backstage view. See Figure 1-1. In the orange bar on the left is a list of recently opened presentations, and on the right are options for creating new presentations.

Figure 1-1	Recent screen in Backstage view

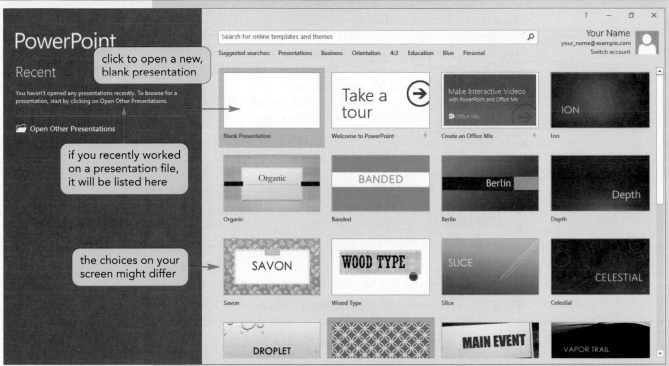

TIP

To create a new blank presentation when PowerPoint is already running, click the File tab on the ribbon, click New in the navigation bar, and then click Blank Presentation.

3. Click **Blank Presentation**. Backstage view closes and a new presentation window appears. The temporary filename "Presentation1" appears in the title bar. There is only one slide in the new presentation—Slide 1.

Trouble? If you do not see the area on the ribbon that contains buttons and you see only the ribbon tab names, click the Home tab to expand the ribbon and display the commands, and then in the bottom-right corner of the ribbon, click the Pin the ribbon button 📌 that appears.

Trouble? If the window is not maximized, click the Maximize button ☐ in the upper-right corner.

When you create a new presentation, it is displayed in Normal view. **Normal view** displays the selected slide enlarged so you can add and manipulate objects on the slide. The Slides pane on the left side of the program window displays **thumbnails**—miniature images—of all the slides in the presentation. The Home tab on the ribbon is selected when you first open or create a presentation. The Session 1.1 Visual Overview identifies elements of the PowerPoint window.

Working in Touch Mode

In Office 2016, you can work with a mouse or, if you have a touch screen, you can work in Touch Mode. In **Touch Mode** the ribbon increases in height so that there is more space around each button on the ribbon, making it easier to use your finger to tap the specific button you need. Also, in the main part of the PowerPoint window, the instructions telling you to "Click" are replaced with instructions to "Double tap." Note that the figures in this text show the screen with Mouse Mode on. You'll switch to Touch Mode and then back to Mouse Mode now.

Note: The following steps assume that you are using a mouse. If you are instead using a touch device, please read these steps but don't complete them, so that you remain working in Touch Mode.

To switch between Touch Mode and Mouse Mode:

1. On the Quick Access Toolbar, click the **Customize Quick Access Toolbar** button ▾. A menu opens. The Touch/Mouse Mode command near the bottom of the menu does not have a checkmark next to it.

Trouble? If the Touch/Mouse Mode command has a checkmark next to it, press the Esc key to close the menu, and then skip Step 2.

2. On the menu, click **Touch/Mouse Mode**. The menu closes and the Touch/Mouse Mode button appears on the Quick Access Toolbar.

3. On the Quick Access Toolbar, click the **Touch/Mouse Mode** button 👆. A menu opens listing Mouse and Touch, and the icon next to Mouse is shaded orange to indicate it is selected.

Trouble? If the icon next to Touch is shaded orange, press the Esc key to close the menu and skip Step 4.

4. On the menu, click **Touch**. The menu closes and the ribbon increases in height so that there is more space around each button on the ribbon. Notice that the instructions in the main part of the PowerPoint window changed by replacing the instruction to "Click" with the instruction to "Double tap." See Figure 1-2. Now you'll change back to Mouse Mode.

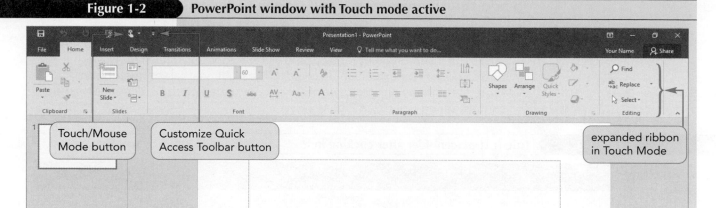

Figure 1-2   **PowerPoint window with Touch mode active**

Trouble? If you are working with a touch screen and want to use Touch Mode, skip Steps 5 and 6.

5. Click the **Touch/Mouse Mode** button 🖑, and then click **Mouse**. The ribbon and the instructions change back to Mouse Mode defaults as shown in the Session 1.1 Visual Overview.

6. Click the **Customize Quick Access Toolbar** button ⭳, and then click **Touch/Mouse Mode** to deselect this option and remove the checkmark. The Touch/Mouse Mode button is removed from the Quick Access Toolbar.

Creating a Title Slide

The **title slide** is the first slide in a presentation. It generally contains the title of the presentation plus any other identifying information you want to include, such as a company's slogan, the presenter's name, or a company name. The **font**—a set of characters with the same design—used in the title and subtitle may be the same or may be different fonts that complement each other.

The title slide contains two objects called text placeholders. A **text placeholder** is a placeholder designed to contain text. Text placeholders usually display text that describes the purpose of the placeholder and instructs you to click so that you can start typing in the placeholder. The larger text placeholder on the title slide is designed to hold the presentation title, and the smaller text placeholder is designed to contain a subtitle. Once you enter text into a text placeholder, it is no longer a placeholder and becomes an object called a **text box**.

When you click in the placeholder, the **insertion point**, which indicates where text will appear when you start typing, appears as a blinking line in the center of the placeholder. In addition, a contextual tab, the Drawing Tools Format tab, appears on the ribbon. A **contextual tab** appears only in context—that is, when a particular type of object is selected or active—and contains commands for modifying that object.

You'll add a title and subtitle for Caitlin's presentation now. Caitlin wants the title slide to contain the company name and slogan.

To add the company name and slogan to the title slide:

1. On **Slide 1**, move the pointer to position it in the title text placeholder (where it says "Click to add title") so that the pointer changes to I, and then click. The insertion point replaces the placeholder text, and the Drawing Tools Format contextual tab appears as the rightmost tab on the ribbon. Note that in the Font group on the Home tab, the Font box identifies the title font as Calibri Light. See Figure 1-3.

Figure 1-3 | **Title text placeholder after clicking in it**

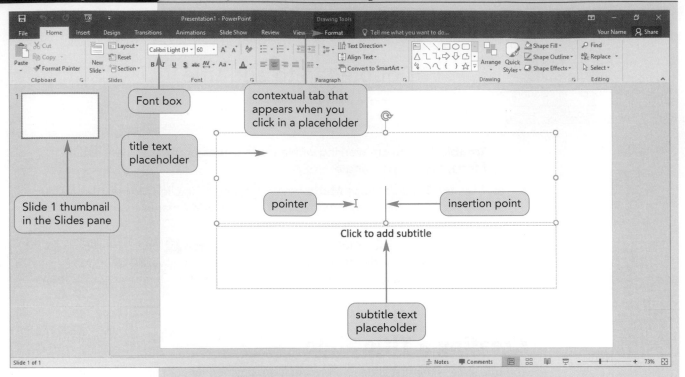

2. Type **Lakeside Event Hall**. The placeholder is now a text box.

3. Click a blank area of the slide. The border of the text box disappears, and the Drawing Tools Format tab no longer appears on the ribbon.

4. Click in the **subtitle text placeholder** (where it says "Click to add subtitle"), and then type **Perfect venue for all occasions!**. Notice in the Font group that the subtitle font is Calibri, a font which works well with the Calibri Light font used in the title text.

5. Click a blank area of the slide.

Saving and Editing a Presentation

Once you have created a presentation, you should name and save the presentation file. You can save the file on a hard drive or a network drive, on an external drive such as a USB drive, or to your account on OneDrive, Microsoft's free online storage area.

To save the presentation for the first time:

1. On the Quick Access Toolbar, point to the **Save** button 🖫. A box called a **ScreenTip** appears, identifying the button.

2. Click the **Save** button 🖫. The Save As screen in Backstage view appears. See Figure 1-4. The **navigation bar** on the left contains commands for working with the file and program options. Recently used folders on the selected drive appear in a list on the right.

Figure 1-4   Save As screen in Backstage view

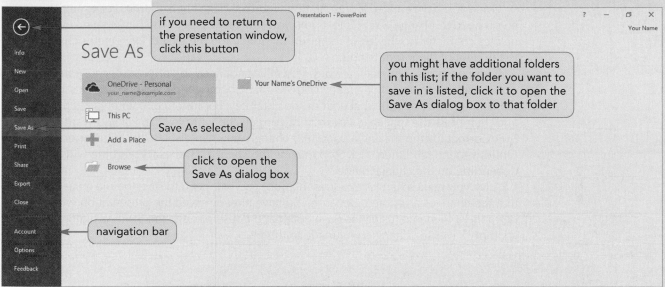

3. Click **Browse**. The Save As dialog box opens, similar to the one shown in Figure 1-5.

Figure 1-5   Save As dialog box

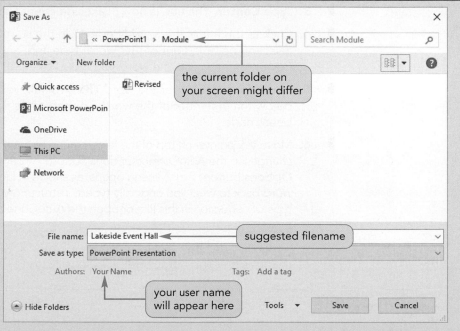

4. Navigate to the drive and folder where you are storing your Data Files, and then click in the **File name** box. The suggested filename, Lakeside Event Hall, is selected.

5. Type **Convention Presentation**. The text you type replaces the selected text in the File name box.

6. Click the **Save** button. The file is saved, the dialog box and Backstage view close, and the presentation window appears again with the new filename in the title bar.

Once you have created a presentation, you can make changes to it. For example, if you need to change text in a text box, you can easily edit it. The Backspace key deletes characters to the left of the insertion point, and the Delete key deletes characters to the right of the insertion point.

If you mistype or misspell a word, you might not need to correct it because the **AutoCorrect** feature automatically corrects many commonly mistyped and misspelled words after you press the spacebar or the Enter key. For instance, if you type "cna" and then press the spacebar, PowerPoint corrects the word to "can." If you want AutoCorrect to stop making a particular change, you can display the AutoCorrect Options menu, and then click Stop making the change. (The exact wording will differ depending on the change made.)

After you make changes to a presentation, you will need to save the file again so that the changes are stored. Because you have already saved the presentation with a permanent filename, using the Save command does not open the Save As dialog box; it simply saves the changes you made to the file.

To edit the text on Slide 1 and save your changes:

1. On Slide 1, click the **title**, and then use the ← and → keys as needed to position the insertion point to the right of the word "Hall."

2. Press the **Backspace** key four times. The four characters to the left of the insertion point, "Hall," are deleted.

3. Type **Center**. The title is now "Lakeside Event Center."

4. Click to the left of the word "Perfect" in the subtitle text box to position the insertion point in front of that word, type **Teh**, and then press the **spacebar**. PowerPoint corrects the word you typed to "The."

5. Move the pointer over the word **The**. A small, very faint rectangle appears below the first letter of the word. This indicates that an AutoCorrection has been made.

6. Move the pointer on top of the faint rectangle that appears under the "T" so that it changes to the AutoCorrect Options button ⬚▾, and then click the **AutoCorrect Options** button ⬚▾. A menu opens, as shown in Figure 1-6. You can change the word back to what you originally typed, instruct PowerPoint to stop making this type of correction in this file, or open the AutoCorrect dialog box.

   Trouble? If you can't see the AutoCorrection indicator box, point to the letter "T," and then slowly move the pointer down until it is over the box and changes it to the AutoCorrect Options button.

Figure 1-6 ▶ AutoCorrect Options button menu

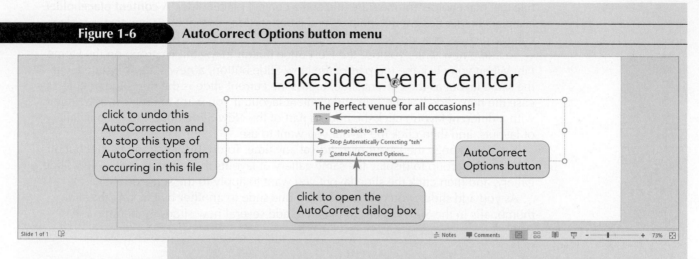

7. Click **Control AutoCorrect Options**. The AutoCorrect dialog box opens with the AutoCorrect tab selected. See Figure 1-7.

Figure 1-7 ▶ AutoCorrect tab in the AutoCorrect dialog box

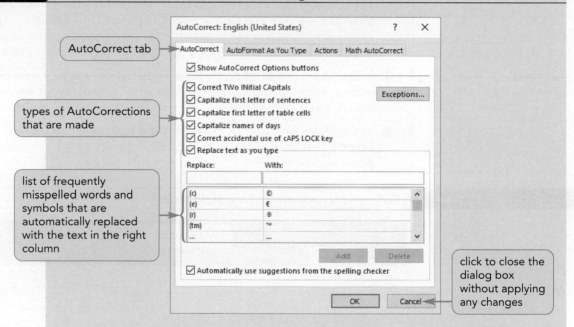

8. Examine the types of changes the AutoCorrect feature makes, and then click the **Cancel** button.

9. Click to the left of the "P" in "Perfect," if necessary, press the **Delete** key, and then type **p**. The subtitle now is "The perfect venue for all occasions!" Now that you have modified the presentation, you need to save your changes.

10. On the Quick Access Toolbar, click the **Save** button 🖫. The changes you made are saved to the Convention Presentation file.

Adding New Slides

Now that you've created the title slide, you need to add more slides. Every slide has a **layout**, which is the arrangement of placeholders on the slide. The title slide uses the Title Slide layout. A commonly used layout is the Title and Content layout, which contains a title text placeholder for the slide title and a content placeholder. A **content placeholder** is a placeholder designed to hold several types of slide content including text, a table, a chart, a picture, or a video.

To add a new slide, you use the New Slide button in the Slides group on the Home tab. When you click the top part of the New Slide button, a new slide is inserted with the same layout as the current slide, unless the current slide is the title slide; in that case the new slide has the Title and Content layout. If you want to create a new slide with a different layout, click the bottom part of the New Slide button to open a gallery of layouts, and then click the layout you want to use.

You can change the layout of a slide at any time. To do this, click the Layout button in the Slides group to display the same gallery of layouts that appears in the New Slide gallery, and then click the slide layout you want to apply to the selected slide.

As you add slides, you can switch from one slide to another by clicking the slide thumbnails in the Slides pane. You need to add several new slides to the file.

To add new slides and apply different layouts:

1. Make sure the Home tab is displayed on the ribbon.

2. In the Slides group, click the top part of the **New Slide** button. A new slide appears and its thumbnail appears in the Slides pane below Slide 1. The new slide has the Title and Content layout applied. This layout contains a title text placeholder and a content placeholder. In the Slides pane, an orange border appears around the new Slide 2, indicating that it is the current slide.

3. In the Slides group, click the **New Slide** button again. A new Slide 3 is added. Because Slide 2 had the Title and Content layout applied, Slide 3 also has that layout applied.

4. In the Slides group, click the **New Slide button arrow** (that is, click the bottom part of the New Slide button). A gallery of the available layouts appears. See Figure 1-8.

Figure 1-8 ▶ **Gallery of layouts on the New Slide menu**

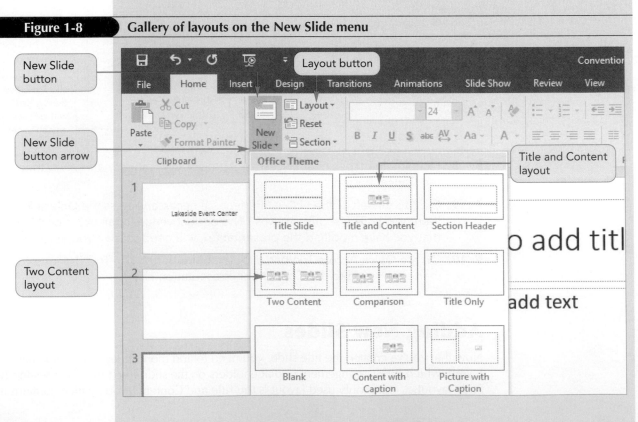

▶ **5.** In the gallery, click the **Two Content** layout. The gallery closes and a new Slide 4 is inserted with the Two Content layout applied. This layout includes three objects: a title text placeholder and two content placeholders.

▶ **6.** In the Slides group, click the **New Slide** button. A new Slide 5 is added to the presentation. Because Slide 4 had the Two Content layout applied, that layout is also applied to the new slide. You need to change the layout of Slide 5.

▶ **7.** In the Slides group, click the **Layout** button. The same gallery of layouts that appeared when you clicked the New Slide button arrow appears. The Two Content layout is selected, as indicated by the shading behind it, showing you that this is the layout applied to the current slide, Slide 5.

▶ **8.** Click the **Title and Content** layout. The layout of Slide 5 is changed to Title and Content.

▶ **9.** In the Slides group, click the **New Slide** button twice to add two more slides with the Title and Content layout.

▶ **10.** Add a new slide with the Two Content layout. There are now eight slides in the presentation. In the Slides pane, Slides 1 through 3 have scrolled up out of view, and vertical scroll bars are now visible in both the Slides pane and along the right side of the program window.

▶ **11.** In the Slides pane, drag the **scroll box** to the top of the vertical scroll bar, and then click the **Slide 2** thumbnail. Slide 2 appears in the program window and is selected in the Slides pane. See Figure 1-9.

| Figure 1-9 | Slide 2 with the Title and Content layout |

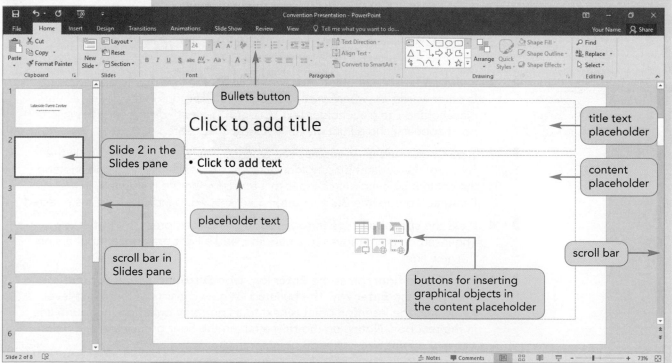

▶ **12.** On the Quick Access Toolbar, click the **Save** button 🖫. The changes you made are saved in the file.

If you accidentally close a presentation without saving changes and need to recover it, you can do so by clicking the File tab, clicking Open in the navigation bar, and then clicking the Recover Unsaved Presentations button.

Creating Lists

One way to help explain the topic or concept you are describing in your presentation is to use lists. For oral presentations, the intent of lists is to enhance the oral presentation, not replace it. In self-running presentations, items in lists might need to be longer and more descriptive. However, keep in mind that PowerPoint is a presentation graphics program intended to help you present information in a visual, graphical manner, not create a written document in an alternate form.

Items in a list can appear at different levels. A **first-level item** is a main item in a list; a **second-level item**—sometimes called a **subitem**—is an item beneath and indented from a first-level item. Usually, the font size—the size of the text—in subitems is smaller than the size used for text in the level above. Text is measured in **points**, which is a unit of measurement. Text in a book is typically printed in 10- or 12-point type; text on a slide needs to be much larger so the audience can easily read it.

Creating a Bulleted List

A **bulleted list** is a list of items with some type of bullet symbol in front of each item or paragraph. When you create a subitem in the list, a different or smaller symbol is often used. You need to create a bulleted list that describes the amenities of the Lakeside Event Center and one that describes the catering packages available.

To create bulleted lists on Slides 2 and 3:

1. On **Slide 2**, click in the **title text placeholder** (with the placeholder text "Click to add title"), and then type **Amenities**.

2. In the content placeholder, click any area where the pointer is shaped as Ⅰ— in other words, anywhere except on one of the buttons in the center of the placeholder. The placeholder text "Click to add text" disappears, the insertion point appears, and a light gray bullet symbol appears.

3. Type **Comfortable**. As soon as you type the first character, the icons in the center of the content placeholder disappear, the bullet symbol darkens, and the content placeholder changes to a text box. On the Home tab, in the Paragraph group, the Bullets button ▤ is shaded to indicate that it is selected.

4. Press the **spacebar**, type **indoor seating**, and then press the **Enter** key. The insertion point moves to a new line, and a light gray bullet appears on the new line.

5. Type **Dance floor**, press the **Enter** key, type **Surround sound for music**, and then press the **Enter** key. The bulleted list now consists of three first-level items, and the insertion point is next to a light gray bullet on the fourth line in the text box. Notice on the Home tab, in the Font group, that the point size in the Font Size box is 28 points.

6. Press the **Tab** key. The bullet symbol and the insertion point indent one-half inch to the right, the bullet symbol changes to a smaller size, and the number in the Font Size box changes to 24. See Figure 1-10.

Figure 1-10   **Subitem created on Slide 2**

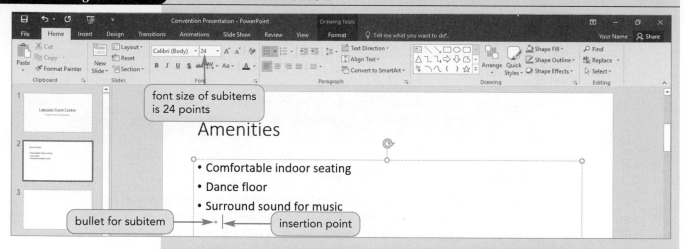

font size of subitems is 24 points

Amenities

• Comfortable indoor seating
• Dance floor
• Surround sound for music

bullet for subitem → • | ← insertion point

7. Type **DJs can easily plug in** and then press the **Enter** key.

8. Type **Live bands have plenty of room** and then press the **Enter** key. A third subitem is created. You will change it to a first-level item using a key combination. In this book, when you need to press two keys together, the keys will be listed separated by a plus sign.

TIP

You don't need to press the keys at exactly the same time—press and hold the first key, press and release the second key, and then release the first key.

9. Press the **Shift+Tab** keys. The bullet symbol and the insertion point shift back to the left margin of the text box, the bullet symbol changes back to the larger size, and 28 again appears in the Font Size box because this line is now a first-level bulleted item.

10. Type **Optional outdoor seating on patio**, press the **Enter** key, and then type **Additional appetizers and pasta stations available as add-ons**.

11. In the Slides pane, click the **Slide 3** thumbnail to display Slide 3, click in the **title text placeholder**, and then type **Packages**.

12. In the content placeholder, click the **placeholder text**, type **Basic--5 hours, standard catering package**, press the **Enter** key, and then type **Special--5 hours, deluxe catering package**. When you pressed the spacebar after typing 5, AutoCorrect changed the two dashes to an em-dash, a typographical character longer than a hyphen.

If you add more text than will fit in the text box with the default font sizes and line spacing, **AutoFit** adjusts these features to make the text fit. When AutoFit is activated, the AutoFit Options button appears below the text box. You can click this button and then select from among several options, including turning off AutoFit for this text box and splitting the text between two slides. Although AutoFit can be helpful, be aware that it also allows you to crowd text on a slide, making the slide less effective.

PROSKILLS

Written Communication: How Much Text Should I Include?

Text can help audiences retain the information you are presenting by allowing them to read the main points while hearing you discuss them. But be wary of adding so much text to your slides that your audience can ignore you and just read the slides. Try to follow the 7x7 rule—no more than seven items per slide, with no more than seven words per item. A variation of this rule is 6x6, and some presenters even prefer 4x4. If you create a self-running presentation (a presentation file others will view on their own), you will usually need to add more text than you would if you were presenting the material in person.

Creating a Numbered List

A **numbered list** is similar to a bulleted list except that numbers appear in front of each item instead of bullet symbols. Generally you should use a numbered list when the order of the items is important—for example, if you are presenting a list of step-by-step instructions that need to be followed in sequence in order to complete a task successfully. You need to create a numbered list on Slide 5 to explain how clients can reserve the event center for a function.

To create a numbered list on Slide 5:

1. In the Slides pane, click the **Slide 5** thumbnail to display Slide 5, and then type **Reserve Lakeside Event Center for Your Function!** in the title text placeholder.

2. In the content placeholder, click the **placeholder text**.

3. On the Home tab, in the Paragraph group, click the **Numbering** button. The Numbering button is selected, the Bullets button is deselected, and in the content placeholder, the bullet symbol is replaced with the number 1 followed by a period.

   Trouble? If a menu containing a gallery of numbering styles appears, you clicked the Numbering button arrow on the right side of the button. Click the Numbering button arrow again to close the menu, and then click the left part of the Numbering button.

4. Type **Specify date of function**, and then press the **Enter** key. As soon as you start typing, the number 1 darkens to black. After you press the Enter key, the insertion point moves to the next line, next to the light gray number 2.

5. Type **Choose package**, press the **Enter** key, type **Submit deposit**, and then press the **Enter** key. The number 4 appears on the next line.

6. In the Paragraph group, click the **Increase List Level** button. The fourth line is indented to be a subitem under the third item, and the number 4 changes to a number 1 in a smaller font size than the first-level items. Clicking the Increase List Level button is an alternative to pressing the Tab key to create a subitem.

7. Type **Credit card**, press the **Enter** key, type **Debit from checking account**, and then press the **Enter** key.

8. In the Paragraph group, click the **Decrease List Level** button. The sixth line is now a first-level item, and the number 4 appears next to it. Clicking the Decrease List Level button is an alternative to pressing the Shift+Tab keys to promote a subitem.

9. Type **Confirm**. The list now consists of four first-level numbered items and two subitems under number 3.

10. In the second item, click before the word "Choose," and then press the **Enter** key. A blank line is inserted above the second item.

11. Press the ↑ key. A light-gray number 2 appears in the blank line. The item on the third line in the list is still numbered 2.

12. Type **Specify number of guests**. As soon as you start typing, the new number 2 darkens in the second line, and the third item in the list is numbered 3. Compare your screen to Figure 1-11.

Figure 1-11 **Numbered list on Slide 5**

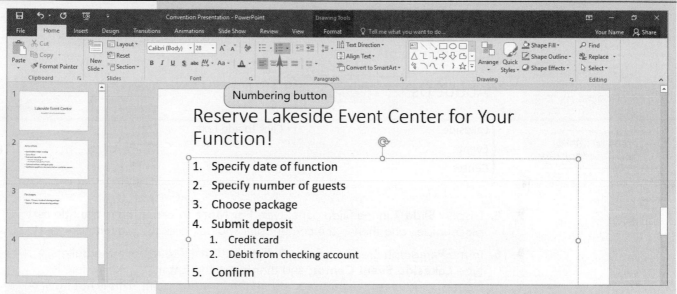

Creating an Unnumbered List

An **unnumbered list** is a list that does not have bullets or numbers preceding each item. Unnumbered lists are useful in slides when you want to present information on multiple lines without actually itemizing the information. For example, contact information for the presenter, including his or her email address, street address, city, and so on, would be clearer if it were in an unnumbered list.

As you have seen, items in a list have a little extra space between each item to visually separate bulleted items. Sometimes, you don't want the extra space between lines. If you press the Shift+Enter keys instead of just the Enter key, a new line is created, but it is still considered to be part of the item above it. Therefore, there is no extra space between the lines. Note that this also means that if you do this in a bulleted or numbered list, the new line will not have a bullet or number next to it because it is not a new item.

You need to create a slide that explains the event center's name. Also, Caitlin asks you to create a slide containing contact information.

To create unnumbered lists on Slides 4 and 7:

1. In the Slides pane, click the **Slide 4** thumbnail to display Slide 4. Slide 4 has the Two Content layout applied.

2. Type **About Us** in the title content placeholder, and then in the left content placeholder, click the **placeholder text**.

3. On the Home tab, in the Paragraph group, click the **Bullets** button ⊞. The button is no longer selected, and the bullet symbol disappears from the content placeholder.

4. Type **Lakeside**, press the **Enter** key, type **Event**, press the **Enter** key, and then type **Center**. Compare your screen to Figure 1-12.

Figure 1-12	Unnumbered list on Slide 4

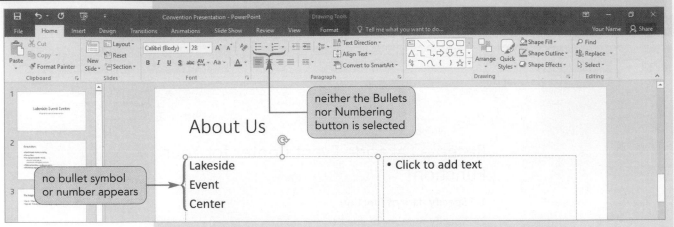

5. Display **Slide 7** in the Slide pane, type **For More Information** in the title text placeholder, and then in the content placeholder, click the **placeholder text**.

6. In the Paragraph group, click the **Bullets** button ⊞ to remove the bullets, type **Lakeside Event Center**, and then press the **Enter** key. A new line is created, but there is extra space above the insertion point. This is not how addresses usually appear.

7. Press the **Backspace** key to delete the new line and move the insertion point back to the end of the first line, and then press the **Shift+Enter** keys. The insertion point moves to the next line, and, this time, there is no extra space above it.

8. Type **15680 Shore Drive**, press the **Shift+Enter** keys, and then type **Lake Havasu City, AZ 86403**. You need to insert the phone number on the next line, the general email address for the group on the line after that, and the website address on the last line. The extra space above these lines will set this information apart from the address and make it easier to read.

9. Press the **Enter** key to create a new line with extra space above it, type **(928) 555-HALL**, press the **Enter** key, type **info@lec.example.com**, and then press the **Enter** key. The insertion point moves to a new line with extra space above it, and the email address you typed changes color to blue and is underlined.

When you type text that PowerPoint recognizes as an email or website address and then press the spacebar or Enter key, the text is automatically formatted as a link that can be clicked during a slide show. To indicate this, the color of the text is changed and the text is underlined. Links are active only during a slide show.

▶ **10.** Type **www.lec.example.com**, and then press the **spacebar**. The text is formatted as a link. Caitlin plans to click the link during her presentation to show the audience the website, so she wants it to stay formatted as a link. However, there is no need to have the email address formatted as a link because no one will click it during the presentation.

▶ **11.** Right-click **info@lec.example.com**. A shortcut menu opens.

▶ **12.** On the shortcut menu, click **Remove Hyperlink**. The email address is no longer formatted as a hyperlink. Compare your screen to Figure 1-13.

| Figure 1-13 | List on Slide 7 |

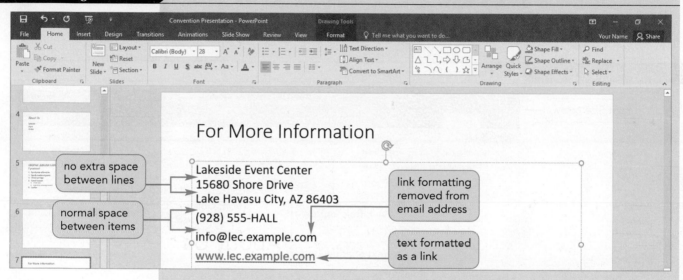

▶ **13.** On the Quick Access Toolbar, click the **Save** button 🖫 to save the changes.

Formatting Text

Slides in a presentation should have a cohesive look and feel. For example, the slide titles and the text in content placeholders should be in complementary fonts. However, there are times when you need to change the format of text. For instance, you might want to make specific words bold to make them stand out more.

To apply a format to text, either the text or the text box must be selected. If you want to apply the same formatting to all the text in a text box, you can click the border of the text box. When you do this, the dotted line border changes to a solid line to indicate that the contents of the entire text box are selected.

The commands in the Font group on the Home tab are used to apply formatting to text. Some of these commands are also available on the Mini toolbar, which appears when you select text with the mouse. The **Mini toolbar** contains commonly used buttons for formatting text. If the Mini toolbar appears, you can use the buttons on it instead of those in the Font group.

Some of the commands in the Font group use the Microsoft Office **Live Preview** feature, which previews the change on the slide so you can instantly see what the text will look like if you apply that format.

Caitlin wants the contact information on Slide 7 ("For More Information") to be larger. She also wants the first letter of each item in the unnumbered list on Slide 4 ("About Us") formatted so they are more prominent.

To format the text on Slides 4 and 7:

1. On **Slide 7** ("For More Information"), position the pointer on the border of the text box containing the contact information so that it changes to ✛, and then click the border of the text box. The border changes to a solid line to indicate that the entire text box is selected.

2. On the Home tab, in the Font group, click the **Increase Font Size** button A⁺ twice. All the text in the text box increases in size with each click, and all the text in the text box is now 36 points.

3. Display **Slide 4** ("About Us").

4. In the unnumbered list, click to the left of "Lakeside," press and hold the **Shift** key, press the → key, and then release the **Shift** key. The letter "L" is selected. See Figure 1-14.

Figure 1-14   **Text selected to be formatted**

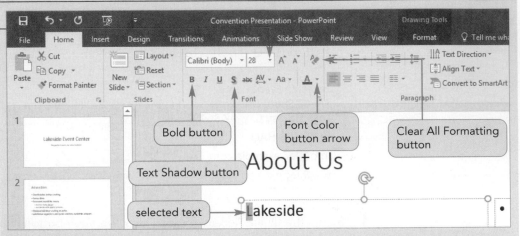

5. In the Font group, click the **Bold** button B . The Bold button becomes selected, and the selected text is formatted as bold.

6. Make sure the letter "L" is still selected, and then in the Font group, click the **Text Shadow** button S . The selected text is now bold with a slight drop shadow.

7. In the Font group, click the **Font Size arrow** to open the Font Size menu, and then click **48**. The selected text is now 48 points.

8. In the Font group, click the **Font Color button arrow** A ⁻ . A menu containing colors opens.

9. Under Theme Colors, move the pointer over each color, noting the ScreenTips that appear and watching as Live Preview changes the color of the selected text as you point to each color. Figure 1-15 shows the pointer pointing to the Orange, Accent 2, Darker 25% color.

Figure 1-15	Font Color menu

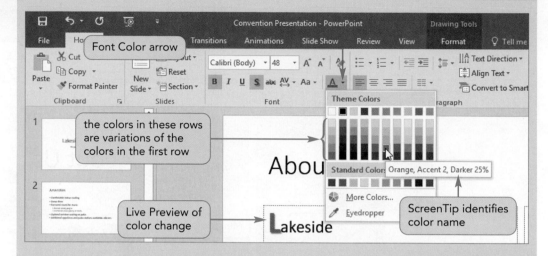

10. Using the ScreenTips, locate the **Orange, Accent 2, Darker 25%** color, and then click it. The selected text changes to the orange color you clicked.

Now you need to format the first letters in the other words in the list to match the letter "L." You can repeat the steps you did when you formatted the letter "L," or you can use the Format Painter to copy all the formatting of the letter "L" to the other letters you need to format.

Also, Caitlin wants the text in the unnumbered list to be as large as possible. Because the first letters of each word are larger than the rest of the letters, the easiest way to do this is to select all of the text, and then use the Increase Font Size button. All of the letters will increase in size by four points with each click.

To use the Format Painter to copy and apply formatting on Slide 4:

1. Make sure the letter "L" is still selected.

2. On the Home tab, in the Clipboard group, click the **Format Painter** button, and then move the pointer on top of the slide. The button is selected, and the pointer changes to .

3. Position the pointer before the letter "E" in "Event," press and hold the mouse button, drag over the letter **E**, and then release the mouse button. The formatting you applied to the letter "L" is copied to the letter "E," and the Mini toolbar appears. See Figure 1-16. The Mini toolbar appears whenever you drag over text to select it.

| Figure 1-16 | The Mini toolbar |

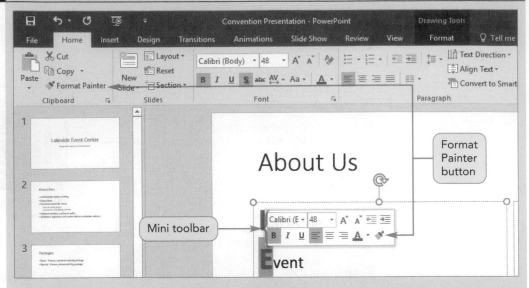

4. On the Mini toolbar, click the **Format Painter** button, and then drag across the letter **C** in "Center."

5. Click the border of the text box to select the entire text box, and then in the Font group, click the **Increase Font Size** button five times. In the Font group, the Font Size button indicates that the text is 48+ points. This means that in the selected text box, the text that is the smallest is 48 points and there is some text that is a larger point size.

6. On the Quick Access Toolbar, click the **Save** button to save the changes.

INSIGHT

Undoing and Redoing Actions

If you make a mistake or change your mind about an action as you are working, you can reverse the action by clicking the Undo button on the Quick Access Toolbar. You can undo up to the most recent 20 actions by continuing to click the Undo button or by clicking the Undo button arrow and then selecting as many actions in the list as you want. You can also Redo an action that you undid by clicking the Redo button on the Quick Access Toolbar.

When there are no actions that can be redone, the Redo button changes to the Repeat button. You can use the Repeat button to repeat an action, such as formatting text as bold. If the Repeat button is light gray, this means it is unavailable because there is no action to repeat (or to redo).

Moving and Copying Text

You can move or copy text and objects in a presentation using the Clipboard. The **Clipboard** is a temporary storage area available to all Windows programs on which text or objects are stored when you cut or copy them. To **cut** text or objects—that is, remove the selected text or objects from one location so that you can place it somewhere else—you select the text or object, and then use the Cut button in the Clipboard group on the Home tab to remove the selected text or object and place it on the Clipboard. To **copy** selected text or objects, you use the Copy button in the Clipboard group on the Home tab, which leaves the original text or object on the slide and places a copy of it on the Clipboard. You can then **paste** the text or object stored on the Clipboard anywhere in the presentation or, in fact, in any file in any Windows program.

You can paste an item on the Clipboard as many times and in as many locations as you like. However, the Clipboard can hold only the most recently cut or copied item. As soon as you cut or copy another item, it replaces the previously cut or copied item on the Clipboard.

Note that cutting text or an object is different from using the Delete or Backspace key to delete it. Deleted text and objects are not placed on the Clipboard; this means they cannot be pasted.

Caitlin wants a few changes made to Slides 5 and 3. You'll use the Clipboard as you make these edits.

To copy and paste text using the Clipboard:

1. Display **Slide 5** ("Reserve Lakeside Event Center for Your Function!"), and then double-click the word **Reserve** in the title text. The word "Reserve" is selected.

2. On the Home tab, in the Clipboard group, click the **Copy** button. The selected word is copied to the Clipboard.

3. In the last item in the numbered list, click after the word "Confirm," and then press the **spacebar**.

4. In the Clipboard group, click the **Paste** button. The text is pasted and picks up the formatting of its destination; that is, the pasted text is the 28-point Calibri font, the same font and size as the rest of the first-level items in the list, instead of 44-point Calibri Light as in the title. The Paste Options button 📋 appears below the pasted text.

5. Click the **Paste Options** button 📋. A menu opens with four buttons on it. See Figure 1-17.

| Figure 1-17 | Buttons on the Paste Options menu when text is on the Clipboard |

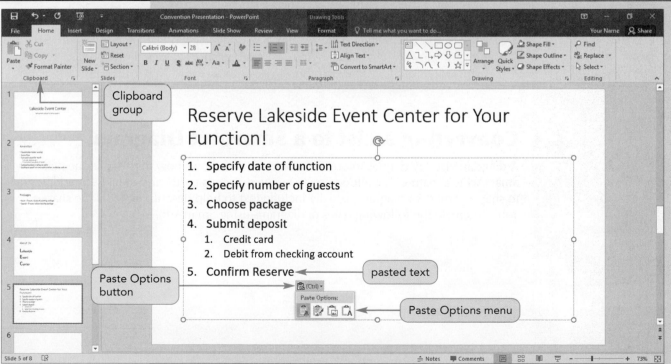

6. Point to each button on the menu, reading the ScreenTips and watching to see how the pasted text changes in appearance. The first button is the Use Destination Theme button 📋, and this is the default choice when you paste text.

7. Click a blank area of the slide to close the menu without making a selection, press the **Backspace** key, type **ation**, click to the left of "Reservation," press the **Delete** key, and then type **r**. The word "reservation" in the numbered list is now all lowercase.

8. Display **Slide 2** ("Amenities"). The last bulleted item (starts with "Additional appetizers") belongs on Slide 3.

9. In the last bulleted item, position the pointer on top of the bullet symbol so that the pointer changes to ✛, and then click. The entire bulleted item is selected.

TIP

To cut text or an object, you can press the Ctrl+X keys; to copy text or an object, press the Ctrl+C keys; and to paste the item on the Clipboard, press the Ctrl+V keys.

10. In the Clipboard group, click the **Cut** button. The last bulleted item is removed from the slide and placed on the Clipboard.

11. Display **Slide 3** ("Packages"), click after the second bulleted item, and then press the **Enter** key to create a third bulleted item.

12. In the Clipboard group, click the **Paste** button. The bulleted item you cut is pasted as the third bulleted item on Slide 3 using the default paste option of Use Destination Theme. The insertion point appears next to a fourth bulleted item.

13. Press the **Backspace** key twice to delete the extra line, and then on the Quick Access Toolbar, click the **Save** button 💾 to save the changes.

INSIGHT

Using the Office Clipboard

The **Office Clipboard** is a special Clipboard available only to Microsoft Office applications. Once you activate the Office Clipboard, you can store up to 24 items on it and then select the item or items you want to paste. To activate the Office Clipboard, click the Home tab. In the Clipboard group, click the Dialog Box Launcher (the small square in the lower-right corner of the Clipboard group) to open the Clipboard task pane to the left of the displayed slide.

Converting a List to a SmartArt Diagram

A **diagram** visually depicts information or ideas and shows how they are connected. **SmartArt** is a feature that allows you to create diagrams easily and quickly. In addition to shapes, SmartArt diagrams usually include text to help describe or label the shapes. You can create the following types of diagrams using SmartArt:

- **List**—Shows a list of items in a graphical representation
- **Process**—Shows a sequence of steps in a process
- **Cycle**—Shows a process that is a continuous cycle
- **Hierarchy** (including organization charts)—Shows the relationship between individuals or units
- **Relationship** (including Venn diagrams, radial diagrams, and target diagrams)—Shows the relationship between two or more elements
- **Matrix**—Shows information in a grid
- **Pyramid**—Shows foundation-based relationships
- **Picture**—Provides a location for a picture or pictures that you insert

There is also an Office.com category of SmartArt, which, if you are connected to the Internet, displays additional SmartArt diagrams available in various categories on Office.com, a Microsoft website that contains tools for use with Office programs.

A quick way to create a SmartArt diagram is to convert an existing list. When you select an existing list and then click the Convert to SmartArt Graphic button in the Paragraph group on the Home tab, a gallery of SmartArt layouts appears. For SmartArt, a **layout** is the arrangement of the shapes in the diagram. Each first-level item in the list is converted to a shape in the SmartArt diagram. If the list contains subitems, you might need to experiment with different layouts to find one that best suits the information in your list.

REFERENCE

Converting a Bulleted List into a SmartArt Diagram

- Click anywhere in the bulleted list.
- In the Paragraph group on the Home tab, click the Convert to SmartArt Graphic button, and then click More SmartArt Graphics.
- In the Choose a SmartArt Graphic dialog box, select the desired SmartArt type in the list on the left.
- In the center pane, click the SmartArt diagram you want to use.
- Click the OK button.

Caitlin wants the numbered list on Slide 5 changed into a SmartArt diagram.

To convert the list on Slide 5 into a SmartArt diagram:

1. Display **Slide 5** ("Reserve Lakeside Event Center for Your Function!"), and then click anywhere in the numbered list to display the text box border.

2. On the Home tab, in the Paragraph group, click the **Convert to SmartArt** button. A gallery of SmartArt layouts appears.

3. Point to the first layout. The ScreenTip identifies this layout as the Vertical Bullet List layout, and Live Preview shows you what the numbered list will look like with that layout applied. See Figure 1-18. Notice that the subitems are not included in a shape in this diagram.

Figure 1-18 Live Preview of the Vertical Bullet List SmartArt layout

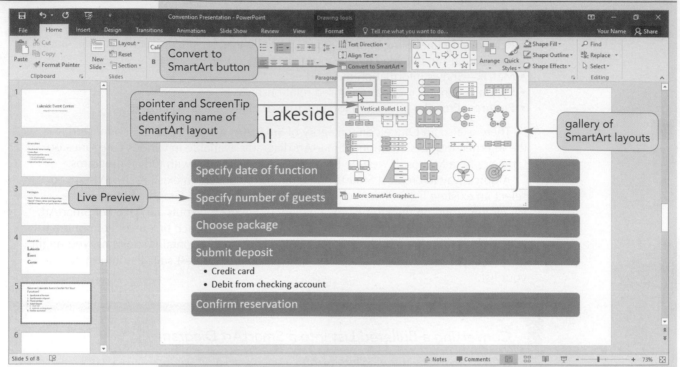

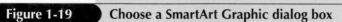

4. Point to several other layouts in the gallery, observing the Live Preview of each one. In some of the layouts, the subitems are included in a shape.

5. At the bottom of the gallery, click **More SmartArt Graphics**. The Choose a SmartArt Graphic dialog box opens. See Figure 1-19. You can click a type in the left pane to filter the middle pane to show only that type of layout.

Figure 1-19 Choose a SmartArt Graphic dialog box

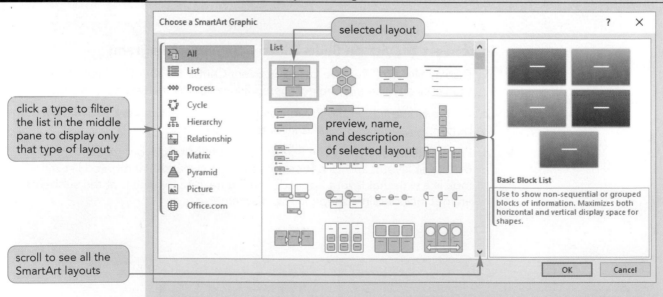

6. In the left pane, click **Process**, and then in the middle pane, click the **Step Up Process** layout, using the ScreenTips to identify it (it's the second layout in the first row). The right pane changes to show a description of that layout.

7. Click the **OK** button. The dialog box closes, and each of the first level items in the list appears in the square shapes in the diagram. The items also appear as a bulleted list in the Text pane, which is open to the left of the diagram. The SmartArt Tools contextual tabs appear on the ribbon. See Figure 1-20.

Figure 1-20   SmartArt diagram with the Step Up Process layout

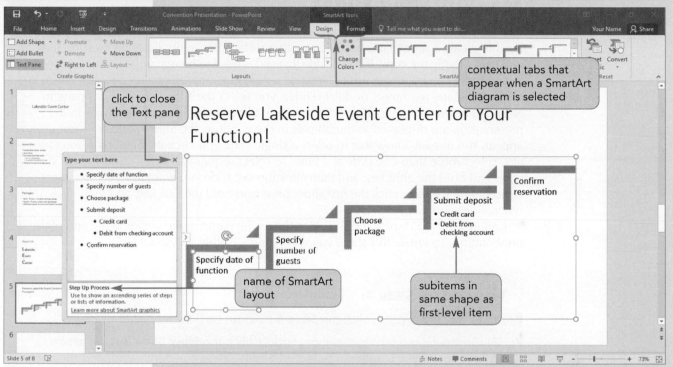

Trouble? If you do not see the Text pane, click the Text pane button ⟨ on the left border of the selected SmartArt diagram.

In this layout, the subitems below "Submit deposit" are included in the fourth step shape; they are not placed in their own shapes in the diagram. Caitlin decides the information in the subitems does not need to be on the slide because people will see those options on the website when they submit their deposit.

8. In the "Submit deposit" shape, select **Debit from checking account**, and then press the **Delete** key. The text is deleted from the shape and from the Text pane.

9. In the Text pane, click to the right of the word "card," press the **Backspace** key as many times as necessary to delete all of the bullet text, and then press the **Backspace** key once more. The bullet changes to a first-level bullet and a new square shape is inserted in the diagram.

10. Press the **Backspace** key one more time. The empty bullet and the blank line are deleted in the Text pane, and the newly added shape is removed from the diagram. The "Submit deposit" shape now contains only the first-level item. Notice that AutoFit increased the size of the text in all the shapes so that the text still fills the shapes and is as large as possible. The "Submit deposit" shape is still selected. This shape should appear after the "Confirm reservation" shape.

▶ **11.** On the SmartArt Tools Design tab, in the Create Graphic group, click the **Move Down** button. The selected "Submit deposit" shape moves down one spot in the bulleted list in the text pane and one shape to the right in the SmartArt graphic on the slide.

▶ **12.** Click a blank area of the slide to deselect the diagram, and then on the Quick Access Toolbar, click the **Save** button 🖫 to save your changes.

Manipulating Slides

You can manipulate the slides in a presentation to suit your needs. For instance, if you need to create a slide that is similar to another slide, you can duplicate the existing slide and then modify the copy. If you decide that slides need to be rearranged, you can reorder them. And if you no longer want to include a slide in your presentation, you can delete it.

To duplicate, rearrange, or delete slides, you select the slides in the Slides pane in Normal view or switch to Slide Sorter view. In **Slide Sorter view** all the slides in the presentation are displayed as thumbnails in the window; the Slides pane does not appear. You already know that to select a single slide you click its thumbnail. You can also select more than one slide at a time. To select sequential slides, click the first slide, press and hold the Shift key, and then click the last slide you want to select. To select nonsequential slides, click the first slide, press and hold the Ctrl key, and then click any other slides you want to select.

Caitlin wants to display the slide that shows the name of the center at the end of the presentation. To create this slide, you will duplicate Slide 4 ("About Us").

To duplicate Slide 4:

▶ **1.** In the Slides pane, click the **Slide 4** ("About Us") thumbnail to display Slide 4.

▶ **2.** On the Home tab, in the Slides group, click the **New Slide button arrow**, and then click **Duplicate Selected Slides**. Slide 4 is duplicated, and the copy is inserted as a new Slide 5 in the Slides pane. Slide 5 is now the current slide. If more than one slide were selected, they would all be duplicated. The duplicate slide doesn't need the title; Caitlin just wants to reinforce the center's name.

▶ **3.** On Slide 5, click anywhere on the title **About Us**, click the **text box border** to select the text box, and then press the **Delete** key. The title and the title text box are deleted and the title text placeholder reappears.

You could delete the title text placeholder, but it is not necessary. When you display the presentation to an audience as a slide show, any unused placeholders will not appear.

Next you need to rearrange the slides. You need to move the duplicate of the "About Us" slide so it is the last slide in the presentation because Caitlin wants to leave it displayed after the presentation is over. She hopes this visual will reinforce the company's name for the audience. Caitlin also wants the "Packages" slide (Slide 3) moved so it appears before the "Amenities" slide (Slide 2), and she wants the original "About Us" slide (Slide 4) to be the second slide in the presentation.

To rearrange the slides in the presentation:

1. In the Slides pane, scroll up, if necessary, so that you can see Slides 2 and 3, and then drag the **Slide 3** ("Packages") thumbnail above the Slide 2 ("Amenities") thumbnail. As you drag, the Slide 3 thumbnail follows the pointer and Slide 2 moves down. The "Packages" slide is now Slide 2 and "Amenities" is now Slide 3. You'll move the other two slides in Slide Sorter view.

TIP

You can also use the buttons in the Presentation Views group on the View tab to switch views.

2. On the status bar, click the **Slide Sorter** button ⊞. The view switches to Slide Sorter view. Slide 2 appears with an orange border, indicating that it is selected.

3. On the status bar, click the **Zoom Out** button ➖ as many times as necessary until you can see all nine slides in the presentation. See Figure 1-21.

Figure 1-21   Slide Sorter view

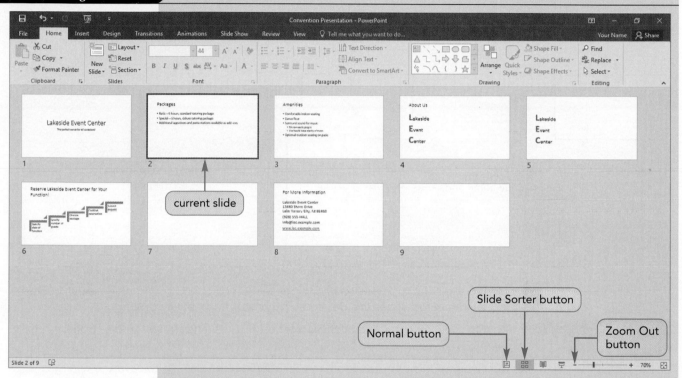

4. Drag the **Slide 4** ("About Us") thumbnail to between Slides 1 and 2. As you drag, the other slides move out of the way. The slide is repositioned, and the slides are renumbered so that the "About Us" slide is now Slide 2.

5. Drag the **Slide 5** thumbnail (the slide containing just the name of the company) so it becomes the last slide in the presentation (Slide 9).

Now you need to delete the two blank slides. To delete a slide, you can right-click its thumbnail to display a shortcut menu.

To delete the blank slides:

1. Click **Slide 6** (a blank slide), press and hold the **Shift** key, and then click **Slide 8** (the other blank slide), and then release the **Shift** key. The two slides you clicked are selected, as well as the slide between them. You want to delete only the two blank slides.

2. Click a blank area of the window to deselect the slides, click **Slide 6**, press and hold the **Ctrl** key, click **Slide 8**, and then release the **Ctrl** key. Only the two slides you clicked are selected.

3. Right-click either selected slide. A shortcut menu appears. See Figure 1-22.

Figure 1-22   **Shortcut menu for selected slides**

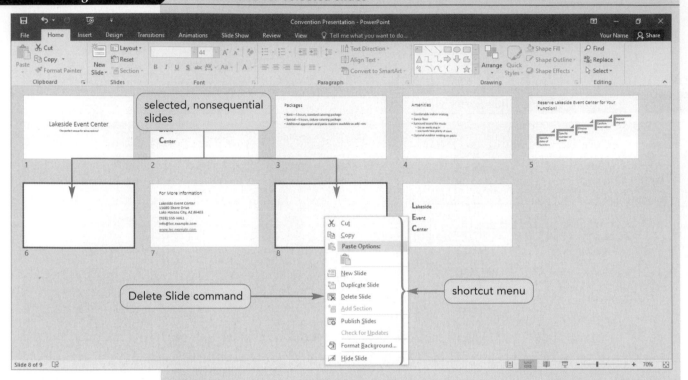

4. On the shortcut menu, click **Delete Slide**. The shortcut menu closes and the two selected slides are deleted. The presentation now contains seven slides.

5. On the status bar, click the **Normal** button 🔲. The presentation appears in Normal view.

6. On the Quick Access Toolbar, click the **Save** button 🔲 to save the changes to the presentation.

TIP

You can also double-click a slide thumbnail in Slide Sorter view to display that slide in Normal view.

Closing a Presentation

When you are finished working with a presentation, you can close it and leave PowerPoint open. To do this, you click the File tab to open Backstage view, and then click the Close command. If you click the Close button ✕ in the upper-right corner of the PowerPoint window and only one presentation is open, you will not only close the presentation, you will exit PowerPoint as well.

You're finished working with the presentation for now, so you will close it. First you will add your name to the title slide.

To add your name to Slide 1 and close the presentation:

1. Display **Slide 1** (the title slide), click the **subtitle**, position the insertion point after "occasions!," press the **Enter** key, and then type your full name.

2. Click the **File** tab. Backstage view appears with the Info screen displayed. See Figure 1-23.

Figure 1-23   **Info screen in Backstage view**

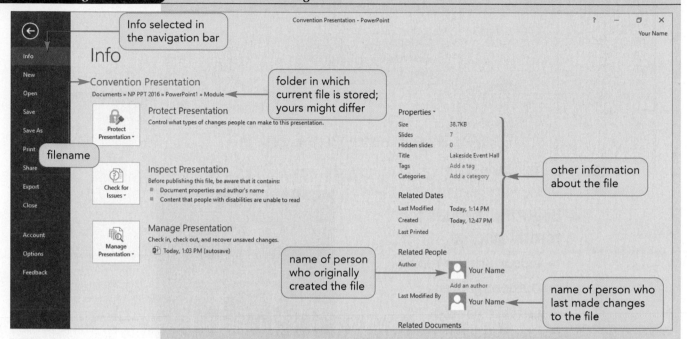

3. In the navigation bar, click **Close**. Backstage view closes, and a dialog box opens, asking if you want to save your changes.

4. In the dialog box, click the **Save** button. The dialog box and the presentation close, and the empty presentation window appears.

Trouble? If you want to take a break, you can exit PowerPoint by clicking the Close button ☒ in the upper-right corner of the PowerPoint window.

You've created a presentation that includes slides to which you added bulleted, numbered, and unnumbered lists. You also formatted text, converted a list to SmartArt, and manipulated slides. You are ready to give the presentation draft to Caitlin to review.

REVIEW

Session 1.1 Quick Check

1. Define "presentation."

2. How do you display Backstage view?

3. What is a layout?

4. In addition to a title text placeholder, what other type of placeholder do most layouts contain?

5. What is the term for an object that contains text?

6. What is the difference between the Clipboard and the Office Clipboard?

7. How do you convert a list to a SmartArt diagram?

Session 1.2 Visual Overview:

In **Slide Show view**, each slide fills the screen, one after another.

Benefits of Lakeside Event Center

▶ Beautiful venues for formal photos

  ▶ Indoor private rooms

  ▶ Outdoor gardens

  ▶ Outdoor gazebo

▶ Friendly and accom

The pointer is not visible in Slide Show view until you move it or right-click it. When you move the pointer, this faint row of buttons appears in the lower-left corner of the screen. All of these buttons are also available in Presenter view.

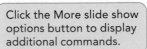

Click the More slide show options button to display additional commands.

Click the Zoom into the slide button to zoom into a portion of the slide during the slide show.

Click the Return to the previous slide and Advance to the next slide buttons to move from slide to slide in Slide Show view.

Click the See all slides button to display all the slides, similar to Slide Sorter view.

©iStock.com/bloggityblog

Slide Show and Presenter Views

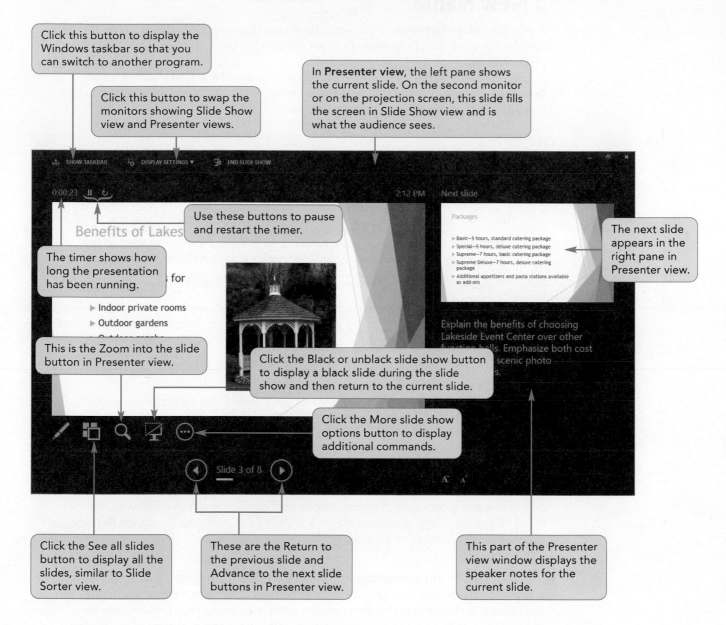

Click this button to display the Windows taskbar so that you can switch to another program.

Click this button to swap the monitors showing Slide Show view and Presenter views.

In **Presenter view**, the left pane shows the current slide. On the second monitor or on the projection screen, this slide fills the screen in Slide Show view and is what the audience sees.

Use these buttons to pause and restart the timer.

The timer shows how long the presentation has been running.

The next slide appears in the right pane in Presenter view.

This is the Zoom into the slide button in Presenter view.

Click the Black or unblack slide show button to display a black slide during the slide show and then return to the current slide.

Click the More slide show options button to display additional commands.

Click the See all slides button to display all the slides, similar to Slide Sorter view.

These are the Return to the previous slide and Advance to the next slide buttons in Presenter view.

This part of the Presenter view window displays the speaker notes for the current slide.

©iStock.com/bloggityblog

Opening a Presentation and Saving It with a New Name

If you have closed a presentation, you can always reopen it to modify it. To do this, you can double-click the file in a File Explorer window, or you can open Backstage view in PowerPoint and use the Open command.

Caitlin reviewed the presentation you created in Session 1.1. She added a slide listing the benefits of using Lakeside Event Center and made a few additional changes. You will continue modifying this presentation.

To open the revised presentation:

▶ **1.** Click the **File** tab on the ribbon to display Backstage view. Because there is no open presentation, the Open screen is displayed. Recent is selected, and you might see a list of the 25 most recently opened presentations on the right.

   Trouble? If PowerPoint is not running, start PowerPoint, and then in the navigation bar on the Recent screen, click the Open Other Presentations link.

   Trouble? If another presentation is open, click Open in the navigation bar in Backstage view.

   Trouble? If you are storing your files on your OneDrive, click OneDrive, and then log in if necessary.

▶ **2.** Click **Browse**. The Open dialog box appears. It is similar to the Save As dialog box.

▶ **3.** Navigate to the drive that contains your Data Files, navigate to the **PowerPoint1 > Module** folder, click **Revised** to select it, and then click the **Open** button. The Open dialog box closes and the Revised presentation opens in the PowerPoint window, with Slide 1 displayed.

   Trouble? If you don't have the starting Data Files, you need to get them before you can proceed. Your instructor will either give you the Data Files or ask you to obtain them from a specified location (such as a network drive). If you have any questions about the Data Files, see your instructor or technical support person for assistance.

If you want to edit a presentation without changing the original, you need to create a copy of it. To do this, you use the Save As command to open the Save As dialog box, which is the same dialog box you saw when you saved your presentation for the first time. When you save a presentation with a new name, a copy of the original presentation is created, the original presentation is closed, and the newly named copy remains open in the PowerPoint window.

To save the Revised presentation with a new name:

▶ **1.** Click the **File** tab, and then in the navigation bar, click **Save As**. The Save As screen in Backstage view appears.

▶ **2.** Click **Browse** to open the Save As dialog box.

▶ **3.** If necessary, navigate to the drive and folder where you are storing your Data Files.

▶ **4.** In the File name box, change the filename to **Convention Final**, and then click the **Save** button. The Save As dialog box closes, a copy of the file is saved with the new name Convention Final, and the Convention Final presentation appears in the PowerPoint window.

Changing the Theme and the Theme Variant

A **theme** is a coordinated set of colors, fonts, backgrounds, and effects. All presentations have a theme. If you don't choose one, the default Office theme is applied; that is the theme currently applied to the Convention Final presentation.

You saw the Office theme set of colors when you changed the color of the text on the "About Us" slide. You have also seen the Office theme fonts in use on the slides. In the Office theme, the font of the slide titles is Calibri Light, and the font of the text in content text boxes is Calibri. In themes, the font used for slide titles is the Headings font, and the font used for the content text boxes is the Body font.

In PowerPoint, each theme has several variants with different coordinating colors and sometimes slightly different backgrounds. A theme and its variants are called a **theme family**. PowerPoint comes with several installed themes, and many more themes are available online at Office.com. In addition, you can use a custom theme stored on your computer or network.

You can select a different installed theme when you create a new presentation by clicking one of the themes on the New or Recent screen in Backstage view instead of clicking Blank Presentation, and then clicking one of the variants. If you want to change the theme of an open presentation, you can choose an installed theme on the Design tab, or you can apply a theme applied to another presentation or a theme stored on your computer or network. When you change the theme, the colors, fonts, and slide backgrounds change to those used in the new theme.

Caitlin wants the theme of the Convention Final presentation changed to one that has more color in the background. First you'll display Slide 2 so you can see the effect a different theme has on the text formatted with a theme color.

To examine the current theme and then change the theme and theme variant:

▶ **1.** Display **Slide 2** ("About Us"), and then, in the unnumbered list select the orange letter **L**.

▶ **2.** On the Home tab, in the Font group, click the **Font Color button arrow** $\boxed{\text{A}}$ ·. Look at the colors under Theme Colors, and note the second to last color is selected in the sixth column, which contains shades of orange. Notice also the row of Standard Colors below the theme colors.

▶ **3.** In the Font group, click the **Font arrow**. A menu of fonts installed on the computer opens. At the top under Theme Fonts, Calibri (Body) is selected because the letter L that you selected is in a content text box. See Figure 1-24.

Figure 1-24   Theme fonts on the Font menu

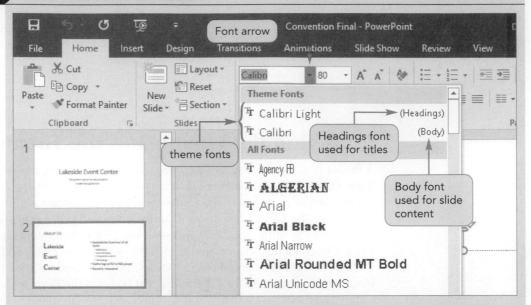

4. On the ribbon, click the **Design** tab. The Font menu closes and the installed themes appear in the Themes gallery on the Design tab. See Figure 1-25. The current theme is the first theme listed in the Themes group on the Design tab. The next theme is the Office theme, which, in this case, is also the current theme.

Figure 1-25   Themes and variants on the Design tab

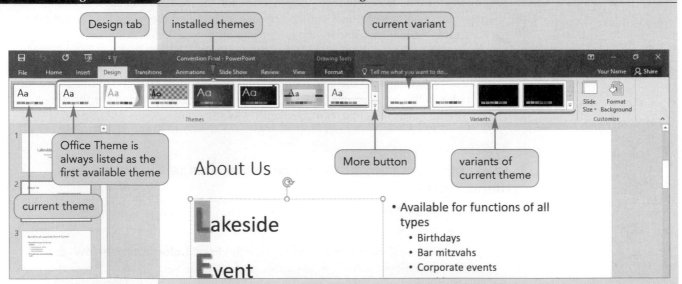

To see all of the installed themes, you need to scroll through the gallery by clicking the up and down scroll buttons on the right end of the gallery or clicking the More button to expand the gallery to see all of the themes at once. The **More button** appears on all galleries that contain additional items or commands that don't fit in the group on the ribbon.

5. In the Themes group, click the **More** button ▼. The gallery of themes opens. See Figure 1-26. When the gallery is open, the theme applied to the current presentation appears in the first row. In the next row, the first theme is the Office theme, and then the rest of the installed themes appear. Some of these themes also appear on the Recent and New screens in Backstage view.

Figure 1-26   **Themes gallery expanded**

6. Point to several of the themes in the gallery to display their ScreenTips and to see a Live Preview of the theme applied to the current slide.

7. In the first row of the Office section of the gallery, click the **Facet** theme. The gallery closes, and the Facet theme is applied to all the slides with the default variant (the first variant in the Variants group). The title text on each slide changes from black to green, the letters that you had colored orange on Slide 2 are dark green, the bullet symbols change from black circles to green triangles, and in the Slides pane, you can see on the Slide 6 thumbnail that the SmartArt shapes are now green as well.

8. In the Variants group, point to the other three variants to see a Live Preview of each of them, and then click the **second variant** (the blue one).

   Trouble? If there are no variants, your installation of Office might have an extra version of the Facet theme installed. In the Themes group, click the More button, and then make sure you click the Facet theme in the first row.

9. Click the **Home** tab, and then in the Font group, click the **Font Color button arrow** ⬛▾. The selected color—the color of the selected letter "L"—is now a shade of blue in the Theme Colors of the Facet theme. Notice also that the row of Standard Colors is the same as it was when the Office theme was applied.

10. In the Font group, click the **Font arrow**. You can see that the Theme Fonts are now Trebuchet MS for both Headings (slide titles) and the Body (content text boxes).

11. Press the **Esc** key. The Font menu closes.

After you apply a new theme, you should examine your slides to make sure that they look the way you expect them to. The font sizes used for the text in lists in the Facet theme are considerably smaller than those used in the Office theme. You know that Caitlin wants the slides to be legible and clearly visible, so you will increase the font sizes on some of the slides. The title slide is fine, but you need to examine the rest of the slides.

To examine the slides with the new theme and adjust font sizes:

1. On **Slide 2** ("About Us"), in the bulleted list, click the **first bulleted item**. In the Font group, the font size is 18 points, quite a bit smaller than the font size of first-level bulleted items in the Office theme, which is 28 points. You can see that the font size of the subitems is also fairly small.

2. In the bulleted list, click the **text box border** to select the entire text box. In the Font group, 16+ appears in the Font Size box. The smallest font size used in the selected text box—the font size of the subitems—is 16, and the plus sign indicates that there is text in the selected text box larger than 16 points.

3. In the Font group, click the **Increase Font Size** button $\boxed{A}$ twice. The font size of the first-level bulleted items changes to 24 points, and the font size of the second-level bulleted items changes to 20 points.

   Trouble? If the Drawing Tools Format tab becomes selected on the ribbon, click the Home tab.

4. Display **Slide 3** ("Benefits of Lakeside Event Center"), click the **bulleted list**, click the **text box border**, and then in the Font group, click the **Increase Font Size** button $\boxed{A}$ three times. The font size of the first-level bulleted items changes to 28 points, and the font size of the second-level bulleted items changes to 24 points.

5. On **Slide 4** ("Packages") and **Slide 5** ("Amenities"), increase the size of the text in the bulleted lists so that the font size of the first-level items is 28 points and of the subitems is 24 points.

6. Display **Slides 6, 7, 8,** and then **Slide 1** in the Slide pane. These remaining slides look fine.

7. On the Quick Access Toolbar, click the **Save** button $\boxed{\blacksquare}$. The changes to the presentation are saved.

INSIGHT

Understanding the Difference Between Themes and Templates

As explained earlier, a theme is a coordinated set of colors, fonts, backgrounds, and effects. A **template** has a theme applied, but it also contains text, graphics, and placeholders to help direct you in creating content for a presentation. You can create and save your own custom templates or find everything from calendars to marketing templates among the thousands of templates available on Office.com. To find a template on Office.com, display the Recent or New screen in Backstage view, type keywords in the "Search for online templates and themes" box, and then click the Search button in the box to display templates related to the search terms. To create a new presentation based on the template you find, click the template and then click Create.

If a template is stored on your computer, you can apply the theme used in the template to an existing presentation. If you want to apply the theme used in a template on Office.com to an existing presentation, you need to download the template to your computer first, and then you can apply it to an existing presentation.

Working with Photos

Most people are exposed to multimedia daily and expect to have information conveyed visually as well as verbally. In many cases, graphics are more effective than words for communicating an important point. For example, if a sales force has reached its sales goals for the year, including a photo in your presentation of a person reaching the top of a mountain can convey a sense of exhilaration to your audience.

Inserting Photos Stored on Your Computer or Network

Content placeholders contain buttons that you can use to insert things other than a list, including photos stored on your hard drive, a network drive, a USB drive, an SD card from a digital camera, or any other medium to which you have access. You can also use the Pictures button in the Images group on the Insert tab to add photos to slides.

Caitlin has photos that she wants inserted on three of the slides in the presentation. She asks you to add the photos to the presentation.

To insert photos on Slides 3, 5, and 8:

▶ 1. Display **Slide 3** ("Benefits of Lakeside Event Center"), and then in the content placeholder on the right, click the **Pictures** button ◻. The Insert Picture dialog box opens. This dialog box is similar to the Open dialog box.

▶ 2. Navigate to the **PowerPoint1 > Module** folder included with your Data Files, click **Gazebo**, and then click the **Insert** button. The dialog box closes, and a picture of a gazebo appears in the placeholder and is selected. The contextual Picture Tools Format tab appears on the ribbon to the right of the View tab and is the active tab. See Figure 1-27.

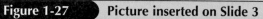

Figure 1-27   **Picture inserted on Slide 3**

©iStock.com/bloggityblog

▶ 3. Display **Slide 5** ("Amenities"). This slide uses the Title and Content layout and does not have a second content placeholder. You can change the layout to include a second content placeholder, or you can use a command on the ribbon to insert a photo.

▶ 4. Click the **Insert** tab, and then in the Images group, click the **Pictures** button. The Insert Picture dialog box opens.

5. In the PowerPoint1 > Module folder, click **Tables**, and then click the **Insert** button. The dialog box closes and the picture is added to the slide, covering the bulleted list. You will fix this later.

6. Display **Slide 8** (the last slide). This slide has the Two Content layout applied, but you can still use the Pictures command on the Insert tab.

7. Click the **Insert** tab on the ribbon.

8. In the Images group, click the **Pictures** button, click **Wedding** in the PowerPoint1 > Module folder, and then click the **Insert** button. The picture replaces the content placeholder on the slide.

Cropping Photos

Sometimes you want to display only part of a photo. For example, if you insert a photo of a party scene that includes a bouquet of colorful balloons, you might want to show only the balloons. To do this, you can **crop** the photo—cut out the parts you don't want to include. In PowerPoint, you can crop it manually to any size you want, crop it to a preset ratio, or crop it to a shape.

Caitlin wants you to crop the photo on Slide 5 ("Amenities") to make the dimensions of the final photo smaller without making the images in the photo smaller. She also wants you to crop the photo on Slide 8 (the last slide) to an interesting shape.

To crop the photos on Slides 5 and 8:

1. Display **Slide 5** ("Amenities"), click the **photo** to select it, and then click the **Picture Tools Format** tab, if necessary.

2. In the Size group, click the **Crop** button. The Crop button is selected, and crop handles appear around the edges of the photo just inside the sizing handles. See Figure 1-28.

Figure 1-28 Photo with crop handles

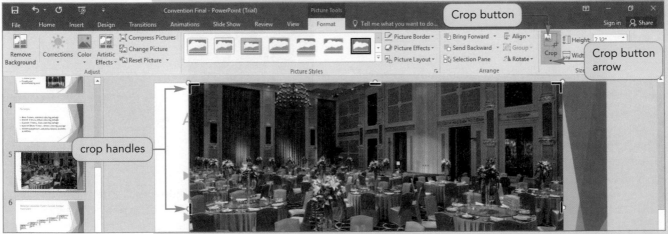

©iStock.com/kai zhang; ©iStock.com/bloggityblog

3. Position the pointer directly on top of the right-middle crop handle so that it changes to ⊢, press and hold the mouse button, and then drag the crop handle to the left approximately two inches. See Figure 1-29.

Figure 1-29   Cropped photo

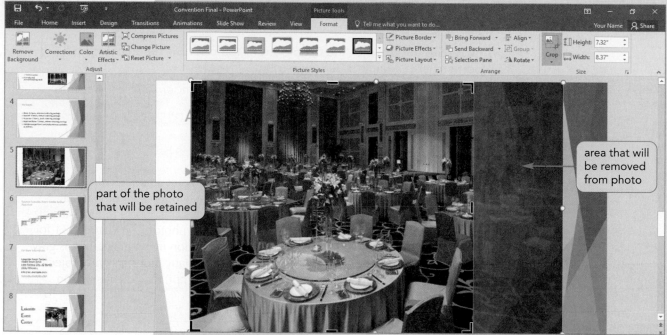

part of the photo that will be retained

area that will be removed from photo

©iStock.com/kai zhang; ©iStock.com/bloggityblog; Courtesy of Dina White

> 4. Click the **Crop** button again. The Crop feature is turned off, but the photo is still selected and the Format tab is still the active tab.

> 5. Display **Slide 8** (the last slide), click the **photo** to select it, and then click the **Picture Tools Format** tab, if necessary.

> 6. In the Size group, click the **Crop button arrow**. The Crop button menu opens. See Figure 1-30.

Figure 1-30   Crop button menu

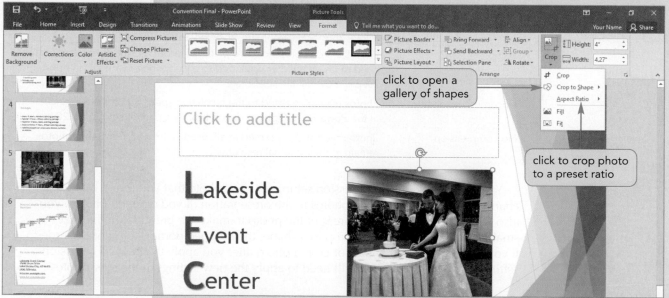

click to open a gallery of shapes

click to crop photo to a preset ratio

Courtesy of Dina White; ©iStock.com/kai zhang; ©iStock.com/bloggityblog

7. Point to **Crop to Shape** to open a gallery of shapes, and then in the second row under Basic Shapes, click the **Plaque** shape. The photo is cropped to a plaque shape. Notice that the rectangular selection border of the original photo is still showing.

8. In the Size group, click the **Crop** button. You can now see the cropped portions of the original, rectangle photo that are shaded gray.

9. Click a blank area of the slide. The picture is no longer selected, and the Home tab is the active tab on the ribbon.

Modifying Photo Compression Options

When you save a presentation that contains photos, PowerPoint automatically compresses the photos to a resolution of 220 pixels per inch (ppi). (For comparison, photos printed in magazines are typically 300 ppi.) Compressing photos reduces the size of the presentation file, but it also reduces the quality of the photos. See Figure 1-31 for a description of the compression options available. If an option in the dialog box is gray, the photo is a lower resolution than that setting. Note that many monitors and projectors are capable of displaying resolutions only a little higher (98 ppi) than the resolution designated for email (96 ppi).

Figure 1-31 Photo compression settings

Compression Setting	Description
330 ppi	Photos are compressed to 330 pixels per inch; use when slides need to maintain the quality of the photograph when displayed on high-definition (HD) displays. Use when photograph quality is of the highest concern and file size is not an issue.
220 ppi	Photos are compressed to 220 pixels per inch; use when slides need to maintain the quality of the photograph when printed. This is the default setting for PowerPoint presentations. (Note that although this is minimal compression, it is still compressed, and if photograph quality is the most important concern, do not compress photos at all.)
150 ppi	Photos are compressed to 150 pixels per inch; use when the presentation will be viewed on a monitor or screen projector.
96 ppi	Photos are compressed to 96 pixels per inch; use for presentations that need to be emailed or uploaded to a webpage or when it is important to keep the overall file size small.
Document resolution	Photos are compressed to the resolution specified on the Advanced tab in the PowerPoint Options dialog box. The default setting is 220 ppi.
No compression	Photos are not compressed at all; used when it is critical that photos remain at their original resolution.

You can change the compression setting for each photo that you insert, or you can change the settings for all the photos in the presentation. If you cropped photos, you also can discard the cropped areas of the photo to make the presentation file size smaller. (Note that when you crop to a shape, the cropped portions are not discarded.) If you insert additional photos or crop a photo after you apply the new compression settings to all the slides, you will need to apply the new settings to the new photos.

REFERENCE

Modifying Photo Compression Settings and Removing Cropped Areas

- After all photos have been added to the presentation file, click any photo in the presentation to select it.
- Click the Picture Tools Format tab. In the Adjust group, click the Compress Pictures button.
- In the Compress Pictures dialog box, click the option button next to the resolution you want to use.
- To apply the new compression settings to all the photos in the presentation, click the Apply only to this picture check box to deselect it.
- To keep cropped areas of photos, click the Delete cropped areas of pictures check box to deselect it.
- Click the OK button.

You will adjust the compression settings to make the file size of the presentation as small as possible so that Caitlin can easily send it or post it for others without worrying about file size limitations on the receiving server.

To modify photo compression settings and remove cropped areas from photos:

1. On **Slide 8** (the last slide), click the **photo**, and then click the **Picture Tools Format** tab, if necessary.

2. In the Adjust group, click the **Compress Pictures** button. The Compress Pictures dialog box opens. See Figure 1-32. Under Target output, the Use document resolution option button is selected. Other than that option button, only the E-mail (96 ppi) option button is selected. This is because the currently selected photo's resolution is higher than 96 ppi but lower than the next largest photo size, Web (150 ppi).

Figure 1-32   **Compress Pictures dialog box**

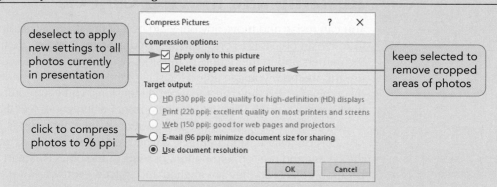

3. Click the **E-mail (96 ppi)** option button. This setting compresses the photos to the smallest possible size. At the top of the dialog box under Compression options, the Delete cropped areas of pictures check box is already selected. This option is not applied to cropped photos until you open this dialog box and then click the OK button to apply it. Because you want the presentation file size to be as small as possible, you do want cropped portions of photos to be deleted, so you'll leave this selected. The Apply only to this picture check box is also selected; however, you want the settings applied to all the photos in the file.

Be sure you deselect the Apply only to this picture check box, and be sure you are satisfied with the way you cropped the photo on Slide 5 before you click OK to close the dialog box.

▶ **4.** Click the **Apply only to this picture** check box to deselect it.

▶ **5.** Click the **OK** button.

The dialog box closes and the compression settings are applied to all the photos in the presentation. You can confirm that the cropped areas of photos were removed by examining the photo on Slide 5. (The photo on Slide 8 was cropped to a shape, so the cropped areas on it were not removed.)

▶ **6.** Display **Slide 5** ("Amenities"), click the **photo**, and then click the **Picture Tools Format** tab, if necessary.

▶ **7.** In the Size group, click the **Crop** button. The Crop handles appear around the photo, but the portions of the photo that you cropped out no longer appear.

▶ **8.** Click the **Crop** button again to deselect it, and then save the changes to the presentation.

INSIGHT

Keeping Photos Uncompressed

Suppose you are a photographer and want to create a presentation to show your photos. In that case, you would want to display them at their original, uncompressed resolution. To do this, you need to change a setting in the PowerPoint Options dialog box before you add photos to slides. Click the File tab to open Backstage view, click Options in the navigation bar to open the PowerPoint Options dialog box, click Advanced in the navigation bar, and then locate the Image Size and Quality section. To keep images at their original resolution, click the Do not compress images in file check box to select it. Note that you can also change the default compression setting for photos in this dialog box—you can increase the compression or choose to automatically discard cropped portions of photos and other editing data. Note that these changes affect only the current presentation.

Resizing and Moving Objects

You can resize and move any object to best fit the space available on a slide. One way to resize an object is to drag a sizing handle. **Sizing handles** are the circles that appear in the corners and in the middle of the sides of the border of a selected object. When you use this method, you can adjust the size of the object so it best fits the space visually. If you need to size an object to exact dimensions, you can modify the measurements in the Size group on the Format tab that appears when you select the object.

You can also drag an object to reposition it anywhere on the slide. If more than one object is on a slide, **smart guides**, dashed red lines, appear as you drag to indicate the center and the top and bottom borders of the objects. Smart guides can help you position objects so they are aligned and spaced evenly.

In addition to using the smart guides, it can be helpful to display rulers and gridlines in the window. The rulers appear along the top and left sides of the displayed slide. Gridlines are one-inch squares made up of dots one-sixth of an inch apart. As you drag an object, it snaps to the grid, even if the grid is not visible.

Resizing and Moving Pictures

Pictures and other objects that cause the Picture Tools Format tab to appear when selected have their aspect ratios locked by default. The **aspect ratio** is the ratio of the object's height to its width. When the aspect ratio is locked, if you resize the photo by dragging a corner sizing handle or if you change one dimension in the Size group on the Picture Tools Format tab, the other dimension will change by the same percentage. However, if you drag one of the sizing handles in the middle of an object's border, you will override the locked aspect ratio setting and resize the object only in the direction you drag. Generally you do not want to do this with photos because the images will become distorted.

You need to resize and move the photos you inserted on Slides 3, 5, and 8 so the slides are more attractive. You'll display the rulers and gridlines to help you as you do this.

To move and resize the photos on Slides 3, 5, and 8:

1. Click the **View** tab, and then in the Show group, click the **Ruler** and the **Gridlines** check boxes. Rulers appear above and to the left of the displayed slide, and the gridlines appear on the slide.

2. On **Slide 5** ("Amenities"), click the **photo**, if necessary, and then position the pointer on the top-middle sizing handle so that the pointer changes to ↕.

3. Press and hold the mouse button so that the pointer changes to ┼, drag the top-middle sizing handle down approximately two inches, and then release the mouse button. The photo is two inches shorter, but the image is distorted.

4. On the Quick Access Toolbar, click the **Undo** button ↩. You need to resize the photo by dragging a corner sizing handle to maintain the aspect ratio.

5. Click the **Picture Tools Format** tab, and then note the measurements in the Size group. The photo is 7.32 inches high and about 8.4 inches wide. (The exact width on your screen might differ depending on how much you cropped.)

6. Position the pointer on the bottom-left corner sizing handle so that it changes to ⤢, press and hold the mouse button so that the pointer changes to ┼, and then drag the bottom-left sizing handle up. Even though you are dragging in only one direction, because you are dragging a corner sizing handle, both the width and height are changing proportionately to maintain the aspect ratio.

7. When the photo is approximately 4.5 inches high and approximately 5 inches wide, release the mouse button. Note that the measurements in the Height and Width boxes changed to reflect the picture's new size.

8. Drag the photo to the right so that the right edge of the photo aligns with the 6-inch mark on the horizontal ruler above the slide, and drag it down so that smart guides appear indicating that the bottom and top of the photo is aligned with the bottom and top of the text box that contains the unnumbered list as shown in Figure 1-33.

TIP

If you don't want objects you are moving to snap to the grid, press and hold the Alt key while you are dragging.

Figure 1-33	Repositioning photo on Slide 5 using smart guides and gridlines

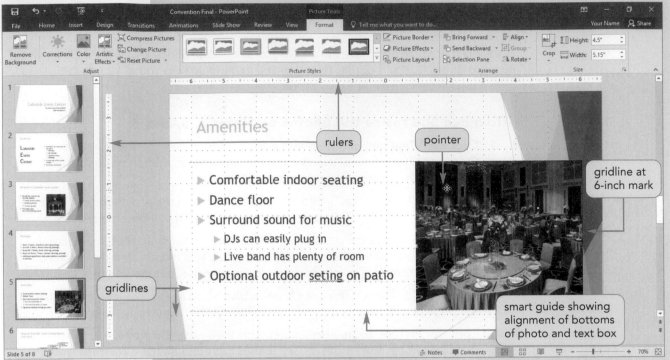

©iStock.com/kai zhang; ©iStock.com/bloggityblog

9. Release the mouse button. The photo is repositioned.

10. Display **Slide 3** ("Benefits of Lakeside Event Center"), click the **photo** to select it, and then click the **Picture Tools Format** tab if necessary.

11. In the Size group, click in the **Height** box to select the current measurement, type **4.5**, and then press the **Enter** key. The measurement in the Width box in the Size group changes proportionately to maintain the aspect ratio, and the new measurements are applied to the photo.

12. Drag the photo up and to the right until horizontal smart guides appear above and below the photo indicating that the top and bottom of the photo and the top and bottom of the text box containing the bulleted list are aligned, and so that the right edge of the photo aligns with the right edge of the title text box (at the 3.5-inch mark on the ruler), as shown in Figure 1-34.

| Figure 1-34 | Moving resized photo on Slide 3 |

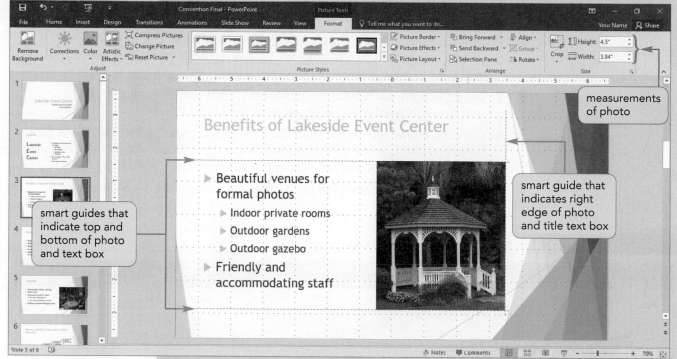

©iStock.com/bloggityblog; ©iStock.com/kai zhang

13. When the photo is aligned as shown in Figure 1-34, release the mouse button.

14. Display **Slide 8** (the last slide), resize the photo so it is 5.9 inches high and 6.3 inches wide, and then position it so that its bottom edge is aligned with the gridline at the 3-inch mark on the vertical ruler, and its right edge is aligned with the gridline at the 6-inch mark on the horizontal ruler.

15. Click the **View** tab, and then click the **Ruler** and **Gridlines** check boxes to deselect them.

Resizing and Moving Text Boxes

The themes and layouts installed with PowerPoint are designed by professionals, so much of the time it's a good idea to use the layouts as provided to be assured of a cohesive look among the slides. However, occasionally there will be a compelling reason to adjust the layout of objects on a slide, by either resizing or repositioning them.

Text boxes, like other objects that cause the Drawing Tools Format tab to appear when selected, do not have their aspect ratios locked by default. This means that when you resize a text box by dragging a corner sizing handle or changing one dimension in the Size group, the other dimension is not affected.

Like any other object on a slide, you can reposition text boxes. To do this, you must position the pointer on the text box border, anywhere except on a sizing handle, to drag it to its new location.

To improve the appearance of Slide 8, you will resize the text box containing the unnumbered list so it vertically fills the slide.

To resize the text box on Slide 8 and increase the font size:

1. On **Slide 8** (the last slide in the presentation), click the unnumbered list to display the text box border.

2. Position the pointer on the top-middle sizing handle so that it changes to ↕, and then drag the sizing handle up until the top edge of the text box is aligned with the top edge of the title text placeholder.

3. Drag the right-middle sizing handle to the right until the right edge of the text box is aligned with the left edge of the photo.

4. Click the **Home** tab, and then in the Font group, click the **Increase Font Size** button A̅ three times. Even though the title text placeholder will not appear during a slide show, you will delete it to see how the final slide will look.

5. Click the **title text placeholder border**, and then press the **Delete** key. See Figure 1-35.

| Figure 1-35 | Slide 8 with resized text box |

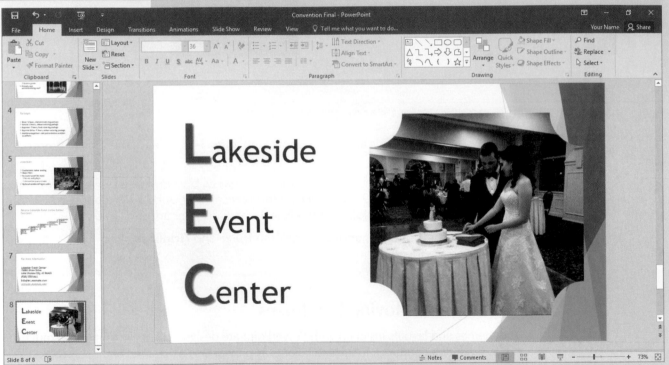

Courtesy of Dina White; ©iStock.com/bloggityblog; ©iStock.com/kai zhang

6. Save the changes to the presentation.

Adding Speaker Notes

Speaker notes, or simply **notes**, are information you add about slide content to help you remember to bring up specific points during the presentation. Speaker notes should not contain all the information you plan to say during your presentation, but they can be a useful tool for reminding you about facts and details related to the content on specific slides. You add notes in the **Notes pane**, which you can display below the displayed slide in Normal view, or you can switch to **Notes Page view**, in which an image of the slide appears in the top half of the presentation window and the notes for that slide appear in the bottom half.

To add notes to Slides 3 and 7:

▶ **1.** Display **Slide 7** ("For More Information"), and then, on the status bar, click the **Notes** button. The Notes pane appears below Slide 7 with "Click to add notes" as placeholder text. See Figure 1-36.

Figure 1-36	Notes pane below Slide 7

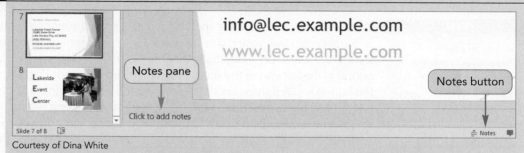

Courtesy of Dina White

▶ **2.** Click in the **Notes** pane. The placeholder text disappears, and the insertion point is in the Notes pane.

▶ **3.** Type **Hand out contact information to audience. Use the link to demonstrate how to use the website.**

▶ **4.** Display **Slide 3** ("Benefits of Lakeside Event Center"), click in the **Notes** pane, and then type **Explain the benefits of choosing Lakeside Event Center over other function halls.**

▶ **5.** Click the **View** tab on the ribbon, and then in the Presentation Views group, click the **Notes Page** button. Slide 3 is displayed in Notes Page view. See Figure 1-37.

Figure 1-37	Slide 3 in Notes Page view

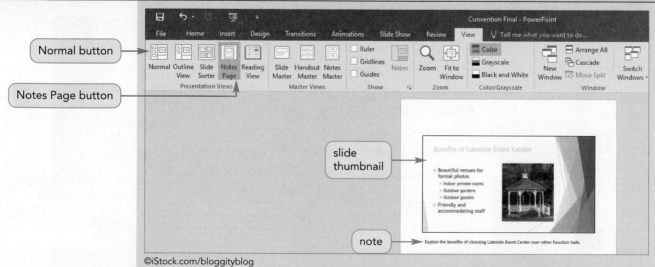

©iStock.com/bloggityblog

6. In the note, click after the period at the end of the sentence, press the **spacebar**, and then type **Emphasize both cost benefits and scenic photo opportunities**.

7. In the Presentation Views group, click the **Normal** button to return to Normal view. The Notes pane stays displayed until you close it again.

8. On the status bar, click the **Notes** button to close the Notes pane, and then save the changes to the presentation.

Checking Spelling

You should always check the spelling and grammar in your presentation before you finalize it. To make this task easier, you can use PowerPoint's spelling checker. You can quickly tell if there are words on slides that are not in the built-in dictionary by looking at the Spelling button at the left end of the status bar. If there are no words flagged as possibly misspelled, the button is ▯; if there are flagged words, the button changes to ▯. To indicate that a word might be misspelled, a wavy red line appears under it.

To correct misspelled words, you can right-click a flagged word to see a list of suggested spellings on the shortcut menu, or you can check the spelling of all the words in the presentation. To check the spelling of all the words in the presentation, you click the Spelling button in the Proofing group on the Review tab. This opens the Spelling task pane to the right of the displayed slide and starts the spell check from the current slide. A **task pane** is a pane that opens to the right or left of the displayed slide and contains commands and options related to the task you are doing. When a possible misspelled word is found, suggestions are displayed for the correct spelling. Synonyms for the selected correct spelling are also listed.

To check the spelling of words in the presentation:

1. Display **Slide 4** ("Packages"), and then right-click the misspelled word **Delux** in the fourth item in the list. A shortcut menu opens listing spelling options. See Figure 1-38.

| Figure 1-38 | Shortcut menu for a misspelled word |

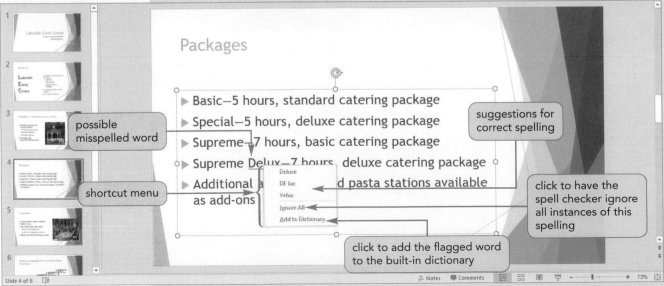

2. On the shortcut menu, click **Deluxe**. The menu closes and the spelling is corrected.

3. Click the **Review** tab, and then in the Proofing group, click the **Spelling** button. The Spelling task pane opens to the right of the displayed slide, and the next possible misspelled word on Slide 5 ("Amenities") appears with the flagged word, "seting," highlighted. See Figure 1-39. In the Spelling task pane, the first suggested correct spelling is selected. The selected correct spelling also appears at the bottom of the task pane with synonyms for the word listed below it and a speaker icon next to it.

Figure 1-39	Spelling task pane displaying a misspelled word

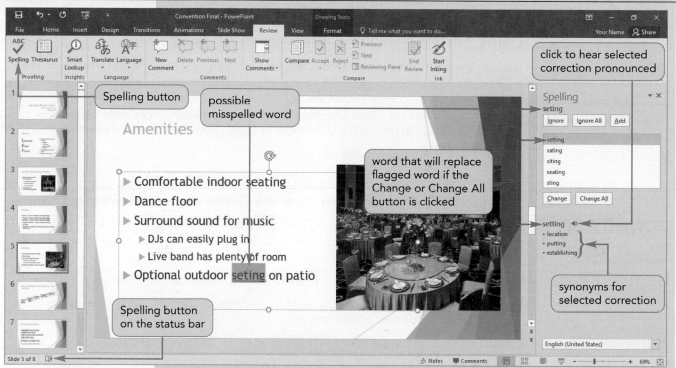

©iStock.com/kai zhang; ©iStock.com/bloggityblog

4. In the Spelling task pane, click the **speaker** icon 🔊. A male voice says the word "setting."

5. In the list of suggested corrections, click **sting**. The word at the bottom of the task pane changes to "sting," and the synonyms change also.

6. In the list of suggested corrections, click **setting**, and then click the **Change** button. The word is corrected, and the next slide containing a possible misspelled word, Slide 1, appears with the flagged word, "Keough," highlighted and listed in the Spelling task pane. This is part of Caitlin's last name so you want the spell checker to ignore this.

7. In the task pane, click the **Ignore All** button. Because that was the last flagged word in the presentation, the Spelling task pane closes, and a dialog box opens telling you that the spell check is complete.

Trouble? If the spell checker finds any other misspelled words, correct them.

8. Click the **OK** button. The dialog box closes. The last flagged word, "Keough," is still selected on Slide 1.

9. Click a blank area of the slide to deselect the text, and then save the changes to the presentation.

Running a Slide Show

After you have created and proofed your presentation, you should view it as a slide show to see how it will appear to your audience. There are several ways to do this—Slide Show view, Presenter view, and Reading view.

Using Slide Show View and Presenter View

You can use Slide Show view if your computer has only one monitor and you don't have access to a screen projector. If your computer is connected to a second monitor or a screen projector, Slide Show view is the way an audience will see your slides. Refer to the Session 1.2 Visual Overview for more information about Slide Show view.

Caitlin asks you to review the slide show in Slide Show view to make sure the slides look professional.

TIP

To start the slide show from the current slide, click the Slide Show button on the status bar.

To use Slide Show view to view the Convention Final presentation:

1. On the Quick Access Toolbar, click the **Start From Beginning** button 🖵. Slide 1 appears on the screen in Slide Show view. Now you need to advance the slide show.

2. Press the **spacebar**. Slide 2 ("About Us") appears on the screen.

3. Click the mouse button. The next slide, Slide 3 ("Benefits of Lakeside Event Center"), appears on the screen.

4. Press the **Backspace** key. The previous slide, Slide 2, appears again.

5. Press the **7** key, and then press the **Enter** key. Slide 7 ("For More Information") appears on the screen.

6. Move the mouse to display the pointer, and then position the pointer on the website address **www.lec.example.com**. The pointer changes to 🖑 to indicate that this is a link, and the ScreenTip that appears shows the full website address including "http://". If this were a real website, you could click the link to open your web browser and display the website to your audience. Because you moved the pointer, a very faint row of buttons appears in the lower-left corner. The buttons provide access to commands you need in order to run the slide show. See Figure 1-40.

Figure 1-40   Link and row of buttons in Slide Show view

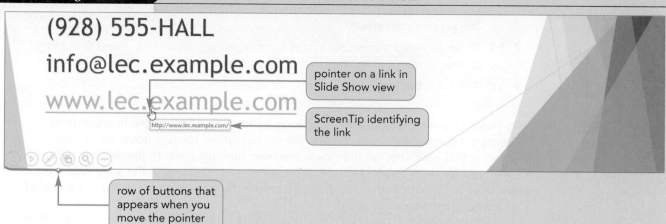

7. Move the pointer again, if necessary, to display the buttons that appear in the lower-left corner of the screen, and then click the **Return to the previous slide** button ⊙ four times to return to Slide 3 ("Benefits of Lakeside Event Center").

Trouble? If you can't see the buttons at the bottom of the screen, move the pointer to the lower-left corner so it is on top of the first button to darken that button, and then move the pointer to the right to see the rest of the buttons.

8. Display the buttons at the bottom of the screen again, and then click the **Zoom into the slide** button ⊙. The pointer changes to ⊕, and three-quarters of the slide is darkened. See Figure 1-41.

Figure 1-41   Zoom feature activated in Slide Show view

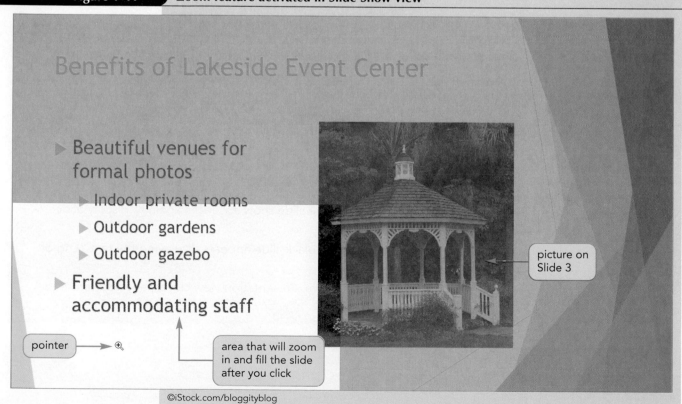

©iStock.com/bloggityblog

9. Move the pointer to the picture, and then click the **picture**. The view zooms so that the part of the slide inside the bright rectangle fills the screen, and the pointer changes to 🖐.

10. Press and hold the mouse button to change the pointer to ✊, and then drag to the right to pull another part of the zoomed in slide into view.

11. Press the **Esc** key to zoom back out to see the whole slide.

Presenter view provides additional tools for running a slide show. In addition to seeing the current slide, you can also see the next slide, speaker notes, and a timer showing you how long the slide show has been running. Refer to the Session 1.2 Visual Overview for more information about Presenter view. Because of the additional tools available in Presenter view, you should consider using it if your computer is connected to a second monitor or projector.

If your computer is connected to a projector or second monitor, and you start a slide show in Slide Show view, Presenter view starts on the computer and Slide Show view appears on the second monitor or projection screen. If, for some reason, you don't want to use Presenter view in that circumstance, you can switch to Slide Show view. If you want to practice using Presenter view when your computer is not connected to a second monitor or projector, you can switch to Presenter view from Slide Show view.

Caitlin wants you to switch to Presenter view and familiarize yourself with the tools available there.

To use Presenter view to review the slide show:

1. Move the pointer to display the buttons in the lower-left corner of the screen, click the **More slide show options** button ⊙ to open a menu of commands, and then click **Show Presenter View**. The screen changes to show the presentation in Presenter view.

2. Below the current slide, click the **See all slides** button 🎞. The screen changes to show thumbnails of all the slides in the presentation, similar to Slide Sorter view.

3. Click the **Slide 4** thumbnail. Presenter view reappears, displaying Slide 4 ("Packages") as the current slide.

4. Click anywhere on Slide 4. The slide show advances to display Slide 5 ("Amenities").

5. At the bottom of the screen, click the **Advance to the next slide** button ⊙. Slide 6 ("Reserve Lakeside Event Center for Your Function!") appears.

6. Press the **spacebar** twice. The slide show advances again to display Slides 7 and then 8.

7. Press the **spacebar** again. A black slide appears displaying the text "End of slide show, click to exit."

8. Press the **spacebar** once more. Presentation view closes, and you return to Normal view.

PROSKILLS

Decision Making: Displaying a Blank Slide During a Presentation

Sometimes during a presentation, the audience has questions about the material and you want to pause the slide show to respond. Or you might want to refocus the audience's attention on you instead of on the visuals on the screen. In these cases, you can display a blank slide (either black or white). When you do this, the audience, with nothing else to look at, will shift all of their attention to you. Some presenters plan to use blank slides and insert them at specific points during their slide shows. Planning to use a blank slide can help you keep your presentation focused and remind you that the purpose of the PowerPoint slides is to provide visual aids to enhance your presentation; the slides themselves are not the presentation.

If you did not create blank slides in your presentation file, but during your presentation you feel you need to display a blank slide, you can easily do this in Slide Show or Presenter view by pressing the B key to display a blank black slide or the W key to display a blank white slide. You can also click the More button—⬤ in Slide Show view, ⬤ in Presenter view—or right-click the screen, point to Screen on the menu, and then click Black Screen or White Screen. To remove the black or white slide and redisplay the slide that had been on the screen before you displayed the blank slide, press any key on the keyboard or click anywhere on the screen. In Presenter view, you can also use the Black or unblack slide show button ▨ to toggle a blank slide on or off.

An alternative to redisplaying the slide that had been displayed prior to the blank slide is to click the Advance to the next slide button ⬤. This can be more effective than redisplaying the slide that was onscreen before the blank slide because, after you have grabbed the audience's attention and prepared them to move on, you won't lose their focus by displaying a slide they have already seen.

Using Reading View

Reading view displays the slides so that they almost fill the screen, similar to Slide Show view; however, in Reading view, a status bar appears, identifying the number of the current slide and providing buttons to advance the slide show. You can also resize the window in Reading view to allow you to work in another window on the desktop.

To use Reading view to review the presentation:

▶ 1. Display **Slide 2** ("About Us"), and then on the status bar, click the **Reading View** button ▨. The presentation changes to Reading view with Slide 2 displayed. See Figure 1-42.

Figure 1-42 **Slide 2 in Reading view**

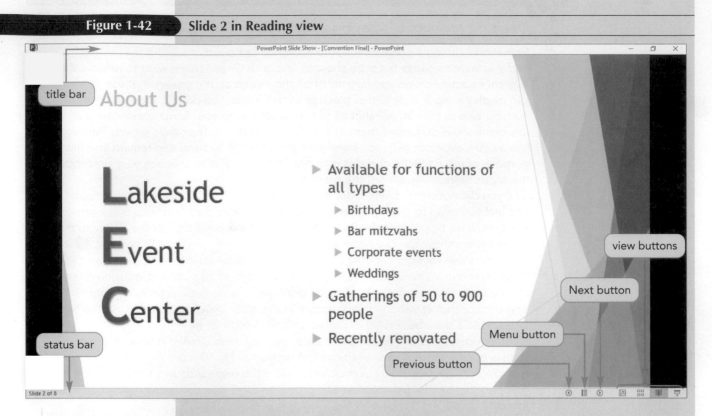

2. On the status bar, click the **Menu** button. A menu appears with commands for working in Reading view, some of which are also available in Slide Show and Presenter views.

3. Click **Full Screen**. The presentation switches to Slide Show view displaying the current slide, Slide 2.

4. Press the **Esc** key. Slide Show view closes, and you return to Reading view.

5. On the status bar, click the **Next** button. The next slide, Slide 3 ("Benefits of Lakeside Event Center"), appears on the screen.

6. On the status bar, click the **Normal** button to return to Normal view with Slide 1 displayed in the Slide pane.

Printing a Presentation

Before you deliver your presentation, you might want to print it. PowerPoint provides several printing options. For example, you can print the slides in color, grayscale (white and shades of gray), or pure black and white, and you can print one, some, or all of the slides in several formats.

You use the Print screen in Backstage view to set print options such as specifying a printer and color options. First, you will add your name to the title slide.

To add your name to the title slide and choose a printer and color options:

1. Display **Slide 1**, click after Keough-Barton in the subtitle, press the **Enter** key, and then type your full name.

2. Click the **File** tab to display Backstage view, and then click **Print** in the navigation bar. Backstage view changes to display the Print screen. The Print screen contains options for printing your presentation, and a preview of the first slide as it will print with the current options. See Figure 1-43.

Figure 1-43   **Print screen in Backstage view**

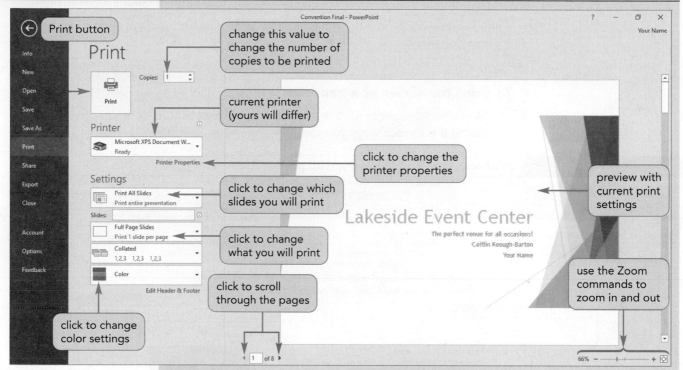

Trouble? If your screen does not match Figure 1-43, click the first button below Settings, and then click Print All Slides, and then click the second button below Settings and then click Full Page Slides.

3. If you are connected to a network or to more than one printer, make sure the printer listed in the Printer box is the one you want to use; if it is not, click the **Printer** button, and then click the correct printer in the list.

4. Click the **Printer Properties** link to open the Properties dialog box for your printer. Usually, the default options are correct, but you can change any printer settings, such as print quality or the paper source, in this dialog box.

5. Click the **Cancel** button to close the Properties dialog box. Now you can choose whether to print the presentation in color, black and white, or grayscale. If you plan to print in black and white or grayscale, you should change this setting so you can see what your slides will look like without color and to make sure they are legible.

6. Click the **Color** button, and then click **Grayscale**. The preview changes to grayscale.

7. At the bottom of the preview pane, click the **Next Page** button ▶ twice to display Slide 3 ("Benefits of Lakeside Event Center"). The slides are legible in grayscale.

8. If you will be printing in color, click the **Grayscale** button, and then click **Color**.

In the Settings section on the Print screen, you can click the Full Page Slides button to choose from among several choices for printing the presentation, as described below:

- **Full Page Slides**—Prints each slide full size on a separate piece of paper.
- **Notes Pages**—Prints each slide as a notes page.
- **Outline**—Prints the text of the presentation as an outline.
- **Handouts**—Prints the presentation with one or more slides on each piece of paper. When printing four, six, or nine slides, you can choose whether to order the slides from left to right in rows (horizontally) or from top to bottom in columns (vertically).

Caitlin wants you to print the slides as a one-page handout, with all eight slides on a single sheet of paper.

To print the slides as a handout:

▶ **1.** In the Settings section, click the **Full Page Slides** button. A menu opens listing the various ways you can print the slides. See Figure 1-44.

Figure 1-44	Print screen in Backstage view with print options menu open

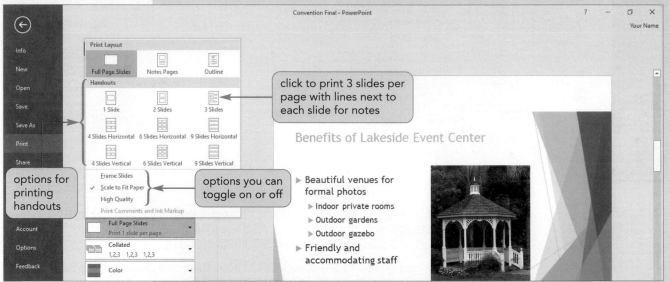

©iStock.com/bloggityblog

▶ **2.** In the Handouts section, click **9 Slides Horizontal**. The preview changes to show all eight slides in the preview pane, arranged in order horizontally, that is, in three rows from left to right. The current date appears in the top-right corner, and a page number appears in the bottom-right corner.

▶ **3.** At the top of the Print section, click the **Print** button. Backstage view closes and the handout prints.

Next, Caitlin wants you to print the title slide as a full-page slide so that she can use it as a cover page for her handouts.

To print the title slide as a full-page slide:

▶ **1.** Click the **File** tab, and then click **Print** in the navigation bar. The Print screen appears in Backstage view. The preview still shows all eight slides on one page. "9 Slides Horizontal" appears on the second button in the Settings section because that was the last printing option you chose.

 ▶ **2.** In the Settings section, click **9 Slides Horizontal**, and then click **Full Page Slides**. Slide 1 (the title slide) appears as the preview. Below the preview of Slide 1, it indicates that you are viewing Slide 1 of eight slides to print.

 ▶ **3.** In the Settings section, click the **Print All Slides** button. Note on the menu that opens that you can print all the slides, selected slides, the current slide, or a custom range. You want to print just the title slide as a full-page slide.

 ▶ **4.** Click **Print Current Slide**. Slide 1 appears in the preview pane, and at the bottom, it now indicates that you will print only one slide.

 ▶ **5.** Click the **Print** button. Backstage view closes and Slide 1 prints.

Recall that you created speaker notes on Slides 3 and 7. Caitlin would like you to print these slides as notes pages.

To print the nonsequential slides containing speaker notes:

 ▶ **1.** Open the Print screen in Backstage view again, and then click the **Full Page Slides** button. The menu opens.

 ▶ **2.** In the Print Layout section of the menu, click **Notes Pages**. The menu closes, and the preview displays Slide 1 as a Notes Page.

 ▶ **3.** In the Settings section, click in the **Slides** box, type **3,7** and then click a blank area of the Print screen.

 ▶ **4.** Scroll through the preview to confirm that Slides 3 ("Benefits of Lakeside Event Center") and 7 ("For More Information") will print, and then click the **Print** button. Backstage view closes, and Slides 3 and 7 print as notes pages.

Finally, Caitlin would like you to print the outline of the presentation. Recall that Slide 8 is designed to be a visual Caitlin can leave displayed at the end of the presentation, so you don't need to include it in the outline.

To print Slides 1 through 7 as an outline:

 ▶ **1.** Open the Print tab in Backstage view, click the **Notes Pages** button, and then in the Print Layout section, click **Outline**. The text on Slides 3 and 7 appears as an outline in the preview pane.

 ▶ **2.** Click in the **Slides** box, type **1-7** and then click a blank area of the Print screen. See Figure 1-45.

3. At the top of the Print section, click the **Print** button. Backstage view closes, and the text of Slides 1–7 prints on two sheets of paper.

Exiting PowerPoint

When you are finished working with your presentation, you can exit PowerPoint. If there is only one presentation open, you click the Close button ☒ in the upper-right corner of the program window to exit the program. If more than one presentation is open, clicking this button will only close the current presentation; to exit PowerPoint, you need to click the Close button in each of the open presentation's windows.

To exit PowerPoint:

1. In the upper-right corner of the program window, click the **Close** button ☒. A dialog box opens, asking if you want to save your changes. This is because you did not save the file after you added your name to the title slide.

2. In the dialog box, click the **Save** button. The dialog box closes, the changes are saved, and PowerPoint exits.

Trouble? If any other PowerPoint presentations are still open, click the Close button ☒ on each open presentation's program window until no more presentations are open to exit PowerPoint.

In this session, you opened an existing presentation and saved it with a new name, changed the theme, added and cropped photos and adjusted the photo compression, and resized and moved objects. You have also added speaker notes and checked the spelling. Finally, you printed the presentation in several forms and exited PowerPoint. Your work will help Caitlin give an effective presentation to potential clients of Lakeside Event Center.

Session 1.2 Quick Check

REVIEW

1. Explain what a theme is and what changes with each variant.
2. Describe what happens when you crop photos.
3. Describe sizing handles.
4. Describe smart guides.
5. Why is it important to maintain the aspect ratio of photos?
6. What is the difference between Slide Show view and Presenter view?
7. List the four formats for printing a presentation.

PRACTICE

Review Assignments

Data Files needed for the Review Assignments: DJ.jpg, Musicians.jpg, Photog.jpg, Vendor2.pptx

In addition to booking new clients, Caitlin Keough-Barton, the event manager at Lakeside Event Center, maintains a preferred vendors list for providing additional services of entertainment, music, photography, and so on that clients might want. If clients who book the hall use a preferred vendor, they receive a discount on the price of the vendor's services. Caitlin wants to create a presentation that she can use when she meets with new vendors to describe their responsibilities to both the function hall and to the clients. She asks you to begin creating the presentation.

1. Start PowerPoint and create a new, blank presentation. On the title slide, type **Information for Vendors** as the title, and then type your name as the subtitle. Save the presentation as **Vendor Info** to the drive and folder where you are storing your files.

2. Edit the slide title by adding **Lakeside Event Center** before the word "Vendors."

3. Add a new Slide 2 with the Title and Content layout, type **Types of Vendors We Partner With** as the slide title, and then in the content placeholder type the following:
   - **Photographers**
   - **Videographers**
   - **Florists**
   - **Music**
     - **DJs**
     - **Bands**

4. Create a new Slide 3 with the Title and Content layout. Add **Requirements for Vendors** as the slide title, and then type the following as a numbered list on the slide:
   1) **Supply advertisement for brochure**
   2) **Pay annual fee by January 15**
   3) **Submit availability schedule for clients**
   4) **Contact Caitlin Keough-Barton**

5. Create a new Slide 4 using the Two Content layout. Add **Questions?** as the slide title.

6. Use the Cut and Paste commands to move the last bulleted item on Slide 3 ("Contact Caitlin Keough-Barton") to the left content placeholder on Slide 4.

7. On Slide 4, remove the bullet symbol from the text you pasted, and then add the following as the next two items in the unnumbered list:
   Email: c.keoughbarton@example.com
   Cell: 602-555-8723

8. Click after "Keough-Barton" in the first item in the list, and then create a new line below it without creating a new item in the list and so that there is no extra space above the new line. On the new line, type **Events Manager**.

9. Remove the hyperlink formatting from the email address.

10. Create a new Slide 5 using the Title and Content layout. Delete the title text placeholder. In the content placeholder, type **Thank You!** as a single item in an unnumbered list. Increase the size of the text "Thank You!" to 96 points, and then change the color of this text to Blue, Accent 1.

11. On Slide 3 ("Requirements for Vendors"), change the numbered list to a SmartArt graphic. Use the Vertical Circle List layout, which is a List type of diagram.

12. Save your changes, and then close the presentation.

13. Open the file **Vendor2**, located in the PowerPoint1 > Review folder included with your Data Files, add your name as the subtitle on the title slide, and then save it as **LEC Vendor Information** to the drive and folder where you are storing your files.

14. Change the theme to Basis and choose the third variant. On Slide 2, change the size of the text in the bulleted list so that the size of the text of the first-level items is 28 points and the size of the text of the second-level items is 24 points.

15. Change the layout of Slide 4 ("Photographers") to Title and Content, and then duplicate Slide 4. In the title of Slide 5 (the duplicate slide), replace the slide title with **Music Vendors**.

16. On Slide 4, insert the photo **Photog**, located in the PowerPoint1 > Review folder. Resize the photo so it is five inches high, maintaining the aspect ratio, and reposition it so its top and right edges are aligned with the top and right edges of the slide title text box.

17. On Slide 5, change the layout to Two Content, and then in the content placeholder on the left, insert the photo **DJ**. Crop the photo from the right about one-half inch and from the top about one-quarter inch. Resize the cropped photo so it is 2.4 inches high, maintaining the aspect ratio, and then reposition the photo so its left edge is aligned with the left edge of the slide title text box and its middle is aligned with the middle of the content placeholder on the right.

18. On Slide 5, in the content placeholder on the right, insert the photo **Musicians**. Resize it so that it is 2.5 inches tall. Position it so that its right edge is aligned with the right edge of the slide title text box and its middle is aligned with the middle of the photo on the left.

19. Move Slide 5 ("Music Vendors") so it becomes Slide 7.

20. On Slide 9 ("Questions?"), crop the photo to the Oval shape. Increase the size of the text in the unnumbered list to 20 points, and then resize the text box to make it wide enough so that the line containing the email address fits on one line. Remove the hyperlink formatting from the email address.

21. Compress all the photos in the slides to 96 ppi and delete cropped areas of pictures.

22. On Slide 4 ("Photographers"), add **Must be available for the entire event. Should be able to take both formal portraits and candids.** in the Notes pane. On Slide 7 ("Music Vendors"), add **Must be available for the entire time during the event. Should be versatile and be able to play music for all audiences.** as a note on this slide.

23. Delete Slide 3 ("Vendor Requirements") and the last slide (the blank slide).

24. Check the spelling in the presentation. Correct the two spelling errors on Slide 7, ignore all instances of Caitlin's last name, and ignore the flagged instance of "candids" in the Notes pane on Slide 3 ("Photographers"). If you made any additional spelling errors, correct them as well. Save the changes to the presentation.

25. Review the slide show in Slide Show, Presenter, and Reading views.

26. View the slides in grayscale, and then print the following in color or in grayscale depending on your printer: the title slide as a full-page-sized slide; Slides 1–9 as a handout on a single piece of paper with the slides in order horizontally; Slides 3 and 6 as notes pages; and Slides 1–8 as an outline. Save and close the presentation when you are finished.

Case Problem 1

APPLY

Data Files needed for this Case Problem: After.jpg, Before.jpg, Clients.pptx, Team.jpg, Windows.jpg

Cleaning Essentials Suzanne Yang owns Cleaning Essentials, a home cleaning company in New Rochelle, New York. She markets her company at home shows in Westchester County and in New York City. She asks you to help her create PowerPoint slides that she will use at the home shows. Complete the following steps:

1. Open the presentation named **Clients**, located in the PowerPoint1 > Case1 folder included with your Data Files, and then save it as **New Clients** to the drive and folder where you are storing your files.

2. Insert a new Slide 1 that has the Title Slide layout. Add **Cleaning Essentials** as the presentation title on the title slide. In the subtitle text placeholder, type your name.

3. Create a new Slide 2 with the Title and Content layout. Add **What Is Cleaning Essentials?** as the slide title, and **An affordable door-to-door cleaning service designed to make a homeowner's life easier.** as the only item in the content placeholder. Change this to an unnumbered list.

4. Apply the Savon theme, and then apply its second variant. (If the Savon theme is not listed in the Themes gallery, choose any other theme and variant that uses a white or solid color background, places the slide titles at the top of the slides, uses bullet symbols for first-level bulleted items, and positions the content in the bulleted lists so it aligns to the top of the content text box, not the middle.)

5. On Slide 2 ("What Is Cleaning Essentials?"), increase the size of the text in the text box below the slide titles to 28 points.

6. On Slide 3 ("What Services Do We Provide?"), Slide 7 ("Extra Services Offered"), and Slide 9 ("Book Us Now!"), increase the size of the text in the bulleted list so it is 28 points.

7. On Slide 4 ("Why Choose Cleaning Essentials?"), increase the size of the text in the bulleted list so that the first-level items are 24 points.

8. On Slide 2 ("What Is Cleaning Essentials?"), insert the photo **Team**, located in the PowerPoint1 > Case1 folder. Resize the photo, maintaining the aspect ratio, so that it is 3.6 inches wide, and then use the smart guides to position it so that its center is aligned with the center of the text box above it and its bottom is aligned with the bottom border of the text box.

9. On Slide 3 ("What Services Do We Provide?"), add the speaker note **All clients are welcome to request extra services needed to completely clean their homes.**

10. On Slide 6 ("Picture Proof"), change the layout to the Comparison layout, which includes two content placeholders and a small text placeholder above each content placeholder. In the small text placeholder on the left, add **Before**, and then in the small text placeholder on the right, add **After**. Change the font size in both text boxes to 24 points.

11. In the left content placeholder, insert the photo **Before**, and in the right content placeholder, insert the photo **After**.

12. On Slide 5 ("Polish wood floors"), cut the slide title, and then paste it in on Slide 3 ("What Services Do We Provide?") as the fifth bulleted item. If a blank line is added below the pasted text, delete it.

13. On Slide 7 ("Extra Services Offered"), add **Laundry** as a third bulleted item in the list, and then add **Use in-home machines** and **Send out and pick up dry cleaning** as subitems under the "Laundry" first-level item. Change the layout to Two Content.

14. On Slide 7, in the content placeholder, insert the photo **Windows**, located in the PowerPoint1 > Case1 folder. Resize the photo so it is 5 inches high, maintaining the aspect ratio, and then reposition it so that the top of the photo and the top of the title text box are aligned and the right edge of the photo is aligned with the right edge of the title text box.

15. Compress all the photos in the presentation to 96 ppi.

16. On Slide 8 ("Cleaning Visit Options"), add **Once a week** as the second item in the list, and then add **Most popular option** and **Visit is the same day each week** as subitems below "Once a week."

17. On Slide 8, convert the bulleted list to a SmartArt diagram using the Vertical Bullet List layout, which is a List type of diagram. In the Text pane, click before "Still produces a clean and uncluttered home," and then press the Tab key to make it the second subitem under "Once a month."

18. Delete Slide 5 (a blank slide). Move Slide 4 ("Why Choose Cleaning Essentials?") so it becomes Slide 6, and then move Slide 5 ("Extra Services Offered") so it becomes Slide 4.

19. Check the spelling in the presentation and correct all misspelled words.

20. Save the changes to the presentation, view the slide show in Presenter view, and then print the title slide as a full-page slide, print Slides 2–8 as a handout using the 9 Slides Horizontal arrangement, and print Slide 3 as a notes page.

TROUBLESHOOT

Case Problem 2

Data Files needed for this Case Problem: Keyboard.jpg, Music.pptx, Richard.jpg

Dillaire Music Richard Dillaire has owned Dillaire Music in Easton, Pennsylvania, since 1991. He sells, rents, and repairs musical instruments, and he teaches students how to play instruments. He wants to expand his business and attract new students, so he asks you to help him create a presentation. He created slides containing text and a few photos that he wants to include, and he wants you to finish the presentation by inserting additional photos and formatting the presentation. Complete the following steps:

1. Open the file named **Music**, located in the PowerPoint1 > Case2 folder included with your Data Files, and then save it as **Music School** to the drive and folder where you are storing your files. Add your name as the subtitle on Slide 1.

⚙ **Troubleshoot** 2. Review the presentation to identify the two slides that contain information that is repeated on another slide in the presentation, and delete those slides.

3. Display Slide 1 (the title slide), and then apply the Headlines theme to the presentation. Change the variant to the second variant.

⚙ **Troubleshoot** 4. Evaluate the problem that the theme change caused on Slide 1 and fix it.

⚙ **Troubleshoot** 5. Consider how changing the theme affected the readability of the lists on the slides and the size of the photos in the file. Make the appropriate changes to the slides. (*Hint:* On the slides that have pictures of a child playing an instrument on them, the first-level items should not be larger than 24 points.)

6. On Slide 8 ("Contact Info"), in the first item in the bulleted list, move "Easton, PA 18042" to a new line below the street address without creating a new bulleted item.

7. Move Slide 7 ("Lessons") so it becomes Slide 4.

8. On Slide 7 ("How to register online"), change the bulleted list to a numbered list. Add as a new item 2 **Click the green Apply button**.

9. Change the layout of Slide 8 ("Contact Info") to Two Content, and then insert the photo **Richard**, located in the PowerPoint1 > Case2 folder, in the content placeholder. Crop off about one-half inch from the top of the photo, and then increase the size of the picture, maintaining the aspect ratio, so that it is 3 inches wide. Reposition the photo so it is vertically centered below the slide title and bottom aligned with the bottom of the slide title text box.

10. On Slide 1 (the title slide), insert the photo **Keyboard** located in the PowerPoint1 > Case2 folder. Resize the photo so it is 5.25 inches square, and then position it so it is aligned with the right and bottom edges of the slide.

11. Compress all the photos in the presentation to 96 ppi and delete cropped portions of photos.

12. Check the spelling in the presentation, and then save the changes.

13. View the slide show in Presenter view, zooming in on the pictures in the presentation.

14. Print the title slide as a full-page slide in grayscale, and then print the entire presentation as an outline.

CREATE

Case Problem 3

Data Files needed for this Case Problem: Beach.jpg, House1.jpg, House2.jpg, House3.jpg, House4.jpg, House5.jpg, Realty.pptx

Shoreside Realty Karen Bridges owns Shoreside Realty, a real estate company in Scarborough, Maine, that specializes in selling and renting homes in local beach communities. As part of her marketing, she attends local events, such as the farmers' market, weekly summer concerts, and chamber of commerce events, and shows photos of houses near beaches for sale or rent. She created a presentation with slides containing the addresses and brief descriptions of newly listed properties. She asks you to finish the presentation. The completed presentation is shown in Figure 1-46. Refer to Figure 1-46 as you complete the following steps:

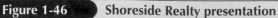

Figure 1-46   **Shoreside Realty presentation**

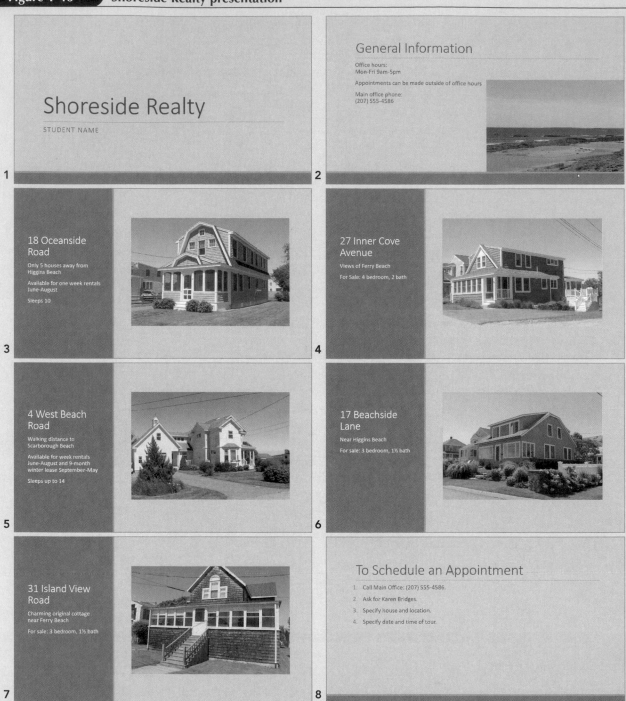

Courtesy of Helen M. Pinard

1. Open the file named **Realty**, located in the PowerPoint1 > Case3 folder included with your Data Files, and then save it as **Shoreside Realty** to the drive and folder where you are storing your files.

2. Add a new slide with the Title Slide layout, and move it so it is Slide 1. Type **Shoreside Realty** as the title and your name as the subtitle.

3. Move Slide 8 ("General Information") so it becomes Slide 2, and then delete Slide 3 ("Newest Homes on the Market").

4. Change the theme to Retrospect, and the variant of the Retrospect theme to the seventh variant. (Note that in this theme, bulleted lists do not have any bullet symbols before each item.)

5. On Slide 2 ("General Information"), in the first item in the list, move the phone number so it appears on the next line, without any additional line space above the phone number. Then move the text "Mon–Fri 9am–5pm" so it appears on the next line, without any additional line space above it.

6. On Slide 2, move the "Main office phone" list item and the phone number so these appear as the last list items on the slide.

7. On Slide 2, insert the photo **Beach**, located in the PowerPoint1 > Case3 folder. Crop two inches from the top of the photo, and then resize the photo so that it is 3.4 inches high.

8. On Slide 2, position the photo so that its right edge is flush with the right edge of the slide and so that its bottom edge is slightly on top of the lighter blue line at the bottom of the slide.

9. Change the layout of Slides 3 through 7 to Content with Caption. On all five slides, move the unnumbered list from the content placeholder on the right to the text placeholders on the left, as shown in Figure 1-46, and then change the font size of the text in the unnumbered lists you moved to 16 points. Then insert the photos named **House1** through **House5** provided in the PowerPoint1 > Case3 folder on Slides 3 through 7, using Figure 1-46 as a guide.

10. Compress all the photos in the presentation to 96 ppi.

11. On Slide 8 ("To Schedule an Appointment"), change the list to a numbered list, and then add **Specify house and location.** as a new item 3.

12. Save the changes to the presentation, and then view the presentation in Reading view.

Case Problem 4

CHALLENGE

Data Files needed for this Case Problem: Ballet.jpg, Dancing.mp4, HipHop.jpg, Jazz.jpg, Jump.jpg, Leap.jpg, Modern.jpg, and Tap.jpg

Greater Dayton Dance Academy Paul LaCroix owns Greater Dayton Dance Academy, a dance studio that teaches students ages two through adult. He has an open house every September to attract new students. He asks you to help him create a presentation that includes photos and video that he can show at the open house. Complete the following steps:

Explore 1. Create a new presentation using the Striped black border presentation template from Office.com. (*Hint:* Use "striped black border" as the search term. If you get no results, type **white** as the search term, and then choose a template with a simple theme.)

2. Replace the title text on the title slide with **Greater Dayton Dance Academy**, and replace the subtitle text with your name. Save the presentation as **New Students** to the drive and folder where you are storing your files.

3. Delete all the slides except the title slide.

4. Add a new Slide 2 with the Two Content layout. Add **About Us** as the title, and then type the following as a bulleted list in the left content placeholder:

   • **Recreational classes meet once a week**

   • **Competitive classes meet 3 to 5 times a week**

   • **Private lessons available**

   • **Annual winter and spring productions**

5. On Slide 2, in the right content placeholder, insert the photo **Leap**, located in the PowerPoint1 > Case4 folder included with your Data Files. Resize it, maintaining the aspect ratio, so it is 3.8 inches high, and then reposition it so that the top edge of the photo is aligned with the top edge of the text box and the left edge of the photo is aligned with the right edge of the text box.

6. Add a new Slide 3 with the Title and Content layout. Add **Styles Offered** as the title, and then type the following as a bulleted list in the content placeholder:
   - **Ballet**
   - **Modern**
   - **Jazz**
   - **Tap**
   - **Hip Hop**

7. On Slide 3, convert the bulleted list to a SmartArt diagram with the Bending Picture Semi-Transparent Text layout, which is a Picture type of diagram.

✪ **Explore** 8. Change the colors of the diagram to Colorful Range – Accent Colors 3 to 4 by using the Change Colors button in the SmartArt Styles group on the SmartArt Tools Design tab.

✪ **Explore** 9. Insert the following pictures, located in the PowerPoint1 > Case4 folder, in the appropriate picture placeholders in the SmartArt diagram: **Ballet**, **Modern**, **Jazz**, **Tap**, and **HipHop**.

10. Add a new Slide 4 with the Two Content layout. Add **Call Today!** as the title. In the content placeholder on the left, type the following as an unnumbered list (no bullets) without extra space between the lines:
    Greater Dayton Dance Academy
    1158 North St.
    Dayton, OH 45417

11. On Slide 4, add the phone number **(937) 555-1254** and the website address **www.daytondance.example.com** as new items in the unnumbered list. Press the spacebar after typing the website address to format it as a link.

12. On Slide 4, change the size of the text in the unnumbered list to 22 point. (*Hint:* Click in the Font Size box, type **22**, and then press the **Enter** key.)

13. On Slide 4, add the photo **Jump**, located in the PowerPoint1 > Case4 folder, to the content placeholder on the right. Resize it so it is 3.6 inches high, maintaining the aspect ratio, and then position it so the top edge aligns with the top edge of the text box on the left and there is approximately one inch of space between the right side of the photo and the right edge of the slide.

14. Compress all the photos in the presentation to 96 ppi, and then save the changes.

15. Add a new Slide 5 with the Two Content layout. Add **Classic Ballet Technique Emphasized** as the title. In the content placeholder on the right, add **Because ballet is the foundation of all dance, all students are required to take ballet technique classes.** Remove the bullet from this item.

16. Move this slide so it becomes Slide 4.

✪ **Explore** 17. On Slide 4 ("Classic Ballet Technique Emphasized"), insert the video **Dancing**, located in the PowerPoint1 > Case4 folder, in the content placeholder.

✪ **Explore** 18. Open the Info tab in Backstage view. Use the Compress Media command to compress the videos to the lowest quality possible. Use the Back button at the top of the navigation bar in Backstage view to return to Normal view.

19. Save the changes to the presentation, and then run the slide show in Slide Show view. When Slide 4 ("Classic Ballet Technique Emphasized") appears, point to the video to make a Play button appear, and then click the Play button to play the 20-second video. (*Hint:* Point to the video as it plays to display the play bar again.)

OBJECTIVES

Session 1
- Explore the Outlook window
- Navigate between Outlook elements
- Set up Outlook for email
- Create and send email messages
- Create and edit contact information

Session 2
- Read and respond to email messages
- Attach files to email messages
- File, sort, and save messages
- Delete items from Outlook folders

Communicating with Outlook 2016

Sending and Receiving Email Messages

OUTLOOK

Case | *Musical Notes*

Musical Notes is owned by Rivi Stein, a registered piano technician in Arlington, Texas, who travels from location to location to tune, service, and repair pianos. Her clients range from organizations with many pianos that require regular tunings, such as at schools, concert halls, and community centers, to individuals with a single piano at home that require periodic tuning. Rivi also gives voice, piano, violin, guitar, and ukulele lessons to teenagers and adults. She teaches both individual and group lessons. To communicate with her clients, Rivi relies on **Microsoft Outlook 2016**, or **Outlook**, an information management and communication program.

You will use Outlook to help Rivi with a variety of tasks. In this module, you'll explore the Outlook window and its elements. You'll use email to send messages for Rivi. You'll set up contact information for vendors and students. You'll receive, read, and respond to email messages. Finally, you'll organize messages by filing, sorting, and archiving them.

STARTING DATA FILES

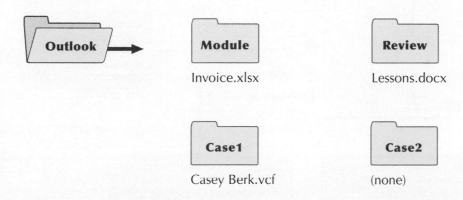

Outlook →

Module
Invoice.xlsx

Review
Lessons.docx

Case1
Casey Berk.vcf

Case2
(none)

Session 1 Visual Overview:

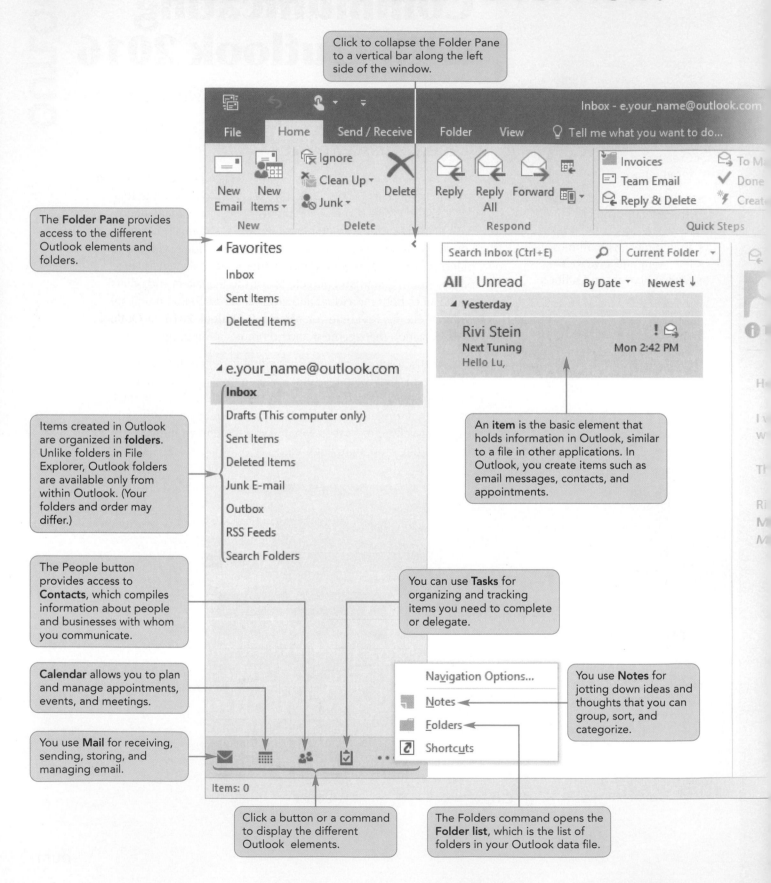

Click to collapse the Folder Pane to a vertical bar along the left side of the window.

The **Folder Pane** provides access to the different Outlook elements and folders.

Items created in Outlook are organized in **folders**. Unlike folders in File Explorer, Outlook folders are available only from within Outlook. (Your folders and order may differ.)

The People button provides access to **Contacts**, which compiles information about people and businesses with whom you communicate.

Calendar allows you to plan and manage appointments, events, and meetings.

You use **Mail** for receiving, sending, storing, and managing email.

An **item** is the basic element that holds information in Outlook, similar to a file in other applications. In Outlook, you create items such as email messages, contacts, and appointments.

You can use **Tasks** for organizing and tracking items you need to complete or delegate.

You use **Notes** for jotting down ideas and thoughts that you can group, sort, and categorize.

Click a button or a command to display the different Outlook elements.

The Folders command opens the **Folder list**, which is the list of folders in your Outlook data file.

Outlook Window

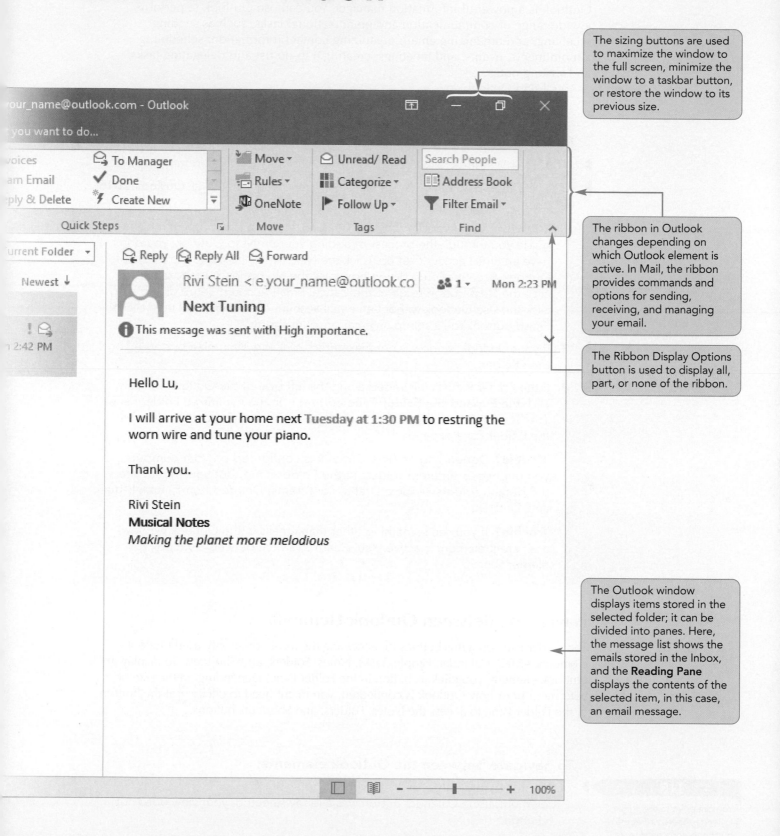

The sizing buttons are used to maximize the window to the full screen, minimize the window to a taskbar button, or restore the window to its previous size.

The ribbon in Outlook changes depending on which Outlook element is active. In Mail, the ribbon provides commands and options for sending, receiving, and managing your email.

The Ribbon Display Options button is used to display all, part, or none of the ribbon.

The Outlook window displays items stored in the selected folder; it can be divided into panes. Here, the message list shows the emails stored in the Inbox, and the **Reading Pane** displays the contents of the selected item, in this case, an email message.

Exploring Outlook

Outlook is a powerful information manager. You can use Outlook to perform a wide range of communication and organizational tasks, such as sending, receiving, and organizing email; organizing contact information; scheduling appointments, events, and meetings; creating a to-do list and delegating tasks; and writing notes.

You'll start Outlook now.

To start Outlook:

▶ 1. On the Windows taskbar, click the **Start** button ⊞. The Start menu opens.

▶ 2. Click **All apps** on the Start menu, scroll the list, and then click **Outlook 2016**. Outlook starts.

   Trouble? If the Welcome to Microsoft Outlook 2016 dialog box opens to guide you through the process of adding your email to Outlook, you don't have an email account set up. Click the Next button to go to the Microsoft Outlook Account Setup dialog box, click the No option button, and then click the Next button to go to the Cancel Email Account Setup dialog box, click the Use Outlook without an email account check box, and then click the Finish button. You'll set up an email account shortly.

▶ 3. If your Outlook window is not maximized, click the **Maximize** button ❐ on the title bar.

▶ 4. If the Folder Pane is minimized along the left side of the Outlook window, click the **Expand the Folder Pane** button ❯ in the minimized Folder Pane. The Session 1 Visual Overview shows the maximized Outlook window with the Folder Pane expanded.

   Trouble? Depending on how Outlook is configured on your computer, you might see different folders in the Folder Pane, but you should see the default folders—Inbox, Drafts, Sent Items, Deleted Items, Junk E-mail, and Outbox.

   Trouble? If you see something other than emails in the Outlook window, a different element is active. You'll learn to switch between Outlook elements next.

Navigating Between Outlook Elements

The Folder Pane contains buttons for accessing the most commonly used Outlook elements—Mail, Calendar, People, Tasks, Notes, Folders, and Shortcuts. To display an Outlook element, you click its button in the Folder Pane. Depending on the size of your monitor or how Outlook is configured, you might need to click ⋯ at the bottom of the Folder Pane to access the Notes, Folders, and Shortcuts buttons.

To navigate between the Outlook elements:

TIP

You can point to the Calendar, Tasks, or People button to get a peek of its contents.

▶ 1. In the Folder Pane, click the **Calendar** button ▦ to display the Calendar element. If the Calendar button was already selected, your view does not change.

2. On the Home tab, in the Arrange group, click the **Work Week** button, if necessary. The planner appears and the Date Navigator with calendars for the current month and next month appears at the top of the Folder Pane. See Figure 1.

Figure 1   **Calendar**

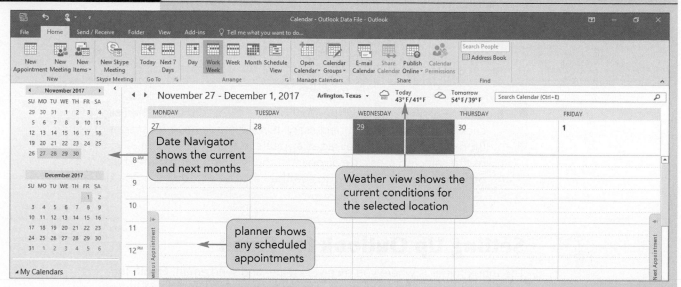

3. In the Folder Pane, click the **People** button 👥 to display the Contacts element.

4. On the Home tab, in the Current View group, click the **People** button, if necessary. The contacts list appears in the center pane; if you don't have any contacts entered, you see only the buttons that you use to display the contacts that start with the selected number or letter. If you have contacts in your list, information about the selected contact appears in the Reading Pane. See Figure 2.

Figure 2   **Contacts**

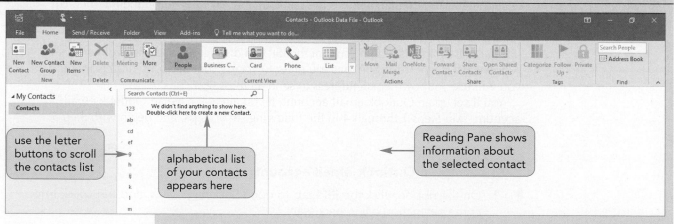

5. In the Folder Pane, click the **Tasks** button 📋 to display the Tasks element. The to-do list appears in the center pane. If you have tasks on your to-do list, information about the selected task appears in the Reading Pane. See Figure 3.

Figure 3 Tasks

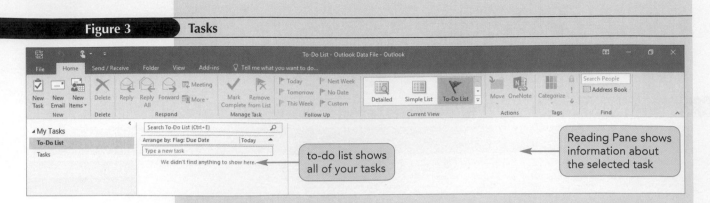

to-do list shows all of your tasks

Reading Pane shows information about the selected task

6. In the Folder Pane, click the **Mail** button ✉, and then in the Folder Pane, click the **Inbox** folder, if necessary. If you already have messages in your Inbox, a list of email messages appears in the middle pane, and the content of the selected message appears in the Reading Pane. Refer back to the Session 1 Visual Overview to see the Inbox selected in the Folder Pane.

Setting Up Outlook for Email

The Inbox folder is where you receive, create, and send email. **Email**, the electronic transfer of messages between computers, is a simple and inexpensive way to communicate with people near or far. The messages you send are delivered immediately and stored until recipients can read those messages at their convenience. Rivi uses email to correspond with her suppliers and students because it is fast, convenient, and inexpensive. It is also portable, as she can access her email from her cell phone, laptop, and tablet.

Before you can send and receive email messages with Outlook, you must have access to an email server or Internet service provider (ISP), an email address, and a password. An **email address** is a username and a domain name separated by @. A **username** (or account name) is a unique name that identifies you to your mail server. A username can include uppercase and lowercase letters, numbers, and periods; although symbols are allowed, you should avoid them because some ISPs may not accept them. The **domain name** is the name of your ISP's server on the Internet. For example, in the email address "name@example.com," "name" is the username and "example.com" is the domain name. Although many people might use the same ISP, each username is unique, so that the ISP can distinguish one user from another. A **password** is a private code that you enter to access your account. (In this module, you will use your own email address to send all messages.)

You'll set up an Outlook email account. If you already have an Outlook email account, skip Steps 1 through 4 in the following set of steps, and begin with Step 5.

To set up an Outlook email account:

1. On the ribbon, click the **File** tab to open Backstage view, and then click **Info** in the navigation bar, if necessary.

2. On the Account Information screen, click the **Add Account** button. The Add Account dialog box opens. See Figure 4.

Figure 4   **Add Account dialog box**

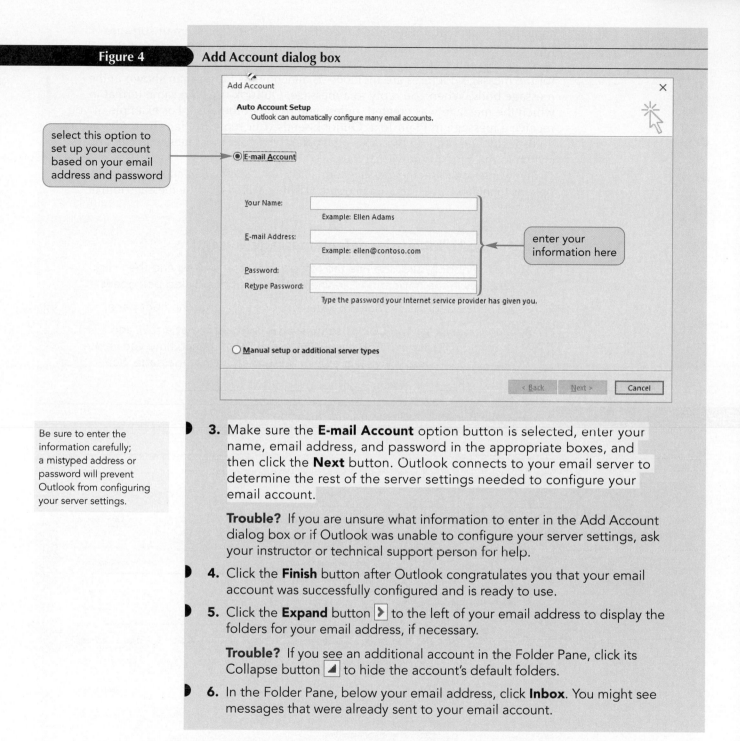

select this option to set up your account based on your email address and password

enter your information here

Be sure to enter the information carefully; a mistyped address or password will prevent Outlook from configuring your server settings.

3. Make sure the **E-mail Account** option button is selected, enter your name, email address, and password in the appropriate boxes, and then click the **Next** button. Outlook connects to your email server to determine the rest of the server settings needed to configure your email account.

Trouble? If you are unsure what information to enter in the Add Account dialog box or if Outlook was unable to configure your server settings, ask your instructor or technical support person for help.

4. Click the **Finish** button after Outlook congratulates you that your email account was successfully configured and is ready to use.

5. Click the **Expand** button ⏵ to the left of your email address to display the folders for your email address, if necessary.

Trouble? If you see an additional account in the Folder Pane, click its Collapse button ⏴ to hide the account's default folders.

6. In the Folder Pane, below your email address, click **Inbox**. You might see messages that were already sent to your email account.

Choosing a Message Format

Outlook can send and receive messages in three formats: HTML, Rich Text, and Plain Text. HTML provides the most formatting features and options (text formatting, numbered and bulleted lists, alignment, horizontal lines, backgrounds, and HTML styles), and shows pictures in the message body. Rich Text provides some formatting options (text formatting, bullets, and alignment), and allows linked objects. Rich Text Format can be read only by Outlook and Microsoft Exchange Client versions 4 and 5. Outlook converts Rich Text messages to HTML, which retains the formatting, for any other recipients. With both HTML and Rich Text, some recipients will not be able to see the formatting if their email software is not set up to handle formatted messages. All email applications support Plain Text messages, which include no formatting; the recipient specifies which font is used for the message. Pictures are included as attachments rather than shown in the message body. When you reply to a message, Outlook uses the same format in which the message was created, unless you specify otherwise. For example, if you receive a message in Plain Text, Outlook sends your reply in Plain Text. Although you specify one of these formats as the default for your messages, you can always switch formats for an individual message.

Rivi wants you to set the message format to HTML so you can apply formatting options to the messages. You'll make sure HTML is selected as the message format.

To choose HTML as the default message format:

1. On the ribbon, click the **File** tab to open Backstage view, and then click **Options** in the navigation bar. The Outlook Options dialog box opens.

2. In the left pane, click **Mail**. The Mail options appear in the right pane.

3. If necessary, click the **Compose messages in this format** arrow, and then click **HTML**. Outlook will use the HTML format each time you create a message, unless you select a different format for that message. See Figure 5.

Figure 5   **Mail options in the Outlook Options dialog box**

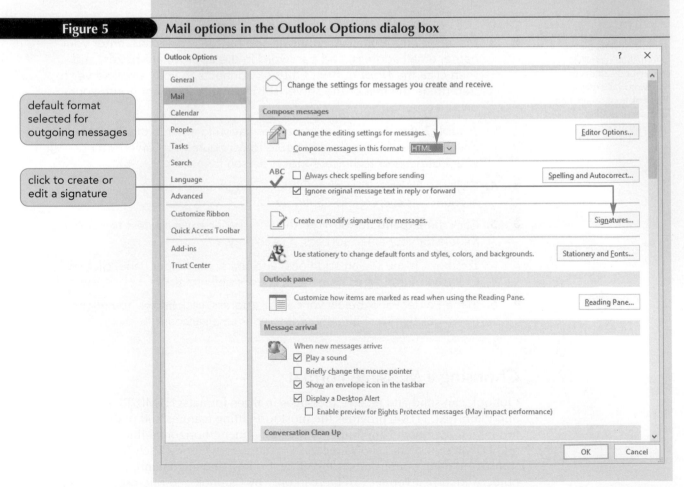

Adding a Signature

A **signature** is text that is automatically added to every email message you send. A signature can contain any text you want. For example, you might create a signature with your name, job title, company name, and phone number. Rivi might create a signature containing a sentence that describes the services she offers. You can create more than one signature for an email account, and you can create different signatures for each email account you have. Although you can attach a signature to a message in any format, the HTML and Rich Text formats enable you to apply font and paragraph formatting.

You can customize your messages with a signature. Because you selected the HTML message format, you can add formatting to the signature. You'll create a formatted signature.

Note: The figures in this module show the name Rivi Stein, and the email address e.your.name@outlook.com.

To create a formatted signature:

1. In the Outlook Options dialog box, click the **Signatures** button. The Signatures and Stationery dialog box opens with the E-mail Signature tab displayed.

2. Click the **New** button. The New Signature dialog box opens.

3. In the Type a name for this signature box, type **Musical Notes**, and then click the **OK** button. The signature name is selected in the Select signature to edit box.

4. Click in the **Edit signature** box, type your name, press the **Enter** key to move the insertion point to the next line, and then type **Musical Notes**, press the **Enter** key to move the insertion point to the next line, and then type **Making the planet more melodious**.

5. Select the text **Musical Notes**, click the **Font** arrow, click **Calibri Light (Headings)**, and then click the **Bold** button B.

6. Select the text **Making the planet more melodious**, and then click the **Italic** button *I*. The selected text is reformatted.

7. Click the **E-mail account** arrow, and then click your email address, if necessary.

8. Click the **New messages** arrow, and then click **Musical Notes** (the name of the signature you just set up). Leave the Replies/forwards box set to (none). The Musical Notes signature will be added to new messages you create, but not to messages you respond to. See Figure 6.

Figure 6   **Signatures and Stationary dialog box**

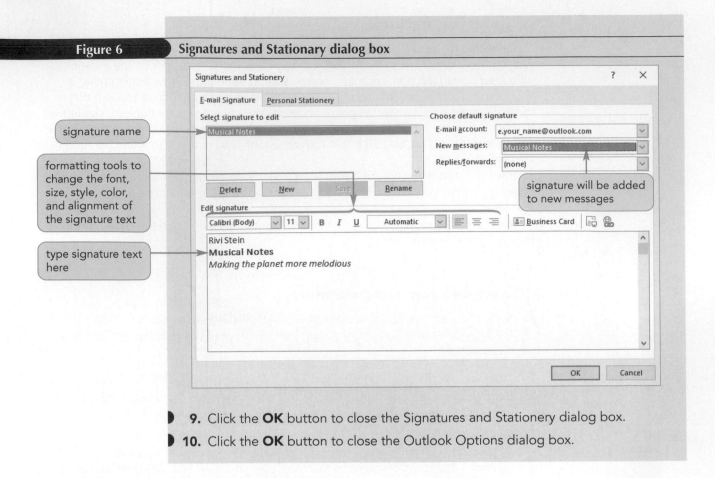

signature name

formatting tools to change the font, size, style, color, and alignment of the signature text

type signature text here

signature will be added to new messages

9. Click the **OK** button to close the Signatures and Stationery dialog box.

10. Click the **OK** button to close the Outlook Options dialog box.

Using Stationery and Themes

Stationery and themes are a way to quickly distinguish your HTML messages with a preset design. **Stationery** is an HTML file that includes complementary background colors, images, or patterns. A **theme** includes complementary backgrounds as well as other design elements such as fonts, bullets, colors, and effects. Stationery and themes increase the size of the outgoing message. Stationery uses HTML message format, so recipients whose email programs don't read HTML email will see the message but not the stationery.

To add stationery or a theme to a message, click the New Items button in the New group on the Home tab, point to E-mail Message Using, click More Stationery to open the Theme or Stationery dialog box, and then select the one you want to use. To add the same stationery or theme to all your outgoing messages, you can click Mail in the left pane of the Outlook Options dialog box, click the Stationery and Fonts button in the right pane, and then click the Theme button on the Personal Stationery tab of the Signatures and Stationery dialog box. Select the theme in the Theme or Stationery dialog box, and then click the OK button in each dialog box. You also can create your own stationery.

TIP

Previously applied stationeries and themes appear above the More Stationery command.

Creating and Sending Email Messages

An email message includes Date, To, From, Cc, and Subject lines followed by the message. Outlook fills in the Date line with the date on which you send the message and the From line with your name or email address; these lines are not visible in the window in which you create your email message. You complete the other lines. The To line lists the email addresses of all recipients. The Cc line lists the email addresses of anyone who will receive a courtesy copy of the message. An optional Bcc line lists the email addresses of anyone who will receive a blind courtesy copy of the message; Bcc recipients are not visible to each other or to the To and Cc recipients. The Subject line provides a quick overview of the message topic, similar to a headline. The main part of the email is the message body.

REFERENCE

Creating and Sending an Email Message

- On the Home tab, in the New group, click the New Email button.
- In the To box, type the recipient email address; for each additional recipient type a semicolon and then the email address.
- In the Cc box and the Bcc box, type recipient email addresses, as needed.
- In the Subject box, type the topic.
- In the message body, type the message text and then format it as needed.
- Click the Send button.

You'll create an email message to Lu Chan, who owns a piano that Rivi tunes periodically. You usually send messages to other people; in this module, you will send messages to yourself so you can practice sending and receiving messages.

To create an email message to Lu Chan:

1. On the Home tab, in the New group, click the **New Email** button. An Untitled - Message window opens with the insertion point in the To box. Your signature appears in the message body; you'll type your message above the signature.

2. In the To box, type your email address. To send an email message to multiple recipients, you type a comma or semicolon between addresses.

3. Click in the **Subject** box, type **Next Tuning** and then press the **Tab** key. The insertion point moves to the message body just above the signature. As soon as you move the insertion point out of the Subject box, the title bar shows the subject of the message.

4. Type **Hello Lu,** as the salutation, press the **Enter** key twice, **I will arrive at your home next Tuesday at 1:30 PM to restring the worn wire and tune your piano.** (including the period), press the **Enter** key twice, and then type **Thank you.** (including the period).

You don't need to type your name because you included it as part of the signature. Before sending this message, you will add some text formatting. You have access to the standard text formatting features available in all the Office programs. For example, you can apply bold, underline, and italics; change the font, font size, and font color; align and indent text; create a bulleted or numbered list; and even apply paragraph styles. People whose email programs cannot read formatted email will still be able to read your messages in plain text.

To format text in the message body:

1. Select **Tuesday at 1:30 PM** in the message body. You'll make this text bold and orange.

2. On the Message tab, in the Basic Text group, click the **Bold** button **B**. The text changes to boldface.

3. In the Basic Text group, click the **Font Color button arrow** [A ·], and then click the **Orange, Accent 2** color (the sixth color in the first row of the Theme Colors section in the Font Color gallery). The text changes to orange.

4. Press the ↓ key to deselect the text and move the insertion point to the next line.

Rivi's message conveys the day and time for Lu's appointment, and the formatting helps these details stand out from the rest of the message.

Setting the Importance and Sensitivity Levels

You can add icons that appear in the message pane of a recipient's Inbox to provide clues to the recipient about the importance and sensitivity of the message. You can specify an importance level of High or Low or leave the message set at the default Normal importance level. High importance tells the recipient that the message needs prompt attention, whereas a Low importance tells the recipient that the message can wait for a response. Use the importance level appropriately. If you send all your messages with a High importance, recipients will learn to disregard the status.

You'll change the message importance level to High.

To change the message importance level to High:

1. On the Message tab, in the Tags group, click the **High Importance** button. The button remains selected to indicate the importance level you selected for the message. See Figure 7.

Figure 7   Completed email message

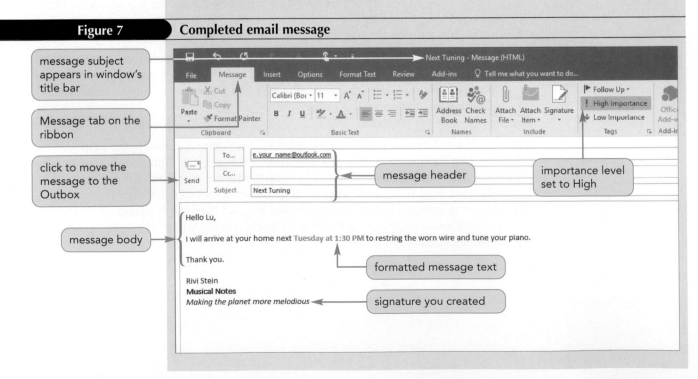

You can also change the normal sensitivity level for the message to Personal, Private, or Confidential. This is another way to help recipients determine the content of a message before reading it. To set the sensitivity level, click the Dialog Box Launcher in the Tags group on the Message tab to open the Properties dialog box, click the Sensitivity button in the Settings section, select the sensitivity level for the message, and then click the Close button. You'll leave the sensitivity set to Normal for this message.

INSIGHT

Creating Effective Messages

Keep the following guidelines in mind to create effective, professional messages:

- **Focus on one topic per email.** A distinct conversation thread makes it simpler to find messages related to a topic.
- **Include a short, descriptive subject line.** A clear subject quickly tells recipients the main point of a message (and reminds you when they reply). Also, some people decide whether to read a message based on its subject line.
- **Write a concise, complete message.** An effective message conveys information quickly and fully, so the entire contents appear in the Reading Pane. People receive many messages each day and tend to save poorly written or rambling messages to deal with later.
- **Format to enhance rather than decorate.** Recipients may see a message that looks very different from the one you sent with variations in colors or fonts. Add emphasis with bold, italic, and other basic formatting as needed. Use white or a light-colored background with black or a dark-colored text. Choose common fonts and sizes, such as 10- or 12-point Arial and Times New Roman.
- **Use an attachment for complex content.** If you want to send a more elaborately formatted message, an attached Word document or PDF file might be a better option.

Sending Email

When your computer is connected to the Internet, the messages you write are sent immediately when you click the Send button in the Message window. After you send the message to your email server, a copy of the message is stored in the Sent Items folder, which provides a record of all the messages you sent. The time your email takes to arrive at its destination varies, depending on the size of the message, the speed of your Internet connection, and the number of other users on the Internet.

If you are working **offline** (not connected to the Internet), the messages you write move to the Outbox folder when you click the Send button in the Message window. The outgoing messages remain in the Outbox until you choose to send them. You can set a schedule for Outlook to automatically send and receive messages at regular intervals that you specify (such as every 15 minutes or every few hours). You must then click the Send/Receive All Folders button in the Send & Receive group on the Send/Receive tab to check for and deliver new messages.

To send the completed message:

1. Click the **Send** button in the message header area. The message is sent to your email server, and you return to the Inbox. You could receive the email message you sent at any point; if a notification box appears or a sound plays informing you of incoming mail, ignore it for now. You'll work with the received message in the next session.

2. Click **Sent Items** in the Folder Pane. The message in the Sent Items folder appears in the message list and Reading Pane. See Figure 8.

Figure 8   **Sent Items folder with the sent message**

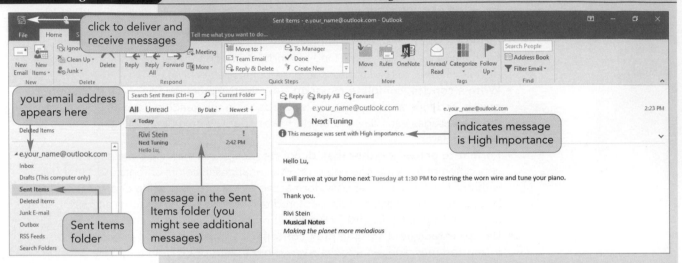

Trouble? If the message wasn't sent, you are probably working offline. On the Send/Receive tab, in the Preferences group, click the Work Online button. In the Send & Receive group, click the Send/Receive All Folders button to send all the messages in the Outbox to your email server. The Outlook Send/Receive Progress dialog box remains open until all the messages in the Outbox are sent. You can tell when the messages are sent because the Outbox will be empty.

Trouble? If Outlook requests a password, you need to enter your password before you can send and receive messages. Type your password, and then click the OK button.

The message is sent to Lu to confirm her piano tuning.

Written Communication: Following Netiquette Guidelines

Email, like other types of communication, is governed by its own customs of behavior, called **netiquette** (short for Internet etiquette), which helps prevent miscommunication. As you write and send email messages, keep in mind the following guidelines:

- **Think before you send.** Your words can have a lasting impact. Be sure they convey the thoughts you intend and want attributed to you. Your name and email address are attached to every message you send, and your message can be forwarded easily to others.
- **Be concise.** The recipient should be able to read and understand your message quickly.
- **Use standard capitalization.** Excessive use of uppercase is considered shouting, and exclusive use of lowercase is incorrect; both are difficult to read.
- **Check spelling and grammar.** Create and maintain a professional image by using standard spelling and grammar. What you say is just as important as how you say it.
- **Avoid sarcasm.** Without vocal intonations and body language, a recipient may read your words with emotions or feelings you didn't intend. You can use punctuation marks and other characters to create **emoticons**—also called **smileys**—such as :-), to convey the intent of your words. (Tilt your head to the left to look at the emoticon sideways to see the "face"—in this case, a smile.) To learn additional emoticons, search the web for emoticon or smiley dictionaries.
- **Don't send confidential information.** Email is not private; once you send a message, you lose control over where it may go and who might read it. Also, employers and schools usually can legally access their employees' and students' email messages, even after a message is deleted from an Inbox.

For more email netiquette guidelines, search the web for email etiquette or netiquette websites.

Organizing Contact Information

The Contacts element is an address book where you store information about the people and businesses with whom you communicate. Each person or organization is called a **contact**. You can store business-related information about each contact, including job title, phone and fax numbers, postal and web addresses, and email addresses, as well as more personal information, such as birthdays, anniversaries, and spouse and children's names.

Each piece of information you enter about a contact is called a **field**. For example, a complete contact name, such as Mr. Charlie P. Zang, Sr., consists of a Title field, First field, Middle field, Last field, and Suffix field. The field's name, or label, identifies what information is stored in that field. You can use fields to sort, group, or look up contacts by any part of the name.

Creating Contacts

You can create contacts for anyone you communicate with. To create a contact or access information for existing contacts, you click the People button in the Folder Pane. Rivi asks you to create new contacts for several vendors.

To create the first vendor contact:

1. In the Folder Pane, click the **People** button 👥. The Folder Pane changes to display the Contacts element, and the ribbon changes to provide the commands and options for working with contacts.

2. On the Home tab, in the New group, click the **New Contact** button. A Contact window opens in which you can enter the contact information.

The Contact window provides options for entering and working with information about a contact. Contact information is divided into a General page and a Details page, available by clicking the corresponding buttons in the Show group on the Contact tab. The General page includes the most pertinent information about a contact, including the contact's name, job title and company, phone numbers, and addresses. The Details page includes fields for less frequently needed items, such as the names of the contact's department, manager, assistant, and spouse/partner, as well as the contact's birthday, anniversary, and nickname.

REFERENCE

Creating a Contact

- In the Folder Pane, click the People button.
- On the Home tab, in the New group, click the New Contact button to open the Contact window.
- Enter the contact's name, job title, company, email and webpage addresses, phone numbers, and mailing addresses.
- On the Contact tab, in the Show group, click the Details button, and then enter other business or personal data as needed.
- In the Actions group, click the Save & New button to create another contact or click the Save & Close button if you have no other contacts to create.
- If the Duplicate Contact Detected dialog box opens, select whether to add the contact anyway or merge with existing contact, and then click the OK button.

Rivi wants you to create a contact for Mr. Charlie P. Zang, Sr. at the Piano Parts store she frequents for parts she needs to repair pianos. You'll start by entering his name and company.

To enter the first contact's name and company:

1. In the Full Name box, type **Mr. Charlie P. Zang, Sr.** and then press the **Enter** key. The insertion point moves to the Company box, and the contact name appears in the File as box as "Zang, Charlie P." By default, Outlook organizes contacts by their last names.

The contact's name also appears at the top of the business card on the right and in the title bar of the Contact window. The business card is a graphic that displays all of the contact information as you enter it in a standard business card format.

2. Click the **Full Name** button. The Check Full Name dialog box opens. Although you entered the contact name in one box, Outlook stores each part of the name as a separate field. See Figure 9.

| Figure 9 | Check Full Name dialog box |

3. Click the **Cancel** button to close the dialog box without making any changes.

4. In the Contact window, click in the **Company** box, and then type **Piano Parts**.

5. Press the **Tab** key to move to the Job title box, and then type **Sales Manager**.

Next, you'll enter Charlie's contact information. You can enter up to three email addresses for each contact in the Internet section of the Contact window. In most cases, each email address would be unique. For this module, you'll use your email address for all of the contacts.

In the Phone numbers section, you can display only four phone fields at a time, but you can use any of the four available phone number boxes to continue to enter and store up to 19 phone numbers per contact. No matter how you enter the numbers—with or without spaces, hyphens, or parentheses—Outlook formats them consistently in the format (817) 555-1234. Next to each phone number box is an arrow you can click to change the name of the phone field to help you identify the phone number. For example, you could choose Home Fax as the third type of phone number instead of Business Fax if the contact had only a home fax number.

In the Addresses section of the window, you can enter a business, home, and other address for each contact. As soon as you start typing the first address, a checkmark appears in the "This is the mailing address" check box. Outlook sets the first address you enter for a contact as the mailing address. However, you can specify any one of the addresses you enter as the mailing address.

To enter Charlie's email address, phone numbers, and mailing address:

1. Click in the **E-mail** box, type your email address, and then press the **Tab** key to move the insertion point to the Display as box. The email address you typed is underlined in the E-mail box and appears in both the Display as box and on the business card in the Contact window.

The Display as box shows how the email address will appear in the To box of email messages as well as how it will be displayed within Outlook. Rivi prefers to display with the contact's name. You'll edit the address in the Display as box to include the contact's name.

2. Select the text in the Display as box, and then type **Charlie Zang**.

TIP

The Auto-Complete List displays suggested names and email addresses as you begin to type. To select a suggested name or address, click it.

3. In the Phone numbers section, click in the **Business** box, type **817 555 8365** and then press the **Tab** key. Outlook formats the phone number with parentheses around the area code and a hyphen between the main parts of the number, even though you didn't type these punctuation symbols, and underlines it. Note also that the phone number appears on the business card with the label "Work" because you entered the phone number in the Business box.

4. Click the **Home button arrow** to display a menu of phone number field labels, click **Assistant** to change the field label, type **817-555-3491** for the phone number of Charlie's assistant, and then press the **Tab** key. The phone number is formatted to match the business phone number and appears on the business card with the label "Assistant."

   Rivi wants you to store the name of Charlie's assistant, so you need to switch to the Details page.

5. On the Contact tab, in the Show group, click the **Details** button. The Details page appears in the Contact window.

6. Click in the **Assistant's name** box, and then type **Anna Gomez** as the name of Charlie's assistant.

7. In the Show group, click the **General** button to return to the General page.

8. In the Addresses section, click in the **Business** box, type **1800 E Park Row**, press the **Enter** key to move the insertion point to the next line within the box, and then type **Arlington, TX 76010**. You could verify that Outlook recorded the address in the correct fields by clicking the Business button, but you don't need to do so for a simple address.

9. Press the **Tab** key. The address appears on the business card. See Figure 10.

Figure 10	Completed Contact window for Charlie P. Zang, Sr.

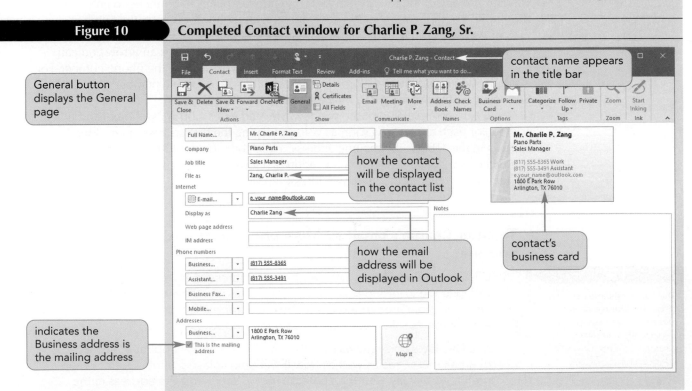

You have completed the contact information for Charlie. Rivi asks you to create additional contacts. You can close Charlie's Contact window and open a new Contact window in the same step.

To create additional contacts:

▶ 1. On the Contact tab, in the Actions group, click the **Save & New** button to save Charlie's contact information and open a new Contact window.

▶ 2. Enter the following information: full name **Cy Murphy**, company **Sheet Music Galore**, job title **Owner**, your email address, display as **Cy Murphy**, business phone **817-555-1224**, business fax **817-555-4331**, and business address **2177 Roundrock Rd., Arlington, TX 76014**.

   Trouble? If your email address or the "Display as" entry is shown with the text "Charlie Zang" at the beginning, edit the entry to delete this text. This text might appear because of the "Display as" entry you completed for the contact Charlie Zang earlier. Because you are using your email address for multiple contacts, this could happen each time you add a new contact. Continue to edit the email and "Display as" entries so they match those provided in the steps. When doing so, you might not be able to press the Tab key after typing in the Email box; you might need to click in the "Display as" box to be able to enter your email address correctly.

▶ 3. In the Actions group, click the **Save & New** button. Outlook detects that another contact already has the same email address as Charlie Zang and opens the Duplicate Contact Detected dialog box. You can add the contact as a new contact or update the information of the selected contact.

▶ 4. Click the **Add new contact** option button, and then click the **Add** button. The new Untitled - Contact window appears.

▶ 5. Enter the following new contact information: full name **Quint Tomas**, company **The Music Rental Place**, your email address, display as **Quint Tomas**, business phone **817-555-6382**, and business address **4207 E. Mayfield Rd., Arlington, TX 76011**.

▶ 6. In the Actions group, click the **Save & New** button, click the **Add new contact** option button in the Duplicate Contact Detected dialog box, and then click the **Add** button to add Quint Tomas as a new contact and open a new Untitled - Contact window.

   For your work in this module, you need to create a contact for Rivi as well.

▶ 7. Enter the following new contact information: full name **Rivi Stein**, company **Musical Notes**, your email address, and display as **Rivi Stein**.

▶ 8. In the Actions group, click the **Save & Close** button, click the **Add new contact** option button in the Duplicate Contact Detected dialog box, and then click the **Add** button to add Rivi Stein as a new contact. Rivi's contact information is saved, and you return to the Contacts folder. The four contacts you added appear in the Contacts list sorted alphabetically by last name. See Figure 11.

Figure 11   **Contacts in People view**

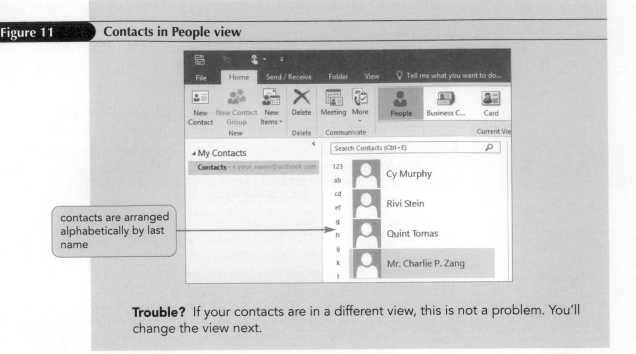

contacts are arranged alphabetically by last name

Trouble? If your contacts are in a different view, this is not a problem. You'll change the view next.

Switching Contact Views

Views specify how information in an Outlook element is organized and which details are visible. Each Outlook element has a set of standard views from which you can choose. There are a variety of ways to look at the information in Contacts, for example. All of the information about a contact is called a **contact card**. People view displays the names in a contacts list and the information for the selected name appears in the Reading Pane. Business Card view displays the names and addresses in a standard business card format. Card view displays names and addresses in blocks. Phone view displays details about your contacts, such as name, company, and telephone numbers, in columns. List view displays additional information in column format but grouped by company name.

Currently the contacts are shown in People view. Rivi wants to see how the contact information appears in different views. You'll change the Contacts view.

To change the view of Contacts:

1. On the Home tab, in the Current View group, click the **Business Card** button. Business Card view displays a business card for each contact. Unless you customize it, the business card includes the contact's name; company; job title; department; phone numbers for work, home, mobile, and assistant; email address; and mailing address.

2. Click the **Card** button. Card view displays more contact information than is shown in Business Card view, such as the business fax number.

3. If you cannot see all of the address text in the contact cards, point to the vertical bar to the right of the contact cards until the pointer changes to ↔, and then drag the vertical bar to the right until the cards to display all of the address text. See Figure 12.

| Figure 12 | Contacts in Card view |

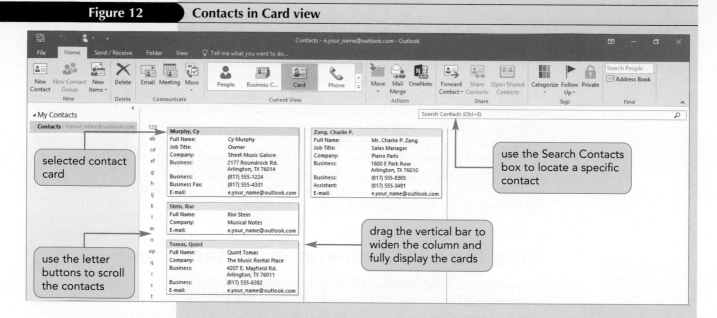

In the People, Business Card, Card, and List views, your contacts appear in alphabetical order by last name, as specified by the information you entered in the File as box in when you created each contact. When you have many contacts, you can find a specific contact quickly by typing the contact's name in the Search Contacts box, which appears below the ribbon, and then click the Search button. This **Instant Search** feature finds all items in the selected folder that match the keywords you enter. You can also click the letter button in the middle pane that corresponds to the first letter of a contact's last name and then scroll as needed to display that contact.

Editing Contacts

Many aspects of a contact's information might change over time, or you might discover that you entered information incorrectly. Rather than deleting the contact and starting over, you can update the existing contact. You can double-click the contact to open its Contact window and then edit the information as needed.

The zip code for The Music Rental Place was entered incorrectly; it is 76014. Rivi asks you to correct the zip code. You'll make this change in Card view.

To edit Quint Tomas's contact card:

1. Click the **t** button along the left side of the Contacts list to select the first contact card that starts with the letter *T*—in this case, Quint Tomas's contact card.

   Trouble? If your contacts list has additional contacts, the first contact beginning with "t" will be selected. Scroll until you can see contact card for Quint Tomas.

2. Double-click Quint Tomas's contact card. The Quint Tomas - Contact window opens.

3. In the Address box, select the final **1** in the zip code, and then type **4**. The zip code is corrected.

4. In the Actions group, click the **Save & Close** button to save and close Quint's contact card.

Sending Contact Information by Email

If you need to send some of your contacts to others, you can forward the contact information. When you forward contact information as a business card, it includes only the data displayed in Business Card view. The file that is created is known as a vCard (short for virtual business card), and is in Internet Format, which is compatible with popular communication and information management programs. If you forward the Outlook contact, it contains all the information in the contact card. The recipient can then drag the contact into his or her Contacts folder to create a new contact card with all the forwarded information. Keep in mind that the recipient must use Outlook to open and read the contact information.

To forward a contact, select the contact, click the Forward Contact button in the Share group on the Home tab, and then click As a Business Card or As an Outlook Contact. A new Message window opens with the contact included as an attachment to the message in the format you specified.

Creating and Modifying a Contact Group

Sometimes you need to repeatedly send one email message—such as a weekly progress report or company updates—to the same group of people. Rather than selecting the names one by one from the Contacts list, you can create a contact group. A **contact group**, also called a distribution list, is a group of people to whom you frequently send the same messages, such as all clients or all vendors. A contact group saves you time and ensures that you don't inadvertently omit someone. You can create multiple contact groups to meet your needs, and individuals can be included in more than one contact group. You send a message to a contact group just as you would to an individual contact.

REFERENCE

Creating a Contact Group

- In the Contacts window, on the Home tab, in the New group, click the New Contact Group button to open the Contact Group window.
- Click in the Name box, and then type a name for the contact group.
- On the Contact Group tab, in the Members group, click the Add Members button, and then click From Outlook Contacts.
- In the Select Members: Contacts dialog box, click the Address Book arrow, and then click Contacts, if necessary.
- Double-click each contact in the list to add to the contact group, and then click the OK button.
- On the Contact Group tab, in the Actions group, click the Save & Close button.

Rivi asks you to create a contact group with the three vendors so she can send messages to all of them using the contact group instead of individual email addresses.

TIP

To open the Contact Group window when working with other Outlook elements, click the New Items button in the New group on the Home tab, point to More Items, and then click Contact Group.

To create the vendors contact group:

1. On the Home tab, in the New group, click the **New Contact Group** button. The Contact Group window opens.

   Trouble? If the New Contact Group button is grayed out, then you cannot create a contact group. This may occur if you are using a live.com or outlook.com email address. Read, but do not perform, this set of steps.

2. In the Name box, type **Vendors** as the name for the contact group.

3. On the Contact Group tab, in the Members group, click the **Add Members** button, and then click **From Outlook Contacts**. The Select Members: Contacts dialog box opens. A separate entry is listed for each email address and fax number for each contact.

4. Click the email address entry for **Charlie P. Zang, Sr.**, if necessary, to select it and then click the **Members** button to enter this contact in the Members box.

   Instead of using the Members button to move a selected entry to the Members box, you can also double-click a name to move the entry to the list in the Members box.

5. Double-click the email address entry for **Cy Murphy**, and then double-click the email address entry for **Quint Tomas**. Both email addresses are added as members of the Vendors contact group, which now includes the three email addresses separated by semicolons. See Figure 13.

Figure 13	Select Members: Contacts dialog box

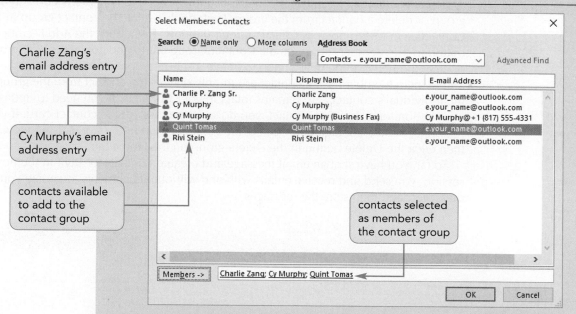

6. Click the **OK** button. The three vendors appear as members of the Vendors contact group in the Contact Group window. Note that the names appear in alphabetical order by first name. See Figure 14.

| Figure 14 | Vendors – Contact Group window |

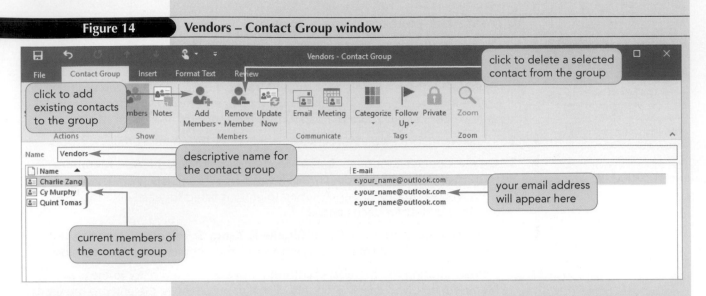

Figure 14   Vendors – Contact Group window

TIP

To send a message to all members of the group, type the contact group name in the To or Cc box of the message.

7. In the Actions group, click the **Save & Close** button. The contact group is filed as "Vendors" in Contacts. The group icon in the upper-right corner of the contact card indicates that this is a contact group rather than an individual contact.

Modifying a Contact Group

At times, you'll need to update a contact. You might need to add a new contact to the group or delete a contact from the group. First, double-click the contact group in the Contacts window to open its Contact Group window. Then, click the Add Members button in the Members group on the Contact Group tab to add contacts to the group, or click the Remove Member button to delete a selected contact from the group. Removing a member from a contact group only deletes the contact from the group; the individual's contact card remains intact in your Contacts. If you need to update the information for an existing contact, you do so in the individual's contact card. If you no longer need a contact group, select the contact group in the Contacts window, and then click the Delete button in the Delete group on the Home tab.

So far, you have sent an email message and created contacts for Rivi. In the next session, you send and receive emails with and without attachments, organize your messages, and then store the messages.

Session 1 Quick Check

REVIEW

1. Describe the purposes of the Inbox and the Outbox.
2. Define email.
3. What are two benefits of using email?
4. What is a signature?
5. List five types of contact information that you can store in Outlook.
6. Explain the purpose of a contact group.

Session 2 Visual Overview:

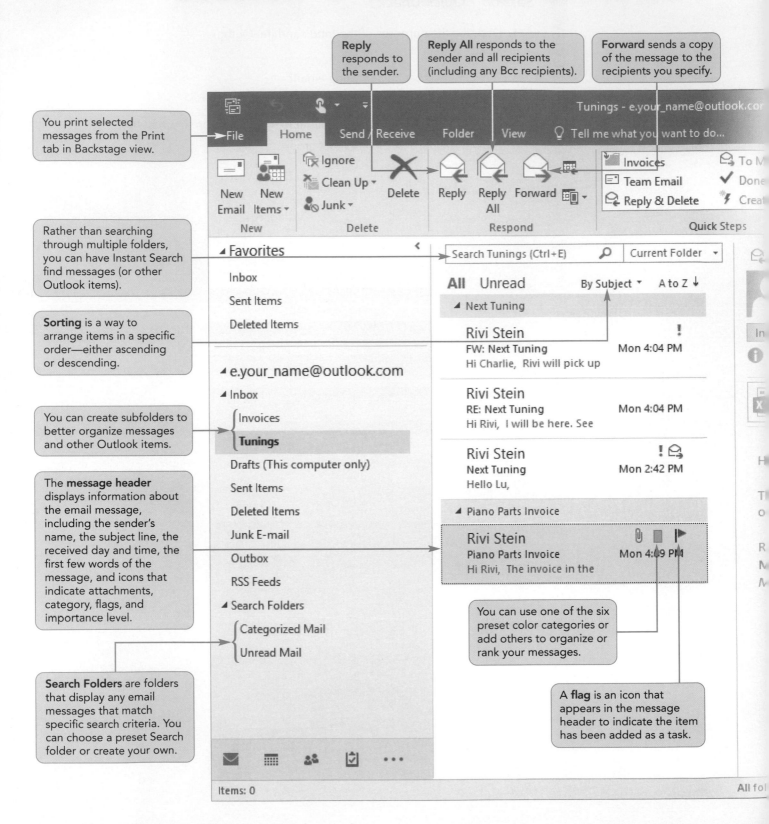

Reply responds to the sender.

Reply All responds to the sender and all recipients (including any Bcc recipients).

Forward sends a copy of the message to the recipients you specify.

You print selected messages from the Print tab in Backstage view.

Rather than searching through multiple folders, you can have Instant Search find messages (or other Outlook items).

Sorting is a way to arrange items in a specific order—either ascending or descending.

You can create subfolders to better organize messages and other Outlook items.

The **message header** displays information about the email message, including the sender's name, the subject line, the received day and time, the first few words of the message, and icons that indicate attachments, category, flags, and importance level.

Search Folders are folders that display any email messages that match specific search criteria. You can choose a preset Search folder or create your own.

You can use one of the six preset color categories or add others to organize or rank your messages.

A **flag** is an icon that appears in the message header to indicate the item has been added as a task.

Email Messages and Attachments

Rather than manually filing messages, you can create **rules** that specify how Outlook should process and organize them.

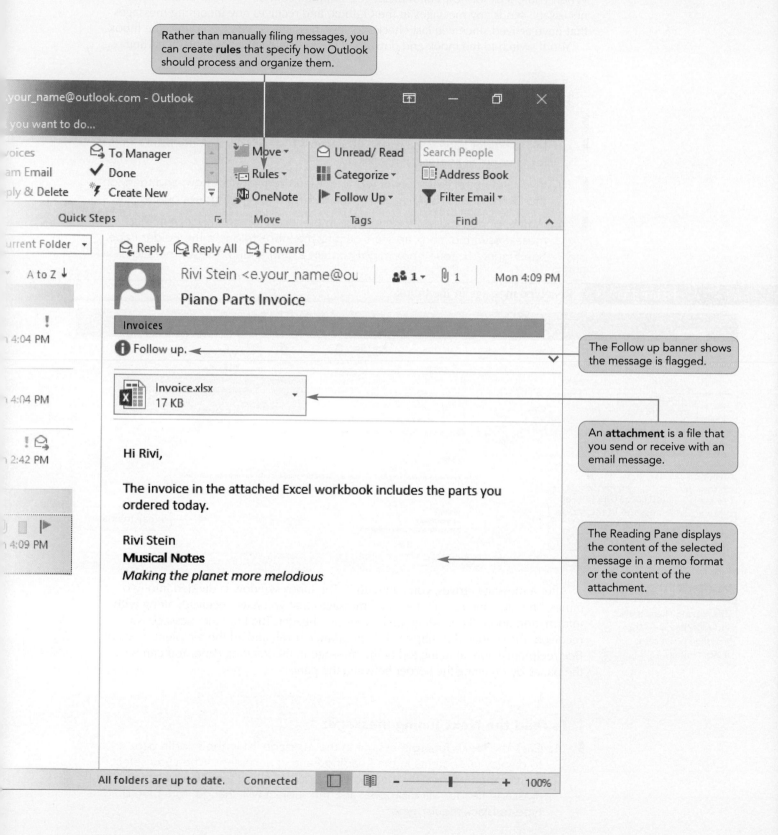

The Follow up banner shows the message is flagged.

An **attachment** is a file that you send or receive with an email message.

The Reading Pane displays the content of the selected message in a memo format or the content of the attachment.

Receiving Email

When you check for new email messages, Outlook connects to your email server, if necessary, sends any messages in the Outbox, and receives any incoming messages that have arrived since you last checked. New messages are delivered into the Inbox. You'll switch to the Inbox and download the message you sent yourself earlier.

To receive the Next Tuning email you sent earlier:

1. If you took a break after the previous session, make sure Outlook is running.

2. In the Folder Pane, click the **Mail** button ✉, and then click the **Inbox** folder for your email address, if necessary.

3. If you are not already connected to the Internet, connect now, and then, on the Quick Access Toolbar, click the **Send/Receive All Folders** button 🖥.

4. Watch for new messages to appear in the Inbox. The number of unread messages in the Inbox appears next to the Inbox folder in the Folder Pane. See Figure 15. Your Inbox might contain a different number of messages.

Figure 15   Received message in the Inbox

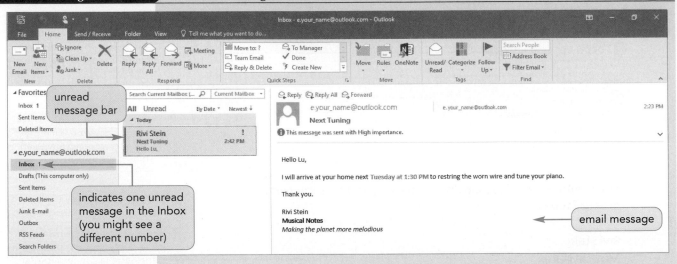

TIP

The message header also includes the date if the message was received on a different day.

After a message arrives, you can read it. The Inbox window is divided into two panes. The left pane lists all the email messages that you have received, along with information about the message in the message header. The time the message was received, the sender, the subject, the importance level, and all the recipients (except Bcc recipients) appear at the top of the message in the Reading Pane. You can resize the panes by dragging the border between the panes.

To read the Next Tuning message:

1. Click the **Next Tuning** message in the message list in the middle pane to display its contents in the Reading Pane, if necessary. When you select a different message, the Unread message bar along the left side of the message header will disappear and the subject will change from blue bold type to black regular type.

> **Trouble?** If the Reading Pane does not appear on the right side of the window or if it appears at the bottom of the window, you need to set it. On the ribbon, click the View tab. In the Layout group, click the Reading Pane button, and then click Right.
>
> ▶ **2.** Read the message in the Reading Pane. Because Outlook can view HTML messages, the formatting added to the message is visible.
>
> **Trouble?** If you don't see the HTML formatting, your email server might not preserve the HTML formatting in email messages; continue with the module.

After you read a message, you have several options—you can leave the message in the Inbox and deal with it later, reply to the message, forward the message to others, print it, file it, or delete it.

Replying To and Forwarding Messages

Many messages you receive require some sort of response—for example, confirmation you received the information, the answer to a question, or sending the message to another person. The quickest way to respond to messages is to use the Reply, Reply to All, and Forward features. Reply responds to the sender, and Reply to All responds to the sender and all recipients (including any Bcc recipients); Outlook inserts the email addresses into the appropriate boxes. Forward sends a copy of the message to one or more recipients you specify; you enter the email addresses in the To or Cc box. With both Reply and Forward, the original message is included for reference, separated from your new message by a line and the original message header information. By default, new text you type is added at the top of the message body, above the original message. This makes it simpler for recipients to read your message because they don't have to scroll through the original message to find the new text.

You'll reply to the Next Tuning message, as if you were Lu, the recipient, responding to Rivi.

To reply to the Next Tuning message:

▶ **1.** On the Home tab, in the Respond group, click the **Reply** button. The Reading Pane changes to show a new message header with the recipient's name and email address in the To box (in this case, your address) and RE: (short for Regarding) inserted at the beginning of the Subject line. The body of the original message appears in the message body pane below a divider line, and the insertion point is above the message, ready for you to type your reply.

▶ **2.** Type **Hi Rivi,** as the salutation, press the **Enter** key twice, type **I will be here. See you then.** as the reply message, press the **Enter** key twice, and then type your name (remember that your signature is not added for replies). Your reply message may appear in blue or another color because you selected HTML format. Notice in the message list in the left pane that [Draft] appears in the message header.

Trouble? Depending on how your computer is configured, you might not see the HTML formatting.

▶ **3.** Click the **Send** button to send the message. In the message list, the icon appears in the upper-right corner of the message header to indicate you replied to this message.

> **TIP**
>
> You can also click the Reply, Reply All, or Forward button above the message header in the Reading Pane to respond to the message.

Next, you'll forward the message for Lu to Charlie Zang at Piano Parts. Because Charlie's contact information is in your Contacts, you can address the message to him quickly.

To forward the Next Tuning message:

1. On the Home tab, in the Respond group, click the **Forward** button. This time, in the Reading Pane, the insertion point is in the empty To box and FW: (for Forward) is inserted at the beginning of the Subject line.

2. In the To box, type **Charlie Zang**.

3. Click at the top of the message body, above the forwarded message, and then type **Hi Charlie,** as the salutation, press the **Enter** key twice, type **Rivi will pick up hammer felt and a replacement piano string before the appointment listed below.** as the message, press the **Enter** key twice, and then type your name.

4. Click the **Send** button to send the message. In the message list, the icon now appears in the upper-right corner of the message header to indicate that this message has been forwarded.

5. On the Quick Access Toolbar, click the **Send/Receive All Folders** button to send the messages to your email server, if necessary. The messages you just sent might appear in your Inbox.

Printing Messages

Although email eliminates the need for paper messages, sometimes you might require printed documentation of a correspondence or you want to read your email when you're away from your computer. You can use the Print screen in Backstage view to preview and print a selected message. From the Print screen, you specify a printer and select settings such as the print style. Memo Style prints the contents of the selected item—in this case, the email message. Table Style prints the view of the selected folder—in this case, the Inbox folder. Other Outlook elements have different print style options. The Print Options button opens the Print dialog box, where you can select the page range, number of copies, and other options for printing.

Rivi asks you to print the Next Tuning message for future reference.

To print the Next Tuning message:

1. On the ribbon, click the **File** tab to open Backstage view, and then click **Print** in the navigation bar.

2. In the Printer section, make sure that the printer you want to use is listed.

3. In the Settings section, click **Memo Style** to select it, if necessary.

4. If you are instructed to print, click the **Print** button to print the message and return to the Inbox folder; otherwise, click the **Back** button to return to the Inbox folder.

Working with Attachments

You'll often want to send information that is stored in a variety of files on your computer. Some of this information could be typed into an email message, but the original file might be long with complex formatting that is inappropriate for email. Also, some kinds of files (such as photos and spreadsheets) cannot be inserted into email messages. Instead, you can send files as attachments.

Attachments can be any type of file, including documents (such as a Word document, Excel workbook, or PowerPoint presentation), images, sounds, and programs. Recipients can then save and open the file; the recipient must have the original program or a program that can read that file type. You'll send an attachment containing the cost for the replacement parts that Rivi ordered.

TIP

Many ISPs don't accept messages with attachments over a certain size. You might not be notified that the recipient didn't receive your message.

To attach the replacement parts invoice file to the email message:

1. On the Home tab, in the New group, click the **New Email** button to open a Message window.

2. Click the **To** button. The Select Names: Contacts dialog box opens. You will select the contacts you want to receive the message.

3. Click **Rivi Stein** in the list of contacts (if necessary), and then click the **To** button at the bottom of the dialog box. Rivi Stein is added to the To list.

4. Click the **OK** button. The To box in the Message window now contains Rivi's name, which you specified as the Display as name when you created her contact card.

5. In the Subject box, type **Piano Parts Invoice**.

6. In the message body, type **Hi Rivi,** as the salutation, press the **Enter** key twice, and then type **The invoice in the attached Excel workbook includes the parts you ordered today.** as the message.

7. On the Message tab, in the Include group, click the **Attach File** button. A menu opens with a list of Recent Items, which are the latest files that were opened and saved on your computer.

   If you see the file you want to include as an attachment, you can click its filename to attach the file to the message. Otherwise, you need to locate it.

8. On the Attach File menu, click **Browse This PC**. The Insert File dialog box opens, which functions like the Open dialog box.

9. Navigate to the **Outlook > Module** folder included with your Data Files.

   Trouble? If you don't have the starting Data Files, you need to get them before you can proceed. Your instructor will either give you the Data Files or ask you to obtain them from a specified location (such as a network drive). If you have any questions about the Data Files, see your instructor or technical support person for assistance.

10. Double-click **Invoice** in the file list. The file is attached to your email message. See Figure 16.

| Figure 16 | Email message with an attached file |

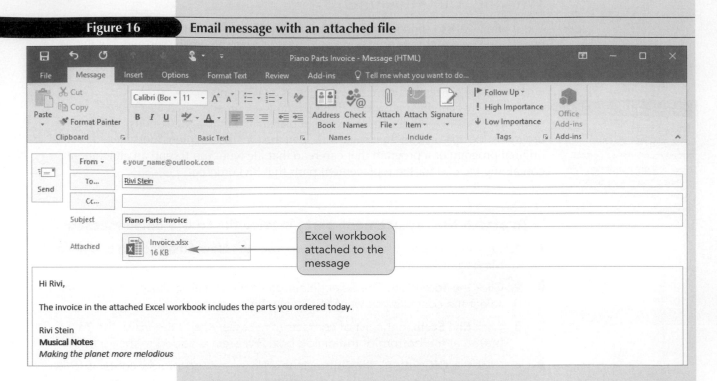

11. Click the **Send** button to send the message.

A message with an attachment might take a bit longer to send and receive because its file size is larger than an email message without an attachment. Messages with attached files display a paper clip icon in the message header. If the appropriate program is installed on your computer, you can open the attached file from the message itself. You can also save the attachment to your computer and then open, edit, and move it like any other file on your computer. You can reply to or forward any message with an attachment, but the attachment is included only in the forwarded message because it's unlikely that you'll want to return the same file to the sender.

After you receive the message with the Invoice workbook attachment, you'll save the attachment and then view it.

To save and view the Piano Parts Invoice message attachment:

1. If the Piano Parts Invoice message (with the attachment) is not already in your Inbox folder, on the Quick Access Toolbar, click the **Send/Receive All Folders** button.

2. Click the **Piano Parts Invoice** message in the message list for the Inbox. The attachment icon appears in the upper-right corner of the message header. The message is displayed in the Reading Pane, and the attached file's icon and name appear below the message header. See Figure 17.

| Figure 17 | Invoice.xlsx attachment displayed in the Reading Pane |

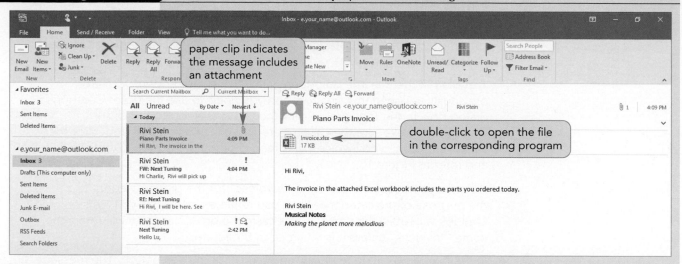

3. In the Reading Pane, double-click **Invoice.xlsx** below the message header. Excel starts and displays the Invoice file in Protected View.

4. On the message bar that appears below the ribbon indicating the file is in Protected View, click the **Enable Editing** button.

5. On the Excel ribbon, click the **File** tab to open Backstage view, and then click **Save As** in the navigation bar. The Save As screen appears.

6. Click the **Browse** button to open the Save As dialog box, navigate to the location where you are storing your files, change the filename to **Piano Parts Invoice** and then click the **Save** button. The attached file is saved. You can work with this file just as you would any other file on disk.

7. On the Excel title bar, click the **Close** button ☒.

Flagging and Color Coding Messages

Some messages you receive require a specific response or action. Although the subject should be informative and the message can provide explicit instructions, often a more obvious reminder would better draw attention to messages that require action. A flag in the message header indicates that the item has been added as a task; text appears in the Reading Pane with a reminder of the start date and deadline. To add a flag, point to the upper-right area of the message header and click the flag icon that appears. You can click the flag icon in the message header to mark the flag as complete. You can also choose from six preset color categories or add others to better organize or rank your messages.

Rivi asks you to flag the message with the invoice and add it to the green color category. Rivi wants to use the green color category for all messages related to invoices. The flag will cause Outlook to display a reminder of the item that needs your attention on the date specified.

To flag and color-code the Piano Parts Invoice message:

1. In the message list, point to the **Piano Parts Invoice** message header, and then click the gray **flag** icon ▷ that appears. The gray flag icon changes to red, and a Follow up banner is added to the message header in the Reading Pane.

2. On the ribbon, click the **Home** tab.

3. In the Tags group, click the **Categorize** button, and then click **Green Category** in the menu. If this is the first time you have assigned this category, the Rename Category dialog box opens. You can choose to enter a descriptive category name or keep the default name.

   Trouble? If the Rename Category dialog box doesn't open, you have previously assigned this category and you need to use the Color Categories dialog box. In the Tags group, click the Categorize button, click All Categories, make sure the Green Category check box is selected, click the Rename button, type Invoices, and then click the OK button. Skip Step 4, and refer to Figure 18.

   Rivi asks you to specify the name "Invoices" for the green category to clarify the purpose of the category. When you rename a category, your version of Outlook will retain the name; in this case, the green category will retain the name "Invoices" unless it is renamed in the future.

4. In the Name box, type **Invoices**, and then click the **Yes** button. The message has a green category icon in the message header. Also, a green bar labeled "Invoices" appears at the top of the message in the Reading Pane; this indicates that the message is in the Invoices category. See Figure 18.

Figure 18 Piano Parts Invoice message with a flag and green color category

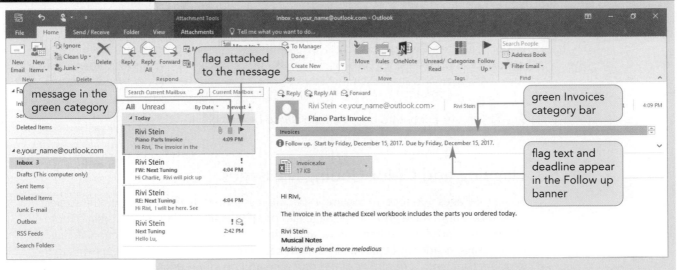

Organizing and Managing Messages

So far, all the messages you received are stored in the Inbox folder. As you can see, messages can collect quickly in your Inbox. Even if you respond to each message as it arrives, all the original messages still remain in your Inbox folder. Some messages you'll want to file and store; other messages you'll want to delete.

Creating a Folder

The Folder List acts like an electronic file cabinet. You should create a logical folder structure in which to store your messages. For example, Rivi might create subfolders named "Tunings" and "Invoices" within the Inbox folder. You can create folders at the same level as the default folders, such as Inbox, Outbox, and Sent Messages, or you can create subfolders within these folders. For now, you'll create one subfolder named "Tunings" in the Inbox folder.

Note: If you are using a web-based email account and store messages on your mail server, you will not be able to create folders in Outlook. Please read the following sections related to creating folders, but do not attempt to complete the steps.

To create the Tunings subfolder in the Inbox:

1. On the ribbon, click the **Folder** tab. The ribbon displays options for working with the selected folder—in this case, the Inbox.

2. In the New group, click the **New Folder** button. The Create New Folder dialog box opens.

3. In the Name box, type **Tunings**. Because you opened the dialog box from the Inbox, the Folder contains box lists Mail and Post Items. You can also create subfolders to store other items, such as contacts, notes, and tasks.

4. In the Select where to place the folder box, click **Inbox** if it is not already selected.

5. Click the **OK** button. The new folder appears indented below the Inbox folder in the Folder Pane.

   Trouble? If you don't see the Tunings folder, the Inbox is probably collapsed. Click the Expand button next to the Inbox.

   Trouble? If a dialog box opens to notify you that you cannot create the folder, you are probably using a web-based email account. Click the OK button, and then read but do not complete the steps in the next two sections.

Moving Messages into Folders

One method for keeping messages organized and the Inbox uncluttered is to move a message out of the Inbox as soon as you have dealt with it. This leaves the Inbox folder filled only with messages you still need to deal with. You'll file messages related to piano tuning and repairs in the new subfolder.

To move messages into the Tunings folder:

1. On the ribbon, click the **Home** tab.

2. In the message list, make sure the **Piano Parts Invoice** message is still selected. It is the first message that you will move.

TIP

You can also drag selected messages from one folder to another.

3. On the Home tab, in the Move group, click the **Move** button, and then click **Tunings**. The selected message moves to the Tunings subfolder.

   You could continue to move each message individually, but it is faster to move all of them at once. You press the Ctrl key to select nonadjacent messages in the message list and the Shift key to select a block of adjacent messages.

4. Click the **Next Tuning** message header, the first message you want to file.

5. Press and hold the **Ctrl** key, click the **RE: Next Piano Tuning** message header, click the **FW: Next Piano Tuning** message header, and then release the **Ctrl** key. The three messages are selected.

6. In the Move group, click the **Move** button, and then click **Tunings**. The three selected messages move from the Inbox into the Tunings subfolder. You might see a number next the Tunings subfolder, depending on whether any messages in the folder remain unread.

The Inbox folder is now empty of messages related to Musical Notes. However, the Piano Parts Invoice message does not belong in the Tuning folder. You'll create a new folder named "Invoices" to store that message.

To create a subfolder named Invoices:

1. In the Folder Pane, right-click the **Inbox** folder, and then click **New Folder** on the shortcut menu. A box for the subfolder name appears in the Folder Pane below the Inbox folder. Because you created this folder as a subfolder within the Inbox, it is already set for storing mail and post items.

2. In the box, type **Invoices** as the folder name, and then press the **Enter** key. The Invoices subfolder appears indented below the Inbox folder. Note that subfolders you create are listed in alphabetical order below the main folder.

Creating Rules

Rather than manually filing messages, you can create rules that specify how Outlook should process and organize them. For example, you can use rules to move messages to a folder based on their subjects, flag messages about a particular topic, or forward messages to a person or a distribution list.

Each rule includes three parts: the conditions that determine if a message is to be acted on, the actions that should be applied to qualifying messages, and any exceptions that remove a message from the qualifying group. A rule might state that all messages you receive from Charlie Zang (condition) are moved to the Tunings folder (action) except for ones marked as High importance (exception). Outlook can apply rules to incoming, outgoing, or stored messages.

You can create a simple rule from common conditions and actions in the Create Rule dialog box. Or you can use the Rules Wizard, which is a feature that steps you through the rule-writing process, to write more complex rules that also include exceptions.

Rivi asks you to create a rule to move all messages related to invoices to the Invoices subfolder. A message must be selected in order for the Create Rule button to be available. You can select any message to create a rule. Note that the information from the selected message automatically appears as conditions in the Create Rule dialog box.

To create a rule to move all invoice messages to the Invoices subfolder:

1. In the Folder Pane, click the **Tunings** subfolder, and then click the **Piano Parts Invoice** message in the message list to select it, if necessary.

2. On the Home tab, in the Move group, click the **Rules** button, and then click **Create Rule**. The Create Rule dialog box opens. You need to create a rule that will move any message that includes "Invoice" in the subject into the Invoices subfolder.

3. Click the **Subject contains** check box to insert a checkmark. The Subject contains box already contains the subject from the selected message.

4. Delete **Piano Parts** from the Subject contains box. You've specified the first part of the rule, the condition—the Subject of the message must contain the text "Invoice."

5. Click the **Move the item to folder** check box. The Rules and Alerts dialog box opens.

6. In the Choose a folder box, expand the Inbox folder for your email account, click the **Invoices** folder, and then click the **OK** button. You've specified the second part of the rule, the action—move the message to the Invoices folder. There are no exceptions needed for this rule, so the settings are complete. See Figure 19.

Figure 19	Completed Create Rule dialog box

set conditions for the rule

set actions for the rule

rule will move all messages that meet conditions to this folder

rule will search for this text in the Subject field of messages

click to open the Rules Wizard

7. Click the **OK** button. The Success dialog box opens, indicating that the rule "Invoice" has been created.

   Trouble? If a dialog box opens and displays the message, "This rule is a client-only rule, and will process only if Outlook is running," you are set up to run Outlook with Exchange Server. This message appears because Outlook has determined that the rule requires access to your computer to run. Click the OK button. Outlook saves the rule and adds "(client only)" after the name of the rule in the Rules and Alerts dialog box to remind you that your computer must be logged on to Exchange Server for the rule to be run. If you have any questions about Exchange Server, ask your instructor or technical support person for assistance.

   So you can see how to run a rule at any time, you'll deselect the option for running the rule immediately and then use another option to run it.

8. Click the **Run this rule now on messages already in the current folder** check box to remove the checkmark, if necessary, and then click the **OK** button.

You'll use the Rules and Alerts dialog box to run the Invoice rule on the messages in the Tunings subfolder. The dialog box gives you options for running the rule on specified folders as well as any subfolders.

To run the Invoice rule:

1. On the Home tab, in the Move group, click the **Rules** button, and then click **Manage Rules & Alerts**. The Rules and Alerts dialog box opens with the E-mail Rules tab displayed.

2. On the E-mail Rules tab, click the **Run Rules Now** button. The Run Rules Now dialog box opens.

3. Click the **Invoice** check box to insert a checkmark, and then read the rule description.

4. Click the **Run Now** button. The rule runs on the messages in the Tunings folder and the Piano Parts Invoice message is moved to the Invoices folder.

5. Click the **Close** button in the Run Rules Now dialog box, and then click the **OK** button in the Rules and Alerts dialog box.

6. In the Folder Pane, click the **Invoices** folder to see that the Piano Parts Invoice message is now in the Invoices folder, having been moved there from the Tunings subfolder.

Rearranging Messages

As your folder structure becomes more complex and you have more stored messages, it might become difficult to locate a specific message you filed. Searching, sorting, and changing views provide different ways to locate and organize your messages.

Searching for Messages

Rather than searching through multiple folders, you can use Instant Search to find the desired message (or any other Outlook item). You select the folder you want to search and then enter search text in the Search box. As you type, items with that search text appear in the message list with the search text highlighted. Attachments are also searched, but the search text is not highlighted in them. To narrow your search, you can select additional criteria in the Refine group on the Search Tools Search tab, which appears on the ribbon when you click in the Search box.

REFERENCE

Searching for Messages

- Display the Outlook element you want to search.
- Type search text in the Search box.
- To narrow your search, select additional criteria in the Refine group on the Search Tools Search tab.
- To clear a search, click the Close Search button next to the Search box.

You'll use Instant Search to look for messages containing the word "replacement" in the Tunings folder.

To search for messages with the word "replacement":

1. In the Folder Pane, click the **Tunings** subfolder to list its contents in the message list.

2. Click in the **Search Tunings** box above the message list. The Search Tools Search tab appears on the ribbon with tools for searching Outlook items.

3. Type **replacement** in the Search box. As you type, any text in the message headers and the Reading Pane that matches the search text is highlighted. Only one message contains the search text. See Figure 20.

Figure 20 — Instant Search results

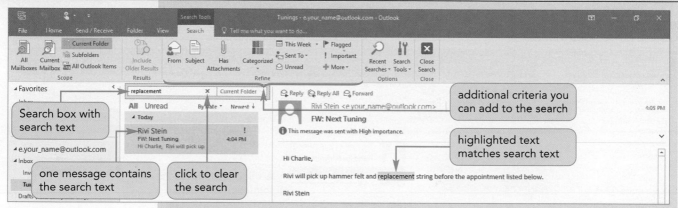

4. In the Search box, click the **Close Search** button ☒. The highlighting is removed and the message list once again lists all of the messages in the Tunings folder.

Using Search Folders

Another way to find specific messages is with Search Folders. Outlook has preset Search Folders. For example, the Categorized Mail Search Folder displays messages grouped by their color categories, the Large Mail Search Folder displays any messages larger than 100 KB, and the Unread Mail Search Folder displays all messages that have an unread icon. Messages that meet a Search Folder's criteria are displayed in that Search Folder but remain stored in their current folders. This lets you open one folder to view messages with similar characteristics but store them logically in other folders based upon their contents. A message can appear in more than one Search Folder. For example, a message in the blue category that is 200 KB and marked as unread will appear in at least three Search Folders: Categorized Mail, Large Mail, and Unread Mail. You can use the preset Search Folders, customize them to better fit your needs, or create your own Search Folders.

If you delete a Search Folder, the messages that were displayed in that folder are not deleted because they are actually stored in other Outlook folders. However, if you delete an individual message from within a Search Folder, the message is also deleted from the folder in which it is actually stored.

You'll use Search Folders to look for categorized messages and unread messages.

To use the Categorized Mail and Unread Mail Search Folders:

1. On the ribbon, click the **Folder** tab. In the New group, click **New Search Folder**. The New Search Folder dialog box opens.

2. Scroll down the Select a Search Folder box until you see the Organizing Mail section, and then click **Categorized mail**.

3. Click the **OK** button. The Categorized Mail Search Folder appears in the Folder Pane below Search Folders.

4. In the Folder Pane, click the **Categorized Mail** Search Folder if it is not already selected. In the message list, one message header appears under the green group heading "Invoices." See Figure 21.

Figure 21   **Categorized Mail Search Folder**

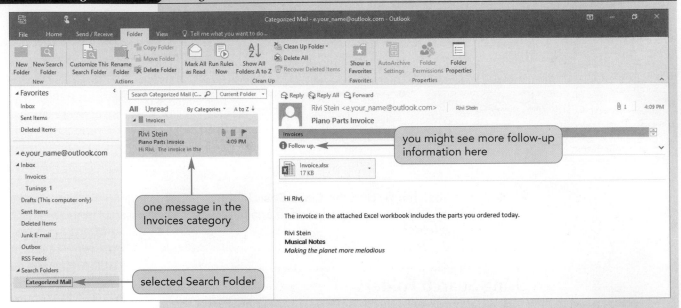

If you had more than one message categorized and used different colors, the messages would appear grouped according to their color categories.

5. In the New group, click the **New Search Folder** button, click **Unread mail** in the Reading Mail section of the Select a Search Folder box, and then click the **OK** button. The Unread Mail Search Folder is added to the Folder Pane. Any messages you haven't yet read appear in the message list when the Unread Mail Search Folder is selected.

Switching Views and Arrangements

Another way to manage messages is to change the view or arrangement. You are already familiar with views, which specify how items for an Outlook element are organized and which details are visible. Each Outlook element has a set of standard views from which you can choose. An **arrangement** is a predefined organization of how items in a view are displayed. Views and arrangements enable you to see the same items in different ways.

To switch the arrangement of the Tunings folder:

1. In the Folder Pane, click **Tunings** to display the contents of this folder in the message list. The messages are listed according to the date and time they were received.

2. Click the **View** tab, and then, in the Arrangement group, click **Subject**. All of the messages appear in the message list grouped according to the text in their Subject boxes. Because there are three messages with Next Tuning as the subject, they appear in the message list under the Next Tuning heading.

3. Above the message list, click the **By Subject** arrow to display the list of default arrangements, and then click **Importance**. The messages are now grouped according to their importance levels, in this case High or Normal. The messages with High importance appear first in the list, followed by messages with Normal importance.

Sorting Messages

Sorting arranges items in either ascending or descending order. **Ascending order** arranges messages alphabetically from A to Z, chronologically from earliest to latest, or numerically from lowest to highest. **Descending order** arranges messages in reverse alphabetical, chronological, or numerical order. By default, all messages are sorted in descending order by their Received date and time. You can, however, change the field by which messages are sorted; for example, you might sort email messages alphabetically by sender. You can also sort messages by multiple fields. For example, you might sort email messages alphabetically by sender and then by subject.

To sort the messages in the Tunings folder by importance:

1. On the View tab, in the Arrangement group, click the **Reverse Sort** button. The Importance sort order changes to ascending, as indicated by the text "Low" above the message list. See Figure 22.

Figure 22	Messages in the Tunings folder sorted in ascending order by importance

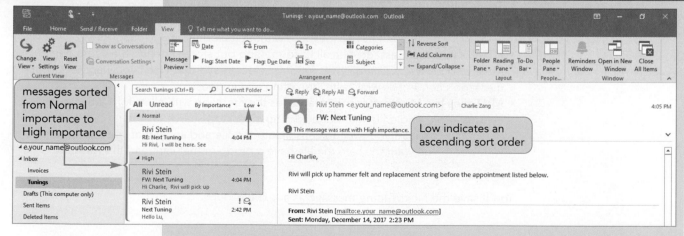

Trouble? If the text changes to "High," the sort order was already ascending. Repeat Step 1.

> **2.** Above the message list, click **Low**. The Importance sort order returns to descending (High on top), as indicated by the text.

> **3.** Above the message list, click **By Importance**, and then click **Date** on the menu. The messages are listed again in the original order.

Storing Messages

After a time, you might not need immediate access to the messages you have compiled in the Outlook folders. You can store messages by saving them in other file formats.

Saving Messages

You can use the Save As command to save messages and other Outlook items in other file formats so that you can store them separately from Outlook in a specific location on your hard drive or removable storage device (such as a USB flash drive) just as you save other files, and then delete them from Outlook. You can open such messages with other programs. For example, you can save an email message as a Text Only (.txt) file that most word processing programs can read. You can also save HTML messages as HTML (.htm) files to preserve their original formatting.

INSIGHT

Understanding Save As File Formats in Outlook

Sometimes you will want to work with items created in Outlook using other programs, or you might want to share items created in Outlook with others who might not have Outlook installed on their device. To be able to do this effectively, you need to understand the types of file formats available and some of the limitations associated with each.

- **Outlook Template, Outlook Message Format, Outlook Message Format – Unicode** are Outlook formats that can be read only by Outlook. These formats limit your options in sharing your saved files.
- **Text Only** saves the message as plain text but loses any formatting and images. Most word processing programs can read this format. Select this format when you want to save the content of a message without its formatting or images.
- **HTML** saves the message with all its formatting but stores images in a subfolder. Most web browsers can read this format. Select this format when you want to save a message's content as well as its formatting and images.
- **MHT files** is a Microsoft format that saves the message with all its formatting and images into a single file that Edge and most desktop search programs can read. Select this format if you want to consolidate the file and know that you and others with whom you want to share the file have a program that can read this format.

You'll save the Next Tuning message as a text file.

To save the Next Tuning message as a text file:

> **1.** Click the **Next Tuning** message in the message list to select it.

TIP

To save a message as a Word document, select and copy the message, paste it into an open document, and then save the document from Word.

2. On the ribbon, click the **File** tab to open Backstage view, and then click **Save As** in the navigation bar. The Save As dialog box opens, with the message's subject in the File name box.

3. Navigate to the location where you are saving your files.

4. Click the **Save as type** button to display the available file formats from which you can choose, and then click **Text Only** to select that file format.

5. Click the **Save** button. The message is saved as a text file.

You can open, edit, and print the email you saved as a text file just as you would any other text file.

INSIGHT

Archiving Mail Messages

Eventually, the messages in your subfolders can become too numerous to manage easily. Rather than reviewing filed messages and moving older ones to a storage file, you can archive them. When you **archive** a folder, you transfer messages or other items stored in a folder (such as an attachment in the email folder) to an Outlook data file when the items have reached the age you specify. Outlook calculates the age of an email message from the date the message was sent or received, whichever is later. An **Outlook data file** (which has the file extension .pst or .ost, depending on your email account type) can be accessed only from Outlook, and stores folders, messages, files, and other items.

When you create an archive, your existing folder structure from Outlook is recreated in the archive file and all the messages are moved from Outlook into the archive file. If you want to archive only a subfolder, the entire folder structure is still recreated in the archive file; however, only the messages from the selected subfolder are moved into the archive file. For example, if you archive the Tunings folder, the archive file will include both the Inbox folder and the Tunings subfolder, but only the messages in the Tunings subfolder will be moved. Any messages in the Inbox folder remain in the Outlook Inbox. All folders remain in place within Outlook after archiving—even empty ones.

You can manually archive a folder at any time, such as when you finish a project or event. You specify which folders to archive, the age of items to archive, and the name and location of the archive file in the Archive dialog box. To open the Archive dialog box, on the ribbon, click the File tab, and then click Info in the navigation bar, if necessary. Click the Cleanup Tools button, and then click Archive. Once a folder is archived, it appears at the bottom of the Folder Pane under an Archive heading, thereby providing you access to the archived item. If you don't need immediate access to an archive, you can close it by right-clicking it in the Folder Pane, and clicking Close Archives on the shortcut menu. You can access items in a closed archive from the Open screen in Backstage view. To work with the files from the Folder Pane, use the Open Outlook Data File command to open the file, and then drag the items you need from the archive to a current folder. To restore all of the items in the archive file, use the Import command.

When you no longer need to keep items you have created in Outlook, you can delete them permanently.

Deleting Items and Exiting Outlook

After you finish working with Outlook, you should exit the program. Unlike with other programs, you don't need to save or close any files. Before you exit, however, you'll delete the rule and each of the items you created in this module. Deleted items are moved into the Deleted Items folder. This folder acts like the Recycle Bin in Windows. Items you delete stay in this folder until you empty it.

To delete the rule, items you created, and your signature:

1. On the Home tab, in the Move group, click the **Rules** button, and then click **Manage Rules & Alerts**. The Rules and Alerts dialog box opens with the E-mail Rules tab active.

2. In the Rule box, click **Invoice** to select the rule if necessary, and then click the **Delete** button on the toolbar above the Rule box.

3. Click the **Yes** button to confirm the deletion, and then click the **OK** button to close the Rules and Alerts dialog box.

4. In the Folder Pane, click the **Invoices** folder.

5. On the ribbon, click the **Folder** tab. In the Actions group, click the **Delete Folder** button. A dialog box opens to confirm that you want to move the folder and all of its messages to the Deleted Items folder.

6. Click the **Yes** button.

7. Repeat Steps 4 through 6 to delete the **Tunings** folder, the **Categorized Mail** folder, and the **Unread Mail** folder.

8. In the Folder Pane, click the **Sent Items** folder, click the first message you sent in this module, press and hold the **Ctrl** key as you click each additional message you sent in this module, and then release the **Ctrl** key. All of the messages you sent in the module are selected.

9. On the ribbon, click the **Home** tab, and then in the Delete group, click the **Delete** button. The selected messages move to the Deleted Items folder.

10. In the Folder Pane, click the **People** button 👥, press and hold the **Ctrl** key as you click each of the four contacts and the Vendors contact group you created in this module, release the **Ctrl** key, and then click the **Delete** button in the Delete group. The contacts you created for this module are deleted.

11. On the ribbon, click the **File** tab to open Backstage view, and then click **Info** in the navigation bar, if necessary.

12. On the Account Information screen, click the **Cleanup Tools** button, click **Empty Deleted Items Folder**, and then click the **Yes** button to confirm that you want to permanently delete all the items and subfolders in the Deleted Items folder.

13. Click **Options** in the navigation bar to open the Outlook Options dialog box, and then click **Mail** in the left pane.

14. Click the **Signatures** button in the right pane, click **Musical Notes** in the Select signature to edit box, and then click the **Delete** button.

15. Click the **Yes** button to confirm that you want to delete this signature.

16. Click the **OK** button in the Signatures and Stationery dialog box, and then click the **OK** button in the Outlook Options dialog box.

You have deleted all of the items you created in this module—email messages, contacts, Search Folders, a rule, a signature, and emptied the Deleted Items folder. You will now exit Outlook.

To exit Outlook:

▶ **1.** In the upper-right corner of the Outlook window, click the **Close** button ⊠. The Outlook window closes.

The next time you start Outlook, any email messages, contacts, Search Folders, rules, and signatures that weren't deleted will still be available.

PROSKILLS

Teamwork: Communicating Effectively with a Group

Email is a common way for team members to communicate. As teams work on a project, many messages about a variety of topics related to that project will be exchanged. When you are part of a team (or communicating with a group for a one-time purpose), keep in mind the following guidelines as you send and receive messages:

- **Check the recipient list.** Are all team members are included? Has anyone else has been added to the exchange? If so, should that person be part of the ongoing communication? For example, a customer should be removed from the internal discussion about how to deal with the customer's complaint, and be sent only the resolution.
- **Reread the message chain.** Is the entire conversation appropriate for all recipients? For example, an upcoming surprise retirement party should not be mentioned in an email chain that includes the retiree. Also, is the message chain getting very long? If so, it might be appropriate to delete the earliest part of the chain.
- **Use one subject per message chain.** Is the discussion veering to a new topic? Start a new email with an appropriate subject line to reflect the new topic. This makes it simpler to track the different conversations.
- **Check attachment content.** Is the attachment appropriate for all recipients? For example, you want to make sure that confidential or proprietary information, such as budgets and items under development, are not forwarded to customers or competitors.
- **Understand Reply vs. Reply All vs. Forward.** Who do you want to include in the message chain? Use Reply when you want to respond only to the sender. Use Reply All when you want to respond to everyone who received the message chain. Use Forward when you want to send the message chain to someone not already on the list. Keep in mind that you can add or remove recipients each time you send a response.

Thanks to your help, Rivi is set up to use Outlook to communicate more effectively with her clients and students, and manage the email messages that she sends and receives.

REVIEW

Session 2 Quick Check

1. Explain the difference between Reply and Reply All.
2. What is an attachment?
3. How do you move an email message from the Inbox to a subfolder?
4. What is a Search Folder?
5. What is the purpose of a rule?
6. What does it mean to archive a folder?

Review Assignments

Data File needed for the Review Assignments: Lessons.docx

Rivi Stein asks you to help her communicate with her students who come to her for music lessons at Musical Notes. Complete the following steps:

1. Create a signature that uses your name and the company name **Musical Notes**. Format the company name with bold and italics. Apply the signature to new messages and replies and forwards.

2. Create a new email message addressed to your email address with the subject **Lesson Reminder** and the message **Hello, Your lesson is next Saturday at 10 AM. Please confirm.**

3. In the message body, format "10 AM" with bold and a red font.

4. Send the email.

5. Create a contact card for **Rivi Stein** at **Musical Notes** using your email address, an appropriate display as entry, a fictional business phone number, and a fictional business mailing address.

6. Create contact cards for the following three students at their home addresses and phone numbers, using your email address and an appropriate display as entry. (*Hint*: Click the arrow button in the address section, and then click Home.)

   - **Alaina Redmund, 32948 W Abram Street, Arlington TX 76018, 817-555-4291**
   - **Porter Garrison, 381 Secret Drive, Arlington TX 76015, 817-555-0907**
   - **Vijay Gupta, 8201 Kelly Terrace, Arlington TX 76010, 817-555-6497**

7. Create a contact group named **Students** that includes Alaina Redmund, Porter Garrison, and Vijay Gupta.

8. Edit Porter's contact card to change the address to **381 Secretary Drive**.

9. Create an email message addressed to **Rivi Stein** with **Singing Lessons** as the subject and **Hi Rivi, Do you have any upcoming group singing lessons?** as the message body. Send the message.

10. Download your messages. If the Singing Lessons message hasn't arrived, wait a few minutes and try again.

11. Reply to the Singing Lessons message with the text **The attached flyer describes the upcoming group lessons. Let me know if you are interested in signing up.**

12. Attach the **Lessons** document located in the Outlook > Review folder included with your Data Files to the file, and then send the message.

13. Forward the **Singing Lessons** message to Rivi Stein with the message **The group singing lessons are starting to fill up.** Mark the message as High importance. Send the message.

14. Create a new folder named **Students** that contains Mail and Post Items placed in the Inbox folder.

15. Create a rule to move messages you receive from yourself to the Students folder. Run the rule now.

16. Download your messages, and verify that the Lesson reminder message and the three Singing Lessons messages were filed in the Students subfolder.

17. Add a blue color category to the Singing Lessons message, using the default category name.

18. Find the three messages in the Students folder that contain the word **singing**.

19. Save each message that was found in HTML format using the subject as the filename.

20. Review the attachment in the RE: Singing Lessons message, and then save the attachment as **Group Lessons** in the location where you are saving your files.

21. Delete each Outlook item you created: the signature, the rule, the subfolder, the four messages in the Sent Items folder, the four contacts, and the contact group, and then empty the Deleted Items folder.

Case Problem 1

Data File needed for this Case Problem: Casey Berk.vcf

Cedar Park Neighborhood Association   Cedar Park, Texas, is divided into different neighborhood zones. Each zone has a neighborhood association that residents can join to participate in discussions and events focused on their neighborhood. The group meets monthly to discuss current events such as traffic issues, local crime, and neighborhood beautification projects. They also plan events throughout the year, including a neighborhood cleanup, a fall harvest festival, and a summer ice cream social. You'll use Outlook to send email to some of Neighborhood Association members. Complete the following steps:

1. Display the Contacts window, and then create the following new contacts, using the Save & New button to create each new contact:

   - Full name **Kara Wendel**; company name **Mulberry Elementary School**; job title **Principal**; your email address; an appropriate display as entry; mobile phone **512-555-8712**; home mailing address **17 Old Mill Rd., Cedar Park, TX 78613**; spouse **Pat**

   - Full name **Darren Morely**; home phone **512-555-6741**; home mailing address **841 Old Mill Rd., Cedar Park, TX 78613**

   - Full name **Philip Worthington**; job title **Student**; your email address; an appropriate display as entry; mobile phone **737-555-2145**; home mailing address **8 Goldfinch Dr., Cedar Park, TX 78613**; nickname **Phil**

   - Full name **Tracy Peterson**; company name **Cedar Park Neighborhood Association**; job title **President**; your email address; an appropriate display as entry; business phone **512-555-9797**; business fax **512-555-9701**; pager **737-555-2157**; business mailing address **2949 Sycamore St., Cedar Park, TX 78612**

2. View the contacts in Card view.

3. Edit Darren Morely's contact card to add **512-555-6110** as his mobile phone number.

4. Create a contact group called **Association Members** that includes all members with an email address; do not include Tracy Peterson.

5. Send Tracy Peterson's contact information as a business card. Select Tracy's contact card. On the Home tab, in the Share group, click the Forward Contact button, and then click As a Business Card. A Message window opens with the contact card included as an attachment. Send the message to the Association Members contact group, use **Tracy Peterson** as the subject, and include the message **Attached is Tracy's contact information. Please direct any questions or comments about the Association to her.** followed by your name on a separate line.

6. Send a new email message to Tracy Peterson with the subject **Casey Berk's contact** and no message; attach the vCard file **Casey Berk** located in the Outlook > Case1 folder included with your Data Files.

7. Download your messages, select the Casey Berk's contact message, click the business card attachment to view it in the Reading Pane, click the Copy button in the Selection group on the Attachment Tools Attachments tab, switch to the Contacts folder, press the Ctrl+V keys to create a contact card based on the attachment, and then save and close the new contact card.

8. Create a new folder named **Association** that contains Mail and Post Items placed in the Inbox folder.

9. Search for all messages in the Inbox related to the subject **contact**.

10. Save the two messages you found as HTML files, and then file them in the Association folder.

11. Delete the Association folder, the two messages in the Sent Items folder, and the five contacts and the contact group, and then empty the Deleted Items folder.

CHALLENGE

Case Problem 2

There are no Data Files needed for this Case Problem.

Children's Theater Group   Fay Leander owns Children's Theater Group, which provides performing arts programming for youth. In addition to providing classes and camps, CTG presents four shows a year using a mix of youth and adult participants. Fay has collected a list of youths who have expressed interest in auditioning for the next show, a series of fractured fairytales. Production Manager Ally Jeralds is managing the auditions, which will occur the last week of the next month. Youth actors need to be accompanied by their parent or guardian and be prepared to perform a three-minute song and dance routine and a two-minute monologue. Complete the following steps:

1. Create contact cards for five youth actors. Include their names, mailing addresses, phone numbers, email addresses (using your email address for each contact), and appropriate display as entries. Create a contact card for Ally Jeralds that includes her name, company name, your email address, and an appropriate display as entry.

2. Create a contact group named **Potential Actors** that includes the contact cards of all the youth actors.

3. Edit at least two contacts to include one item of personal information, such as a birthday or nickname.

⊕ **Explore** 4. Create an email message using stationery for the audition announcement.

5. Address the audition announcement to the Potential Actors contact group. Type an appropriate subject. Enter an appropriate message for the audition; be sure to include the day, time, and place of the audition. Format the message text appropriately. Send the message.

6. Switch to Contacts, and then change the view to Business Card.

⊕ **Explore** 7. Create a new folder named **Actors** that contains Contact Items placed in Contacts, and then move the contact cards you created for this Case Problem into it. (*Hint:* If you have an Exchange ActiveSync account, you cannot create this folder. In Step 8, select Contacts folder.)

⊕ **Explore** 8. Export your contact list. Click the File tab on the ribbon, click Open & Export in the navigation bar, and then click Import/Export. In the Import and Export Wizard, click Export to a file, and then click the Next button. Click Comma Separated Values as the file type, and then click the Next button. If necessary, expand the Contacts folder, select the Actors subfolder, and then click the Next button. Use the Browse button to save the file as **Actors List** to the location specified by your instructor. Click the Next button, and then click the Finish button. The contact list is exported.

9. Create a new folder named **Audition** that contains Mail and Post Items placed in the Inbox folder, and then move the invitation email into the subfolder.

10. Save the audition email as an HTML file in the location where you are saving your files. (You might receive only one message because you used the same email addresses for all your contacts.)

11. Delete the Audition subfolder and the messages in the Sent Items folder, delete the Actors subfolder and the contacts, and then empty the Deleted Items folder.

INDEX

A

abbreviations, using consistently, AC 12

absolute cell references, EX 154, EX 161–163, EX 165–166

.accdb files, AC 9

Access, AC 1
backward compatibility, AC 9
comparison operators (fig.), AC 142
data limits, AC 7
vs. Excel, when to use which, AC 44
exiting, AC 22–23
Help, AC 40–41
maintaining databases, AC 42–43
starting, AC 7–8

Access 2016 Help, AC 25

Access tables, modifying structures of, AC 68–71

Access window (visual overview), AC 2–3

Accounting format, EX 66, EX 80

active cell, changing, EX 10–11

active sheet, EX 2, EX 8–9

Add & Delete group, AC 2, AC 14

Add Account dialog box (fig.), OUT 7

adding. See inserting

Address bar, FM 10

Address Quick Start selection, AC 87

addresses
adding sentence including email, WD 12
inside, in block-style letters, WD 11

Advance to the next slide button, PPT 32

aggregate functions, AC 161
frequently used (fig.), AC 161
query with (fig.), AC 165
using record group calculations, AC 166–167
working with using Total row, AC 162–163

aligning
cell content, EX 84–85
text, WD 43–44

alignment
buttons (fig.), EX 84
of field values in reports, changing, AC 213–214
options, Format Cells dialog box, EX 89

Alignment buttons, WD 30

Alignment group, EX 66

All Access Objects, Navigation Pane, AC 40, AC 167, AC 169

And logical operator
described, AC 149–151
vs. Or logical operator, AC 153

animation emphasis effects, PA-8

annotating webpages (Microsoft Edge), PA-15

apostrophes ('), displaying numbers as text, EX 21

approximate match lookup, EX 171

apps, productivity, PA-1–4

archive described, OUT 43

archives, FM 28

archiving email messages, OUT 43

arguments
and function syntax, EX 141–142
required and optional, EX 133, EX 146

arithmetic. See aggregate functions

arithmetic operators, EX 32

arrangement described, OUT 40

ascending sort order, OUT 41, AC 134

aspect ratio, PPT 44, PPT 47

Associated Press Stylebook, WD 94

attachments, OUT 27
using email, OUT 13
visual overview, OUT 26–27
working with, OUT 31–32

AutoComplete
described, EX 20–21
entering dates using, WD 10

Auto-Complete List, OUT 17

AutoCorrect, PPT 10, WD 14–15

AutoCorrect Options button menu (fig.), PPT 11

AutoCorrect Options dialog box, PPT 10–11

AutoFill, EX 155
exploring options, EX 158–159
filling a series, EX 156–158
series patterns extended with (fig.), EX 157
used to fill series (fig.), EX 156

AutoFill Options menu (fig.), EX 158

AutoFilter
described, AC 131
sorting data using, AC 131–132

AutoFit
autofitting worksheet column contents, EX 27
described, PPT 15, EX 27

automatic page breaks, EX 95

AutoNumber, AC 13

AutoSum, EX 79
described (fig.), EX 31
and SUM function, EX 35–38

Available Fields box, Simple Query Wizard dialog box, AC 31

Average aggregate function, AC 163

AVERAGE function, EX 35, EX 96, EX 132
described, EX 142
nested, EX 143–145

averages, calculating, EX 96–98

B

Back button, FM 8

background images, adding, EX 74–75

backgrounds, cell, EX 72–75

backing up
databases, AC 43
described, AC 43

backslashes (\\) in file path, FM 10

Backspace key
deleting characters with, PPT 10
using to delete, WD 15

Backstage view, PPT 5, AC 8
Print screen in (fig.), PPT 57
print settings in (fig.), WD 26
Recent screen in (fig.), EX 4
recent screen in (fig.), WD 4
Recent screen in (fig.), AC 8
Save As dialog box in, PPT 9
Save As screen in (fig.), WD 7

Bcc line, email, OUT 10–11, OUT 29

Berlin theme, WD 88–90

bibliography, WD 100
formatting as MLA-style works cited list, WD 112
generating, WD 108–110
updating, finalizing, WD 111–112

Bibliography button, WD 93

Black or unblack slide show button, PPT 33, PPT 55

Blank workbook template, EX 14–15

block-style letter (fig.), WD 9

bold, WD 41
applying to text, WD 42–43
italic, EX 68
text, AC 191, OUT 11

Bold button, PPT 20

Border gallery (fig.), WD 45

Border tab, Format Cells dialog box, EX 97

borders
adding cell, EX 49
adding double, EX 97–98
adding paragraph, WD 45–47
adding to cells, EX 85–87
illustrated (fig.), EX 30
options, Format Cells dialog box, EX 90

Borders button, WD 31

browsers. See Microsoft Edge

bulleted lists
creating, PPT 14–15, WD 62, WD 70–72
described, PPT 14, WD 70

bullets
applying to paragraphs, WD 71–72
illustrated (fig.), WD 62
replacing type of, WD 71–72

Business Communication: Process & Product (Guffey), WD 9

business letters, creating block-style, WD 9

buttons, WD 2
  organized on tab in groups (fig.), EX 2
  on ribbon, AC 13
  window, AC 2

C

Calculated cell style, EX 132

calculated fields, AC 156
  creating, using, AC 156–160
  creating using Expression Builder, AC 157
  formatting, AC 160
  vs. using calculated field data type, AC 161

calculated values, EX 140–141

calculating averages
  described, EX 96–98
  and maximum amounts, AC 164–165

calculations
  with blank cells and zero values (fig.), EX 145
  performing with formulas, EX 32–35

Calendar
  described, OUT 2
  displaying, OUT 4–5

caption property
  setting for fields, AC 58
  values, and importing, AC 80

Caption property, setting for fields, AC 91–92

capturing video clips, PA-11

Card view, OUT 21

cards (Sway), PA-6–7

Cascade Delete Related Records option, AC 99

Cascade Update Related Fields option, AC 99

cases
  Backspace Gear, EX 187
  Game Card customer order report, EX 1
  Lakeside Event Center, PPT 1
  Miami Trolleys, FM 1
  Morning Bean shops, EX 65
  Musical Notes, OUT 1
  Quincy Rivers College handout, WD 61
  Villa Rio Records, cover letter, flyer, WD 1
  Vista Grande Neighborhood Center, WD 119
  Wingait Farm, EX 131

category values, EX 180

Cc line, email, OUT 10–11, OUT 29

cell content
  aligning, EX 84–85
  formatting, EX 68
  indenting, EX 85
  rotating, EX 88–89

cell ranges, EX 2
  cells inserted into (fig.), EX 46
  dragging and dropping, EX 40–41
  formatting copied and pasted (fig.), EX 101

inserting, deleting, EX 45–46
selecting, EX 11–13
setting printing to exclude, EX 114–115

cell references, EX 9
  changing in formulas, EX 165–167
  mixed, EX 155, EX 163–164, EX 166
  navigating within worksheets using, EX 11
  relative and absolute, EX 154, EX 161–163, EX 165–166
  visual overview, EX 154–155

cell styles, EX 95, EX 98–100, EX 140–141

Cell Styles button, Styles group, Home tab, EX 106

Cell Styles gallery, EX 98–99

cells
  adding borders, EX 49
  borders, adding, EX 85–87
  changing active, EX 10–11
  conditional formatting, EX 107–113
  with conditional formatting (fig.), EX 109
  described (fig.), EX 3
  displaying formulas, EX 55–56
  displaying significant digits, EX 140
  editing text in, EX 19–20
  formatted worksheet (fig.), EX 91
  formatting text selections within, EX 72
  formatting text strings within, EX 66
  formatting text within, EX 68–75
  formatting worksheet, EX 84–89
  formula being entered in (fig.), EX 34
  highlighting based on their values, EX 107–109
  highlighting with Top/Bottom rule, EX 109–111
  inserted into ranges, EX 45
  locking, hiding, EX 90
  merged (fig.), EX 88
  merging, EX 87–88
  moving and copying, EX 39–41
  styles. *See* cell styles
  wrapping text within, EX 27–28

Center button, WD 30

centering text, WD 43–44

character-level formatting, WD 84

characters
  deleting, WD 13, PPT 10
  nonprinting, WD 2
  wildcard (fig.), AC 195

chart area, EX 180

chart elements
  illustrated (fig.), EX 180
  visual overview, EX 180–181

chart sheets
  described, EX 7
  'Expenses' example (fig.), EX 9

charts, EX 180

checking spelling, grammar errors, WD 34–37, PPT 50–52

Choose a SmartArt Graphic dialog box (fig.), PPT 26

Citation Options menu (fig.), WD 105

citations, WD 94
  creating, WD 100–107
  creating bibliography with, WD 108–110
  editing, WD 103, WD 105
  illustrated (fig.), WD 92

Clear All Formatting button, Font group, Home tab, WD 41

clearing described, EX 44

Click to Add column, AC 2

Clipboard, FM 19, PPT 22, EX 35
  copying and pasting, PPT 23–24
  copying and pasting formulas using, EX 35
  copying multiple files using, FM 22–23
  moving and copying text using, PPT 22–23
  moving files using, FM 20–21

Clipboard task pane, WD 75, WD 76–77

clips, PA-11

Close (relationships) button, AC 76

Close button, PPT 60

closed-captioning tools, Office Mix, PA-11

closing
  databases, AC 28
  Mini toolbar, WD 19
  presentations, PPT 30–31
  Print Preview, AC 207
  reports, AC 39
  tables, AC 22–23
  workbooks, EX 13

cloud described, FM 5

coloring fonts, WD 42–43, WD 46, PPT 20–21

colors
  applying font, EX 70–71
  changing font, in reports, AC 217–218
  changing of text on forms, AC 191–192
  coding email messages, OUT 33–34
  creating custom, EX 71
  fill. *See* fill colors
  previewing in grayscale, PPT 57
  ranking email messages by, OUT 26
  shading paragraphs, WD 30, WD 45–47
  standard, EX 70
  Theme, Standard, WD 46, WD 87
  using with highlights, EX 113

column headings, EX 3

column selector, AC 16

Columnar form layout, AC 180, AC 183–184

columns, datasheet, AC 2

columns, resizing in reports, AC 36–37

columns, worksheet
  changing widths, EX 25–27
  deleting, EX 43–45
  formatting titles, EX 90
  hiding, unhiding, EX 47
  inserting, EX 42–44
  navigating within worksheets, EX 9–11
  resizing, EX 25–29

Comma style, EX 67, EX 81–82

commands
See also specific command
Key Tips, EX 6

comments, WD 65
adding, WD 69–70
attached to document text (fig.), WD 68
displayed in document (fig.), WD 66
reviewing and responding to, WD 67–69
working with, WD 67–70

common field, AC 4

Compact & Repair Database button, File tab, AC 42

Compact on Close option, AC 42–43

compacting
described, AC 42
and repairing databases, AC 42–43

comparison operators, AC 140, EX 175
described (fig.), AC 142
using to match range of values, AC 147–149

Compress Pictures dialog box (fig.), PPT 43

compressed (zipped) folders, FM 3

compressed files, working with, FM 28–30

compressing
files, folders, FM 28–30
photos, PPT 42–44

computers
exploring with File Explorer, FM 7–8
as file cabinets (fig.), FM 4

conditional formatting, EX 95, AC 218
creating legend, EX 111–112
highlighting data with conditional formats, EX 107–113
options, EX 111
using effectively, EX 113
using in reports, AC 218–220

conditions described, AC 140

Confidential sensitivity level of email, OUT 13

constants
described, EX 136
using in formulas, EX 136–139

contact cards, OUT 20

Contact Group window, OUT 23, OUT 24

contact groups, OUT 22
communicating effectively within, OUT 45
creating, modifying, OUT 22–24

contacts, OUT 15
in Card view (fig.), OUT 21
completed contact window (fig.), OUT 18
creating, OUT 15–20
editing, OUT 21
illustrated (fig.), OUT 5
sending information by email, OUT 22
switching contact views, OUT 20–21

content control
bibliography displayed in (fig.), WD 110
described, WD 93

Content view, FM 11

contextual tabs, PPT 7, AC 13, PPT 27

control layouts, AC 190

converting
bulleted lists into SmartArt diagrams, PPT 25
handwriting to text, PA-3–4
lists to SmartArt diagrams, PPT 24–28

copy described, WD 75

copying
See also filling
and applying formatting using Format Painter, PPT 21–22
described, FM 18
files, FM 19–23
formats, EX 100–102
formatting, with Format Painter, WD 30, WD 47–48
and moving cells, EX 39–41
and pasting formulas, EX 35
records from another Access database, AC 26–29
slides, PPT 28
text, PPT 22–24
text to paste into new document, WD 76–77

correcting
errors as you type, WD 14–15
spelling, grammar errors, WD 15–16

Cortana, FM 24
locating information with, PA-14–15
Notebook, FM 26–27
setting up, FM 25–26
voice controls, FM 25

COUNT function, EX 35, EX 41–42, EX 132, EX 142–143

COUNTA function, EX 41

Create Rule dialog box, OUT 36–37

Create Source dialog box (fig.), WD 104, WD 107

Create tab illustrated (fig.), AC 24

Create tab options (visual overview), AC 24–25

creating
bibliography, WD 108–110
bulleted lists, PPT 14–15, WD 62, WD 70–72
business letters, WD 9
calculated fields, AC 156–160
calculated fields vs. using calculated field data type, AC 161
citations, WD 100–107
conditional formatting legend, EX 111–112
contact groups, OUT 22–24
contacts, OUT 15–20
custom colors, EX 71
databases, AC 7–9
documents with templates, WD 29
email messages, OUT 10–13
envelopes, WD 26–29
error values, EX 152–153
expressions, AC 156
folders, FM 17–18, OUT 35
form with main form and subform, AC 200–204
forms, AC 33–35
forms using Form Wizard, AC 182–185

headers, footers, EX 118–120
larger databases, AC 104
multitable queries, AC 129–130
new presentations, PPT 5–7
new workbooks, EX 14–17
numbered lists, PPT 16–17, WD 70–73
queries, AC 30–33, AC 125–127
queries with aggregate functions, AC 163–165
queries with Group By operator, AC 166–167
reports, AC 35–39
reports based on query, AC 208
rules for organizing email messages, OUT 36–37
series with AutoFill, EX 157
subforms, AC 201–204
Sway presentations, PA-6–7
tables by importing existing table, table structure, AC 83–86
tables in Datasheet view, AC 11
tables in Design view, AC 59–68
title slides, PPT 7–8
unnumbered lists, PPT 17–18

Creative Commons license, PA-7

Crop button menu (fig.), PPT 41

crop described, PPT 40

cropping photos, PPT 40–42

Currency format, EX 80

currency format, AC 160

Current Record box, AC 22, AC 29

customer orders, EX 23–24

Customize Quick Access Toolbar button, PPT 2

customizing
colors, EX 71
margins, WD 24–25

Cut button, Clipboard group, PPT 22

cut described, PPT 22

cutting
or copying and pasting cell contents, EX 41
and pasting text using Clipboard, WD 75–78

D

data
adding to tables by importing text files, AC 95–97
filtering, AC 136–138
finding in datasheets, AC 194
finding using forms, AC 194–196
highlighting with conditional formats, EX 107–113
importing from Excel worksheets, AC 80–83
maintaining table data using forms, AC 197–198
organizing, AC 4
planning workbook, EX 13–14
searching in tables for, AC 121–122
sorting in queries, AC 131–135
storing in separate tables, AC 6
summarizing with Quick Analysis tool, EX 167–169

text, numeric, date and time, EX 17
types. *See* data types
updating using queries, AC 128–129
Data Files, FM 2, FM 10–11, PPT 34
data files, Outlook, OUT 43
data labels, EX 180
data redundancy
avoiding, AC 55
described, AC 55
data series, EX 180
data sources, EX 180
Data Type column, Table window, AC 52
Data Type gallery
adding fields using, AC 86–88
described, AC 86–88
data types, AC 13
assigning field, AC 56–57
calculated field, vs. using calculated field,
AC 161
changing for fields in Design view, AC 90
changing of primary key field, AC 13–14
common (fig.), AC 57
sorting results for different (fig.), AC 131
database concepts, AC 4–7
database management system (DBMS), AC 6–7
database objects
See also objects
applying themes to, AC 185–188
saving, AC 35
viewing in Navigation pane, AC 221
databases, AC 4
backing up and restoring, AC 43
closing, AC 28
copying records from another Access
database, AC 26–29
creating, AC 7–9
creating larger, AC 104
design guidelines, AC 54–56
file types, AC 9
forms. *See* forms
maintaining, AC 41–43
opening, AC 26
and relationships, AC 4–5
saving, AC 23
tables. *See* tables
updating, AC 118–124
Datasheet form layout, AC 183
Datasheet view, AC 2
changing format properties in, AC 71–73
creating tables in, AC 11
modified table in (visual overview), AC 76–77
selectors in, AC 16
Datasheet View button, AC 117
datasheets, AC 2
changing alternate row colors in,
AC 154–156
changing appearance of, AC 154–155
displayed after running query (fig.), AC 127
displaying calculated field (fig.), AC 160

displaying selected fields, records (fig.),
AC 144
finding data in, AC 194
navigating, AC 29–30
with records added (fig.), AC 21
sorted on two fields (fig.), AC 135
sorting query, AC 133
viewing, AC 96–97
date data, EX 17
date format symbols (fig.), AC 65
date formats, EX 22
date functions (fig.), EX 169
Date line, email, OUT 10
Date Navigator, OUT 5
dates
entering in various formats, EX 22–23
formatting, EX 83
inserting, WD 10–13
symbols for some custom formats (fig.),
AC 65
working with, EX 169–170
Date/Time fields, displaying available formats
(fig.), AC 64
decimal places, EX 67, EX 81
decision making
Access vs. Excel, when to use which, AC 44
creating effective documents, WD 33
determining where to store files, FM 7
displaying blank slides during presentations,
PPT 55
methods of adding fields to design grid,
AC 128
specifying field size property for number
fields, AC 58
Default Value property
described, AC 93
setting for a field, AC 93–94
defining database table fields, AC 59–66
Delete button, Records group, Home tab,
AC 122
Delete key, WD 15
Delete key, deleting characters with, PPT 10
deleting, EX 44
See also removing
blank slides, PPT 29–30
cell ranges, EX 45–46
characters, words, paragraphs, WD 13
characters with Backspace or Delete keys,
PPT 10
comments, WD 69
email items, OUT 43–44
fields from table imported structures,
AC 88–89
files, folders, FM 23
records, AC 122–124
rows, columns, EX 43–45
Search Folders, OUT 39
worksheets, EX 16–17
descending sort order, OUT 41, AC 134

Description property, AC 53
design grid, AC 116
after adding fields from two tables (fig.),
AC 143
columns in, AC 117
field added to (fig.), AC 126
methods of adding fields to, AC 128
moving fields in, AC 145–146
Total row inserted in (fig.), AC 164
Design tab, themes and variants on (fig.), PPT 36
Design view, AC 52
adding fields in, AC 69–71
changing field properties in, AC 73–74
changing field's data types, AC 90
creating tables in, AC 59–68
criteria entry (fig.), AC 140
defining fields, AC 59
moving fields in, AC 69
Query window in (visual overview),
AC 116–117
renaming fields in, AC 90
selecting two sort fields in (fig.), AC 134
sorting on multiple fields in, AC 132–133
specifying primary key in, AC 67
Table window in (visual overview), AC 52–53
designing
databases, AC 54–56
forms, AC 183–193, AC 193
headers, footers, EX 118–120
printouts (visual overview), EX 94–95
reports, AC 212–218
detail records, AC 207, AC 210
Details view, FM 11, FM 13
diagrams, PPT 24
converting lists to SmartArt, PPT 24–28
SmartArt, PPT 24
Dialog Box Launcher, WD 63, WD 76
disks described, FM 2
Display for Review button, WD 67
displaying
See also showing, viewing
available Date/Time field formats (fig.),
AC 64
cell formulas, EX 55–56
nonprinting characters, WD 6
numbers as text, EX 21–22
ribbon, PPT 3
ruler, WD 6
selected records, AC 142
significant digits, EX 140
Styles gallery, WD 84–85
Docs.com public gallery, PA-8
documenting formulas, EX 135
documents
comments displayed in (fig.), WD 66
copying text to paste into new, WD 76–77
creating with templates, WD 29
entering text, dates, WD 10–13
formatting (visual overview), WD 30–31
formatting professional, WD 49

grammar checking, WD 34–37
hyperlinks. *See* hyperlinks
moving text in, WD 73–78
navigating through page by page,
WD 78–79
opening existing, WD 32–33
previewing, WD 25–26
proofreading, WD 17–18
reviewing, WD 33, WD 64–67
saving, WD 7–8
saving with new name, WD 32–33
searching for words in, WD 79–81
spell-checking, WD 34–37
with title and heading styles (fig.), WD 86
Documents folder, FM 9
dollar sign ($) and cell references, EX 111
domain name, OUT 6
double-spacing, WD 18
drag and drop, EX 39, WD 73
moving text using, WD 73–74
outlines into Sway, PA-7
dragging
and dropping cell ranges, EX 40–41
files to copy, move, FM 19–20
Draw tab tools (fig.), PA-3
drawing canvas, PA-3
duplicating
folders on multiple computers, FM 23
See also copying

E

Edge, OUT 42
Edit Citation dialog box (fig.), WD 105
Edit mode, EX 19, EX 72
Edit Relationships dialog box (fig.), AC 101
editing
cell content, EX 19–20
citations, WD 103, WD 105
contacts, OUT 21
headers, footers, EX 119
presentations, PPT 10–11
sources, WD 110–111
Sway presentations, PA-8
editing mode, keyboard shortcuts (fig.), AC 118
email, OUT 6
adding sentence including email address,
WD 12
attachments. *See* attachments
automatic formatting of addresses, PPT 18
choosing message format, OUT 7–8
contacts. *See* contacts
deleting items, OUT 43–44
hyperlinks, WD 12
importance, sensitivity levels, OUT 12–13
messages. *See* email messages
netiquette guidelines, OUT 15
receiving, OUT 28–34
sending contact information, OUT 22
setting up Outlook for, OUT 6–10

signatures, adding, OUT 9–10
email addresses, OUT 6
email messages
archiving, OUT 43
with attached file (fig.), OUT 32
color categories, OUT 26
completed (fig.), OUT 12
creating, OUT 10–13
creating effective, OUT 13
creating rules for organizing, OUT 36–37
flagging, color coding, OUT 33–34
in Inbox (fig.), OUT 28
moving into folders, OUT 35–36
organizing, managing, OUT 34–38
printing, OUT 30
rearranging, OUT 38–42
replying to, forwarding, OUT 29–30
saving, OUT 42–43
searching for, OUT 38–39
sending, OUT 13–14
sorting, OUT 41–42
storing, OUT 42–43
switching views, arrangements of,
OUT 40–41
visual overview, OUT 26–27
emoticons, OUT 15
entity integrity, AC 68
envelopes, creating, WD 26–29
Envelopes and Labels dialog box (fig.), WD 28
equal sign (=) and formulas, EX 30, EX 32, EX 34
error values, EX 151
creating, EX 152–153
Excel (fig.), EX 152
managing with IF function, EX 179
errors
correcting as you type, WD 14–15
correcting spelling, grammar, WD 31
exact match lookup, EX 171, EX 172
exact matches, specifying, AC 142–144
Excel, EX 1
error values (fig.), EX 152
formulas. *See* formulas
function categories (fig.), EX 145
functions. *See* functions
introduction to, EX 4, EX 6–7
keyboard shortcuts (fig.), EX 6
moving from Touch Mode to Mouse Mode,
EX 6–7
navigation keys (fig.), EX 10
Excel 2016
See also Excel
using in Touch Mode, EX 6–7
Excel workbooks
See also workbooks
described (fig.), EX 2–3
Excel worksheets, importing data from,
AC 80–83
exiting
Access, AC 22–23

Outlook, OUT 43–45
PowerPoint, PPT 60–61
Expression Builder
creating calculated fields with, AC 157
described, AC 156
expressions, AC 156
for calculated field (fig.), AC 158
creating using Expression Builder, AC 157
extending (filling) formulas, EX 159–161
Extract button, FM 29
extracting compressed files, FM 29–30

F

F1 Help, EX 6, AC 40–41
F2 key, AC 118
field lists
Query window, AC 116
Relationships window, AC 77
Field Name column, Table window, AC 52
field properties
determining, AC 56
modifying, AC 71–74
setting, AC 56–58
Field Properties pane
described, AC 53
moving from Table Design grid to, AC 52
field selector, AC 16
Field Size property, AC 57–58
field value, AC 4
fields, WD 108
adding in Design view, AC 69–71
adding to design grid, AC 128
adding to tables, AC 14–16
adding using Data Type gallery, AC 86–88
calculated. *See* calculated fields
Caption property, AC 58
changing alignment of values, AC 213–214
condition for (fig.), AC 140
contact, OUT 15
defining, AC 59–66
Description property, AC 53
Field Size property, AC 57–58
grouping related, into tables, AC 54
hiding, AC 119
identifying all needed, AC 54
including common, in related tables, AC 55
modifying properties, AC 71–74
moving, AC 69
moving, resizing on reports, AC 214–216
moving in design grid, AC 145–146
Quick Start selection, AC 87
renaming in Design view, AC 90
secondary sort, AC 133
setting Default Value property, AC 93–94
sort, AC 131
unhiding, AC 119
Fields tab, AC 2
File Explorer
changing view in, FM 12–13

deleting files, folders, FM 23
  illustrated (fig.), FM 2–3
  moving, copying files and folders, FM 18–20
  opening, FM 9
  opening files, FM 14
  viewing files in (fig.), FM 8
file extensions in Cortana, FM 27
file formats, OUT 42
file icons, FM 3
file paths, FM 2, FM 10
file system, FM 5, FM 6
file types, database, AC 9
filename extensions, FM 15
filenames, FM 3
files, FM 3
  copying, FM 19–23
  deciding where to store, FM 7
  deleting, FM 23
  exploring, FM 7
  finding with Cortana, FM 24–27
  in a folder window (visual overview), FM 2–3
  managing, FM 13–14
  opening, FM 14
  organizing, FM 4–7
  Outlook data, OUT 43
  PowerPoint, PPT 2
  renaming, FM 24
  saving, FM 15–16
  searching for without Cortana, FM 27
  selecting multiple, FM 22
  working with compressed, FM 28–30
fill colors, EX 67, EX 72–75
fill handles, EX 156
fill options, Format Cells dialog box, EX 90
filling
  formulas, EX 159–161
  a series, EX 156–158
Filter By Form, AC 136
Filter By Selection
  described, AC 136
  using, AC 136–138
filtering data, AC 136–138
filters described, AC 136
Find and Replace commands, EX 95
Find and Replace dialog box, WD 81–83, EX 104–105
Find and Replace dialog box (fig.), AC 121, AC 195
Find button, AC 181
Find command, EX 103, AC 121
finding
  data in tables, AC 121–122
  data using forms, AC 194–196
  files and information with Cortana, FM 24–27
finding and replacing
  text, WD 81–83
  text and formats, EX 103–105
First Line Indent marker, WD 96, WD 97

First record button, AC 30
first-level items in lists, PPT 14
Fit slide to current window button, PPT 3
flagging email messages, OUT 26–27, OUT 33–34
flags, OUT 26
Flash Fill
  described, EX 47
  using, EX 47–48
flyers, WD 32
Folder List, OUT 2, OUT 35
Folder Pane, OUT 2
folder window, files in (visual overview), FM 2–3
folders, FM 2
  archiving, OUT 43
  creating, FM 17–18, OUT 35
  deleting, FM 23
  duplicating on multiple computers, FM 23
  exploring with File Explorer, FM 8–9
  managing, FM 13–14
  moving email messages into, OUT 35–36
  organizing, FM 4–7
  Outlook, OUT 2
  Search. *See* Search Folders
  selecting multiple, FM 22
  ways of viewing, FM 11–13
  zipped, FM 3, FM 28
Folders command, OUT 2
Font Color gallery (fig.), WD 43, EX 71
Font Color menu (fig.), PPT 21
font color on reports, AC 217–218
Font commands, and Live Preview, PPT 19
Font gallery (fig.), EX 69
Font group, Home tab, WD 30, EX 66
Font list (fig.), WD 40
Font menu (fig.), PPT 36
font size, EX 30, EX 50, AC 154
fonts, EX 66
  applying colors, EX 70–71
  for Berlin theme, WD 90
  changing, sizing, WD 39–41
  changing colors, EX 73–74
  choosing theme, WD 87, WD 90
  coloring, WD 42–43, WD 46, PPT 20–21
  options, Format Cells dialog box, EX 89
  setting, sizing, WD 30
  sizing, PPT 20
  using complementary, PPT 19
Footer dialog box (fig.), EX 120
footers, WD 98
  described, EX 118
  designing, creating, EX 118–120
foreign key, AC 5
form design, AC 193
form objects, name displayed on tab for the form, AC 180
form records
  displayed in Print Preview (fig.), AC 199

  previewing and printing selected, AC 198–200
form titles, AC 180
Form tool
  creating forms using, AC 33–35
  described, AC 24
Form view
  forms displayed in (visual overview), AC 180–181
  main form with subform in (fig.), AC 202
Form Wizard, AC 24
  creating forms using, AC 182–185, AC 200–204
  described, AC 181
Form Wizard dialog box (fig.), AC 182
Format Cells dialog box, EX 89–91
Format Painter, EX 94
  copying and applying formatting using, PPT 21–22
  copying formats with, EX 100–101
  copying formatting using, WD 47–48
Format Painter button, WD 30
formats
  Accounting, EX 66, EX 80
  copying and pasting, EX 100–102
  Currency, EX 80
  currency, AC 160
  dates, EX 83
  displaying available Date/Time field (fig.), AC 64
  file for Outlook, OUT 42
  finding and replacing, EX 103–105
  General, EX 79, EX 83
  recognized by Excel as date, EX 22
  symbols for some custom date (fig.), AC 65
formatting
  automatic, of email or website addresses, PPT 18
  bibliography as MLA-style works cited list, WD 112
  calculated fields, AC 160
  cell content, EX 68
  cell text, EX 68–75
  conditional, EX 95
  conditional, in reports, AC 218–220
  copying and applying using Format Painter, PPT 21–22
  copying with Format Painter, WD 30, WD 47–48
  dates and times, EX 83
  documents (visual overview), WD 30–31
  email messages, OUT 13
  forms, subforms, AC 201
  MLA-style research papers, WD 94
  monetary values, EX 80
  numbers, EX 79–83
  paragraph, WD 31
  paragraph-level, character-level, WD 84
  professional documents, WD 49
  searching for, in documents, WD 84
  text, PPT 19–21

text in email message, OUT 11–12
text selections within cells, EX 72
text strings within cells, EX 66
worksheet cells, EX 84–89
worksheets, EX 48–50
worksheets (visual overview), EX 66–67
worksheets for printing, EX 113–121
forms, AC 24
   adding pictures to, AC 189–191
   applying themes to, AC 185–188
   changing color of text on, AC 191–192
   created by Form tool (fig.), AC 34
   creating main, with subform, AC 200–204
   creating simple, AC 33–35
   creating using Form Wizard, AC 182–185
   displayed in Form view (visual overview), AC 180–181
   displayed in Layout view (fig.), AC 186
   finding data using, AC 194–196
   icon (fig.), AC 40
   importance of design, AC 193
   maintaining table data using, AC 197–198
   modifying design in Layout view, AC 185–193
   navigating, AC 34–35, AC 193–194
   with picture added (fig.), AC 190
   saving, AC 35
   themes, working with, AC 189
Forms group, AC 24
formula bar, EX 2, EX 30
formulas
   being entered in a cell (fig.), EX 34
   breaking up, EX 39
   calculating sales data using, EX 75–79
   and cell references, EX 161–163
   changing cell references in, EX 165–167
   constants, using, EX 136–139
   copying and pasting, EX 35
   documenting, EX 135
   in effective workbooks, EX 14
   entering, EX 32–34
   entering with mouse, EX 34
   and equal sign (−), EX 30, EX 32
   filling (extending), EX 159–161
   and functions (visual overview), EX 30–31
   with multiple operators, EX 33
   simplifying with functions, EX 36–38
   using absolute references (fig.), EX 163
   using mixed references (fig.), EX 164
   using relative references (fig.), EX 162
   viewing worksheet, EX 55–56
   visual overview, EX 154–155
Forward, OUT 26
Forward button, FM 8
forwarding email messages, OUT 29–30
free-response quizzes, PA-12
From line, email, OUT 10
Function Library group, EX 132
Function Library, using, EX 145
function syntax, EX 35

functions
   See also specific function
   AutoSum, EX 31
   calculating sales data using, EX 75–79
   common math, trig, and statistical (fig.), EX 142
   described (fig.), EX 31
   Excel function categories (fig.), EX 145
   and formulas (visual overview), EX 30–31
   logical, EX 174–179
   simplifying formulas with, EX 35
   syntax, EX 35, EX 141–142
   using Excel, EX 141–149
functions, aggregate. *See* aggregate functions
Functions Arguments dialog box, EX 133
   for IF function (fig.), EX 176
   with VLOOKUP function (fig.), EX 173

G

Gallery of layouts, New Slide menu (fig.), PPT 12
Game Card customer order report (case), EX 1
General format, EX 79, EX 83
General tab, AC 52
Get External Data - Excel Spreadsheet dialog box (fig.), AC 81
gigabytes (GBs), FM 4
Go To command, EX 11
Go To dialog box (fig.), EX 11
Goal Seek
   described, EX 150
   what-if analysis using, EX 150–151
grammar
   checking, PPT 50
   Spelling and Grammar settings, WD 34–37
Grammar Settings dialog box (fig.), WD 35
Grammar task pane, WD 31
graphic elements, adding, AC 180
graphs described, EX 180
grayscale, previewing in, PPT 57
green triangles, EX 22
gridlines
   illustrated (fig.), EX 30
   repositioning objects using, PPT 46
   turning on, PPT 45
Group By operator, AC 166–167
grouped reports, AC 206
grouping
   objects, AC 167–169
   related fields into tables, AC 54
Growing Degree Days (GDD), EX 166–169
Guffey, Mary Ellen, WD 9

H

handles, WD 49
handouts
   draft of (fig.), WD 64–65
   printing slides as, PPT 58

handwriting, converting to text, PA-3–4
Hanging Indent marker, WD 96
hanging paragraphs, WD 95
hard disks, FM 4
hard drive, FM 5
Header & Footer Tools Design contextual tab, WD 99
Header and Footer view, WD 98
Header dialog box (fig.), EX 119
headers, WD 98
   described, EX 118
   designing, creating, EX 118–119
heading styles, WD 85–86, WD 94
headings
   column, EX 3
   row, EX 2
Help
   accessing Access, AC 25
   getting Excel, EX 6
   getting Word, WD 31
   with Office.com, WD 52–54
   using Access, AC 40–41
   windows (fig.), AC 25
Hide Fields command, AC 119
hiding, EX 47
   comments in documents, WD 69
   display of group's objects in Navigation Pane, AC 167
   ribbon, PPT 3
   rows and columns, EX 47
   and unhiding fields, AC 119
   worksheets, EX 47
High importance, email, OUT 12–13
Highlight Cells rules (fig.), EX 107
highlighting
   cells based on their values, EX 107–109
   cells with Top/Bottom rule, EX 109–111
   using with colors, EX 113
Hoisington, Corinne, PA-1
Home tab, WD 2
horizontal lookup tables, EX 171
HTML email format, OUT 7, OUT 8, OUT 42
hyperlinks
   removing, PPT 19
   typing, WD 12

I

icons, Word, WD 3
ID field (primary key field), AC 2
IF function, EX 174–176
   described, EX 155
   managing error values with, EX 179
images
   See also photos, pictures
   adding background, EX 74–75
import described, AC 80
Import Objects dialog box (fig.), AC 85

Import Spreadsheet Wizard dialog box (fig.), AC 82
Import Wizard dialog box (fig.), AC 96
importance levels of email, OUT 12–13
importing
    data from Excel worksheets, AC 80–83
    tables, table structures, AC 83–86
    text files to add data to tables, AC 95–97
Inbox
    checking, OUT 7
    received message in (fig.), OUT 28
indenting
    bullets, WD 72
    cell content, EX 85
    paragraphs, WD 95–98
    paragraphs to create outline, WD 73
indents, common paragraph (fig.), WD 96
Info screen in Backstage view (fig.), PPT 31
information, finding using Cortana, FM 24–27
Ink to Text button, Convert group, Drawing tab, PA-3
inked handwriting, PA-3
inking toolbar, Make a Web Note button (Microsoft Edge), PA-15
inline pictures, WD 52
Input cell style, EX 132
input values, EX 140–141
Insert Function button, EX 132
Insert Function dialog box, EX 145–146, EX 148
inserting
    bibliography, WD 109–110
    cell ranges, EX 45–46
    citations, WD 106–107
    columns or rows, EX 42–44
    copied text into new documents, WD 76–77
    dates in documents, WD 10
    inside addresses in block-style letters, WD 11
    page breaks, WD 108, EX 115–116
    page numbers, WD 98–100
    pictures in documents, WD 49–50
    pictures in reports, AC 217–218
    stored photos, PPT 39–40
    table rows, AC 70–71
    videos into OneNote notebooks, PA-4
    worksheets, EX 15–16
insertion point, PPT 7
    described, WD 2
    keystrokes for moving (fig.), WD 15
inside addresses in block-style letters, WD 11
Instant Search, OUT 21, OUT 26
Integral theme, WD 88
international date formats, EX 22
Internet Explorer, PA-14
interpreting error values, EX 151–153
INT(number) function, EX 142
italic, WD 41, EX 68
italicizing text, OUT 11, AC 191
items described, OUT 2

J
join line (fig.), AC 77
justified alignment, WD 43–44

K
Keep Text Only, Paste Option, WD 75
key combinations, copying folders using, FM 24
key symbol, AC 76
Key Tips, EX 6
keyboard shortcuts, AC 79
    cutting and pasting, PPT 24
    navigation mode (fig.), AC 118
    using, EX 6
    using in Tell Me box, PPT 3, WD 31

L
labels
    extending a series of, with AutoFill, EX 157–158
    moving, resizing on reports, AC 214–216
    on ribbon, AC 13
Lakeside Event Center (case), PPT 1
landscape orientation, EX 53, AC 207
    changing, WD 38
    illustrated (fig.), WD 30–31
Large icons view, FM 11, FM 13
Large icons view button, FM 3
Last record button, AC 30, AC 204
Layout view, AC 34
    displaying forms in, AC 181
    form displayed in (fig.), AC 186
    modifying design of forms in, AC 185–193
    modifying forms in, AC 202–204
    modifying report design in, AC 212–218
layouts, PPT 11
    changing slide, PPT 12
    choosing for forms, AC 183–184
    SmartArt, PPT 25
lectures, recording, PA-4
left alignment, WD 43–44
Left Indent marker, WD 96
legends, creating conditional formatting, EX 111–112
letters, block-style, WD 8–9
Line and Paragraph Spacing button, WD 19
line spacing
    adjusting, WD 18–21
    described, WD 18
List view, FM 11
lists
    bulleted. See bulleted lists
    converting to SmartArt diagrams, PPT 24–28
    creating bulleted, PPT 14–15
    creating numbered, PPT 16–17
    creating unnumbered, PPT 17–18
    numbered. See numbered lists
    organizing information in, WD 70
    using in presentations, PPT 14
    visual overview (fig.), WD 62–63

Live Preview, EX 68
    of changed fonts, WD 40
    of Droplet theme (fig.), EX 106
    and Font commands, PPT 19
    of Less Than conditional format (fig.), EX 108
    and Theme Colors, PPT 20
    of vertical bullet list, SmartArt layout (fig.), PPT 26
live webpages, PA-12
locking cells, EX 90
logical comparison operators (fig.), EX 175
logical functions, EX 174–179
logical operators, AC 149
Long Date format, EX 83
lookup tables, EX 171

M
Mail described, OUT 2
main form, AC 200
maintaining, AC 118
    databases, AC 41–43
    table data using forms, AC 197–198
managing
    email messages, OUT 34–38
    files, folders, FM 13–24
manipulating slides, PPT 28–30
manual line breaks, WD 21
manual page breaks, EX 94, EX 115–116
margins, WD 2, EX 120
    and Alignment buttons, WD 30
    changing, WD 38
    changing report's, AC 212
    described, adjusting, WD 22–25
    gallery (fig.), WD 24
    setting page, EX 120–121
marking comments, WD 69
matches
    of range of values, AC 147–149
    specifying exact, AC 142–144
MAX function, EX 35, EX 132, EX 142, EX 147
Maximize button, EX 3, WD 3
maximizing Outlook window, OUT 4
Maximum aggregate function, AC 163
MEDIAN function, EX 132, EX 142, EX 147–148
Medium icons view, FM 11
Memo Style, OUT 30
menus
    See also specific menu
    shortcut, AC 12, WD 12–13
Merge Formatting, Paste Option, WD 75
merging cells, EX 87–88
message headers, OUT 26, OUT 28
MHT files, OUT 42
Miami Trolleys (case), FM 1
Microsoft Access 2016, AC 1
    See also Access
    .accdb files, AC 9

Microsoft Access Help button, AC 25

Microsoft account, accessing information about, WD 3

Microsoft accounts
    and OneDrive, FM 15
    signing in, PPT 3

Microsoft Edge, browsing the web with, PA-14

Microsoft Edge tools (fig.), PA-14

Microsoft Excel. *See* Microsoft Excel

Microsoft Excel 2016
    See also Excel
    described, EX 1

Microsoft Office Word 2016
    See also Word
    described, WD 1

Microsoft OneNote Mobile app, PA-2, PA-3

Microsoft Outlook 2016
    See also Outlook
    described, OUT 1

Microsoft PowerPoint 2016
    See also PowerPoint
    described, PPT 1

MIN function, EX 35, EX 132, EX 142, EX 146–147

Mini toolbar, WD 12, PPT 19, WD 19, EX 72

Minimize button, EX 3, WD 3

minimizing Outlook window, OUT 4

Minimum aggregate function, AC 163

misspellings
    and AutoCorrect, WD 14–15
    correcting, PPT 50–52
    shortcut menu with suggested spelling (fig.), WD 16
    suggested corrections, WD 31

mixed cell references, EX 155, EX 163–164, EX 166

MLA formatting guidelines (visual overview), WD 92–93

MLA Handbook for Writers of Research Papers, WD 94, WD 101

MLA style
    guidelines for citing books, journals, WD 101
    reviewing, WD 94–95
    style research papers, formatting, WD 94

Modern Language Association (MLA) style
    See also MLA style
    described, WD 94

monetary formats, EX 80

More slide show options, PPT 32–33

Morning Bean shops (case), EX 65

mouse, entering formulas using, EX 34

Mouse Mode
    described, EX 6–7
    switching with Touch Mode, WD 5, AC 10, PPT 6–7

Move Items dialog box (fig.), FM 21

Move to button, FM 21

moving
    and copying cells, EX 39–41
    and copying text, PPT 22–24
    described, FM 18
    email messages into folders, OUT 35–36
    fields in design grid, AC 145–146
    fields in Design view, AC 69
    fields in reports, AC 214–216
    files by dragging, FM 19
    insertion point, WD 15
    from one fields to another, AC 18
    and resizing pictures, PPT 44–47
    and resizing text boxes, PPT 47–48
    text in documents, WD 73–78
    texting using cut and paste, WD 75
    worksheets, EX 16

multiple selection criteria, defining queries for, AC 149–153

multitable queries, creating, AC 129–130

Music folder, FM 9

Musical Notes (case), OUT 1

N

Name box, EX 2, EX 11

naming
    See also renaming
    documents, WD 32–33
    fields, AC 12
    fields, objects, AC 56
    fields vs. setting Caption property, AC 57
    presentations, PPT 34–35
    queries, AC 116
    tables, AC 2
    workbooks, EX 56–57

navigating
    Data Files, FM 10, FM 10–11
    datasheets, AC 29–30
    forms, AC 34–35, AC 193–194
    between Outlook elements, OUT 4–5
    through documents page by page, WD 78–79
    within worksheets, EX 9–11

navigation bar, Backstage view, PPT 9

navigation buttons, AC 29, AC 180, AC 203, AC 206

navigation keys (fig.), EX 10

navigation mode
    described, AC 118
    keyboard shortcuts (fig.), AC 118

Navigation Pane, AC 2, WD 62
    File Explorer, FM 2
    menu (fig.), AC 168
    opening, WD 63
    tables listed in, AC 22
    using, WD 78–81
    viewing database objects in, AC 221
    viewing objects in, AC 40
    working with, AC 167–169

navigation techniques, FM 9

nested functions, EX 143

nesting ROUND and AVERAGE functions, EX 143–145

netiquette guidelines, OUT 15

networks described, FM 5

New Contact button, OUT 16

New folder button, FM 17

New Formatting Rule dialog box (fig.), AC 219

Next record button, AC 30, AC 203

nonadjacent ranges, EX 2, EX 12–13

nonprinting characters, WD 2, WD 6, WD 10

nonunique (sort field), AC 132

Normal view, PPT 6, EX 31

Notebook
    accessing Cortana, FM 26–27
    described, FM 25

notebooks, OneNote, PA-2–3

notes, PPT 48, PA-3

notes, speaker, PPT 48–50

Notes described, OUT 2

Notes Page view, PPT 49

Notes pane, PPT 48

null value, AC 68

Number group, EX 67

numbered lists
    creating, PPT 16–17, WD 70–73
    described, PPT 16, WD 70

Numbering button, WD 62, WD 72–73

numbering styles gallery, PPT 16

numbers
    applying to paragraphs, WD 72–73
    displaying as text, EX 21–22
    displaying significant digits, EX 140
    entering, EX 24
    formatting, EX 79–83, EX 89
    formatting options, Format Cells dialog box, EX 89

numeric data, EX 17

O

Object Type, Navigation Pane, AC 167

objects
    database. *See* database objects
    grouping, AC 167–169
    opening Access, AC 22
    resizing and moving, PPT 44–48

Office accounts, Sign in link, AC 2

Office Clipboard, PPT 24, WD 75

Office Mix, PA-10

Office theme, PPT 35, WD 87–88

Office.com
    category of SmartArt, PPT 25
    getting Word Help, WD 52–54
    online templates, PPT 38
    online themes, PPT 35

offline, OUT 13

OneDrive, FM 5, FM 6
database backups, AC 43
described, FM 2
saving files to, WD 7, FM 15
saving presentations to, PPT 8–9
saving workbooks on, EX 17
and Share link, PowerPoint window, PPT 3
storing Sway sites on, PA-6
syncing with OneNote notes, PA-2
OneNote, PA-2
creating notebook, PA-2
syncing notebooks to the cloud, PA-2–3
one-to-many relationships, AC 98–99, AC 200
defining, AC 102
described, AC 76
opening
Access objects, AC 22
Contact Group window, OUT 23
databases, AC 26
existing documents, WD 32–33
existing workbooks, EX 4–5, EX 134
File Explorer, FM 9
files, FM 14
Navigation pane, WD 63
presentations, PPT 34
Query window in Design view, AC 125
tables, AC 22, AC 119
Themes gallery, WD 88–89
operators, EX 32
arithmetic (fig.), EX 32
comparison. See comparison operators
logical. See logical operators
logical comparison (fig.), EX 175
optional arguments, EX 133, EX 146
Or logical operator, AC 149, AC 152–153
vs. And logical operator, AC 153
order of operations, EX 32, EX 33
organizing
data, AC 4
data into smallest part(s), AC 54
email messages, OUT 34–38
files and folders, FM 4–7
orientation, page, EX 52–53, EX 53
characters, WD 38
landscape, illustrated (fig.), WD 30–31
OS (C:), FM 7
outlines
dragging into Sway, PA-7
printing slides as, PPT 59–60
Outlook, OUT 1
exiting, OUT 43–44
exploring, OUT 4–6
file formats, OUT 42
setting up for email, OUT 6–10
window (visual overview), OUT 2–3
Outlook data files, OUT 43
Outlook Options dialog box, Mail options (fig.),
OUT 8
OwnerData form, AC 181, AC 184

P

Page Break Preview, EX 31, EX 50, EX 95,
EX 113–114
page breaks
automatic, EX 95
inserting, WD 108, EX 115–116
manual (fig.), EX 94
removing, EX 116
Page Layout tab, EX 30, EX 94
Page Layout view, EX 31, EX 50–52, EX 119
page margins, setting, EX 120–121
page number fields, WD 98
page numbers
adding for citations, WD 105
inserting, modifying, WD 98–100
on reports, AC 37–38
styles gallery, WD 99
page orientation
changing, WD 38, EX 52–53
changing report's, AC 212
landscape, illustrated (fig.), WD 30–31
portrait and landscape, AC 207
Page Setup dialog box (fig.), EX 117
pages
changing margins, WD 23–24
line and paragraph spacing, WD 20–21
panes. See specific pane
paragraph borders, WD 45
paragraph marks (¶), WD 2, WD 6
paragraph spacing, WD 18, WD 48
paragraph-level formatting, WD 84
paragraphs
adding borders, shading, WD 45–47
adjusting, WD 18–21
applying bullets to, WD 71–72
deleting, WD 13
described, WD 18
formatting, WD 31
indenting, WD 95–98
spacing between, WD 21
parentheses (()) in formulas, EX 33
password-protecting OneNote notebooks, PA-4
passwords described, OUT 6
paste described, WD 75
Paste Options button, WD 75–78
Paste Options button, copying formats with,
EX 101–102
Paste Options menu (fig.), PPT 23, WD 77
Paste Special, copying formats with, EX 102
Paste Special dialog box (fig.), EX 102
pasting
formats, EX 100–102
formulas, EX 35
records into databases, AC 28
text using Clipboard, WD 75–78
pencil symbol, AC 17
People button, OUT 2, OUT 5

Percent style, EX 67
percentages, EX 82–83
Personal sensitivity level of email, OUT 13
photo compression settings (fig.), PPT 42
photos
See also images, pictures
adding styles to, WD 51–52
compressing, PPT 42–44
cropping, PPT 40–42
inserted on slide (fig.), PPT 39
inserting stored, PPT 39–40
keeping uncompressed, PPT 44
modifying compression options, PPT 42–44
and Pictures button, Word window,
WD 30
removing cropped areas, PPT 43
resizing, WD 50–51
selecting, WD 49–50
working with, PPT 38
picture styles, WD 51–52
Picture Styles gallery, WD 51–52
pictures
See also images, photos
adding to forms, AC 189–191
described, WD 49
inline, WD 52
inserting in reports, AC 217–218
resizing and moving, PPT 44–48
working with, WD 49–52
Pictures button, WD 30
Pictures folder, FM 9
placeholders, PPT 2
buttons on content, PPT 39
for list bullets, numbers, PPT 16
text, PPT 7
plagiarism, citations, WD 102
Plain Text email format, OUT 7–8
planning
database backups, AC 43
presentations, PPT 4
tables, AC 11–12
workbooks, EX 13–14
plus sign, in keyboard shortcuts, EX 6
point, WD 18
pointer in Slide Show view, PPT 32
points, PPT 14, EX 28
portrait orientation, AC 207
pound sign (#####) errors, EX 24, EX 81
PowerPoint, PPT 1
adding Office Mix to, PA-10
exiting, PPT 60–61
starting, PPT 5–6
PowerPoint files, PPT 2
PowerPoint Option dialog box, PPT 44
PowerPoint window
with Touch mode active (fig.), PPT 7
visual overviews, PPT 2–3
presentation media, PPT 4

presentations, PPT 4
  adding new slides, PPT 11–14
  closing, PPT 30–31
  creating new, PPT 5–7
  creating Sway, PA-6–7
  displaying blank slides during, PPT 55
  editing, PPT 10–11
  Office Mix, PA-12
  opening, PPT 34
  planning, PPT 4
  printing, PPT 56–58
  publishing Sway, PA-8
  rearranging slides in, PPT 29
  saving, PPT 8–9, PPT 11
  spell-checking, PPT 50–52
  title slides, PPT 7–8
Presenter view
  using, PPT 52, PPT 54
  visual overviews, PPT 33
previewing
  documents, WD 25–26
  email messages, OUT 30
  reports, AC 220
  selected form records, AC 198–200
Previous record button, AC 30, AC 204
primary key, AC 5
  changing data types of, AC 13–14
  determining each table's, AC 54–55
  importance of, AC 68
  renaming default field, AC 12–13
  specifying, AC 67
primary sort field, AC 133
primary tables, AC 77
print area
  defining, EX 114–115
  described, EX 95
Print Layout view, WD 3, WD 26, WD 94
Print option in Backstage view, WD 25
Print Preview
  closing, AC 207
  finished report in (fig.), AC 220
  first page of report in (fig.), AC 38
  form records displayed in (fig.), AC 199
  report displayed in (visual overview),
    AC 206–207
Print screen, Backstage view, PPT 56–57
Print tab, Backstage view, OUT 26
print titles, EX 94, EX 117–118
Printer Properties, PPT 57
printing
  email messages, OUT 30
  formatting worksheets for, EX 113–121
  presentations, PPT 56–58
  reports, AC 39–40, AC 220–221
  scaling printed output, EX 53
  selected form records, AC 198–200
  setting print options, EX 54–55
  slides as handouts, PPT 58
  slides as outlines, PPT 59–60
  workbooks, EX 50–55, EX 121

printouts, designing (visual overview), EX 94–95
Private sensitivity level of email, OUT 13
problem solving, writing effective formulas, EX 39
productivity apps
  creating OneNote notebook, PA-2
  recording lectures, PA-4
  syncing OneNote notebooks to the cloud,
    PA-2–3
proofreading
  documents, WD 17–18
  your document, WD 37
properties, AC 56
  determining field, AC 56
  setting field, AC 56–58
Property Sheet for calculated field (fig.), AC 159
publishing Swap presentations, PA-8

Q
queries, AC 24
  with aggregate functions entered (fig.),
    AC 165
  creating and running, AC 125–127
  creating multitable, AC 129–130
  creating new, AC 157–158
  creating reports based on, AC 208
  creating simple, AC 30–33
  creating with aggregate functions,
    AC 163–165
  creating with And logical operator,
    AC 149–151
  creating with Group By operator, AC 166–167
  creating with Or logical operator, AC 152–153
  defining multiple selection criteria for,
    AC 149–153
  defining record selection criteria for,
    AC 142–149
  designing, vs. using Query Wizard, AC 124
  icon (fig.), AC 40
  introduction, AC 124–125
  matches, specifying exact, AC 142–144
  modifying, AC 144–147
  naming, AC 116
  results (fig.), AC 141
  saving, AC 35
  selection criteria in (visual overview),
    AC 140–141
  sorting data in, AC 131–135
  updating data using, AC 128–129
Queries group, AC 24
query by example (QBE), AC 117
query datasheets, sorting, AC 133
query results (fig.), AC 32, AC 141, AC 165
Query Tools Design tab, on ribbon, AC 117
Query Type group, active Select button, AC 116
Query window
  in Design view (visual overview), AC 116–117
  opening in Design view, AC 125
  with Or logical operator (fig.), AC 152
Query Wizard button, AC 24

Query Wizard vs. designing queries, AC 124
Quick access list, FM 2, FM 9
Quick Access Toolbar, PPT 2, WD 2, PPT 22
  described, AC 2, FM 2
  Save button on, WD 7, AC 23, AC 74
  Undo, Redo buttons, WD 13–14
Quick Analysis tool, EX 109
  summarizing data with, EX 167–169
  using, EX 109–111
Quick Print, AC 39
Quick Start selection, AC 87
Quincy Rivers College handout (case), WD 61
quizzes, adding to slides, PA-12

R
ragged (text alignment), WD 43–44
RAND() function, EX 142
range references, EX 12
ranges. See cell ranges
readability, formatting workbooks for, EX 92
Reading Pane, OUT 3, OUT 27, OUT 33
Reading view, PPT 55–56
Reading view (Microsoft Edge), PA-14
rearranging
  email messages, OUT 38–42
  slides in presentations, PPT 29
receiving email messages, OUT 28–34
Recent locations button, FM 8
Recent screen in Backstage view (fig.), EX 4,
  PPT 5, AC 8
record selector, AC 16
recording lectures, PA-4
records, AC 4
  adding to new tables, AC 78–80
  adding to tables, AC 94
  adding using forms, AC 198
  copying from another Access database,
    AC 26–29
  creating based on query, AC 208
  defining record selection criteria for queries,
    AC 142–149
  deleting, AC 122–124
  detail, AC 207, AC 210
  display, and primary key, AC 68
  entering, AC 16–19
  entering new (fig.), AC 20
  finding using wildcard characters,
    AC 195–196
  modifying, AC 118–119
  previewing and printing selected form,
    AC 198–200
  sorting with AutoFilter, AC 131–132
recordsets, AC 124
Recycle Bin, FM 23
red wavy underlining for misspellings, WD 18
Redo button, using, WD 13–14
redoing, undoing actions, EX 19, PPT 22

redundancy. *See* data redundancy

References tab, WD 93, WD 103

referential integrity, AC 99, AC 101, AC 103

related tables, AC 77

relational database management system, AC 6

relational databases, AC 4

relationships
defining between two tables, AC 99–103
one-to-many, AC 76

Relationships window, AC 76
adding tables to, AC 100
defined relationship in (fig.), AC 102

relative cell references, EX 154, EX 161–163, EX 165–166

reminders using Cortana, FM 26–27

Removable Disk (D:), FM 7, FM 10

removing
See also deleting
cropped areas, PPT 43
hyperlinks, PPT 19
page breaks, EX 116

renaming
See also naming
default primary key field, AC 12–13
documents, WD 65
fields in Design view, AC 90
files, FM 24
worksheets, EX 15–16

repairing databases, AC 42–43

Replace and Find commands, EX 95

Replace tab, Find and Replace dialog box, WD 81

replacing text, WD 81–83

Reply, Reply All, OUT 26, OUT 29

replying to email, OUT 29–30

report objects, AC 206

report titles, AC 206

Report tool, AC 25

Report Wizard, AC 25, AC 207
creating report using, AC 208–212
starting, AC 208

reports
changing page orientation, margins, AC 212
conditional formatting, using, AC 218–220
created by Report tool (fig.), AC 36
creating, AC 35–39
creating using Report Wizard, AC 208–212
displayed in Print Preview (visual overview), AC 206–207
finished, in Print Preview (fig.), AC 220
first page, in Print Preview (fig.), AC 38
grouped, AC 206
inserting pictures, AC 217–218
modifying design in Layout view, AC 212–218
previewing, AC 220
printing, AC 39–40, AC 220–221
saving, AC 35
themes, applying to, AC 212–213

Reports group, AC 25

required arguments, EX 133, EX 146

research papers
acknowledging sources, WD 102
inserting citations, bibliography, WD 100–112
MLA style, WD 94

resizing
See also sizing
columns, AC 36–37
fields in reports, AC 214–216
and moving pictures, PPT 44–47
and moving text boxes, PPT 47–48
photos, WD 50–51
worksheet columns, rows, EX 25–29

resolution, and photo compression settings (fig.), PPT 42

responsive design, PA-6

Restore Down button, EX 3, WD 3

restoring
databases, AC 43
search options to original settings, WD 83

Return to the previous slide button, PPT 32

return values described, EX 155

reviewing
documents, WD 33, WD 64–67
MLA style, WD 94–95
slide shows, PPT 54

RGB Color model, EX 71

ribbon, WD 2, AC 2, PPT 2, OUT 3
buttons and labels on, AC 13
displayed in Touch Mode (fig.), AC 10
hiding, displaying, PPT 3
tabs on (fig.), EX 2

Ribbon Display Options button, EX 3, OUT 3, PPT 3, WD 3

Rich Text email format, OUT 7

right alignment, WD 43–44

Right Indent marker, WD 96

right-clicking to display shortcut menus, WD 12

Riverview Veterinary Care Center (case)
creating and modifying tables, AC 51
creating database, AC 1
updating tables, retrieving information, AC 115
using forms, reports

root directory, FM 5, FM 6

rotating cell content, EX 88–89

ROUND function, EX 132, EX 149
described, EX 142
nesting, EX 143–145

rounding, methods of, EX 149

row headings, EX 2

row selector, AC 16

rows, datasheet, AC 2

rows, inserting table, AC 70–71

rows, worksheet
changing heights, EX 28–29
deleting, EX 43–45
formatting titles, EX 90–91

hiding, unhiding, EX 47
inserting, EX 42–44
navigating within worksheets, EX 9–11
resizing, EX 25–29

ruler, WD 2
displaying, WD 6
indents on, WD 96

rules
conditional formatting, AC 218–220
for organizing email messages, OUT 27, OUT 36–37
running, OUT 36–37

Rules Wizard, OUT 36

Run button, AC 116

running
queries, AC 125–127, AC 147
rules, OUT 36–37
slide shows, PPT 52–56

running totals, EX 167–169

S

sales
average results (fig.), EX 97
data, calculating, EX 75–79
formatted monthly gross (fig.), EX 87
formatted values (fig.), EX 82
statistics (fig.), EX 77

salutation in block-style letters, WD 12

sandbox (Microsoft Edge), PA-15

Save As command, PPT 34, OUT 42

Save As dialog box, WD 7–8

Save As dialog box (fig.), PPT 9, FM 16

Save button, Quick Access Toolbar, AC 23

Save command, EX 6, PPT 10

saving
database objects, AC 35
databases, AC 23
documents, WD 7–8
documents with new name, WD 32–33
email attachments, OUT 32–33
email messages, OUT 42–43
files, FM 15–16
presentations, PPT 8–9, PPT 11
presentations with new name, PPT 34–35
table structures, AC 68
tables, AC 19–20, AC 74
themes, EX 106
workbooks, EX 17, EX 121
workbooks with new filenames, EX 56–57

scaling printed output, EX 53

school, productivity apps for, PA-1–4

screen recordings, PA-11

ScreenTips, EX 6, WD 10
file details, FM 11
illustrated (fig.), FM 2
for links, PPT 52

scroll arrows, WD 3

scroll box, WD 3

scrolling through worksheets, EX 10

Search box, FM 3, FM 8, AC 25, AC 180

Search document box, Navigation pane, WD 79

Search Folders, OUT 26, OUT 39–40, OUT 40

Search for more things button, WD 62

search results, WD 78

Search results (fig.), FM 27

search text, WD 62, WD 78

searching
Cortana, locating information with, PA-14–15
for email messages, OUT 38–39
for files without Cortana, FM 27
restoring search options to original settings, WD 83
for templates online, WD 29
the web for information on word, phrase, WD 53
the web with Microsoft Edge, PA-14
for words in documents, WD 79–81

secondary sort field, AC 133

second-level items in lists, PPT 14

section tabs, OneNote, PA-2

See all slides button, PPT 32

Select Members: Contact dialog box (fig.), OUT 23

selecting
multiple files, folders, FM 22
photos, WD 49–50
text, methods for (fig.), WD 22

selection criteria in queries (visual overview), AC 140–141

sending email messages, OUT 13–14

sensitivity levels of email, OUT 12–13

Sent Items folder with sent message (fig.), OUT 14

series (of data values)
extending labels with AutoFill, EX 157–158
filling, EX 156–158
patterns extended with AutoFill (fig.), EX 157

Series dialog box (fig.), EX 159

servers described, FM 5

setting up
Cortana, FM 25–26
custom margins, WD 25
Outlook for email, OUT 6–10
Word window, WD 6

settings
photo compression, PPT 43
printing, PPT 58

shading, WD 45, AC 211
paragraphs, WD 45–47
using, AC 207

Shading button, WD 30

Shading gallery with Live Preview (fig.), WD 46

Share link, PowerPoint window, PPT 3

sharing
Office Mix presentations, PA-12
styles, themes, EX 106
Sway sites, PA-8

sheet tabs, active sheet, EX 8

sheets
changing active, EX 8–9
chart sheets. See chart sheets
work. See worksheets
in workbook sheet tab (fig.), EX 3

Short Date format, EX 83, EX 170

Short Text data type, AC 13, AC 14, AC 57, AC 60, AC 61

shortcut menus, AC 12
accessing, WD 12–13
for applying themes (fig.), AC 188
for selected slides (fig.), PPT 30
with suggested spelling (fig.), WD 16

shortcuts, keyboard, EX 6, AC 79

Show Table button, AC 76

Show Table dialog box (fig.), AC 100, AC 125

Show Tabs and Commands, WD 3

Show/Hide button, WD 3, WD 6

showing
See also displaying, viewing
comments in documents, WD 69

Shutter Bar Open/Close Button, AC 2

Sign in link, AC 2

signatures, adding to email, OUT 9–10

Signatures button, OUT 9

Simple Query Wizard
described, AC 24
using, AC 31–33

Simple Query Wizard dialog box (fig.), AC 31

single-spacing, WD 18

size, changing font, AC 154

sizing
See also resizing
fonts, PPT 20, WD 30, WD 39–41, EX 50
and moving pictures, PPT 44–47

sizing button, Outlook window, OUT 3

sizing handles, PPT 44

Slide Notes, PA-11

slide recordings, PA-11

Slide Show view
using, PPT 52–53
visual overview, PPT 32

slide shows
reviewing, PPT 54
running, PPT 52–56

Slide Sorter view, PPT 28, PPT 29

slides
See also slide shows
adding company name, slogan to, PPT 8
adding new, PPT 11–14
creating lists, PPT 14–19
displaying blank during presentations, PPT 55
duplicating, PPT 28
manipulating, PPT 28–30
PowerPoint files, PPT 2
printing as handouts, PPT 58
printing as outlines, PPT 59–60

rearranging in presentations, PPT 29
shortcut menu for selected (fig.), PPT 30
in Slides pane, PPT 2

Slides pane, PowerPoint window, PPT 2, PPT 6

Small icons view, FM 11

smart guides, PPT 44, PPT 46

SmartArt diagrams
converting bulleted lists into, PPT 25
converting lists to, PPT 24–28
illustrated (fig.), PPT 27

SmartArt layouts, PPT 25

smileys, OUT 15

snap to grid, PPT 45

soft returns, WD 21

sort field, AC 131

sort order, AC 209

sorting, FM 13, OUT 26
data in queries, AC 131–135
email messages, OUT 41–42
files, folders, FM 13
query datasheets, AC 133

sources
acknowledging your, WD 102
Create Source dialog box (fig.), WD 104
modifying existing, WD 110–111

space between words, character marking, WD 6

spaces in field names, AC 12

spacing
line. See line spacing
line and paragraph options, WD 20–21
paragraph, WD 18, WD 48
between paragraphs, WD 21

speaker notes, PPT 48
adding, PPT 48–50
printing, PPT 59

spell-checking, WD 34–37

spelling, checking, PPT 50–52

Spelling & Grammar button, WD 31

Spelling and Grammar settings, WD 34–37

Spelling task pane, WD 31, WD 36, PPT 50, PPT 51

spreadsheet programs vs. DBMSs, AC 7

spreadsheets described, EX 4

Standard Colors, WD 46. WD 87, EX 70, AC 155

star symbol, AC 17

starting
Access, AC 7–8
Form Wizard, AC 182
new workbooks, EX 14–17
Outlook, OUT 4
PowerPoint, PPT 5–6
Report Wizard, AC 208
Simple Query Wizard, AC 31
Word, WD 4

stationery, using with email, OUT 10

status bar, AC 2, EX 2, FM 2, WD 2, PPT 2

status bar view buttons, AC 117

storing email messages, OUT 42–43

Storylines (Sway), PA-6

strikethrough, EX 68

strings, text, EX 17

Style box, WD 93

Style button, Citations & Bibliography group, WD 103

style guides, WD 94

styles, WD 63, WD 84
See also specific style
adding to photos, WD 51–52
block-style letters, WD 9
cell, EX 95, EX 98–100
page number, WD 99
sharing, EX 106
visual overview (fig.), WD 62–63
working with, WD 84–87

Styles gallery, WD 84–85

subfolders, FM 5, OUT 26

subforms
creating, AC 201–204
described, AC 200–204

subitems in lists, PPT 14, PPT 15

SUM function, EX 35–39, EX 76, EX 78, EX 142

summarizing
data with logical operators, EX 177–178
data with Quick Analysis tool, EX 167–169

Sway
adding content to build stories, PA-7
creating presentations, PA-6–7

Sway sites, PA-6, PA-8

Sways, PA-2

switching
contact views, OUT 20–21
between navigation and editing mode, AC 118
between Touch and Mouse mode, WD 5, PPT 6–7
between Touch Mode and Mouse Mode, AC 10
views, PPT 29
views and arrangements of email messages, OUT 40–41

symbols
currency, EX 80
not allowed in filenames, FM 15
for some custom date formats (fig.), AC 65

syncing
described, PA-2
OneNote notebooks to the cloud, PA-2–3

syntax, function, EX 35, EX 141–142

T

table data, maintaining using forms, AC 197–198

Table Design grid, AC 52

table relationships
introduction, AC 97–98
one-to-many, AC 98–99

table structures
creating by importing existing, AC 84–86
deleting fields from, AC 88–89
modifying imported, AC 88–92

Table window in Design view (visual overview), AC 52–53

Table window, table with three fields (fig.), AC 63

tables, AC 4
adding data from imported text files, AC 95–97
adding fields to, AC 14–16, AC 86–88
adding records to, AC 94
adding records to new, AC 78–80
with all fields entered (fig.), AC 16
closing, AC 22–23
creating by importing existing, AC 83–86
creating in Datasheet view, AC 11
creating in Design view, AC 59–68
in database (fig.), AC 27
in Datasheet view (visual overview, AC 76–77
default name of, AC 2
defining relationship between two, AC 99–103
entering tables, AC 16–19
finding data in, AC 121–122
icon (fig.), AC 40
importing, AC 86
after importing data (fig.), AC 83
modifying field properties, AC 71–74
modifying structures of Access, AC 68–71
naming, AC 52
opening, AC 22
organizing related fields into, AC 54
planning, AC 11–12
primary. *See primary tables*
related, AC 77
renaming default primary key field, AC 12–13
saving, AC19–20
saving structure, AC 68
storing data in separate, AC 6

Tables group options, AC 24

tabs, WD 2
See also specific tab
contextual, PPT 7, AC 13
OneNote section, PA-2
on ribbon, PPT 2

Tabular form layout, AC 183

task panes, WD 31, PPT 50

Tasks
described, OUT 2
displaying element, OUT 5–6

teamwork, communicating effectively within groups, OUT 45

Tell Me box
using keywords in, WD 31
Word Help, WD 52–53
PowerPoint window, PPT 3

Tell me what you want to do box
described (fig.), EX 3
getting Help, EX 6

templates, AC 8, WD 26, PPT 38
creating documents with, WD 29
meeting notes, PA-3
obtaining online, WD 29
OneNote, PA-2
vs. themes, PPT 38

templates described, EX 4

Templates.office.com, WD 87

testing
formulas, EX 39
workbooks, EX 14

text
adding sentence including email address, WD 12–13
aligning with Alignment buttons, WD 30
alignment types, WD 43–44
applying effects, font colors, font styles, WD 41–43
AutoComplete, using, EX 20–21
being entered with Flash Fill (fig.), EX 47
bolding, italicizing, underlining, AC 191
centering, WD 44
changing color of on forms, AC 191–192
converting handwriting to, PA-3–4
counting, EX 143
cutting and pasting using Clipboard, WD 75–78
deleting characters with Backspace or Delete keys, PPT 10
displaying numbers as, EX 21–22
entering, WD 10–13
entering in worksheets, EX 17–18
finding and replacing, WD 81–83, EX 103–105
fonts, WD 39–41
formatting, PPT 19–21
formatting cell, EX 68–75
formatting selections within cells, EX 72
formatting with Format Painter, WD 30
justified, right, left, alignments, WD 43–44
methods of selecting (fig.), WD 22
moving and copying, PPT 22–24
moving in documents, WD 73–78
points, PPT 14
proofreading, WD 17–18
search, WD 62, WD 78
shading, WD 30
undoing entry, EX 19
wrapping within cells, EX 27–28

text boxes
AutoFit options, PPT 15
described, PPT 7
resizing and moving, PPT 47–48

text data, EX 17

Text Effects and Typography button, Font group, Home tab, WD 41–42

text effects, applying, WD 41–42

text files, adding data to tables by importing, AC 95–97

text placeholders, PPT 7

Text Shadow button, PPT 20

text strings
    described, EX 17
    formatting within cells, EX 66
Theme Colors, WD 46, WD 87, EX 70, AC 155, PPT 20
theme families, PPT 35
theme fonts, PPT 36, EX 68
themes, EX 68, WD 87, AC 154, AC 181, OUT 10, PPT 35
    adding to reports, AC 212–213
    applying to database objects, AC 185–188
    applying to forms, AC 181
    changing, PPT 35–36
    changing alternate row colors in datasheets, AC 154–156
    obtaining online, WD 87
    sharing, EX 106
    vs. templates, PPT 38
    working with, WD 87–90, EX 105–106, AC 189
Themes button, WD 87
Themes gallery (fig.), PPT 37, AC 187
Thesaurus button, Proofing group, Review tab, PPT 50
This PC, FM 9
thumbnail images (fig.), FM 3
thumbnails
    described, PPT 6
    in Slides pane, PPT 6
Tiles view, FM 11
time data, EX 17
timer, PPT 33
times, formatting, EX 83
Title and Content layout, PPT 13
title bar, AC 2, EX 2, WD 2, PPT 3
title slides, PPT 7
    adding company name, slogan to, PPT 8
    adding name to, PPT 30–31
    creating, PPT 7–8
    printing, PPT 58–59
    printing as full-page slides, PPT 58–59
Title style, WD 63
titles, adding print, EX 117–118
To Do tags, PA-2
To line, email, OUT 10–11
TODAY function, EX 154, EX 169–170
Top 10% dialog box (fig.), EX 110
Top/Bottom rule, EX 109–111
Total row
    and aggregate functions, AC 162–163
    inserted in design grid (fig.), AC 164
Touch Mode, WD 5, EX 6–7
    described, working in, PPT 6–7
    ribbon in (fig.), AC 10
    switching to, AC 10
    working in, AC 9
Touch/Mouse mode command, WD 5

U

underline, EX 68
underlining text, OUT 11, AC 191
Undo button, EX 19
Undo button, using, WD 13–14
undoing, redoing actions, EX 19, PPT 22
Unhide Columns dialog box (fig.), AC 120
Unhide Fields command, AC 119
unhiding, EX 47
    fields, AC 119
    rows and columns, EX 47
unique (sort field), AC 132
unnumbered lists
    creating, PPT 17–18
    described, PPT 17
Up to button, FM 8
updating, AC 118
    bibliographies, WD 111
    data using queries, AC 128–129
    databases, AC 118–124
    workbook files, EX 56
USB drives, FM 6, PPT 8–9, FM 23
USB flash drives, FM 4
user-friendly workbooks, making, EX 134–141
usernames described, OUT 6

V

#VALUE! error value, EX 151–153
variants, theme, PPT 36–37
verbal communication, planning presentations, PPT 4
vertical lookup tables, EX 155, EX 171
video clips, capturing, PA-11
videos, inserting into OneNote notebooks, PA-4
View buttons, WD 3, AC 116
view buttons on status bar, AC 117
View tab, FM 2
viewing
    See also displaying, showing
    datasheets, AC 96–97
    objects in Navigation Pane, AC 40
    reports in Print Preview, AC 211–213
    sheets in workbook, EX 8–9
    tables in Datasheet view, AC 74–75
    worksheet formulas, EX 55–56
views
    See also specific view
    changing, FM 11–13
    changing worksheet, EX 50–52
    switching, OUT 40–41
    switching between, PPT 3
    switching contact, OUT 20–21
Villa Rio Records (case), WD 1
Vista Grande Neighborhood Center (case), WD 119

visual overviews
    Access window, AC 2–3
    cell references and formulas, EX 154–155
    chart elements, EX 180–181
    Create tab options, AC 24–25
    designing printouts, EX 94–95
    email messages and attachments, OUT 26–27
    files in a folder window, FM 2–3
    formatting worksheets, EX 66–67
    formatting documents, WD 30–31
    forms displayed in Form view, AC 180–181
    formulas and functions, EX 30–31, EX 132–133
    lists and styles, WD 62–63
    MLA formatting guidelines, WD 92–93
    modified Visit table in Datasheet view, AC 76–77
    Outlook window, OUT 2–3
    PowerPoint window, PPT 2–3
    Query window in Design view, AC 116–117
    report displayed in Print Preview, AC 206–207
    selection criteria in queries, AC 140–141
    Slide Show and Presenter views, PPT 32–33
    Table window in Design view, AC 52–53
    workbook window, EX 2–3
VLOOKUP function, EX 154, EX 171–173, EX 177
voice, setting up Cortana to respond to your, FM 25

W

wavy underlines, correcting, WD 15
web, searching for information on words, phrases, WD 53
web hyperlinks, WD 12
Web Note tools (Microsoft Edge), PA-15
webpages
    annotating, PA-15
    live, PA-12
website, automatic formatting of addresses, PPT 18
what-if analyses, EX 149
    performing using Goal Seek, EX 150–151
    performing using trial and error, EX 149–150
wildcard characters (fig.), AC 195
window, Access (visual overview), AC 2–3
window buttons, AC 2
windows
    completed contact (fig.), OUT 18
    maximizing, minimizing, OUT 4
    Outlook (visual overview), OUT 2–3
    sizing button, OUT 3
    task panes, WD 31
    workbook (fig.), EX 3
Windows 10, symbols not allowed in filenames, FM 15
Windows file system, FM 6
Wingait Farm (case), EX 131
wizards. See specific wizard

Word, WD 1
See also specific feature
dragging outlines into Sway, PA-7
features, learning about, WD 54
formatting document to match MLA style, WD 95
Help, getting, WD 31, WD 52–54
starting, WD 4
Word Help window (fig.), WD 53
Word Options dialog box, ribbon, WD 34
Word window
reducing to smaller size or icon in taskbar, WD 3
setting up, WD 6
visual overview, WD 2–3
words
deleting, WD 13
searching for, in documents, WD 79–81
work, productivity apps for, PA-1–4
Work Week button, OUT 5
workbook window (visual overview), EX 2–3
workbooks
blank (fig.), EX 15
changing themes, EX 105–106
closing, EX 13
colors, using to enhance, EX 73
documenting contents of, EX 135
entering text, data, numbers, EX 17–24
exploring, navigating within worksheets, EX 7–11
illustrated (fig.), EX 2–3
making user-friendly, EX 134–141

opening existing, EX 4–5
planning, EX 13–14
previewing, printing, EX 54–55
printing, EX 50–55, EX 121
saving, EX 17
saving with new filenames, EX 56–57
starting new, EX 14–17
templates described, EX 4
working offline, online, OUT 13–14
works cited lists, WD 101, WD 109, WD 112
worksheets
See also sheets
adding print titles, EX 117–118
changing views, EX 50–52
contents in workbook window (fig.), EX 3
deleting, EX 16–17
editing cell content, EX 19–20
entering text, data, EX 17–24
with font, fill, and border formatting (fig.), EX 98
formatted cells (fig.), EX 91
formatting, EX 48–50
formatting (visual overview), EX 66–67
formatting cells, EX 84–89
formatting for printing, EX 113–121
hiding, unhiding, EX 47
importing Excel, AC 80–83
modifying, EX 39–47
moving, EX 16
navigating within, EX 9–11
numbers, entering, EX 24

in Page Break Preview (fig.), EX 52
in Page Layout view (fig.), EX 51
renaming and inserting, EX 15–16
switching to different views, EX 50–52
viewing formulas, EX 55–56
wrapping text within cells, EX 27–28
written communication
acknowledging your sources, WD 102
creating a business letter, WD 9
creating effective workbooks, EX 14
displaying significant digits, EX 140
effective conditional formatting, EX 113
formatting monetary values, EX 80
formatting workbooks for readability, appeal, EX 92
how much text to include, PPT 16
netiquette guidelines, OUT 15
organizing information in lists, WD 70
proofreading your document, WD 37

Z

Zip button, FM 28
zipped folder icon, FM 3
zipped folders, FM 28, FM 29–30
Zoom box, AC 156
Zoom controls, EX 3, PPT 3
Zoom into the slide button, PPT 53–54
zooming
changing zoom level, WD 23
described, WD 3